A LONG, DEEP FURROW

THE UNIVERSITY PRESS OF NEW ENGLAND

Sponsoring Institutions

Brandeis University

Clark University

Dartmouth College

University of New Hampshire

University of Rhode Island

University of Vermont

A Long, Deep Furrow

THREE CENTURIES OF FARMING

IN NEW ENGLAND

BY

HOWARD S. RUSSELL

University Press of New England

HANOVER, NEW HAMPSHIRE

1976

Foreword

I COMMEND this volume to the general reader as well as the serious historian. Howard Russell's carefully constructed narrative, a pleasure to read, is based upon both early published literature and, to a large extent, local manuscripts. In going to the sources, Mr. Russell has given us a documentary history, as it were, which makes New England's rural past come alive.

The book spans a three-hundred-year period of great importance to the nation. Only a few other volumes—by Percy Bidwell, Clarence Day, Carl Woodward—cover reasonably large areas of New England or long periods of time. None is so comprehensive as this one. Equally important, *A Long, Deep Furrow* locates New England's agriculture within the framework of the nation's agriculture, contributing significantly to both.

The wealth of detail, as revealed by the index—for example, when a particular crop, breed, animal, tool, or machine became part of our agricultural heritage—will prove invaluable to those concerned with preserving or reconstructing our past in agricultural museums and in living, historical farms, which are becoming an important educational force in our nation. One of the most neglected aspects of agricultural history, the place of women in farm life, receives careful attention. No aspects of rural life are overlooked.

American farmers and consumers alike owe much to New England agriculture. The New Englanders' township system of land settlement led to an emphasis upon family-operated and family-owned farms, and the pattern of local village self-government proved so successful that after the Revolution it spread half way across the continent, providing a workable base for a productive, expanding agriculture.

Even before the Revolution, a number of New Englanders

were concerned with developing a more productive agriculture. These leaders knew changes were taking place in English farming that were increasing production and making better use of land and labor. The first influential reformer was Jared Eliot, a Connecticut pastor and farmer. His *Essays upon Field Husbandry* were published in the mid-1700's. These essays were followed by Samuel Deane's *New England Farmer* in 1790 and Manasseh Cutler's systematic botanical classification at about the same time. The *Farmer's Almanac* by Robert B. Thomas first appeared in 1793.

Agricultural organizations in New England became another force for improved farming. The Kennebec Agricultural Society was formed in 1787, the Massachusetts Society for Promoting Agriculture came in 1794, and others followed. The Berkshire Agricultural Society, organized in Pittsfield, Massachusetts, in 1811, had as its primary purpose the sponsorship of local agricultural fairs. Eventually, this idea spread throughout the United States.

Agricultural education, though opposed by some farmers, began in New England and then spread throughout the United States. In 1822, Maine incorporated the nation's earliest school for teaching agriculture, chemistry, and the mechanic arts: the Gardiner Lyceum. The culmination of the movement for establishing agricultural education of college grade came in 1862 when Representative Justin S. Morrill of Vermont sponsored the law endowing every state with a generous land grant from the national domain to establish colleges to teach agriculture and the mechanic arts. In the same year the United States Department of Agriculture was established as an outgrowth of the activities of Henry L. Ellsworth of Connecticut. Later, in 1875, Connecticut became the first state in the nation to appropriate public funds for an agricultural experiment station. The idea was widely adopted and received Federal support in 1887.

Meanwhile, a young man from Westborough, Massachusetts, Eli Whitney, after graduating from Yale went south in 1793 and invented the cotton gin. This, more than any other single factor, turned the South to dependence upon cotton and ensured the continuation of slavery until it was ended by the Civil War and the thirteenth amendment to the Constitution. Ingenious Yankees were inventing and improving other horse-powered equipment such as mowing machines, hay rakes, and threshing machines, from about 1830 on.

The new inventions were not widely adopted until the Civil War, when high prices and seemingly unlimited demand for farm products, combined with labor shortages, triggered the first American agricultural revolution. This thrust the American farmers—New Englanders with the others—into full-scale commercial agriculture. As Mr. Russell develops in detail, the thirty years that followed 1870 were close to disastrous for New England farmers.

In 1874, the United States Commissioner of Agriculture asked of several New England farmers: "Does farming in New England pay?" Among the conclusions reached were: "Farming in New England pays well if conducted with skill and enterprise, combined with the use of sufficient capital. . . . Proximity to numerous markets compensates for lower natural fertility; contiguity to the sea-coast renders available large supplies of cheap marine fertilizers, and the manufacturing villages furnish equivalent advantages to interior farms; and while the average yields of crops are thus made equal to those of the most fertile portion of the country, the prices obtained are greater." Some 61 percent of New England's farm land was improved, and its average price was $29.90 per acre. New England's average yields of corn, wheat, rye, oats, and potatoes equaled or exceeded those of most states.

In spite of these brave words, the number of farms and total farm production continued to decline. Many New Englanders continued the trend that had developed before the Civil War of moving to new farm lands in the west and to factories in the towns and cities. Those moving west carried with them improved types of livestock, particularly sheep, as well as a strong feeling for the family farm. Thus New England continued to contribute to the agricultural development of the nation.

Those remaining in farming in New England turned to specialization, particularly in dairying, poultry, and fruits and vegetables for the growing urban population. The state experiment stations gave particular attention to bettering the quality and increasing the production of milk, eggs, broilers, potatoes, sweet corn, oats, apples, blueberries, cranberries, strawberries, and other products that could be marketed in the urban areas in, and bordering, New England. These studies had impacts on other parts of the United States. For example, work at the Connecticut station led directly to the commercial development of hybrid seed corn.

The value of careful marketing, particularly through cooperatives, was emphasized by the state experiment stations and many farm organizations. Again, the New England experience in this area was carefully studied throughout the United States.

New England farms in recent years have been a haven for such men and women as (in Mr. Russell's apt phrasing) "look to the soil for life as well as for a living." Some of these farmers have been nationally known in other fields, such as the poet Robert Frost. Others are families finding a livelihood on farms that their ancestors had originally acquired from the Indians or hewn out of the green forest. Again, this concept of making farm life a viable alternative to life in the city is one that is urged by exponents of rural development and that has been adopted by many younger people as the way in which they wish to live.

New England farmers, in sum, have made substantial contributions to the nation. They began in 1621 and are continuing. It is fitting that these contributions and the place of New England agriculture in the development of both New England and the United States be, at long last, the subjects of a comprehensive, scholarly history.

Washington, D.C.   Wayne D. Rasmussen
January 1975

Acknowledgments

IT WOULD BE a delight to thank here by name all who have contributed to the preparation of this book. Their number is legion, for it has been a half-century in the making. Visits to unnumbered farms, markets, and county and state agricultural offices have enriched and broadened personal farming experience. At least two-score reference librarians, of every New England state and elsewhere, have helped; so have numerous correspondents, official and lay, from the most diverse places. Farm people and agricultural officers beyond computation, including the older generations of my own family, have provided information, wit, and wisdom; hired men, and knowledgeable chauffeurs encountered on trips through the English countryside where New England farming had its roots, have had their part, along with published writers and historians, some of whom are recognized by specific citation.

Clearly, an attempt from memory or inadequate files to thank certain individuals by name would be unjust to a host of others, living and departed, whose assistance might chance to be overlooked. This, therefore, is my comprehensive expression of appreciation and gratitude to all who have in any way helped.

Aside from persons, a book of this scope would have been impossible without the resources of Boston's great libraries. The riches of the Athenaeum year after year have generously been made available to me, as has the assistance of its competent staff. Across the street the enormous collections of local and governmental history at the Massachusetts State Library with its helpful corps of workers have been an invaluable resource. Harvard's stacks were used for several years. The specialized collections of the Massachusetts Historical Society, the Massachusetts and the Worcester Horticultural societies, the American

Antiquarian Society, Old Sturbridge Village Library, the Essex Institute, and Peabody Museum have all contributed, together with at least twenty state, college, and local libraries and museums, including Boston's great Public Library. My local Wayland library has with cheerful courtesy obtained scarce volumes by interlibrary loan. To all of these, my gratitude.

As with libraries, so with scholars and friends. Especial appreciation, however, goes to Dr. Wayne D. Rasmussen, Executive Secretary of the Agricultural History Society for advice and encouragement; to his associate, David Brewster; to Henry Bailey Stevens, retired Editor and Extension Director Emeritus of the University of New Hampshire; and to Clarence S. Day, historian of Maine's agriculture (whose works, as a dependable resource, have made a more extended Maine bibliography superfluous). All these have read the manuscript and made valuable suggestions. Nor should encouragement from friends now deceased be forgotten, especially that of the late George L. Moore, for thirty years creator of that sparkling, history-rich house organ *Food Marketing in New England*, and James Watson, for some decades editor of the century-old *New England Homestead*.

Beyond all these, if this history is readable, may I pay tribute to the suggestions, patient proofreading, and indexing of Mrs. Russell, Radcliffe honor graduate and former English teacher; to our daughter Constance S. Russell, long in publishing; to my editor, David Horne, for his contributions of wisdom and experience; and to my typist, Mrs. Kathryn Maher, for patient struggles with bad handwriting and frequent revisions.

Finally, may I acknowledge the encouragement of the numberless friends who along the way have helped make of a long, demanding task its own reward.

Wayland, Massachusetts   Howard S. Russell
March 1975

Note: Although great care has been taken to verify the many dates that appear in the text and the words "first" and "earliest" have been applied with discretion to invention, discoveries, and new procedures, I make no guaranty, explicit or implied, that such dates and statements are not subject to correction.

Contents

Contents   xiii

Illustrations

I. THE ROOTS

I

New England's First Farmers

LONG BEFORE any white settler brought the first plow, tillage of
New England soil for food was an old story. Archaeological
evidence leads to the conclusion that its beginning may well date
back a millennium: others place the advent of flint corn, at any
rate, as recently as A.D. 1400. Before agriculture was developed,
men are believed to have inhabited parts of the New England
area perhaps ten thousand years earlier still.[1]

When Roger Williams talked farming with his Indian
friends in Rhode Island, they told him that in the beginning the
crow brought their ancestors "a graine of corne in one Eare, and
an Indian or French Beane in another from the great God
Kantantowit's field in the Southwest, from whence come all their
Corne and Beanes." [2] Recent plant research confirms this
tradition, at least as to the origin of maize.

However crude these agricultural beginnings may have
been, by the time white explorers were able to observe and record
their agriculture New England natives were growing for food not
only corn and beans in substantial quantities, but also squashes,
pumpkins, watermelons, and Jerusalem artichoke roots, as well
as tobacco for smoking and gourds for utensils. Some tribes at
least appear to have encouraged desirable grapevines, nut and

1. Nauset, Cape Cod.
In 1605 Champlain found this Indian village on Cape Cod's east shore well
peopled, surrounded by cabins and cornfields—the corn, in late July, 5½ feet tall.
"L" on his map, he states, denotes "dwellingplaces of the savages that till the land."
Champlain, Voyages *(1878), courtesy of Boston Athenaeum.*

acorn-bearing trees, and berries, and developed deer pasture as a
source of meat.

When in 1524 the Florentine navigator Giovanni de Verrazano visited the coast and left the first credible account of the
countryside, he found it well populated and far from a wilderness. "We often went five or six leagues [12–15 miles] into the
interior and found the country as pleasant as it is possible to
conceive, open plains twenty-five or thirty leagues in extent
entirely free from trees." [3]

In the next century other observers add details. On the
southern Maine and New Hampshire coast, all about Massachusetts Bay, at Plymouth, and on Cape Cod in 1604–06 Champlain
saw "a great deal of country cleared up and planted," and left
several local charts to prove it. Captain John Smith circled much
the same territory in 1614, counted forty villages, saw hillsides
and "many iles all planted with corne," and remarked on the

numerous cabins and gardens.[4] When the Pilgrims arrived in 1620, not only did they find a large area of open, previously cultivated land at Plymouth and more on Cape Cod, but later noticed some of Boston Harbor's islands cleared from end to end and formerly cultivated. Their inhabitants, like Plymouth's, had been wiped out by a deadly sickness, three years after Smith's visit.

"Pity it was to see so many goodly fields, and so well seated, without men to dress and manure the same," was Edward Winslow's lament as he and another Pilgrim headed inland, following the Nemasket and Taunton rivers, to visit Massasoit at his seat to the southward on Narragansett Bay.[5]

Like those on Cape Cod and further north, the native Indians on the Rhode Island and Connecticut coasts who had escaped the plague were farming busily. Captain John Endecott, who fought some of them in 1636, commented on their many cornfields. He laid waste 200 acres of their corn on Block Island. In the Pequot War the next year, Captain John Mason of Connecticut, finding the Pequot village by the Pawcatuck River with its wigwams full of corn, loaded his ship with it before burning their wigwams.[6] Up the Connecticut River, Dutch Captain David De Vries was surprised at the great amount of open land suitable for cultivation. William Pynchon, after he arrived at Springfield in the Connecticut Valley, was glad to buy 500 bushels of corn from the Pocumtucks upriver at Deerfield. Inland, between this river and Massachusetts Bay, the Nipmucks had cornfields and villages alongside every large pond or stream; while in the Merrimack, Androscoggin, and Kennebec valleys to the north of the Bay Colony's bounds, cultivated fields were also numerous. One Maine field alone, it was estimated, covered over 600 acres.[7]

These fields were largely of light upland or silt soil, easier to clear and cultivate with hand tools than richer lowlands. Indian tools were crude but effective. For breaking ground, a pointed three-sided stone hoe or the shoulder blade of deer or moose bound to a long handle served as a mattock. A hoe made from a large clamshell on a wood handle or some similar light sharp instrument did the weeding. In a new field the natural fertility might be sufficient. In an old field herring rotted in the hill would bring the crops to successful maturity. Conveniently close to spring planting time these herring and other fish rushed up the rivers and brooks to spawn at their headwaters and were taken in weirs for fertilizer. In the fall the harvest was stored near the cabins in spacious underground barns dug in dry banks or knolls, for the Indians were a long way from being improvident.

So far as is known, the local type of corn was the hard northern flint, often white but grown in many separate strains and colors.[8] Beans were of the climbing type, also well varied. Seeds of all these and of the other vegetables were carefully selected and the strains kept pure. Indian crops were often sizable. Both Pilgrims and Puritans sought and followed native advice on cultivation practices and for some years were happy to add to their own meager food supplies by repeated purchases of native corn, in more than one case like Winthrop's and Pynchon's to the extent of hundreds of bushels.[9]

The Indian women were the planters and cultivators, helped by the children and old men. The single exception was tobacco growing, which was the province of the men. The natives planted their corn in hills three to four feet apart and after the corn had a good start, put in beans among them to twist up the stalks. Skipping to every fourth or fifth hill, the squaws then planted squash and pumpkin seeds, the vines of which would cover the ground completely.

Hoeing was done at least twice, sometimes three times. Cultivation was so clean as to draw the settlers' admiration, while the squaws poked fun at the slovenly fields of some of the English.[10]

These crops—corn, beans, squash, pumpkins, and arti-chokes—furnished a substantial part of the native food. The rest of the vegetable portion of their diet and much of their pharmacopoeia came from nuts, acorns, roots, berries, and wild plants. To some of these, even though not domesticated, they gave calculated attention and help, as they did also to hunting grounds, so that they would be attractive to deer and game. Fish of many kinds and meat from hunting balanced their menu. The skins from wild animals provided clothing, materials for snowshoes, and many other necessities.[11]

Such was the condition of New England agriculture when the first farmers from Europe reached its coasts.

2

Corn: Teachers and Pupils

Iт was in April of 1621 when the Pilgrims first turned New England soil for planting, yet they were far from the earliest Europeans to eye the land and weigh its possibilities for agriculture. Verrazano a century before had found the country "adapted to cultivation . . . and of so great fertility that whatever is sown there will yield an excellent crop." [1] As the century advanced, other explorers from France and scores of fishermen visited the "New Lands" of eastern Canada, and English fishermen began making Monhegan Island off the Maine coast their summer headquarters. In 1602 Captain Bartholomew Gosnold, in the ship *Concord* out of Falmouth in Cornwall, looked in on Maine and Cape Cod, and in late May tried some seeds at Cuttyhunk, on one of the Elizabeth Islands off Buzzards Bay. "Touching the fertility of the soil," he reported, ". . . we found it to be excellent for sowing some English pulse; it sprouted out in one fortnight almost half a foot." [2]

The next year, 1603, Captain Martin Pring in the *Speedwell* out of Milford Haven in Wales inspected the Maine coast and then spent considerable time at Plymouth. While loading a cargo of sassafras there to pay his passage, he tested the soil, watching for several weeks the results of sowing wheat, barley, oats, peas, even garden seeds. A year later, Sieur de Monts, a French explorer, tried a garden patch and sowed wheat on an island in the estuary of the St. John River, which two centuries later by a nineteenth-century treaty was to become State of Maine territory. Other Frenchmen, landing in a succeeding season, found excellent wheat and some vegetables growing.[3]

The next visiting gardener-sailor, this one from Devonshire, was Captain George Waymouth. On a spring day in 1605, in Maine, he and his crew "digged up a plot of ground wherein among some garden seeds, we sowed peaze and barley, which in sixteen days grew eight inches above the ground, and so continued growing every day a half an inch." Also in Maine, the unsuccessful Popham colony of 1607 tried agriculture. They left behind "Rootes and Garden Hearbes and some old walls" to be observed by a visitor a decade and a half later.[4]

So far as is now known, New England soil remained thereafter undisturbed by visiting agricultural experimenters until 1613, when two French Jesuits, Fathers Biard and Masse, started a mission garden on Mount Desert Island, only to have the English turn them out. The next spring Captain John Smith, farmer's son turned soldier, put in a garden out on rocky Monhegan Island off Pemaquid, Maine. It "served us for sallets in June and July," he records.[5] More important, Smith made a detailed map and wrote a book that was to have wide influence, describing the whole coast, including the gardens of the native inhabitants which he noted along the shores of southern New England.

These assays at farming had all been tentative. If gardening failed, there remained the ships' stores for the few weeks before a return to the homeland. But by 1621 a group of people had settled for whom the bounty or poverty of New England soil was to be a matter of life or death, and farming an experiment that must succeed. Fortunately for them, and for New England, they fell upon soil that was cultivable, and into the hands of an apt instructor who schooled them in the kind of farming for which their own modest agricultural knowledge had only partially fitted them.

Persons lacking extensive agricultural experience are apt to

2. *Plymouth's future site, 1605.*
A deadly pestilence, sweeping away the Indian inhabitants, had left open for the Pilgrims this long-tilled site, which they named Plimoth. When Champlain mapped it fifteen years earlier, only the two points were forested. "F" on the map refers to "Cabins where the savages till the ground." Voyages *(1878), courtesy of Boston Athenaeum.*

think farming a simple operation; that anyone can tickle the soil or raise an animal and secure a living thereby. They little realize the vast differences in soils, climate, and types of crops and animals; nor can they readily appreciate the importance of accumulated knowledge inherited locally from previous generations of husbandmen, lack of which can make farming an especially hazardous and unfruitful operation. It is important to examine each of these factors as they relate to the enterprise of the passengers of the *Mayflower* which on December 21, 1620, dropped anchor in Plymouth Harbor to open the agricultural annals of New England.

First as to the terrain. If any single factor proved the key to the eventual success of the Pilgrim enterprise, it was that their exploring party found at Plymouth not merely a sheltered harbor but a tract of tree-cleared hillside, long farmed, but whose numerous farmer cultivators had been completely swept away by a recent pestilence. Had the newcomers been forced to chop their way to their first few acres of cropland and harvest or to fight the original occupants for possession, it is hard to see how they could have survived.

Plymouth soil was and is poor; but on the other hand it was what farmers call "old land" and of a character unusually easy to work. This proved another most fortunate circumstance; for the *Mayflower* lading included not a single plow—everything had to be done with clumsy hand tools, and years were to pass before this soil would feel the tread of an ox to draw a plow of any kind.

The climate at the beginning was also favorable. The mild winter of 1620–21 was succeeded by an early spring; and the summer season proved normally productive, untroubled by the long weeks of drought that in some succeeding seasons were to plague the cultivators, accustomed as they were to the frequent showers of England and the cool, gray skies of Holland. Moreover, New England's was in the main a healthy climate, without the deadly chills and fever of the lowland colonies of Virginia and Guiana.

But it was in the knowledge of local crops and practices which is essential to agricultural success in any part of the world that the newcomers were most handicapped. Just how much farming experience did the Pilgrims bring with them to the New World, and how valuable was it to their survival?[6] First to be considered is the background of those who were to become their leaders: Bradford, Brewster, Carver, Winslow, and Standish.

William Bradford's grandfather and the uncles who brought him up were substantial farmers at Austerfield, on the border between Yorkshire and Nottingham. As a lad they had "devoted him like his ancestors unto the affairs of husbandry," though the youth's health was frail. However, at about the age of seventeen he came under the influence of Reverend John Robinson and the congregation of Separatists in the neighboring village of Scrooby. When these were soon forced by government persecution to flee to Holland, young Bradford went with them, ending any agricultural training.

William Brewster, considerably older than Bradford and a leader in the Scrooby congregation, was the village postmaster and bailiff (or superintendent) of the manor there. Since a major route of travel passed through Scrooby, the postmastership was of some importance; but the manor area was chiefly fenland and wash, a district of very limited, poor farms.

John Carver, who backed the Pilgrim enterprise financially and became the colony's first governor, had always been a businessman. Such were the original leaders. So far as records show, none of them nor any others from the Leyden group were in any way connected with agriculture while they were exiled in Holland.

At Southampton, among the seventeen persons from London who there joined the Pilgrim party, was Edward Winslow, destined eventually to become a governor of the colony. He was a printer, though in station describing himself as a yeoman. Myles Standish was and remained a professional soldier. So much for the persons of prominence. Some of the passengers who joined the Pilgrim company at Southampton came from Kent and rural areas of southern England. All in all, however, though Bradford says that many of the Pilgrims came originally from a plain country life,[7] actual agricultural experience among the 102 people who embarked in the *Mayflower* was apparently not great.

In any case farming in the mild, showery climate of southeast England or beneath the overcast skies of Holland could have scarcely prepared the voyagers to grow crops in the burning drought and heat of New England's summer, with neither plow nor ox. Nor would experience in livestock-raising among lush English meadows be of much value in a country where the chief meat source for some time was to be wild deer. As Roland Usher has truly said, the Pilgrims lacked everything but virtue.[8]

So it was incredible good fortune when with a "Welcome, Englishmen," out of the woods stepped an English-speaking Indian, Hobomok (or Samoset), who had learned the language from fishermen frequenting Monhegan Island off the Maine coast, and when on March 22 he returned with Squanto, a native born on this very soil. Captured by an English ship captain and forcibly removed to Europe, Squanto had been spared from the sickness that took off every other inhabitant of Plymouth's Indian village. In England he had learned to speak the Pilgrims' tongue. Wise in the ways of New World agriculture, Squanto has properly been called the first of America's "agricultural advisers."

Fortune had smiled on the newcomers in another respect. The exploring party that in the preceding November had landed at Truro on Cape Cod had run into several underground Indian barns filled with corn, some of it seed ears in various colors. Of this they had kept as much as they could carry away, intending at a later day to satisfy its owners (as eventually they did, Bradford states).

Thus Squanto could instruct them how to burn the four or five years' accumulation of weeds, poverty grass, and hardhack from the old fields; and how with mattocks and grubhoes to break up the soil on as much as twenty-six acres. Next, following the Indian custom, they manured twenty with the herring (or shad) that almost filled the Town Brook at the time of their spring migration, and then planted this twenty with the confiscated maize seed, a grain which they confessed they had never before known. On the other six acres they broadcast English barley and pease, which they must have "hacked in" with pickaxes or heavy hoes.

For only twenty-one men and six grown boys, as Usher points out, to loosen and prepare twenty-six acres; to seine the fish, carry them up from the stream, and distribute two or three to each of the thousands of cornhills; then to draw up earth over them, drop the seed and cover it—all without a vehicle and with only hand tools—was a tremendous job.[9]

The twenty acres of corn brought a considerable harvest; a little barley and no pease at all was the result from the six acres of European grain. Altogether, the crop was sufficient, nevertheless, to enable the Pilgrims, Squanto, and other Indian friends whom the settlers by this time had made from Massasoit's village on Narragansett Bay thirty miles away, to celebrate with a bounteous Thanksgiving feast, complete with games and merriment. Moreover, each man, woman, and child who had survived the winter's deadly fevers could thereafter be rationed a peck of cornmeal a week. With shellfish and wild fowl this would keep all alive and in health. This first harvest had not been gained without tragedy, however. Unaccustomed to field work or physical toil and under an unseasonably hot April sun, Governor John Carver collapsed and died of a stroke, the first casualty of New England agriculture that history records.

The planting of the first two years was done on a joint or communal basis, and so was the trading that the group soon began with Indian tribes along the shore. This communal farming had its origin in the type of joint-stock business organization which had been necessary to secure capital for the voyage. The harvests secured might have sufficed, had not the arrival of two additional groups sent by the London backers of the colony doubled the mouths to be fed; for the newcomers brought no provisions with them. Once landed, some of the new arrivals were not even willing to work for the common good. A starving time ensued. The supply of food, no more than enough even for the original group, had to be rationed very closely, and general discontent and privation followed. Hungry persons even stole green corn from the stalks before it could mature.

A change in method was clearly necessary. With the spring of 1623, after a petition from the planters, the colony's General Court dropped the communal system and assigned each family its own parcel of tillable land, one acre for each person, to cultivate for its sole benefit. The new plan brought prompt improvement: it "made all hands very industrious, so as much more corne was planted than other waise would have bene. . . . The women now went willingly into ye feild, and tooke their little-on(e)s to set corne . . . whom to have compelled would have been thoughte great tiranie and oppression."

Though there were still no oxen to plow with, that season's harvest was so much better that all had enough to eat, and things began to look up. By 1625 the colony could even load a small vessel with corn and send it eastward to be traded with the Kennebec Indians for furs to be sold in Europe to pay debts. This date is one to be remembered. It marks the first instance of commercial agriculture in New England, and the first agricultural export by its people.

The colony had previously sent Edward Winslow to England to deal with the joint-stock company that had so far financed the enterprise; for the company's stockholders were pressing for income on the money they had advanced. When he returned in 1624, Winslow brought along three heifers and a bull, the first neat or cloven-footed cattle known to have come to New England. More followed, red and black, from time to time. In 1626 a Plymouth vessel again sailed down east on a trading voyage. At Monhegan Island, a trading and fishing settlement (off what is today Boothbay Harbor), the crew swapped corn for trading goods and acquired "a parcell of goats," dairy animals for whose milk Governor Bradford yearned. Meanwhile, hogs and poultry had increased (though information appears lacking as to when and how they first arrived), while breeding had added five young native-born cattle.

By 1627 the colony had been successful enough in trade with the Indians for furs so that a deal could be made to buy out its complaining English backers. Outstanding obligations were compromised for a fixed amount, and eight of the leading men, acting on behalf of all, assumed the debt remaining.

Relieved thus of uncertainties, these leaders called the colonists together and outlined a new plan for the farming on which everything depended. They proposed a division by families of the available arable or planting land, and of the livestock. It was to be on a share basis; both types of property were to become individual possessions. Each man was to be allotted one share of land. If married, he was to be entitled to an extra share for each member of his family. Each share was to be good for twenty acres, so that a whole family might readily receive as much as a hundred acres. The entire area of "settable or tillable" land was to be laid out fairly by a committee, and evened as to quality. Each tract would have some frontage on the shore or a stream. Then the tracts were to be distributed by lot. It was even arranged that people might exchange land so as to be with congenial neighbors. By 1638, Usher calculates, Plymouth had 356 fields covering five square miles between the Jones River on the north (now in Kingston) and the Eel River to the south.

The livestock was divided also. One cow and two goats were allotted for each six shares, so that every family could have its own milk, butter, or cheese. In addition the hogs, now increased to 146, were proportionately divided.

During the years when there had been no cattle, lack of grassland fit to mow had been unimportant. We wish we had one beast for every hundred that there is grass to keep, Governor Bradford had lamented. Now, with a considerable herd, it seemed best to hold all meadowland in common ownership and assign areas for mowing to each householder annually according to his need, an old English custom. All woodland and unallotted land remained in direct control of the colony.

The plan, which was not far from the traditional arrangements of an English village, was hailed as fair by all, and for some time content reigned. As one result, by 1629 Plymouth was not only profitably trading surplus corn for furs with Maine Indians but exchanging corn and tobacco for needed commodities with the Hollanders who had now begun the colony of New Netherland at the mouth of the Hudson.

Thus at the end of its first decade of struggle, New England's earliest colony, though still poor, was settling successfully into a new way of life. No plow had yet turned a furrow. The hoe remained the chief agricultural tool. No power mill had yet sawed a board or ground a grist. All was done by hand. Not a sheep had been shorn, if indeed any had yet arrived. An order of the General Court in 1633 implies that sheep were still scarce. Yet the Pilgrims had plenty to eat and a surplus to exchange for clothing and indispensable supplies. In this single decade they had learned from the natives the essential lessons of practical food production and by costly trial and error some features of agricultural trade as well. Each family had been settled in possession of what is today known as a family farm and had been provided foundation livestock. The arrangements reflected to some extent customs remembered from English village life; yet to a substantial degree they foreshadowed something quite different: the course that farming, in New England and later in the United States, was destined to follow for the next three centuries.

Meanwhile a few scattered homesteaders had filtered in at inviting spots along the shore to the north, while on a harbor fifty miles northeast the seed was already sown for a vigorous new colony, far better financed, and equipped with substantial agricultural experience.

3

Massachusetts Bay

CAPTAIN JOHN SMITH's MAP and published book and similar descriptions of the world beyond the Atlantic influenced others besides the Leyden exiles who settled Plymouth. More fishermen continued to appear seasonally on the northern New England coast where cod were so plentiful. More adventurers began to attempt other settlements. Thomas Weston tried a colony at Weymouth on the shore north of Plymouth in 1622, but it lasted less than a year. The next year Robert Gorges took over in the same general location. This group broke up, yet from an agricultural viewpoint it proved not altogether in vain, for Reverend William Blaxton, probably from Gorges' company originally, in 1625 or 1626 put down roots on open and empty Shawmut Peninsula in what was to become Boston Harbor and soon had an orchard and garden started on the southwest slope of the Trimountain. Across the harbor, Samuel Maverick, from Weston's or Gorges' group, sat down on Noddle's Island and later was found farming there. In a separate enterprise a Captain Wollaston with thirty or forty others made a beginning on the open hillsides of what was to become Quincy.

Meanwhile, hoping for profits in the waters toward Maine, where fish were extraordinarily abundant, merchants and fishermen had started small settlements to replace their former seasonal fishing stages. By 1623 a Scot, David Thomson, had begun a stay at the mouth of the Piscataqua in what is now

Portsmouth, New Hampshire, which lasted three years. Edward Hilton and companions landed that year also and founded a permanent settlement beside the river at Dover Point. On Maine shores, a few people had moved in at York and at the Saco River and Pemaquid areas. In 1623 a mercantile company from Dorchester, England, landed fourteen men on Cape Ann to pass the winter there, and increased the group by thirty-two the next year. Roger Conant, formerly at Plymouth, next at Nantasket in Boston Harbor, was called to become manager of this Cape Ann enterprise. In 1626 he transferred its operations to Naumkeag, now Salem.

Who of these various groups may have been first to break up the soil, or what they planted, no record states; but by 1632 the settlement on the Piscataqua had a sufficient start in planting to sail sixteen hogsheads of grain, apparently Indian corn, by boat to Watertown on the Charles River to be ground at a new mill there.

Evidence as to livestock beginnings is more exact. The merchants from southern England who financed the Cape Ann project must have realized that families a long way from home (for Conant's wife was with him and other wives began to arrive) could scarcely survive contentedly on fishing alone. Reverend John White's "Brief Relation" of the enterprise of the Dorchester Company of Adventurers mentions a small vessel bearing "kine" sent to Conant at Cape Ann in 1625. Part of the men stationed there returned to England that fall, but Conant and some conscientious ones stayed to look after the cattle. After removal of the experiment to Naumkeag in 1628, twelve more cattle arrived, bulls among them.[1]

Conant was by occupation a salter or ship chandler; among his group only one, Thomas Gardner, was listed as "agriculturist." Before long, however, they were trying tobacco as well as corn, apparently in old Indian fields. To grow these they must have observed the methods of Indian neighbors and obtained Indian seed. Though agriculture was not their primary interest, a few of them persevered as farmers for the rest of their lives.

The Naumkeag project took on a much more ambitious aspect in 1628 when Master John Endecott arrived to act as

governor under commission from six gentlemen who with others
had recently acquired the rights to the area from the earlier
Council for New England and taken over the interests of the
Dorchester Adventurers, for whom Roger Conant had been
superintendent. He and the other "Old Planters," as they came
to be called, already experienced on the soil, were scarcely
pleased to be superseded, but Conant fortunately was a mild man
and his objections moderated as Endecott assigned each of them
200 acres of good land. The name Salem, given the new
settlement, signified peace.[2]

Wealthy capitalists from London and the east part of
England were now behind the Naumkeag venture: merchants,
clothiers, leather dealers. They began to ship over substantial
supplies of cattle, horses, tools, and seeds, in addition to fishing
gear. They also sent additional colonists. Governor Endecott and
his neighbors could soon count at least forty dairy cattle besides
young stock, forty milch goats, a dozen mares—with John
Woodbery, a horse fancier, to watch over their foaling. There
were also increasing numbers of rabbits. There may have been
poultry, too, for tame turkeys are listed in the items the
Massachusetts Bay Company ordered to be sent to Endecott.[3]

With all this livestock, plus hogsheads of oats and dried pea
seed, farming now began in earnest; so that when the next season
Reverend Francis Higginson arrived in a shipload of settlers, he
could write home enthusiastically of the "Abundance of corne
planted by them, very good and well liking." This language
sounds as though he meant Indian corn, for he mentions it
elsewhere with admiration. He rejoiced also to see green peas
growing, as good as ever he ate in England. Endecott soon started
a vineyard and began to try out berries, fruits, and nuts, both
native and imported.[4] It was only four years until, at his 300-acre
Orchard Farm in Danvers, he set out his famous pear tree. For
three centuries it bore fruit; eventually it was but a stone's throw
from Boston's roaring circumferential highway, Route 128.
Judging from the English records, potatoes may have been sent
Endecott to try, also, though so far as is known without practical
result. As "The Governor and Company of Massachusetts Bay,"
the English sponsors of the infant settlement in 1629 secured

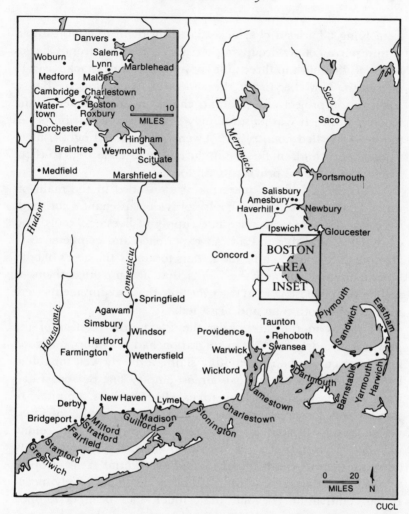

3. Apart from access by water, two factors appear to have governed the choice by New England's colonizers of sites for their towns. This map illustrates one: the availability of an open area already cultivated or at least cleared by the native Indians. Such clearings offered the settlers a ready-made site for home lots (dwelling, outbuildings, garden, orchard, night pasture) together with nearby land cultivable for grain. According to credible evidence, every town named on this map (all settled by 1650) had such a precleared area as a nucleus. Some early settled towns—for example, Newport and Middletown, R.I., and Sudbury, Mass.—are not included. Despite circumstantial evidence, diligent inquiry has turned up no adequate proof. Cartography Laboratory, Clark University.

from King Charles a charter authorizing them to establish and administer a colony occupying territory stretching from Charles River on the south to three miles beyond the Merrimack River to the north. Now began on the shores of Massachusetts Bay a colonization project of a size and character unparalleled in the modern world. It was painstakingly geared to the possibilities of the newly settled countryside. Twenty thousand English, men, women, and children, flooded in during the decade 1630 to 1640. These had all to be provided with food.

Success in such an undertaking depended in the main on three factors: a soil that could provide sustenance for both livestock and crops; an adequate supply of livestock, tools, and equipment; and, beyond all, an experience and competence in farming that would enable the settlers to supply the needs of both human immigrants and the beasts that accompanied them. It will be the purpose here to discover how these requirements were satisfied and both man and beast fed.

First as to the land. Like the Plymouth colonists of the previous decade, the Puritan migration had the enormous good fortune to enter upon an inviting shore, formerly well inhabited by native Indians but in 1630 almost empty. The Bay coast had the advantage of affording several excellent harbors, a number of small rivers for access to the interior, and a wealth of forest within reach. Besides all these, the site awaiting the colony included thousands of acres of natural grass, of types reasonably adequate for the needs of cattle, and substantial areas of open, tillable land. Parts of this land had been in comparatively recent Indian cultivation: beyond that, much had been kept open purposely by seasonal Indian fires. In general the soil was of considerably better quality than that found by the Pilgrims at Plymouth. Yet the same strange circumstance prevailed as at Plymouth—considered by the colonists to be providential: the scourge of illness that had wiped out Plymouth's Indians had likewise left only three or four small and weak Indian villages anywhere about Boston Bay, well populated as it must formerly have been.

A second advantage for the Massachusetts Bay Colony was in adequate leadership, capital, and preparation. Much was by this time known of the possibilities of the new land, and the directors of the enterprise planned carefully. The financial backing of the sponsoring company was sufficient; the most important needs of the venture could be adequately met. The tools, seeds, plants, and animals that were thought most necessary were provided in liberal quantities almost from the beginning.

From the records it becomes clear at once that the Bay company management expected farming in the new colony to be carried on as far as possible after the English manner. Livestock and grain were to be its main props; supplemented by fruits, vegetables, and cultivated fibers. There was no intention to let the colonists be dependent on Indian practices alone, helpful as those had been to the impoverished Pilgrims at Plymouth. Livestock in quantity came with the first ships, and continued coming. So did European seeds and plants.

All such supplies might have been thrown away, however, had the Bay Colony immigration not included a substantial proportion of persons of seasoned agricultural experience. Because the farm-trained portion among the newcomers proved so important in shaping not only the agricultural but the commercial and political future of Massachusetts Bay and every one of the colonies that eventually fanned out from it, the English origins of these farm people deserve particular attention, together with the agricultural traditions and practices in which they had been trained.

To begin with, the new governor of the Massachusetts Bay Colony, John Winthrop, besides being able in the field of law, was a countryman and had been lord of the manor of Groton in Suffolk. In New England he from the first became a farm proprietor, acquired an orchard (perhaps previously set by Conant) on Governor's Island in Boston Harbor, and promptly stocked his Ten Hills farm beside the Mystic just north of Boston with cattle and tools brought from England.

Among the long list of passengers who filled the Winthrop fleet arriving with him in 1630 or who landed during the next decade, the occupations of over 300 males (other than servants), chiefly heads of families, have been determined as a result of the

painstaking research of Charles E. Banks.[5] Among these immigrants, but seventy-five, fewer than one fourth, are listed as
yeomen (who were not necessarily farmers) or as husbandmen.
One in six was from London and unlikely to have had farm
experience, though of these some may originally have been from
the country. Aside from these city dwellers, the immigrants listed
included numerous merchants; armourers, bakers, carpenters,
shoemakers, smiths, tanners, weavers, and other tradesmen, as
well as the large number of servants and laborers. Of these,
weavers and tanners were most likely to have been rural dwellers,
and as tenants on some manor to have at least possessed a
garden, a cow, and a few sheep or poultry. Yet useful as the
industrial skills of all such craftsmen might prove for the success
of the Bay Colony, any important contribution from them to the
settlement's agricultural success could scarcely be expected.

It appears a tribute, then, to the modest number of
husbandmen, in particular to the livestockmen among them, as
well as to the careful preparations by the Company for provisioning the colony from England, that only the first two or three
years of the venture were seasons of real want for the newcomers.
Once these years were over, the colony seldom failed to be
adequately fed and eventually in part clothed by the production
of its professional farmers, with such supplements as the rest
might be able to provide. Indeed, hardly had the first decade
ended before merchants would find it possible to accumulate
surplus grain and provisions to be shipped abroad in order to
obtain in return needed salt, apparel, and manufactured goods.

Turning then to this important minority of yeomen and
husbandmen, so vital to the success of the whole enterprise, what
sort of ideas and traditions did they bring with them? In what
type of agriculture were they likely to succeed? To answer this
requires a look to Old England and its agriculture at the time.[6]

The foundations of English farming were dual: first, livestock, with grassland to feed it; second, bread-grain for the
family. It had been England's good fortune since William the
Conqueror's time not to have been invaded except across
the Scottish border, nor ravaged by the hungry armies that
decimated the livestock of Europe's mainland. Hence for centu-

ries stock breeders over most of the kingdom had been freely able to select and gradually to improve their cattle, sheep, and hogs, feeding and fattening them on the green grasses that good soil and long, mild, damp summers encouraged. The livestock also provided manure on which to grow the needed grain, or "corn," as it was called, for bread: wheat for the better-off, and barley, rye, or a mixture known as meslin for the rest. Yet livestock was the chief basis for the farming of the east part of England from which so many New England colonists came. Joan Thirsk's study of fenland farming shows scarcely a farmer without stock, though many had no arable land.

Across the greater part of England an "open field" or community type of farming prevailed. In certain counties close to big markets or influenced by trade with Europe, however, this had given way to an individual type of ownership and management often described today by the words "severalty" and "enclosure." Both types merit attention.

In the majority of English counties each town or manor had for centuries pastured its cattle on common land in a common herd, and its sheep in a common flock. By day a common herdsman watched over the cattle as they fed on the village meadow or "waste." At sunset he returned each one to its owner's gate. The town shepherd likewise took the village sheep to pasture. When he returned them at evening, however, he customarily "folded" the whole flock on some acre of the village's "arable" (cultivated fields) for the night. By means of movable fences, a new acre could be folded each night, so that at length the whole field was fertilized for the next season's grain. Under a common swineherd, the village hogs rooted for food in the common woodland and waste, where ancestral oaks, preserved generation after generation, dropped their acorns.

In the common lands of the village, each freeholder or tenant had certain rights, well known and strictly enforced. One of these, where land was limited, was the "stint," which defined the exact number of each sort of beast he was entitled to pasture. The stint was usually proportioned to the number of his acres, whether owned outright or held as a long-term tenant of the lord of the manor. Even though a villager should possess or rent no land whatever, custom might allow him to pasture a cow or two, or a half dozen sheep, maybe a hog, on the common lands of the village, and to gather faggots there for his fire: all in order that he and his family might have means of subsistence. The details of all this were discussed and settled at regular annual meetings or "courts," attended by the lord of the manor, his bailiff, and all the villagers.

In the tilled fields each farmer holding land cultivated his own narrow slice or slices in accordance with an agreed program. If the land were poor or the neighborhood backward, the plan might call for only a two-year rotation: grain one season, fallow the next. On good soil and with advanced practices, however, the land might be cropped for two, three, or four successive years. Nevertheless the crop and the time of sowing and reaping would be the same for all cultivators.

After harvest the grain fields were opened for pasturage to the beasts of the entire village. To the laborer or very small farmer for whom life was hard, this was a boon indeed. With a garden and poultry besides his few animals, he might even have something to trade at the nearest of England's three hundred market towns. On the other hand, under this system the freeholding yeoman or copyholder with many acres and a substantial stint of livestock might not only live well but have surplus fleeces, wheat, and beef to market in big towns like York, Bristol, or London. This was the situation in the majority of English counties.

In a few areas, however, important changes in farm practice had been under way for a century or more. The East Anglian counties of Norfolk, Suffolk, Essex, as well as Kent and the neighborhood of London, were the most heavily populated and were most accessible to markets. The growing cities bought the fruits and hops of Kent, the butter and cheese of the Essex dairies, the poultry of Norfolk and Suffolk, the grain and vegetables of Middlesex and Norfolk, and the mutton and fleeces of the downs counties. From the sheep farmers of Wiltshire and Dorset wools went to nearby clothmakers, who wove them for export abroad. Cornwall likewise had good local trade.

Where large markets were within reach, sales of farm

produce were more likely to be for money rather than by means of the usual barter. Thus what is today called commercial farming, not unknown even before the Roman invasion, had been on the increase for several generations. Old communal customs in farming crumbled. Farmers found it profitable by exchange to consolidate their narrow strips from many fields into a single field, and to add to them by purchase. More and more land passed into individual ownership, was enclosed with hedges or fencing, and thereafter cultivated or pastured by the owner according to his individual desires. Larger markets and bigger farms brought wealth to ambitious yeomen and husbandmen; their sons in time might rise in the social scale to become gentry.

These developments were to prove of particular importance to New England, where communal customs were to give way eventually to independent farming and where growing animals and crops for sale abroad was soon to be a means of livelihood. Analysis of place of origin of the yeomen and husbandmen arriving in New England in this decade of 1630–40 shows that at least one third of those for whom information is available came from the very counties in the east and south of England where old custom was most widely shattered. It will become evident as this study proceeds to what degree each influence, communal and individual, affected the course of New England's farm life.

At least one further question arises. Why did English farmers and their wives and children risk all by leaving their pleasant ancestral homes and fields for a new and little-known world? Three reasons are usually offered. One is religious: the attempt by the Crown and the Established Church to suppress exercise of the Puritan faith and practice. The second is economic: the hard times of the decade 1620–30 in Old England, and in particular a fall in the price of wool and farm produce. The third is the human desire to better one's fortunes.

It is not the province of this book to discuss the religious motives that impelled the mass movement of English Puritans to the shores of Massachusetts Bay, a subject covered with distinction by many historians; nor is it pertinent to our purpose to assess the economic strains that caused unease and financial distress in many parts of King Charles's realm, or the commer-

cial motives underlying formation of the Massachusetts Bay
Company and the emigration to New England's shores. The first
motive, religious, was long held unquestioned as the great cause
of migration: the second, economic, has loomed large with recent
historical writers. To become enmeshed in a debate as to which
element, religious or economic, was decisive would be unproductive, and unnecessary for an agricultural history. Yet it should be
pointed out that although an unemployed spinner or weaver of
woolens or even an enterprising London merchant might be led
by alluring reports into adventuring in a new country, it would
ordinarily take more than a year or two of poor markets or low
income to uproot country gentlemen such as Winthrop and
Endecott, or yeomen and husbandmen with fertile lands, ancestral rights, and assured position in Essex, Norfolk, Lincoln, or
Middlesex.[7]

Consider what was involved in so momentous a change.
Each such countryman had to sell or lease his land, or if a tenant
abandon his copyhold, renouncing cherished ancestral or acquired rights and privileges. He had then to provide himself with
tools and equipment for his new enterprise; and pay the heavy
cost of transporting household, goods, and livestock three thousand miles to a new and uncertain world. Beyond this, he had to
provide in advance supplies for the subsistence of his family,
servants if he had them, and stock, for many months at least after
arrival.

To these financial considerations must be added a farmer's
inborn conservatism, and the uncertainties connected with the
practice of agriculture anywhere, any time, but especially in an
unknown land and climate. This may well explain why, in the
passenger lists, the number of farmers appears proportionately
small.

Clearly, many of these farm persons were men of character
and local standing at home. Some had been bailiffs, church
wardens, constables, surveyors of highways, overseers of the poor
in their English parishes. They knew livestock and markets. They
were established. Their wives were skilled in churning butter,
pressing cheese, setting a hen—even selling fruit and produce in
a market stall. To such it must have been a wrench indeed to sell

all, to leave the known, the established, the familiar, for the difficulties and dangers of a new life in a new world.

Yet leave they did; and many of them were destined to serve in their new townships as in their old ones, as mainstays of community life. When, during anxious discussions between husband and wife across the trestle table and by the fire in a hundred East Anglian farmhouses, descriptions of the faraway new land were read and proposals for emigration pondered, it must, at least sometimes, have been listening to a higher voice than man's which overweighed the powerful ties of home and kin, and brought the decision to leave behind so much for what might prove to be so little.

4

Livestock the Key

LATE IN JUNE 1630, the eleven vessels of Governor Winthrop's fleet dropped anchor in Boston Harbor and began setting ashore their 700 passengers, with livestock and supplies, on the peninsula of Mishawum, soon to become Charlestown. On hand to greet them were blacksmith Thomas Walford, its original settler, snug "in a palisadoed and thatched house," and ten families who had been sent over from Salem in 1629 by Governor Endecott. Each of these ten had been provided a two-acre home lot, with instructions to fence in common.[1]

The newcomers set up tents and booths along the ways of a town plot laid out the year previous by Thomas Graves, Endecott's surveyor. Mishawum was a narrow, hilly peninsula, however, short of fresh water and able to accommodate only a limited number of persons or cattle, despite its marshes. Exploring parties began to examine prospects up the valleys of the four principal streams that enter Boston Harbor. Sir Richard Saltonstall, a Yorkshireman become London merchant, ascended the Charles River to what was to become Watertown; Governor John Winthrop and others went up the Mystic. Extensive salt marshes fringed the banks of each and fresh marshes bordered the entering brooks, offering the prospect of herbage for a large number of cattle. William Pynchon, an Essex County squire, and friends from a party of settlers sponsored by Reverend John White of Dorchester, England, explored the harbor shore southward, viewing the neck of high land that was to become a new Dorchester and Roxbury.[2] With the wide marshes of Great Neck and the Neponset River, this promised for their livestock safety from wolves as well as fodder. To the eastward, beyond Noddle's Island, where Samuel Maverick had some years before installed himself, stretched more miles of salt marsh bordering what were to be called Malden River and Saugus Creek. Marshes such as these had been prized resources for cattlemen in Old England's shore counties.

Besides their human freight, the ships of the fleet had landed 170 cattle, survivors of 240 originally driven aboard. Governor Winthrop counted at least 15 cows of his own, plus young stock and 14 she-goats, and is recorded as buying two sows from Plymouth for his farm. Milk and cheese from cows and goats were valuable food, but even more important, if tillage was to be attempted, would be young male calves which at the age of two years might be trained to the plow and oxcart. Meanwhile, the goats would clear the weeds and brush that had pushed up in the old Indian fields which their former proprietors had left vacant. The fleet had started with 60 horses.[3] These would be valuable for travel and to carry burdens in panniers, but were not expected to draw heavy, clumsy wooden seventeenth-century plows or carts.

Not long after landing in Charlestown, Governor Winthrop received an invitation from Reverend William Blaxton, who had his cabin and young orchard across the river on the Shawmut Peninsula. Shawmut was largely cleared land watered by copious springs, which Charlestown lacked. The hillsides sloped chiefly south and west, and the whole was almost surrounded by tidewater, hence defensible. They struck a bargain and soon transfer of the new arrivals with their goods to the more favorable location was under way. Thus amicably was the townsite for the future Boston acquired and its settlement begun.

During the remaining weeks of an all too short summer and fall the most that could be done was to throw up makeshift shelter for the new population. Tillage was out of the question.[4] With winter's dearth ahead and seed needed for the following spring it was ordered that no Indian corn be given away or sold without permission. There was no time to provide warm cover for animals. When the end of December came, Governor Winthrop lamented that many of the cattle and goats brought over at such great cost were without shelter.[5] Wolves had already feasted on precious calves and hogs.

The winter proved sharp, the cold intense, at least to people used to the mild weather of southern England. Nearly 200 of their original number had already died, and scores more failed to live till spring. Providentially, in February a ship arrived loaded with meat, pease, oatmeal, butter, and cheese.

With spring's advent, the cattle and goats that had managed to survive could browse and gain strength. At least one Watertown cow dropped a calf. A young heifer, lost and supposed by its owner to have been eaten by a wolf, returned, to his great joy. Meantime at Salem some of Endecott's cattle almost died from being fed nuts by an ignorant herdsman. Hogs had looked after themselves, digging through the snow for acorns and roots and for clams along the beaches. No person was permitted to kill any of the hogs, now running wild, without leave. With food for humans so scarce, three hungry men received a public whipping for making away with a pig apiece.

Some colonists may have dug gardens in this first spring, for it was decreed on May 3 that trespassing or doing "hurte in the corne of another" by cows, horses, goats, or swine would result in having to satisfy the person damaged: but this order, a traditional precaution, may well have been intended to keep good relations with the few neighboring Indians.

The spring of 1631 brought other ships with more red cows and heifers, as well as goats and hogs. A Barnstaple ship landed five sheep. With numbers of stock thus increasing and herbage scanty it was ordered that no cattle be put on any harbor island except by permission of the authorities.[6]

More cattle still were landed in 1632. The *Whale* brought 70 cows, losing only two; the *Charles*, of Barnstaple, nearly 80 and 6 mares. The large 300-ton *James* from London brought 61 heifers but lost 40 others.

As to whether any new-come husbandman actually planted English grain in that first spring of 1631, the record is silent, though rye and barley seed had arrived in February. At the start the rough Indian fields about Boston Harbor were far better suited for goats. Nor is there any record as to whether the Salem settlers taught the newcomers to drop and fertilize Indian corn, except as this may be indicated by the order protecting gardens already referred to. Indian corn was undoubtedly scarce, for on September 27, 1631, for the crime of stealing two baskets of corn from Indian Chief Chickatawbut who farmed on Milton Hill, Josiah Plaistowe was fined and degraded from his status as "gentleman," and two of his servants were sentenced to be whipped.[7]

The settlers were very short of food. Two thousand bushels of corn were purchased from Virginia in a single shipment. Chief Chickatawbut donated a welcome present, a hogshead-full, to the governor. Ships from England brought supplies, but not enough, and the summer of 1632 was cool and wet.

The winter of 1632–33 set in with terrible cold. Boston Harbor froze over. Englishmen were not used to such weather; neither were their cattle; and both still lacked adequate shelter. Death was the result. It was fortunate that some persons, discouraged, had headed back to England or left for other colonies, and that few new settlers arrived.

Things looked a little better by the summer of 1633. More cattle kept coming, including 60 for Salem in another trip of the ship *James*; 100 for Boston the next year in the *Griffen* and 50 in the *Regard*. Dorchester with plentiful salt hay had so many cattle that the town needed four bulls to service its herd. It was bad luck, though, that the wolves were learning to enjoy calves. Some sheep were coming, 34 in one Dutch ship. Swine multiplied almost too fast. In November the General Court decreed that no person might feed corn to hogs unless it was too poor for humans; and the following fall keeping young pigs beyond the roasting stage of one month was forbidden lest they eat settlers out of house and home before spring.

Goats take care of themselves and are excellent at clearing land. The records tell of 42 milch goats coming to Salem in one 1629 shipment. A French ship brought six to Boston the next year; the *Thunderer* brought more from Virginia in 1634, and

Samuel Maverick returned from that colony in 1636 with 80. Plenty of others must have arrived, and their young increased, for in three years, William Wood guesses, perhaps wildly, that there were a total of 4,000 in the colony.[8] So plentiful did they become that at one time later the Narragansett Indians were said to have killed 200 of Winthrop's goats. Goats provided a certain amount of milk and excellent cheese but were prone to get into gardens. Within three decades, though "once in great esteeme" they "are now almost banished." Hogs, still running free, were able to find plenty of food without attention. In the Mystic Valley they plundered the underground barns of the Indians, who complained to the Governor and had to be compensated.

While cattle, swine, and goat numbers-continually mounted, sheep increased but slowly. Following the early shipments, 40 more from New Netherland were landed in 1634; the next year, 88 from Holland. These were sent down the coast to newly settled Newbury, where herbage was plentiful. But sheep require skillful handling, by men with affection for them. They also need good, smooth, grass pasture rather than the rough browse goats can live on: "Until the land be often fed with Cattell, Sheepe cannot live."[9] Not fighters as pigs and goats soon became, they were helpless against the wolves that infested the woods; so their increase was very slow.

Horses were being bred. The *James*, a frequent livestock carrier, besides cattle brought 8 mares, and in 1635 Dutch ships landed 27 Flanders mares and three stallions. These last were larger than the small horse-kind, mostly from southern England, that had so far been received. They must have helped toward progeny more suited to New England conditions.

With domestic animals so numerous, good fencing became necessary to keep stock out of corn land and kitchen gardens. Newe-Towne (Cambridge), where planters had already impaled much ground by the spring of 1633, decreed penalties that season for failure to mend corn fencing. How farmers from the West Country of Old England must have sighed for the tall banks of earth and stone crowned with hedges which protected the fields of Cornwall, Devonshire, and Dorset!

The winter of 1633–34 was fortunately much milder. Food

was still scarce. Massachusetts had to buy 400 bushels of corn from the Narragansetts, while complaining that the Indians had promised a full thousand.[10] To grind the grain a windmill was set up at Cambridge (soon taken to Boston) and watermills at Roxbury and Dorchester. New shiploads of immigrants arrived all that summer, adding hundreds more mouths to feed. No one was permitted to take grain out of the colony, under penalty. By the end of this fourth summer, settlements surrounded Boston Bay.

In an enterprise such as starting a New England colony, many things had to be done all at once. What would now be called farm work formed only a small proportion of the essential tasks. The first need was shelter. Carpenters and servants had come in the ships, and the wealthier planters hired them for building. Others who lacked wealth had to put together make-shift shelters, until such time as each family could provide squared timbers, split clapboards or weatherboarding, and build properly. Then the house would be perhaps a two-room peaked-roof dwelling of the type long used in England. Roofs were of thatch at first, chimneys often of plank.

While this and similar essential work went on, someone had to look after the stock. Old English custom set the example. Each town hired its cowherd. In 1635 Newe-Towne employed a goatherd also, and Salem needed two such. These herdsmen picked up the animals of a whole village in the morning, drove them to pasture, and delivered each to its owner's lot at evening, when the householder or some of his family could milk cows and ewe goats.

Weatherboard shelters for such milking cattle began to appear, similar to those of Old England's eastern counties. Dry stock and young cattle, however, still had to grow long coats and shift largely for themselves even after several years. To secure the weaker animals from wild beasts, wealthy Cambridge proprietors had their servants surround hundreds of acres of ground with one general fence a mile and a half long. William Wood records that at Master Matthew Cradock's plantation on the Mystic in Medford, "he hath impaled a park where he keeps his cattle till he can store it with deer." [11] With much stock by necessity

4. Pounds for stray livestock. Howard S. Russell collection.

5. A tight pale fence with split pickets driven deep kept hungry animals out of gardens and orchards. Perley, History of Salem *(1924).*

grazing at large, fencing was as necessary to keep them out of tilled land as the wild beasts. One or more common fields were usually completely enclosed as soon as possible by the whole village. Thereafter, under the eyes of the town's fence viewers, each landholder was required to keep up his share of the common fence. In addition each family had also to protect its individual garden and orchard. With so much fencing done in haste and of rough materials, and so many animals grazing and rooting, fencing complaints and damage suits for animal trespass for years constantly harassed town officials and courts.

Wealthy homesteaders on the cramped Boston peninsula, lacking space and meadow to keep stock properly, were granted grazing land across the Back Bay in Muddy River (now Brookline) or got permission to pasture their animals on islands safe from wolves.

Hungering for vegetables, villagers had early begun gardens. Newe-Towne in 1634 granted a garden plot near the meeting house to "Mr. Stone"; and the Proprietors' Records of 1635 describe several more. Alvan Ervington and others were allowed timber from the common for fencing theirs. Roxbury and Dorchester settlers planted vegetable gardens near their dwellings. Amongst the puddingstone on their hillsides, apple and pear seeds and cherry stones were soon sprouting from the soil. In each of the dozen new villages that before long ringed Boston Bay and dotted the North Shore, colonists were trying out fruit. They planted the Indian's corn, bean, and pumpkin as well

as their own carrots, parsnips and turnips, all of them roots that
do well in spaded ground. To protect these, Cambridge in 1636
ordered fines levied whenever cocks, hens, and turkeys damaged
gardens. Some settlers wished to grow tobacco, but the General
Court frowned. A special dispensation allowed the "Old Planters" such as Roger Conant, who had grown it all along, to have
"tobacco yeards."

Altogether, agriculture was looking up. Boston decreed a
market for every Thursday, indicating that produce and animals
were for sale. For several years after 1635 farmers did very well,
and when Stephen Daye set up his Cambridge printing press, the
first booklet printed (1639) was that useful agricultural item, an
almanac. New colonists came in every ship. Before starting
across, many had sold out in England and had money in their
pockets. From the planters already established at the Bay and in
Plymouth they bought stock at high prices. Plymouth stockmen
took in newly arrived English cattle and bred and fed them, in
consideration of a share of their offspring.

Each year the General Court laid out fresh townships and
arranged for them to be peopled. In the older towns at the Bay
good herbage was already at a premium; people left, saying that
the plowable plains were too dry and sandy. In some towns,
Cambridge for example, religion and politics bred disagreements,
and the discontented and the unsuccessful were already looking
toward fresh horizons. Such property as they left behind was
readily salable to new arrivals from the ships. So soon after the
beginning, emigration had started. On the destinations and the
fortunes of these migrants a later chapter will report.

5

Stirring the Soil

LIVESTOCK, DESIRABLE AS IT WAS, met the food needs of the colonists only in part. If the newcomers were to have bread, land must be broken up at once, and in the beginning nearly all the work had to be done by hand. Except on fields that the Indians had quite recently cultivated, this was no easy task, even where, as Edward Johnson later put it, "The Lord [had] mitigated their labors by the Indians' frequent firing of the woods." Yet, in his words, "Standing stoutly to their labours [they] tare up the roots and bushes which the first yeare bears them a very thin crop till the soard of the earth be rotten, and therefore they have been forced to cut their bread very thin for a long season." [1]

Where and how the people at the Bay began to grow the Indian corn that was to become New England's staple is not always clear, for in English speech of that time the word corn might include any grain. At Naumkeag the original old planters had learned to plant maize, taught either by neighbor Indians or Plymouth Colony visitors. Pastor Higginson, arriving in 1629, was struck with wonder at the tremendous increase in kernels, so far beyond that of any European grain which was the fruit of a single seed. In 1633 he mentions that the settlers there had grown corn for seven seasons. Reverend John White, the pastor in old Dorchester, England, declared in 1630 in his tract, *The Planter's Plea*: "The Corne of Countrey (which it produceth in good proportion with reasonable labour) is apt for nourishment and agrees . . . very well with our health; nay, is held by some Physitians to be restorative." Roger Clap of the new Dorchester, reminiscing in old age, declared: "it was not accounted a strange thing in those days to eat samp or hominy" (both Indian corn dishes), and Johnson, also looking back, recorded that the chief "corn they planted before they had plows was Indian grain."

For Boston planters perhaps the lessons on how to grow it came from the Squaw Sachem of the Mystic Valley or from Chief Chickatawbut's womenfolk. William Wood paid the native teachers this tribute in 1634: "Maney wayes hath their advice and endeavour been advantageous to us; they being our first instructors for the planting of their Indian Corne, by teaching us to cull out the finest seed, to observe the fittest season, to keep distance for holes, and fit measure for hills, to worme it, and weede it; to prune it, and dress it as occasion requires." [2]

During these earliest years of scarcity only a small beginning could be made toward preparing ground properly for European grain. Later, as the colony developed, a plowman might be engaged with his team of four or six oxen to break up the land, but for a considerable time plows, plowmen, and oxen were very few. Regardless of this lack, to most of the newcomers producing grain appeared a necessity, and almost as much for beer as for bread. At Plymouth the Pilgrims had sown English grain the very first season, as has already appeared; but lacking animal manure and the plow they had to learn that the lean sandy soil of their Indian fields was too poor for wheat and barley. Grain enough they did secure, however, even without plowing, by following Squanto's directions and fertilizing Indian corn with fish directly in the hill. At the Cape Ann settlement later in the 1620 decade, native Indian corn seems also to have been the chief cereal.

About Boston Bay, whether the soil had been prepared well or ill, sowing of European grain must have begun in the autumn of the second full season of the Winthrop colony. Autumn would have been the normal time at home. At any rate during the next summer, in 1633, according to Johnson, "a small glean of rye" was brought to the governor and the General Court as "the first fruits of English grain, at which the poor people greatly rejoiced to see that the land would bear it." Actually it was barley and oats, if Winthrop's account is correct, and reaped at Rumney Marsh or "Sagus," where, Wood boasted, there was more English tillage than in all the rest of New England and Virginia besides. The settlers there, chiefly farmers by calling, had harvested twenty acres of grain. They had plowed in the seed, so Winthrop said, apparently after the English custom by which a light crossplowing and seeding followed the original soil breaking. By 1636 Governor Winthrop himself was putting rye in the ground. The next year beans, millet, and vetch were sown, and all seemed to prosper.[3]

Individual householders tried wheat in their gardens, the only spots safe from hogs and larger animals, but Salem's order passed in 1639 that fences be kept up "forasmuch as divers of our town are resolved to sow English grain this spring," shows that progress was slow, for a dozen years had passed since Salem's founding. Wheat seldom took kindly to soils along the coast, nor did barley become of importance in early times except in a few areas. Opinions differed as to quality. "Wheat and barley are not thought to be as good as these grains in England," wrote a Bay colonist to an English friend, "but Rye and Pease are as good as the English. Beans also there are very good." Captain John Underhill was of a different mind. In 1638 he reported "in the Bay as good English grain as can grow in any part of the world." [4]

Regardless of ill success, farmers continued to experiment with wheat as soon as land could be got into fit condition, for that was the grain for which English stomachs hankered. Wheat had a second merit. As soon as necessity drove the colony to exporting, it became a staple that traders could readily sell: so it was made receivable for taxes. As a result, even Salem farmers eventually began to harvest some wheat. On Cape Cod also wheat was sown: the better fields there might yield 15 to 20 bushels to the acre. Nevertheless conditions on the coast were seldom fully congenial for it. In 1646 caterpillars attacked both wheat and barley; deer trespassed upon the fields; and after a few years black stem rust appeared. By mid-century it had become clear that for the great part of the colonies the

combination of "rye and Injun" must become New England's
main reliance for bread. It was a combination that proved
satisfactory and remained popular into the twentieth century.

Before the end of the first decade the towns earliest settled
had encouraged millers to construct wind and water mills. Town
meetings offered special inducements in land grants and tax
exemption, for millers and millwrights were never plentiful. Yet
a century and a half would have to pass before the quern or
Indian mortar in which grain was pounded by hand, as well as
the hand sieve to sift out the flour, could be completely given up
in frontier settlements.

At least one belt of soil did prove well fitted for European
grains, however: the many miles of alluvial terraces bordering
the Connecticut River from Middletown north. As this rich
valley began increasingly to draw settlement, the dream of the
colonies' governing bodies of wheat as an exportable staple, to be
sold for silver and gold or imported commodities, became more
fully a practical reality. The Pynchons, traders of Springfield,
might sometimes ship as much as 2,000 bushels to Boston, a large
amount when reaped with a sickle and threshed by hand. The
Connecticut Valley, therefore, has been called the continent's
first wheat belt. As time passed, the Valley's wheat area was to
shift steadily northward. In 1644 "the blast took hold of
Connecticut and New Haven" and wheat spoiled, but Indian
corn, barley, pease, and rye were spared. Since the disease spread
slowly, new land up river continued for several decades to grow
wheat to be shipped to Boston and elsewhere. Hadley, Massachusetts, for example, raised wheat: scarcely sowed rye at all until
1685.[5]

Next to wheat, barley was the desired crop. Englishmen felt
that they must have beer, though after a generation or two in
New England the settlers decided that cider would do as well.
Barley was also good for bread and broth. Oats did only fairly;
less adaptable than rye, it filled out poorly.

Despite success here and there, it took only a few years of
disappointment with European cereals, during which the native
maize provided regular harvests, to prove without question that

Indian corn was to be king in New England. Englishmen might not take to it with enthusiasm, but from necessity all the settlements learned to grow and eat it. Their hogs and poultry, less finicky, enjoyed it whenever they could get at it. Not only was maize a reliable yielder of grain, excellent food for man and a superior ration for poultry and animals, but its stalks if cut at the proper time could furnish palatable winter fodder for the cattle that were so important to New England farming.

A special advantage to corn growing was that alewives to fertilize it found their way naturally far inland, up every stream with a pond at its head; while at the shore it would thrive on either fish or king crabs. Wherever animal manure was available, this likewise grew good corn.[6] In new settlements the ability of corn to do well on unplowed fields under hoe culture alone was especially valuable. "The chiefest Corne they planted before they had Plowes was Indian Graine," said Johnson; but, he added, at first anything beyond four or five acres was rare.

Corn did have disadvantages. Dogs played havoc with fish in the fields and had to be hobbled for three or four weeks till the fish rotted. The fence around the common cornfield must be kept tight or cattle would spread ruin. Important officers in each town, therefore, were the haywards (hedge wards) or fence viewers, already mentioned, who saw to it that each villager kept his section of fence in sound condition. Birds did such damage that town authorities required each householder to kill a dozen blackbirds and three crows annually.

Yet corn was not hard to raise. Like their Indian tutors, the settlers waited till the white oak leaves reached the size of a mouse's ear before planting. After it was up, cultivation was the next step, to control the inevitable weeds. At first, and in primitive settlements for a long time, tillage was by hoe alone; but by 1637 the Bay Colony could count up to thirty-seven plows, each able to turn over an acre or more a day of tilled land, and oxen had been trained to draw them. After the corn was up, where plows were available, two successive light plowings, the furrow thrown toward the row, would cover the weeds.[7] Harvesting was simple: ears were left on the stalk till well ripened, picked at a convenient time and drawn to the farm yard for husking, and the stock then turned into the field to clean up all that was left.

Growing grains and planting gardens and orchards were by no means the only pressing early duties. Another immediate need was fuel. Since most villages were laid out as far as possible on or adjoining land left open by the Indians, the nearest firewood might well be at a distance, an eighth of a mile, for example, at Plymouth's beginning. Thus getting fuel for daily cooking and enough for the winter fireplace was in itself no small task. A second essential was water for household needs, often from a common spring. The cutting and curing of salt and fresh meadow hay for winter feed for stock was another absolutely necessary labor, and still no place to store it when secured except in stacks in the open. Truly the burdens of existence must have appeared endless.

To carry out such tasks some of the better-off colonists had brought along young relatives, or indentured servants who had bound themselves to work for seven years for board, lodging, and a modest reward at the end. Others bought from shipmasters the terms of service of persons who had indentured themselves to the captain to pay their passage. Some free laborers had come also; but wages were high, and it was chiefly wealthy planters such as those at Cambridge and New Haven who could afford to hire them. At both Plymouth and the Bay some proved too lazy to work voluntarily and had to be forced to do so.[8]

Getting in the harvest was of such vital public importance that the authorities were obliged to step in, as they had on occasion done in Old England, and order mechanics and artisans to assist. The Bay General Court notified local constables in 1646 that because the harvest times of hay, corn, flax, and hemp usually came so close together, they were authorized to impress labor. In every town where the request was made to them, artificers and handicraftsmen could be required to work by the day for neighbors needing them, to mow, reap, and get the crops (for wages, however,) on penalty of a fine equal to two days' pay.[9]

Most farmers, nevertheless, depended on their own labor and that of their boys and girls, and on the help of neighbors.

Governor Winthrop set the example at the Bay, as had the Plymouth leaders. Says one of his friends, the governor "was a discreet and sober man . . . putting his hand to any ordinary labor with his servants." Roger Williams at Providence tells of his own work at planting.[10] Leading men in Connecticut likewise worked in their own fields, and so did many ministers.

Ordinary farmers shared with neighbors in the heavier tasks also, although this had disadvantages, one of which was offered by John Josselyn: "Many hands make light work . . . But many mouths eat up all." [11]

One sufferer in such a situation might well be the farm wife. The custom of English yeomanry was that she should not be called on to help in the field.[12] Her hands were already full with kitchen, dairy, perhaps poultry, and the vegetable garden. As wool-growing gradually increased and the colony authorities called for a flax patch in every household, the spinning wheel and weaving frame were added to her domain. Without running water, sometimes at first without even a fireplace chimney for cooking, and working largely with only wooden utensils, woman's lot was hard indeed.

So in this new land, despite the shirkers who distressed Governor Winthrop, hard manual labor was at first the lot of nearly all. Some, both women and men, died young. Yet a surprising number found both life and labor bearable, as a recent study of Plymouth Colony and another at Andover show, and some lived to a remarkable age.

Thus early began in New England the habit of industry on the part of all—a force that was to become a transcendent regional characteristic. By the end of the first decade the need for shelter was being met more satisfactorily. There were still temporary hovels in Bay Colony towns, dug into the sides of banks or hills and roofed over; and there were "wigwams," perhaps round, dome-roofed cabins like those of the Indians. Many families, however, had built framed houses, often of but one or two rooms yet with chimneys of plank or stone. Roofs at first were of thatch, till frequent fires caused authorities to ban them. Some householders, already established in larger dwellings and with wide acres and numerous cattle, were called rich.

Here and there mechanics were at their tasks. Smiths shaped iron tools on forges, tanners conditioned hides, cobblers tapped shoes, coopers hooped buckets and barrels. Village life was well begun.

6

Distance Beckons the Uneasy

ALL ALONG the winding Massachusetts Bay shore, wherever salt grass caught the eye, exploring stockmen were petitioning the General Court to be allowed to set up new townships. The adjoining upland might be only moderately fertile, even chiefly ledges and woods, yet cattlemen brought up amid England's grassy vales and tidal marshes coveted the salt hay in the lowlands. At Weymouth and Braintree on Massachusetts Bay's south shore and at Ipswich, Newbury, and Salisbury to the north, a list of applicants was assembled—heads of families of known good character and standing, who would agree to live there and support a town and minister—and the General Court had its commissioners mark out towns. Some of the planters of a new township were from older settlements, some newly arrived by ship. All had to be well vouched for. After the site had been examined by a trusted committee, the General Court formally authorized the town grant. Squatting and haphazard settlement were not permitted.[1]

Fresh-water marshes exhibited drawing power also. In addition to Concord, founded in 1635, and Sudbury on the Musketahquid in 1638, the alluvial grasses of the Charles brought Dedham into being in 1636, and later Medfield, further up river. Charlestown farmers followed the fertile Mystic Valley north to begin Medford and Woburn. The Nashua River meadows soon enticed settlers inland to Lancaster.

In Plymouth Colony the same magnet drew ambitious men toward new locations. Reluctantly the Plymouth authorities permitted their neighbors to leave the close-knit mother town and its scant fertility and set up new and distant farmsteads beside inviting hay lands. Duxbury, Green Harbor (Marshfield), and Hingham, their tidal marshes rich in salt hay, drew planters northward. The miles of green salt meadow on the Cape Cod shore and Indian fields there open for tillage beckoned still others to plant Sandwich, Barnstable, and Yarmouth, and to move inland to Taunton at the head of Mt. Hope Bay.[2]

It has already been recorded how, before the Massachusetts Bay migration, the trade in fish had caused commercial interests to locate agents and employees at the outlet of the Piscataqua River at what were to become Portsmouth and Dover, New Hampshire, and the nearby Maine coast. Speculative eyes soon turned to the neighboring forests also. In the early 1630's sawmills were set up and a start made in turning the splendid pine and oak of the Piscataqua watershed into merchantable lumber and spars.

Agriculture came as a natural development from all this. A London fish merchant, David Hilton, and his brother William had sat down at Dover Point beside the Piscataqua under a patent from the Council for New England. They raised grain on both the Maine and New Hampshire sides, and by 1632 had hogs also. That year two Piscataqua men, Thomas Commack and Edward Godfrey, freighted sixteen hogsheads of corn to Watertown in the Bay Colony for grinding.[3] In 1631 Mason and Gorges, as the Laconia Company, after vainly trying to develop Indian trade in the interior, received a patent in the same area. Eventually twenty-two women were numbered among the settlers. A company agent wisely wrote home that the capitalists could hardly expect good returns unless they furnished cattle as well as hired hands.[4]

In the course of three years the company landed several score of large yellow cattle at Cow Cove. A Virginian captain also arrived at Boston in 1633 with a load of 100 young cattle from St. Christopher, some of which he sold at Piscataqua, some at York, Maine. Unfortunately the chief mover of the Laconia enterprise, Captain John Mason, died. When his estate came to be settled, a hundred of the big yellow cattle were herded over the paths to Boston for sale by the manager of Mason's property (a fraudulent act on the part of Mason's agents, Sanborn's *History of New Hampshire* claims). There they brought twenty-five pounds sterling each, a price above the ordinary. A 1635 inventory of the Mason assets included, besides cattle, 40 horses, almost 200 sheep, and 54 goats. More cattle from Bristol reached this northeastern coast in 1636 and 1638. A deposition of a somewhat later period was to the effect that most of the cattle then found in Maine inherited some of the Mason cattle's blood.[5]

In 1638 the pleasant lands on the river entering Great Bay from the south attracted thirty-six families from Boston, among them at least two husbandmen. With their dissident pastor John Wheelwright, they founded Exeter, (New Hampshire). About the same time cattlemen newly arrived from England took over the immense salt marshes and inviting upland of what was to become Hampton, New Hampshire. In 1641 Dover and Portsmouth, till then self-governed, placed themselves under Massachusetts' jurisdiction.[6]

Further east, the Saco Valley soon counted 150 people. Near what is now Portland, Maine, Richmond Island and Cape Elizabeth had for a decade been harboring white inhabitants who raised Indian corn and pumpkins. They also tried vegetables and English grain—all cultivated by hand behind high, tight fences to keep out wild animals. Pigs multiplied, fed largely on fish waste. John Winter had seventy on Richmond Island in 1634 in connection with his fishing and farming enterprise and had provided shelter for them. But wolves and Indians made swine-keeping difficult except on islands offshore. Two years later Winter claimed that between them they had cost him two hundred porkers. Maine's earliest local court decreed death for either wolf or Indian if discovered and convicted. Though considerable farming went on, fish and timber were to remain for many years the chief props for people of the New Hampshire and Maine coasts.[7]

Estimable and high-principled as were the Massachusetts Bay leaders, they ruled with so stiff a hand that not all could bear it, and the Puritan hive around Boston and the Bay began early to swarm south to Rhode Island and inland to the Connecticut Valley. The first to leave had been the gentleman who bid Winthrop welcome, peace-loving Reverend William Blaxton, planter of New England's original orchard on the Shawmut peninsula that was to become Boston. In 1634 he sold his property on Trimountain's southwest slope to the newcomers, and, buying "a stock of cows" with the money, and taking with him apple seeds and little trees, found a new haven to the southward under the Plymouth Colony's patent.[8] On a hillside in what is now Cumberland, Rhode Island, at the foot of which flowed the river that today honors his name, Blaxton planted his second orchard. Sprouts from certain trees that he set out were still bearing Rhode Island Sweetings two centuries later. As time went on and he occasionally went in to Providence to preach, this good man would fill his saddlebag with apples to delight the children of that primitive settlement who had never before tasted them.[9]

Blaxton left Massachusetts Bay voluntarily, but others were pushed out. The year after he departed, the magistrates banished Roger Williams, teacher beloved by his Salem church. He headed southwest, first to Seekonk, where he did planting on Plymouth Colony soil. Then, following a friendly warning from Plymouth, he abandoned his venture there and with five companions in a canoe paddled west to found the town of Providence, not far from Blaxton's seat. A Londoner, Williams may never previously have farmed; but his friends the Indians must have taught him the necessary skills. Many a time, he wrote, "was my time spent at the hoe . . . for bread." [10] It is recorded that he planted with his own hands two former Indian fields, one in today's Roger Williams Park at Providence. Other malcontents joined him. Soon they had cattle, corn, and tobacco. Governor Winthrop remained his friend, and within a few years he and Williams had a joint herd of hogs rooting and clamming on Prudence Island in Narragansett Bay.[11]

On the excellent soil of the large island of Aquidneck on the Bay's east side, Mrs. Anne Hutchinson of Salem, likewise banished with her followers, sat down; they founded the prosperous farming villages of Portsmouth, Middletown, and Newport. Like the others they had cattle and hogs. For pasture they turned also to Conanicut Island, which the Indians had cleared. Hogs soon grew so numerous and troublesome that they had to be banished to uninhabited islands.[12]

Another restless soul, Samuel Gorton, with associates, by 1643 had settled on the west side of the Bay at Warwick. The Massachusetts Bay authorities claimed jurisdiction, however, and sent soldiers to dislodge him. The invaders found on his farm and those of his friends 80 head of cattle besides swine and goats, "which they divided among themselves." Through various devices a group of merchants had by 1658 acquired much of the land along the west shore of Narragansett Bay, hoping to profit from mining (which proved a chimera) and the pasturage there. In this area, soon to become the famous dairy region of "South County," a single estate was said to extend nine miles long and three wide. From such unrelated and somewhat fortuitous happenings Rhode Island's prosperous colonial agriculture had its beginnings.[13]

The removal of dissidents to Rhode Island was to prove less important agriculturally, however, than the emigration of other uneasy colonists to the wide and fertile intervales of the Connecticut Valley. The Plymouth authorities and the New Amsterdam Hollanders had both been eyeing the river as an opening for settlement, agriculture, and the fur trade. Learning from the visiting sachem Wahquimmacut of the attractions of the broad valley with its open meadows, in the fall of 1632 Plymouth sent Edward Winslow to take a look. In June of the next year the Hollanders from New Amsterdam appeared and built a fort at what was to become Hartford.

Ignoring their threats, a Plymouth expedition sailed by and started a trading post and settlement of their own upriver on land that they bought from the Indians at the confluence of the Farmington River. In the fall of 1634 appeared John Oldham with ten followers from Watertown at Massachusetts Bay and sat down at Wethersfield, below the Dutch. Oldham's group, so far as records show, appear to have been the first Europeans to stir the soil in Connecticut; they sowed rye, presumably "hacking it

in" with hand tools, on one of the untenanted Indian fields. The
next year brought several small groups from the Bay with cattle
and swine, one sitting down close to the Plymouth people at
Windsor. Besides these, others claiming the land under a patent
came up from Saybrook at the river's mouth. Winter drove most
of the adventurers from the Bay back to their old homes.
"Otherwise," explains Winthrop in his history, "they had all
perished as some did." With the help of the Plymouth people and
the local Indians a few hardy ones stuck the winter out. Some of
the cattle, roaming the meadows on the east side, lived well all
winter without human care. Altogether, however, so much stock
perished that the financial loss was heavy.[14]

Undiscouraged, in the following May (1636) a Newe-Towne
(Cambridge) minister, Reverend Thomas Hooker, led out a
hundred of his parishioners to the inviting green valley. His
followers were persons dissatisfied with the shortage of pasture at
Newe-Towne, upset spiritually, or both. They followed the
ancient Indian way that led southwest, known to this day as the
"Old Connecticut Path." The long cavalcade included men,
women, and children, and the pastor's delicate wife in a litter.
They also drove 160 cattle, baiting them on the spring herbage,
their milk sustaining the little ones night and morning. What
with straggling cattle and tender children the procession was
fourteen days on the 120-mile road to their new homes at
Hartford and Windsor. Among the stock were six cows, four
steers, and a bull, that Governor Winthrop sent along to his son
at Saybrook at the mouth of the Connecticut, where he had been
named governor under a patent to Lord Say and Sele.[15]

The first duty of the newcomers before winter was to throw
up palisades and temporary shelter for their families. Man and
beast both found the new life hard going. "Things went not well
at Connecticut," wrote Governor Winthrop at the autumn's end.
Some cattle died and many cast their young, as had the cattle of
the year before. Apparently the new arrivals planted some rye
that fall.

Undaunted, these determined colonizers stuck the next
winter out, and so did their wives and the stock. Building shelters
and caring for families and livestock left little chance that season

for tillage. Women had to be cautioned against feeding seed grain to poultry and hogs. But it all paid off. By 1638 Pastor Hooker could write back to the Bay that his own eight cattle never did better than last year. So things improved. A Hartford farmer who died in 1640 had 13 cattle, 3 horses, 13 goats, and 13 swine, 160 bushels of Indian corn, 30 bushels of summer wheat, and 12 of pease. Another (called "average"), dying in 1641, left 4 cows, 3 goats, 8 hogs, 5 acres of Indian corn, an acre each of wheat, oats, and meslin, and some pease and barley.[16]

More western settlements began. At the mouth of the Quinnipiac River on Long Island Sound wealthy London merchants were attracted by the harbor and the possibilities of trade. Though lacking any patent, in 1638 they built themselves large dwellings, started a mercantile town, New Haven, and set up an independent government. Near them a few Yorkshire farmers established homesteads. West of New Haven, at the mouth of the Housatonic, Hertfordshire families chose tillable fields to begin Milford. To the east, a group of farmers from Kent and Surrey in 1639 sat down beside the shore at Guilford. Both Milford and Guilford were for a time self-governed. A group of restless families from Concord found Fairfield. This town and adjoining Stratford acknowledged the authority of Connecticut, as the three valley towns, now organized as a government, were called. Not until 1662 did Connecticut get a royal charter and annex New Haven and the rest—at which time some dissidents left for New Jersey! Again and again the newcomers began with the benefit of fields long used and fertilized by Indian predecessors, or settled beside natural meadows.[17]

Up the Connecticut at Hartford the earliest settlers, hankering for cider, started apple trees. Among these was an English Pearmain tree that in 1853, two centuries later, still bore fruit. Bent also on improving its neat stock, Hartford soon appointed a committee to pick out promising calves to be saved for breeding. In another important initiative, Hartford, Windsor, and Wethersfield drew up and adopted the famous "Fundamental Orders" that were to protect the political rights of Connecticut citizens for generations.

Further north on the same Connecticut River one of

Massachusetts Bay Colony's enterprising leaders, William Pynchon, with a dozen families, made a bold start on the silt terraces
of Agawam. They had driven stock from Roxbury by Indian
trails the hundred-odd miles across Massachusetts. Almost at
once the cattle and hogs made trouble by feeding on the
unfenced cornfields of the local Indians, and the settlement had
to be moved across the river to the less attractive meadows of the
east bank at what was to become Springfield.

Pynchon's main object was at first not farming but trade
with the Indians for furs. When Connecticut River towns in 1638
ran short of food, he bought 500 bushels of corn for them out of
the surplus of the Pocumtucks, up river at Deerfield, and boated
it down. These Springfield pioneers, however, were good livestock men. Their hogs multiplied. Black pigs, they learned from
experience, had a better chance running loose than those of sand
color: wolves were apt to mistake the cream-colored ones for
fawns. Roaming in the woods and fields, swine soon acquired
speed, and the old boars among them would tackle a wolf with
their tusks and make him sorry. The fur business eventually
proved less of a resource than the traders hoped; but hogs started
to pay, and Pynchon and his son soon were salting pork into
barrels for export to the islands of the far-away Caribbean.[18] His
son John went into cattle also. Settlement continued to push up
the fruitful valley into Northampton, Hadley, Hatfield, Deerfield, and Northfield, eventually to spill over into what is now
Vermont and New Hampshire. Livestock farmers of the Bay
Colony found other promising intervales, and soon towns were
begun at Andover and at Newbury and Haverhill on the
Merrimack.

The continual search for hay had now carried stockmen to
every salt marsh along the Massachusetts Bay coast, across New
Hampshire and well into Maine, to both sides of Cape Cod, both
shores of Narragansett Bay and its islands, and along much of the
Sound shore, as well as into inland valleys.

As the 1630 decade ended, villages dotted southern New
England's coasts and its principal river valleys. Most of them
were small; but with Boston they housed perhaps 20,000 or more
people of English origin. The farmers among them were well

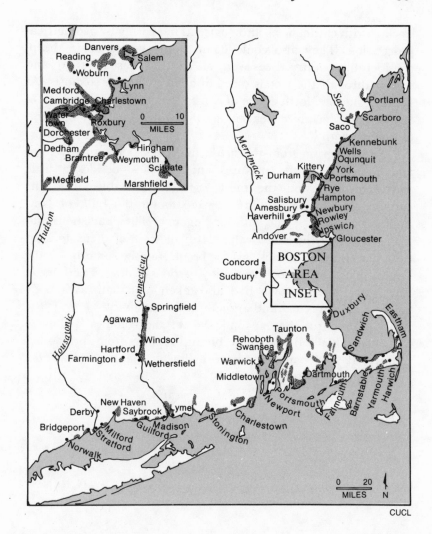

6. *This map (based on U.S. Geodetic surveys) illustrates the importance to the English colonists of available feed for their cattle. The site of every town named (all settled by 1650) adjoined natural salt or fresh hay marsh. The marsh offered the prospect that by breeding livestock the village could live and prosper (as all did). Cartography Laboratory, Clark University.*

stocked with cattle, hogs, and goats, all increasing by geometrical progression. They also could count many horses, some sheep, considerable poultry. Bees were on hand at least by 1639, and spread through the woods often in advance of the colonists. At Rowley, on the North Shore of Massachusetts Bay, from wool of local sheep, Yorkshire weavers in 1638 wove America's first bolt of woolen cloth.[19]

So with grain from the fields, and beef, pork, milk, butter, and cheese from the pastures and marshes, besides a little cultivated fruit and the most essential vegetables from the garden, the end of the first decade found the bulk of New England country people with food enough. They had shelter for themselves and the more valuable or delicate of their stock. A few, like Lady Fenwick at Saybrook by the mouth of the Connecticut, could soon even enjoy gardens of flowers and herbs. The New England town had also taken root, both as a body politic and as a social and agricultural community.

Up to 1640, the economic life of the colonies had been influenced chiefly by immigration and supplies from the mother country. It was soon to undergo a drastic change of direction, and farming with it.

7

To Market, to Market

THE BAY COLONY's first depression was occasioned, though not caused, by tremendous political changes in England. With the problems that the economic crisis brought, the people of New England, including the newly established farmers among them, began to reveal a trait that again and again was to keep them solvent in the centuries to follow. This was the ability to hang on while they adapted practices and products to altered conditions.

About 1640, with the calling of the Long Parliament in England, followed by civil war, immigration of new planters and inflow of their cash capital to New England dropped to a trickle. A speculative market for livestock and commodities created by the sale of these necessaries to newcomers arriving with money to spend had been to the first comers a harvest, to quote William Bradford's words. Now this prosperity collapsed. It became difficult to dispose of goods, cattle, and improved land and buildings. The sale value of animals dropped to a quarter of what they had brought during the great migration, and the General Court had to set a price on corn and make it legal tender. Even at low prices, stock was hard to sell. Plymouth Colony farmers who had prospered by supplying Bay newcomers with stock lost their outlet. Butter and cheese had for some time been cheaper than in England, but now grain that settlers had begun to find profitable fell in price. Merchants could no longer move imported goods. Everywhere trade languished.[1]

Yet in real assets—available timber, fish, livestock, and

agricultural produce which, rather than currency, constituted true wealth—the country still abounded. Moreover, as always, low prices opened possibilities. Though England itself offered a poor market, due in part to political troubles, the wars in Europe which disrupted business for merchants of that continent opened opportunities to New World traders. The eyes of the leaders of the Bay Colony turned southward. Virginia, first settled in 1607, had begun to raise tobacco by 1612 and to export it a few years later. It soon became that colony's almost sole crop. The rapid increase of plantations in the West Indies concentrating on sugar offered ambitious New England traders a market for surplus meat, grain, and livestock. Ships were needed to develop such a commerce; but New England was favored with a wealth of shipbuilding resources, as well as with a great number of safe, deep, and accessible harbors.

Its colonists, not only merchants by profession but farmers and tradesmen, had come to the New World experienced in buying, selling, and trading grain, wool, horses, stock, poultry, dairy products, and other produce at the 800 fairs and markets held regularly in every part of the English realm. Many a New England settlement was named after such a market town. In easttern England, at places where marsh hay was abundant, stockmen had made a business of buying in cattle from a distance to fatten, then selling them to drovers and butchers for the London market. In England's eastern and southern counties, a constant trade in wool and cloth for export had gone on for generations. Buyers regularly came to Kent and the Severn Valley for fruit.[2]

So trade in stock and produce was an old story to many a New Englander. Already a lively commerce had grown up between the well-established planters of Plymouth Colony and the new arrivals at the Bay, and both had carried on frequent transactions with New Amsterdam. Thus when the local economy languished, nothing could be more natural than to look abroad for markets, as well as to consider what imports could be dispensed with.

Governor Winthrop's journal recites the measures adopted. "These straits set our people on work to provide fish, clapboards, plank etc. and to sow hemp and flax (which prospered very well) and to look out to the West Indies for a trade for cotton. The general court also made orders about payment of debts, setting corn at the wonted prices, and payable for all debts which should arise after a time prefixed." [3] With matters at home thus stabilized, the colony looked abroad for new income.

In 1641 enterprising men at Salem, Charlestown, and New Haven began to build vessels. With ships on the stocks, the numerous ship carpenters and mechanics whose names had appeared in the rosters of immigrant passengers had a chance to use their skills. Already Salem had a ropewalk to provide rigging. Alert Connecticut speculators began to scar the bark of the trees of its pine forests to gather tar and pitch for the ships. At Amesbury in 1641 Sam Winslow started work on a contract for 30,000 pipestaves each year, presumably to be shipped to Spanish ports for wine. Connecticut that same year authorized Wethersfield to ship out 30,000; Hartford and Windsor, 20,000 each. To ensure uniformity in their export as shooks (the pieces to form a complete barrel or box assembled in a bundle), Connecticut in 1641 and Massachusetts two years later established standards of quality.

Sawmills were at work. One is reported very early at York, Maine; by 1660 Maverick tells of mills at Manchester in Massachusetts and at Exeter, Dover, and on the branches of the Piscataqua River in New Hampshire. The area thus had lumber, spars, and masts for export along with fish and farm produce. Connecticut woodsmen split oak and pine for clapboards which New Haven merchants sent to the Canary Islands. Salt fish for the Catholic countries of Europe and for the West Indies went to market in barrels, the staves and hoops for which were cut not far inland. By 1643 a Boston ship set sail for Spain loaded with New England grain.

Nature gave assistance to budding trade. A drought in the West Indies brought demands for foods that New England was happy to supply. As Winthrop put it in his *History* in 1647: "It pleased the Lord to open to us a trade with Barbados and other islands . . ." That year Boston sent Barbados a deckload of horses; the next year one of cattle; in the same year New Netherland came to New Haven for beef. Meanwhile, in 1645,

20,000 bushels of grain had gone out, and export of grain grew so vigorous that in the spring of 1648 Massachusetts had temporarily to forbid its shipment to the West Indies, Portugal, and the Spanish islands in order not to go short herself. The ban was soon lifted, but the next year the colony had to stop export of mares, lest its reservoir of horseflesh dry up. Through the 1650's trade in commodities of many sorts grew fast. Providence merchants, for example, sent tobacco to Boston, which reshipped it to London. A whole ton went to Newfoundland, the settlers there finding it more advantageous to fish than to farm in the island's brief summer.

The result of all this enterprise soon showed in work for all and a market for every type of farm produce. Carpenters and mechanics were fully employed on dwellings, barns, shipping. "Now it is wonderfull," exclaimed Maverick in 1660 (he had preceded the Puritans to Boston Harbor), "to see the many Vessels belonging to the Country of all sorts and seizes from Shipps of some reasonable burthen to Skiffes and Cannoes, many other great Shipps of Burthen from 350 Tunns to 150 have been built there, and many more in time may be." Merchants were taking in European coined money and Spanish bar silver. They bought lumber for sale. They collected flour, meat, and vegetables from the country to provide food for the crews, whether engaged in distant foreign trade, or manning the hundreds of smaller vessels that were soon taking fish off Cape Sable. Bakers set up shop not only to bake bread from the farmers' grain for townspeople, but to bake hard "bisquits" to feed sailors and residents of tropic islands a thousand miles away.[4] For the sale of animals and farm produce towns like Hartford, Charlestown, Salem, Lynn, and others authorized local market days weekly or oftener.

In 1652 Massachusetts even set up its own mint. The early days of scarcity were over. Domestic animals of all kinds had increased remarkably. The tropical islands and the tobacco plantations of the southern colonies offered established markets for salt beef and salt pork, and the Catholic countries of Europe bought quantities of salt fish. Even a small farm could turn an extra cow or two into imported clothing for the family. Some beasts were slaughtered in the towns where they grew, but from the Ipswich and Newbury meadows, drovers brought fat cattle to Salem to be butchered.

In the Connecticut Valley the Pynchons of Springfield dealt in hogs and cattle, stall-feeding the latter. They drove some stock down river to slaughter them and pack their meat on Warehouse Point, at the edge of salt water, where it was made ready for shipment to the West Indies. From the prolific pastures and grain fields of Hadley and Hatfield, they herded other beef cattle overland to the Bay's busy markets. Stockmen drove in animals from New Hampshire, and others came by sea from as far west as Milford, Connecticut. From his farm at Stonington, in eastern Connecticut, Thomas Minor drove a mixed herd up to Boston. Some of them never reached the slaughterhouse, for his diary records that in a thunderstorm four of his swine took refuge under a tree where lightning forestalled the butcher.

Cattle had now become plentiful everywhere, though it was an unusual farmer whose total including young stock exceeded twelve or fifteen. Dorchester, Dedham, and Watertown counted 400 each, and soon Watertown had enough to compose four town herds. Cambridge, with over 600, was the leading cow town of the Bay Colony. Even Charlestown, busy with commerce, had 400. To the eastward, Hampton with its marsh hay herded 450 cattle. Johnson, in 1654, estimated for the Bay Colony a total of 12,000 kine. Swine, he said, were innumerable. (The correct word would have been unnumbered.) All in all, "It is a wonder," comments Maverick in 1660, "to consider how many thousand neat beasts and hogs are yearly killed and have been for many years past for Provision in the Country and sent abroad to supply Newfoundland, Barbados and Jamaica." [5]

Boston and Salem people needed other supplies besides meat. Winthrop farmers, for example, sent butter and cheese across the harbor on a regular schedule. Cheese and sometimes even butter, presumably well salted, were included in the supplies of ships destined for far ports.

The effect of this burgeoning trade is described by Samuel Maverick from his farm on Noddle's Island, as he looks across at Boston: "The Towne is full of good shopps well furnished with all kind of merchandize and many Artificers and Trad'smen of all sorts." The influence of improved trade, he notes, has spread into the smaller towns. A dozen miles to the north, at "Wooburne" "They live by furnishing the Sea townes with Provisions as Corne and Flesh and also furnish the Merchants with such goods to be exported." To the southwest: "in Dedham live many Bisquett makers and Butchers and have vent enough for their Commodities in Boston."

Braintree raises provisions and furnishes Boston with wood; Weymouth likewise. Neighboring Hingham is already "a handsome Towne" supplying Boston with wood, timber, leather, boards, masts, and provisions. Even from Rehoboth in Plymouth Colony, 40 miles to the south on waters opening into Narragansett Bay, "there is a Comon trade, carrying and recarrying goods by land in Cart and on Horseback, and they have a very fayre conveyance of goods by water also," despite the long voyage around Cape Cod.

In the Old Colony of Plymouth, farmers of late-settled towns such as Duxbury and Barnstable, fortified by their wide stretches of salt marsh, have built up large populations of cattle, the chief market for which is with their northern neighbors.[6]

In the Connecticut Valley grain abounded. Some stockmen had embarked on the profitable English custom of finishing the hogs of others for market. Western Rhode Island by 1661 had horses as a staple exportable to the West Indies, often through Boston, the chief horse mart. In June 1669 Thomas Minor of Stonington recorded in his diary, how he set forth for Boston on a Monday, sold his string of horses and got home Saturday. Such horses for the West Indies were intended not to draw plows but to transport people and goods on their backs or to power treadmills for crushing sugar cane.[7]

Massachusetts, Plymouth Colony, Rhode Island, and Connecticut all raised horses for export. In Massachusetts two farmers out of three had horses, at least a mare. Horses at first were small, perhaps such as today's visitor to England finds grazing wild in the New Forest near Southampton, but better blood was introduced. Grown often cheaply by running more or less wild in pasture, they had to be identified by the owner's brand, required by law. A considerable number could be packed on the deck of a moderate-sized "horse jockey," as the export vessels came to be called. The animals sold so well in the tropics that it became profitable to steal and drive them to some sequestered landing for export.[8]

In 1652, besides horses, pease, beef, pork, and dairy products, Rhode Island was raising tobacco. Connecticut was growing tobacco as well as cattle for sale in New Amsterdam and Newfoundland.

From New England, Manhattan was receiving in 1661 beef, sheep, flour, biscuit, malt, butter, cider apples, iron, tar, and wampum. When a British naval expedition set out to capture Jamaica in 1655, New England was able to provision the ships.

So agricultural trade built up. Small packets plied from inland estuaries and every little harbor along the coast to Boston, Charlestown, Newport, and Manhattan, where larger ones assembled cargoes for distant markets. Almost every day two packets sailed between Scituate and Boston. New London, New Haven, and Milford, Connecticut, traders sent vessels to both Boston and Manhattan. New London gathered hides, furs, and the skins of wild animals, and ordinary farm produce. Wethersfield's chief product so far was pipestaves. Warehouse Point at the Connecticut River falls received the produce of the upper valley. Boston and Plymouth merchants complained that Connecticut Valley grain flooded their markets, and in 1650 New Netherland's Secretary reported to Holland that the Dutch colonists could buy all kinds of livestock from New England more cheaply than from overseas. Little coasting boats carried almost everything. A Martha's Vineyard vessel wrecked among the Elizabeth Islands in 1667 had aboard, according to William Weeks, its commander, "48 bu. Indian corne, fower barrels of pork, 4 hydes, 1 firkin of buter, 1 small casks of suett about 40ᵉ, on(e) barrel of tobacco, about 34 or 35 cotton wool; 26 bushells meale, 8 bushells of it wheate meale, the rest Rye or Indian meale; 1 bushell wheate, 1 bushell of Rye, 2 bushells turnepps, one bushell of Inions." [9]

All this active trade had wide ramifications, with eventual results not then to be imagined. While Boston and Salem built their trade in beef and pork for the West Indies, the wealth of hides and skins accumulated by slaughterhouses close by led readily, as it had in Old England, to tanning, the making of shoes, and their export, so that it was natural that Massachusetts should become shoemaker to the new continent.

Export of pipestaves became inextricably tied to imports of molasses, and its distillation into rum; which became the staple of the African slave trade. Thus do the patterns of history become woven and interwoven.

Besides the animals and crops that farmers grew, the third crop, wood and lumber, deserves further discussion. The forest was especially helpful because it furnished winter employment. Timber was sometimes the product of individual properties but was often cut legally by permission or illegally without it, from undivided town commons, even from highways. Its first use, naturally, was at home for building materials, fencing, and farm tools, and for the needs of local artisans—the bark, for example, was used by tanners. Immense quantities of wood were burned in fireplaces for heating and cooking.

Shipbuilders of Portsmouth, Medford, and New London required the best of oak and pine for their vessels. As time went on, newly built vessels replaced wrecked and wornout ships; others were sold abroad. As New England's trade expanded, shipbuilding offered a growing market for forest products.

Lumber went as cargo also: barrels in which salt fish, beef, pork, and many other goods were exported; shooks and hoops for hogsheads, in which to bring back molasses; or pipestaves for Madeira wine. Entire cargoes were of clapboards. With other cargo in the hold, a deckload of sawn boards and plank—even the frame and siding of an entire house—might be added. Long spars were cut not merely to rig the ship itself but for sale to foreign riggers. Maverick tells, for example, how the town of Hingham in 1660 was supplying Boston with not only wood, timber, and boards but masts as well, from its pine plains.

With the straight, tall pine of southern Maine and New Hampshire to draw on (Maine's first sawmill is said to date from 1633 or 1634), Portsmouth became a great lumber port. An incoming vessel might leave its imported cargo at Boston, then at Portsmouth take on a new lading of lumber and perhaps cattle, together with furs, salt meat, and salt fish. England's timber was becoming scarce. The war with Holland in 1652, which cut off her Baltic Sea sources of wood, gave an extra fillip to New England's lumber trade. Merchants began to buy into sawmills. The less valuable cordwood went to Boston and Salem to keep town dwellings warm and their bread baked. Firewood might come direct from nearby towns by oxcart, or from all along the shore in little wood boats that sailed for fish in summer.[10]

A further source of forest income was the preparation of charcoal for the furnaces of the iron bloomeries that soon developed at Saugus, Taunton, and other locations where bog iron ore was found. These furnaces bought enormous amounts of wood, to be turned into charcoal by professional colliers.[11] As early as 1643 another industry had opened: tapping evergreen forests for naval stores: pitch and tar.

Yet such wholesale use of wood already caused misgivings. The notion that in colonial New England the forest was wantonly destroyed is completely contradicted by the public records of the time. On the contrary, measures were taken almost from the beginning to conserve the woodlands. Many settlers had come from areas of England where wood was scarce and furze and faggots had to be used to cook the meals. Fifteen English counties were practically destitute of timber by the time of New England's settlement, and forest laws were strict and penalties severe.[12] By English standards, the woodland of New England's shore was truly plentiful. Yet the settlers deliberately chose for their early towns sites such as Plymouth, Boston, Cambridge, Concord, Hartford, Milford, Fairfield, Springfield, and Newport, to name but a few where the Indians had cultivated or at least partially deforested. The newcomers therefore acted almost at once to preserve a resource the value of which for farming, shipbuilding and commerce they well knew from experience.

Plymouth Colony levied duties on the export of boards, plank and staves. The Bay towns promptly established public controls to regulate the cutting of wood on their undivided common land: Cambridge and Watertown, for example, in 1634; Salem in 1636; Springfield, 1638; Boston, 1639; Amesbury and Exeter (New Hampshire), 1640; the General Court of New Haven, 1641. In Plymouth and in Connecticut Colony indiscriminate cutting was forbidden. Collection of pitch and tar was permitted by towns only for a consideration; it was allowed at Simsbury by 1643, but many towns forbade it altogether. Towns were especially strict with regard to cutting for fencing, staves and hoops and stripping bark for tanning where export from the town was intended. A river town, Medfield, beside the Charles, by 1664 went to the extent of forbidding the fencing of meadow land if a ditch would serve to control the stock. Official wood-reeves enforced local wood-cutting orders. Shade trees on highways were often especially protected.[13]

On the other hand, some towns authorized burning under control at particular periods to keep pasture land clear for stock feeding. In 1665 John Kilburne was employed to burn the woods along the Connecticut River from Wethersfield to Middletown "at such a time as may be most convenient for the advantage of the town."[14] Plymouth also allowed discreet woods burning. Yet all in all it is clear that seventeenth-century towns considered their woodlands valued assets. With livestock and fish, the woods became a cornerstone of New England's trade and prosperity for two centuries.

One more facet of economic life needs explanation. Increasing trade required market places and some medium of exchange. Sale of cargoes to Spain, Portugal, and the West Indies brought considerable hard currency into the ports, but little of it filtered through to farming towns. With no banks and no local currency except beaver-skin tokens (in the Connecticut Valley) and wampum, which served the Valley and the Long Island Sound area into the eighteenth century, most transactions were by exchange of goods and notes. In 1640 Zaccheus Gould of Salem leased 300 acres from John Humfrey, agreeing to pay as rent 400 bushels of rye, 300 of wheat, 200 of barley, 8 oxen, 5 cows, 2 heifers, 4 calves, and 2 mares. On March 6, 1676, William Prichard of Quaboag Plantation agreed to drive two cattle to Boston to pay part of his father's debt to John Pynchon. In 1662 a bushel of turnips at Newbury would pay for a cord of oak firewood. In 1668 Peleg Sanford, Newport merchant, shipped pork, beef, peas, butter, and four horses to his brother in Barbados, to be paid for in rum, molasses, and cotton wool. From

Connecticut, John Winthrop Jr.'s passage to England cost 500 bushels of wheat and 300 of pease. In Rhode Island tobacco served as a useful medium, in Plymouth Colony, corn.[15]

During the crisis of 1640, when the depression struck, the Massachusetts Bay General Court attempted to establish prices for the exchange of produce, commodities, and labor. When this proved difficult, the burden was passed on to town authorities. Thereafter each town set values for the chief items involved in mercantile transactions, wages, and the payment of taxes.

In Amesbury, for example, the town meeting or selectmen the next year set legal prices on butter, milk, grain, clapboard, sawn board, labor, and other commodities. Ministers and schoolmasters received their pay in corn, wheat, meat, and fuel; town taxes were payable in grain at fixed ratios. Roxbury in 1667 set Indian corn at 3 shillings a bushel, peas at 3 shillings 8 pence, rye at 4 shillings, barley and malt at 4 shillings 6 pence.[16] Differences in weight and quality of grain and commodities made for uncertainties and disagreements, and as time went on, inflation or surpluses of produce caused further difficulty. To make easier the settlement of such disagreements, Massachusetts in 1652 set up a Council For Trade; but suits for unpaid balances and disputed amounts remained common. To make trade fairer, the General Courts of Connecticut and Massachusetts required towns to appoint sealers of weights and measures and examiners of all commonly traded commodities such as pipestaves, biscuits, fish, hides, leather, and lumber; and of containers such as casks for pitch and turpentine. By 1660 Connecticut provided that every horse exported be registered.[17]

These measures were far from adequate, yet despite all difficulties trade in farm produce grew and prospered, so that in his almanac of 1648 Samuel Danforth crowed:

> Few think, who only hear, but do not see
> That plenty groweth much upon this tree . . .
> That heaps of wheat, pork, bisket, beef and beer
> Masts, pipestaves, fish should store both far and near
> Which fetch in wines, cloth, sweets and good tobacc
> O be contented then, you cannot lack[18]

8

Patterns from Home

CHAPTER 7 HAS SHOWN the effect of one sort of experience that New England's settlers, farmers and nonfarmers alike, had brought with them from across the sea: the ability when the need appeared to adapt themselves to trade and to an increasingly commercial type of agriculture such as many of them must already have been well accustomed to in their old homes in Essex, Kent, and close to busy London. Almost from the outset a controlling factor in New England farm economy was the available markets.

A second important factor in shaping the character of rural New England, also founded on the colonists' experience in Old England, was the laying out and distribution of the land, and the methods developed for stocking and managing it. For these, certain immemorial customs still powerful at the time in much of England, especially in Wiltshire and the midland counties, set the general pattern. This pattern was destined to be modified by more recent developments in the land tenure and practice of East Anglia, Kent, and similar progressive areas from which part of the settlers had emigrated. To these traditional methods, trial and error under New World conditions were bound to bring certain modifications. In New England as in Old, however, village government was one important basis of the whole.

New England settlement, except for the earliest founded communities and Rhode Island, went on according to well-

defined plans. In all the territory under control of the Massachusetts Bay and the Connecticut colonies, once the original
landings were over, the pattern was set by the colony's General
Court. Plymouth Colony also did its best to keep a tight rein on
where its people lived and farmed, though its land system tended
at an early date more to individual than to community
management. In no colony were would-be settlers expected or for
long permitted to squat in spots of their own choosing.

The underlying principle was that title to the whole
country, both land and water, rested in the king. Out of his
bounty he made grants, not always carefully defined as to extent,
to certain corporations and individuals, the latter generally
highly placed. These persons or corporations in turn were to
provide capital and inhabitants to develop their territories, and
decide terms of settlement not specified in the charter. Charter
terms varied from one colony to another, being quite different in
the southern colonies from those of New England.

Since the present treatise is primarily agricultural, legal
details of the various charters granted for New England will be
omitted except as they directly concern farm people and their
livelihood. The charter of the Massachusetts Bay Colony and the
actions taken under it will serve as the prototype, since it not
only affected the organization of most of New England but
produced a pattern that for two centuries was to exert wide
influence on the development of communities in much of what
became the northern United States.

Absence of one customary provision from its charter made
the Massachusetts Bay Company decisively different from earlier
colonization enterprises. The location for the conduct of the
company's affairs was not specified. The colony was therefore
doubly fortunate. Not only were the leaders of the migration
persons of superior character and experience, but they brought
their charter, the document itself, with them to the New World.
Citing its authority as they interpreted it, they at once established the colony's governing body on the new soil, instead of
attempting, as had other grantees, to control its operations from
England. The effects were immediate.[1]

From Boston, the capital of the actual territory to be

administered, the Company's General Court authorized and directed the establishment of each new town; specified its limits; decided who the proprietors of its lands should be; and set forth the powers and duties of its inhabitants and local magistrates. The Court's control was extended at first even to the towns that the Court authorized in Connecticut, later to New Hampshire and Maine, and the attempt was made to include Rhode Island.

Concord, first town to be established inland on fresh water, may serve as an example of how the Court proceeded with the settlement and organization of a township. An adventurous trader, Simon Willard, had followed an Indian trail northward in the quest for furs. He returned to Boston with the tale of an extensive tract of open Indian fields, beside a wide stretch of grassy river meadow that looked good as a locality for cattle. The explorer and others, including friends newly arrived in the colony, petitioned the General Court to grant them this site for settlement. The Court appointed a committee of trusted persons to investigate. They reported favorably. The Court then directed them to lay out a village and to allot lands to prospective settlers who agreed to inhabit. The result was the town of Concord.[2]

In carrying out such a mission in a virgin, unsettled countryside, the planners would naturally follow the familiar pattern of an English village.[3] In most English villages the houses with their garden plots and stables stood close together, facing one or more highways, within easy reach of the church and not far from the manor with its green or park. So for their New World town, the committee or its surveyor would first trace on a suitable location the outline of "The Street," as it was often designated, with perhaps another joining it at an angle. Facing this highway, sometimes on one side only, perhaps on both, they marked out a series of contiguous home- or house-lots, usually of similar proportions. One purpose was to establish a congenial community, each household with neighbors, friends, and church close by; another was to provide for close supervision by authority; a third was mutual protection.

In the new colony of Massachusetts Bay, in Plymouth Colony, and in Connecticut, the General Courts insisted that a bargain agreeable to both sides be made with any Indians who inhabited or claimed title; and Rhode Island colonists made similar bargains. Having compensated them for the land, a deed of the land of the new township was formally signed and recorded.

A closely settled village was almost uniformly the pattern. To a majority of the newcomers, the idea of scattered farmsteads on outlying disconnected sites would have been strange and repugnant. In most districts of England the villagers had been used to living sociably alongside one another, the byres (barns or sheds) for their stock adjoining each dwelling; a croft or nightpasture and their gardens and fruit trees in the rear. From these home lots they were accustomed to go out to the fields to cultivate their crops. These crops were usually planted under an agreed-on pattern in individual strips in large common fields. A common herdsman led or drove the stock of all to pasture in the common "waste" or woods.

In Massachusetts Bay, therefore, the public commission, acting under authority of the colony's General Court, arranged the preliminaries for the new township after a similar model, and reported to the Court as to its investigation and recommendations. Next, the heads of families who proposed to become the proprietors of the new settlement each certified to that intention. If their number was sufficient (usually at least forty were required) and they satisfied the Court that they were responsible persons, intending to occupy, they were assigned a specific tract and accorded the powers of a body politic, and the Court gave the new town a name. The General Court ordinarily endowed such a town with at least thirty-six square miles of territory and often much more. The intending settlers then chose their homesteads according to the plan already prepared, often by drawing lots.

From that point on, those whose names had been included could and did elect their local officers, pass bylaws, and handle the town's affairs more or less after the fashion of the English town or parish they had known at home; except that in their new situation, with no bishop to appoint a rector, they chose their minister. They were now proprietors of their home lots and any meadow or plowland assigned them individually, and from that time forward they had power over all the rest of the common and undivided land within the township limits.

In early days the townsite chosen was likely to be on or adjoining a tract left clear by the Indians. In Concord and in neighboring Sudbury alike, it ran along the south or west side of a protecting hill; near a river ford and a small entering stream, at a spot where the intersection of Indian paths or a ford offered logical choices for proposed highways.

In a few towns a home lot was as small as an acre or even less, at the beginning. Ordinarily, however, its size was four or five acres, and it might be as much as ten, even twenty acres. In any case it would be enough, as in Old England, for a dwelling, garden, fruit orchard, and buildings for the family's stock, plus an exercise ground or small night pasture for the animals. The house lots were frequently all of the same size but sometimes varied according to investment and social order, and were set up side by side in one unified plan. At the start of the division one suitably located lot was reserved for the meetinghouse, one or more "glebe" lots for the ministry, and, as time went on, other lots for education and a burying ground.

To every occupying family went also title to certain "rights," including a share in the village's most important asset, meadows, which were to furnish hay for its cattle; a share in its arable or plow land for growing "corn" or grain for food; and a share in its woodland and waste, to provide necessary pasture, building materials, fencing, and fuel to cook with and to keep the family warm.

Whether the prospective settler were farmer, sailor, tailor, or tanner, each head of a family who was to become a proprietor in the new community was entitled to such a home lot and the rights that appertained to it. No one paid for his lot, but in return for the privileges granted him, the General Court expected each to become a partner in the town and a builder of its communal life.

Economic equality was by no means intended or expected. Aside from the home lot, some persons received much more than the minimum allotment of meadow and "arable." This might be in recognition of the larger capital or estate that they were prepared to invest in the new community. Thus, if a "planter" brought with him a dozen cattle rather than a single cow, naturally he would need more meadow or mowing to carry them through the winter, plus other things in proportion. In the division, therefore, he was accorded extra rights. If the new proprietor had a wife, or if an additional asset was several sons, he would require extra land to feed and support them. On the other hand, it was clear that with such a number of helpers, a head of household should be able to handle more land to advantage. A large family, therefore, as a rule got proportionately extra rights.

This was the general pattern for Massachusetts Bay and Connecticut, with certain variations in Plymouth Colony after its first decade. It was familiar to everyone, for the roots of the township and agricultural systems ran back in Britain across medieval times into Scandinavian, Saxon, Roman, and Celtic customs through at least two thousand years.

One basic difference in the terms of settlement compared to common Old World practice was that once a settler was received as a member of the group under the required conditions of character and residence, all land and rights allotted were ordinarily held in fee simple: no rents to pay, no lord or bailiff to placate. Every proprietor became a freeholder, and could sell or bequeath his property, subject only to the customary requirement that it be first offered to the town, unless disposed of to a new owner approved by the community as suitable to become one of its members. The latter provision was to discourage absentee ownership.

Other customs brought from the homeland prevailed. Allotments of plow land (called arable) were usually portions in one or more large town fields, often former Indian-cleared tracts, the planting of which was according to a single pattern determined seasonally by the town. Town meeting or town selectmen set the date by which fence was to be mended alongside and proportionate to each man's cultivated section. When the crop was grown, the town determined how soon harvest should be finished, so that the town's cattle could be turned in to feed off the straw, stalks, and weeds. Town authority decided the number or "stint" of animals each was entitled to pasture, according to his agreed-on "rights."

Often the town provided one or more town bulls, and employed one or more herdsmen to gather at each man's gate his stinted number of cattle, goats, or sheep, drive them as a single herd or flock to pasture, and return them. Each morning the cowherd blew his horn for the householders to bring their creatures to their gates. He watched the animals through the day in the woods and meadows, and returned them at sundown to their owners. Horses, hogs, turkeys, geese, and fowl were in most places allowed to run at large, but the town set the beginning and duration of periods during which they must be yoked or hobbled to prevent their damaging gardens and cornfields.

As the generations passed and more and more of the town's common lands came to be divided and assigned to individuals, this ancient system was gradually modified and eventually outgrown. Crops were thereafter planted according to each man's pleasure, and stints of all sorts were done away with. Yet because of the convenience of the system, common herding and pasturage persisted in some towns even to the twentieth century. In these later times, and quite soon in Plymouth Colony, houses began to go up on outlying land; and a system of scattered and individually owned and operated farms at length took over. Even so, the close-knit village remained and in hundreds of towns exists today, its highways and lots little altered.

One factor that modified the general rule of land proprietorship in all the colonies was the occasional grant of a large acreage as compensation or as an honorarium to some public official or prominent personage. Moreover, as time went on, fiscal necessities, land speculation, and political pressures brought about changes in the original pattern.

Since agriculture was for generations to be closely interwoven with the political life of the New England town, a closer look at the town's civil and political structure, its relation to farming, and how it operated will be helpful.[4]

Who composed the town? Here five words become of particular importance: proprietor, commoner, freeholder, freeman, and inhabitant. At a town's beginning, as has been noted, the head of each of the families agreeing to settle there drew or was assigned a house lot and became a proprietor. By this act, without payment or financial commitment, he gained title to his home lot. Sometimes with the latter a tract of meadow was specifically granted him, even several such pieces. He also obtained a share in such common fields as might then or later be laid out for tillage or pasture; and gained a proportionate right or rights in the undivided woods and other lands of the township which in England would have been termed forest and waste.

Thus he became a freeholder and a commoner, legally owning and able to dispose of his real estate and appurtenant rights, rather than a tenant holding his "messuage" or dwelling and rights in the commons by custom or copyright, as many had in England. Being a freeholder did not, however, make a person a freeman. This was a superior type of citizenship, usually granted only to specified individuals of good character and reputation, members of the church. Freemanship carried with it the right of voting in colony as well as local elections, and holding office. Commoners not so designated were "inhabitants."

An important change from English practice was the abolition, in most colonies, of entailment, by which in England (except in a few localities like Kent, for example), real estate and property rights went by descent to the eldest son. Sooner or later all the New England colonies came to provide for proportionate distribution of a deceased person's estate to his widow and children or kin. This change from usual English practice was destined to have a marked influence not only on local farming and land use but on rural society as a whole, even on emigration and the founding of new communities.

The limitation brought from Old England that if the proprietor desired to sell and remove, he must offer his property to the town, avoided absentee landlordism and outside control and made it more likely that the forty or fifty families who made up the struggling new village would be responsible and congenial neighbors in an often isolated, unpopulated area. The custom also kept out persons likely to become a burden to the town, another common English usage.

Not all "proprietors" granted land and common rights were

by occupation or social status yeomen or husbandmen. One exception was the minister for whom the town plan set aside not only a home lot but usually, as in England, special glebe land for his support. In addition to his religious duties, however, the parson often proved himself a capable farmer and businessman. Other types of inhabitant especially desired in a new town were a miller and a tanner. To persuade these to settle, a town frequently offered extra inducements of land and other privileges, and even built the mill.

Salem granted land to glassmakers; Roxbury and Haverhill, to brickmakers; Ipswich, to a potash and soapmaker; Plymouth Colony, to ironworkers. Windsor, Connecticut, even provided a site for a barber. Carpenters, smiths, wheelwrights, and other tradesmen received a welcome. In Charlestown, a port town, for example, besides farmers the following additional tradesmen are mentioned by 1640: tailors, coopers, ropemakers, glaziers, tilemakers, anchor-smiths, collar makers, charcoal burners.[5] Most such mechanics would live on what would now be called "a little place," dig a garden, plant a few fruit trees; perhaps keep poultry, a cow and a hog or two, maybe a cosset sheep, all the large animals to join the herd or flock cared for by the village herdsmen. The mechanic might also cut his hay on the village meadow and bring in his firewood, building timber, and tool handles from the common woodland.

The town meeting ran the town, under the statutes of the General Court. Following ancient English usage, after warning by a constable, the heads of families gathered at the hour appointed, at first in some central tavern or dwelling, or even outdoors under a tree. As soon as time and increase of wealth permitted, the town would vote to erect a meetinghouse to be used both for this local assembly and for worship. "All triveall things e. c. shall be ordered in the towns," the General Court of Massachusetts Bay decided in 1635. In time it became burdensome for the citizens to leave their work for the frequent decisions required to handle ordinary business of the community. Hence they came to elect three, five, seven, sometimes more, "chosen men" or "townsmen," who eventually received the title of selectmen. Not seldom it was hard to find persons willing to accept such offices, almost all unpaid and time-consuming, and penalties were set for refusing.

In disposing of common lands and common property, only proprietors could vote. In other town matters eventually all male inhabitants possessing a certain modest amount of personal property or land, the "inhabitants," came to receive the privilege. At first only the "freemen," persons selected and named by the General Court of the Commonwealth as worthy, members all of them of the established Congregational Church, might vote on the election of magistrates and representatives to the General Court. This also was liberalized. However, in the Body of Liberties adopted by the Massachusetts General Court in 1641, an essential ancient English right was reaffirmed. "Every man whether Inhabitant or fforreiner, free or not free" is entitled "to come to any publique Court, Council or Towne meeting and either by speech or writing to move any lawful, seasonable, and materiall question, or to present any necessary motion, complaint, Bill or information," though he had to do it in an orderly manner.[6]

The general pattern of the origin of New England town government has been set forth. It is unnecessary to our purpose to trace its beginnings across the sea, point out the differences among the various New England colonies, examine the role of the church in government, or record the modifications that gradually took place over the years—all of which has been many times described and debated in print.

Suffice it to say that as population increased and as ownership of land and other wealth came to be dispersed among many persons, the right to vote, first in town affairs and later in colony affairs, was eventually acquired by almost all male inhabitants who had property worth recording. Sometimes this occurred only after bitter local struggles, especially over land distribution. The village is a small commonwealth, says Maitland, "with an old self-adjusted scheme of common rights and duties," [7] but this ideal often did not evolve in local practice without ferment and strain. Nor is another important consideration to be overlooked: once a person received the right to vote, he was likely to be fined if he neglected to attend town meeting or to assume the duties of an office to which he was elected. Hence many eligible persons failed to aspire to become freemen, and some entitled to vote failed to exercise that right.

How town government and farming were related can scarcely be better told than by specific examples:

In September 1639, Ipswich agreed with William Fellows to keep the town herd from April 20 to September 20, "drive them out to feed before the sunne be half an hour high and not to bring them home before half an hour before sunset." [8]

In 1639, Dedham required that every householder should provide a ladder as fire protection for his house: penalty five shillings. Ipswich made a similar bylaw in 1642, as did many other towns.[9]

At the first meeting of Guilford, Connecticut, on August 14, 1645, one of the most ancient of British institutions, a town pound, was authorized.[10]

On January 13, 1650, and later, Haverhill proportioned out the number of oxen allowed to be pastured on the ox-common by the thirty-five commoners, each of whom was required to help in fencing.[11]

April 20, 1652: Exeter agreed to pay Reverend Samuel Dudley 20 shillings for the use by the town's cattle of his two bulls.[12]

In 1652 Amesbury laid out an ox common and a cow common.[13]

In Cambridge in 1657–58 "Charles Stevens covenanteth with ye selectmen to keep there milch herd . . . and to provide two sufficient Bulls." For each cow the owner was to pay a peck of wheat or two pounds of butter, the rest in any grain except "pease in ye first payment." [14]

In 1661–62 Warwick, Rhode Island, authorized the fencing of an area three fourths of a mile to a mile square for horses.[15]

On November 7, 1663, Portsmouth, Rhode Island, ordered: "For as much as that there is a very greate distruction of sheep by wolves or other . . . vermin . . . it is ordered that upon . . . Satturday next if it be faire the Iland shall be driven" (i.e. hunted by all in concert).[16]

1664: the Greenwich, Connecticut, proprietors voted to "laye down our Rites in common lands lying without fence." [17]

Each town determined the date when its hogs must be

confined or yoked and its dogs hobbled, when its cattle might be turned into its tilled or "Lammas" lands, as they were often termed; what fences should have three rails, what five; the height of fences and stone walls; and the control of poultry.

Each town appointed its committees to lay out highways, saw to their repair, contracted for cartbridges, engaged the town minister, provided his firewood, seated the meetinghouse, paid bounties for destroying predators, collected taxes, and arranged countless other details. Before the fish ran upstream in the spring, the town set the dates for seining them, or let out the privilege of taking them, and appointed fish wardens to supervise the whole.

Certain of the town's duties were prescribed by the General Court. In Massachusetts Bay this included collecting colony taxes, seeing that children received moral training and education, looking after the poor, sealing weights and measures. All the colonies required inspection of export commodities such as staves, bread, salt, meat, fish, and tobacco, packed in kegs. The brands of large animals had to be recorded in a town book before they were permitted to be at large, shipped, or sold. The selectmen received also the duty of setting a fair value on staple commodities for purposes of exchange or barter, and for paying taxes and debts.

About much of these and similar procedures little was new. Most found English precedents in the customs of the manor or parish, and the statutes of the several King Henrys, King John, even back through William the Conqueror to Celtic, Saxon, and Danish customs.

Two duties were building fences and roads. Every man was bound to improve the road against his "tenement," and keep up his portion (often several portions) of the town hedge, wall, or fencing. This had been the rule in England for at least four centuries. In the colonies, fencing was required not only to keep animals in but, more importantly, to keep them outside cultivated fields and gardens. The painted and sometimes artistically ornamental white picket fences with gates that line old New England village streets are reminders that once cattle and hogs were frequent passersby, unwelcome in gardens.

The colonies' first roads were poor but laid out by town committees wide enough for the passage of cattle and so that riders might as far as possible avoid boulders and sloughs. Before long they had to be improved for the passage of oxcarts and hayricks. Periodically all able-bodied men were called out to labor on them, on pain of a fine.

Each town elected one, later two, representatives to the General Court or assembly of the colony. With the magistrates, these formed its governing body, under the Crown. However, a town entitled to two frequently sent but one. Many times, pleading poverty, towns asked to be excused altogether.

To the ordinary farmer, however, the local town government and its ordering of local matters were for a long time his chief concern with public affairs. One such concern was the local sale of produce, livestock, and mercantile goods.

From the earliest times the colonial governments authorized leading towns to hold market days. Thursday was market day in Plymouth. Duxbury and other Plymouth Colony towns had their own days, set by the Colony Court. In the Bay Colony Wednesday, "Lecture Day," was market time for Boston, Salem, and Lynn; while Charlestown, Watertown, and Dorchester each got its day. New Haven cleared the woods from the site of its famous Green to serve as the town's market place. Hartford in 1643 was permitted a Wednesday market for cattle and every kind of merchandise. New London and Fairfield likewise were market towns. In Rhode Island, Newport and Providence were the leaders. In addition each colony authorized annual or semiannual "fairs" of one or two days in leading towns. These were intended to bring together a wider assortment of livestock and merchandise than was offered at weekly markets.

All this was on the pattern by which for centuries grain, livestock, wool, cheese, and other farm products had been bought and sold in England. Nevertheless, except for Boston, Charlestown, Newport, Hartford, New Haven, and a few others, little evidence remains that market days and fairs became of great importance. At Salem, for example, the caustic observer Ward saw nothing in the market but pumpkins, and a local historian says that little was ever heard of the market.[18] In every town where trading was carried on, the local authorities appointed a clerk of the market to keep order, test scales, and settle disputes.

9

A Few Tools

DURING THE FIRST few decades the two chief branches of New England's agriculture, livestock and grain (the latter chiefly Indian corn), with work in the woods as a corollary, required neither many nor elaborate tools. As farming was practiced in the seventeenth century it has been aptly said that a strong man might carry on his shoulder all his ordinary farm implements.[1] Tools and tillage were both designed chiefly for "old" land, previously tilled. In former Indian fields and burned-over areas customarily cultivated by preference at the beginning, plowing was not essential. In fields where the timber had been newly cut, it was impossible, and under early rough planting methods, unnecessary. For some years Plymouth Colony, Cape Ann, Rhode Island, and southern New Hampshire each grew crops with only hand tools. Governor Endecott is said to have held Salem's first plow in 1633, a decade after the coming of the "Old Planters." Six years after Winthrop's arrival in 1630, the whole Bay Colony counted only thirty-seven plows.[2]

Since tillage in the early decades was largely for bread, not export, and carried on in communal fields, ownership by each farmer of a large, expensive plow was unnecessary. Instead, a town might reward a professional plowman who maintained a plow and team of oxen for the benefit of the whole neighborhood. The plow itself was universally constructed of wood, preferably ash or oak. There was no such thing as a strict design or interchangeable parts. Each mouldboard was an individual production, its shape depending on the portion of a tree from which it was hewn and the skill of the maker; and not all places were as fortunate as New London, Connecticut, in having a "ploowright." To save wear, the point of the plowshare was likely to be shod with iron, and bits of iron sheeting or old hoe blades attached to the mouldboard where wear was greatest. Occasionally the beam was fitted with a coulter or wheel.[3]

Plows were so heavy and unwieldy as to require four or even six oxen to draw them in difficult ground. At least two men were needed, better three and a boy—one to hold the handle or handles, one to press down on the beam to keep the plow in the ground, a third with a shovel to pull back the soil from the sticky mouldboard, and a boy to drive. Even then the furrow was shallow, and an acre was a day's work.[4] Like the plow, the wooden harrow used to break up clods had changed little since the Middle Ages. It might be either square or A-shaped, with teeth more often of wood than iron.[5] The ox-yoke was of wood; the chains by which the power was transmitted were iron. Contemporary inventories of estates include plow chains far oftener than plows, indicating that a farmer might use his own oxen but borrow or hire the large tools, perhaps with a second team.

The wealthier farmers soon had wheelwrights build them ox-wains or tumbrils. The wheels were solid cross-sections cut from large hardwood tree trunks. They turned on wood axles spread with animal grease. As time went on, blacksmiths rimmed the wheels with iron. Horse wagons would be unknown for longer than another century. In Plymouth Colony, in 1644, when William Hanbury rented out a farm complete with oxen and plows, a "weane" (hay vehicle) was part of the bargain. Captain Keayne of Boston, dying in 1656, left among his assets three "old waines" and two dung carts. Such roughly made carts were likely to injure the backs of the cattle that drew them. The poorer farmer used a wooden sled or drag pulled by one or more oxen, or got along without.[6]

For small farmers the mattock and grubhoe served to break up land and "hack in" seed of small grain. The wooden spade or shovel, sometimes iron-tipped, and the broadhoe remained the chief reliance for stirring the soil afterward. To reap his patch of Old-World bread-grain, a harvester was likely to use a saw-edged iron hook not too different from an Old Testament flint sickle. The manure fork was of iron, and so might be the hayfork—both prone to be loose in the handle. The hayfork, however, was more likely to be of wood, and cut from a suitably branched sapling. Thomas Minor of Connecticut mentions in 1654 in his diary a "leading rake" as though pulled by a draft animal, but such a tool would certainly be unusual.

One ingenious mechanic, Joseph Jenckes of the new Saugus ironworks, by trade a swordmaker and die-cutter, offered a foretaste of what was to happen in New England in a later era with respect to farm tools by inventing a greatly improved scythe. His blade was longer than that of the English scythe, yet rendered lighter and more effective by fastening the strip that furnished the cutting edge to a slender reinforcing bar. This light, sharp scythe proved superior to the former one forged of solid metal. For encouragement the General Court of Massachusetts Bay in 1646 awarded him the first American patent. The privilege was to run for fourteen years, later extended to twenty-one. Whether as a result or not, New England was to become for two centuries a center of scythe manufacture.[7]

Other hand farm tools recorded in inventories and similar lists during the first half-century or more include broad, narrow, and stubbing hoes; the shovel, spade, pickaxe or mattock, hatchet, sledge, crowbar, flail, fan, sieve, hand rake, hay knife, shears, trowel, lantern, currycomb, branding iron, and cowbell. Among larger tools were the yoke, wheels, "horse tackling," ladder, vise, cider press, mortar and pestle, grindstone, and wheelbarrow. Some of these, however, were uncommon. Dairy utensils such as churns, cheese presses, milk tubs, noggins, keelers, pails, trays, bowls, and firkins appear in some lists; occasionally, carpenter's and glazier's tools; and saddles, bridles, and harness for horses are mentioned.[8]

Production of lumber, fencing, firewood, and turpentine required the axe, adze, saw, and special tools such as the frow (slicer), which was employed to split shingles and clapboards.

The seventeenth-century straight-handled axe was much less effective in the woods than the modern axe with its artistically curved helve and weighted bit. Moreover, few of the newcomers had been experienced in their English home in felling large, tall trees; so much needed to be learned. As a later commentator astutely points out, it takes as many generations to make a woodsman as a gentleman. The Puritan immigration had no excess of either.

Large timbers for framing buildings were always hewn to size with axe and adze. So also at first, before sawn lumber was available, were the planks used for siding on dwellings. Almost at once, however, towns began to grant permission to sawyers to operate sawpits. In 1631 Obadiah Turner recorded in his diary: "In Salem they now have some bigge saws, wherewith to make boards." A pit was about twelve feet long and five feet deep. It might be arranged for convenience by cutting into the side of a knoll to provide the two necessary levels. The tree-trunk or bole was rolled onto supports at the upper level and secured so as to lie horizontally. With one man stationed above and one in the pit below, powerful muscles drove the great whipsaw up and down, up and down, through the trunk. About a hundred running feet of board or plank rewarded a day's labor. Crosscut saws also appeared occasionally in the inventories of large farms.[9]

Rough siding and flooring as well as fence rails were fashioned by splitting small tree trunks, with a bit of dressing from axe or adze as needed. To obtain shingles, clapboards, fence pales, and staves, suitable lengths were cut from the boles of straight-grained pine, ash, or oak. A blow of a hammer on a thin metal frow would cleanly split off a sheet of wood of the desired thickness. Shingles and clapboards split thus acquired a reputation for lasting a lifetime.

Reviewing such processes and assessing the amount of physical labor involved sheds light on the reasons for the small size of the early dwellings of ordinary families, and on why livestock had at first only makeshift shelter or none.

10

Settling In

THE FIRST NECESSITY for every family, once its head had
acquired home lot and appurtenant farming rights, was a
dwelling. What were the earliest habitations like?

At Plymouth the twelve original dwellings are described as
built of hewn plank, gardens growing about them, and the whole
surrounded by a wooden stockade. Once the settlement had
taken root and lots were assigned to individual families the
poorer ones began with small "booths" or cottages of light
framework, their walls of intertwined branches or sedge filled up
with clay. Sometimes these first dwellings were set into an
excavation in the protecting side of a hill to help keep out cold.
When able to do better, Pilgrim families put up more substantial
framed dwellings, still of only a room or two for most, with loft
above reached by a ladder. In the new towns soon begun along
the shore to the north and on Cape Cod, the style still popular as
the Cape Cod cottage became widely used, its form suggested, it
appears, by dwellings remembered from the Pilgrims' Holland
sojourn. Other houses were reminiscent of the wood-framed
homesteads of East Anglian towns.[1] As population grew and new
farms were opened in inland towns, another custom developed.
At Middleboro, pioneered in the 1660's after the colonists had
become more expert with the axe, the first houses are said to have
been built of squared logs, fitted at the corners, with doors of
plank.[2]

In the Bay Colony—except for the rich and prominent, who had ready cash, servants, perhaps even a house frame shipped from England—housing at the beginning was flimsy and meager indeed. At Charlestown in 1629 and 1630 many had to live in tents, or booths built of branches. In Cambridge and Watertown a year or two later some had to be content with what were termed wigwams, roofed with cattail stalks or thatch like shepherds' huts in England.[3] At Concord, Newbury, and other of the earliest villages new settlers burrowed into sandy hillsides, set up corner posts, and filled in the framework with rushes. With no chimney, the fire was at first built old-Saxon fashion against the bank of earth at the rear, smoke escaping through the roof, a method still used in parts of England at least as late as 1600.[4] "Poor hovvils," Benjamin Tompson called them, and so they were.

In the earliest Connecticut settlements about Hartford the first habitations were similar. As late as 1679 settlers in Enfield, like those at the first settlement of Concord, are said to have built into the sides of hills. Further down the valley on its flat, sandy, river terraces, and at New Haven, one method was to dig a square pit six or eight feet deep in dry ground, increase its height a little, line the sides with rushes, cover the whole with a roof of bark or sods, and floor it by hardening the earth or laying split saplings. Protected thus from winter winds, the family subsisted till they could do better. In legal documents of the time these are sometimes described as "cellars."[5] Such habitations were not unique. Similar dwellings were a holdover from before the Christian era in some districts of England and parts of Europe.

As in the other colonies, as soon as the Connecticut settler could find time, tools and capital, he hewed timber for a frame and plank for vertical siding, had boards sawed for floors, split pitch pine for siding or oak for clapboards, and built himself a one-room house. Later he would add another room alongside; next a kitchen lean-to behind, such as he recalled from Old England.[6] In interior Connecticut at least one original farmhouse remained into the twentieth century (built probably in 1671), of squared oak logs, halved at the corners, and so tightly fitted inside that a knife blade could scarcely be entered between them.[7]

In both Massachusetts and Connecticut almost from the first, the better-off, with the aid of carpenters, were able to build the larger structures of several rooms still exhibited in numerous towns as "typical" colonial. Frames were of oak and ash, walls at first of wattle, "noggin" or sunbaked clay, similar to half-timbered English dwellings; or of two- or three-inch plank set upright. To withstand New England's weather, both types were soon made tight outside with split clapboards.

At Providence Plantation, Newport, and Narragansett, housing followed a similar pattern; one- or two-room cottages at first, more elaborate clapboarded structures later. Weeden believed that the earliest Providence houses were of squared logs.[8] Hewn logs with fitted ends formed the original dwellings at Exeter, New Hampshire, as well as at North Berwick and Cape Porpoise in what was to become southern Maine. At Newmarket, New Hampshire, three-inch vertical planks are mentioned.[9] However, the popular conception of early dwellings built of logs is for the most part without historical foundation.

Roofs in all the settlements were at first of thatch, boughs, or rushes; chimneys were of plank, sometimes plastered over with clay. Because of the number of fires that resulted from these methods, both were speedily forbidden. Cleft wood shingles took the place of thatch; masonry replaced plank for chimneys. To enforce the regulations, chimney viewers were appointed. Yet thatch persisted in some instances as late as 1671. Good brick clay was scarce, however, and stone was often substituted for brick. To lay up either, lime for the mortar had to be burned from seashells,[10] usually at the heaps accumulated by generations of Indians at clam and oyster banks.

Such living quarters meant a hard life at first, especially for women. What with rough food, water only from a spring or brook, exposure to rain, snow, cold, and heat, together with leaks in roofs that were made of sod or rushes—not to mention the mosquitoes—many women died, including some the colony was least able to spare. But most got used to housing, climate, and hardships and made a go of it. "After the first winter we were very healthy," recalls old Roger Clap of Dorchester. Of the original settlers at Plymouth, once the first tragic winter was past, most lived to a good old age. Among the fifty-odd families, many of them young people, who in 1638 set their faces to found Sudbury, second inland town in the Bay Colony, not a single death occurred in the first two hardest years. Moreover, recent population studies for others of the original towns show the settlers to have been remarkably long-lived, as local historians have often claimed.[11]

In the beginning the farm animals suffered even more than the farm people. Most colonists, accustomed to letting stock remain on pasture or with only slight cover in the milder English winter, at first failed to realize the importance of shelter from New England's severe cold and storms. In the first winters a large proportion of the cattle and horses died, Johnson states, until there was time and capital to house and feed them properly. Yet a few such seasons taught livestock how to stand the climate; and soon barns, hovels, and outhouses began to appear for them.[12]

Cambridge Proprietors' Records mention a cowhouse by 1635, and by 1642 at least eight barns, plus numerous outhouses, are recorded there. The Connecticut Colony's first barn is said to have been built by Lt. Col. John Talcott at Hartford in 1636. If farm buildings were framed, the outside walls were likely to be split weatherboarding or clapboards, a fashion then (and still in use) on farms in English counties blessed with forests to draw on. In 1664 Thomas Minor of Connecticut was "clobboarding" his barn, presumably one already standing.[13]

Dwellings and other farm buildings followed traditional dimensions. They were of one or more "bays" measuring a rod of 16 or 16½ feet, or of some proportion of this ancient English farm dimension. Thomas Lechford describes an early Massachusetts Bay house 16 × 14 feet, with chimney outside. In Concord, Elisha Jones' house of two rooms, one above the other, built in 1640, had a 12 × 8 foot fireplace. In a fairly large house built at Sandwich on Cape Cod in 1642, the front room measured 16 feet square. Edmund Rice's house at Sudbury, put up in 1647, was planned 30 × 16; and the "Peak House," still standing at Medfield, was laid out 24 × 14½, and 10 feet to the eaves, with four very small windows. At Sudbury Edmund Rice's barn was 50 feet long with a 12-foot stud.[14] Cambridge Records of the 1670's mention barn lengths of 17, 18, and 30 feet; a lean-to (1683) was to be 30 × 10 feet with a 4-foot stud. As to the outhouses and hovels where young stock, goats, and poultry must have found shelter, very little is recorded, though tax lists often mention them.

As part of the home lot each household soon had its "pleasant gardens with kitchin gardens," to borrow Wood's words. In Cambridge in 1635 house after house is listed as having a garden and "backside," though lots there were small compared to those in most towns. Manured with fish at first, gardens had to be well enclosed by pales (closely spaced vertical stakes driven into the ground, or slats fastened to two rails), to prevent dogs from making a meal of the fertilizer. For his fence, the householder got permission of the selectmen or timber warden to cut posts and pales from the common woodland. (On Cambridge's "Tory Row" fences of pales today still enclose a few front yards.)[15]

Until fruit trees had time to reach bearing, "instead of Apples and Pears they had Pomkins and Squashes of divers kinds," Johnson records. One visitor likewise wrote that pumpkins and squash were the chief fruit that supported the English when they first settled; in fact, pumpkins were all this man saw in the market at Salem. More than one colonist was enthusiastic about the way vegetables grew, especially the roots. "Our turnips, parsnips, and carrots are here both bigger and sweeter than is ordinary to be found in England," boasted Pastor Higginson of Salem: "Pease of all sorts and the best in the World." In his *New England's Rarities Discovered,* Josselyn declares, "I never heard of, nor did see in eight year's time one worm eaten pea."

Old customs endured. A Medford gardener notes in 1648: "Sown one peck of pease, the moon in the full." The muskmelons and watermelons were especially juicy, Josselyn thought, and cabbages grew "exceeding well." At Plymouth, besides the usual roots, Bradford's poem tells of cucumbers, radishes, coleworts, and cabbages.[16]

As to fruit, John Endecott's seeding of apples was so successful that in 1648 he traded 500 three-year apple whips with William Trask for 200 acres of land, not a bad bargain either way. The age of the saplings is notable, because four years earlier Endecott had suffered a catastrophe. "My children," he wrote Governor Winthrop, "burnt mee at least 500 trees this spring by setting the ground on fire neere them." [17]

Governor Winthrop too was strong for fruit. From trees on Governor's Island in Boston Harbor, perhaps started by Roger Conant before Winthrop's advent, he was delighted eight years after his arrival to be brought ten very fair pippins; and he planted more at his "Ten Hills Farm" on the Mystic.[18]

Householders everywhere were soon planting seeds of apples, pears, cherries, and other fruits about their dwellings. By 1646–47 Reverend Mr. Danforth of Roxbury could record: "Aug. 1. The great pears ripe." "Aug. 3, The long apples gathered." "Aug. 12 Blackstone's apples gathered." "Aug. 15 Tankerd apples gathered." "Aug. 18, Kretoin pippins and long red apples gatherd." and by 1649, on July 20 he had "apricocks ripe." [19]

In the fall of 1646 Reverend John Eliot, at Nonantum (now Newton), rewarded each Indian child in his catechism class with an apple. The famous Roxbury Russet, still the best apple for cider and one of the longest winter keepers, is thought to have originated about 1647 in the town for which it was named. Fruit added to property values. In 1648 the will of John Balch of Beverly left to his widow one-half of "the great fruit trees," the other half to his oldest son, and to his younger sons the younger trees.[20] An orchard is mentioned at Amesbury in the Merrimack Valley in 1649.

Though much of Plymouth Colony's soil was less well adapted to fruit than that of Massachusetts Bay, Governor Thomas Prence, elected in 1634, set pear trees in Eastham on Cape Cod about 1640, one of which was still capable of yielding 15 bushels of fruit 200 years later. A pear tree set at Yarmouth and another at Truro were likewise fruiting bountifully at ages well beyond two centuries. Kentish cherries and plums did well in Plymouth Colony, also.

In what is now Rhode Island some of the Reverend Mr. Blaxton's original Yellow Sweetings at his Study Hill home in Cumberland, then under the Plymouth patent, were called the richest and most delicious apples of the whole kind. They were reported thrifty still in 1765, and at least two trees of his orchard were fruiting in 1830, almost two centuries after he started them. At Newport in 1639 six acres were granted to William Coddington for an orchard, the second recorded in what was to become Rhode Island.[21]

Connecticut's first comers from The Bay had scarcely sat down before they were starting apples. One tree at Hartford, said to date from 1638, was still bearing in 1853. Hedrick credits George Fenwick of Saybrook with the first New England nursery, well started by 1641. He had cherry and peach trees as well as apples. Henry Wolcott of Windsor, a magistrate there, had 32 orders for trees from 25 customers in 1641; and a decade later sold 500 apple trees in one lot, to be paid for half in wheat, half in pease. In the Connecticut Valley, however, Hollanders seem to have been ahead of their rivals, the English. When de Vries in 1639 visited their fort near Hartford, he saw forty or fifty cherry trees near the redoubt full of fruit (but possibly native rum cherries). After the English settled the Connecticut shore, Thomas Minor at Stonington recorded grafting 100 trees in 1663, and the next year gathered in all 120 bushels of apples and "pounded 6 barrels of sider."

A desire for cider and vinegar was the chief reason for the planting of apples that went on everywhere. The English found that barley for their customary beer grew poorly, but that apples for cider, which had been a beverage only in the fruit-growing counties at home, would thrive almost universally. Henry Wolcott of Connecticut in 1671 boasted to John Josselyn that in one year he made 500 hogsheads. A hogshead of cider ordinarily sold at 10 shillings. Some pears went into another alcoholic drink, perry. Josselyn made cherry wine, and so, he said, did many others.

By 1643 Johnson claimed that there were as many as 1,000

acres of orchards and gardens in the Bay Colony, and in 1660
Maverick commented: "The great abundance of English Fruite,
as Apples, Pears, Apricocks, Cherries, Muskmellons, Watermel-
lons &c is not to be believed but by those that have seene it." [22]
He might have added gooseberries and barberries, both brought
from England.

For most families the orchard, like the vegetable garden,
was one of the features of the home lot, where the apple yard was
companion to the turnip yard and tobacco yard, each fenced
against wandering stock. If Johnson is to be believed, on village
home lots it was not long before the flower garden became
companion to the vegetable garden. When the lilac appeared
beside the front door no diarist records.

II

The Farm Family

How, in general, was the farm family getting along at the end of the first half century?

As to food, it was eating heartily and wholesomely by the standards of that century, though not always daintily. Gone were the early days of dependence on biscuits and beer out of English ships, corn bought of Indians, and clams dug on the shore. Indian corn was indeed still a mainstay of the colonists' diet, but it was corn of their own raising, and in the older settlements corn ground by a water mill rather than pounded in a quern or mortar to be mixed with water into cakes called bannock.

"I could not eat the bread made from ye maise," wrote home a lady in 1632, "but now I find it very good." [1] Josselyn and later John Winthrop, Jr., tell how corn bread was best made. Josselyn's method was to form the loaf in a deep basin, then turn it out in the oven before the mixture spread. Winthrop said it should be stirred into a thin batter, then turned into a wooden dish fixed on the end of a long handle from which it was poured onto the floor of a clean, very hot oven, where it spread out thin. Layer after layer was added till it became a large but not very thick loaf. As English grain became more common the mixture came to include rye and even wheat flour, resulting in a lighter but still brownish bread. Some might prefer to "make a kind of loblolly [of cornmeal] to eat with milk," said Josselyn; or after sifting out the flour, to "boyle it upon a gentle Fire till it be like a

Hasty Pudden" also eaten with milk.[2] Rhode Islanders developed
their own "jonnycake" with special characteristics. By 1642
Johnson states that "good white and wheaten bread is no
dainty." Farm wives were at least as well off for cereals as they
had been in England, where wheat, barley, and rye flour for
bread were often filled out with pease, and where among small
farmers the common pottage was pot liquor thickened with
oatmeal or barley.[3]

A second food soon adopted from the native Indians was
beans. No Boston baked beans for a considerable time, but beans
or peas cooked soft in pork or beef pot liquor (as in the famous
pease porridge of the children's rhyming chant) and eaten hot or
allowed to jell. In winter it might be frozen and a section cut off
as needed. Beans boiled with corn kernels into Indian succotash
made a popular combination.[4]

Added to corn and beans, two other Indian vegetables,
squash and pumpkin, became a great resource. "Pumpkin
Porridge being as much in esteem with New England Saints as
Jelly broth with Old English sinners," as jocular Ned Ward put
it. In 1674 Benjamin Tompson looked back on the time "When
Cimnels [summer squashes] were accounted noble bloud among
the tribes of common herbage Food". "For pottage and pudding
and custards and pies our pumpkins and parsnips are common
supplies," as the popular Forefathers' Song put the situation in
rhyme.[5] Even more common than the parsnip among vegetables
of English origin were the turnip, the onion, and in time the
cabbage.

As has been noted, for meat no animal furnished so much so
quickly and cheaply as the porker. Hunting his own acorns,
groundnuts, Jerusalem artichokes, and other roots, with shellfish
to eke out in winter near the shore, the hog grew with little
expense except perhaps for some grain at the end. A fat little pig
made a good roast, as John Dunton recorded in his journal. Hog
weights at killing time in the fall ran low by modern standards,
seldom up to two hundred pounds. Nevertheless the animal
provided hams, bacon, lard, and barreled salt pork. Salt meat
had been the winter dish most relished in the old country. Salt

pork became for two centuries in all seasons the chief reliance of the farm wife in the new.[6]

Getting a supply of beef involved much more time and trouble than one of pork, since good hay was as yet scarce. Yet practically every farmer, and even the village mechanic, tried to keep a few cows. The cow furnished milk, in summer at least, to eat with his gruel, plus butter and cheese for his family. Before long there might even be a surplus for sale. A calf could be killed for veal, or occasionally an older animal to supply the corned beef barrel.

Sheep were scarce at first and provender suitable for them lacking; but immigrants from English sheep counties began rearing them on disforested islands or in niches safe from wolves. Well before the end of the half century Reverend Edmund Browne could report for Massachusetts that mutton as well as pork was usually eaten there.[7] Yet even in Essex County, despite its plentiful meadow hay, midcentury inventories list sheep in considerably fewer than half the farm estates.

Hunting might help to vary the farm family's diet, though as early as 1646 Portsmouth and Newport on Aquidneck Island (now Rhode Island) were limiting the deer-hunting season to winter. A thief who entered a house at Truro on Cape Cod in 1647 made away with venison, along with such usual products of the farm as beef, bread, butter, cheese, and tobacco. At Oxford in central Massachusetts, at a date much later, a farmer claimed that it was as easy to bring in a fawn from the woods as to get a lamb from his sheepfold. Migrating fowl, especially wild pigeons, were a common table delicacy in spring and fall. Fish, too, were good food in the short period in spring when they pushed up the streams to spawn in their headwaters.

Yet it is easy to overemphasize the value of game as a colonial food resource. The old-fashioned muzzle-loading flint-lock, clumsy and inaccurate, was far from the efficient modern shotgun or a rifle with telescopic sight. In addition, the ordinary English settler, even if in the old country he had lived near a forest, had been forbidden to hunt, that privilege in England being reserved for the gentry—hence most colonists lacked experience in the art of hunting. Beyond this, once extensive farming began, the most desirable types of game were apt to depart. It was chiefly the nuisance animals and birds that remained—those which preyed on livestock, poultry, and crops.[8]

Though wild birds might not often be on the table, barnyard fowl are reported to have increased rapidly. They were kept for spring and summer eggs more than for meat, however. At Plymouth, Captain John Smith reports many poultry in 1624; yet of 88 early inventories, Langdon states, only 6 listed them. At Wethersfield, Connecticut, the earliest mention of poultry is in 1644. Josselyn says the Massachusetts Bay people had "good store" of poultry, and Johnson calls them plentiful. Both were writing later in the century.

The wild berries and grapes that do so well over most of New England helped satisfy the newcomers' taste for fruit. In June wild strawberries were common. Josselyn called the numerous "Skyecoloured" or blue-berries "a most excellent summer dish." "They usually eat of them put into a Bason, with Milk and sweeted a little more with Sugar and Spice." Dried berries were mixed into puddings. Bees from across the seas were soon on hand to fertilize the blossoms of fruit trees. As bees began to provide honey, tarts made from apple, pear, and quince were added to the diet. Pumpkins, eaten at first as vegetables, eventually went into pies also.[9]

By the end of the half-century sugar was being imported in such quantity that ordinary people could afford it. One Essex County farmer in 1651 sold a Salem merchant 12 bushels of rye and took home sugar; along with it went a doll and a bird-whistle. (This incident is to be recalled when it is argued that all Puritans were hardhearted and severe.)

Farm people ate from wooden trenchers or bowls, sitting at a wood trestleboard according to English custom. Everybody used knives, wooden spoons, and their fingers. Crockery, glassware, and pewter began to come in, but for the ordinary family these for the most part were still in the future.

For clothing farm people were likely to go short. Imported cloth was expensive. The spinning wheel and the loom would not for a considerable time become part of every household's furnishings. "The Farmers," says Johnson, "deemed it better for their profit to put away [sell] their cattel and corn for cloathing, than to set upon making of cloth . . ." So they were likely to sell a cow or two for something to wear. At first all clothing was worn to shreds. Then as hides and skins were tanned and cured right on the farm or by the village tanner, these became raw material for leather coats, breeches, and aprons for the men. Shirts and women's wear were apt to be of coarse gray cloth, sometimes cotton, sometimes woolen. The first American center for cloth manufacture was Rowley, in Massachusetts Bay, settled by experienced Yorkshire textile workers. Here in 1638, from the wool of local sheep, they wove the first bolt of woolen cloth in America, 83½ yards long. Except for the men, the members of the family would spend most of the summer barefoot. Soon, however, the village cobbler made them boots or shoes from the hides of their stock for Sabbath and winter wear.[10]

Within a decade or two the English were settling in, their most pressing needs met, and many achieved a fair degree of comfort. Their dwellings were small and not infrequently crowded, but at least they afforded shelter. The more valuable stock was housed also. Towns had put up small, plain meeting-houses to which all went for worship, and the men for town meetings. They had begun to lay out highways and had long since been collecting taxes. Already the general level of welfare was such that the Colony's magistrates were worried about the idleness of some who along with the "saints" had been attracted to the new land.

Johnson's *Wonder Working Providence* summed up the situation in 1654: "There are not many towns in this country, but the poorest person in them hath a house and land of his own, and bread of his own growing if not some cattel; besides flesh is now no rare food, beef, pork and mutton being frequent in many houses . . ."[11] Johnson was overoptimistic, but in the main his description was justified.

One other important point he makes. The artisans, who at first had almost perforce tried their hands at a modest amount of agriculture, now with commerce flourishing were busily employed at their own trades. Coopers, tanners, and shoemakers were doing especially well in the export field; but a long list of other tradesmen found paying occupations. As a result, instead of growing food, many of them had turned into food consumers. Hence, Johnson declares, "they have left the husbandman to follow the plow and cart," a development that was to have an important bearing on farming's future.[12]

In thinking of the seventeenth century farm it is essential largely to discard the picture of the modern, self-contained farmstead. Except in the very smallest operations, as towns over the years divided their reserves of common land among the proprietors, the farmer's holdings would come to include, besides the home lot, several separate pieces of meadow or salt marsh from which he got his winter hay, plus upland scattered among various locations, often at a considerable distance from his dwelling. All this would be in addition to his one or several pieces or "gates" in the common or cultivated fields. There he grew his grain, and had pasturage rights to follow.

The harvest from his cultivation was ordinarily of small proportions by modern standards. Although a large percentage of early inventories contain items of Indian corn, very seldom does the total count run as high as 50 or 60 bushels; or, if standing in the field, five or six acres is a notably high figure. The majority of inventories are much smaller. Not over half the inventories mention the English bread grains: wheat, rye, or barley, except perhaps for a little in the house for cooking. Anything over five or ten bushels of such grain is highly unusual, though an occasional large farm with several yoke of oxen and presumably hired labor may have as high as 200 bushels. Generally the harvest is on a small scale.

Moreover carts and wains are few on farms for the first forty years and plows even less common. Such heavy work as was essential would seem to have been arranged for with professional plowmen and teamsters who did such operations for many others, perhaps plowing the entire common arable with some equivalent manual labor by the individual farmers in return.

Livestock numbers for a whole town might be impressive, as Johnson and others added them up, but from today's point of view the numbers per individual farm were far from weighty. A dozen cowkind, even when it included not only mature animals but younger ones from one, to three years old, was a large herd for the first fifty years of the New England colonies. With sheep the situation was similar. In Newbury at the mouth of the Merrimack by 1660, John Cutting's total of 47 sheep in all, or John Dowlett's flock of 76 plus 10 lambs at Rumney Marsh in 1681, were enormous compared to the usual flock of from three to a dozen. Hog numbers on individual farms ran from a single sow to a total of perhaps a dozen swine in all, in some cases including young pigs. Once more Dowlett at Rumney Marsh heads the list of those surveyed, with 29. Livestock numbers in Connecticut appear similar.[13]

Such statistics do not imply incompetence, lack of ambition, or idleness, nor do they suggest any lack of good food for the farm family or preclude the possibility of a salable surplus to be traded to some merchant. They merely illustrate the immense expenditure of labor and time involved in farming before the advent of modern machinery and chemical fertilizers. To support a family of five to a dozen with only the hoe, scythe, sickle, axe, and spinning wheel for tools required not only knowledge of farming but continuous labor for the whole family through all daylight hours, which often provided no more than the simple necessities of shelter, food, fuel, and clothing that modern Americans are apt to regard as their rightful minimum.

So with unending labor the first dwellings had been built, and makeshift shelters for the stock arranged. Gardens had been laid out, manured, and planted, and apple and pear trees set. Indian corn, rye, and wheat had been grown, harvested, and ground for the family's food. At winter's beginnings hogs and beef were ready to be slaughtered, portions exchanged with neighbors or sold, and the balance salted. Trees had been cut, fuel hauled, highways laid out, meetinghouses provided.

By the end of the colonies' first half century, the old folks had mostly died, and the next generation had taken over the farms. Persistent, intelligent application had brought to farm families adequate food, shelter, and means not only of existence but of a considerable degree of comfort. In some few cases wealth had begun to accumulate.

How then are the accomplishments of the farmers of New England's first half century and their agriculture to be assessed?

First and most essential, the new colonies were fed. There was no starvation such as plagued Virginia's earliest years. It was done at the beginning by breeding livestock in plenty; and not long afterward sufficient harvests of grain, fruits, and vegetables were added.

In part this achievement resulted from adequate planning by the sponsors of the Massachusetts Bay Colony across the seas. In part it rested on the preparation of much of the landscape by the colony's vanished Indian predecessors. In part the outcome was the fruit of the settlers' own heavy toil and struggle. Yet the success of these first New England farm people went beyond essentials. Before even the second decade was complete, they were helping to provide masts and plank for shipbuilding and lumber and livestock to accompany the fisherman's contribution to the cargo. Thus they supplied a foundation for the foreign trade that helped the colonies to achieve an economically sound life.

This, however, was not the whole achievement. Following principles ingrained from a millennium and more of English rural experience, they bore the strain of transplanting and adapting an ancient system of local village self-government to rough new circumstances in a rough new land. They did this with success so complete that the pattern then established was to prove not only adequate but adaptable enough to serve with only minor changes for three and a half centuries to come. Indeed eventually in essence it would spread half way across the continent, to govern much of the rural heart of a nation then undreamed of.

Now, at the end of their first half century, the first generation had completed the foundation. A second generation, no longer transplanted Englishmen but native to the soil, had begun to build thereon. The work of both was to be tried by the fire of Indian warfare. On these country-born farm people the brunt of the death and destruction of King Philip's War was about to fall.

II. WAR AND TRADE, 1675–1775

12

Toil and Trouble

As THE NEW YEAR of 1675 came in, the inhabitants of no farming town in New England could escape dread of trouble close at hand. But it was June before Philip, son of Massasoit and chief of the Wampanoags who inhabited the western shore of Mt. Hope Bay, with his allies, launched his desperate attempt to drive the white men from the planting fields and hunting grounds which these Indians and their forefathers had cleared: fields and forests which for generations had furnished the natives with food, clothing, shelter, and fuel.

Though not the immediate occasion of the outbreak, the underlying causes were the continued spread of white settlement and the white men's restrictions on the way of life of the local Indians. Added to these was a marked difference between English and Indians in their conception of land tenure, use, and trespass. Moreover, the natives had suffered losses from the Englishman's livestock, failed to find what they considered justice in his courts, and experienced not only indignities but fraud and robbery at the hands of some unscrupulous newcomers.

Philip and his counselors determined to stand such abuses no longer. Forming a league with other tribes, eventually to include the natives of most of southern New England except western Connecticut, Cape Cod, and the islands, Philip began a series of staggering blows. His hope and purpose was to exterminate the English or drive them from the land.

The plan nearly succeeded. The two years of dreadful pillage and carnage in 1675 and 1676 fell with particular force on the farms. It was farm people and their families that the Indians murdered or carried off. It was their homes, in large part, that the raiders burned, their cattle and hogs that were slaughtered, their harvests destroyed. The people of the coast towns and of the parts of Connecticut that went unscathed had to furnish soldiers and contribute to the common defense, but they were spared the worst horrors and losses.

The detailed story of King Philip's War, a tragedy told and retold many times, is not necessary here; a summary from the farm point of view will suffice. In June 1675 came the first open outbreak, with several whites slain at Mattapoisett and Swansea in Plymouth Colony (today southeastern Massachusetts), not far from Philip's headquarters at Mt. Hope, now in Rhode Island. The next month raiders descended with slaughter on Dartmouth, burned thirty dwellings, and seared Middleboro, both of Plymouth Colony. Then the Nipmucks fell on Mendon, a farm village in south central Massachusetts. August brought widely scattered raids, the heaviest on Brookfield and Lancaster in central Massachusetts. In September the Piscataqua region and coastal New Hampshire suffered destruction; next, the Falmouth (now Portland) area, where, by the middle of December, eighty inhabitants had been slain. The often described ambush of Captain Lathrop's Essex company at Bloody Brook near Deerfield in the Connecticut Valley in September was followed by raids on Hatfield, Northfield, and Springfield. In December the "Great Swamp Fight" in South County, Rhode Island, with its terrible losses to the Narragansetts, brought the year to a close.[1] The widespread field of action, including the domain of the Narragansetts themselves and their allies, was farming territory.

Midwinter afforded a slight surcease, but in February 1676 Lancaster was sacked, Medfield burned; then in March farming towns as far separated as Northampton in Massachusetts, Simsbury in Connecticut, Providence and Warwick in Rhode Island, Rehoboth close by in Plymouth Colony, and Groton in Middlesex County, Massachusetts, suffered heavy blows or were totally destroyed. On April 19 Sudbury, twenty miles from Boston, was attacked. The "Wadsworth Massacre" there attested to the fury of the Indians. Within a few weeks Marlboro, Andover, Chelmsford, Bridgewater, Wickford (R.I.), and other towns were raided. Though the tide of war soon turned that summer with defeats for the Indians in the Connecticut Valley, and though Philip was slain at Rehoboth in August, yet in 1677, a year later, the flames had still not completely died. Indians fell on Wells, York, Sheepscot, and Falmouth; and much of the southern Maine coast was abandoned. In the Connecticut Valley, attacking Hatfield a second time, they killed or captured twenty. These form only a partial list of towns raided and farms destroyed, but from it may be gathered something of the anxiety, peril, and loss that country people suffered in those three dreadful years.[2]

Estimates of the cost of the struggle to the white population put the total destruction at not fewer than 600 killed (Leach's, the most recent estimate, is close to 1,000), twelve or thirteen towns wiped out, at least 600 houses burned (one historian says 1,200), 8,000 cattle slaughtered, and thousands of bushels of grain and innumerable haystacks destroyed. These figures tell only part of the loss. For example, "the histories of those times rarely mention the barns, stores and outbuildings burned," warns Trumbull, the Connecticut historian. "The loss of buildings must therefore have been much greater." Only occasionally is the destruction of harvests considered.[3]

One of the few such records is found in a book by Wilbur O. Spencer, a Maine historian, taken from the annals of Scituate, Massachusetts. To that town some of the farm people from Sheepscot, Maine, fled in August 1676, leaving their farms and herds to the enemy. "William Dyer, besides 56 cattle, and 30 swine, had left fields back in Maine seeded with 16 bushels of wheat, 1½ bushels of corn and 9 bushels of peas. John White, besides leaving 17 head of cattle and 16 swine, had sown 10 bushels wheat, 1½ bushel Indian corn, and 5 bushels peas; P. Bendall had planted 9 bushels peas, 50 of wheat. The widow Cole, besides losing cows, heifers and a pair of oxen, had planted

6 bushels wheat and 3 of corn in her fields." [4] All these plantings were abandoned in a single area, and scores of other hamlets were left similarly tenantless.

Official archives contain communications like the following, in which Major Pynchon reports to Governor Leverett of Massachusetts Bay: "We found all [Springfield] in flames, & about 30 dwelling houses burnt downe & 24 or 25 Barnes, my Corn Mills, Sawmill & other buildings. Generally, mens hay & corne is burnt & many men, whose houses stand, had their goods burnt in others houses wch they had carried ym too." [5]

Rhode Island, with a Quaker governor, did not organize resistance, "so that their towns, goods, corn, and cattle were by the savage natives burned and destroyed." [6]

From Maine, Major Waldron writes: "Nov. 11th: 2 men more killed at Wells"; "12th: 2 men one woman and 4 children killed at York & 2 houses burnt at Kittery and 2 old people taken captive"; 14th, "a house surprised on the south side Piscataway and 2 young women carried away there." [7]

In a Connecticut Valley burying ground Verrill records a rude and weathered headstone that commemorates a simple tragedy of that day's farming: "Mary Du . . . who in her sixteenth year was killed by ambushed Indians while on her way To bring home the cow." [8]

Financial woe was one result, so complete that in Dartmouth (now in part New Bedford) and other towns taxes had to be suspended for several years. Even in Connecticut, least affected of the colonies, field work had to be done in companies, arms at the ready. The Council there directed that one-fourth of each town's manpower be under arms daily.

Only a few areas in New England—such as Cape Cod, the offshore islands, southwestern Connecticut (which enjoyed excellent crops that helped supply the troops), Boston, and its nearby towns—escaped the awful destruction of life and property. Yet even these places suffered heavy losses of men sent as soldiers— the Dedham company at Sudbury and "the flower of Essex" at Bloody Brook in Deerfield, for example. All had to bear the burdensome charges for the war.

To this tale of disaster, human and agricultural, must be

added a sorrowful supplement, from the point of view of the Indians and their farming. As New England's original cultivators, they had introduced the whites to the husbandry of corn, beans, and squash and taught them the preparation of these crops as food. The first conflict to cause loss of planting fields to the native Indians concerned the numerous, powerful Pequots who lived and farmed along the eastern Connecticut shore and on Block Island. The trouble started in 1636 following the murder of a white trader and his crew. Connecticut and Massachusetts troops with Mohegan assistance ended it the next year by almost complete destruction of the tribe, its forts, and its villages. The tribe's extensive cornfields and hunting grounds were expropriated by Connecticut. For the next four decades, marred though they were by local disputes, the rest of southern New England's Indians continued to farm and hunt on their ancestral lands.[9]

It would serve no purpose to detail the long series of transactions, sometimes friendly and honorable, sometimes fraudulent, by which gradually the Indians relinquished planting fields and hunting grounds to the whites; or to go into their disputes with the colonial officials and governments. After a half-century, despite white encroachments, there still remained land enough for all. At the time of King Philip's War, records show, for example, extensive Indian planting fields adjoining Lake Quinsigamond in central Massachusetts, (including apple trees obtained from the whites), and in the Merrimack and Connecticut valleys. Near Woodstock, Connecticut, Gookin says in his *Historical Account of the Christian Indians*, that on their fertile lands the Indians were raising forty bushels of corn to the acre, an excellent yield. At Natick, Nashoba, and John Eliot's other Christian villages, they were also doing well, while if we are to believe Samuel Drake, King Philip's company at their seat on the Mt. Hope peninsula (now Bristol, Rhode Island) had "a thousand acres of noble corn." Yet the handwriting was on the wall, and Philip could read it. Friction over violent deaths, differing conceptions of justice, and demands for submission to English decisions were finally too much. The Wampanoags and the Narragansetts rose and others joined them.

Philip's bowmen had begun their rampage in late June 1675, and it was August 1676 when he was betrayed and killed. One of the objectives of the whites during the war was to destroy the crops of the hostile Indians, not only in Philip's domain but in the Nipmuck country of central Massachusetts and up into the Merrimack Valley, home of the Pennacooks. They succeeded, and other disasters for the Indians followed. At the war's end Plymouth Colony sold Philip's wife and son and the male captives into West Indian slavery, their women and children desolate. Even the Christian Indians, helpful as they were to the whites in several important actions of the war, did not escape. The Nashoba and Natick villagers, despite guarantees that they were not to be molested, were illegally herded in winter onto an island in Boston Harbor, where many died. Those who survived returned to find their buildings wrecked, their tools, carts, and swine gone. From blows like these their diminished numbers could not recover.

Further, Plymouth Colony sold the Indian lands at Mt. Hope to Boston capitalists and distributed the proceeds to the towns to help pay the expenses of the war. Within two decades these fields, again fruitful, were growing onions and feeding horses for export to the West Indies. Except on Cape Cod, Martha's Vineyard Island, and a few areas in Connecticut, the agriculture of the small number of native Indians who survived in southern New England was never again to be of consequence. Many a field of theirs, however, is still fertile and productive in other hands. To quote J. Lewis Diman at the bicentennial of the town of Bristol in 1880: "We are standing on soil that was wrested from him [Philip]: we are enjoying privileges that were purchased by his ruin." And that was true of hundreds of other Indians, including many who never adhered to his cause, even helped the colonists.

With final scattering of the remnants of the defeated Indians the farm people who had escaped reoccupied the frontier towns but settled no new ones. Even with adequate capital it might take years for a farmer to breed and raise replacement stock; and money as well as time is needed to rebuild burned houses and barns. These war years were a period of deep discouragement.

More, however, was soon to follow. Not much over a decade later the countryside had to arm once more. The new struggle was not of the colonists' making but had its roots in great part in national ambitions and dynastic conflicts in Europe. This time it was not local Indians of southern New England but those of Canada and eastern Maine who pillaged, burned, and killed. They hit chiefly outlying frontier towns in the Connecticut Valley, New Hampshire, and Maine.

The destruction commenced with scattered raids on North-field in the Connecticut Valley and along Penobscot Bay in Maine, followed in 1689 by the burning of Dover, New Hampshire, and captivity for many of its people. In 1690 other towns in that area and in southern Maine suffered heavily: 34 killed and 54 taken captive at Salmon Falls in March; Falmouth, Maine, attacked in July. From Newington in southern New Hampshire devastation extended south into Amesbury in Massachusetts, and by 1691 all Maine settlements but four had been wiped out.

These attacks were but the prelude to three quarters of a century of bitter struggle with Indians, French, or both, lightened by only a few brief intervals. Like the seventeenth century, the eighteenth, up to 1763, brought slaughter, flame, pillage—and abandonment or poverty—to outlying towns in Massachusetts, to almost the whole settled area of New Hampshire, and once more to the entire Maine coast. As war proceeded, blows by the French extended to farms on the offshore islands and to coastal towns untouched in King Philip's War.

Striking stealthily from the forest the Indians added a new tactic: they carried victims back with them to Canada, to be held there for money ransom. Of those captured, many perished from exposure and hunger. Some, more fortunate, their liberty bought by ransom, eventually returned. A few of the youngest married or were adopted and remained in Canada.

Again and again through the decades from 1690 on, death or captivity, fire and pillage, descended on Brookfield, Hadley, Deerfield, and other villages in Western Massachusetts. Lancaster and vicinity in its center; Andover, Dunstable, Haverhill, and Newbury in the Merrimack Valley; and up the Connecticut

Valley to Charlestown, New Hampshire—the whole of settled New Hampshire was swept with fire and blood. On the Maine coast "not a house from Wells to Casco was passed by." Fire destroyed standing grain. To quote Sanborn, a New Hampshire historian: "Land and property were everywhere insecure. No one knew an hour beforehand where the next blow would strike. No person could enjoy a quiet meal or an hour's rest." [10]

Uneasy intervals of relative peace intervened from 1709 to 1713, from 1714 to 1723, and from 1750 to 1754. Treaties made in Europe, to which the Indians frequently paid no heed, gave some relief. A longer period from 1725 to 1744 did allow two decades of substantial material progress; otherwise the outlying parts of New England knew little quiet until the Peace of Paris in 1763, when Canada came wholly under the sovereignty of Great Britain.

If the wars did not depopulate frontier towns they stunted their growth. Wrote Thomas Wilder from the Massachusetts town of Harvard, in 1704, in a petition to the colony government: "Most of ye Inhabitants have been necessitated to watch and ward a third part of their time at least besides Rangeing the woods often where Rumorns and Allarms have happened, so that near halfe our time is spent in actuall service and when we are about our own worke we cannot keep to it . . . being forced to get our bread with ye periol of our Lives which hang in doubt continually & but little peace day and night." [11]

Colonel Partridge sent a message to Governor Dummer of Massachusetts from the Connecticut Valley in 1723 declaring that these towns could not stand the strain upon them to "watch and ward, scout and fort" without pay, and their spring work was pressing to be done. A Lancaster historian lists the many oxen, cows, sheep, and horses besides a new barn and twelve loads of English hay lost in attacks there on July 31, 1704.[12] A New Hampshire local historian details how in 1751 cattle were slaughtered "to furnish provision for the skulking savage." With crops unharvested and currency depreciated, poverty came to the rich intervale of Keene, New Hampshire, and many another town.[13] In June 1755 the hundred settlers at Ashfield, in the Berkshire foothills of Massachusetts had left everything for a place of safety. Public treasuries were emptied, and taxpayers bowed down with expenses and debts, taxes falling almost wholly on polls and property. Calls for army service, to which the towns loyally responded, depleted the countryside.

The burden on the colonies might have been too heavy to bear had not actual devastation been confined largely to frontier settlements, leaving older agricultural areas with unimpaired production, while New England's commercial life was bolstered by expanding commerce and the outfitting and provisioning from time to time of troops and fleets, largely on credit. Such extraordinary public exertions created demands for farmers to supply, and for some at least the resulting trade offset the financial losses the wars brought on.

13

A Surplus to Sell

A PHRASE THAT HISTORIANS have frequently used to describe the agriculture of New England's early generations is "subsistence farming." The words imply that the early farmer, once he had chopped out a spot in the forest, spent the rest of his life and energies barely keeping himself and his family in food—planting just sufficient grain and raising only enough animals to furnish milk for their porridge, wool for their backs, and shoes for their feet. There were many such, but a more accurate description even for this type of agriculture is "self-sufficient farming," as some historians have more precisely described it.

Self-sufficiency certainly was the first objective of nearly all early farmers. Because of inadequate capital, distance from markets, or poor land, some never got beyond it. Included in this category of farming might be the tradesmen, fishermen, and sailors who on their village lot had a cow and a sow, who grew a little corn or wheat, set a dozen fruit trees, and perhaps dug a kitchen garden while for the most part pursuing their primary occupations. Yet the phrase "self-sufficient farming" affords only a partial picture of what in numerous instances actually went on almost from the beginning, and especially after the first decade when it became clear that if they were to survive economically, the Bay Colony and its neighbors had to find products that could be sold outside New England. As decades passed, to grow and dispose of at least some farm produce beyond the family's requirements became more and more the goal of New England farm people. As Governor Thomas Hutchinson later put it, they gradually fell into the trade most natural to the country.

In the very year 1676 when King Philip and his allies were harassing the outlying towns of Massachusetts and Rhode Island, Edward Randolph, the English customs collector sent out by Charles II, made a detailed report, perhaps a trifle inflated, to the Committee For Trade and Plantations across the sea regarding New England's economic situation, in particular its exports. In addition to the cod, mackerel, large fat herring, furs, and bar iron, all of which he mentions, he gives a list of other exportable commodities, the fruits of agriculture and lumbering.

Among those he counted: all things necessary for shipping and naval furniture; pines for masts the best in the world, pitch, tar and hemp; clapboards, pipestaves, planks and dealboards; horses, beefs, sheep, hogs, and goats; great plenty of wheat, rye, barley, oats and pease. Of agricultural products, he states, salt beef and pork, pease, flour, biscuit, and malt had long been going to Virginia, Maryland, Jamaica, and the West Indies; together with horses, dealboards, pipestaves, and houses ready framed. Ship's masts, timber, and wood products were exported to England, Spain, Portugal, their islands, and Gibraltar; and to other parts of Europe were sent "such commodities as are vendible." Some New England ships, he says, have recently sailed as far as Guinea, Madagascar, and those coasts. Thirty master-builders put together ships from the native lumber and sell several yearly in England and other parts, for they build them well and at low cost.[1]

This trade affected individual areas in differing ways. New Hampshire, which until well into the eighteenth century was settled chiefly along the coast with its great salt marshes, abounded in cattle. Along Great Bay and the Piscataqua River its towns had also developed an important lumber trade; as much as 20,000 tons of boards and pipestaves a year was claimed.[2] Cattle, hogs, and horses were driven over the road from coastal points and the interior to Boston; salted beef went by coaster.

From Bristol and Newport, Rhode Island, onions locally

grown started for Guiana with a load of horses and lumber. Rhode Island's fat sheep went overland to market in Boston. New London and Milford, Connecticut, shipped horses, cattle, and salt meats to Boston, Newfoundland, and the West Indies, and soon added wool, hemp, flax, cider, boards and staves, tar, and pitch.[3]

At the head of the Connecticut River estuary, Wethersfield exported wheat and other grains grown on alluvial valley soils, and after 1700 was a famous source of onions. Upriver in Massachusetts John Pynchon and others did a thriving business growing pork and beef to send down the great river to salt water, whence it went packed in barrels either to Boston or directly abroad. When New Jersey suffered a drought in 1687 New England supplied Indian corn. Wool crossed the sea to France, Spain, and Portugal; New England soap helped keep Virginians clean.[4] Some merchant families raised cattle and horses for export on farms of their own. The variety and volume of exports from the score of New England ports is amazing.

Johnson in an earlier decade had exclaimed, "Nor could it be imagined that this Wilderness should turn a mart for Merchants in so short a space. Holland, France, Spain and Portugal coming hither for trade . . ."[5] All the commerce mentioned was developed before the 1600's were over, while the first generation of colonists were little more than in their graves.

With the coming of the eighteenth century, agricultural exports increased. Country produce flowed to the merchants of Boston, Salem, Newport, New London and New Haven by coaster and oxteam and on the hoof, to be sent wherever it might bring a good return. For example, a daily packet sailed between the South Shore town of Scituate and Boston. On one June day in 1724 six separate "horse jockeys" sailed out of New London for the West Indies, each ship loaded, in addition to other cargo, with a score or more of the animals that traders had collected. The horses were destined for sugar mills or for saddle and pack animals. An ordinary freighter might carry up to 45 horses, in addition to its main cargo of hoops and staves below deck. A large ship with built-in pens might accommodate 150 to 200.[6]

Other livestock went also. On December 5, 1730, a neigh-

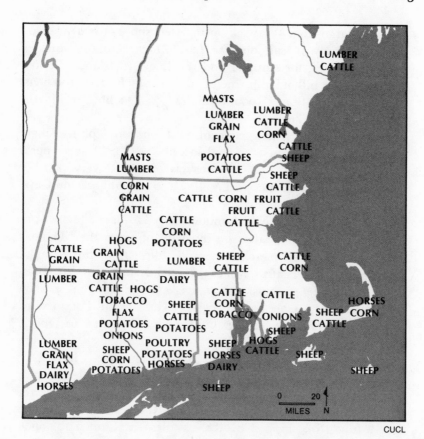

7. *Principal eighteenth-century farm productions, by area. Cartography Laboratory, Clark University.*

borhood cargo from Warwick on the west shore of Narragansett Bay was ready to sail on *The Little Mary*, Captain Stuckley Stafford, master, for Antigua and the Leeward Islands. Besides five horses, the bill of lading included "56 hogs, 84 gees, 190 hens, Boards 4460 ftt. Staves 1900, Shingles 5500, 11 bbls. fish, 7 BB apples, 1700 lb. Cheese." [7]

To Virginia, which concentrated on tobacco, its single money crop, Boston in 1711 sent in one vessel $5\frac{1}{2}$ tons of pork, 690 bushels of corn, and 207 bushels of wheat, very possibly originating in the Connecticut Valley and brought around Cape Cod. [8]

The lading of the New London sloop *Fox* for St. Thomas, in November 1759, illustrates the diversity of cargo that Thomas Allen, New London merchant, could collect from the farms of Connecticut and central Massachusetts. It included "10 bbls. Pork, 8 bbls. Beef, 14 bbls. Fish, 14 casks Bread, 800 Staves, 6500 ropes Onions, 55 Cheeses, 16 kegs Briskets, 50 bu. Potatoes, 10 boxes Sope, 50 Shoats, 32 Gees, 7 Duz $\frac{1}{2}$ of Fowls, 1 Duz Ducks, 47 Turkeys, 13 bbls. Apples." [9]

How such a cargo could be brought together is hinted by intermittent entries from the diary of Joshua Hempstead, farmer-trader of New London. Here are a few samples: "June 18, 1714 I shipped a bl of Tallow on bord Capt. Boss, weight 159 lbs"; "July 16 I shipped 82 lbs. candles—a Ram, 6 lb. Shoe Thread for Barbados." On one Madeira voyage he sent 10 pounds of tobacco and $28\frac{1}{2}$ pounds of beeswax; on another, $41\frac{1}{2}$ pounds of bayberry tallow that his son had gotten of a neighbor. Small items like these might be entrusted for sale to friendly captains. On the last day of December 1718, Hempstead wrote in his diary: "I sent 2 Geese 82 ganders by Jonathan Bailey to St. Citts" (St. Christopher). On June 3, 1719, he records the result: "Jonat Bailey hath been over & brought Some Cotton ye Effects of ye Geese I sent by him Last Winter. Still due 2 to 3." Just what was still due is lost to us! At times shipments might even be the result of an order from abroad. William B. Weeden tells of a Surinam planter in 1763 ordering beef, pork, flour, mackerel, fish, tobacco, a bull, two cows and two heifers, and also peacocks, six tame geese, and one dozen ducks. [10]

Trade to the north was of a slightly different character. On Oct. 20, 1764, after the end of the French war, the Massachusetts sloop *Fannie and Jennie*, loaded with 38 tons of brick and tile, also carried 2 chaises, 20 boxes of candles, 40 dozen cabbages, 22 cattle, and 70 sheep. On the 31st the schooner *St. Elizabeth*, in the same brick trade, had on board 5 barrels of apples, 12 dozen cabbages, 44 oxen, 40 sheep, and 5 hundred weight cheese.[11]

As the eighteenth century advanced, additional products from the country found a market. Ships and ship timber went to England, to the other American colonies and the West Indies. Stands of forest too far from coast or river to be sold as timber were now being burned and turned into potash and pearlash, chemical products which were light, easily transported, and in demand in Great Britain. Salt hay went to the South along with beef, pork, dairy products, and apples. Rhode Island had long been exporting its tobacco, and tobacco-growing in Connecticut must also have been considerable.[12] In 1742 Providence cargoes for the West Indies listed up to 5 tons per ship.

Flax was becoming important. The Scotch-Irish, settled in New Hampshire in 1718, began at once to grow it and make it into very good thread and linen. More valuable for trade than the fiber was the seed, which was shipped in bulk from the Connecticut Valley to Ireland, to be sown in that linen center where seed did not mature well. By the middle of the eighteenth century Connecticut was shipping out flaxseed to a value of 80,000 pounds a year, much of it to Ireland, as Victor Clark notes.[13] In more modest amounts seed went to market from small country towns such as Chatham on Cape Cod, Hingham in the Massachusetts Bay Colony, and Peacedale, Rhode Island. It passed as currency in country stores. The local product was not always received with enthusiasm. In 1774 a Philadelphia merchant wrote to Newport complaining that from experience they had found the seed from New England and Rhode Island to run short.

How much, in relation to agriculture, did all this commercial activity actually amount to? Gleanings from contemporary documents help toward an estimate. Boston, leading port of the entire seaboard, is said to have cleared 40 vessels a month in

1714; in 1730 the Massachusetts colony was estimated to be employing 500 ships and 5,000 sailors. In 1740 Boston alone was reported to be sponsoring three to four hundred ships great and small, and in 1750 clearances of vessels from Boston and Charlestown ran to a thousand a year. Newport claimed in 1718 to have exported 100,000 pounds of wool and eventually had 200 vessels in foreign trade, with twice as many smaller ones in coast traffic. Between March 1757 and March 1758, Ezra Stiles says, New Haven from chiefly agricultural Connecticut, cleared 168 coasters and 53 vessels for foreign ports. (New London records were destroyed by fire.) From Providence during this period the Browns were sending out mixed cargoes, including beef, pork, lumber and staves, tobacco, and sheep. Even Wells (Kennebunk) and York in Maine had vessels in foreign trade. York, with twenty, by 1745 was carrying cattle, horses, lumber, vegetables, meat, soap, and candles, as well as fish, largely to Halifax and Montreal. Yet the trade of none of these ports compared with that of Boston and Salem. Boston was shipping even salt hay, cut on Chelsea marshes, to the South! Massachusetts is estimated to have been putting to sea half the carrying capacity of the American colonies together.[14]

Active commerce bred thriving markets for farm produce, not merely to lade the ships but to provision them. The hundreds of fishing vessels from Marblehead, Gloucester, and Cape Cod towns consumed quantities of salt pork, beef, biscuit, and other food both when fishing in the summer and when carrying cargo in winter. Another modest type of traffic easy to overlook is the great number of boats supplying wood fuel to the port towns, the crew of each of which required provisions.

Whaling, by the middle of the eighteenth century, was also thriving and by the 1770's Massachusetts alone counted over 300 vessels which had to be provisioned for considerable voyages. For example, the sloop *Susannah*, out of Martha's Vineyard, Captain Pease master, heading for whales in the West Indies, in 1763 took on board "7 bbls. beef, 4 bbls. pork, 3 bbls. flour, ½ firkin butter, 1 side good leather, 1100 lbs. bread, 50 lbs. cheese, 4 bu. beans, 3 bu. meal, 4 bu. turnips, 2 bu. potatoes, 16 bu. corn, 14 lbs.

candles." The Vineyard and Nantucket between them had 60 whalers out that year; 101, two years later; and 125, in 1768. In 1767 the sloop *Betsey* was fitted for a short whaling voyage at Dartmouth, Massachusetts. Her supplies included "4 bbls. pork, 60 lbs. tallow, 60 lbs. butter, 45 bu. corn, three hundred weight of bread, 66 gr. of flour, 1 cheese, 2 bu. beans, and 166 lbs. beef." [15]

The live freight carried on merchant vessels consumed farm produce. For each horse, cow, ox, or sheep bound for the West Indies, a vessel had to take aboard 200 to 500 pounds of hay according to destination; for each horse, 10 to 15 bushels of oats also. A ship loading 50 horses might need as much as 10 to 12 tons of pressed hay and 500 or more bushels of oats, in addition to food for the crew. Hogs and poultry, to arrive at market in good condition, required grain. In 1768 the New London sloop *Sally* stocked 23 bushels of corn, presumably for its 73 turkeys.[16]

The recurring eighteenth-century wars with the French and Indians swelled demands for market produce. The garrisons of forts had to be provisioned. The colonies outfitted thousands of men for land campaigns and hundreds of ships for the expeditions against Port Royal, Louisburg, and Quebec which dominate the history of this century. The Louisburg troops, for example, numbered over 4000, sent in small vessels; both soldiers and crews had to be fed.[17]

Even though New England early in the eighteenth century was importing flour and other supplies from colonies further south, it becomes clear that the salable surplus its farm people produced beyond subsistence requirements played an important part in the region's foreign commerce and in its income from abroad.[18]

Without entering into the economics of the rise and fall of prices, inflation from paper money, harassing difficulties of exchange and credit, or the limiting acts of Great Britain and the colonists' evasions of them, it becomes apparent how intertwined agricultural production and commerce were. Despite the newness of the country, despite wars that so frequently impinged on orderly progress, all through this century of 1675–1775 New England farmers to a considerable degree enjoyed that essential of a successful agriculture, substantial markets, and they produced the commodities to meet the demands.[19]

Two forces influenced the farmer's choice of what to grow for sale. One was his estimate of what the drover or the merchant shipping to southern or foreign trade would buy for resale at some river port or West Indies island or in Europe. The other was the needs of the people of his market town nearby. From the beginning the colony governments had tried to encourage trade of both kinds by providing local market places and making regulations to ensure fair trade.

For Boston, back in 1633 the Court of Assistants had made Thursday the weekly market day, and in 1635 they designated a market site at the head of what is now State Street. They ordered the land cleared and the pits that pockmarked it, formerly used by sawyers producing plank and boards, to be filled.[20]

In 1656 the will of Captain Robert Keayne, a wealthy Boston merchant, left 300 pounds for a market house and conduit, the latter to serve as a safeguard against fire. Up to that time both market facilities and fire protection must have been poor, for the will read: "I having long thought and considered of the want of some necessary things of public concernment which may not be only commodious, but very profitable and usefull for the Town of Boston, as a market place and cundit, the one a good help in danger of fyre, . . . the other usefull for the country people who come with their provisions for the supply of the towne, that they may have a place to sett dry in and warme, and . . . leave their corne or other things safe that they cannot sell, till they come again, which would be both an encouragement to come in and a great means to increase trading in the Towne also."

Two years later the Court had fruitlessly authorized erection of a townhouse at the marketplace, the lower part to be free for a market, as was common practice in English towns. In 1696, Tuesday, Thursday, and Saturday were named market days, trade to open at seven from March to May and six from May to September. Housekeepers were to buy in the morning, traders in the afternoon. The Clerk of the Market was to enforce the rules. The plan did not take hold, however, till 1734.

Such regulations failed to control buyers with money or such farmers as preferred quick action, though many were ready to spend all day trying to sell their produce. Hucksters found it profitable to intercept incoming farmers, buy the contents of their panniers or carts, and resell them at higher prices. Traders met farmers from the north at Medford and Charlestown, and those from the south and west beyond Roxbury Neck, sole land entrance to the town. They dickered by the roadside or at taverns, and often bought the load, though such "forestalling" was illegal and rules were frequently reenacted forbidding the practice. Many countrymen preferred to peddle their goods direct to the consumer rather than sell in the market, and continued to do so.

A visitor to the town in 1709 offers this picture of how Boston was eating: "The town of Boston is plentifully supplied with good and wholesome provisions of all sorts . . . Though the town is large and populous they could never be brought to establish a market in it . . . the country people always oppose it. Their reason is, if market days were appointed all the country people coming in at the same time would glut it."

At length Peter Faneuil, a rich merchant, thought to make marketing more effective for both buyers and sellers by offering the gift of a new market building. Whether to accept it or not brought on a battle at town meeting. The crowd was so great that the session had to adjourn to the town's largest church, and the margin for acceptance was only seven votes out of 747. A site was picked on town-owned land close to the dock.

Faneuil's offer to add to his gift a second story for use as a town hall turned the tide of sentiment; and when the building was opened two years later on September 16, 1742, he received the thanks of the town, and the hall was named for him. Provision dealers rented a few market stalls on the street level, but public acceptance was lacking and the market was closed in 1747. It opened again the next spring, closed in 1752, then opened once more. In 1761 fire burned all but the outer walls. With funds from a lottery it was rebuilt two years later, stood through the lean days of the Boston Port Bill and the War for Independence, and today Seth Drowne's grasshopper vane still looks down from the cupola on visitors from every part of the continent.[21]

Providence completed a market house in 1775 and two years later installed scales and rented ten stalls to produce merchants. How New England's other large ports must have been supplied is indicated by the comment of James Birket at Portsmouth, New Hampshire, in August 1750: "Country people come to town as it suits them with such Commodities as they have for Sale by which the Town is pretty well supplied with Beefe, Mutton, Veal and other Butcher's Meat. they have plenty of large Hoggs and very fat bacon . . . abundance of good fish of many different kinds, And abundance of Garden culture as Beans, Peas, Carrots, Parsnips, Turnips, Radishes, Onions, Cabages, Colliflowers, Asparagus, English or whats commonly called Irish Potatoes . . . they have also Apples, Pears, Plumbs, Cherries & Peaches in Abundance [also various berries] Water and Muskmellions, Squashes." [22] Londonderry, New Hampshire, for much of this century, conducted a May and an October fair that drew 10,000 people and all sorts of traders from both farms and towns, even Boston.[23] In 1762 Massachusetts authorized a fair at Hardwick, in Worcester County, which continued for many years. Wethersfield in Connecticut held three-day fairs in the years succeeding the Revolution. A half-year cattle fair is said to have been held at Watertown, in the Bay Colony, up to the Revolution, and a similar fair was authorized for Dorchester.

When demand was good, merchants sent their own buyers direct to the farm districts. These dealt with the country stores that began to appear and act as collection centers. A merchant might set up a branch of his own to exchange imported household needs, rum, and molasses for meat, grain, and cheese. Toward the middle of the eighteenth century agents of the Browns, Providence merchants, rode north into interior Massachusetts picking up meat, grain, and other country produce to turn over at a profit. The Allens of New London had a store at Shrewsbury, near Worcester, Massachusetts; the Trumbulls one at Lebanon, Connecticut. Agents for merchants shipping horses scoured Rhode Island and Connecticut bargaining for strings of nags for the West Indies.

After the end of the French wars, as demand for butter and eggs increased, itinerant collectors began to travel the back towns assembling dairy and poultry products for sale in Boston and other markets. Drovers brought cattle over the road to the slaughterhouses in Essex County, Massachusetts, and elsewhere, at which both hides and meat were salable. Cow traders visited the farms in the Connecticut Valley and other interior points and picked up cheap animals to fatten where provender was plentiful; the meat, after slaughter, was barreled for the export trade.

Concentration of agricultural products gave birth to what today might be termed infant industrial complexes. Did the introduction of shoemaking at Lynn fill Danvers, next door, with tanneries? or did the plentiful hides from the cattle of the Merrimack Valley, New Hampshire, and Maine, brought to Topsfield and Danvers for slaughter, make practical Lynn's commercial shoe industry? At any rate at least by 1739 Danvers was tanning large numbers of hides, while at Lynn cordwainers were busy fashioning shoes of textiles and leather for sale in quantity and for export, a marriage of supply and demand that was to continue there for over two centuries. Roxbury, whither cattle converged from south and west, was another tanning center.

The presence near the rivers to the eastward of an immense supply of forest products especially of oak and pine, much of it the fruit of the winter labor and ox teams of farmers, made possible expansion in shipbuilding, at as little as three fifths of English costs. Not only did this become a great industry itself, but the ships furnished the vehicles for both the fisheries and the export trade that were for so long mainstays of the New England economy. Conversely, the return lading of molasses supplied the New England distilleries. Hogsheads and barrels in which fish, molasses, rum, and tobacco were handled were also products of winter employment for local farmers.

Important relationships such as these between farming and trade were foundation stones for the prosperity of the area which are too often ignored altogether or taken for granted. More than one similar close interconnection of local agriculture with manufacturing and commercial enterprise, frequently over-looked, appeared in the period of industrialization that followed the Revolution.

14

Growth of the Land:
Grass and Grain

"I<small>T IS INDISPUTABLE</small> that fresh Grounds are full of Riches," wrote the English farm and garden adviser Richard Bradley in 1724. The relative leanness of southern New England soils did not unduly handicap New England farmers in the eighteenth century, except in some older, settled regions, for the aphorism of another English writer of that century applied to the New World: "Good markets make good farmers." [1]

Soil quality varied greatly from one colony to another, and even more between areas within each colony. Reverend William Hubbard in his *General History of New England*, written about 1680, summed it up: "For the generality of the soyle, it is of a lighter sort of earth, whose fruitfulness is more beholding to the influence of the heavens, advantages of the seasonable skill and industry of the husbandmen, than the strength of its own temper." [2]

Travelers from elsewhere have left their assessments. Near Boston, James Birket about 1750 thought Cambridge and vicinity "very promising for corn and grass," while in Dorchester "the land seems to Exceed any that I have seen in this Country." Fruit trees in orchards were very large. Newport Island was throughout like a garden, he said, but at New London, Connecticut, large and immovable stones made it mighty difficult to plow.[3] Doctor Alexander Hamilton in 1744 thought Stonington, the next town, aptly named.

To a hilltown Connecticut parson, the Connecticut River Valley of Massachusetts looked, in 1760, like a beautiful garden: "Hundreds of acres of Wheat, Rye, Pease, Flax, Oats, Corn &C." The Housatonic Valley in the Berkshires Lord Adam Gordon in 1764 called a delightful vale, well planted and thickly inhabited, with orchards to every house. Further north Theodore Atkinson in 1752 considered the Coos country, at the Connecticut River's oxbow, a tract of the finest land on the continent.[4]

Central Massachusetts received both credits and demerits, but in eastern New Hampshire the historian Daniel Neal considered the soil very rich. It produced English grass naturally and in great plenty; James Birket, of Antigua, by contrast, judged what he saw there light and gravelly, not capable of bearing much dry weather. Cape Cod soils drew little praise from any traveler.[5]

The learned Jared Eliot of Killingworth in Connecticut wrote about the same time. If he is to be believed, the originally fertile soil there was badly handled. Planted to wheat, it gullied. When a piece no longer produced well, the owner cleared another, as wheat farmers were to do across the entire continent. Eliot deplored the lack of manuring.[6] In Rhode Island at the beginning of the eighteenth century, Governor Cranston also was saying that the soil was exhausted.

Perhaps careless soil mining, scarcely to be called agriculture, was to be expected in newly opened frontier towns where, at first, crops could feed on centuries of accumulated fertility in forest soil or river silt; yet the painstaking habits of English farming and soil enrichment and lessons in fertilizing derived from Indian tutelage were continued in the settlements, especially where markets were available.

The supply of manure was often inadequate, but the need for hauling and spreading it was recognized early. As far back as 1641 at Marblehead, Archibald Thomson drowned when his boat sank while he was moving dung. This circumstance was a matter of particular note, because it was a Sabbath. In 1676 Samuel Richardson of Woburn and his little son were carting manure to a field and returned to find that the Indians had murdered his wife and daughter. Entry after entry in Joshua Hempstead's early eighteenth-century diary notes how this Stonington farmer carted dung and spread it, as much as fifteen loads in a single day, and seaweed also. In Hingham in the Bay Colony, on March 13, 1757, Joseph Andrews recorded that he began to sled dung. Reverend Timothy Walker, first minister of Concord, New Hampshire, began to sled dung early each March. Zaccheus Collins of Lynn was hauling dung all the first week of May 1762, his diary states. After it had been dumped on the fields, it had to be beaten up.[7] As it had been in England sheep manure was especially prized where available. In an accounting that apparently included other farmers besides the diarist, Hempstead paid "ye Shepard . . . wt was due for ye Dung."

Along the shore farmers fertilized with humus cast up by the sea. At Hingham on March 23, 1756, Andrews gathered 18 loads of rockweed, spread it, then hauled more still; and did the same again a week later. Hempstead brought home seaweed loads each December to stop up the cellar doorway outside and each January carted load after load to fertilize his land for the next spring. He tells on May 6, 1746, of fetching a stout load of rotten seaweed, apparently for immediate use.

In Connecticut shore towns the early settlers also dug peat out of swamps, carted it to their fields and piled it to crumble under the weather. At Narragansett, Rhode Island, Rev. Jared Eliot saw swamp mud carted into a cow yard to increase the dung, and was told it served the purpose very well. On his own place he had success with what he called "shell sand," and with seaweed. Cape Cod farmers and others on the southeast shore fertilized with herring; but apparently with time the runs decreased, for in 1718 Sandwich ordered its herring reserved for food. On the Bay side of the Cape farmers chopped up horseshoe crabs to fertilize corn hills.

Despite such additions it can scarcely be doubted that by the middle of the eighteenth century much land, of only moderate original fertility, particularly in areas distant from the shore and herring rivers, had been cropped and pastured until yields were small, or it was left for pasture alone. This may have been a reason why some farmers, or at least their younger sons, were anxious to find new land, and awaited only the end of Indian warfare to venture into the wilderness to secure it.

"To what produce is your climate best adapted?" asked King George III of Governor Thomas Hutchinson of Massachusetts. "To grazing, sir; your majesty has not a finer colony for grass in all your dominions; and nothing is more profitable in America than pasture, for labor is very dear." [8] The governor's reply illuminates two fundamental facts governing New England agriculture for the century 1675–1775. First, cheap and productive pasturage plus available native hay, fresh and salt, offered a chief reason why New England could profitably raise beef and pork and horses for the export market. His second reason, dearness of labor, helps explain the colonists' emphasis on livestock in preference to cultivated crops that had to be harvested by hand. It also had a bearing on the careless type of field husbandry that critics often noted and sometimes condemned.

Pasturage and hay, nevertheless, were not abundant in heavily wooded New England. Hence, with the exception of a few settlements like Plymouth (founded by refugees without cattle), New Haven (founded by merchants for trade), and Marblehead (peopled by fishermen), the towns set up in New England's first century were invariably seated beside stretches of natural grassland.

Expeditions from the first Puritan vessels to reach Boston had set off almost at once to seek haylands and pasture. The search continued through the years. When in 1633 settlers looked northward from Salem, it was the 20,000 acres of Plum Island salt and fresh marsh at Ipswich and Newbury that caused them to sit down there. That same year under another patent, Captain John Mason sent his first neat cattle into New Hampshire to take advantage of the immense natural hay lands about Great Bay. Not long after began the hegira of Hooker's congregation from the Bay towns of Dorchester and Cambridge to the fresh intervale meadows of the Connecticut Valley, driving their cattle with them. Within a decade, the Musketahquid River, bordered by thousands of acres of grassy marsh, invited settlements at inland Concord and Sudbury, which soon found it profitable to winter cattle from less favored towns. The old town of Plymouth saw its hillsides become depopulated as, with the increase in their herds of livestock, farmers moved north to the wide salt marshes of Duxbury and Marshfield, and southeast to the salt grass of Eastham and the great silted bay that the Pilgrims named for Barnstaple, Devonshire, which it still resembles. A group of Plymouth's leading men bought the great salt hay marshes on the west side of Buzzards Bay, the adjoining upland, with its pines, and the swampland, with its valuable cedars.

Cattle enjoyed also such natural grasses as they found in the woods and beaver meadows; but some of the hay from the fresh meadows beside the rivers, though it grew tall and bulky, was disappointing as fodder. "Our beasts grow lousy with feeding upon it, and are much out of heart and liking", wrote one stockman.[9] If cut at the proper stage the "bluejoint" of the Sudbury meadows and the fowl meadow grass that appeared beside the Charles River at Dedham proved better. Certain types of salt hay also kept cattle in good heart; other types were eaten by stock only to keep alive. But none of this native herbage quite equaled the hay and pastures remembered from Old England. Both fresh and salt hay had the advantage of not requiring fertilizing. The river floods and seasonal high tides provided that.

Almost from the beginning, fortunately, English grasses began to creep in. The most obvious source is the hay that came with every shipment of stock. Chaff from it and the manure of the animals brought ashore contained seeds of all the pasture grasses and weeds of the south of England. Many of both took heart at their new environment.

Just when seed began to be purposely sown appears unrecorded. In response to Winthrop's request, Roger Williams wrote from Providence to John Winthrop, Jr., at New London in 1647 in great detail about handling a certain type of grass seed, perhaps the one now known as Rhode Island bent grass. His letter indicates that several persons had been growing the grass he recommended and finding it valuable. In 1650 William Pynchon brought 30 bushels of grass seed up to Springfield from down river; and in the spring of 1654 a hundred pounds of seed in chaff were said to be for sale at Hartford.[10]

Meanwhile, Thomas Minor at New London in 1653 was putting a picket fence of 500 pales around a patch of clover, a type of plant that became so prolific on Long Island that two Dutch travelers found it a quarter-century later filling the air with scent. Pynchon, who was doing extensive hay-raising, was by then selling "Flanders grass seed," a title that sounds like clover, for red clover was known in Belgium at least by 1605.[11]

The use of cleaned seed rather than chaff must soon have become widespread. In 1666 the town of Fairfield, Connecticut, was collecting money to pay for grass seed that had been furnished by a Mr. Burr to sow the common meadows. A few years later an official report from Rhode Island records that "in this Province is also the best English grass," and a Swiss who visited the province tells about the loading of the ship on which he sailed with pressed hay for 35 horses, though its type is uncertain.

John Josselyn in 1663 observed that "our English Clover-grass thrives very well" in New England. So well indeed that the Winthrops in 1684 were corresponding about having their clover, grown on Naushon Island off Buzzards Bay, thrashed in order to sow the seed at Tarpolin Cove, on old Indian fields. They planned to get Indian women and children to thrash it out. If cleaned well it "is worth half a crown or three shillings the pound . . . redy money." [12]

J. Hempstead was sowing white clover in Connecticut in 1725. He must have liked it, for two decades later he was still curing clover hay, and in February ten years later still he was buying 13 pounds of clover seed. After another decade Thomas Hutchinson, in his *History of Massachusetts Bay*, remarked that white clover was so widespread that "our farmers affirm, and there is no doubt of the fact, that if they break up new ground in the woods where no dung has ever been spread, and give it a thin coat of ashes, the white honeysuckle comes in as thick as if the seed had been sown." Clover seed was offered in Boston in 1730. Jared Eliot of Connecticut wrote learnedly about both white and red clover in his first essay in 1747, and Peter Kalm saw both growing in profusion on the hills above Albany, New York, in 1749.[13] William Logan of Pennsylvania in 1755 bought 200 pounds of red clover seed in Rhode Island to be shipped to him at Philadelphia by vessel. Enterprising Western Massachusetts farmers by 1657 were sending to Boston for it. In England the use of clover had been spreading westward from East Anglia for a century and a half.[14] In a letter to Eliot in 1761 a Marshfield gentleman is even reported to have two acres of "Lucern grass," presumably alfalfa, which had stood drought well.

By 1757 Hempstead was sowing clover and herdsgrass together, a combination that was to become a standby in New England for two centuries. Herdsgrass, *Phleum pratense*, had long been a constituent of English meadows, but seems not to have been selected or propagated there. A New Hampshire man named Heard is said to have found it growing in a moist spot at Piscataqua and propagated it. About 1720 Timothy Hanson took seed of it to the Carolinas, where it was called by his first name. The use of this handsome, erect, and nutritious timothy spread across the colonies.[15]

Herdsgrass, as New Englanders called it, was the favorite hay to feed with oats, to keep horses in top condition. Sown with red clover, likewise tall and vigorous, it gained an equal reputation as top feed for cattle. From America it was introduced as a separate variety back into England and Europe, from which its seed had once crossed the sea.

Timothy likes strong soil, but a more modest grass, redtop, was also making a place for itself in the eighteenth century. Though it does best on good manuring, redtop is adaptable: it will furnish grazing and a moderate amount of hay on rather poor and sour New England soils. Today it is to be found nearly everywhere, even when it receives no artificial encouragement whatsoever.

Two further notes on hay. The haybaler is a modern invention, but pressing or twisting hay for space saving and transportation by vessel was well known by the early 1700's, and very likely earlier. Pressed hay was regularly loaded on vessels to feed New England's livestock on their way to foreign markets.

Along with the original hay supplies arriving with stock in

vessels at the Bay had come seeds of the Old Country's weeds—and most of them flourished. Josselyn listed over twenty immigrants of varying degrees of nuisance, including couch grass and knot grass, shepherd's purse, dandelion, nettle, plantain, chickweed, sorrel, daisy, mullin, nightshade, and dock. Botanists have debated whether purslane was native or introduced. Champlain in 1605 saw what he called purslane abundant in Maine Indian fields.[16] Among native plants that Plymouth explorers recorded as head high in Indian lands must have been those hayfield nuisances, goldenrod and ragweed.

Although the farmers among the English settlers of New England appear in the main to have been livestock men, they and others experienced in different branches of agriculture had come expecting to grow wheat, rye, barley, and other grains, at least for their own use. As soon as plows and oxen were available they set about it. Massachusetts exported wheat in bulk even in the 1640's, largely to Europe. Within a half century, however, the spread of smut or mildew, particularly in spring-sown wheat, had discouraged many, especially those near the sea. "We Reapt ye yard of wheat: it is blasted," laments a farm diarist. A manuscript diary of 1663 quoted by C. L. Flint states that the best wheat and some other grain was so blasted in many places that whole acres were not worth reaping.[17]

Yet at Stonington, Connecticut, beside Long Island Sound, on August 16, 1663, Thomas Minor wrote: "We had 700 sheaves of wheate, 13 score without the Barne," which appears to spell abundance. A decade later on January 2 he noted: "I had threshed Two Ackers of winter wheate wee had in all 38 bushells," not a bad yield for any farm. In other coast towns some farmers continued to raise the crop. In that fateful year 1676 when Philip's Indians were abroad, John Jacob of Hingham, south of Boston, went to his wheat field on Glad Tidings Plain to try to shoot a trespassing deer, and was himself shot by Indians.[18] This was the very period when Josselyn was recording mildew and blasting.

As natural fertility decreased and disease increased, farmers seeded rye and wheat together. The resulting harvest and the bread made from it, an accustomed combination in England, was called maslin or meslin. Eventually the hardier rye took over for the most part in the older sections of the colonies, although on April 19, 1775, when the British troops marched through the Lexington countryside, the tradition is that spring was so far advanced that the young wheat ruffled in the breeze.

The Connecticut Valley became the breadbasket of New England: first the area about Hartford, then the middle section, and finally the intervales in Vermont and New Hampshire. A woman who grew up in Hatfield, Massachusetts, but had removed in 1767, recalled in her old age that the fields of grain there were immense, without fences. Northfield, Massachusetts, on the New Hampshire line, had a good wheat crop in that year 1767 when the province was offering a bounty for wheat. Meslin, then rye, took over here also, and the wheat center moved still further north. In the years before the Revolution the Coos meadows at the oxbow of the Connecticut, to quote their historian Reverend Grant Powers, "became to other infant settlements, north and south of them what the granaries of Egypt were to Canaan . . . in the . . . seven years of famine." An aged man later recalled the time when those in necessity carried up their silver shoe buckles to the Coos and exchanged them with farmers there for wheat.[19]

It took about two generations for farmers in the older towns to decide what caused the blight of their wheat crop. They noticed that the rust was most destructive in the neighborhood of barberry bushes, a fruit introduced from England. In 1726 Connecticut ordered the bushes destroyed. In 1758 Massachusetts followed, though Salem had been ahead with a local bylaw in 1747. At least one Salem grain grower was pulling up the bushes the year before that. Doubters remained until scientists showed in the nineteenth century that the farmers' observations had been correct.

Barley was scarcely the common crop that it had been in England, but some farmers grew it for barley "fire-cake" and to brew beer. An occasional inventory records fifty to a hundred bushels. On April 13, 1708, the Reverend Joseph Green of Salem, a considerable farmer, recorded brewing three barrels of beer. During the siege of Boston in 1775, a lady entered in her journal for July 21: "Major Vose having returned from an expedition to Nantasket reports that they took off about a thousand bushels of barley . . . besides the hay," indicating heavier production than has been ordinarily suspected.[20]

In Connecticut, Hempstead grew oats alone or with barley from time to time through thirty years from 1711. So did others. But Doctor William Douglass called New England barley a hungry, lean grain that made no good malt liquor. The oats too were lean, chaffy, and dark in color, he said. Peas were sometimes a companion crop to oats, sometimes separate. Lord Adam Gordon commented on the country about Boston: the soil, he said, was kindly, producing every European grain and root in plenty and perfection besides Indian corn.

For barley to become beer, hops were necessary. Woburn, north of Boston, made these a specialty. Judge Samuel Sewall visited the noted hopyards there in 1702. A Massachusetts cargo for Newfoundland in 1718 included hops. Joshua Hempstead in Connecticut was fencing his hopyard and poling his hops between 1735 and 1743; Birket saw hops growing near New Haven in 1750; on February 26, 1763, the schooner *Bernard* took 3,000 pounds of hops and 400 bushels of barley from Massachusetts to New York. Yet, judging from the evidence of estate inventories, neither hops nor barley appear to have been widely grown in New England before the Revolution. Lord Gordon remarked one cause: "although they grow good barley, and . . . hops grow there everywhere, with little trouble or culture, more large and high than any I remember in Surrey," they were little valued. "Cyder is their common drink." [21]

Yet, however much European grain some farms and certain areas might grow, and even export, it was not enough. Long before the Revolution the port towns were importing breadstuffs from the Middle Colonies for their growing populations.

"Besides Indian Corn." That phrase of Lord Gordon's points to the mainstay of New England's cereal production all through the sixteen and seventeen hundreds. Maize was thoroughly at home in New England. It was immune to wheat blast and most diseases. Even on poor land it yielded some grain and fodder. Most farm inventories include it, either harvested or by the acre. Paul Dudley told the Royal Society that one seed grain "commonly produces 1200 and often 2000 grains . . . 6 quarts plants an acre and it is not unusual for an acre of good ground to produce fifty bushels of corn." On sandy Cape Cod, William Douglass in 1750 put the ordinary production at 25 bushels. Benjamin Bangs is said to have recorded in 1742 a harvest of 177 bushels from six acres; and at Truro on the Cape, with sufficient crab underneath for fertilizer, Dudley's boast of fifty might be reached.[22]

The South Shore town of Hingham, in 1749, harvested a total of 11,693 bushels. Using Douglass' average, this would indicate 466 acres of corn in that one town. Twenty-six of its farmers raised 100 bushels each; one reached 225 bushels. (In all such figures the bushel may refer to ears in bulk, not shelled corn.) That corn production was substantial almost everywhere becomes clear from the diary of a lady exiled by the siege of Boston to Nantucket. The chief produce of the island was corn, she said, and one field of it (presumably a common field) was six miles long! [23]

One of corn's virtues is that the grain is equally nourishing and healthful for man and beast. For livestock, Thomas Anbu-rey, a British army officer in the Revolution sized it up: "Indian corn is certainly the heartiest and most strengthening food for cattle and poultry, and gives their meat firmness and excellent flavor." [24]

On old land the best culture practice was to plow, crossplow, harrow smooth; then furrow and crossfurrow at intervals of from 3 to 4½ feet according to the quality of soil, and plant at the intersections. After the corn plants came up, light furrows plowed lengthwise between the rows threw the earth toward the hill, followed by hoeing to kill or cover weeds. After these first cultivations the hoe was used once, sometimes twice, according to need. Bean vines twined up the cornstalks, and pumpkin seeds planted at intervals provided foliage to cover the ground for the final few weeks, smother weeds, and produced welcome addi-tional food.

A much less elaborate method developed as new settlements in the eighteenth century reverted to an Indian practice:

planting, with a hoe only, in the fresh soil between tree trunks and burnt logs—rough culture but successful. In August cornstalks might be lopped early to cause the ears to mature, or left on the field after harvest for stock to browse on.

When the harvest was ready and the ears had been drawn in from the field, it was husking time. Joshua Hempstead of New London, Connecticut, and his boys in the fall of 1711 husked corn at night till 10 o'clock, his diary records. On another October day he picked more for the boys to carry to the garret for storage. A week later, he turned all the corn in the chamber garret. As the years went by he changed his method, spent some days cutting poles, and made a "Cribb" the last week in October. On November 4 his diary records: "I finished Cribbing the Corn." One year, with a neighbor's oxen, his sons carted in "1 Load of Corn and 1 of pumpkins."

Connecticut liked its corn yellow, Rhode Island liked it white. It was, in any color, New England's most valuable grain.[25]

15

Growth of the Land: Vegetables and Fruits

OF ALL plant immigrants to arrive in New England after the early 1600's, none was more welcome or proved more important to its economy than that which accompanied the influx of Scotch-Irish settlers toward the end of the second decade of the 1700's. The potato, a Peruvian vegetable sent back to Spain by de la Vega or some other conquistador in the previous century, had been shipped to Virginia in 1622 and included among a list of plants and seeds ordered shipped to Governor Endecott in 1628; but if the tubers arrived and he planted them, nothing seems to have come of it. He may have preferred the other roots: parsnips, carrots, and turnips, all of which promptly took hold in their new surroundings. It was not long, however, before potatoes were imported for food, 15 tons from Bermuda in one shipment in 1636, "which were a great relief to our people," said Winthrop. But like the oranges and lemons that came with them, they must all have been eaten; no planting is mentioned. In Pennsylvania a rich merchant is said to have tried potatoes in his garden in or about 1685. At a Harvard Commencement in 1707 potatoes appeared on the menu, perhaps also from Bermuda.[1]

The first potatoes of any historic consequence to arrive in the English colonies, however, came with five shiploads of families of Scottish blood from Londonderry, Ireland, immigrants from the colony of that race domiciled in northern Ireland during the previous century. Some of these immigrants spent the winter in Portland. A few settled permanently at nearby Cape Elizabeth and about Casco Bay. Sixteen families were granted land in the Merrimack Valley in southern New Hampshire, and on April 11, 1719, began settlement there, naming their town Londonderry for their Irish home. Others dispersed into central and western Massachusetts. The next year, 1720, more came to settle on the Maine coast and plant potatoes at Wells, while others sat down about the mouth of the Kennebec.

Whether the New Hampshire group of immigrants in the spring of 1719 grew the first Irish tubers in North America, as the potato monument at Derry states, or whether the first seed planted was in Nathaniel Walker's garden at Andover, Massachusetts, or that put in the ground by the Youngs who journeyed west to Worcester, is a matter of debate. There is credit enough for all.[2] Potatoes are said to have been introduced in Connecticut the following year and by 1735 were being sold in Rhode Island. It seems to have been 1750 before the Connecticut Valley took up the new crop.

What is clear is that within two decades New England farmers were harvesting the tubers not only in those areas but in places as scattered as Norwich, Connecticut; Warwick, Rhode Island; Arundel (Kennebunk), Maine; Lynn, on the coast; and Westborough in central Massachusetts. Moreover, by 1745, at least, New England had begun to export potatoes. Following the middle of the century its potatoes were being shipped south to Virginia in vessels from New Hampshire, Salem, and Boston; and from New York as well. In 1759 the cargo of the New London sloop *Fox*, for St. Thomas, included fifty bushels. Not long after that a Martha's Vineyard whaler listed two bushels for its crew. In Connecticut the new crop proved so satisfactory that in 1767 Reverend John Devotion, writing from Westbrook on Long Island Sound, was enthusiastic: "We improve in Potatoes in this Colony exceedingly. Many farmers raise 500 bushels pr. An. I don't think myself stored without 150 Bush per. An." [3]

Apparently several varieties were tried, for Douglass in 1755 writes: "Irish potatoes . . . is much planted in New England, thrives well and is of good use; varieties here are the rough coat, red coat, flat white and long white: my taste prefers the rough coat." A correspondent of a Boston paper tells of one type which, though inferior, proved a godsend. The summers of 1761 through 1763 were seasons of intense drought (the Connecticut Valley in 1761, an exception). Almost no rain fell in 1762 from June until the last week of September. "In 1761," the informant writes, "we began to plant the Spanish potato, corn etc. being so scarce. 1762 and 1763 were years of scarcity: they would have been years of famine had not this despised root been providentially brought among us." Why it should have been despised is hinted by Samuel Deane of Maine in his *Georgical Dictionary*. Though extremely prolific, he says, the Spanish potato was fit only for cattle and swine. It was probably the small red kind of a rank taste which was the first Deane grew, in 1740, presumably at Portland, where he was long a pastor and farmer; but a white kidney sort soon appeared. His diary records experiments with several other varieties and various methods of culture. Like Pastor Devotion of Connecticut, he liked the rough coat, and also the "winter white." [4]

Difficulties similar to the ones that were to plague potato growers in the next century appeared early. One was price fluctuation. In Weeden's "Table of Prices," printed in the supplement to his *Economic and Social History of New England*, potato values vary widely from year to year. The second hazard is mentioned in a local history. Just before the Revolution a potato disease prevailed extensively in eastern Massachusetts which the author judged to have been similar to the blight that was to prove so devastating in the middle of the next century.

All in all it is not too much to say that the arrival of the Scotch-Irish with their potatoes proved one of the most important events of New England's whole agricultural history, with an influence that was to spread much farther still. Yet that was only one of their contributions. Almost from the beginning, colonial governments considered cultivation of flax important to provide linen. In 1640 Connecticut directed its inhabitants to plant either flax or hemp and tend and husband both. Attempts must have been made to grow it further up river, for in 1646 Springfield

8. Breaking and swingling flax. From flax harvest to linen thread there were twenty hard, dirty steps. Chase, History of Old Chester *(1889).*

forbade washing flax in a brook used for dressing meat. The Valley soils proved adaptable and flax became a staple commodity in trade there. Clark estimates that by the middle of the century Connecticut's export trade in the seed alone was worth 80,000 pounds sterling a year. It was three fourths of a century later when in 1718 a mill to press out linseed oil, a flaxseed derivative important for paint, medical, and industrial uses was opened at New Haven. Others followed, one at Hatfield, Massachusetts, another at Derby, Connecticut, at the confluence of the Housatonic and Naugatuck rivers, which prospered for a considerable time. Silas Deane of Connecticut told John Adams in 1774 that 35,000 bushels of flaxseed went to New York yearly in exchange for salt. In eastern Massachusetts flax is occasionally included in inventories in Essex, Middlesex, and Suffolk counties. Hingham on the South Shore grew 1735 pounds in 1773; Cape Cod also grew considerable just before the Revolution, as did the Germans who in 1748 had colonized Broad Bay in Maine. In Rhode Island, South County raised it in great quantity.

It appears to have been the settlers who came to New Hampshire from the north of Ireland, however, expert in textile experience, who opened the full possibilities of growing flax, twisting its fibers into thread, and producing fine linens, as Yorkshire weavers had been doing with woolens at Rowley in Massachusetts since the previous century. To grow and harvest the crop, "ret" or rot the stems, separate the fibers, and comb them out were matters of skill as well as long, smelly, hard, and dirty work. Spinning the thread and turning it into fine linens or even coarse tow cloth for rough work required more skill and more labor. James Birket in 1750–51 had this to say of the New Hampshire colonists' success at it: "This province also produces . . . exceeding good flax of which the Irish settled at Londonderry make very good Cloth & fine Ounce thread . . . and I'm informed this little town increases very much." [5]

New England flax growing, however, was mostly on a small scale. For example, Reverend Timothy Walker of Concord, New Hampshire, in general quite a large farmer, on May 5, 1764, sowed a bushel of seed and harrowed it in. Matthew Patten of Bedford, also in that province's moderately fertile Merrimack

Valley on September 7 and 9, 1765, cleaned his harvest of 64 pounds of flax seed. Joseph Andrews of Hingham, Massachusetts, took only a day or two each fall to thresh out his flax seed. Traders took flax in barter, had machines to beat out seed, and assembled many small amounts at export points.

Colonial authorities also tried by bounties to encourage hemp growing, since cordage was so important for the rigging of ships. Whether soils were not well adapted for it, manure scarce, experience lacking, or the cost of labor too high, its cultivation made little headway. Both large and small farmers tried the crop, however. On May 13, 1767: "Between the house and barn I sowed about 3 quarts of hemp seed in all," Patten records. By contrast, in 1764, Stiles states in his "Itineraries," Captain Stevens of Boston, with 6,000 acres of new land in the hills of Ashford, Connecticut, seeded thirty acres, tended by a man and a boy who cultivated by plowing between rows. It took thirty hands to pull the crop. He expected to harvest twenty tons of hemp worth 60 pounds sterling, besides 200 bushels of seed worth 20 shillings per bushel: its total value was 1,400 pounds, Dr. Stiles estimated.[6] Clearly agricultural speculation is of ancient origin! Yet so far as any record shows, despite bounties, hemp growing remained a very minor practice.

Tobacco growing, forbidden at first in both Massachusetts and Connecticut, got a slow start, though Plymouth was selling some to the Hollanders by 1628. By 1657, however, Milford, Connecticut, town meeting was granting liberty to Charles Deal to purchase Milford Island with its buildings for a tobacco plantation, and three years later the colony's governor, John Winthrop the younger, wrote that tobacco had brought some good crops. Soon items of tobacco were appearing in Rhode Island inventories. By 1682 Ipswich records indicate that tobacco "yards," fenced for protection, were common in Essex County, Massachusetts. In 1694 it was being grown in Deerfield, for a daughter of the Belding family escaped the Indians by hiding among tobacco hanging in the garret. By the end of the century Connecticut was exporting it.[7]

Windsor and the other Connecticut Valley towns around Hartford became the center of cultivation. Wethersfield in 1704 had to forbid encroachment on public land by persons wishing to grow it. After the French wars eastern Connecticut also got into tobacco growing. The product went abroad packed in barrels and tierces as well as in hogsheads, 400 pounds to the cask. Some went to the West Indies to be made into cigars, some to England, some to Europe. Shipments varied all the way from a lot of 31 pounds that Joshua Hempstead in 1712 sent, along with 7½ pounds of beeswax, by his friend Captain Mainwaring to "Madara" (the Captain brought him a cask of wine when he returned), or the four tierces that Thomas Allen shipped in the schooner *Triumph* from New London to the West Indies in 1759, to cargoes of 12,000 to 21,000 pounds that Elizabeth Ramsey records.[8]

The trade became so important that in 1753 the Connecticut General Court made it mandatory for each town to choose at least two surveyors and packers to make sure that no tobacco went out unless well ripened, sufficiently cured, and in every way good and merchantable. Massachusetts in 1724 made tobacco a commodity in which taxes could be paid, and tobacco growing crept up the Connecticut Valley (Ramsey estimates fifteen acres in Hatfield, Massachusetts, by 1771); but the crop was not yet of commercial importance in that colony.

Rhode Island was in the business early. By 1727 James Brown was shipping tobacco from Providence to Martinique; Obadiah Brown in 1734 sold a shipment of 8 hogsheads at St. Eustatia, but a lot sent to France in 1764 received a cold reception because its variety was unsuitable. Eventually the Rhode Island province is said to have produced 200,000 pounds a year, though dark colored and not of the best quality. In 1766, with tobacco in over supply, by a secret agreement the Browns and other Rhode Island firms formed what today would be called a cartel to allocate quotas and maintain export prices in the West Indies. Rhode Island tobacco is said to have been packed in empty molasses barrels, often returning to the area from which the molasses had been imported.[9]

Growing this crop had all the present-day hazards. In August 1731, Hempstead noted "a very great Hail" at Norwich, severe enough to break windows and ruin the delicate leaves of the tobacco in the fields. In the middle of September 1764, frost took much of the Rhode Island crop. However, from small beginnings, for some parts of New England the future of tobacco was to prove bright indeed.

The first vegetables to become of importance in the new colonies appear to have been the roots. Parsnips were a popular garden vegetable from the beginning. Turnips, at first grown in gardens or from seed scattered among squash hills, were sometimes sown with wheat in new ground. They were useful also to fill spots in fields where corn had failed to germinate. They came to be very abundant. In July 1722 Hempstead was plowing for them as a field crop, but had to fence them. Along with potatoes they were among supplies furnished at public expense to Acadian refugees in 1757. Douglass wrote that the best New England turnips were from new lands northeast of Boston. Numerous cargo lists include "roots."

Onions, a garden crop at the beginning in the Bay Colony, were grown also at Plymouth, and by John Winter in 1634 on Richmond Island, Maine. They had been a commercial crop in Lincolnshire, England, before the Puritan settlement and they did not wait long to be produced for market in New England, for the cargo list of a coaster on Long Island Sound in 1667 included a bushel of them. By 1686, a decade after the death of King Philip, Colonel Byfield, one of the purchasers of this chief's fertile Mt. Hope lands in what is now Rhode Island, was exporting them from Bristol. Deacon Bosworth of the same town in 1691 sent off 540 ropes grown on his farm. (Onions had been woven together into "ropes" in England.) By 1707 a Boston-built vessel listed 25 barrels in its cargo for Surinam. In the summer and fall of 1718 Boston vessels carried onions to Surinam, Barbados, Newfoundland, and South Carolina. At Wethersfield, Connecticut, which was soon to become a very large producer, Benjamin Adams sold 71 bushels in 1710. By the middle decades of the eighteenth century vessel after vessel from this port, New London, and Boston, bound for the West Indies, carried shipments of from 1,000 to 6,500 ropes of commercial-sized onions. The largest onions went loose in barrels. In 1760 Connecticut recognized the importance of the crop by setting standards for bunched onions.[10]

The Indian vegetables—squashes, pumpkins, and beans— continued popular among the colonists. Paul Dudley of Massachusetts tells how in 1699 a single pumpkin dropped by accident in a small pasture where cattle had been fed produced 260 fruits as big as a half-peck measure, which helps explain their general cultivation. "The inhabitants plant great quantities of squashes," observed the British officer Thomas Anburey in 1777. "The seed [is] cultivated with assiduity." Even in rural Rhode Island where vegetables were few, summer squashes were often on the table.

Besides the roots commonly found in gardens, gentlemen, ministers, and farmers near the port towns, perhaps with an eye on the market, were raising certain green vegetables, peas, cauliflower, and melons, and trying out asparagus and others. In Connecticut a 1655 hog-damage complaint had included cabbages. Thomas Minor was setting plants three years later. Hempstead raised them in an enclosure in 1713. Benoni Waterman, storekeeper of Warwick, Rhode Island, sold cabbages in 1735; and the Germans at Waldoboro, Maine, grew them from the first.

Seed merchants appeared. By 1719 Evan Davies, a Boston importer, was advertising in the *Boston Gazette* all sorts of fresh garden seeds as well as "English Sparrow-grass Roots." In 1768 William Davidson, a gardener on Seven Star Lane, one of several Boston dealers previous to the Revolution, offered 56 varieties of vegetable and herb seeds. Nathaniel Bird, a Newport bookseller, dealt in garden seed in 1763, Charles Dunbar in 1764, and in the same town Gideon Welles had Connecticut onion seed for sale. Field and garden seed advertisements appeared in the *New Hampshire Gazette* in 1766 and 1770.[11]

These dealers must have found customers, for on April 23, 1742, Dr. Holyoke's Salem diary tells of planting mushrooms, and in other springs appear such items as peas, beans, and onions. On February 19, 1753, he sowed gourds, cucumbers, and lettuce under glass in his "hotbed," and in June 1763 he was cutting asparagus, "1836 heads in all." Hotbeds must have caught on, for in 1762 windows suitable for them were advertised in Boston. Andrew Faneuil, Peter's uncle, is credited with New England's earliest greenhouse. When he died in 1737, his nephew Peter continued to grow fruits and other rarities in it. A royal official named Hulton put up another in Brookline in 1768. Hulton's sister, who wanted to try out such things as artichokes and broccoli, wrote a friend in England of putting 500 heads of the finest celery into it in the fall. But she added: "It is strange what little improvements are made in gardening here." Marked improvement was to wait largely till after the Revolution, though at Saybrook, Connecticut, Jared Eliot was already trying a new garden plant, rhubarb, started from seed that Benjamin Franklin sent from London in 1760. Green peas, at least, were plentiful in the early market: in the warm spring of 1775 by June 17.[12]

Among vegetable enemies the pea weevil appeared, spreading north from Philadelphia to infest field peas and cut down their production in the Connecticut Valley; and Jared Eliot at Killingworth in the Connecticut province in order to anticipate losses from the turnip fly felt obliged to sow turnip seed at three-inch intervals.

If there was one European crop to which New England soil and climate proved especially adapted, it was the apple. The ease of its production, the generous crops, and the juiciness of the fruit not only caused it to fill a need in the diet but within a generation or two from the first landing made cider the common beverage in place of the beer the colonists had at first considered almost indispensable.

How readily the apple took to its new environment is revealed by an observation from the Berkshire Hills just before the Revolution. By 1770 the whole length of the Indian path between the settlement of the Stockbridge tribe at Great Barrington, Massachusetts, and the Scaticoke village at Kent, Connecticut, nearly 40 miles along the Housatonic, was said to be lined with apple trees. They stood at irregular intervals, sprung from apple cores thrown away by traveling natives who had promptly learned to enjoy the Englishman's fruit.[13]

Parson Joseph Green of Salem grafted 59 "cyons" onto 24 of his trees on an April day in 1701, his diary tells us. On April

9. At a cider mill: tuns of cider, New England's favorite drink. Howard S. Russell collection.

11, 1709, Nehuman Hinsdale was driving a cartload of apple whips from Northampton to the newer town of Deerfield. Most such activities went unrecorded. In 1730 the century-old trees started by Boston's original settler, William Blaxton, were still bearing. Diarist Joshua Hempstead set out over sixty Sweetings as a nursery behind his stable at Norwich, Connecticut, on April 17, 1742. Perhaps this number was more or less a standard planting, for on April 24, 1764, Reverend Timothy Walker of Concord, New Hampshire, entered in his diary this notation: "Set about 60 young apple trees in ye house lot." The next day he "Made log fence around my young orchard," an essential precaution in a new area where cattle and deer roamed free. Lord Adam Gordon, just before the Revolution, exclaims that every road is lined with apples and pears: even the poorest farmer has at least one orchard.[14]

Some of the fruit went into pies, dried apples, and apple molasses, an excellent source of sweetening, which may explain why Sweeting trees were especially popular. Some were fed to fatten hogs. Most were crushed and turned into cider and vinegar. One village of forty families near Boston made 3000 barrels in 1721. Judge Joseph Wilder of Lancaster is said to have made 616 barrels in 1728. As part of the normal yearly supplies to be furnished his widow, a Worcester County farmer in the Bay Colony about 1750, included three barrels of cider. How the totals could mount may be gathered from an estimate taken from the valuation lists for Middlesex County, Massachusetts Bay, for 1764. The county's total is 33,436 barrels of cider, or seven per family, well over a barrel for every man, woman, and child.[15]

Export of apples, even of cider apples, was not uncommon; but most of the cider and the vinegar made from it must have been consumed in New England, for at this period neither appears often in cargo lists. Some was distilled into brandy or applejack. Torrington, Connecticut, for example, had four cider mills and one brandy still in 1774. Cider appears also as an accepted medium of exchange. In 1762 Ruel Baldwin of Woburn, in Massachusetts Bay, picked up a load of earthenware at the Charlestown port of entry, paying for it in cider.

Considerable attention was centered on varietal quality in the fruit, perhaps from the fact that so many trees were seedlings. The Roxbury Russet, which had originated on the Ebenezer Drew farm in that town close to Boston and then been taken to Connecticut about 1649, was and still remains a favorite for late winter and for cider. On another farm in the same town the handsome and delicious early Williams was noticed and propagated about 1750, to become for the next century and a half a favorite dessert apple.

The Rhode Island Greening, a famous pie apple ever since, may have come from an orchard set in 1640 by Governor Brenton, and been spread in 1748 by scions from an especially popular tree, at Green's Inn on Brenton's Neck near Newport. In the Connecticut Valley a dozen years later the Westfield Seek-No-Farther began two centuries of popularity for both cooking and cider. The original Baldwin tree at Wilmington must have dated from before the middle of the eighteenth century.[16]

Pears, too, were planted plentifully—along roads, in gentlemen's orchards, and in backyards; peaches also. The Bartlett pear is said to have been propagated in Roxbury in 1770. Judge Paul Dudley of Roxbury, who was fond of tall stories, claimed to have picked 800 peaches from a single tree, as well as pears eight inches across.

Josselyn back in the seventeenth century had rejoiced in all the wealth of fruit. "The Quinces, Cherries, Damsons set the Dames at work. Marmalade and preserved Damsons is to be met with in every house . . . I made Cherry wine, and so many others for there is good store of them both red and black." Maverick, scarcely less enthusiastic, added "Apricocks, Musk Mellons and Water Mellons" to his fruit list. John Hancock's famous garden included nectarines, quinces, limes, and mulberries, as well as peaches.[17] Among bush fruits barberries and currants, both brought over from Europe for cultivation, were the most widely grown—the former so numerous that near Dover, New Hampshire, a Mrs. Heard escaped the Indians in 1689 by hiding in a barberry thicket.

Caterpillars were already a nuisance. Miss Hulton described how at the beginning of the season they ate so much of the foliage that the trees had "a most dreary aspect in the summer." Hempstead's diary tells of his staying home in April 1712 to pick caterpillars off his trees. Whether these were tent caterpillars or canker worms is not clear; probably they were both. The year 1771 is said to have been an exceptionally bad cankerworm year, and in Westfield, Massachusetts, the next spring, Reverend John Ballantine's diary tells how a multitude of caterpillars stripped the orchards. On May 29, 1750, Hempstead found the wild pigeons feasting on canker worms in his bare trees. A "peach worm," perhaps the borer, had already put in an appearance.

Evidence that the practice of mulching orchards, which might be considered modern, is really of long standing is afforded by a letter of Ephraim Williams of Northampton, founder of Williams College, to his sons, who were managing his home farm at Stockbridge in the Berkshires. He tells them to get some buckwheat straw from the Stockbridge Indians, whose plantings adjoined, and scatter a good cock of it about each apple tree. If they will do this, he tells them, they will never bother to plow again. However, they must keep the straw a couple of feet away from the trunks for fear that field mice will strip the bark.[18] For the same reason, Eliot advised tramping down the snow about the trees.

16

Growth of the Land:
Livestock

Writers on colonial New England, if they pay more than cursory attention to its agriculture, have often treated farming as though it were a single comprehensive occupation, carried on practically everywhere according to a uniform pattern. Yet almost from the beginning the types of agriculture varied in response to natural conditions of soil and surroundings, available markets, and the experience an individual farm family brought or inherited from England.

At least by the end of the first half century, farming was dividing into two major categories: crop production and livestock and its products. Important as were the field, vegetable, and fruit crops in the century of 1675–1775, livestock production in its several branches, and the products and industries connected with it, were in this period of at least equal historical consequence. Not only did crops and livestock vary in importance from one district to another, however, but the livestock industry itself became concentrated in certain areas.

The one animal raised nearly everywhere, though not most important in numbers or value, was the hog. How important swine were in the New England economy is illustrated by the well-known story of Reverend Eleazar Wheelock, who in 1770 removed his Indian school from Lebanon, Connecticut, to

Hanover, New Hampshire, there to found Dartmouth College. The cavalcade consisted of seventy persons: family, students, and neighbors; but ahead of it was driven the herd of Connecticut hogs that was to help put the enterprise on a practical basis in its new home.[1]

In early settled towns hogs ranged the woods, according to the custom of forested districts in England (though by contrast with Old England, in New England their number was usually unstinted). They lived on acorns, nuts, and roots; and in the fall the family would gather additional bushels of nuts and acorns for their winter feed. Wolves and bears took toll, but an old boar, if allowed to grow tusks, was a match for almost any wild marauders. Moreover when winter storms arrived, he would lead the herd back to the shed, where he knew that corn and slops would be waiting.

Yet it is scarcely true, as has been asserted, that every farm had four or five hogs. Some did, and some had one or two; but others, even in early days, had none and must have relied on beef or mutton for meat. A random sampling of figures from a variety of sources, and not precisely comparable, illustrates sufficiently the wide variations between localities, as inventories do between farms.

Place	Year	Size of Town	No. Swine
Woodstock, Conn.	1718	100 dwellings	80
Sudbury, Mass.	1771	250½ "	464
Dartmouth, "	1764	772 "	383
Harvard, "	1771	163 "	276
Amherst, "	1779	134 "	206
Harwich, "	1781	273 "	193
Cape Elizabeth (Me.)	end of Revolution	1469 population	178

It should be noted that Dartmouth, Harwich, and Cape Elizabeth undoubtedly contained many sailors, and that in all towns there lived various mechanics, millers, and other tradesmen.

As a matter of comparison, Woodstock in 1718 listed three times as many cows as hogs and a hundred oxen besides. Its sheep numbered five and one half times its swine. Even

Woodstock's horses outnumbered its hogs. Amherst in 1779 counted between two and two and a half times as many cows and steers as swine and more than four times as many sheep; while the number of Sudbury's and of Harvard's oxen alone approximately equaled their swine, and the total of their milch cows was close to double. Relative to population, in 1735 the Bay Colony had 18 swine to each hundred persons. In 1767 for the three most populous counties, the proportion was nine per hundred persons.[2] A sampling of 86 eastern Massachusetts farm inventories, mostly in the 1700's, however, shows that five out of six of these farms had at least one hog, and one large estate counted 18.[3] There was no town, even the ports, without its hogs. Local by-laws required that swine running at large be ringed and yoked to prevent their being a nuisance in gardens and cornfields. Even so, fences had to be built strong and tight.

"Wood hogs," when butchered near the end of the year, were apt to be light in weight, from 100 to 150 pounds. On November 27, 1712, Reverend Joseph Green of Salem Village (Danvers) recorded in his diary: "Cut up and salted 7 hogs, 648 pounds." Two years before, three yielded 316 pounds. Even when well fatted with corn, wood hogs would run considerably lower in weight than hogs fed constantly on the home farm. The latter would usually weigh out at 150 to 250. Anburey saw cornfed hogs, which he called particularly excellent, which he said weighed twenty-five score. Salt pork from hogs fatted on Indian meal was said to be the best in America.[4] Connecticut farmers had a reputation for putting a good finish on their hogs: hence any fat, corn-finished pork came to be known in the trade as "Connecticut pork", even if it came from the Middle Colonies. Large amounts of pork of varying quality went into provisioning ships and into export trade. When a West Indies market appeared to promise well, vessels sometimes carried live shoats and fat hogs as cargo.

Hog growers in colonial times, as ever since, faced losses not easy to explain. Matthew Patten of Bedford, New Hampshire, on October 10, 1767, sorrowfully recorded: "The boys found our barrow hog dead who had been missing . . . and we missed our grown sow this morning, what the distemper I know not."

Sometimes it might have proved better not to find them. On a May day in 1635 a farmer named Clough, at Kingston in the east part of the New Hampshire colony, found a hog dead and examined a swelling on its throat. Within three weeks he was dead and three children of the neighborhood likewise from what was thought to be a similar throat distemper.[5]

Hogs might be driven over the road to market or, if their number was small, be killed at home. Home slaughter was most likely after cold weather began—often in early January, with some neighbor to help in return for a share in the pork. Cut into merchantable pieces and salted, barreled pork was a local medium of exchange as well as an export commodity. A Milford, Connecticut, receipt dated December 26, 1723, records payment by John Holbrook of Derby of 136 pounds of pork at three cents a pound "upon the account of the Bridge Logs of Derby," presumably a tax payment. A Rehoboth, Massachusetts, merchant's account in 1719 charges for killing one hog a shilling sixpence: equivalent in the account to 40 pumpkins or 2 pounds of butter. Merchant Jonathan Trumbull, later Connecticut's governor, packed pork at Lebanon. He bought hogs in the fall and shipped the barreled pork to several ports.[6]

Sheep raising is a specialized calling. Sheep require good pasturage free from thickets and briers likely to catch and tear their wool coats, protection from predatory animals, and careful, knowledgeable attention on the part of man. Much of New England's surface, even in the 1700's, was still too untamed for their somewhat fastidious appetites. Most of Maine and New Hampshire was not yet sheep country. After three fourths of a century many towns held yearly wolf hunts and offered rewards for wolf heads. Dedham, only 10 miles south of Boston, began to keep sheep in 1667. The town put its bounties high, but it took three decades before every wolf was gone.

Despite such drawbacks, as time passed, the number of sheep in the colonies showed substantial increase. Partly this was due to inducements offered by colony and town governments, their economies short on cash and overdependent on woolen imports. To improve and add to the sheep pasture available, and to prevent damage to the fleece of the sheep, Connecticut required every adult male to work a day each year at clearing brush from the commons. Northampton, Massachusetts, followed Connecticut's example. Springfield in 1654 gave John Pynchon ownership of Round Hill for bringing in forty sheep for sale, and in 1680 decreed that every inhabitant keep at least three sheep. Weymouth, also in the Bay Colony, in 1673 limited the number of horses allowed on its commons to afford better grazing for its sheep. New Hampshire offered tax benefits for sheep raising.

A dog that killed sheep was treated as a murderer and hanged. Northampton fined owners of "Large Doggs Going at Large." By contrast, one Buzzards Bay town kept four dogs especially trained to protect its flocks from foxes.

Well into the decades preceding the Revolution, sheep towns followed Old England custom and as in East Anglia employed municipal shepherds to take charge of town flocks. Newbury, at the outlet of the Merrimack River, with 5,635 sheep, toward the end of the seventeenth century gathered most of them into four flocks. Ipswich on Massachusetts Bay's North Shore had nine such in 1702. Branford, Connecticut, in 1770, had two. Its shepherds took each flock to its own sheepwalk on the common undivided lands of the town. Every commoner was permitted to pasture the number of sheep to which his rights of common entitled him. At night, according to old English custom, the shepherd brought the flock back from its own course to the arable common field. There movable fencing was changed each day so that each commoner's cropland eventually had the benefit of a night's manuring, one of the traditional objects of sheep raising. This enriched plot was often sowed to turnips, sometimes planted to potatoes. At Deerfield a particular part of the arable thus fertilized was known long after as "The Turnip Field." In the fall, if the field was cultivated in common, as at Deerfield, the crop of roots was divided in proportion to each commoner's stint of sheep. (In Essex County a bushel of turnips was worth a cord of wood.) So that a stockman might know his animals, and also to prevent theft, each sheep was marked with pitch on its wool, its ear, or both, with the earmark of its owner, registered with the town clerk.

Although sheep raising had at first been largely confined to islands and points safe from wolves and stray dogs, as more pasture was cleared, wolves decreased, and the demand for wool kept growing, sheep men were led to increase their flocks. Of the 86 Massachusetts inventories mentioned in connection with swine, 28 had sheep, six of them with over 50 mature animals each. Besides the large flocks of such towns as Newbury and Ipswich in the Bay Colony, by 1678 Rumney Marsh (Chelsea) and the Boston Harbor islands sheltered 1,544. Across the harbor by 1773 Hingham's sheep numbered 3,162. At Reading, north of Boston, the commons were thick enough with sheep to remind Daniel Neal of Devon's fields in England.

Dartmouth on Mt. Hope Bay in 1768 counted 7,108 sheep and goats (probably few of the latter). When Governor William Brenton of Rhode Island died, he left 1,500 sheep, according to his estate inventory; but on his Rocky Farm at Newport he is said to have had at one time 11,000.[7] South Kingstown on the westerly shore of Narragansett Bay, Rhode Island, first entered sheep marks on its records in 1696, but long before the Revolution the great South County landowners counted individual flocks in thousands.

In Connecticut Ezra Stiles, preaching here and there, found in 1770 in Branford a flock of 3,000, and one of the town's shepherds thought the entire township's total to be 10,000. In New Haven a flock numbered 1,300 out of an estimated 4,000 in the First Parish—and there were two other parishes.

Yet the numbers in such towns were less than those on the grassy islands off the coasts: Nantucket with 15,000 in 1773; Martha's Vineyard with 20,000 is called a vast sheep pasture. All sent their surplus wool to the mainland for sale. Such totals were often the sum of many farm flocks. As an example of a small flock, on June 30, 1756, Joshua Hempstead brought back from shearing at Stonington "2 Baggs of wool my 9 fleeces & 12 lb & 7 fleeces of Christophers 13 lb ¾." Where the sheep ran in town flocks, as in Nantucket, the number allowed each owner was likely to be strictly stinted, and at intervals the excess was slaughtered and sent to market as mutton.

From the localities mentioned it is clear that in this century up to 1775 sheep raising on a large scale more or less followed the

coast and the offshore islands, all with wide marshes or grass-
lands. It also extended up rivers where towns such as Deerfield in
the Connecticut Valley, Dedham on the Charles, and Reading
on the Ipswich River provided broad grassy intervales.

The sheep business appears to have been influenced considerably by economic conditions and the bounties offered by the
colonies. Clark, in his *History of Manufactures*, states that prices of
wool fell by half in the depression years following the end of the
French Wars.

"Wool . . . is pretty plenty where I live," wrote Reverend
James McSparran, of Rhode Island about 1753, "yet if you
throw the English America into one Point of View there is not
half enough to make Stockings for the inhabitants." [8]

From the foregoing it should not be inferred that all sheep
were herded in town flocks. Entries in journals such as those of
Joseph Andrews of Hingham, Zaccheus Collins of Lynn, Reverend Joseph Green, Reverend William Bentley, and others show
that in the eighteenth century at least, where wolves had been
killed off, sheep were often pastured on or near the home farm.

As to the quality of the fiber, Andrew Burnaby, just before
the Revolution, called it coarse and short, not over seven inches,
only a third the length of the best in England. To improve
quality some surreptitious importing of well-bred rams took place
despite English prohibition; but since nearly or quite all the wool
was made into yarn and cloth locally, competition as an
incentive was lacking. The wool was only tolerably good, in
Burnaby's opinion. Bennett's "Historical Account" judged the
clothing made from it pretty good for ordinary uses.[9]

Two types of animal are said to have composed the sheep
population. One was a breed with dark or spotted faces and legs,
from England's south coast; the other, a larger and longer type
with white faces, originating in Holland, from which numerous
purchases were made in the early years of the colonies.

An occasional cargo for the West Indies from Boston or New
London included sheep, often designated as "fat sheep," apparently to be sold live for food, since unlike beef and pork, mutton
was not satisfactory either salted or smoked. Birket liked the
mutton for eating. Visiting New Hampshire in 1750, he said:

"Their Sheep are Small but the meat very Sweet, fat & well tasted."

Unlike sheep, cattle were to be found in every town and in nine out of ten farm inventories. Nearly every farm, even those of village tradesmen, had at least a family cow for milk and perhaps butter or cheese. Seldom were herds large, often four to eight plus young stock—except in Rhode Island's southerly towns, where they might number 50 to 100 on great estates. The size of herds was kept modest not solely from absence of a large local market for milk and cheese but, for a long time, by the lack in all but a few localities of sufficient hay to carry dairy stock productively through the winters. In old, settled, eastern Massachusetts there were, in 1767, about two cows for each five persons.

Oxen had a special place and value. They moved heavily loaded drays in port towns. On the farm they pulled the plow, hauled grain to the mill, delivered ship timber and logs, jockeyed boulders out of the grain field, and drew in hay, apples, and firewood. Equally important, after a few years of such labor, at the end of some season's toil the ox would be put in a yard or stall, offered several weeks of rest and princely feed, then slaughtered in cold weather, for the family's winter meat or to go as barreled salt beef to the West Indies. For such reasons, in a new town like Ashfield in the Berkshires, in 1766 settled only two decades, oxen outnumbered milch cows: 35 oxen to 31 milkers. Long-settled Haverhill, on the other hand, had 716 cows to 252 oxen, and in the three eastern Massachusetts counties as a whole the ratio was nearly three cows to one ox.

What little breeding or selection of cattle there was in most of New England tended to produce a modest-sized, hardy, willing type of animal better designed for pulling loads and fattening into beef quarters than for strictly dairy purposes. Birket commented in New Hampshire in 1750: "Their Cattle [meaning oxen] are small but seemingly very strong, having Short thick bodies and Short Limbs." [10]

Great improvement in breeding could scarcely be expected while cows were served by common town bulls running with the town herds, though it was an immemorial custom brought from

England. Braintree, in the Bay Colony, in 1710 appropriated six pounds "for keeping bulls to run at large" at not over 20 shillings per bull, each "to be a good sufficient bull of 2 years old." The town operated on a similar basis for the next forty years. Durham, Connecticut, selectmen were directed in 1716 to provide good bulls, three years old, for only 15 shillings each. In 1728 Springfield paid from 10 to 40 shillings each to twenty citizens for use of their bulls to breed the town's cattle. With over 52,000 cows three years old in the Bay province alone in 1735, to say nothing of those younger, how many cheap bulls must have fathered how many nondescript young stock in the whole of New England! [11] One advantage New England did have: it seems to have escaped the enormous losses of cattle from disease that plagued Europe in the eighteenth century.

Cattle had to be hardy to survive. It was not till November 11 that Reverend Ebenezer Parkman, pastor at Westborough in the Bay Colony, in 1737 recorded: "We first tyed up our Cattle in ye Barn." Life for cattle was even more rugged in new settlements. Like many another, the earliest settler at Marlboro in southern Vermont, named Whitmore, carried his cow through the first winters on wild grass and hay from a beaver meadow helped out with "browse," the tender foliage of evergreen trees. At Cornwall in Connecticut's northwest hills, settled 1738 to 1740, early comers kept their cows alive at times with venison broth. In even older communities where hay land was limited, cattle might get little but corn husks and corn fodder in winter. No wonder an outside observer wrote in a book published in 1775 that in the management of cattle, New England farmers had the worst imaginable notions. It was true of some, though writers in parts of England were making similar complaints of the farmers of that country at the same time.[12]

Where there was plenty of good pasture and hay—either natural or English—or other fodder, stockmen found profit in buying lean animals from the back country and fattening them for market. Indirect evidence of the financial benefit derived comes from the records of towns with good meadows. Again and again, to save pasturage and hay for their own stock, they forbade bringing in cattle from outside to feed, or, if it was permitted, they set a high price on such pasturage. Stock-feeders in the Connecticut Valley, in Essex County on Massachusetts Bay, and other favored places gained reputations that lasted for generations for fattening stall-fed cattle. Northampton and Hatfield feeders drove some over the road to Boston; others they slaughtered locally. Average Northampton fat animals might dress at 769 pounds. Compare this with the weights achieved by Zaccheus Collins in Lynn, who in 1726 got from two cows 682 pounds of beef; in 1727 "from my two creatures a cow & ox . . . 660 lb."; and in 1729 from "my two fat Cows—my (w)hole Beef 780 lbs. this year." An ox that Matthew Patten butchered on October 29, 1762, in Bedford, New Hampshire, yielded 367 pounds of beef plus a hide of 53½ pounds. Another in 1770 yielded 292 pounds of beef, 50 pounds of hide, and 10 pounds of tallow. These animals must have been very small by modern standards, weighing no more than a six-month-old baby beef of today. For butchering a cow Ezekiel Read of Rehoboth in 1725 got 2 shillings sixpence, equal more or less to the value of 3 fowls, 3 to 4 pounds of butter, or the use of a pair of oxen for two days (as shown in his accounts).[13]

As to the dairy side of livestock farming, welcome as milk was for making palatable the common breakfast of corn mush and the evening meal of bread and milk, as well as for butter and cheese, little was expected from a milch cow except during the warm months. Butter and cheese of the best quality were for a long time imported from England for the well-to-do. The only true dairy section was southern Rhode Island, where in 1750 J. Birket reported that they had excellent grass and fine cattle. Burnaby a decade later concurred: the whole province, he said, was laid out in pasture or grazing ground, the oxen were the largest in America, the butter and cheese excellent. Really good cheese from any part of New England, when exported to the Middle Colonies or the South, was likely to be called Rhode Island cheese. Writing from Charleston, South Carolina, in 1766, Israel Brayton told his Newport shippers that cheese sold well there.

These Rhode Island farms were no minor affairs. "College Tom" Hazard's farm made 3,627 pounds of cheese in 1754, which sold at three shillings a pound; in 1763, 2,830 pounds brought ten shillings each. William Douglass, describing the largest single dairy, said that it ordinarily milked about 110 cows, cut 200 loads of hay, made about 13,000 pounds of cheese in addition to butter, and sold a considerable number of calves and fatted bullocks. Such an enterprise would scarcely have been possible except for black slaves, which Newport traders had been bringing in from Africa, and Indian labor. In 1730 South Kingstown counted 333 Negroes and 223 Indians. By 1748 the Negroes had increased to 380 and the Indians had dropped below 200. One dairy is said to have been staffed by 24 Negro women. Though regulation of the slaves was very strict, the Quakers who owned many of the estates are credited with treating them well. Many were set free even before the Revolution.[14]

Most New England cattle farming, however, was on a very different scale, with a few kine to each farm. In the back towns beef for the farm family's eating was a thing to be looked forward to as a treat. All the local milch cows were assembled in one or more town herds, the young animals and dry cows put in another. Milkers got the best pasture. The rest might not even have a herdsman but be branded and left to range wherever they could find feed. In the Connecticut Valley near Northampton, this meant the woods and burned-over areas that stretched east for twenty to thirty miles to the Ware River Valley.

In towns where the arable was in common, each owner of cow rights was required to keep his proportionate share of the fence in repair or be presented to the court and fined for any damage arising from his neglect. After the crops had been harvested from the enclosed and tilled area, on a date set in October the beasts were permitted to enter and for six weeks pick up the herbage inside the fence, at the end of which they were housed: all according to Old English custom. In late fall many animals were turned over to merchants to help balance farmers' store accounts. The merchants in turn would herd them to Boston or some other port for slaughter, to pay their own bills.

Rhode Island's South County excelled in still another type

of livestock: horses. There and in nearby Connecticut a highly valued horse of this era, the Narragansett Pacer, had its home.

The Pacer's origin is a moot question. One story traces it to an Andalusian mare, imported by Governor William Robinson, who died in 1751. Another credits it to one of a choice breed of coach horses that Captain John Hull of Boston, a shrewd and far-sighted merchant, planned, back in 1677, to introduce onto Point Judith, where a stone wall from shore to shore would keep out common animals. Something of the sort appears likely to have been done, for Hull and his associates are said to have rounded up thirty horses in the tract a decade later to meet the cost of a jail. Another ancestor of the Pacer is reputed to have been "Old Snip," a fabled wild horse of unusual characteristics who sired many colts. A still further source offered is the Irish Hobbies. All accounts agree on the superior qualities of the horses that were developed and on the insistent demand for them, especially for the export trade to the West Indies.[15]

Pacers were a sort of bright sorrel color and, except for a fine forehead, about as homely as a horse can be; but their smooth, steady gait, their speed and sure-footedness, and their intelligence and stamina earned their high reputation. Their gait was a swift amble, so even that at high speed a rider could carry a pail of water without spilling. Numerous instances are recorded of their great endurance. Eighty-year-old Captain Charles Goodrich, so a Pittsfield, Massachusetts, historian says, left Pittsfield, Vermont, on a Narragansett Pacer one summer morning after sunrise. He reached the mother town, Pittsfield, Massachusetts, that evening, a journey of 104 miles, neither horse nor rider tuckered out.[16] Their smooth gait made Pacers favorites with ladies. A Mrs. Lee of Rhode Island, traveling into Connecticut in 1791 made thirty to forty miles daily for a week, with a two-day stopover in the middle, and both horse and rider arrived home in good condition.

Planters in the West Indies and horse breeders in Virginia at length became so anxious to obtain Pacers, especially mares, that rather than depend on shipments of export merchants they maintained local buyers at Narragansett to snap up the best animals.

To meet the demand, breeders increased their foalings. From 1700 on, a farm inventory might include as many as 30 to 60 "horsekind." A single breeder might have as many as 87 mares. Robert Hazard, of that great land-owning family, is said to have shipped a hundred Pacers a year to Cuba. Apparently there was rivalry among breeders to produce speedy colts. Joshua Hempstead's diary makes clear that horse racing in New England has a long history. On October 19, 1724, "I went to Groton to See ye Horse Pacing between ye Horses of William Wheelock & James Harris 100 rod for £5. Harris gained about 3 foot but they Daveled & then yeilded ye Wage[r] but drew Stakes & afterwards went down twice for Nothing. Harris gained." Douglass says colts gained speed from running in the same pasture with cows.[17] For such horses, three miles in seven minutes, at "cow-run" speed, was claimed, but steadiness and stamina were of at least equal importance.

An extra-fine animal might bring 300 to 400 pounds. In 1718, long before prices reached their height, Hempstead traded his pacing mare's colt for a cow and calf. With such demand and with many horses running at large, horse stealing grew rampant. For identification, Connecticut required each to be branded by a public brander with a mark for the town as well as the owner, and registration in the town record book. No sale was legal unless recorded. For stealing a horse the penalty was ten pounds and ten lashes the first time, doubled the second, tripled the third. By 1700 every Massachusetts horse exported had to be described and the dealer identified in a toll book kept at each port. "Horse constables" are among officers mentioned in the records of Dighton, Massachusetts. Yet despite all precautions, rustlers would raid a pasture by night, capture loose animals, remove the owner's brands, and from some small harbor on a dark night load them on a vessel and set sail.

With a hungry market, in time pure seed stock dangerously diminished. Then came the disruptions of the Revolution, especially severe along the Rhode Island and Connecticut coasts where the British controlled the sea. Breeding farms were broken up and the pure Pacer lines interrupted, till finally there were no more.

Meanwhile, other parts of New England were raising and exporting horses of various sorts, most of them inferior by today's standards. Horses were numerous, John Josselyn commented in 1673, "and here and there a good one; they let them roam all the year abroad and seldom provide any fother for them." Watertown people in 1669 were angry at roaming horses that damaged cornfields, meadows, and pastures, and decreed iron fetters for all over a year old. On Cape Cod, in 1691, they ran so wild that their owners had to hire Indians to catch them. The town fathers of Harwich complained that they suffered great damage from having their feed eaten by horses from outside. Their fences were broken and their colts drowned, they claimed, when Indians employed by these outsiders tried to hunt down these intruders. At the mouth of the Merrimack the Newbury selectmen sought help from the General Court, because roaming horses and cattle ate their town's herbage and stirred up Plum Island sand so that when the wind blew, sand dunes buried valuable hay marshes.[18]

Many horses were of a small breed not much larger than Welsh horses, one visitor to New Hampshire noted, but very hardy and strong. Another saw beasts with a long switch tail and mane down to the horses' knees. Lest the progeny become too small, the Bay Colony ordered "that no stone horse (stallion) be allowed at liberty unless he be of comely proportions and . . . not less than fourteen hands high, reckoning four inches to the hand full." In the Connecticut Valley, Hatfield and Hadley—the river between them no barrier—in 1700 appointed a joint committee to regulate the breed. The results of indiscriminate breeding were scarcely favorable to quality. Thomas Anburey, a British officer in the Revolution, opined that of all the various breeds of that noble animal, New England horses were certainly the most peculiar and diabolical to ride; and his description of their physical characteristics is far from complimentary.[19]

In 1715 the total export value of horses was 25,000 pounds, almost five sixths of the amount of New England's lumber sales abroad. By 1763 exports of horses and livestock were estimated at a value of 37,000 pounds, considerably more than that of pickled beef and pork exports that year, and one third the value of all the codfish, mackerel, and shad exported.[20] At home Pacers and ordinary nags bore the family on their backs to church, carried travelers from inn to inn, and in their panniers carried surplus vegetables, eggs, and cheese to market; but horses were seldom used for draft purposes.

A few breeders outside Rhode Island and Connecticut were careful in their selections. A Dr. Clarke, physician and horse-lover of Newbury, Massachusetts, started a line known long after by his name. After the end of the final French war, thousands of excellent horses of French breeding were brought from Montreal and Quebec through a roadless wilderness by way of Richelieu River and Lake Champlain ice, some for export, others to mingle their blood in the stud farms of southern New England.[21] Horse totals reported in Connecticut Valley towns in Massachusetts at the time of the Revolution do not, however, suggest marketable surpluses there. In 1767 the three northeast counties of the Bay province were estimated to have four cows to each horse, and oxen outnumbered horses three to one.

Poultry keeping seems never to have reached large propor-tions before the Revolution or to have become of marked economic importance, although domesticated turkeys, and dung-hill fowl, as hens were still termed, had come to New England with both Pilgrims and Puritans.

Judge Samuel Sewall, for one, discovered the value of Indian corn as poultry feed. On January 13, 1676/7, he writes: "Giving my chickens meat, it came to my mind that I gave them nothing save Indian corn and water, and yet they eat it and thrive very well." [22] If the well-to-do judge kept hens, many ordinary people must have done so, and for the same purpose: to have eggs to eat, at least in spring and fall. Benoni Waterman's account-book at Warwick, Rhode Island, in 1739 put the price of a dozen eggs at a shilling (perhaps in Rhode Island paper); of a fowl at a shilling and a half. At Amherst, inland in the Bay Colony, eggs sold about the year 1700 for threepence a dozen. Ezekiel Read at Rehoboth in 1719 charged two and sixpence for killing three fowls (size and type not noted), close to the equivalent of three pounds of butter.

The word "fowl" was sometimes used to include turkeys or

geese. Geese were not plentiful at first, but on December 31, 1718, that versatile Connecticut farmer and trader, Joshua Hempstead, "sent 2 Geese & 2 ganders by Jonathan Bayly to St. Cits." On the following March 20th his diary shows that the "Goose Sett 11 Eggs"; April 28, "Goose hatched 9 goslings." As the century advanced, the number of geese apparently increased. When James Birket visited Bristol, Rhode Island, in the middle of the century, he commented that the only remarkable things there, according to a local saying, were the town's women and its geese. In New Hampshire he found poultry plentiful: geese, turkeys, ducks, and dunghill fowl, besides wild turkeys in the woods. William Douglass about the same time added to this list fatted wild pigeons that country people caught with nets, fed on Indian corn, and brought to market: "delicate good eating," he considered them.[23]

Live turkeys appear in many West Indies cargoes out of New London in the years preceding the Revolution, in numbers running from 10 to 60 or more per shipment, occasionally with geese (32 in one 1759 shipment), ducks, and other fowl. Turkeys sold at a higher price than geese. Tame turkeys were to be found even in Maine, where Falmouth parson Samuel Deane wrote on the 24th of October 1775: "I had seven turkies stole out of the yard." A Doctor Honyman, in Boston that year, three weeks before the fateful April 19th, found turkeys priced upward of a dollar each, at least four times the price of a pullet.[24]

Numerous enemies preyed on crops and stock. The Indians for centuries had grown field crops but had kept no domestic animals except the dog. When the Europeans appeared with their cattle, sheep, and hogs, the flesh of all these new animals at once appealed to the taste of wild predators. Chief among them were wolves and bears. As domestic animals increased, this new source of food seems to have caused their enemies to concentrate and multiply. For the next two centuries the settlers had a continual struggle to destroy them. Records seldom if ever tell of wolves attacking humans, though bears, especially those with cubs, sometimes did so. Loss and damage to sheep and calves never ceased, however. Every forested town in every New England colony offered bounties for wolves' heads. The struggle continued for a century even in old seacoast towns, and inland till after the Revolution. Wildcats and foxes were also pests for generations. During the quarter century of 1698–1722 the town of Lynn paid bounties on most of the 428 foxes killed in its woods. In Harvard, Massachusetts, a hunter collected bounties in 1732 on 16 wildcats and 10 wolves. Hadley, beginning in 1727, in seven years paid bounties on 2,275 wildcats.

Reverend Henry White tells of the ingenuity of a Connecticut bear in 1766. With a taste for calf, the bear tried to tunnel into the byre, dug out two or three bushels of earth, but struck boulders. He then went at the door, drew the tenpenny nails from its wooden hinges, got his paws underneath the door, pried it open, and made off with the "best of 2 calves." Three times this same bear was driven from a flock of sheep. He enjoyed the honey from a beehive. With a taste for dairy products also, he took bars from the window of the milk room, drank a tray of milk, ate three quarts of solid cream from a punchbowl and carried the bowl five yards. When his career was ended, he weighed out at 162 pounds.[25] In the new community of Thetford, Vermont, Joel Strong, who came in 1768, killed two bears in his cornfield in a single night. Local histories abound in such tales.

Gray squirrels, raccoons, crows, and blackbirds found Englishmen's corn as attractive as they had that of Indians, and there was much more of it. Birds enjoyed the new grains: wheat, barley, and rye. Neither rewards for destroying these pests nor penalties for not destroying them seemed to reduce their numbers more than temporarily. Reverend Joseph Green in his Salem diary in 1711 despaired of the squirrels: "They have eaten one-quarter of my corn. It is said that there are millions of them in this village." John Ballantine's Westfield, Massachusetts, diary in the summer of 1758 complained of woodchucks as superabundant, along with squirrels and bears.[26]

To add to the natural destroyers, ships that brought settlers and supplies brought also rats. They spread inland to reach Pomfret, Connecticut, in 1740. They were borne from Providence to Wilbraham, Massachusetts, in the Connecticut Valley in a sack of wool. The black rat is said to have come early, the gray rat not till later, about 1800.

Domestic animals brought their own diseases and pests from Europe. Hog cholera was recorded by the middle of the seventeenth century. In 1708 an imported infectious disease of sheep called scab caused Massachusetts Bay to notify all towns to be on the lookout. In the third quarter of the century a fatal disease of the nose and throat, doubtless glanders or farcy, spread among horses in the Bay Colony. Bot flies also did their deadly work on horses. Just before the Revolution an unidentified distemper visited neat cattle. Rabies appeared for the first time about 1760, killing dogs and swine. A letter to Ezra Stiles in 1761 declared that up to that time New England had known angry dogs and sad dogs but never mad dogs. What seems to have been cat distemper occasioned orders to bury bodies of those afflicted, both dogs and cats. Josselyn in 1660 mentioned roup, brought over with domestic poultry. The extent of such imported diseases and their virulence are subjects that need fuller exploration.

Crops had enemies, too. Among them were insects, both native and imported. Canker worms have already been described. Other enemies that did great damage and caused privation were the army worm and the seventeen-year locust, destroyers that never failed to cause amazement among the colonists. These and forest caterpillars made enough havoc to cause the years 1646, 1649, 1665, and 1666 in the seventeenth century to be especially remembered.

In 1735 worms ate clean thousands of acres of the woods of Essex County, Massachusetts, and reached into New Hampshire. They were smooth on the back with a black streak with white spots. Locusts and grasshoppers caused havoc in Essex County, in Maine, and elsewhere in the years 1734–35, 1743, 1749, 1754, 1756, and 1764, doing their worst in drought seasons.[27]

The year 1770 and the following year saw a species of army worm sweep bare both crops and trees in the upper Connecticut Valley from Massachusetts to the Coos country, and also eastern New Hampshire. Edwin D. Sanborn, a New Hampshire historian, offers a graphic description of the "Northern Army," as it was named. Brown, with a yellow stripe on each side, and the size of a finger, "they marched from the north and northwest . . . to the east and south." So numerous were the worms that they hid the ground completely. They "crawled over houses and barns, covering every inch of the boards and shingles. Every stalk of corn and wheat was doomed. The inhabitants dug trenches, but they soon filled them . . . and the remaining army marched over . . ." They "devoured most of the standing crops and reduced the people nearly to starvation." Timothy Dwight, Yale President, offers his remembrance of this season.[28] The palmer worm, as he calls it, acted largely as Sanborn described it, but to Dwight it was brown and white striped, about two inches long, and marched west to east. In the Oxbow or Coos country wheat and corn were ruined, but peas, potatoes, and pumpkins were not to the worms' liking. Where pumpkins had been planted among the corn a tremendous crop of these matured to provide winter supplies. Great flights of wild pigeons, returning south in September, arrived to gorge on the worms, and the settlers caught and dried the pigeons for winter food to replace meat from hogs and cattle that died for lack of fodder. One family captured 500 of these birds. In older areas, where canker worms were enemies of fruit trees, wild pigeons were likewise welcome.

All through this period weeds spread and increased. Connecticut wheat was full of cockle, Douglass noticed. Near port towns weed plants accidentally imported from Europe had become a great nuisance. He saw the buttercup, white daisy, and fall dandelion thirty miles inland from Boston. The many weeds that Josselyn had earlier listed were the advance guard of a thousand unneeded visitors still arriving in the twentieth century.

17

Wealth from Forests

THOUGH NEW ENGLAND'S SOIL was in general of only fair quality and its climate rigorous, a splendid growth of forest covered its western and northern mountains and valleys, and such parts of its south and east, especially Maine, as had not been cultivated, cleared, or fired by the Indians for their own purposes.

By the colonies' second half-century, harvesting the forest riches had become a mainstay of agricultural and commercial economy in many settlements. Without sturdy natural "knees" for the frame and stout plank for siding harvested from wide-branched white oaks, the vessels that carried New England's booming commerce could scarcely have been launched. Its pines wept pitch to make tight the seams of ships and to render their rigging weatherproof. White pines were perfect for tall, erect masts to bear the sails: "The Treasure and glory of the woods," the eighteenth-century historian Daniel Neal called such trees. The fish, beef, and pork that filled the vessels' holds were barreled in native staves, and packaged staves and hoops accompanied them as exports. A deckload of spars and lumber often completed the cargo.

In frontier towns, the laborious up-and-down whipsaws were still slicing the boles of trees in the middle of the eighteenth century. Elsewhere they had given way to water mills. Sometimes a town obtained a mill by offering inducements in land and tax exemptions. The sawyer was likely to take half the lumber as his toll.

With ship timber, lumber, and staves thus valuable, towns protected their common woodlands. The permission of selectmen or forest warden was necessary to cut timber for a dwelling, barn, or farm implement, just as had been a custom of Old England. Outside speculators as well as thieves got stern warning. Thought for the future was evident. Malden in the Bay Colony in 1689 forbade felling for firewood any trees of less than one foot girth. Hadley forbade cutting young oak and walnut, and selling timber out of town. Watertown in 1649 appointed two citizens to mark trees to be left in the highway "that shall continue for shade." Groton in 1665, only thirty years from founding, had officials designate shade trees to be protected along its ways; Ipswich did the same the next year. On December 16, 1735, Guilford, Connecticut, with few exceptions required liberty from the selectmen to fell or destroy "any Tree or Trees that are now standing or that shall be set out on the . . . Highways of this Township."[1] In 1685 Job Pilsbury petitioned Newbury's select-men to forbid anyone's cutting a white oak standing on the highway near his father's barn and asked that he might have liberty to preserve it. In 1716–17 the town appointed officers to prosecute any who cut or defaced trees in any highway.[2] Thus early was New England valuing its street trees. Salem, short on shade for cattle, went further. In 1747 the commoners voted bounties for anyone who would set locust trees on its highlands.

Massachusetts had already forbidden tree-cutting on the Province Lands near the tip of Cape Cod, where drifting sand was silting up Cape Cod Harbor at Provincetown, probably a result of burning wood as fuel in the process of making lime from Indian shell heaps. Plymouth Town in 1702 made it illegal to cut pines at its beach, presumably in order to prevent the sand from blowing.

Protective measures were needed also to regulate burning over woodland. In neighborhoods where grazing was of special importance, the English took over the practice of burning large areas, as the Indians had done earlier to furnish deer pasture. In the Connecticut Valley, for example, Hadley burned miles of woods stretching east of the river; on the river's opposite side Northampton burned westward. In 1713 Waterbury, Connecticut, had to forbid burning for seven years, to let young trees get a start. Not long afterward, Block Island, lacking trees, was forced to dig peat to fuel fireplaces. Massachusetts Bay in 1743 passed a general law to regulate woods burning and prevent the destruction that sometimes ensued. Sandwich on Cape Cod in March 1754 selected forty-two citizens to supervise the burning of its woods, the job to be completed by April 16. Public supervision in Plymouth Colony, of which Sandwich had been a part, goes back at least to 1633, when firing after mid-March was banned.

How essential control was appears from the record of destructive forest fires. One started near Lebanon, New Hampshire, in the dry summer of 1761, crossed into Maine, and reached salt water at New Casco after a whole month. Such fires destroyed not only standing trees but laboriously erected fencing. In a similar Cape Cod fire of 1772 great numbers of sheep were lost.[3]

Fires could do especial damage where evergreen trees were tapped for pitch, turpentine, and resin, activities encouraged in the early eighteenth century by an act of Parliament. Towns containing pine forests were tempted to let out the privilege of bleeding or boxing evergreen groves to obtain income. Whether because of their wealth of pines, ease of transportation, or both, the large river valleys and Plymouth County were the focus of this trade. A turpentine distillery was set up in Boston. The business must have begun early in Plymouth Colony, for that colony levied an export tax on tar in 1661,[4] and in 1668 limited its citizens, those who qualified as proprietors, to ten barrels a year. In 1702 the town of Plymouth gave Major John Bradford liberty to "milk" its pines on its commons from Duxbury bounds on the north to Jones River. Sandwich at the head of the Cape in 1707 granted for two years the right to "box" 2000 pines in return for two pounds income, and turpentine rights were valuable along Buzzards Bay in Plymouth Colony.

As to Connecticut, Noah Phelps's history of Simsbury, in the Farmington River Valley, says that pitch and tar began to be made there in 1643. Large amounts came from the valley of the

Quinebaug in northeastern Connecticut about 1700. In 1728 Parson Timothy Woodbridge, Jr. shipped five tons of turpentine to New York. In the Connecticut River Valley the practice was forbidden by Windsor by 1696, Glastonbury by 1700, and Hartford in 1709. Enfield, however, permitted it. Upriver in Massachusetts, Westfield granted the right by 1675; Hadley by 1685. Deerfield acted favorably in 1686 but after 1715 forbade tapping. In the Merrimack Valley, Amesbury forbade gathering pitch, tar, and resin for out-of-town sale, but, like many towns, Chelmsford and Dunstable found the grants too profitable to forego.

By an English law of 1685, as modified five years later, the tallest and straightest pines, unless they stood inside a township and had been in private ownership before 1690, were reserved for the Royal Navy, which needed them as masts and spars for warships. No one was to cut a pine of a diameter of two feet or beyond. Some New England pines were of truly magnificent proportions, without a branch below a hundred feet and according to contemporary accounts reaching even as high as 300 feet into the sky. In 1689 Judge Sewall watched a mast start for England from Salmon Falls, New Hampshire. "Two and thirty oxen before, four yoke beside the mast between fore and hind wheels . . . The forty animals drag the massive load to the shore, where it is set afloat in a home-built vessel." [5] Just before the Revolution, Andrew Burnaby likewise was amazed by the tremendous mast trees: "These are of white pine and are, I believe, the finest in the world, many of them being forty yards long and as many inches in diameter. They never cut these down but in times of deep snow . . . when the trees are fallen they yoke seventy or eighty pair of oxen, and drag them along the snow. It is exceedingly difficult to put them first in motion . . . and . . . they never stop upon any account whatsoever till they arrive at the waterside." If an ox is taken ill, he is cut out of the harness and destroyed, he states. Sometimes the mast was felled into a nest of smaller trees to soften the fall. A straight path had to be cut through the woods to the riverbank or head of tide.[6]

The river valleys of New Hampshire and southern Maine furnished most of the royal mast trees at first, and cutting and hauling them gave farm people work and income in winter. Masts were floated down the Merrimack even from Concord, New Hampshire, and from Wolfeboro on Lake Winnepesaukee, both areas noted for splendid pine forests; likewise down the Connecticut.

Difficulty arose when the English government appointed officials to scout and mark all such two-foot trees with the broad arrow that reserved them for the king's use, then tried to enforce the law through vice-admiralty courts. Officers marked trees throughout southern New Hampshire and across into the Connecticut Valley, but the law was continually violated, as it was with regard to oaks in England itself, by lumbermen and landholders interested in sawing timber into salable boards. In New Hampshire 70 sawmills lined the Piscataqua River in 1720, their annual product six million feet. The king's officers received rough treatment in that colony, as did any who tried to obey the law of the arrow in the northern Connecticut Valley. At Northampton, in the Bay Colony, of 363 trees bearing the king's broad arrow, all but 37 disappeared. At Hadley in 1774 a mob prevented execution of the law. With the Revolution and independence the problem disappeared. A present-day reminder is the rarity in eighteenth century dwellings of any boards over 23 inches wide, a dimension adhered to in order to avoid incriminating evidence. By contrast, in houses of the previous century, boards and wainscot may be found running to 40 inches in width.

Besides lumber and spars, among forest products that enjoyed a good market in England previous to the Revolution were potash and its more refined form, pearlash. To make them, a pile of several cords of wood was burned to ashes. These were shoveled into tubs partly filled with brush and straw, and water was filtered through. The lye that resulted was then boiled in iron kettles till the water evaporated, leaving a hard brown residue. An acre of woods might produce up to two tons of potash. By heating this brown cake redhot in a cast iron kettle, the impurities remaining were largely consumed, and what had been yellow potash became creamy white pearlash[7] Once the peace of Utrecht, in 1713, had ended Queen Anne's War and opened an interval of comparative peace, traders who specialized in potash took advantage by setting up production in interior towns and building shelters to hold their leaching tubs and kettles. The product, broken into small pieces and put up in casks, was sold by the bushel. In comparison to value its bulk was small. It was easy to transport long distances and readily salable in the ports, for it was useful for soap and glass making as well as valuable as a component of medicines.

Another outlet for forest products was the tanneries, many of them local but eventually concentrated at cattle markets in the eastern Bay Colony. Tanners needed bark for processing hides and skins. Sumac and the bark of chestnut oak were especially desirable. By the second century local craftsmen were using native woods, cherry a favorite, to make fine furniture, some of it for export.

Tremendous quantities of wood went into fuel. An ordinary dwelling needed twenty cords a year. The minister and the wealthier families with several fireplaces might each need forty or more. Boston, Salem, and other commercial centers were great consumers of firewood, some from nearby farms, much brought by coastwise wood boats from New Hampshire. In the snowy winter of 1726 hundreds of loads are said to have been sledded daily into Boston.

Biscuit and bread bakers had to heat their ovens. The numerous pig-iron foundries and forges also needed great quantities of fuel, largely charcoal. Ironworks were set up wherever bog iron was to be found. The neighborhood of Taunton in southeastern Massachusetts was one center, but by the time of the Revolution they were found even in Vermont. An iron maker required 130–50 bushels of charcoal, the product of five cords of wood, oak and hickory preferred, for every ton smelted. Once the ore in the iron mountain at Salisbury, Connecticut, began to be worked in 1734, the bloomeries there offered a continuous market for charcoal for the next century. One Salisbury iron product was potash kettles. Other consumers of cordwood were the brickmaker and the lime-burner who turned shell mounds left on the shores by unnumbered generations of Indians into building lime.

Farmers themselves used wood in a great variety of ways besides in the fireplace. It furnished frames, plank, and boards for farm buildings, and furniture for the dwelling. Long fences for fields and pickets for the home lot came from light "staddle" or saplings. Because split chestnut logs or red cedar trunks were resistant to decay, they furnished posts. The oxcart, with its solid wheels, and the plow, harrow, sled, drag, hay rake and fork, flail, shovel, and most other tools were universally of wood, often hardened by charring at the points of wear, or shod with bits of iron. Table dishes, bowls, and spoons were wood at first; cheese vats, firkins to hold butter, milkpans, buckets—all were wood, gouged and whittled out or put together during bad weather by the farmer and his sons.

Local needs for wood and the commercial value of its products made townspeople highly jealous of intrusions on their common woodlands. After these were divided, the woodlots that resulted became valuable personal possessions.

Among the pioneers who, following the French wars began to settle the scores of new towns laid out by New Hampshire, Connecticut, and Massachusetts in the heavily wooded hills and valleys of western New England and inland Maine, a widely different point of view arose. If the settlers and their families were to survive and prosper in such locations, trees had to be destroyed, the land opened to the sun, and crops planted. That would create problems at a later date.

18

Probing the Wilderness

WITH THE RISE of second and third generations, increase in population, and alterations in economic conditions and in farming, the pattern of settlement in New England changed. The original plan of home lots in close-built villages where all lived as a community gave way. In new towns home lots were likely to be larger, of as much as fifty acres or even one hundred acres in some cases. In older towns as the years passed, the outlying common land was distributed in successive allotments. A good deal of buying, selling, and division of property went on. New owners sometimes built homesteads on lots far from the parent village. Moreover the original concept of allotting land without requiring financial payment, and of forming a communal village based to some extent on theocratic principles, yielded to a more materialistic pattern as land gained in value and commerce increased.

Economics caused other changes. In winning the French wars, the New England colonies had made extraordinary efforts and suffered severe losses. These brought on inflation and debts for both colonies and towns, and entailed heavy taxation. Thousands of soldiers had to be paid or otherwise rewarded, and colony treasuries were empty. Debts had to be met, but financial resources were exhausted. The single important available asset of the colonies was unallotted land.

To compensate the soldiers the colonies made grants of land

to them or their heirs in new townships laid out especially for this purpose. Massachusetts Bay began this practice in 1725. Two years later it granted seven townships in Maine, which since the middle of the seventeenth century had been under its jurisdiction, to the soldiers surviving from King Philip's War, or the heirs of those deceased. To pay off war debts the colonies laid out more townships in the wilderness and auctioned them off to the highest bidders. The merchants and speculators who were successful bidders then sought settlers to inhabit them. Several factors—population increase, economic necessity, and outright speculation in land—caused Massachusetts Bay to charter 140 towns during the first half of the eighteenth century. Connecticut doubled the number of its towns. Governor Wentworth of New Hampshire carved out tiers of townships in the Connecticut Valley, on both sides of the river, some in territory where Massachusetts also made grants.[1]

These decades now saw the first large-scale emigration from the earlier settled parts of New England. Massachusetts people spilled over into southern New Hampshire's Monadnock mountain region. Valleys and even some of the hills in the Taconics and Berkshires filled with emigrants from lower Connecticut and eastern Massachusetts. In Connecticut settlers pushed into northern Litchfield County; in Massachusetts, into hill towns like Blandford, Tyringham, New Marlboro, Sheffield, and Great Barrington. Further north they pushed west up the Deerfield Valley to Charlemont and Colrain. About 1764 a group of families from Guilford, Connecticut, started a Guilford in what was to become Vermont; others joined them to form the nucleus of Vermont's Chittenden County. Neighbors in Pomfret and Salisbury, Connecticut, remained neighbors in Pomfret and Salisbury, Vermont. People from Hardwick in the Bay Colony began Bennington. Lancaster, beyond the White Mountains in New Hampshire, was settled from Lancaster, Massachusetts. Londonderry, New Hampshire, though itself not long settled, saw ten different swarms of people leave it before the Revolution.

In Portland, Maine, in 1726 Reverend Thomas Smith wrote: "People constantly flocking down here to petition for lots." Again in 1750, after a quarter-century, he wrote: "There is

news of a brig full of people gone to Penobscot to settle there."
Many of these coastal Maine settlers are said to have come from
inland towns of the Bay Colony and New Hampshire. Such
emigrants did not depopulate the old-settled towns. Rather, they
were overspill from increasing population. If they had held land,
it sold readily. The spill went southward also, emigrants settling
in New Jersey, North Carolina, Georgia, even in what was later
to become Mississippi. It streamed into the Wyoming Valley of
the Susquehanna area and into western New York. It flowed
eastward as far as New Brunswick and Nova Scotia, where New
England people organized numerous towns on New England
models.[2]

The character of the settlers who took up land in the new
towns seems often to have differed somewhat from that of people
who remained in the home towns. They were apt to be the young
and adventurous, ready to take the risk of leaving a comfortable
established community with school, church, and neighbors in
order to acquire farms of their own in new situations, rough
though life there might be. Sometimes, however, a group of
neighbors in the home town acquired the rights to a whole new
township, sent a committee to spy out the land, plotted the house
lots, and in the old town organized a complete town government
for the new a year or more before anyone cleared an acre in it.
Others arranged for new homesteads with some speculative
proprietor who had acquired a large tract and who offered
inducements to get settlers to start in a spot where there was not
even a road, let alone any society.

How an ambitious young man might go about such an
adventure is told by John Adams of West Cambridge, Massachusetts, in a letter to Governor Isaac Hill of New Hampshire, who
had been born in the same neighborhood. "My land was a part
of Cambridge farm in Ashburnham, Mass., fifty miles from my
native place. Early in the spring I took my axe on my back and
set out for my new country . . . began to chop down the timber
on two or three acres . . . went back . . . worked at Medford in
the summer making bricks on shares. In the fall I again went to
my land . . . cleared off my wood . . . sowed two acres of rye
. . . returned to West Cambridge . . . worked through the

winter making shoes with Mr. John Russell; in the spring went and disposed of my bricks . . . went again to my land; my rye looked well; but had no barn, built one that summer . . . saved a little more . . . returned to Mr. Russell's in the winter. In the spring went to my land . . . made some provision for a house; and in the year 1770 hit so that on the 9th of July, my partner being as ready as I was, we were married. Having provided a team to carry her furniture, and a horse for her, and another for myself, we set out for the woods. She had never seen a foot of land within forty miles of our place, but her courage held out till we got home, and then it was better than ever." [3]

William Barker, of Westborough in the Bay Colony, in 1761 explored in southern New Hampshire and picked out a lot on West Hill in what is now Troy. The next year he brought tools and built a hut. Clearing more land in 1764, he built a good house and in the fall brought his wife and three children to the new farm, the last twenty-five miles through roadless forest. Silas Fife of Bolton did the same in 1765 and brought his bride. Many others did likewise. [4]

In 1768 Jonathan Richardson of Newton and his two boys, one aged fourteen, the other nine, came in the spring to the new town of Cheshire in a Berkshire valley, cleared a little land, planted some crops and built a house. The father then left the two youngsters, with the family cow, to manage on their own. Not till the next fall did he return, this time with the rest of the family and their belongings on an oxcart. The brave boys meantime milked the cow, hollowed a soft log for a churn in which they could make butter, and took care of themselves. [5]

A citizen of Pomfret, Connecticut, Bartholomew Durkee, in 1769 acquired title to a lot marked by surveyors on trees at what was to be Pomfret, Vermont. Pomfret's historian tells how, that season, Durkee cleared a piece, put up the walls of a cabin, and roofed one end with elm bark. On the sixth of March the next year, with wife and five children he returned and dug away the snow from the roofed end. They built a fire, cooked food they had brought, and ate it set out on a big stump. When the snow left, they sowed seeds. These grew while he earned something helping the surveyors lay out more lots. It was an example of what Jared

Eliot was writing at this very time of certain original settlers of Connecticut: "Coming from an old cultivated country to thick woods, rough unimproved lands, it may be said that, in a sort, they began the world anew." [6] Such was the general pattern.

These pioneers had an object, and many of them attained it. To quote Samuel Williams, who toward the end of the century wrote of the Vermont settlers: "Amidst the hard living and hard labor that attends the forming of a new settlement the settler has the most flattering prospects and encouragements. One hundred acres in a new town does not generally cost him more than he can spare from the wages of one or two years . . . When he comes to apply his labor to his own land, the produce of it becomes extremely profitable. The first crop of wheat will fully pay for all the expense he has been at in clearing up, sowing and fencing his land, and at the same time increase the value of the land eight or ten times." [7] Such good fortune, however, applied only to the best situations. For most pioneer farmers and their wives the struggle at first was desperate. If they succeeded to some degree, as most of them did, in establishing productive farms and enduring towns, they deserved their modest success.

19

The Ways and the Means

In country cleared only in parts before the arrival of the
English, and without available buildings or livestock, the tools
they first needed had been axes, adzes, saws, and carpenter's tools
to provide shelter; and mattocks or pickaxes, spades, and hoes to
stir the soil and plant and cultivate crops. The Pilgrims had
brought such hand tools with them in their small and crowded
ship. With them they put up their first buildings, and when
spring came planted their hills of Indian corn and a small field of
European grain. Having no cattle, there could be no plowing
even if they had brought a plow. They needed no dairy utensils,
nor fences except pales to keep wild animals from their gardens.

The Puritan colony a decade later was much more adequately equipped, having brought a considerable variety of tools.
The passenger lists had included carpenters, wheelwrights, and
other tradesmen experienced in their use. The numerous cattle
soon made it possible to use plows; but while farm inventories
often include plow chains, few farmers owned plows, a situation
not unusual in Old England at the time. Even after a half
century plows were not plentiful.[1]

As time went on and additional and more varied equipment, especially for transportation, became necessary, carts,
wains, and tumbrils with racks for hay could be built completely
of local oak and ash, their wheels often cross-sections of some
large tough-grained tree with a hole bored through the center of

10. *Early plows were of wood. Added metal patches sometimes protected the mouldboard. Mapes,* Illustrated Catalogue *(1861).*

each to receive the wooden axles. This practice continued for generations. Joshua Hempstead, for example, in his diary on March 22, 1742/3, records that he sawed off a pair of pepperage or ironwood wheels for his stone cart. He rounded them properly and, taking advantage of a hole in the center, shaped each to receive the axle. If a simpler vehicle would do, without a wheelwright's help the farmer could put together a sled useful for both winter and summer with round saplings for runners; or make a flat drag or dray. Both continued for a long time to be used to transport dung to the field, bring home corn or rye, or deliver a load of stone for a wall. On November 5, 1719, Hempstead took his plow to Stonington on such a dray or drag. For bringing in hay, a series of branches bound together horizontally would serve to bear the load.[2]

With iron now more plentiful and some farmers more prosperous, a wheelwright could combine hub, spokes, and felloes, and bind the rims with iron tires to make more elaborate wheels for the cart; or he could shoe the sledge or sled with iron runners. According to Abigail Adams, the useful tipcart, too, was known by the time of the Revolution. By 1762 Amesbury farmers were voting in town meeting that sleds should have a uniform width of 4 feet 2 inches. By that date nearly every farm in Suffolk County, Massachusetts, owned at least one cart.[3]

For the entire first two centuries the plow, if a farmer was fortunate enough to own one (and some well-to-do farmers apparently did not), continued to be of ash or other clear-grained

wood, although the coulter might be iron and the share protected
by narrow flat iron sheets. A good plow-maker gained a
reputation. A single ox or cow might pull a small plow, but
plowing ordinarily took at least two. Large farmers kept two
yokes or more. The most unsatisfactory feature of the wooden
plow was the way damp soil stuck to its mouldboard, requiring
continuous cleaning. At least one early inventory mentions
separately a "breaking-up plow," among several. The heavy "A"
harrow or the square harrow, sometimes double, might be
equipped with imported iron teeth although more likely they
were of native wood. The smoothing harrow that covered grass
and grain seed lightly, and did the job well, was merely birch
brush bound to a crosspiece. Yet it was so efficient a tool that it
persisted into the twentieth century.

Some of these poor wilderness farmers, however, lacking
cattle, as late as the end of the eighteenth century still had only
wooden hand tools to stir the earth. Their shovels were likely to
be fashioned from a thick plank, suitably hollowed at one end
and cut away at the other so as to leave a center handle. It was a
disadvantage in a frontier settlement to own a shovel shod with
iron, because of the temptation for neighbors to borrow it! [4]

Axe, hoe, scythe, and sickle continued to be the most
important tools made of metal. The axe, forged and given an
edge by the local blacksmith, or possibly imported, had a straight
handle. Neither broad axe nor felling axe could compare in drive
or ease of handling with the modern axe. Hoes, also made by the
smith, were of at least three kinds; the grub hoe for breaking the
ground, the broad hoe, and the narrow hoe for weeding. These
were of iron, the two last much heavier than similar modern
hoes.

Joseph Jenckes had made a great improvement to the
scythe, lengthening the blade and at the same time lightening it,
by welding a thin cutting edge to a slender but stiff and strong
iron bar. A century later Hempstead's Connecticut diary notes
purchase of a "Salem Sythe," apparently of this type, for 29
shillings sixpence.[5]

Saws included the long up-and-down two-man blade already mentioned which continued in use even after sawmills

spread widely. The whipsaw and the crosscut saw are also listed in numerous inventories. Matthew Patten's diary at Bedford, New Hampshire, as late as 1784 tells of tribulations caused by the brittle metal of that era, and the hazard of loaning tools: "I brought home my crosscut saw. Robert Gilchrist broke above three inches off one end of her and a tooth out toward the middle."

Wedges used for splitting fence rails, clapboards, and shingles are often mentioned in farm accounts. The larger farmers had grindstones, wheelbarrows, and maybe a vise. The common small hand and dairy tools mentioned in current inventories have already been listed.

Though not customarily included in the category of tools, among the necessities as means of production during this first century and a half were adequate fences, walls, and ditches to keep wandering livestock out of dooryards, gardens, orchards, and cultivated lands, and to fold sheep at night. This was a subject of continuous legislation in every town record generation after generation. With no time in the early years for walls or ditching, farmers turned to wooden fences. At first, and for a long time after in new towns, these might be merely rough-piled stumps or brush; but as one generation succeeded another, four types of fence became common. To protect garden plots and dooryards pales were split and driven into the ground, held together at the top by a rail to which each pale could be fastened. Once sawn lumber became common, the picket fence evolved; later it was painted white. Especially where forest was being cleared, a fence of logs laid one atop the other would serve to protect crop land.

Most common, however, once farming was well established, was the rail fence. It was of two types. Over the greater part of New England a rail fence was built after the following fashion. For posts, the farmer felled foot-thick straight-grained trees (chestnut or red cedar preferred because of their resistance to decay). These he cut to six-foot lengths and split in half; next with auger and chisel he mortised the upper portion every four to six inches. He set them in holes dug 9 to 10 feet apart. For rails he took much larger oak or ash trees, cut their boles into 11-foot

11. Fences and walls, to keep stock in—or out: (a) pole; (b) split-rail; (c) Virginia; (d) half-high wall, with rail; (e) stone wall. Source for a–b, d–e: Perley, History of Salem *(1924). For c: Luigi Castiglioni,* Viaggio Negli Stati Uniti *(1790).*

lengths, and split each length so as to make eight to sixteen rails. Their ends were then slipped into the mortises of one post after another, the post holes filled, and made solid. If properly done, the fence that resulted discouraged even a hog, provided he had been yoked to prevent digging.

A very few writers of the time mention the zigzag Virginia fence, also of rails. This needed less substantial slanted posts, since they were criss-crossed, required less digging, and could be built with only an axe and mattock. An order for such a fence was given at Portsmouth, Rhode Island, in 1671, and one is mentioned by Brissot de Warville in 1788.[6] In the Connecticut Valley above tidewater this type is said to have been unknown. In the Merrimack Valley in New Hampshire, Matthew Patten helped one of his neighbors "set up a rail fence"; but on April 20, 1767, he and his boys "laid up a log fence." (Note the difference in verbs and adjectives.)

Town meetings or selectmen regulated the height and maintenance of fences. Every town chose fence-viewers to see that they were of the required height and strength and to settle disputes as to their upkeep. At Watertown, Massachusetts, in 1647 a fence was required to have four rails; in 1653, to be 3½ feet high. At first, in Guilford, Connecticut, the height was set at 4 feet, but by 1653 a "sufficient fence" there had to be 4½ feet tall. At Salem the requirement at first was 3–4 feet; at Portsmouth, Rhode Island, in 1671, 4½ feet. By that date experience had taught many towns to insist on 5 feet and at least five rails for all cornfields, gardens, and orchards. Before long, however, the need became clear for barriers more permanent than wood fences.

In New England's glacial terrain, where boulders and fieldstone abound, nothing could match the stone wall for permanence. Building walls served a second purpose—to clear fields and make cultivation easier. Moreover, the job was ideal to fill slack time at almost any season. So in 1677 Watertown had to legislate as to how long stones dug from highways, but not removed, might remain the property of the digger. In 1718 we find Joshua Hempstead digging stones in his orchard meadow. That winter in February he was sledding stones "to make wall by the pear tree." The work went on even in hot weather: on July 28, 1721, he was at home all day stacking hay and making a stone wall. Back in 1714 he had built 201 feet, but almost thirty years later he was still at it: "Mar. 26, 1742: Made Six Rod of Stone wall . . . had 3 hands besides my own."

Where moneyed men with servants or slaves had country seats, walls were likely to be ornamental and built in style. Dr. Alexander Hamilton, visiting Boston, headed out to Cambridge on a July morning in 1744. The fields of some country places, he noted, were enclosed by fine stone fences, their gates hung from single stone posts as much as eight feet tall. At Newport Island less than a decade later, described as throughout like a garden, James Birket was especially struck with the stonework about the fields. "Their fences are chiefly of stone made by themselves to save their wood, a piece of industry rarely met with in North America." Sometimes a wall was built on contract.[7] In 1726 Zaccheus Collins of Lynn bargained with Asham Nakus to enclose a newly bought property of a little over 46 acres "to make it a good wall four feet & 3 inches high . . . and dubell at the bottom of hole . . . for about 32 pole" (rods).

The great rocks scattered over the surface near New London caused Birket to feel sorry for the inhabitants. Yet there and elsewhere, farmers like Hempstead were continually building walls: saving out long flat stones suitable for doorsteps and hearthstones (these were valuable); digging great holes in which to sink boulders below plow depth, and tipping loads of smaller stones into miry spots in the highway. Though Birket counted such stony land mighty difficult to plow, he found among the rocks a great plenty of fruit. Fruit trees were likely to line the stone walls.

Hempstead built his walls four feet high. Others with less time or less help were content with a three-foot wall, topped with brush or a single rail if the law allowed. In Rhode Island and southeastern Massachusetts walls were sometimes laid up by Indians, not always willingly. If the Indians did not work according to their contract they were "summarily flagallated." When during the Revolution, Dartmouth (today part of it New Bedford) was raided by the British, one Indian inhabitant at

12. Rhode Island wall in the Portsmouth area on Aquidneck (Rhode) Island, noted for superior wall building. Courtenay P. Worthington photo. Collection of Howard S. Russell.

least regarded it as a deliverance. "I make no more stone wall for Joseph Russell," he chalked on his employer's barn door, before going over to the enemy.[8]

Judd, in his history of Hadley, Massachusetts, mentions a wall built in 1748 of 166 rods in length (over one-half mile). Hauling stone from a distance and building such a wall on Hadley's Connecticut Valley silt or on a tidal marsh by salt water would be a costly project. Yet it was done. In some places stone was valuable. Braintree, south of Boston, rich in seam-faced boulders and easily quarried granite, forbade the removal of stone for sale outside. Windham County towns in northeastern Connecticut protected their quarries. In northwestern Connecticut conditions were otherwise. Ezra Stiles, an eighteenth-century

13. Gundalow of salt hay, waiting for the tide. Society for the Preservation of New England Antiquities, Boston.

president of Yale, quotes a rhyme of his father's about Cornwall, where the parent left him 400 acres.

> Nature out of her boundless store
> Threw rocks together and did no more.[9]

When a group of Cornwall's sons left the town for Vermont, they settled the new Cornwall beside the stone-free meadowlands of Otter Creek.

To build an enduring wall was not only laborious but a work of skill. First the loam was dug out down to the top of the subsoil or the frost line. A bed of small stones, sand, or gravel would replace it where needed. Large boulders, hauled on a stone boat, were next rolled in to serve as a foundation and allowed to settle. Last, field stones of smaller size selected for contour and proportion carried the wall to its intended height of three, four, or five feet. The half-high wall must be topped with a crotch fence and rail. If clearing fields was a main object, the farmer laid up parallel walls a few feet apart, and the interval thus formed provided an excellent dump for still more surplus rocks.

Poorly built walls eventually fell from frost action. The many earthquakes of the colonial period also, as one contemporary writer expressed it, threw down "a vast deal of stone wall." Yet thousands of miles of wall first laid up in the seventeenth and eighteenth centuries still survive two and three centuries later.

In sandy soil and river bottoms it might be much easier and simpler to dig deep ditches three to four feet wide, called ha-has, to keep stray cattle out of meadows or mowings. The soil was thrown up on the far side as a bank, the whole made more secure perhaps, as at Ipswich and Hadley, by a two-rail fence on top. Such ditches and banks are sometimes today mistaken for ancient forts or Indian remains. One ditch in the Hadley area, said to encircle Mt. Holyoke, is the boundary of ancient sheep pasture. Judd states that in that silty soil three rods of digging (about 50 feet) was a day's work for a man. Like fences and walls, ditches had to be "sufficient," and to "be juged according to the [fence] Veiwers Jugments," as records of Portsmouth, Rhode Island, and other towns attest.

20

Life on the Farm

ON MOST NEW ENGLAND FARMS in the century preceding the
Revolution, the farmer and his sons did the field work and cared
for the livestock, sometimes with the help of a neighbor's son
bound out to learn the art of agriculture. For heavy jobs he
exchanged work with other farmers nearby.

Large farmers, merchants, and capitalists employed hired
labor regularly, and some of them used slaves. The great
plantations of southern Rhode Island and adjacent Connecticut,
however, were the only areas where agriculture placed large
dependence on slave labor.

Little overseas immigration occurred during this century.
With fisheries and foreign commerce profitable and frequent
calls for men for military service, ordinary labor was not plentiful
and wages generally high. Moreover, land, especially in a new
town, was cheap and easy to secure. Why, then, should an
able-bodied man work for wages for another except long enough
to get capital to secure a homestead of his own?

No permanent class of agricultural laborers like those to be
found on an English manor existed. Governor Wentworth of New
Hampshire in a report to England commented on the fluidity of
labor in general: "Scarcely a shoemaker, a joiner, or a silver-
smith but quits his trade as soon as he can get able to buy a little
tract of land." [1] Even though the mechanic did not turn into a
full-time farmer, with such a little tract the former apprentice

could plant a garden, set an orchard, get hold of a cow, and exchange his skill with the neighborhood for whatever else he and his family needed. To become a landowner was not difficult. The Governor had land to sell, for in each of the dozens of new towns that he chartered, he reserved for himself a tract of 500 acres. On the other hand, land ownership did not create a leisure class. The dignity of the Governor's station did not render him above severe labor on his own farm at Wolfeboro on Lake Winnepesaukee. General John Stark of Revolutionary fame, who operated mills, like many other leading men was also a practical farmer.

How the work of the ordinary farm got done could scarcely be better illustrated than by excerpts from the journal of Joseph Andrews, a sheep man and general farmer of Hingham, twenty miles south of Boston. Besides all the work he did alone, Andrews gave and received assistance:

Sept. 7, 1753		"Helped Uncle And[rew] about carting some dung"
Oct. 30	″	"Finisht Giting Up my Potatoes & Helpt Uncle take up his Flax"
Nov. 2	″	"Helpt Uncle Sat fence . . . and Git Up Some Potatoes"
Nov. 19	″	"Killing my Beef. Simon Stoddard Helpt me killed three"
Jan. 3	″	"Killed my Pigs today, Knight Sprage Helpt me"
Jan. 15	″	"Threshing my Barly: Uncle And helpt me"
Jan. 30	″	"Spent the day in Reckoning with Uncle And"
April 3, 1754		"Down at Plan hills Picking Up Stones All Day, seven of us in all"
May 3	″	"Helpt Uncle And Plowing & Spreading Rockweed"

The 1726–27 Journal of Zaccheus Collins, a farmer and maltster of Lynn, tells a similar but different tale.

5th month	9	"3 men mowing in feald"
	29	"At Marblehead ye boys got in Barly"
6th month	12	"John Fairn a thrashing my barly"
	16	"Allen Freed faned my barly"
8th month	18	"a killing a pr of Oxen Nathaniel & Jonathan

> Collins and I had between us & my part of it.
> Beef weighed 363"
>
> 1725 5th month "Ezekiel Collins mowed my barly I cleaned out
> my rye" [This farmer also did many jobs alone.]

On the other hand Reverend Timothy Walker, the minister-farmer of Concord, New Hampshire, had a slave, "Prince," who worked on his farms regularly. In haying time as many as six men did his mowing, and in March 1746 he speaks of "my men" swingling (beating and cleaning) flax. He, too, got help from neighbors, however. In April 1764 Deacon Hall sowed his hayseed. In November Timothy Chandler helped him cart dung.

At one time Joshua Hempstead at Stonington, Connecticut, was busy with a big job, breaking up land. On May 17, 1715, he records: "I was all day with all ye boys & benja[min] Fox & Peter Latimer breaking up & planting at Jo Lesters I had Mr. Latimers 6 oxen and uncle foxes 2 oxen & Daniel Lesters Plow." The job took all that day and the next. When he brought home the oxen on the third day, he notes that he had plowed one acre plus 70 rods (160 rods to an acre).[2]

Another type of labor found not infrequently in this period was the bound-out or indentured servant. Many early immigrants, it will be recalled, bound themselves by indentures, ordinarily for seven years, to pay for their passage. That particular bargain was by then usually a thing of the past in New England, but it was not unusual even into the nineteenth century for a boy to be bound out to some neighbor who was a good farmer "to learn the art and mystery of husbandry." Such a boy was likely to be well treated, educated much like a son, and at twenty-one given a good start in life by his employer.

A young farmer starting out on his own got lots of help from others. A young Rhode Islander starting in the Berkshires made a pair of shoes for a neighbor. He was aided with a man and horse for a day on his own lot. John May, Jr., an early comer to Woodstock, Connecticut, planned to build a house. In December 1710 he helped a neighbor named Child at logging and dressing flax. On December 30 Child helped him dig his cellar. The next day Joseph Lyon, Jr., "fetched a load of stone for the walls." In

January 1711 May helped Child fell trees, helped his landlord make a sled, and helped Ichabod Holmes with his rye. Then on the 16th and again on March 22 three neighbors helped May draw timber for his house. In April two helped hew it. More assistance both ways followed. May bought boards and shingles for his dwelling. On September 12 he finished his frame; next day the neighborhood raised it. One neighbor helped with foundation and chimney, another laid floors. Finally the house was done. May next made a bedstead, and bought a mare. On December 18 he recorded "A Great day's work" (he had got married). He loaded his bride's furniture on a cart at Boston. On New Year's Day 1712 the couple reached Woodstock, both bride and groom on the mare. The household goods came with them the seventy-five miles by oxcart, and only a single chair was damaged.[3]

Sometimes a big job enlisted the whole town. Rev. Ebenezer Parkman, minister-farmer at Westboro, Worcester County, Massachusetts, did not need to worry about getting his harvest home. This is his diary entry for October 11, in the Revolutionary year of 1779: "This day we cut up, carted home and husked out our Indian Corn. Ephraim Tucker went with my Team and Deacon Wood with his, about nine dined here. There were forty or more Men and Boys at Eve[ning] and several neighbors were so generous as to contribute to ye Entertainment. Squire Baker above 50 lbs. of Meat; Mr. Eb[eneze]r. Forbes Beef and 3 cabbages; Lt. Bond, Pork; Mr. Barnabas Newton, a Cheese; Breck [the parson's son] sufficient Rum. Through ye Goodness of God we had a good crop of Sound Corn and ye Joy of Harvest . . . We sang latter part of Ps. 65" (certainly an appropriate harvest ode).[4]

Many other ministers farmed. A parson was occasionally to be found in the ranks of the larger farmers, as had been the case in Old England. Reverend Joseph Green of Danvers on June 23, 1712, had ten men at work, eight "about the house" and two mowing. Reverend Timothy Walker of Concord, New Hampshire—to harvest the native grass on his intervale meadow—in August 1746 had six hands to mow for him. Among the large operators were sometimes merchants like John Hull of Boston, who managed livestock ventures in Rhode Island and farms elsewhere in addition to his Boston occupations.

New England farms with the most numerous labor forces were the great estates of the Narragansett planters in southern Rhode Island and nearby Connecticut. These produced livestock and dairy products, and did it with the labor of slaves. Rhode Island ships trading with Africa had brought back enough slaves so that in 1708 the number of "black servants" in that colony is said to have been 426.

By 1748, with prosperity derived from dairying, sheep, and horses, the number had increased to over 3,000; by the end of the next decade, to 4,700. South Kingstown had one negro to each three whites. Twenty-four women slaves did the work of one great dairy. In Connecticut the number of negroes is said to have reached 6,464 in all, part of them free; and, in Massachusetts Bay, 5,235 by 1746.[5]

A Newport planter, Colonel Godfrey Malbone, bought 3,000 acres at Pomfret, Connecticut, in 1766 to be worked by slaves, and they were there during the Revolution, to the worriment of the countryside, which feared them. One historian puts the largest number on any single estate at forty. Edgar Bacon in his *History of Narragansett Bay* calls slave labor in this period as much a part of Rhode Island life as of Virginia's. Since in all four colonies a considerable number were household servants, it is not clear just how large a number were farm workers; still, the proportion must have been considerable.

As time went on, moral scruples caused a number of Rhode Island planters, largely Quakers, to free their slaves. "College Tom" Hazard, from one of the leading families, has been called one of the first American abolitionists. In 1774 the Assembly voted that all blacks imported into the colony thereafter should be free. Connecticut banned the slave trade the same year. Massachusetts in its Revolutionary constitution in 1781 declared all men free. Connecticut at the Revolution's end made free persons of all negro children born after 1784 and eventually abolished slavery. New Hampshire, where slaves were never numerous, took similar action.

All types of labor considered—hired, indentured, and

forced—it was nevertheless on family exertions that the vast majority of farms depended, both for the family's own sustenance and for any produce grown for sale.

Yet life on the farm was by no means unrelieved labor. Diaries of the time tell of such recreations as visiting, quilting parties, husking parties, strawberrying—even "watermeloning" —and fishing.

The health of the colonists during the first few generations appears to have been good.[6] Scurvy and dietary illnesses were rampant during the long ocean voyage and the months of inadequate food and shelter that immediately followed their arrival, causing the death of scores. Of the first settlers of Salem, one in four died the first winter. Of Governor Winthrop's company, arriving in summer, two hundred died like falling leaves before the autumn was over. Such losses must have weeded out the weakest; thereafter the record is favorable. One fortunate circumstance, to which Nathaniel Shaler has called attention was that no new diseases resulted from contact of the English with the native Indians.

Of ailments that the newcomers brought with them, influenza, called in old records "fever and ague" or "epidemical cold with fever," appears again and again. Another complaint common to this age before refrigeration was "malignant dysentery" or "bloody flux." Epidemic "throat distemper" (diphtheria), was often fatal for young people. At Weymouth, Massachusetts, in 1751, the "Throat Distemper Year," 150 died, mostly children. By contrast, for several generations tuberculosis was rare, among the young at least. As one elderly chronicler in a Plymouth Colony town recalled: "In the year 1764 a young man fell into a consumption between twenty and thirty years of age and it passed for a wonder." Michael Wigglesworth's verse seems to bear this out: "New England, where for many years you scarcely heard a cough . . ." A thoughtful local historian suggests that the wide-throated chimneys which so readily ventilated every dwelling may have been a favorable factor in respect to this disease. Helpful also was the practice (though not much considered in the earliest settlements) of choosing elevated locations, airy, with good water drainage and near clear flowing springs, for village sites, in consequence of which, as Worcester County's earliest historian, Peter Whitney, put it, being "to a great degree exempted from fogs, deleterious vapours and exhalations, the inhabitants [of Lunenburg] are remarkably healthy . . ."

Doctors were few, and most of those few ill trained. For seventy-six years, from 1654 to 1730, no surgeon was to be found in the considerable Connecticut Valley town of Northampton. Across the river, neighboring Hadley for thirty-two years had no physician. Ministers' diaries record numerous illnesses and deaths from disease, causes often ill-defined, as well as from what today would be termed industrial accidents.

Every provident country family kept herbs, dry roots, and Indian remedies on hand, and tradition attests to their value. Wild strawberries were a remedy for kidney stone and gout. On October 12, 1715, Joshua Hempstead, his diary tells us, was out on the hills getting wintergreen for his daughter, troubled with what is now termed phlebitis, following childbirth. In 1723, on Cape Cod, a youngster in the Bourne family (missionaries to the Indians), was so ill that the physicians gave her up. An Indian medicine man cured her.

In 1679, Guilford, Connecticut, held a special town meeting "to consider whether the inhabitants would buy Mrs. Corster's Physic and Physical drugs." The vote in favor was unanimous, and the next spring, with only a single person objecting, the town voted a special tax to pay for them.

If professional physicians were few, to the courage of one and the scientific mind of a Boston minister goes the credit for control of one of the scourges of the age, smallpox. New England's wide-spreading ocean commerce brought recurring waves of this disease. It devastated the ports and at times swept inland, local quarantine and isolation in pesthouses the only remedy. The inquiring mind of Reverend Increase Mather happened on a report from the eastern Mediterranean of the value of inoculation as a preventive, and he advocated the practice. Against fierce opposition, political, medical, and physical, Dr. Zabdiel Boylston of Boston on June 26, 1721, successfully inoculated, with live vaccine, first his own six-year-old son,

Thomas, and later the rest of his household; then 246 others. Of the 246 inoculated, according to Dr. Boylston's account, but 6 died, compared to approximately one in seven of the 5,759 uninoculated who came down with the disease in Boston in the course of two years. Though smallpox was less prevalent away from the ports (Northfield, Massachusetts, had but one case in almost a half-century), a few country physicians near Boston took up the practice successfully. It was to be 1796, however, before Edward Jenner in England learned what dairy people there had long known, that cowpox immunized against smallpox. In the United States Dr. Benjamin Waterhouse, young Harvard professor of physic, was first to begin the practice of cowpox vaccination, again on a young son, and the conquest of the disease followed.

New England's climate made unusual the malaria that plagued the southern colonies, but it found its way occasionally into a port. New Haven, especially in 1658 and 1659, was visited by severe epidemics displaying malarial symptoms.

Before the end of the first century a new minor ailment appeared. It was not unusual to see girls of only twenty "pitifully tooth shaken," as John Josselyn phrased it. Tea and hot bread got the blame that today is visited more accurately on sugar. A local rhymester came near to the truth: "From western isles now fruits and delicacies/Do rot maid's teeth and spoil their handsome faces." Joshua Hempstead of Connecticut on September 14, 1718, sent five shillings by John Adams "to buy Some Tooth powder in Boston." Among products of Paul Revere's foundry were false teeth.

Despite lack of professional medical care, and especially in sharp contrast with southern colonization, New England's health record, for the times, is coming to be considered surprisingly good. Two recent studies of rural areas, those of John Demos, of Plymouth Colony, and of Philip Greven, of Andover, offer evidence of the "salubriousness" so often claimed by local town historians. In the Plymouth records but one birth in thirty appears to have been fatal to the mother. In early Andover, up to 1700, only a little over one in five children died before age 20. Half the females and three fifths of the males lived to be fifty;

three in ten men and almost as many women survived to age seventy. Nathaniel Shaler assures us that the size, weight, and beauty of the colonists showed no deterioration from those of Old England, nor did their fecundity. On this important subject much further careful statistical work needs to be done; not only with regard to physical ailments but in the matter of mental illness, for which evidence appears inadequate indeed.

It would be a neat conclusion to this consideration of New England agriculture during the century that ended with the outbreak of the Revolution to offer, as some writers have done, a picture of the "typical farmer" and his family existing on their typical "subsistence" farm. Yet if any judgment were to be drawn from the evidence offered in these pages, it would certainly be that no single, universal, category of farmer and farm existed.

The South County horse breeder, sheep herder and dairy-man, exporting Pacers and cheeses to the West Indies, his stock pastured on a thousand acres or more and cared for by slaves and Indians, was one type. A second was the ambitious young man setting out with a wife and all their belongings in a single oxcart, heading for a hundred acres offered by a township speculator on time payment in the backwoods of Vermont or Maine. The well-fixed grandson of the original owner of a long-tilled and well-manured corn and fat-stock farm, or one near an alewife run and a port market, was a third. Still another was the poor Scotch-Irishman or German with not even an ox or plow, who turned over the southern New Hampshire or Maine soil by hand to start his potato crop.

Besides these there were the Connecticut and Rhode Island farmers who in addition to common crops and animals grew onions, potatoes, tobacco, or flax for export; the Nantucket or Martha's Vineyard flockmaster with a thousand sheep; the innkeeper, grist or saw miller, storekeeper, drover, distiller, or tanner with a farm on the side. (For example, a miller on Cape Cod, dying in 1729, among his assets left a pair of oxen, 22 cattle, 2 horses, and a colt. He was one of many.) The shoemaker, blacksmith, or fisherman who ordinarily worked at his trade, usually farmed a little also to help out.[7]

Variations of other sorts existed. Many farmers enjoyed rights of common in towns where methods of agriculture were still governed by town meeting. Others lacked such rights or set up farming on their own separate tracts, newly divided, or in towns late chartered to which such controls never extended. The historian of Keene, New Hampshire, for example, tells how a settler there might obtain as much as 400 acres of fertile but forested land for $25. Such new farms sometimes made their owners wealthy on wheat alone.

The great majority of farmers kept some cows, often a family horse, an ox or a pair, a pig or two, in some areas sheep or goats. To feed this stock they cut a few tons of English (cultivated) hay and double or triple the weight in meadow or salt hay. In one town they might raise perhaps 30 or 40 bushels of grain per farm for family and stock; in another eight or ten times as much. If the farm was in apple country, the cider could run from 10 barrels up: on Cape Cod it would be very little. For many families a cow and a sow, perhaps a few roots and pumpkins, was as far as farming went; with others, agriculture was merely a side issue to commerce or a foundation on which to build a large estate.

Farm families in some areas, where a storekeeper or merchant offered an outlet, increased their income by making woolens, linens, stockings, caps, mittens, and similar items for market in the New York colony or more distant trade centers. A Northampton merchant in 1762 had a stock of 761 locally made brooms. Along the shore many families gathered wild bayberries and from their wax made candles for export; others hammered out nails or made shoes; still others got extra income from beeswax and honey. These and other sources of family income were to be greatly expanded when the Revolution restricted importation; but even in this early period they added to the wide variety that was to be for so long characteristic of New England agriculture and rural life.

The financial condition of New England's farmers was likewise various. Few were really wealthy, though many were comfortable: yet, except on the fringe of the frontier, scarcely any were poor in the sense of lacking essential food, clothing, or shelter. This was not necessarily the consequence of any virtue of the soil even where it was virgin. Rather, as Robert Honyman phrased the matter in 1775, it was due "to the incomparable industry of the inhabitants," and not least to the severe and exacting labor of farm women and children, though ordinarily they did not do hard field work.

It should always be kept in mind that in the century preceding the Revolution wealth in the form of currency, especially "hard money," was the exception and confined largely to merchants and port towns. In most towns wealth would be measured in land, livestock, and tangible assets together with a balance between a variety of items of all sorts receivable or owed. At any particular date both of the last two, as estate inventories show, were likely to be considerable for with cash scarce, an even settlement between two persons might not be reached readily for years, and no hard feelings either way.

To make up for the shortage of currency the various colonies from time to time made farm products and other commodities legal tender and authorized specific values for them. Wheat, rye, barley, oats, and corn; barreled beef, pork, and fish; flax, hemp, butter in firkins, tobacco, beeswax, boards, and other common items—all appeared on lists of this sort. Such produce was receivable for taxes, for the minister's salary, and similar purposes. As time passed, great variations in values occurred: at New Milford, Connecticut, for instance, between 1715 and 1760, the legal price for wheat went from 4 shillings to 22, and Indian corn from 2½ shillings to 7 in 30 years.[8] This method of placing arbitrary values on commodities not infrequently resulted in disputes over quality. In business transactions such a system made necessary a series of running scores between farmer and farmer, drover and farmer, and merchant and farmer. At infrequent reckonings the balance was often struck by giving orders or notes which, passed from hand to hand, served as a kind of supplementary currency. The problem of exchange was complicated by the issuance of paper money of the various colonies. Fluctuations in value and gains or losses that ensued made barter of one tangible object or product for another likely to be fairer to both parties than the use of the paper script.

A few typical entries in farm and store accounts make this method clear.

From New Hampshire: "I let William Kurr have 3 bushell of potatoes to be paid for in shad or money."

"Amos Gardner got 4 bushels of potatoes for which he is to give me three thousand of shingle nails."

"I got a [plow] shear mould from Thomas McLaughlin . . . toward what he owes me on the fly nets."

Southport, Connecticut, records, as reported by the town's historian Charlotte Lacey, contain this item: "Dec. 16, 1682. Ebenezer Smith hath by way of exchange with Samuel Drake a parcel of fence in quantity five rods, it is made with stones."

From Bristol County, Massachusetts, "Reseeved of Samuel Mason one cheese which waid 7 pounds," balanced by sugar, a whip, and other items.

From Buzzards Bay: "Reckoned with Ebenezer Luce and accounts balanced from the beginning of the world to the date hereof" [9] (a phrase frequently used as a disclaimer of further liability).

Whether agriculture was a vocation or merely a side issue to help feed the household, most farm families lived in decent houses; frame in the villages, of squared logs on the frontier. Almost invariably, except in squatter areas on the fringes in Maine, New Hampshire, and Vermont, they held title to their property in fee simple, and had the right to vote, at least in town affairs. "Everybody has property and everybody knows it," Robert E. Brown quotes a British officer as saying.[10]

All males and many females had some education. Massachusetts Bay had long required public schools in every town, and since 1647 Latin schools in the larger ones. Governor Dummer Academy, a private school at Newbury, Massachusetts, dates from 1762; that same year one was founded at Windham, New Hampshire. In 1771 Braintree was voting tax money for "Women schools." [11] Not infrequently country towns were "presented" to colony governments for not carrying out the law, usually pleading poverty or Indian depredations.

Spelling was often bad, but at the end of the colonial period

nearly all the men could read, and write at least their names, an
unusual distinction for a whole population at that era in history.
Books were to be found in a substantial number of farmhouses,
though perhaps only a Bible and almanac (in three-fourths of
two hundred farm inventories of a Worcester County compila-
tion).[12] The country town of Woburn produced a distinguished
scientist, Benjamin Thompson, later Count Rumford, who
discovered that heat was a form of motion.

Community libraries were appearing here and there
through the countryside. Citizens of Durham in central Connecticut organized a book company in 1733. Nearby Guilford,
Saybrook, Killingworth, and Lyme had begun library associations by 1737; in Connecticut's northeast corner Pomfret,
Woodstock, then Killingly and Lebanon followed within two
years; Milford got under way in 1745 and West Hartford in
1753. At the westerly end of the colony, Danbury had a public
library in 1771, and interior Brooklyn began one in 1775. In the
District of Maine, Falmouth, now Portland, in 1763 led the
library movement. Hingham in the Bay Colony formed a Social
Library in 1771, and a second one in 1773. Newport, Rhode
Island, one of New England's principal ports and a fertile farm
area, in 1747 built its still famous Redwood Library from the
donations of a Quaker of that name, and of others. By 1727
Boston had seen three newspapers started and at Newport one
was begun five years later. Others followed. As to periodicals, by
1775 New England was the best served area of the American
colonies. They carried mostly news of public affairs and commercial information. Editions were not large, but each copy was
likely to have numerous readers.[13]

In 1725 Dr. Nathaniel Ames of Dedham began to offer his
popular *Astronomical Diary and Almanac* (other almanacs had been
printed still earlier) and farmers were eager purchasers. One
Connecticut farm-bred boy, born during the Revolution, tells of
a file of these going back to 1720 as "sources of delight and
instruction." Strictly agricultural books of local origin seem to
have had their inception with the printing in Boston in 1710 by
John Allen of the *Husbandman's Guide*.[14]

The first volume to attain influence, however, and to attack soil fertility and cultivation problems, was Jared Eliot's *Essays upon Field Husbandry*. Originally published serially, 1747–59, the essays were printed in 1760 in Boston as a single volume. Eliot, pastor and farmer at Killingworth, Connecticut, had experimented for years on his farm, had traveled in Europe, and had observed farming methods there. His advice was respected.[15]

The emphasis by modern sociology-conscious historians on class distinctions in eighteenth-century New England tends toward misjudgment of a fundamental characteristic of the New England farming town. When the house lots were originally assigned, it was often by lot, always under basic agreement. The result was that on "The Street," up to the time of the Revolution, the larger house of the wealthy and prosperous was as likely as not to be neighbor to a modest cottage. The children of the two grew up together, worshiped together, studied together, and often intermarried. Charles Grant has well stated in his thoughtful study of Kent, Connecticut, that "in many communities leadership and executive authority go with the man rather than the office," true then in country towns, and still true. Governor Hutchinson complained that the vote of a poor man "will go as far in popular elections as one of the most opulent." Everyone worked, for it was sinful not to, and for the first century and a half nothing that could be called a leisure class existed except in a few port towns.[16]

The whole community had a common descent and a single historical tradition. Church membership was open to the poorest, and skin color was no barrier. Franchise requirements were so modest that almost any self-respecting mechanic or small farmer could meet them. All male inhabitants had their share in providing necessary roads, bridges, and town pounds. In New England as in Old England local public office usually carried no salary, entailed plenty of trouble, and was likely to be regarded less as an honor than as a burden. As such it might be more easily borne by the affluent than by the poorer man, but evidence is lacking that election to town office or continuance in it ordinarily caused either envy or discontent among other inhabitants. On the contrary, town by-laws not infrequently prescribed penalties for refusal of an elective office. In 1682

Amesbury, for example, fined Richard Currier for refusing. Plymouth Colony fined selectmen who declined to serve. Michael Zuckerman shows that persons elected to the post of selectman usually had already filled bothersome and undistinguished minor posts.[17]

The wrangles that eventually arose were occasioned far less by pretensions to social superiority by any group than by differing views of old and new comers, "proprietors" and "inhabitants," as to the ownership and allotment of the town's undivided lands; by disagreements over the site of the meetinghouse; and, as settlement spread to outlying sections, by the determination of proprietors in the new villages to have them made separate parishes, if not separate towns, with their own meetinghouses, pastors, officers, and tax rolls. Each of these involved property, money, or public appropriations and taxation. To most New Englanders, these matters—then as now—loomed as of far greater consequence than such a minor question as the order of seating in the meetinghouse for Sabbath worship.

The century 1675–1775 had again and again brought destruction, misery, and death to New England's farms, especially to those on its northern and western fringes. It had taken thousands of men far from home on expeditions of war and, as captives, women and children also; many of both were never to return.

On the other hand, the accidents of geography plus a powerful commercial instinct had sent exports sea-borne to the West Indies and southern markets: pork, cattle, horses, onions, boards, staves, pitch, and other farm cargo. All this became a basis for economic health at home.

The century had added to New England's list of crops a valuable food and salable commodity, the potato. The vegetable arrived in company with the Scotch-Irish, the first immigrants of consequence to enter since 1640. Though at first shown a cold shoulder, these newcomers, with their Irish potato, as it came to be called, and their art of flax cultivation and linen spinning, all proved valuable additions indeed.

Along with potatoes, dairying and horse breeding found

markets; and tobacco, a crop inherited from the Indians, began to have commercial importance. Nonetheless, because of their adaptability to soil and climate, the hay crop together with pasturage for livestock, corn cultivation, and the apple tree all remained of prime importance to farm well-being. Small grain and certain English vegetables and fruits did well in favorable locations. Meanwhile, New England built ships and loaded them with cargo, including livestock, produce, and wood products of numerous sorts.

Once the French and Indian wars had ended, a burst of emigration headed west and north. On primeval soil the adventurers would build the world anew, creating from the forest new farms, new towns. By 1776 Maine's three organized counties alone reported 47,279 whites.

Back in the old towns the first wealth of fertility was long gone. The soil's heart had to be laboriously renewed each year from any source of fertility at hand. Yet housing for both man and beast improved, and stone walls and new roads crept across the landscape. Continuing concern for the education of all, unique in the world of that day, meant that nearly every man and many women could read and write at least a little. All received continuous moral and political training. Their century and a half of practice in self-government was now to be consummated in a break with the English mother country and establishment of a new nation.

III. THE REVOLUTION AND ITS

AFTERMATH, 1775–1800

21

Patriotic Fervor

THE EVENTS of Lexington and Concord and the deeds of the farmers of Middlesex and neighboring counties on the fateful morning of April 19, 1775, are the province of the political rather than the agricultural historian.[1] Yet certain observations deserve a place here.

Much has been written of the merchants and politicians whose commercial interests and political ambitions are said to have brought on the conflict, and of the Boston mobs whose actions culminated in the Tea Party. Yet the men who first stood their ground and took the bullets in their bodies at Lexington and Concord and Bunker Hill were neither political nor commercial, nor yet a mob. They were mainly sober, responsible farmers and freeholders. Among them were members of the General Court or its temporary provincial successor. They were the product of a century and a half of a vigorous, self-supporting agriculture on this continent, and descendants largely of the independent-spirited yeomanry and countrymen of England.

The Revolution they began would take some of them to their graves, impoverish others, perhaps improve the condition of a few. It was their free choice and sense of duty, however, which brought these farmers swarming down country roads in the unseasonable heat of that April morning to stake their lives and fortunes on the issues of liberty and self-government.

Well in advance of that warm morning the struggle had begun to affect the agriculture of the four New England colonies. The Boston Port Bill, which had become effective in the previous May, had turned that thriving market for farm products to a desert. No more outgoing or incoming cargoes, no more vessels needing provision for their crews; neither merchants nor their workers any longer in a position to buy the country produce of every sort that ordinarily flowed into the capital by oxcart, saddle pannier, and coasting vessel. Marblehead was now designated the port of entry. The local market dried up. With commerce at a standstill, Boston rapidly lost population and the whole coast suffered.

To support the idle workers, soon in want, country towns far and near sent generous donations. Thomas Nowell's diary records a few:[2]

July 8, 1774. "About this time arrived three wagon loads of grain from the towns of Groton, Pepperell and Wrentham, for the poor of this town; and this day 105 sheep from our worthy friends in Pomfret, [Connecticut] for a like purpose."

August 13. "Arrived in town 376 sheep from our sympathizing brethren in Lebanon in the Colony of Connecticut for the benefit of the poor of this distressed town." Two days later Woodstock added 65 sheep.

August 19. "Captain Boyle arrived in Salem from Hartford in Connecticut and has brought some nine hundred bushels of grain for the poor of this town."

September 19. "The following donations received: from Candia Parish in the Province of New Hampshire 3 pounds and 84 sheep; from Concord, in Pennacook River, [New Hampshire] 30 bushels of pease; from Rehoboth [Massachusetts] 14 pounds lawful money; from Rehoboth and East Greenwich [Rhode Island] 112 sheep; from Tiverton [Rhode Island] 72 sheep; from Glassenbury [Glastonbury, Connecticut] 160 bushels of grain; from Southington [Connecticut] 150 bu. do.; from Weathersfield [Connecticut] 73 bu. do.; from Middleto(w)n [Connecticut] 1080 bu. do. and from Mr. Samuel Moody school master at Newbury Falls [Massachusetts] five guineas." Almost every town in the

faraway Housatonic Valley and many others in both Connecticut and Massachusetts sent supplies.

Even Salem felt severely the want of the port for the sale of
its cargoes, wrote Samuel Cooper to Thomas Pownal on August
17, two days before the arrival of Captain Boyle's vessel
mentioned above. "Lord North's Coasters, as the common people
call the Trucks and Waggons, are constantly on the way,
sometimes 40 or 50 in a day," replacing the little vessels, now
forbidden entry, that had formerly plied from every coastal
harbor to Boston.³

When winter impended, nearby towns sent in load after
load of wood "for the suffering industrious poor of Boston."
Lexington contributed 61 cartloads; Medfield, which had earlier
sent in 132 pounds of pork and 402 pounds of cheese, added 22
cartloads of wood. Captain Jeremiah Scott, a Walpole farmer,
was just starting for Boston with a load in April 1775 at the very
moment the news of Lexington arrived.

The imminent struggle generated a variety of side effects.
On Narragansett Bay in 1772 protesting colonists had burned
the customs schooner *Gaspé*. To keep order, the British navy
moved in and had to be fed. On April 6, 1773, for example, H.M.
Sloop *Swan* required "400 pd. beef, 400 pcs. pork, 16 bu. pease,
20 bu. oatmeal, 450 lbs. butter, 30 gals. rum," all supplied
locally;⁴ and the *Swan* was only one of the English naval vessels
that called at Newport or wintered there. Each vessel had a beef
day and a pork day weekly. In earlier years provisions for naval
vessels had been sent around from Boston, but after the Port Bill
took hold, that port was no longer a source of supplies and the
contractor was hard put to get enough animals from the farming
towns to fill out his droves for slaughter.

The Colonial side was also getting ready. Enraged by the
"Boston Tea Party" of December 16, 1773, the British parliament had in early 1774 abrogated the Massachusetts Bay
charter. The royally designated governor was now given sole
power to appoint judges and select also the sheriffs, who in turn
picked the juries. Bitterest pill of all, town meetings were to be
held only with his consent, and to act only as to matters meeting
his approval.

The people of the country towns, not like Boston overawed by British troops, were especially outraged at the suspension of what they regarded as their rights as Englishmen. At western county seats they gathered by thousands, prevented the courts from sitting, and forced the royally appointed judges to resign.

Meantime the House of Representatives had been called by General Gage, Royal Governor, to meet on October 5 at Salem. Disquieted, he now countermanded the call. The members met regardless, organized themselves extralegally into a Provincial Congress of Massachusetts Bay, and set the date for a second meeting for Concord on October 11.

Doubling the usual attendance, 293 town representatives responded. A "Committee of Safety," its actual purpose to gather military supplies and to enlist militia for defense, was set up. In every town, officered by veterans of the recent French wars, militia and minutemen began to drill on village training fields. The farming town of Sudbury, for example, which in 1765 reported 1,773 inhabitants, organized five militia companies and a troop of horse, numbering in all the astonishing total of 348 men. The zeal of other New England provinces almost matched that of Massachusetts Bay.

Supplies of food and clothing were joining munitions at storage points. The account book of John Goddard, a well-to-do farmer of Brookline, just west of Boston, contains the following entry for March 8, 1775: "The Committee For Supplies to Sundry Persons . . . To carting fifty five Barrels of Beef from Boston to Concord at 5 per Barrel £13..15..0." Doubtless this beef was one of the objectives of Lord Percy's troops six weeks later. On March 16 a Sudbury mother wrote in her diary: "But oh! these are troublous times. My son enlisted with about sixty men to go and fight." [5]

Longfellow, in "Paul Revere's Ride," has recorded more memorably than any historical writer how the farmers of Middlesex made history on the morning of April 19, 1775, with those of Essex, Worcester, Norfolk, and the rest of New England only a few hours behind. The sculptor Daniel Chester French, son of a later Middlesex farm owner, has commemorated these men in bronze at Concord Bridge, where thousands of visitors view the memorial each year. The events of that day have been woven into our national folk lore.

From every country village within reach minutemen hastened to Lexington, and then to the rendezvous at Cambridge. Major Aaron Guild, plowing in his field at South Dedham with his son that first morning, left plow and oxen, grabbed his gun, and made the fight before the day was over. Next morning the news reached Connecticut, and at Pomfret Israel Putnam also left his oxen standing in the field. He arrived at Cambridge on the 21st, to meet the New Hampshiremen under farmer John Stark coming in from the north. Soon thousands of men, mostly farmers, were gathered there, effectively shutting the British into Boston from the land side.

Armies require rations. In Brighton, across the Great Bridge from Cambridge, Jonathan Winship arranged to slaughter cattle to furnish fresh beef for the Colonials. He thus laid a foundation for the Brighton Cattle Market, famous for the next two centuries as the focal point for the sale of New England livestock. That fall, however, complaint arose that the Commissary brought in too large a proportion of supplies from Connecticut, whose wheat, ground into flour at Providence, was reaching the army overland. On May 2, 1775, in the Brookline account book of John Goddard an entry for 16 bushels of potatoes "Delivered to the Commasary at the Store in Cambridge" indicates how fresh vegetables were assembled. Another source of food seems to have been the home folks. Bernardston in the Connecticut Valley, for example, sent 445 pounds of bread and 116 pounds of pork to Captain Agrippa Wells's company enlisted from that town. Princeton in Worcester County on May 24 voted to take in twenty-four of Boston's poor, a seldom-mentioned type of patriotic duty.

It was equally important to cut off British supplies. On May 27 a patriot column swung through Chelsea to reach Noddle's Island, across the harbor from British-held Copp's Hill, and from adjoining Hog Island brought off 27 horned cattle, 411 sheep, and 6 horses.

Meantime the British fleet closed Narragansett Bay, shutting off the trade of Newport, Bristol, and Providence; and on

August 20 bombarded Stonington, Connecticut. Six weeks later they bombarded Bristol, Rhode Island, and forced the town to supply them 40 sheep. Boats from men-of-war requisitioned flocks and herds from every Bay shore town, and in December plundered and burned the farms on Conanicut Island, taking sheep, hogs, 6 oxen, and 50 cows. October saw four vessels shell Falmouth—now Portland, Maine—with resulting heavy destruction.

The British army occupied Brenton's Neck at Newport for a long period and before they left had cut all forest trees, "a noble grove of oaks included and made the beautiful park a desolate waste," a local historian lamented.[6] The destruction of war was not the work of one side alone. At Roxbury, during the siege of Boston, on the farm where the Roxbury Russet got its name, lived Mrs. Warren, mourning for her son, General Joseph Warren, killed at Bunker Hill. She suffered the loss of 123 of her apple trees, cut down by the Colonials. New England's foreign trade was ruined, and with it the markets for farm produce laboriously built through generations. Even its coasters suffered continual hazards.

Faced by Washington's guns on Dorchester Heights, the British army sailed to Halifax on March 17, 1776. Of the thousand Loyalists who sailed with them, one historian has calculated that 400 were farmers; another hundred came from country towns. Most of them never returned. Their properties were confiscated, and only a little more than one in ten of the Loyalists from Massachusetts were compensated by the British government. Most of these and the thousands of emigrés from other colonies had to build a new life from the bottom while their former farms passed into other hands.[7]

Once Washington's army had left for New York and the Declaration of Independence had been signed, accounts of the American Revolution are apt to ignore almost completely the direct effects of the war on New England. Yet these effects were numerous and important, at least from an agricultural standpoint.

In April 1777 Royal Governor William Tryon of New York and a British force marched north from Long Island Sound to

Danbury, Connecticut, and destroyed 1800 barrels of beef and pork, 700 barrels of flour, 2,000 bushels of grain, and other supplies collected from the countryside for the American forces, as well as a church and several houses. They also attacked Warren and Bristol in Rhode Island and Fall River in Massachusetts, burning and looting. That same year in the midst of summer, the farmers of Vermont, New Hampshire, and western Massachusetts were summoned to fight under General Stark, to defeat Hessians and British attempting to obtain supplies stored by the Americans at Bennington. The repulse of the attackers helped to bring about Burgoyne's surrender at Saratoga two months later. Meanwhile, however, the families of many soldiers had to bury provisions and flee British foraging parties.

Commanding the sea, vessels of the British fleet in 1778 raided New Bedford and Fairhaven and took 900 sheep and 60–70 cattle from Point Judith, Rhode Island, and appeared at Martha's Vineyard in September. General Gray's raiders cleaned from the island 10,574 sheep, including those of the Gay Head Indians (whom they left destitute), together with 300 oxen, and hay to feed the stock. They destroyed fields of corn and roots for a distance of two miles from Holmes Hole (Vineyard Haven), plus the salt works. Individual farmers lost from one to three cattle and from 15 to 200 sheep each. The next season the raiders returned for more. From Edgartown they requisitioned 900 hogs, 137 bushels of grain, 698 heads of cabbage, lumber, leather, and other provisions. They took stock from Falmouth on the Cape Cod mainland and slaughtered the cattle for fresh meat. At the Manasseh Swift farm there, the story goes, two soldiers stuck their bayonets into cheeses intending to make off with them. Mrs. Swift deftly slipped the cheeses into her checkered apron. "What valiant fellows you are," she taunted. Losses such as those of Martha's Vineyard were crippling. After the war was over, the British government compensated the Vineyard people to the extent of about 30 per cent.[8]

In 1779 British loyalist forces under Tryon raided and burned New Haven, East Haven, Fairfield, and Norwalk, Connecticut. At Greenwich they took all the plunder they could carry off. Though they left the dwellings standing, they cut holes in the attics to cause the stored corn to run down into the cellars, then completed their work by opening the cider casks and letting the cider run out. At Fairfield "2 of the enemy's brigs . . . went to Mill River. It took off 37 sheep & 15 lambs . . . with 4 horses . . . left 7 cattle dead on the shore," a diarist records. It was one of many similar raids. In 1781 Benedict Arnold led a raid on New London and burnt that town and Groton, with terrible loss to the militia defending the latter.

Ruffians, called cowboys, ran riot in southwestern Connecticut, murdering prominent patriots, seizing cattle and other valuable property for sale in British-held New York, and making life miserable and dangerous for farmers sympathetic with the Revolution.[9]

In Maine the British built a fort at Castine in 1779 and from this as a base systematically plundered farms and villages both east and west along the coast and up the Penobscot River. Freebooters seized livestock, food, clothing and valuables. Bucksport, Belfast, Thomaston, Machias, and Mt. Desert all suffered damage or a cutoff of trade.[10]

Vermont endured not only the plottings of vindictive Tories but the raids of Indians under British command. Many settlers had left northern Vermont when the Burgoyne expedition set out for Albany in 1777. The next season farms along Lake Champlain were devastated, cabins and crops destroyed, and 244 farm people, mostly men and boys, made prisoners and taken to Canada. Middlebury's people all fled, and every building in town but three was burned. In 1780 raiders penetrated into the White River Valley, burning as they went. Reaching Royalton, they burned 21 dwellings. To quote the local town history, besides killing several people and carrying off 25 to Canada, the party destroyed "16 new barns filled with hay and grain, slaughtered about 125 cattle and all the sheep and swine they could find." They "destroyed all the household furniture they could not carry away, taking with them about 30 horses laden with the spoil of the settlement." To the end of the war, with local Tories plotting, northern Vermont had to be on constant alert.[11]

Since British war vessels patrolled Long Island Sound,

getting farm produce to market by sea was hazardous. Barnstable on Cape Cod could get its onions and rye to Boston only by running a small coaster close to shore by night. A Fairhaven brig of 160 tons, loaded with staves and beeswax, was spotted by a man-of-war and taken as a prize.

Actions such as these may not have exerted great influence on the outcome of the war, but they did affect materially the livelihood of large numbers of New England's country people. Besides the actual destruction, militia had to be called out again and again to meet alarms, watch the coasts, and provide forces to besiege the enemy at Newport. Hundreds of farmer-sailors went to prison.

After the British fleet returned from Nova Scotia in 1776 and landed troops at Newport, on Long Island, and in New York, the war became a continued grind. The Continental Congress lacked certain powers essential to effective national government, such as the right to tax. Hence, for men and supplies it had to call on the governments of the thirteen individual colonies, now become states. New England state governments in turn made requisitions on the towns. Town meetings and selectmen as a rule did their best to meet the continual demands.

This is one of the fields which historical research has overlooked, except for the authors of local town histories, and information is far from complete. From examination of some local sources, however, it appears that the call-up of men and the assembling of supplies had effects much more far-reaching than historians have sometimes been ready to believe.

Not merely were there continued calls for men to meet the quotas of the Continental armies, but emergencies such as the raids on coasts and frontiers and the need to garrison coastal defenses took men from their farms at seasons when they were most needed at home.

The events of 1775 caused thousands of countrymen to leave their fields that spring, and the emergency continued till the middle of the succeeding March. In the war's second year, Governor Jonathan Trumbull of Connecticut received an appeal from General Washington for troops to protect New York. It was

August—haying time, with harvest just ahead. Five Connecticut regiments were already in service, yet nine more regiments of 350 men each left their farms and responded to their governor's call.[12]

Burgoyne's invasion of the Hudson Valley came at the identical season the following year, taking the militia of New Hampshire, Vermont, and western Massachusetts from their farm work in August before hoeing was finished and holding them through the fall months. In the summer of 1778 came the call for militia for the unsuccessful investment of Newport, to guard Providence, and to meet assaults on the coastal towns of Maine and Connecticut. Again in 1781 a militia garrison that manned Fort Griswold in Groton, Connecticut, beat back the British assaults, and, finally forced to surrender, were massacred by the attackers, who had been enraged by their resistance. Both New London and Groton were burned.

All through the war one quota call for the regular Continental forces succeeded another. Toward the end, with the towns bare of men, special inducements were offered. Chelmsford, Massachusetts, on the Merrimack, in 1781 offered to reward each enlistee with 20 head of cattle, graded by age: one year, two, or older, according to his period of enlistment or the length of the war. In the Connecticut Valley, Montague did the same. Harpswell on the Maine coast promised cows and calves worth five pounds to its enlistees. One recruit at Wells received a bonus of 6 cows and 15 sheep. Ashfield, Massachusetts, voted each man enlisting for three years twenty calves of the following spring, to be kept at the town's expense for the enlistment period.

Such rewards evidence not only the generosity of the towns and the scarcity of available recruits, but the substitution of tangible assets for unreliable and constantly depreciating paper currency. Leominster, Massachusetts, for example, made a combination offer to David Joslin, just about to turn sixteen in the spring of 1781. The town promised him $2,000 in paper currency plus 18 three-year middling cattle if he should stay two and a half years, or two-year-olds if he left at the end of one and a half years. He served till October 18, 1783, and got his cattle: an excellent start in life. In Lancaster, Deacon Moore, one of the town's enlistment committee, deeded to an enlistee a field which the latter had long had his eye on. "Take it," said the Deacon, "for if we lose our liberties it will be of no value to me." [13]

The drain on manpower was particularly hard on new towns, opened since the settlement of the French war, their men mostly young and able-bodied. Their growing families had to have support from the towns during the enlistment of the fathers. This necessity is said to have caused ill feeling against older towns that were wealthier and better established and had fewer young people.[14]

Numerous examples make clearer the contribution of the country towns to the Revolutionary forces. Braintree, Massachusetts, John Adams' home town, from a population of 2,871 recorded about 1,600 enlistments in all, with many enlisting more than once for short terms. In Lancaster one half the rateable polls of 16 years and over served at some time: after the second year of the war, 40 were continuously in service, averaging 27 months each. The little town of Medfield contributed 154 men in all, 42 to the Continental Army. The diary of Parson Thomas Smith of Falmouth, Maine, tells of one draft that required every fourth man. During seven years of war, Connecticut counted 40,000 enlistments from a total population in 1780 of just over 200,000.[15]

New England farms were a reservoir not only of men for the Revolutionary armies, but of food and clothing. Here is the ration that the Massachusetts Provincial Congress voted for the first war year: "Each Soldier in the Massachusetts Army shall have . . . per day: 1 lb. bread, ½ lb. beef and ½ lb. pork [in lieu of pork 1¼ lbs. beef, or on one day in seven, 1¼ lbs. of salt fish instead]; 1 pint milk; if milk cannot be had 1 gill of rice; 1 qt. of good spruce or malt beer; a jill of Pease or Beans or other Sauce equivalent"; plus 6 ounces of good butter and half a pint of vinegar weekly, and for each six men one pound of good common soap.[16]

After the Continental Congress took over the system of supply, state governments were assigned quotas periodically, but they continued to rely on the towns for provisions and clothing to fill them. At first it was not difficult to meet the requisitions.

Before the long war ended, however, towns were at their wits' end to find the necessary supplies. The little central Massachusetts town of Oxford in 1778 voted to raise its quota of 5,760 pounds of beef for the army. When only 2½ months later another requisition of 11,062 pounds came, the town meeting declined.

In 1780 the Massachusetts General Court levied on its towns a requisition of 2,400,440 pounds of beef. Amesbury, on the Merrimack River, met the call with 33 oxen weighing 900 pounds each. The requisition for Barnstable County (Cape Cod) on September 25 was for almost 36 tons of beef (as well as 156 men) from its nine towns. Harwich, asked to furnish 8,350 pounds but suffering from drought, said that more than one fourth of its families had no meat of any kind during the year. By contrast, in 1781 the Merrimack Valley town of Haverhill, to quote its historian, "raised the enormous quantity of 32,256 pounds of beef for the Continental Army," in addition to sending 28 soldiers for whom the town paid the charges.[17] Greenfield in the Connecticut Valley cut its own expenses so as not to fail to meet the quotas laid upon it. Wells in Maine bought 20,000 pounds of beef to fill one requisition; Windham, Maine, voted cash instead. Vermont had its own garrisons to supply. Pomfret, for example, at the end of 1780 collected 1,600 pounds of flour, 532 of beef, 266 of pork, and 67 bushels of grain for this purpose.

Connecticut early adopted an adequate ration for its troops and promptly appointed a Commissary-General to see that they were supplied. During the terrible Valley Forge winter of 1777–78 Connecticut sent drovers with herds of cattle clear to Pennsylvania. Again in early 1780 Washington at Morristown was desperate. He appealed to Governor Jonathan Trumbull. After an exhausting struggle through the snow of that dreadful winter, the Governor's leaders of the supply train got a drove of cattle and 200 barrels of flour, 100 barrels of beef, and 100 barrels of pork across the ice of the Hudson and delivered them at Newburgh on the promised day. Gen. Washington's comment is said to have been: "No other man than Governor Trumbull could have procured them, and no other state than Connecticut would have furnished them." [18]

In June 1777 Litchfield, Connecticut, supplied butter and

cheese enough to provide three tons of iron, presumably from the Salisbury mines. Windsor in 1781 met its clothing quota, also by barter. The town voted to send a thousand bushels of corn or rye flour to Rhode Island as an "equivalent for . . . procuring Linen Cloth for frocks shirts and overalls . . . for this town's quota of clothing for the army agreeable to the acts of the General Assembly." [19] At that very time loyalists in southwestern Connecticut were trading with the British!

The soldiers in the army were not the sole persons in distress. Some of the poor of Boston—its commerce destroyed before the war by the closing of the port, and its resumption barred by the British blockade—were said to be reduced to vegetable food only. The town appealed for help to the country towns, and not in vain. Norton in southeastern Massachusetts, for example, in 1779 appointed a committee to collect sheep and grain for Boston's supply.

Salem also carried a heavy burden: the support of families not only of absent soldiers but of the many sailors removed from its vessels after their capture and held in captivity by the British. Marblehead, its men unable to fish, contributed a disproportionately large number to the army and was forced to assist many of their families. Rhode Island and Philadelphia Quakers sent donations to the town and distributed them. Nantucket, Cape Cod, and New Bedford whalers were unable to sail; Gloucester and Cape Cod fishermen were kept at home. Nantucket set aside 100 acres where the destitute could grow potatoes. A loyalist prisoner in Rhode Island in 1776 tells of grass uncut, corn unhoed.[20]

The attempts by the Continental Congress and the constituent states to pay the costs of the struggle for independence caused endless economic dislocations, some of which fell heavily on the farms. Since the Congress was without power to tax, the province governments had to take up the burden. The New England provinces relied on poll taxes (one third of Massachusetts' revenue was from this source), property taxes, and borrowing. To meet their quotas of food, clothing, and supplies, and the bounties to secure recruits, the towns collected local rates and often borrowed heavily besides. Long-settled, well-to-do farming towns were best off. Recently settled frontier towns suffered. Town after town in Maine and western Massachusetts had to petition the General Court for tax relief. Newly settled northwest Connecticut was in general poor also.

The summer of 1778 was very dry and crops scant. With grain needed for food, Connecticut forbade its distillation into liquor; and Massachusetts for a time in 1779 embargoed export of food and essential commodities. New Hampshire had already put controls on food exports. The severe winters of 1779–80 and 1780–81 and the summer droughts that succeeded in 1780 and again in 1782, made difficulties greater. Corn was extremely scarce and reached $4.00 a bushel in hard money at Boston. Massachusetts had to send supplies to the Maine coast, where the war had prostrated the lumber and spar trade.

Aside from loans arranged with European powers and its requisitions of supplies from the states, the chief reliance of the Congress was on issuance of paper money. Since no adequate resources backed this Continental currency, it fell rapidly in value, in 1781 depreciating to a rate of 1,000 to 1.

Continually rising prices for food and all commodities resulted. To protect persons on wages and to hold down the cost of the war, state legislatures tried setting prices, and towns set values for exchange on all common commodities. These measures, difficult or impossible to enforce, proved futile. The legal price of wheat at Greenfield in the Connecticut Valley rose from 6 shillings 8 pence a bushel in 1776 to 8 pounds 2 shillings (legal) in 1779. At Pittsfield wheat worth $12.00 a bushel in 1779 was valued a year later at nine times as much. Country barter transactions were less affected, however.[21]

For the first few years of the war, shortages and inflated prices often worked to the benefit of a farmer with stock or produce to sell. Taxes were light then, but later became enormous. He received more in shillings or dollars and was thus able to settle old accounts advantageously. In the market towns wages advanced less rapidly than prices, and with many sailors, fishermen, and mechanics out of work, antagonisms arose. People in the ports accused farmers and traders of being cruel profiteers, for, as Reverend Samuel Lane of Stratham, New Hampshire, noted, "people have Such a poor Esteem of paper Money, that they will not carry in their provisions (tho plenty) for it . . . and people were almost in a Starving Condition in the lower Towns: so that they soon broke over the Stated prices." Ministers preached against the farmers for not accepting the legal prices. Even the army is said to have suffered from profiteering by country people. Occasionally a farmer got rough handling. The result was that farmers refused to bring in supplies, or sought other markets. At Salem at least one farmer was posted in a newspaper for selling above legal prices; but the regulations proved unworkable.[22]

In the later years of the war the situation changed. The French alliance brought their fleet and army to Narragansett Bay in the summer of 1780, with headquarters at Newport. These allies required provisions, and repairs to ships, and they paid in hard money. Merchants received contracts to supply them with flour, beef, and beans, opening an important outlet for the farms of southern Massachusetts, Rhode Island, and eastern Connecticut. New England oxen did much of the hauling. (Also in the Yorktown campaign later in the war.) At the same time the American army was still drawing supplies from Connecticut and western Massachusetts. In the winter of 1781, for example, the Connecticut legislature sent 1,000 barrels of beef and pork to the forces.[23]

A second factor aided the market for farm produce, especially along the seaboard. As the war moved south and the blockade relaxed, privateering increased. Scores of ships received authorization as privateers, mounted guns, and set off after British merchantmen. Though it was a dangerous trade, rewards were high. By 1780, American privateers, largely manned by fishermen, had captured prizes totaling 200,000 tons. Ships and their cargoes condemned by United States admiralty courts and sold at auction helped bring once more to port towns a certain prosperity. Over 600 Massachusetts vessels alone sailed under Continental letters of marque, and the newly independent states issued hundreds more letters of their own. New London, Connecticut, in one month saw eighteen prizes brought in.

Samuel Morison calls attention to how the rush for privateers revived shipbuilding, and how emphasis on speed caused ship design to improve, a factor of great importance to postwar New England. From a farm point of view, provisioning the vessels and their builders must have improved the market for produce. Perhaps this may offer a clue to why at Westborough, forty miles inland, Reverend Ebenezer Parkman, a farmer-parson, on December 21, 1778, wrote in his diary: "Mrs. P. kills 5 geese, 26 dunghill Fowls for market with ye Pork. For it appears necessary to make some money of what we raise that we may be able to purchase what is wanting in other respects." Two days later: "Mr. Joseph Harrington goes with his team for Marblehead, and takes my Pork, Geese and Fowls for marketing." [24] As the war went on, however, and the blockade tightened again, privateering became less profitable and resulted in retaliation on the privateers' home ports, such as New London.

Though little is said about this in general histories, it must have been on farm women and children that the war's effects fell hardest. Calls for men came in hoeing time. With men absent, not only had the women to do unaccustomed field work, but much of the burden of providing requisitions for clothing and other supplies for soldiers and for the needs of the people at home fell on them. Spinning wheels whirred, and weaving looms clacked longer than usual. The women of Gloucester, Rhode Island, made hundreds of yards of linen tow cloth. One town in Connecticut furnished 3,000 yards of woolens. Food supplies had to be stretched. Salt for cooking and meat pickling was often almost unobtainable. Severe want sometimes appeared. Parson Parkman's Westborough diary on March 24, 1779, speaks of "ye Straits and Difficulties to which many of ye people of Bolton are reduced, for want of Bread and how scarce Meat is there," as reported by a relative from that town who dined with him. Adding to the housewife's burdens, smallpox and dysentery were epidemic in 1777 and 1778. Worst of all, many a husband and father gone to the army never returned to his farm.

The historian of Westerly, Rhode Island, tells how, in 1778, when the Colonials had the British in Newport under siege, nearly all the males were in the forces trying to capture Newport or doing sentry duty on the coast. Hence the women had to manage horses, cattle, and flocks, husk corn, even plow and reap. They "organized into a band to gather the harvests. They would complete the work on one farm then pass to another." [25] In Hopkinton, Rhode Island, scarcely a man save the aged fathers remained to help them. Women and children had the mean jobs of harvesting flax where that was grown, then retting it and swingling the fibers. Lest this condition appear confined to Rhode Island, the historians of Ashburnham, a hundred miles northwest in central Massachusetts, and others tell of the discouragements of that 1778 summer when the men were absent at the Newport siege. On the coast, tides carried off stacks of unhauled salt hay.

From a historian of the Coos country in the upper Connecticut Valley comes the tale of a Mrs. Wallace of Thetford, in eastern Vermont. Her husband was called in 1777 to join the army opposing Burgoyne. He had planted corn, oats, and potatoes on his new wilderness farm. After his summons, Mrs. Wallace hastened for safety to a Connecticut River settlement; but when she thought the oats must be ripe, she returned to the farm, cut them with a scythe, and bound and stacked them. Then she cut poles and fenced the stacks against the animals. Later in the fall she came back to the clearing, gathered the corn, cut the stalks, and of them made a roof to protect the oats; then dug the potatoes. Finally she cleared the rough from an acre where the trees had been cut the previous season, and before she returned to the settlement seeded this to winter wheat. Moreover, this woman is said to have borne eleven children and eventually to have served as midwife for 1,600 others! [26]

The soil, too, suffered. With labor scarce, proper manuring, cultivation, and fencing were bound to be neglected, while repairs to buildings and tools were postponed. Weeds and brush could take over pastures. The incessant drain of the war depleted the soils and resources of the countryside. Depreciation of the currency and increased taxes impoverished many of its people.

Shortage of food and clothing in the Continental Army had repercussions at home. Some patriotic officers, unable to endure seeing their men unpaid and unclothed by the Continental Congress, hazarded their own property to fill the gap. Lieutenant

John Bolton of Colrain, Massachusetts, a talented army engineer, mortgaged his property to raise money to take care of the men under his command. Neither he nor his men were ever paid. He lost his house as a result and never recovered financially.[27]

Nehemiah Tinkham of Windham, Connecticut, "who had laid out his whole property and pledged his credit in purchasing supplies for the army" was paid in paper. He died suddenly, leaving his widow and eleven children destitute. The town's Baptist minister, out of the goodness of his heart, took them into his home. The careful historian of Windham County asserts: "Many affluent families . . . were reduced to poverty and destitution by the inability of the government to redeem its pledges." In the Berkshires, writes a local historian, many a wealthy Hoosac Valley farmer died in poverty from currency depreciation.[28]

The exhausting struggle was not, however, without plus items for farm people. Of profound importance, though not appearing momentous at the time, was the decline or total prohibition of human slavery in the New England states. Again, the war gave a great impetus to the metal industries, hitherto kept in leash by British restrictions. At Salisbury, Connecticut, for instance, an iron mountain furnished cannon for the Revolutionary armies. Southeastern Massachusetts, long used to working bog iron, before the century's end had 20 blast and air furnaces, 20 forges and slitting mills, and several trip hammers, and was on its way to becoming a center of nail manufacture. Iron works operated all the way from Plymouth County to Vermont, increased the market for charcoal, and laid the foundation for the farm tool and machine manufacture that was to become so important for the economy of New England and the nation in the next century. The cutoff of imports stimulated enterprise and invention.

The first New England woolen mill opened at Hartford in 1788, ushering in a durable union of sheep growing with cloth manufacture. Paper manufacture got a start in western Massachusetts, to become in time a great rural industry and a market for straw and textile waste. In 1780 Zador Benedict established at Danbury, Connecticut, the nation's first factory for making hats, an industry one branch of which was destined later to furnish an extra source of labor income to thousands of farm families.

Salt manufacture from sea water was begun at Dennis on Cape Cod in 1776 by John Sears and carried on in other places. Though comparatively short-lived, it proved of great importance to farmers and others while importation of salt was cut off during the Revolution and the War of 1812.

At Leominster, Massachusetts, the manufacture of horn combs opened an outlet for cattle by-products and laid the foundation of a manufacturing business still of importance. The great Brighton Cattle Market had its inception in the needs of the 1775 Revolutionary army at Cambridge, and by 1790 Jonathan Winship was packing 5,000 barrels of beef annually there for export. And Captain Richard Bagnall brought back from the fighting along the Susquehanna the seed of New England's favorite vegetable of the future, sweet corn.

It was not an enticing prospect that the soldiers of the Revolution faced when the army disbanded on June 13, 1783. Their pay, if they received it, was in Continental currency and nearly worthless. Even so, "the five years' pay granted to the Continental officers is unjust and ought not to be paid them," according to the Plymouth town of Wareham on February 11, 1784. It "was obtained by undue influence & . . . notwithstanding all their good services we shall esteem them Public Nuisances . . ." [29]

Massachusetts, borne down by a tremendous war debt, had learned from French War experience that patriotic service could be paid for in land. As a result, many a Revolutionary soldier headed for the District of Maine, still a part of Massachusetts, where a hundred acres or more were to be had free or for a promise to pay a modest sum. By 1790 twenty-six new towns were incorporated there. Connecticut ex-soldiers moved north into Vermont or went west to the Wyoming Valley, a rich area claimed by Connecticut in what was to become western Pennsylvania. New Hampshire's grant towns in the western part of that state filled up.

Soldiers who returned to their farms were apt to find buildings in disrepair, fields unproductive, and pasturage scant. A series of especially severe winters from 1783 to 1785 killed fall-sown grain. Great freshets in the river valleys added to rural distress. One historian believes that rural New England suffered an actual decline in real wealth in this period.[30]

The heaviest burdens, however, were economic. They hit most severely interior towns, themselves in debt for war expenditures, where hard cash was seldom seen and many transactions involved debts, notes, and open accounts. To ease the payment of obligations, Massachusetts in 1782 passed a legal tender act making cattle, sheep, swine, grain, and pine boards receivable for debt, after appraisal; but many creditors merely held off pressing suit until the act expired a year later.

The end of the war brought a flood of imports to merchants. Prices dropped, collections slowed, depression ensued. Faced with the need to pay their foreign creditors in cash, importers pressed local customers and country storekeepers for money. The situation was most trying in Massachusetts, where hundreds of suits bogged down in the courts. In 1784 Worcester County's Court of Common Pleas alone was faced with 2,000 actions. In Berkshire County even the most prudent people were said to be deeply embarrassed, and a mob estimated at 2,000 prevented the court from sitting at Great Barrington. Taxes had to be collected in cash to meet the state's enormous debt of 1,641,535 pounds. Payment in enumerated commodities was permitted in 1784, but the next year the law became more stringent. With deep depression in trade, daily failures were the rule in Boston: "a horrid and distressing situation," an English visitor called it.[31]

In Vermont in 1785 an armed gathering tried to prevent the court for collections from sitting at Windsor, but was dispersed. In September 1786 in New Hampshire a desperate armed crowd milled about the Exeter church where the legislature sat. The militia was called up, the dissidents dispersed, and arrests followed.

Interior Massachusetts was the area most violently affected. One fourth of the rateable persons in the state were said to be defendants in suits at court. Many debtors went to prison for failure to pay, with no means for their relief. A historian of Pittsfield observes: "in 1786 not a few of these poor creatures, blue with prison mould, were those who had fought for freedom, and were still the creditors of the country whose laws made them tenants of a debtor's jail." [32]

Was this what the war had been endured for: to make business for lawyers? to enable the wealthy to gobble up honest men's farms and stock? Calls went out for Massachusetts towns to appoint delegates to meet in county conventions to seek relief. Conventions assembled in all but the salt water counties. There, with markets close by, farmers appear to have been in less difficult straits.

The conventions forwarded resolutions to the legislature. When these failed to bring relief and seizures of property continued, groups of debt-burdened men, many of them former soldiers, gathered at one county seat after another and prevented the civil courts from sitting. When stock and other property was auctioned to meet debts, neighbors declined to bid. In 1786 the situation reached a point where the governor made a proclamation prohibiting unlawful assemblies. No remedy for the distraining of the property of debtors accompanied it, so the agitation continued.

At length an armed force of the discontented and desperate gathered at Springfield intending to prevent the state Supreme Court from sitting. In January 1787 the rebels, under a Revolutionary Army officer, Captain Daniel Shays, attempted an attack on the federal arsenal there. Massachusetts forces, with artillery, repulsed, pursued, and dispersed them. Many of the attackers were captured and jailed. General Benjamin Lincoln, who commanded the state's forces, was himself a farmer, (he had served through the war and received the surrender of Cornwallis), and loyal farmers served in the forces under his command.

An agricultural history is not the medium to discuss the military aspects of the struggle, the flight through the snow, the arrests and trials that followed, and the eventual amnesty for the rebels.[33] Shays's Rebellion has been studied again and again from legal and military points of view. Most local histories, written long ago by clergymen, are severe on the undisciplined actions of the poverty-stricken "rabble." Yet, recalling the almost parallel response in the 1930's of decent, law-abiding western farmers to the injustice of an unfair and unresponsive economy, the historian is able to view the insurrection and its results with a more sympathetic eye. He can conclude that the farmers were victims of bad economics and unjust legislation rather than being personally wicked or vindictive as was then charged.

In Rhode Island, as Marion Starkey has pointed out, the shoe was on the other foot. The legislature, controlled by farmers, required creditors to accept payment in paper money. If they declined, deposit of the amount of the debt with the town clerk wiped out the obligation. Merchants there avoided those who owed them money, if possible. On the other hand, farmers refused to sell produce for paper money, and want ensued in the towns.[34]

It is notable that Connecticut escaped insurrection. Connecticut farmers had comparatively little mortgage debt, and the tax burden was easier. Most claims there were settled by private agreement or arbitration. The older and more prosperous towns along the coast in eastern Massachusetts, New Hampshire, and in the Connecticut Valley for the most part remained calm, and furnished troops to put down the insurrection. Plymouth, for example, by 1785 was cod-fishing again, and doing well in spite of its poor soil. Vermont, however, showed sympathy for the Massachusetts rebels. Many of the discontented removed to that state, Maine, and the West and started afresh.[35]

Fortunately the disturbances in New England emphasized the necessity for a true national government, able to coin money, levy taxes and imposts, and keep the peace. When the Philadelphia Convention drafted the new United States Constitution and offered it to the states for adoption, in Massachusetts it was a Berkshire countryman, Jonathan Smith of Lanesboro, who persuaded the farmers in the legislature to give it the votes needed to adopt it.

With an effective national government, reviving trade, and a stable currency, the maladjustments and injustices that led to rebellion were gradually corrected. A renewed spirit of enterprise began to surge through New England, and with the opening of the new century, those in agriculture and other occupations took on fresh hope.

22

The New States

A T THE CLOSE of the eighteenth century the heart of Connecticut, and its most fertile area, was the naturally opulent Connecticut Valley. It relied so heavily on wheat production that the appearance of the Hessian fly about 1787 was a disaster. It was also growing rye and Indian corn in abundance. The fat beef that had so helped the Revolutionary armies was now marketed in New York and Philadelphia and sent in barrels to the West Indies. Horses were still a resource. In 1791 New London exported 7,403 horses and mules to the West Indies. Wethersfield, "remarkable for its vast fields uniformly covered with onions," relied on the same markets, and Middletown shipped horses and oxen to similar destinations. The French traveler Brissot de Warville in 1791 admired the "charming cultivated country" about Hartford, its "huge" cattle and swine and its abundant poultry, apples, and potatoes. Another French visitor, the Marquis de Chastellux, called the road from Hartford to Farmington "such a garden, in the English style, as it would be difficult for art to imitate." In northeast Connecticut he described the fertile Woodstock area as "a very gay and well peopled country." In the northwest, about Litchfield, though the area had been poor previously, cheese-making for the southern market was off to a good start, and dairying was destined to enrich it. Charles Grant in his careful study of the Housatonic Valley town of Kent has found that although many farms there were small, six out of ten had something to sell, and the thirty largest kept from six to fifteen cows each.[1]

Yet not all Connecticut was doing so well. Large stretches of light sandy soils near New Haven, once used for grain, had been abandoned and the dust was blowing.[2] Jared Eliot had been distressed at the tree cutting, erosion, and poor management of numerous farms in his neighborhood of Killingworth just off the Sound and elsewhere in the colony. Connecticut was backward also in road building. Even the coast road from Fairfield to New York was called "intolerable bad for horse riders." It must have been impossible for the horse-drawn vehicles just beginning to appear.[3]

In towns recently settled, much land was in the ownership of nonresidents. In older places, their original fertility gone, farms had often become small through divisions from inheritance. And to many natives the future looked better elsewhere. What one writer calls a torrent of emigration headed upriver into Vermont and west into New York State and Pennsylvania's Wyoming Valley: 775 in twenty years from the town of Farmington alone.[4]

Far-sighted Connecticut farmers, however, kept their eyes on the growing markets of New York, Boston, and the South, easily reached by sea. Those beside salt water used fertilizers from the sea in the form of fish and seaweed. All in all, Connecticut agriculture could look to a prosperous period ahead.

Rhode Island, which at the time of the first census in 1790 counted 68,825 inhabitants, had suffered badly. After the British occupation of Aquidneck Island, containing Newport, a 1794 visitor observed that their departing troops, like locusts, had left not a green tree. They had devastated Jamestown Island in the Bay also. Newport's trade was reduced; grass was said to be growing in the public square in 1788; but enterprising merchants there were still combing foreign markets for customers for flaxseed and other exports.[5]

A Spanish-American visitor at the end of the war called Aquidneck, even without trees, "The Paradise of New England." Completely cultivated, to another visitor it appeared like a varicolored map, the richest country he ever saw. Providence was in a bad way, though Brissot de Warville laid its troubles largely to the effect of paper money. Its merchants were aggressive, however, and trade returned. From Providence north, the South American traveler Francisco de Miranda was struck by the abundant orchards.[6]

"South County," bordered by the west side of Narragansett Bay and Long Island Sound, faced transition. When shipping to the West Indies resumed, the trade in horses continued to some extent; but, now without slave labor, the region's preeminence in dairying declined. As an offset, western Connecticut became for the next few generations headquarters for cheese.

Massachusetts, counting close to 400,000 people, in the last decade of the century experienced a mercantile revival. Due to war in Europe, a tremendous spurt in shipping and shipbuilding invigorated Salem, Boston, and seaboard towns well into Maine. In 1787 Salem welcomed its first vessel home from China, the *Grand Turk*, opening what was to become that port's rich Far Eastern trade. The second year afterward, Brissot wrote, Boston sent 44 vessels to the Pacific northwest coast and the Orient, thus adding a new sea-track; and in 1790 the *Columbia* returned, the first American ship to circle the globe. In Maine, demand for lumber and farm produce revived and expanded as New England took a continually larger part in the western world's ocean-carrying trade. Examples of Massachusetts' variegated agricultural exports for 1790 are the following (doubtless originating partly in other states): Indian corn, 69,064 bushels; horns and horntips, 71,281; horned cattle, 652; horses, 324; salt beef, 30,499 barrels; salt pork, 3,174 barrels; fresh beef, 92,269 pounds; fresh pork, 29,334 pounds; hams and bacon, 36,946 pounds; cheese, 23,155 pounds; tallow, 273,641 pounds, together with 12,325,000 shingles and a long list of other items.[7]

Effects soon showed on farming patterns. The demand for butter and cheese caused a town as far out from Boston as Concord, twenty miles, to turn to dairying. Dairy farmers living closer now made daily trips to town, adding their fresh milk to the supply from Boston's own cows. The growing market for fresh fruit and vegetables encouraged their regular production on farms within hauling distance. This farming directly for market, requiring frequent fertilization of the soil, in turn furnished an outlet for the manure that would otherwise pile up in busy Boston from stables housing the horses and dray-oxen that hauled the port's merchandise. In March 1787, however, the Boston selectmen implored the inhabitants who kept horses not to sell such enormous loads of dung to the country people, in order to prevent the injury being done daily to pavements.

One stimulant to market production north of the capital was the 1,800-foot long wooden bridge across the Charles, "well lighted all the way," that was opened in 1798, connecting Boston with Cambridge. This cut several miles from the circuitous route over Roxbury Neck by which Middlesex County produce had previously reached the big town.[8]

With commerce in Salem and Newburyport also booming, the old Essex County towns found markets good for their hay. Drovers brought down fat cattle for slaughter not only from the meadows and salt marshes of the North Shore but also from the newly opened intervales of southern Maine. Salem itself no longer farmed, though home lots were well cultivated and family cows found feed in the municipal pasture. However, Parson William Bentley in July 1790 visited one farm not far off which grew 20 acres of Indian corn, 20 acres of barley and buckwheat (rye blasts, he says), 4 acres of potatoes, and 3 of flax, and milked 29 cows. The highway from Boston east to Portsmouth was better than any he had seen in America, the Italian traveler Castiglioni decided, and the countryside an uninterrupted garden. A visitor from Baltimore a few years later thought this a delightful country.[9]

To the south of Boston along Cape Cod Bay not all was praiseworthy. Barnstable, a lively port, was doing well, cutting plenty of hay from the Great Marsh for its cattle and raising onions for export. At the crook of the Cape and beyond, however, large tracts of land had become unfit for cultivation. Some of Eastham's plains "once fertile were desolation, a prey to the winds, buried under a heap of barren sand." [10]

Toward the end of the eighteenth century, the towns in the center of the state in Worcester County were making great quantities of cheese and butter, growing excellent crops of grain, and from their apple trees producing immense quantities of cider. Barns were likely to contain a central threshing floor. In some towns, a contemporary historian states, "by industry and frugality the people are become wealthy." [11]

Increasing prosperity began to show in the appearance of buildings and property. Now that flax grown in New England's intervales provided seed which when ground by a mill produced linseed oil, it was becoming the custom to paint. People began to "colour" the sides of their dwellings and churches, hitherto left to the action of sun and rain or perhaps coated with pitch. Houses in rural places like Brookfield might show little change, but by 1798 buildings in country towns such as Worcester and Springfield (and across the state line in Windsor, Connecticut) were being protected from weathering. Samuel Davis, riding from Plymouth toward Connecticut, observed weather-boarded houses "neatly painted, some of a free stone colour, others white with green doors and window shutters." He particularly approved the meetinghouse of Spencer, west of Worcester, and Springfield's handsome church building complete with clock and electrical rod.[12]

The Connecticut River Valley drew plaudits from every traveler visiting Massachusetts. Joseph Hadfield, an English merchant who in 1785 rode down from the Berkshires into Southwick and Westfield, speaks of the "charming vale full of settlements. The lands are highly cultivated. Each farm has an extensive orchard." Though the inhabitants "are mostly farmers their houses are really elegant . . . arcadian dwellings in a delightful valley." Fortunate in soil suitable for both grass and grain, the Valley was sending choice meat animals to market in Boston and through the Sound ports into export, and growing grain beyond its own requirements.[13]

Up in the Berkshires in 1764 Lord Adam Gordon had found the Housatonic Valley "a delightful Vale, well planted and thickly inhabited," but at the century's end President Dwight of Yale reported Great Barrington far from thrift and prosperity. The area had been one of the hotbeds of the late rebellion. On the other hand, "a skillful and prosperous farmer" in Pittsfield in 1795, not one of the town's richest, could count this sizable quota of stock: a pair of oxen, five cows, four 3-year olds, nine 2-year

olds, and ten younger, besides a bull; also 30 sheep, plus hogs,
turkeys, geese, and hens; and an apple orchard.

Rochefoucauld's sympathetic eye noted some lands being
manured in interior Massachusetts and fields yielding 200
bushels of potatoes to the acre at Brookfield, a crop, he was told,
that sold readily. At the farm connected with Williams' Inn at
Marlboro, the well-dunged hayfields cut three to four tons per
acre, he said; and if he was truly informed, sixty to seventy
bushels of corn were gathered to the acre.[14] All over the state,
however, were scattered plenty of poorer farmers, like those
Reverend Asa Packard described in that same Marlboro, men
who tried to cultivate too much soil and overstocked both
pastures and buildings. His neighborhood, Packard thought in
1795, produced only two thirds of the crop of three or four
decades earlier. One difficulty, as General James Warren pointed
out in his oft-quoted lament of 1786, was that many farmers had
manure enough from their stock for only their corn, potatoes,
and turnips. With soil already depleted, small grain was starved
and pasture never manured except by cattle droppings. A
remedy was not easy to find, however, unless, like the General's
Plymouth farm, the land was within drawing distance of extra
fertilizing materials like seaweed or herring.

New Hampshire soils were not yet depleted so seriously. The
old towns along the sea and Great Bay had the benefit of
seaweed. Their natural hay from thousands of acres of salt marsh
was refreshed each year by river and tidal silt. When fed to stock,
it was thought to result in manure of high quality, and the
annual addition of this and of the hay itself to upland soils
helped keep them productive. "Cattle here are abundant,"
Chastellux commented in 1782. "This country presents in every
respect, the picture of Abundance and of Happiness." The
interior, too, appealed to him: new houses were being built and
new farms settled every day.[15]

This was especially true of a narrow belt of towns parallel
with the Massachusetts boundary, and another tier near the
Connecticut River to which the Royal Governor, Benning
Wentworth, to increase his own influence at court, had earlier
given names of British noblemen. At Portsmouth, the state's chief

port, Francisco de Miranda records, busy shipyards stretched away as far as the eye could reach.

The Merrimack Valley, too, was well settled north to Concord and beyond. The soil of this valley was less naturally rich than that of the Connecticut, and in 1788 Matthew Patten at Bedford was hauling manure to his fields to grow potatoes, as Reverend Timothy Walker of Concord had been doing forty years earlier. The Scotch-Irish in this lower valley were still prospering on potatoes, flax, and pease. From their "exceeding good flax" they had long been making fine thread and very good cloth. Further north in recently opened towns people were harvesting the splendid pines that clothed the intervales and sawing them into boards. The first house in Wolfeboro beside Lake Winnepesaukee was built of sawn lumber. Beyond Lake Winnepesaukee were only "woods and a wild and horrid country," but north of the mountains, hardy settlers were building houses of hewn logs and packing in families and household goods on horseback.

In the northern intervales of the Connecticut Valley settlers had thronged back after the close of the French wars. More came after the Revolution. The level meadows seemed made for cattle. Corn and wheat also did well on the new lands. A ribbon of towns stretched north to the oxbows and beyond. At the century's end, Lancaster had been populated for thirty-five years. By 1792 the state of New Hampshire was home for 141,885 people, a large proportion of them on farms.

To the four original New England states Congress in 1791 added a fifth by admitting to the Union the independent republic of Vermont. It is unnecessary to go into the bitter struggles between New York, New Hampshire, and Massachusetts—each with adherents among settlers of the Connecticut Valley, the Champlain Valley, and the mountains between—which preceded organization of the new commonwealth. The surge of immigration from Connecticut eventually decided that issue. In the three decades that preceded admission the influx reached such proportions that the new state began its life with 17,000 more inhabitants than Rhode Island could claim after a century and a half. With statehood, numbers continued to grow.

One notable immigrant to be discussed below (page 280) was a horse whose name has come down to us as Justin Morgan.

Vermont differed from the older states not only in its more rugged climate, but in physical conditions. In only a few locations was there any land already cleared by Indians: forest was nearly unbroken. On the other hand the soil that awaited the newcomers was for the most part, rich and undamaged by Indian fires. Twenty bushels of wheat to the acre became common, forty a good crop, with even more possible—all without added fertilizer. But to live and succeed, the settler had to chop. Ezra Stiles, who journeyed north from Connecticut to see what was going on, tells how at Wilmington in southern Vermont "one Man can girdle & clear & fence 3 Acres & sow it to Wheat in a month; can girdle an acre a Day. There is no underbrush" (this was an ash tree region). At Poultney, on Vermont's western line, according to the town's historian, three men started settlement in 1771. They erected a shanty for Thomas Ashley, who had brought his family. Another cleared ground and raised corn sufficient to "bread" his family of seven, then went back and brought them in. A baby son was added to his household that same year. "After the first year, with a little corn, they raised wheat, and some kept a cow. For the first few years they had to go to Manchester to mill, some 30 miles distant." Yet by the time of the first census, 1791, the town had increased to 1,121 people. Often the migration of one family brought relatives and neighbors from the old town to the new.

A Middlebury history describes the removal of Stephen Goodrich and his father, mother, and sister to that Onion River town in 1785, with a cart and oxen, five cows, and five or six swine. The hogs followed the cart, and lay under it at night. On the way the travelers milked the cows, drank what they wished, fed the pigs, and put the rest into a churn on the cart; "and the motion churned it" into butter.

The year 1789 brought a bad season to Vermont: a heavy snow on May eighth and other calamities. Harvests were so poor that for two years families ate wild leeks, even bark. At times famine seemed to be around the corner; but all this passed and better years succeeded. Missionary Nathan Perkins from Connecticut marveled to find the frontier women "cheerful and much more contented than in Hartford." It was "all work" in the log huts "& yet ye women quiet-serene-peaceable-contented-loving their husbands-their home-wanting never to return." "Woods make people love one another & kind & obliging & good natured," was his conclusion.[16]

Not all these Vermont farms were small, however. Reverend Mr. Perkins called at Governor Chittenden's in 1787. He was not highly impressed with the Governor himself and thought his house poor, but his "very great farm" counted a thousand acres. A hundred of it on the Onion River was in wheat, and he had two hundred acres of extraordinary intervale land. At Burlington in 1791 a Scottish visitor looking for land investment found the soil very rich, particularly good for growing wheat, as much as forty bushels to the acre, maize up to seventy bushels. "Their great traffic is with Canada," via the Richelieu River, he said. In the year following his visit the surplus wheat of western Vermont was estimated at 30,000 bushels. Red clover, white clover, and herdsgrass all did well; and hay crops were called prodigious.

In this western area and along the Connecticut River logs could be cut and rafted to market or to sawmills. Away from water transport, however, settlers destroyed the trees and found a salable residue in the ash that remained from burning the felled timber. Either as potash or refined into pearlash, it was in demand in Britain's textile industry as well as locally in New England. Vermont provided official inspection. Traders would accept potash for calico, rum, or almost any purchase; and for a long time potash was a leading cash crop in Vermont. The historian of Hartford in the Connecticut Valley mentions distilleries making potato whiskey and cider brandy, also readily salable, previous to 1800.[17]

At the end of the eighteenth century Maine was still a component of the Commonwealth of Massachusetts but growing as rapidly as Vermont and well on its way to becoming a separate state. The very economic and social upheavals that disturbed Massachusetts and its sister states after the Revolution caused persons and families harried by debts and exactions to look eastward, where unpopulated lands invited settlement. In

Maine's backwoods, land was to be had free or at a dollar an acre, payable later. A healthy, vigorous family could hew out its own future. Such a prospect appealed not only to the alert in the old-settled states but to many living beside Maine's own coastal waters.

Toward the end of the century trade revived and the Maine coast became prosperous again. One stimulus was the wars in Europe. Lumber and ships came once more into tremendous demand, so that the families of seamen, shipwrights, and lumber workers could buy farm produce. Coasting vessels flitted back and forth to Boston with cordwood and agricultural cargo, and Maine merchants engaged larger ships in foreign trade. Many vessels headed for the West Indies, with cargoes of produce that one historian likens to the inventory of a country store.[18] A market was ready for ten times the produce now raised, a ministerial visitor noted in his diary as he rode about among the new towns. He exaggerated, but there was some fact behind his enthusiasm.

Even during the Revolution people had kept coming east, and with its end immigration boiled over. A Penobscot Bay writer of the time marveled because the newcomers who spread farther and farther east had often come from inland towns of the older colonies. In contrast to the carefully laid-out villages they left, they were likely to hunt for some spot in the woods that suited them, clear a few acres, erect buildings from the timber they cut, and wait till later for their entry to be given legal standing after a township had been duly organized by the Massachusetts General Court. Timothy Dwight, from orderly Connecticut, visited the Kennebec region in the early 1800's. He notes that in the town of Litchfield, incorporated in 1795, not one of its more than a thousand inhabitants "has a legal right to the land on which he lives; all of them being what in . . . the Northern and Middle States are called squatters." Yet he was impressed with the thrift, character, and good farming habits they had brought with them.[19]

So was another ministerial visitor, Reverend Paul Coffin, who made a missionary tour into central Maine in 1796, and marveled at the richness of the soil. "Mr. Witham . . . has a very rich farm, with about 30 acres of improved land . . . too rich for wheat until planted once or twice." "Stephen Marden . . . has a pretty farm, has raised 120 bushels of Rye on three acres . . . His corn yields 25 bushels per acre." At Greenfield (near the present Starks) "Capt. Gray has a grand farm . . . Had corn 50 bushels to the acre." At Hebron in western Maine, Mr. Benjamin Spaulding, there thirteen years "owns 800 acres and is from small beginnings advanced to wealth . . . has four barns . . . 40 black cattle with sheep and cattle . . . a grist and sawmill." Remarking how pleasant the country was by nature, "How little do the owners of mean farms in old towns consult their interest by abiding at home," he observed.[20]

By 1790 Maine had seventy-two legally organized towns and nearly a hundred thousand people, not all of them by any means as prosperous as those who entertained the ministers quoted here. On a journey to the Penobscot at the very end of the century Rochefoucauld was far from impressed with the grain-fields he met. He marveled, nevertheless, at how, where woods had been cut by the farmer, sweet-scented native clover luxuriated among the stumps, and at how well sheep and black cattle did on the turf. The pioneer's chief stirring of the soil itself was merely a fenced garden near his house, with potatoes growing in it.[21] Yet the District was doing well agriculturally, growing quantities of corn, wheat, potatoes, flax, and apples and driving fat animals to the Boston market.

23

A New Century Approaches

THE LAST YEARS of the eighteenth century saw a stirring, as of yeast rising, among farm people. In the country towns a multitude of developments, often small in themselves, gave promise of what the next few decades were to bring.

The post-Revolution period is sometimes considered a low point in popular education. If this was true, measures to improve the state of things were already at work. Massachusetts in 1792 offered grants of Maine lands to towns for its encouragement. In 1783 Noah Webster, farmer's son and Connecticut country schoolteacher, published his famous *Spelling-Book*; its circulation would eventually reach twenty million. Next came his *Reader* and two years later his *Grammar for Schools*. Then he went to work on what was to become his greatest achievement, the dictionary. In 1792, nine years after the *Speller*, Jedediah Morse of Woodstock brought out the nation's first geography. This and Webster's three schoolbooks became the foundation of education for the children of all New England. Morse declared: "In New England learning is more generally diffused among all ranks of people than in any other part of the globe, due to the excellent establishment of schools in every township." [1]

Books were becoming common in country towns and among farm people. An analysis of over a hundred inventories of estates of eastern Massachusetts farm operators for the century immediately preceding the Revolution, assembled for other purposes, reveals an item of books in two out of three estates; in some cases apparently little beyond a Bible; in others called a library.[2]

Social library groups which raised funds among members for the purchase of books had been multiplying in country towns for a half century, often under the guidance of the minister. Jeremy Belknap, in his *History of New Hampshire* in 1792, had called village libraries the cheapest and most effective mode of diffusing learning among the people. Even in the war year of 1776, Scituate, Rhode Island, formed one, and within a year of the Revolution's end Wethersfield, Connecticut, had organized its Union Library Association. Late-settled towns like Sutton in central New Hampshire and Brookfield and Peacham in Vermont offered their citizens subscription libraries before the century closed,[3] and battered Castine in Maine organized one in the new century's first year.

More colleges appeared. Brown University began in 1764; Eleazar Wheelock had moved his Connecticut missionary school to Hanover, New Hampshire, in 1769, and so founded Dartmouth College. The University of Vermont at Burlington opened in 1791; Williams, in its Berkshire valley in 1793; and with the founding of Middlebury, Vermont's new century began. In Maine, Bowdoin, at Brunswick, received its first class in 1802. To prepare boys for college, advanced private schools were established, such as Phillips Andover, Phillips Exeter, and Derby Academy at Hingham, even during the Revolution. The people of Deerfield, Massachusetts, "mostly farmers cultivating their own broad acres," set up their famous academy in 1782. Just a decade later at Litchfield, Connecticut, Sarah Pierce opened what is claimed to be the first school for girls in the United States.

Along with the organization of library associations, academies, and colleges, about this time publications relating directly to agriculture began to find a place in farmers' homes. Jared Eliot's *Essays upon Field Husbandry*, which took book form in 1760, was still influential. In 1790 another minister-farmer, Dr. Samuel Deane, put forth America's first cyclopedia of agriculture, his *New England Farmer; or Georgical Dictionary*, destined to go through three editions and to be the standard farm text for several generations. In this same fruitful period a third minister, Reverend Manasseh Cutler of Wenham, in Essex County, Massachusetts, offered the first systematic botanical classification of plants, appearing in Volume I of the *Memoirs* of the American Academy of Arts and Sciences; and at Hartford, New England's first dietitian, Amelia Simmons, in 1796 brought out her 46-page *American Cookery*.

Periodicals also took a hand in agricultural education. Almanacs had long been popular. The year 1793 saw the launching of the most famous and useful of them all, *The Farmer's Almanac* by Robert B. Thomas, offspring of a bookish farm household at Shrewsbury in central Massachusetts and a farm boy turned mathematician. For the next half century he was the New England countryside's farm adviser, philosopher, and sage.[4] In western Massachusetts the *Berkshire Chronicle* was publishing agricultural essays in 1787, and to the north the *Rural Magazine or Vermont Repository* in 1795 introduced articles on agriculture.

Agricultural organizations had their birth in the last years of the century. At Hallowell, Maine, Charles Vaughan and others on July 17, 1787, formed the Kennebec Agricultural Society, later revived in 1832, to continue a further useful life of over a century.[5] Five years later a group of wealthy Bay State men, chiefly farmers by avocation, were impressed with the need for more information as to good farming methods. In 1792 they incorporated the Massachusetts Society for Promoting Agriculture, still active today. Connecticut agriculturists set up a similar body in 1794. The Massachusetts group in 1797 awarded a prize to William D. Peck for his essay on the slugworm. It began in 1798 to circulate its informative periodical, *The Massachusetts Agricultural Repository and Journal*.

In this final decade of the eighteenth century ferment was also stirring in transportation. Boston and Cambridge bridged the lower Charles twice and Beverly and Salem were connected, moves important to farmers to the north in reaching market. New Hampshire bridged the wide Piscataqua. In 1796 the Tucker Toll Bridge between Windsor, Vermont, and Cornish, New Hampshire, began a life of 132 years, in the course of which innumerable Boston-bound animals and vehicles crossed from the farms of Vermont.[6] In the same decade another bridge spanned the stream at Springfield, Massachusetts; and in 1798 a bridge across the Deerfield at Cheapside became a boon to north-south Connecticut Valley traffic, already benefited by boat service which connected this trading point with Hartford. By 1796 the Merrimack was bridged in four places between Newburyport and Concord, New Hampshire.

Highways improved. Borrowing from English experience and urged on by local pride, capitalists began straight, well-drained turnpikes to speed travel. In 1792 the first in New England, some claim in the United States, connected Norwich, Connecticut, with New London. Before the century ended, Massachusetts had chartered three turnpikes and New Hampshire and Vermont each one, a start toward ending the isolation of interior towns. A stone-filled post road had connected Bennington, Vermont, with Albany, New York, since 1791, and progressive communities such as Holliston, Massachusetts, realizing the advantage of a stone foundation, provided an all-season road for swifter travel by the horse-drawn wagons and coaches now beginning to appear.[7]

Population, especially in the newer areas, grew rapidly toward the end of the century. Wilton, in southwest New Hampshire, had 623 inhabitants in 1775; in 1790 it had 1,105, most of the increase having come from Massachusetts. Chesterfield on the Connecticut River, first settled in 1761, counted 150 families a decade later and continued to increase. Peacham, Vermont, founded 1775, contained 1,187 inhabitants by 1800. Ashfield, in the western Massachusetts hills, settled in 1776, had 1,809 in 1800. Maine, with about 42,000 people in 1777, had 151,719 in 1800 and included 126 towns. Nearly all the newcomers to the infant towns did at least some farming. Meanwhile, the population in many of the old communities also continued to grow.

When the British fleet blockaded the New England coast at the start of the Revolution, one unintended effect was to give a tremendous impetus to local manufacture and inventiveness. Distilleries sprang up to turn local grain, potatoes, and cider into strong liquor. Ironworkers and toolmakers were no longer held back by acts of Parliament; war needs cried to be filled, and after the formation of the federal union a tariff on steel and nails gave the iron trade encouragement. Southeastern Massachusetts, for example, was already making ironplated shovels, and scythes and saws. In 1794 Jacob Perkins patented a nail-making machine and began manufacture in a small way at Byfield, Massachusetts, while countless farm people turned nails out by hand. In 1797 Charles Newbold of New Jersey patented a cast iron plow.

A woolen mill began operations at Hartford in 1788, a carding mill at Pittsfield in 1790, and Samuel Slater began American cotton yarn spinning at Pawtucket, Rhode Island, in 1790. In 1795 Arthur Scholfield and John Shaw started carding wool by machine at Byfield, Massachusetts, removing in 1802 to Andover. In 1798 at Providence, Betsey Metcalf plaited her first straw hat. Small beginnings all, but all destined to have marked effect on New England farm life.

Developments of great future importance began to appear in the field of agriculture itself. One was the conversion of considerable areas of interior New England to dairying. With Goshen, Connecticut, as its center, an export business was born that would turn western Connecticut and southwestern Massachusetts to wholesale cheese making, with the South as a market; further north, Cheshire and the northern Berkshire towns in Massachusetts began sending cheeses to Troy, New York, on the Hudson. Butter and cheese became staple products in central Massachusetts also, and were said to have made some farmers there wealthy by the century's end.

At Hadley, Massachusetts, in 1797 Levi Dickinson tried sowing broomcorn seed and opened the way for a new and valuable Connecticut Valley crop and industry. In Newton, John Kenrick began in 1790 to raise peach-tree whips for sale, the start of New England's earliest modern nursery. About that time came the introduction of the Hubbardston apple. To mark the final year of the century Vermonter Eliakim Spooner patented a corn-seeding machine.

What were New England's farm people like as persons, and what position did they hold in the world, as the eighteenth century came to an end? For evidence, to rely either on the addresses of orators at bicentennial celebrations or on the deductions of modern historical writers may be equally dangerous. The former incline toward ancestor worship; the latter, influenced by sociological theory, tend to divide post-Revolution people into sharply defined classes in a manner that would probably have greatly surprised the persons concerned. Records of the time, however, if used with discretion, can tell us a great deal.

In the years following the Revolution there lived on a Connecticut farm, stony like many others, a small family called Nott. The father was helpless from a long illness, and the two boys did the farming. Their mother, when her household tasks allowed, helped in the fields. A dozen sheep and a cow were the entire stock. Besides providing milk, the cow was used for plowing. The staples of the family diet were cornbread and bean porridge. Once, in midwinter, one boy suffered for lack of outer clothing. In the house there was neither money nor cloth, so the mother sheared a sheep, spun and wove its wool, and before long the boy had the needed clothes. Meanwhile, a covering was braided from straw for the shivering sheep. The family lived four miles from the meetinghouse, and walked each Sabbath to service. Yet they survived. Of the Nott boys, Samuel grew up to become a leading preacher. His brother Eliphalet, also a divine, eventually became head of Union College (now University).

Governor Treadwell of Connecticut, writing with regard to Farmington, which as the new century began was still almost wholly agricultural, gives this description of himself and his neighbors: "Industry and economy have characterized the inhabitants; labour has been held in reputation; none, however elevated to office have considered themselves above it. . . . Our magistrates have always been farmers . . . and have derived their support from labor as much as the meanest citizen . . . content . . . to be esteemed the first among equals."

In New Hampshire, according to W. Winterbotham: "Those persons who attend to husbandry are the most thriving and substantial," especially compared to "those who make . . . getting lumber their principal business." [8]

The verdict of one visiting Englishman: "The inhabitants of the country appear to be well-fed, cloathed, and lodged . . . nor is that distinction of the ranks and classes to be found which we see in Britain [and] infinitely more in France." [9] Another says in 1789: "They [the farmers] don't appear to work hard but I am told they live well [and] appear very civil, decent, well instructed people, possess with a spirit of religion." [10] Other similar comments could be cited.

Dr. Samuel Deane at Portland, like many ministers a farmer himself, took a gloomier view. He was troubled by "the low esteem in which husbandry has been held"—this in 1797. He thinks it is because farmers have not made much money and "too many have had the mortification of making but an indifferent figure in life even when they have used the strictest economy . . . The misfortune has been that a great proportion of their toil has been lost by its misapplication." [11] Yet three years later and only fifty miles away, Reverend Paul Coffin is equally impressed at the success of farmers in Androscoggin County. Among others he visits a farmer who had once fled Chelmsford, Massachusetts, to escape the debtors' prison. He now has 800 acres, 4 barns, 40 black cattle, sheep and horses, and two mills, and lives in plenty.[12] Brissot de Warville in 1788 praises the parish pastor at Andover, Dr. Symmes, as "a true model of a minister of religion . . . ; and the cultivation of his farm occupies those moments not necessarily devoted to . . . the care of souls committed to his charge," a double occupation which had marked earlier Symmes generations since the beginning of the colony.[13]

Such part-time farming was common. Brissot noticed that across Massachusetts "almost all the houses are inhabited by men who are both cultivators and artizans; one is a tanner, another a shoemaker, another sells goods, but all are farmers." On Nantucket in 1791 "it was no strange thing to see the same man . . . a merchant, at other times . . . a husbandman . . . or a number of similar occupations," and on Cape Cod both farmers and mechanics were on occasion seamen.

As the century ends it is clear that any swift generalization about the wealth or social status of New England's farm people is bootless. In many of the old settled communities families of well-to-do farm people held their property and stock unencumbered. They owed no man except such current obligations as lack of a reliable circulating medium made customary. In some new towns, on the other hand, there were families working under almost unimaginable handicaps, with barely enough to live on, who like Indians in a similar situation supplemented their few acres of corn and wheat and their hog or two with wild game, nuts, and berries, or went without. Call this poverty, as Kendall did in northern New Hampshire, or call it subsistence farming; it is doubtful if most of those who experienced it thought of themselves as either poor or especially deprived. Rather, as Robert Honyman had put it in 1775, though the land was rough, the people looked well fed and prosperous.[14] To quote a local estimate from an interior town toward the close of the century: "The people . . . have the reputation of being good husbandmen, frugal and industrious, and they live much independent."[15]

The period that succeeded the Revolution had been in general one of fluidity and change. Certain of the less well-established farmers had been dispossessed, partly as a result of the monetary chaos of the period. With the large size of farm families ("They double their numbers every twenty-five years," said the historian of the County of Worcester, describing the hill town of Lunenburg), a periodic swarming from the hive had to take place even from the best-heeled farms and the most fertile towns. Hence this era witnessed a heavy migration of farmers bent on making a new start, often with no great capital and sometimes with small idea of the hardships ahead for themselves, their wives, and children.[16] However, the farms they left went to some other member of the family; or if for sale, a customer, usually some other farmer, took over. Farming, family, and village life continued with little change in the old towns. At the same time new communities on a similar pattern took shape in Vermont, upper New Hampshire, and Maine. Though some farmers would prosper, others had hard work even to fill the mouths of their families.

The Revolution years had been a hard time: divisions between neighbors, continual calls for men and supplies, repeated raids from Canada and on the coasts and islands, neglect of cultivation and upkeep of farms, huge public debts. Then followed economic misery, and in the interior widespread bankruptcy of farmers, which led to Shays's Rebellion.

Offsetting these in part, the four New England colonies, now states, had been joined by a vigorous fifth, Vermont. The confederation of thirteen colonies had become the United States of America.

By the end of the century New England's shipbuilding and foreign trade were expanding at a great rate, opening wider markets than ever for its farm and forest productions. Slavery had been ended. New towns were starting in the wilderness. Colleges were being founded; through highways and great bridges were planned; here and there a society for agricultural improvement born.

Thus after all its wars and turmoil, for the majority of its farm people as well as for the New England community in general, the note on which the eighteenth century ended was one of hope: an expectation of better things to come.

IV. ANOTHER BEGINNING, 1800–1825

24

Lines of Force

IN THE AUTOBIOGRAPHICAL *Education of Henry Adams*, this descendant of two presidents and a line of colonial farmers is struck by the "lines of force" of his era. For New England agriculture in the opening years of the nineteenth century at least four such lines became increasingly powerful; yet in the century's second decade their favorable effect was for a time thwarted by certain opposing events.

The helpful influences included encouraging growth in the market for farm produce; continuous improvement in highways and transport; a wave of intellectual activity; and the beginning of an outburst of mechanical ingenuity, of which the cotton gin of Eli Whitney, born on a Westborough, Massachusetts, farm had already appeared as the forerunner. All stemmed to a considerable extent from country people themselves.

Of adverse factors one was political. To avoid involvement in the Napoleonic Wars, especially with the chief contenders, England and France, Congress, beginning in 1807, passed two measures: the Jefferson Embargo Act and the Enforcement Act. These stifled foreign trade. The War of 1812, which followed, resulted in blockade by the British fleet, the prostrating of New England's shipping and commerce, and the drying up of the market for farm produce. Another blow to New England resulted from natural phenomena: the hurricane of 1815 and the unprecedented low temperatures of the succeeding summer of 1816.

To a farm population, whether working land often of mediocre natural fertility or, at worst, of near sterility, the prime consideration is its market. With good markets keen wits will work out a profitable agriculture on the poorest soils. When farmers lack a market, they soon decide that beyond providing for family needs the game is not worth the candle.

In respect to a market for his surplus, the New England farmer found himself increasingly well off as the new century opened. Despite continued heavy emigration to New York and the Western Reserve, the population of every New England state increased amazingly, with more and more mouths to be fed. Connecticut, with 237,940 people in 1790, by 1830 had added 60,000, bringing the total to 297,675. Rhode Island increased from 68,825 to 97,199. From 378,787, Massachusetts reached 610,408. By 1830 the new State of Maine contained over 300,000. New Hampshire almost doubled, from 141,885 to 269,328. Burgeoning Vermont counted 85,525 by 1790; forty years later this had grown to 280,652. From just over a million inhabitants following the end of the Revolution New England's total was to reach almost $2\frac{1}{4}$ millions by 1840, the completion of a half-century from the first census.[1]

Many of these inhabitants, especially in the three northern states, were farm people, and the new fields and pastures they cleared added to both New England's agricultural capacity and its marketable surplus. Rising export trade, however, and the continual enlargement of the nonfarm population, both in numbers and as a proportion of the community as a whole, soon more than offset increased production.

Samuel Eliot Morison's *Maritime History of Massachusetts* and William Hutchinson Rowe's similar history of Maine vividly portray the expansion of the sea-borne trade of these two areas. Their shipping surged upward after the Revolution to reach by 1810 a registered capacity of 500,000 tons. New Hampshire, Connecticut, and Rhode Island increased their merchant ships proportionately.

A small port like Marblehead besides having its fishing fleet was the home of fifty to sixty merchant vessels; Salem was growing rich on its Oriental trade, and Newburyport was not far behind. Providence and the Connecticut ports were booming. In 1810 Merrimack River yards alone turned out 12,000 tons of vessels. Portsmouth across in New Hampshire, the North River in Plymouth County, and the Sound's shore echoed with shipbuilders' hammers and caulking tools.

Cargo for the West Indies and European ports included such agricultural items as potash and pearlash, lumber, beef, pork, barley, hops, butter, cheese, and beeswax. Outbound vessels from Rhode Island carried grain, flaxseed, lumber, horses, cattle, beef, pork, poultry, onions, butter, cheese, spirits, and linens. In Connecticut—from New London, Wethersfield, and New Haven with its newly opened Long Wharf—merchants shipped similar diversified cargoes; Windsor, Norwalk, Milford, Derby, Fairfield, and other ports forwarded farm produce to New York and southern ports by coasters. How all this might affect the agriculture even of a small town inland from the coast is evidenced by the historian of Ridgefield, Connecticut, fifteen miles north of Norwalk in the southwest corner of the state. Quoting a local minister, Reverend Samuel Goodrich at the opening of the century, he records that from the town's fourteen to fifteen hundred swine the annual export of pork amounted to 150 to 200 barrels (200 pounds each); of beef about the same. Butter sent out yearly reached 250 to 300 firkins, carried fresh to New York (a trade that was increasing); and 9,000 pounds of cheese went with it. That city also got about a hundred of Ridgefield's fat cattle each year. Such a list from a town of small population a half day's journey from salt water casts a clear light on the unsubstantiated statement echoed from one historian to another that New England's early nineteenth-century agriculture was almost entirely subsistence farming.[2]

Though provision for seamen was far from sumptuous, the crews even of coasting vessels and of the whalers from Nantucket, Martha's Vineyard, New Bedford, and New London offered a further substantial market for farm produce. A three-boat whaler carried twenty-one men; Marblehead fishermen off for the Banks carried eight to ten each; a vessel destined for Europe or Asia often had a much larger complement. The ship *Juno*, for Asia from Bristol, Rhode Island, in 1804, for example, took on board 3,800 pounds of salt pork, 8,420 of salt beef, 5,400 of wheat flour, and 10,000 of tobacco, besides Bristol onions and poultry.[3] (The flour may have been either of local Connecticut Valley production or from the Middle Atlantic states.) Crews of fishing schooners found the combination of salt pork and onions with their fish exactly to their taste.

Aside from the food for ships' crews, building and stocking vessels for foreign commerce and the fisheries required great numbers of shipwrights, riggers, blacksmiths, draymen, warehousemen, and others. Though numerous seamen and mechanics were themselves farmers in a small way and during off seasons, their agriculture, especially when times were good, would be chiefly a garden that the wife might attend to, a hog, possibly a cow or two, and a few apples. To supply daily food for the increasing numbers of nonagricultural merchants, tradesmen, and mechanics, market gardens began to appear near Boston, Providence, Hartford, New Haven, and other centers.

Away from the ports still another consuming group began to develop: the small industries springing up under the new republic in all directions. Rumbling charcoal wagons converged to feed the hungry furnaces of the ironworks at Taunton, Massachusetts, and Salisbury, Connecticut; woolen and cotton enterprises sprang up where waterfalls were dammed; paper mills, nailmakers, and shoe and leather enterprises increased. These and other industries, modestly begun, were destined for immense growth in the decades ahead. Added to the needs of the seaport population, they and their workers began to create for farmers a home market of considerable proportions.

Certain of these industries, in addition to the food needs of their employees, offered direct markets for farm products. For in a growing number of cases they added to rural income by "farming out" work to the countryside. For generations, in small shops alongside their homes, the people of Lynn and vicinity had produced shoes for market and export. (By contrast, ordinarily a local or itinerant cobbler made each farm family's boots and shoes to order, perhaps from hides of home production.) In 1800

Lynn turned out 100,000 pairs of women's shoes, a decade later made it a million, and by 1833 reached 1½ million pairs, including 213,000 pairs for men. Leather for such as were not altogether of textiles was tanned largely in neighboring Danvers. The hides were from cattle that drovers brought in from both Essex County and the north. Soon Abington, south of Boston in what was to become the Brockton area, began to make men's boots. Brookfield in western Worcester County also got into shoemaking, the work farmed out in the neighborhood. So did many other towns even up into New Hampshire. All was on a small scale at first, but destined to grow to large dimensions in the second quarter of the century and to furnish a much appreciated income supplement for local farmers in addition to their nearby market for hides.[4] The fat from slaughtered animals went into soap or candles. At the end of the century's first decade a single year's production for Massachusetts was reported to be over two million pounds. Another product was combs made from horns: Worcester County, where the industry centered at Leominster, turned out 440,250 dozen in a year.

Distilling, given momentum by the Revolution, now reached considerable proportions. Entirely apart from the manufacture of rum from molasses at the ports, the distillation of whiskey, gin, and brandy, all merchantable and easily transported, consumed quantities of grain, potatoes, and local cider (especially in the Connecticut Valley), for which a market might otherwise have been wanting. By 1810 Connecticut was said to be furnished with 500 distilleries. Hartford merchants, even in the bad crop year of 1816, paid export duties of $40,000 on liquors from the area's 21 distilleries; East Windsor, itself growing up to 70,000 bushels of rye a year, paid $24,000. Gin and cider were Connecticut's most valuable exports. Four towns in the Springfield, Massachusetts, area in 1826 distilled 100,000 bushels of rye. Vermont counted at least 125 distilleries in 1810 (one writer says 200), of which 10, using grain, were in Putney; several were in Fair Haven. To supplement its income from spirits one distillery kept 40 cattle and fed them on the waste residue of the grain. Two distillers in Townshend, and doubtless others, made potato whiskey. Distilling went on across New

England in places as scattered as Kent and Newtown in western Connecticut, Woodstock in the east, and Granby and South Oxford in Massachusetts. In addition to its local consumption, the product went to New York, Boston, Providence, the South and to foreign ports.[5]

Considerable of the brandy came from apples. Berkshire and Hampshire Counties in western Massachusetts in 1810 distilled 265,000 gallons of spirits from cider. About Windsor, says a Connecticut gazetteer, "Every respectable farmer had a small distillery upon his own premises." Orchards, "a source of profit . . . add greatly to the value of the lands." Newtown reported ten distillers of "apple jack," Canton eight.

Hartford distilleries developed a considerable agricultural by-industry. They fattened a thousand beef cattle yearly on their grain residue, besides a great number of swine.[6] In Vermont the grain residue went chiefly into pork, marketed for the most part to the north in Montreal.

Thus a considerable variety of factors: an expanding population; the increasing proportion of persons engaged in such nonagricultural occupations as fishing, shipping, and mechanical pursuits; the growth in export trade in farm products, and in domestic industries based at least in part on the use of agricultural raw materials—all these had a part in broadening demand for any surplus that the farmer could profitably produce.

Nevertheless, additional possible sources of income were about to appear: the rise of broomcorn growing and broom manufacture, straw-hat making, woolen spinning and weaving, hop growing, silk production, and other new enterprises involving merchantable crops, which had their beginnings in the early years of the century but became of increasing importance in later decades.

25

Turnpikes, Canals, and Bridges

D URING NEW ENGLAND'S first century and a half, most of its towns, established either beside the sea or on navigable rivers, were able to reach markets by water. After the Revolution water transport still offered marked advantages. Take, for example, in the early 1800's, the Connecticut tidewater easterly from the New York line.

Norwalk had a half dozen sloops trading regularly with New York. Stratford, and Derby further up the Housatonic Valley, each employed a fleet of regular New York packets and sloops to carry produce there. In addition each owned a score or so of tall-masted ships for foreign voyages. Fairfield's shipping was similar, New Haven's larger, especially in coastwise vessels. Wethersfield, Hartford, and Enfield at the head of navigation (except by flatboat) in the fruitful Connecticut Valley, boasted 40 to 50 seagoing vessels in addition to their coasters. As for the other states, many of the score of good but minor harbors that indented the coast from Newport east to the Kennebec had similar or greater capacity. "Every farmer of importance was a ship carpenter and had his own vessel," [1] said a historian of New Bedford referring to the century just closed.

With water transportation so convenient, the incentive to improve highways was lessened. Connecticut roads remained so difficult that travelers by the southern route between Boston and New York preferred to board packets on the Sound for the stretch between Newport or New London and New York so as to hold the highway journey to a minimum. However, a public conveyance for passengers by the inland route is said to have begun operation as early as 1772.

Once the French wars had ended and settlements opened farther and farther from salt water, means of inland travel became necessary. In 1767 Simeon Smith had started a freight route by wagon between Amherst and Boston. When the Revolution came and the British blockade forced the use of inland transport almost exclusively, main highways had to be improved and new military roads built. Yet it was said in 1791 that the main east-west link between Worcester and Springfield was still so bad that it would overturn a carriage. In 1794 an English visitor called it nothing but a green lane with one beaten track about midway.

Clearly, better roads were needed. Carriages and horse-drawn wagons were coming into use. A stage between New Haven and Boston had opened in 1783. Yet voters of interior towns remained reluctant to tax themselves to help traveling strangers and freight from elsewhere.

With prosperity returning, however, in the closing decade of the eighteenth century a vigorous movement for better through roads arose. Rather than wait for public appropriations, difficult to obtain and likely to be meager, groups of enterprising citizens began to form turnpike companies modeled after similar bodies in England. These secured charters of incorporation from state legislatures, with power to obtain rights-of-way by eminent domain. The roadways, built from the sale of capital stock, were to be paid for and maintained by tolls.[2]

Rhode Island authorized its first turnpike in 1792 from Chepachet Bridge to the Connecticut line. Connecticut issued a charter in 1795. Governor Samuel Adams in 1796 signed the act establishing the first such body in Massachusetts, empowering it to construct a road from Palmer to Western (Warren) on the important through east-west route. That same year New Hampshire incorporated a company to build a toll road from Durham to Concord. A few others followed. Then in the first decade of the nineteenth century turnpike companies sprouted all over southern New England and up into the mountains. Massachusetts in 1805 passed a general enabling act.

The Boston-Newburyport turnpike opened in 1803, the Salem Turnpike across the Lynn Marshes, the same year. In 1806 the Boston-Hartford pike and the Boston-Providence pike were built, and the Boston-Worcester pike was authorized. Capitalists in Keene, New Hampshire, opened northwest New England with one aimed for Boston through Jaffrey, and constructed another through Winchendon. In 1803 a turnpike headed through the White Mountain Notch toward Portland. These offered access to market for the wool, butter, cheese, and beef of the upper Connecticut Valley and Vermont. Soon turnpikes were building toward all points of the compass. Only in unsettled parts of northern New England were promoters lacking. By 1807 a hard road led west 250 miles from Pittsfield, Massachusetts, into western New York. In Vermont turnpikes tapped at least fifty towns. Connecticut improved its highways to the point that the English traveler John Melish said that turnpikes and other good roads were abundant there.

In turnpike building the general rule of thumb was that a straight road is shortest. Hence marshes had to be filled and hills shaved, but not enough was done always to make the grade comfortable. Inexpert construction and high costs of building often precluded financial success. Yet the pikes, even where financially unsuccessful, opened back country, decreased isolation, reached markets, increased travel, and speeded mail. Many of them are thoroughfares today. Some became chiefly freight roads: six-horse wagon loads replaced plodding ox teams, unreliable in hot weather. Transportation benefited further when Lewis Downing of Concord, New Hampshire, in 1813 built the first of his famed Concord buggies. He followed this two years later with his even more noted Concord coach, the first public vehicle to give passengers a comfortable ride.

This period also saw bridges superseding ferries.[3] The lengthiest, already mentioned, "a most prodigious work 3800 feet long, 34 feet wide," "lighted all night by 40 to 50 lamps and with a draw for vessels," bore traffic from the north across the Charles River from Cambridge into Boston. A second, from Charlestown, soon followed. Not long after, four bridges, all of arched construction, spanned the Merrimack in its course from Concord to the sea. The Connecticut, already bridged at Bellows Falls, was now crossed downstream at Springfield.

While turnpike and bridge builders improved land transportation (fifty turnpikes were incorporated in Connecticut between 1803 and 1808), other entrepreneurs were extending water transportation to interior New England by excavating canals. First in importance was the Middlesex Canal, opened in 1803 from Chelmsford on the Merrimack to Boston. It was extended in 1811 to Manchester. In 1815 the canal transported its first regular freight south from Concord, New Hampshire's capital and its northern terminal. This canal was a marvel, termed the largest engineering work so far undertaken in North America.

In 1823 a canal was completed connecting Lake Champlain with the Hudson via Lake George. Five years later Connecticut opened the Farmington Canal, with one terminus at New Haven, the other at Springfield; and, in central Massachusetts, Worcester in 1828 sent its first freight down through 48 locks the length of the Blackstone Canal to Narragansett Bay at Providence.[4]

The extension of the Middlesex Canal to Concord benefited farmers all across New Hampshire and Vermont, and changed the direction of their shipments. Butter, cheese, and salt meats that once went over the road clear to Boston at high freight charges were routed to the Merrimack Valley terminals as the canal pushed north in successive stages. Each stage cut the expense of teaming, both for farm products and for goods purchased in exchange.[5]

Added together, the new roads, bridges, and canals had a remarkably stimulating effect on the farming of interior New England. Wagons and carriages began to replace saddles, pillions, and panniers. Teams for which a ton was formerly a load could now haul two. How far such inland transport business might extend under necessity is hinted by this item in an Albany newspaper during the blockade of the War of 1812: "Arrived 4 wagons, 4 oxen each, from Dartmouth [New Bedford, Mass.] laden with potatoes for a southern market." [6] By this date the highway from Pittsfield to Albany was of macadam all-weather construction, one of America's earliest stone roads.

Besides growing markets and improved transportation, a third strand of the line drawing agriculture toward a better day was the advance in education. In the new American nation, as Van Wyck Brooks has so well said, farming and learning went together. Nowhere was this so commonly true, every foreign visitor noticed, as in New England. "The education of youth in this state" (Connecticut), commented the critical observer John Harriott in 1815, "seems carried to excess: farmers, tradesmen, and mechanics give their children a college education which is as frequent as that of a common boarding school in England." A Connecticut widow's son bound out in 1786 to a farmer till he should be sixteen got only twelve days of school a year. "But," he wrote later, "I had the good fortune to live in a family where reading and writing were not deemed unimportant . . . I had a disposition for reading and I had the privilege of indulging it." [7]

In Massachusetts a hill farming town such as Harvard, in Worcester County, in 1783 maintained eight district schools and beyond that offered Latin instruction. The Western Massachusetts town of Southampton, between 1765 and 1845, sent 48 boys to college, and its neighbor Easthampton sent 20. Yet as late as 1840 the population of the two did not exceed 2,000. [8]

In 1809 another visitor, Edward A. Kendall, describes some of the means by which country people learned. "There is . . . even in the remote societies and towns . . . a public library . . . common property and purchased by contribution." Education, he notes, is under "school societies," with power to levy taxes, place school buildings, and appoint visitors, and (this in Connecticut) the state turns over a certain proportion of the rates. "Hence every industrious man, who possesses a fair moral character is qualified to fill many important offices in the town, county, and state." [9]

In her *History of Windham County*, Connecticut, Ellen D. Larned tells how Woodstock in the northeast part of that state got its academy building in 1800. To start with, thirty-two townspeople contributed $100 apiece. Then the farmers brought in their best oak lumber, and boards enough were donated "to build a shed from Woodstock to Providence." The building erected, the farmers turned out again with seventy ox teams to haul earth to landscape the grounds. Men too old to shovel smoothed the piles out with hoes. Scores of such country academies in every part of New England got their start during the early decades of the nineteenth century. The whole new township of Houlton in the District of Maine was a grant by the Massachusetts legislature in 1805 as an endowment to fund the academy at New Salem. This was one of several similar township gifts to finance academies.[10]

Yet it would be a mistake to conclude that zest for education was universal. Many towns were far less wealthy than Deerfield and Woodstock. Litchfield and Killingly in Connecticut might each count four library societies, but in new farming areas plucked from the forest and in older towns whose soil was impoverished, sources of strictly agricultural information were scant, education was often neglected, and orders from state governments to provide it ignored. Even so, of New England's country people it could scarcely be said, as Elkanah Watson complained of New York State, "Thus far the German and Dutch farmers have been totally remiss in cultivating the first rudiments of literature." [11]

Education, specifically agricultural, got a slow start. Yale in 1802 did appoint Benjamin Silliman Professor of Chemistry and Natural History. Harvard also made a gesture toward formal agricultural studies in 1804 with the appointment of William D. Peck to a professorship in Natural History, and founded its Botanic Garden three years later.

In 1822 Thomas G. Fessenden began in Boston to publish the area's first farm periodical of importance, the *New England Farmer*, destined for a long and useful life; and James Thatcher of the same town started *The American Orchardist*. Two years later Solomon Drowne & Son published *The Compendium of Agriculture and Farmer's Guide*, and Daniel Adams, M.D., an *Agricultural Reader*.

Touring New England in 1793, John Drayton of South Carolina had observed: "On Sundays, which are days of rest and refreshment, when passing by the farmers' houses, I found many of them reading; and was told that they generally devote those days to reading religious books, the public laws, and the newspapers. Do you think it an easy matter to enslave such a people?" [12]

Newspapers did indeed circulate more widely in New England than in most of the western world. Rochefoucauld wrote, undoubtedly with exaggeration, "Not a house is to be found in the most remote corners of the country [Massachusetts] where a newspaper is not read." [13] Fifty-five are reported as being published in New England at the end of the eighteenth century. In most of these, strictly agricultural news was scant, so that a publication such as that by the *Berkshire Chronicle* in 1782 of essays on agriculture, copied from a New York book, stands out. In 1793 that indefatigable printer Isaiah Thomas established at Walpole, New Hampshire, a *Farmers' Weekly Museum*.

26

Combing the Back Country

IF GOOD MARKETS readily accessible are essential to good farming, New England's widening mercantile pattern was becoming a buttress to its agriculture. Well before the Revolution its merchants, keen on profitable cargoes for foreign trade and for sales through domestic outlets, had pushed their activities inland.

One of the Allen family, New London and Boston merchants, for example, had in 1757 set up a store in the central Massachusetts town of Shrewsbury. Their conveyances supplied the country people of that town and along the way thither with imported necessities; and on the return to New London bore back the farmers' surplus productions. The latter, along with what their coasters brought in, became freight for the firm's West Indies vessels.

What a variety of produce their vessels had carried even before the Revolution! Besides deckloads of horses, cattle, sheep, and hogs, the Allens' invoices included at one time or another (in addition to fish) corn, oats, flour, bread, potatoes, tobacco; fresh, salt, and smoked beef; pork, tallow, soap, lard, cheese, onions, beans, apples, hogs, geese, fowl, ducks, turkeys, tar, pitch, turpentine; together with shingles, hoops, staves, and boards.[1]

In Northampton, in 1780, Nicholas Garrett had acquired 300 bushels of wheat to be delivered for cash to merchant Andrew Lopez at his wharf at Newport. He got another hundred bushels for a barrel of rum, and bargained salt for wheat at the rate of one bushel of salt to four of wheat. At Pittsfield in 1788 Colonel Danforth advertised for lamb's wool and good shipping horses. In return for goods bought, he would take wheat, flaxseed, pork, beeswax, iron, and ashes. A special offer was that farm necessity, salt, for flaxseed. Merchants at Windham in northeast Connecticut just before the Revolution had been buying wool, hemp, flax, tobacco, cheese, and butter.[2]

At Lebanon, New Hampshire, merchant James Duncan built potash facilities and ground flaxseed. He also bought grain and other country produce for export from Haverhill on the Merrimack, to which a continual stream of ox teams delivered his purchases. The conveyances returned loaded with foreign goods and other supplies needed by country people. The historian of Haverhill states that in just over two years shipments of this trader up country amounted to $96,000.

The many merchants who congregated at Deerfield about 1800 exchanged salt for flaxseed or white beans and offered cash for rye and Indian corn, or rum for barreled beef and pork. One ad in the *Greenfield Gazette* that year offered cash for beef bladders in which to pack snuff. Walpole, New Hampshire, stores sought to buy not only butter, cheese, beef, and lard, but mittens, socks, frocking, and tow cloth. A large proportion of such transactions involved little or no cash; entries on opposite sides of the merchant's books sufficed.[3]

All this was in addition to the farm produce that farmers took to market themselves. "Annually in October," said 91-year-old John Morse of Woodstock, Connecticut, regarding the century's early years, "my father went to Providence taking about 50 bushels of walnuts, a good many chestnuts and beans, and driving four or six large fat oxen to be sold for beef." [4] Nearly all histories of the river valleys of up-country New Hampshire, Vermont, and Maine tell of lines of loaded farm sleds on their winter way to Portland and similar markets.

Some merchants specialized in a single commodity, and by their operations influenced agricultural development across a considerable area. During the last decade of the 1700's Alex Norton of Litchfield, Connecticut, sought relief for failing health in a southern trip. Yankee fashion, he took along several thousand pounds of Connecticut cheese to pay his way. Finding the product welcome there, upon his return with health improved he began to buy and pack cheese for the southern market. At first he shipped it in hogsheads, then in specially designed round boxes with covers. His enterprise grew, others copied his methods, and before a decade had passed, the Litchfield County town of Goshen was marketing 270,000 pounds of cheese a year. Northwestern Connecticut and southern Berkshire County in Massachusetts were thus led permanently into extensive dairying. In 1810 Goshen managed to sell 588,124 pounds of cheese and 35,537 of butter. Cheese wagons combed the countryside, and for half a century Goshen remained the cheese capital of the nation.[5]

Across the line in the hills west of Springfield, another cheese operator, Amos W. Collins, in 1807 began to encourage the farmers of the poor Scotch-Irish town of Blandford to go into dairying. He helped them buy cows and taught them cheese making, transforming the economy of the place and causing it to prosper. The broad effect that such an enterprising dealer might exert on a community is evidenced by Jasper H. Stahl in his history of Maine's Waldoboro. Captain Smouse of that town made up a vessel's cargo from lumber purchased from thirty-two separate persons, plus oak staves from eight others. A single family of brokers at North Reading in Middlesex County, Massachusetts, between 1808 and 1837 assembled and sold 16.5 million pounds of hops gathered from a dozen or more towns in northeastern Massachusetts.[6]

Undoubtedly many, though by no means all, of these merchants made money. Some entered the ranks of the wealthy, whom modern economic historians are likely to place at the top of a social pyramid. However, country folks gained from these operations also. Evidences of well-being among the farmers who provided the traders with merchandise are frequently recorded by gazetteers and local observers, who mention some of those who attained wealth measured by the standards of their day.

Political factors, however, soon began to affect agricultural life in this era. The Jefferson embargo on foreign trade and the Non-Intercourse Act that succeeded it cut off New England's foreign trade, tied up its vessels, and idled crews, shipbuilders, supply and mercantile workers, and draymen. They destroyed or greatly impaired the outlets for farm products as exports and ships' stores. Distress resulted for many farmers as well as for the ports.

When 1812 came, the war laid up additional shipping, including fishermen and whalers, both of which had multiplied since 1800. A multitude of persons were left without means even to buy food. On Nantucket real poverty resulted, but a thousand-acre planting of corn gave its inhabitants at least subsistence. Part of the market returned with the commissioning of privateers, but the strict British blockade of 1813 cut even coastal traffic so severely that Maine and Cape Cod packets could scarcely reach Boston. Meanwhile prices of imported commodities and manufactured goods rose. The British occupied eastern Maine and Provincetown and bled Penobscot Bay, Cape Cod, and the offshore islands. In the middle of harvest in 1814, inland New Hampshire militia were called out to defend Portsmouth.

Yet few misfortunes are without gain to someone. With the war unpopular, in some sections of northern Vermont conscience scarcely bothered livestock men when drovers found markets for cattle by the hundreds across the line in Canada. It was reported that two thirds of Britain's Canadian army was living on New York and Vermont beef.[7] Cape Cod people, obliged to supply the British fleet with beef and vegetables, were said not always to do it unwillingly, for the British paid well. Block Island prospered on produce sold to British men-of-war.

To offset the losses, the war gave tremendous impetus to the development of American manufactures, a result from which New England as a whole, including its farmers, eventually was to derive immense benefits. When war ended it appeared for a time that the factories springing up at every waterfall on New England's innumerable rivers would bring unexampled prosperity to the whole region, farms included, but as cheap foreign goods once more poured in, the incipient prosperity collapsed. A money panic in 1819 caused wholesale mill closings. Trade stagnated and prices and wages fell on farms and elsewhere.[8] Before this occurred, however, Congress took one step that was to help invigorate both the industry and the agriculture of New England. In 1816 it enacted the first tariff designed to protect American manufactures and farm products. This, with other acts that succeeded, provided a base on which farmers speedily covered New England's pastures with sheep by the hundred thousand.

In its effect on rural life few events in the century's first quarter had more impact than the remarkable weather of the years 1815 and 1816. The great hurricane gale of September 23, 1815, proved "extraordinarily calamitous," especially in southern New England. It caused immense losses in the cities where trade centered. In the country, even far up into New Hampshire, timber trees were leveled by the millions, the year's crop of fruit was knocked off, and apple orchards destroyed. Stacks of hay and straw floated off the marshes all along the coast and were lost. Corn and grain fields were flattened, farm buildings unroofed and cattle killed. Farmers were especial sufferers from the tremendous gale.[9]

As though this were not enough, the whole year of 1816 which followed was one continuous disaster from cold. In many places frosts blackened vegetation every month of the year. Vermont had a foot of snow on June 8, a little in July and August, and a freeze September 20. Plowed land in Orange, Massachusetts, among Franklin County's eastern hills, was crusted with frost three fourths of an inch deep on June 7. On July 5 and again on August 5, ice formed in Maine. "The year of two winters," 1816 was called, or "Eighteen hundred and froze to death."

In some places drought further aggravated farm calamity. A historian of Keene, New Hampshire, records that in that same year the usual late spring rains failed, and for twelve weeks, while by the calendar spring became summer, no rain fell. Pastures browned, and corn replanted after spring frosts scarcely grew before August frosts cut it down. Distress ensued, for in addition to the bad weather depression came to industry. By 1819 almost every one of the textile mills that had sprouted at every waterfall had closed, and many capitalists lost all.

For a generation, tales of rich, cheap land to the westward

had tempted the less prosperous farm people. Now, with New England experiencing Arctic weather, could they be worse off in the Western Reserve? "The current of emigration from this state has swelled to a torrent," wrote Pease and Niles in their *Connecticut Gazetteer* of 1819. From Maine alone ten to fifteen thousand are thought to have removed between 1810 and 1820. From Vermont, where in some townships actual want and suffering were a consequence of 1816's frigid weather, many families headed for Western New York and Ohio. It was long before the influences of the disastrous years 1815 and 1816 were erased.[10]

27

Ways with Grass and Grain

As THE continuing emigration demonstrated, it has seldom been the nature of New England people generally, whether farmers or others, to rest content with a bare living. To understand how farm families managed in the first half of the nineteenth century it is necessary to consider the basic crops and animals found at least to some degree on nearly every farm, then to explore the specialized avenues along which New England farm people sought means to make a living and achieve economic advancement.

From the first settlement of Massachusetts Bay, the determining factor in New England's agricultural history had been that no crop is better suited to its climate, soil, and terrain than grass. The earliest Puritans rejoiced to come upon the intervales of their new countryside clothed with fresh water grasses, and on salt marshes that ringed shore and estuary to remind many of them of home. Wherever land had been cleared or was naturally open, it appeared designed for sheep and cattle, even as the woods, filled with nuts and acorns, seemed made for swine. To the tall bluejoint of the fresh meadows, nutritious for hay if cut early, fowl meadow grass had been added. This was a superior type of herbage which tradition claims was brought to the Neponset River marshes by a large flock of wild fowl before 1710 (from what source does not appear), and it had spread to other river bottoms.

Countless staddles (wood underpinning) for salt hay still dotted seacoast marshes from southern Maine to Cape Cod, along the shores of the Sound, and up the Connecticut and similar estuaries. In the fall, gundalows ferried the hay up every salt creek to the home farm. On such provender thousands of cattle and horses were wintered every year. The resulting manure, supplemented where possible from other sources, nourished merchantable crops of corn, potatoes, tobacco, flax, onions and other produce. As Lord Adam Gordon in 1765 wrote of similar salt meadows in New Jersey: "It will not fatten either Cattle or Horses, but it will keep them up . . . tis here of [un]Questionable Value for dung [plowed in] and other uses, and conveyed both by Land and Water many miles." One species called blackgrass, found in the upper reaches, was particularly nutritious.[1]

In the valleys of New Hampshire, Vermont, and Maine the beaver meadows, flats, and occasional open uplands that awaited new settlers were often reported to be luxuriant with native grass. Farmers in new country depended on such boggy meadows for scarce winter hay or for pasture. Governor Thomas Hutchinson's answer to King George III that nothing was more profitable in America than pasture, because labor was very dear, remained true in the nineteenth century.

Farmers had long since added nutritious English cultivated hay to the native grass. Well before the end of the eighteenth century timothy, redtop, and red and white clover had spread to every settled part of New England. On new land, crops of two to three tons of hay per acre were not unusual, dropping to less than a ton on old mowings. The latter, growing steadily poorer, were often turned into pasture.

Beginning with Plymouth Colony, Indian corn had been New England's staple grain from the first. In the nineteenth century nearly every farm continued to grow it, though coast-town mills ground large amounts of corn imported from further south. Many farmers continued to follow Indian growing methods, and pioneers in new plantations continued to spot hills between girdled trees or stumps. On Cape Cod and increasingly elsewhere, however, hilling had begun to give place to level culture. Careful cultivators planted corn in rows three feet apart, the hills at five-foot intervals, or vice-versa. The field was hoed three times. After the silk had become well fertilized and the ear had begun to fill, or at least by the time the kernels hardened, the stalk and leaves above the ears were likely to be cut and cured, to furnish a half ton to the acre of excellent winter fodder. Yields ranged from eight bushels an acre on poor, wornout land to the twenty-five to thirty bushel average of Rhode Island, and much higher where the crop had careful attention. Connecticut, with fish for fertilizer, and Massachusetts, under first-class tillage, called forty bushels a good yield.

Indian grain was a favorite food for both man and beast, and nearly always salable. Individual farmers usually saved their own seed; but in 1818 Salmon Dutton of Cavendish, Vermont, perfected and distributed a richly colored glossy flint that received his name.[2] This variety gave very high yields, heralding a long series of improvements by selection. Corn was of particular importance to Connecticut Valley fatteners of beef and hogs, and to Vermont, which besides marketing many in Canada as early as 1806 drove 15,000 cattle a year on the hoof to Boston.

Though not universally grown, wheat remained an important market crop for alluvial valleys and newly cleared towns for as long as their native fertility lasted. On newly cleared land this and other small grains might merely be harrowed in without plowing. On older fields, corn was apt to get the barnyard manure; wheat followed to pick up any residue of fertility. From seacoast areas, however, rust had long since nearly eliminated wheat. These areas now depended for flour chiefly on imports by sea.

The German conscripts of the Revolution have been blamed for bringing to Long Island in imported fodder or straw bedding an insect destined to cause immense damage to America's wheat crops, the Hessian fly. By 1787 it had entered coastal Connecticut. Yet all through the new century's early decades the northern Connecticut, upper Housatonic, and Nashua River valleys continued to grow wheat. Where the insects had spread, the seed was sown late to avoid damage. For the speculative farmer in newly opened Maine lands, for growers in Vermont's Champlain and Otter Creek valleys who found their markets in Canada, and for the more fertile sections of Worcester and Berkshire counties of Massachusetts, the first wheat crops from new land might sometimes pay for the farm.[3] However, if wheat were abundant and the market distant, merchants sometimes fought shy of accepting it in trade.

Where wheat failed, there was always rye to fall back on. On poor soil rye would grow even without manuring if the land were first left fallow for three or four years. Grown properly on good soil, it yielded thirty bushels to the acre. In Maine a common rotation was potatoes, rye or wheat, then seeding to herdsgrass and red clover. Everybody mixed rye meal and flour with corn, barley, and wheat to bake into bread; and distillers bought rye by the thousands of bushels. A Connecticut Valley lady of this time describes the local rye harvest as a notable event and spectacle. She thrills at "the great turnout of reapers with their flashing sickles sweeping up the hills." [4]

Some farms in Rhode Island, others near the Sound in Connecticut, and to a small extent elsewhere still grew barley. Exported, New England barley had a good reputation to the southward. As horses became more numerous and wagons began to take the place of carts, oats came to be a desirable grain; but only where the Scotch influence was active did it become important as food for the table.

28

Horses, Cheese, and Sheep

DURING THE REVOLUTION New England's livestock had been neglected and depleted. Numbers of the best beeves had gone to supply the Continental armies. The British had cleared sheep and cattle by thousands from Rhode Island, Connecticut, the offshore islands, and coastal Maine. With ports closed and foreign commerce almost at a standstill, little incentive had existed for improvement in any branch of livestock. Revival of trade following the peace treaty nevertheless brought renewed interest in stock. Here and there selection or importation of superior animals began. More care came to be shown also in farm products, and pride in their quality was renewed. An example of each will suggest the new trend. Both originated with ordinary country people rather than with wealthy innovators. The first concerns a famous horse.

During the 1790's a horse fancier of West Springfield, Massachusetts, named Justin Morgan, moved north into the new state of Vermont. He took with him to Randolph Center (or returned and took back) a modest-sized clever bay horse with broad forehead, short muscular legs, heavy mane and tail, and pleasant, spirited eyes. This horse's name was "Figure." He was a fast walker, smooth trotter, very strong, intelligent, and willing. In Spooner's *Vermont Journal* in 1793 and 1794 and in the *Rutland Herald* in 1795 Morgan advertised service at stud "by the famous Figure Horse." [1]

14. "Old Green Mountain Morgan," foaled 1834. Thompson, Horses of Woodstock *(1881).*

Just what Figure's ancestry and bloodlines were has been a matter of endless debate and speculation, still unresolved and profitless here. Suffice it to say that the Connecticut Valley had long been breeding horses for export, and that at Cambridge in 1775, the horses of the Western Massachusetts cavalry had aroused General Washington's particular admiration. Figure may have been sired by an English horse owned by a New York loyalist.

What is certain, however, is that this stallion, who after his master's death came to be known by the latter's name, Justin Morgan, possessed precisely the qualities needed for Vermont conditions. Tradition says that he could snake logs out of the woods all day; or just as willingly set off at a smart trot with a rider or two for church or a frolic. Most important of all, in his long life of 29 years he sired a numerous progeny who inherited his characteristics. Many of his descendants, such as "Black Hawk" and "Sherman," became famous sires in their turn. One of the third generation was claimed to be the fastest trotter of his time. Morgan's offspring soon spread through Vermont, across New Hampshire, and into Maine, where conditions were similar, and horsemen bred them there as well.

The Morgans appeared at a time when the Narragansett Pacers were in decline, when wagons were replacing oxcarts on the smooth and speedy new turnpikes, and when the Concord buggy was superseding saddle and pillion. Stage drivers all over New England came to swear by Morgans. Soon the new West also, to which many New England people emigrated, turned to Vermont breeders, and was willing to pay high prices.

During the Civil War, U.S. Cavalry buyers very nearly denuded Vermont of Morgans. The 1st Vermont Cavalry charged at Gettysburg on Morgan mounts. It is said to have been a Morgan that bore General Sheridan on his famous ride in 1864 to turn the tide of battle at Winchester.

New England was not destined to be a wholesale breeder of horse-kind, but with Narragansetts, Morgans, and certain others to be later cited, it has no call to hang its head in the matter of horseflesh. In fact, in Vermont itself the original Morgan horse

"Figure" was only one of a number of excellent stallions, some imported, advertised for breeding in this period.

A second example of the spirit of ambition among ordinary farm people of the time is the story of "The Great Cheshire Cheese."

In February 1801 Thomas Jefferson of Virginia was chosen president over John Adams of Massachusetts. Surprisingly, this was a cause of rejoicing in the Western Massachusetts dairy town of Cheshire among the Berkshire Hills, for a majority of its farmers were Democrats. Most ardent Democrat of all was Elder John Leland, who for a decade had been pastor of the town's Baptist church. He admired Jefferson among other things for his Virginian policy of separation of church and state, a hot subject then in Massachusetts. Why not celebrate Jefferson's election, asked Leland, and also call the attention of the nation to Cheshire and its chief product, by presenting to the president a cheese of a size never before seen on this side of the Atlantic?

The pastor talked up the plan; the farmers and their wives responded. On a certain July day, it was decided, each farmer would bring in his whole milking. The curds from every cow in Cheshire would be merged into one giant cheese and that cheese transported to the nation's capital. How large a container would be needed to hold this mammoth? The town counted its milkers and calculated the result. Darius Brown prepared the materials and built a round wooden case four feet across and eighteen inches deep, to hold the product of 1,200 cows.

On July 20 the whole town brought in its milkings. The most skillful dairy women mixed the curds, sifted in their choicest herbs, primed and salted the mass to perfection. For eighteen days a cider press squeezed the cheese within iron bands. Then it was left to ripen. When ready for the journey it weighed 1,235 pounds.

The route took the giant cheese west across the hills to Hudson, New York, then by water to the nation's year-old capital, Washington. On New Year's Day in 1802 a six-horse team drew the gift through the streets of the new capital. Elder Leland proudly presented it to the nation's chief executive; and

15. Self-governing cheese press: curds are pressed into wooden hoop. Newell,
Catalogue *(1836).*

the assembled cabinet, diplomats, and distinguished guests
partook of bread garnished with slices of Cheshire's pride.[2]

The productive limestone lands of the Taconics and the
Berkshires were now permanently committed to dairying. Western Connecticut exported its cheeses through the Sound ports,
Western Massachusetts via Troy and the Hudson. Williamstown,
for example, by 1829 had deserted winter wheat, its former
staple, and marketed 200,000 pounds of cheese that year.

Though farms with perhaps four or five milkers were the
rule, by 1830 herds of 15 to 30 cows were becoming common in
Berkshire valleys, and some ran beyond 50.[3] Farmers were
building dairy houses and diverting springfed streams through
wooden pipes to large tubs where night and morning milkings
could promptly cool.

Goshen, Connecticut, the great cheese center, marketed 380,236 pounds—$38,000 worth—in 1811. Lewis M. Norton had in 1808 introduced there the pineapple cheese, and patented it two years later.[4] A second Norton manufactured circular boxes for ordinary cheese, their sides bent like a half bushel measure. For a limited time Rhode Island, where John Harriott reported the best milch cows he had seen in America, and neighboring Connecticut towns, such as Pomfret, could retain their reputation for export butter and cheese of superior quality. The rest of New England, however, was catching up. In any case a Northern visitor to the South at this period thought New England cows far superior as butter producers to any he saw there. Country merchants began to buy butter, heavily salted, as well as cheese; they cased it in firkins and sent it to market packed in straw. In winter, butter reached Boston safely even from northern Vermont.

Where dairy products had an outlet, better care was given the stock. Farmers began to provide more adequate shelter. One town after another voted not to leave its cattle and the town bull free to roam. Some farmers with a milk market had even decided that it was more profitable to turn their calves into veal than to raise them, and bought young animals, "springers," in the fall to serve as next year's milch cows. Stockmen began to take more pride in their animals. The Berkshire County Society's first exhibition in 1811 brought out sixty yoke of prime oxen. The French officer Marquis de Chastellux had been struck with admiration at the fine cattle he saw on the meadows at Greenland, New Hampshire; and the Connecticut Valley became noted for fat stock which another French observer, Brissot de Warville, called enormous. When slaughtered, such beeves helped the Boston market acquire a reputation for the high quality of beef offered there.

The Massachusetts Agricultural Society imported two Alderney bulls and two cows in 1816, and here and there a wealthy farmer tried improvement by importation from Europe of superior animals. Samuel and Lemuel Hurlburt, of Winchester, Connecticut, in 1819 brought from England a choice Devon bull, and the next year added two heifers. During his thirty-seven years of breeding, Lemuel was said to have distributed 1,500 of his Devons. About the same time Samuel Williams, Cornelius Coolidge, and a few other Massachusetts breeders began importing English Shorthorns. In 1810 William Jarvis brought two Holstein-Friesians to his Weathersfield, Vermont farm. About 1823 Henry W. Hills sent to Hezekiah Hills of Windsor, in Hartford County, Connecticut, several Ayrshire imports, and the following year a Hereford bull and heifer were forwarded to Northampton by the Massachusetts Society. Others followed.

Such innovators were the exception, however. On most farms native red cattle made up the herd. Dickinson's 1819 *Geographical View* said that Massachusetts cattle resembled those of northern France. In the western counties they were excellent, in the rest of the state ordinary, it stated. Care and fodder ranged from good to downright poor. The *Massachusetts Agricultural Journal* in 1819 reported enough "provident farmers" raising roots in quantity as winter food for their cattle to call this practice a common thing. Yet another writer two years later told how, in new settlements, "the young cattle are with few exceptions without any kind of shelter during the whole of our severe winters . . . foddered with poor hay, straw and husks, and suffered to browse in the woods." Feeble in the spring, the luxuriant honeysuckle clover soon restores them, he continues, and by fall they are fat again. But, he adds, they can scarcely be expected to make good milkers.[5] Moreover, as the *New Hampshire Agricultural Repository* warned in 1822, a common error was overstocking.

From the viewpoint of the family larder, the most necessary farm animal was the hog: few meals of this period anywhere were complete without some pork product. Nearly every farmer and some villagers had at least one or two. Concord, Massachusetts, in 1801, with 227 dwellings, counted 290 hogs. Dairymen making cheese or butter might have skim milk or whey enough to grow several, and a distiller could feed hundreds on mash. Thomas Badger, one of Boston's garbage contractors, in the early years of the century maintained a considerable herd right on Prince Street and fed them on garbage collected from among the town's 20,000 people.[6] Colonel Ethan Allen, one year, brought a

Vermont herd down into the Franklin County hills of Western Massachusetts to fatten there on beechnuts.

In country towns swine, yoked or ringed, still ran at large and were expected to pick up a living in woods and from highways. More than one town maintained a swineherd still to look after the local herd during the warm months. In Vermont swine might be expected to forage for their living even into winter.[7] With such treatment hogs were apt to become bony and tough, and though perhaps fed some corn in the fall would dress only 150 to 175 pounds at slaughter, a total not much above a year's ration of pork for one person. Good farmers, however, fed their swine not only dairy and kitchen waste, but beans, pumpkins, sweet apples, small potatoes and other roots and vegetables; then finished them off with plenty of corn meal, beechnuts (for taste) collected by the family, or both. The bristles were sometimes the perquisite of the boy of the household, to be sold for pocket money.

Good feeding was the practice likewise in the older farming regions, especially Connecticut. "Connecticut pork" gained a reputation both locally and in distant markets for being of the highest quality. As a result any superior salt pork, even if grown in Pennsylvania, was likely to be given a Connecticut label by the trade.[8] In contrast to the contempt properly visited on the "slab-sided sharpnosed, subsoiling" animals of rough-forested townships, traveler after traveler in the early nineteenth century speaks of Connecticut and Rhode Island pork as the best in America, and their hogs "as large as can be had in any part of the globe." John Harriott in 1815 saw four killed in Rhode Island that ran over 600 pounds apiece. An ordinary Essex County, Massachusetts, farmer, Deacon Amos E. Jewett of Rowley, in 1820 and 1821 weighed his hogs at a respectable 320, 350, and 342 pounds. Captain Benjamin Parker slaughtered one at Concord, New Hampshire, weighing 639½ pounds. A Brookline, Massachusetts, garden farmer in January 1812 records assisting at the killing of "a noble fellow" who weighed 402 pounds. Thus the time was near when good markets were bound to stimulate better breeding and feeding of hogs along with other animals. As one corollary, the slaughter of fat hogs, sheep, and oxen was reported in 1810 to have provided the four northeastern counties of Massachusetts 1,332,550 pounds of tallow.[9]

Poultry for the table and for sale was a resource for numerous farm families. The rooster and his harem continued to be called "dunghill fowls." The clutch of eggs yielded in the warm months was scant indeed by modern standards, yet some farms must have found poultry profitable. W. Winterbotham, the Englishman, visiting New Hampshire in 1796, had found "poultry of all kinds . . . raised in great plenty and perfection." [10] He recognized in the lower towns the characteristics of a large-sized breed imported from England twenty years earlier, indicating that some attention was being paid to breeding.

In some sections of New England—the Connecticut Valley, southeast Massachusetts, and Rhode Island, for example—nearly every family raised geese. They scrounged their own food, ridding cultivated fields of bugs and weeds in the process. Geese were a source of valuable feathers, plucked two to five times a season (a merry time amid flying feathers for the children), to fill up the omnipresent feather beds. They also furnished quills for pens. Feathers and quills were each salable. The sloop *Toleration*, from Stratford, Connecticut, for Boston in 1825, carried an item of 10 bags of feathers. Geese were a favorite export from Bristol, Rhode Island, proverbial according to Birket, for "its plenty of [beautiful] women and geese." The Wolfeboro, New Hampshire, farm wife "from the profitable goose obtained for herself and her daughters many of the extras for their wardrobes." [11]

Turkeys were likewise a source of farm income. Reverend William Bentley's diary tells of his seeing a drive of several hundred turkeys reach Salem market on January 11, 1802. Guinea hens were in places still bred. Peacocks had been among Rhode Island's earlier exports, and Germans at Waldoboro, Maine, continued to raise them all through the nineteenth century.

Poultry, whatever the sort, were likely to be the province of the farm woman, even if she were the minister's wife; and income from them helped supply household needs. Plenty of poultry, live and slaughtered, went to market on the carts and sleds of Northern New England merchants and farmers. Substantial numbers went out by ship, also. In a series of Massachusetts cargo entries from 1784 to 1801, now at the Peabody Museum in Salem, "fowles" occur frequently. The Rhode Island ship *Juno*, leaving Bristol in 1804 for a Pacific voyage, took on board live poultry. Visitor John Melish included poultry in a list of Rhode Island's more important exports when he passed through the state in 1810–11. Historian Percy Bidwell states that in 1810 New England sent to three southern states alone 4,000 dozen poultry. For ordinary marketing, up-country people might pack the dressed meat in snow until it could be forwarded.

Small woolen mills were appearing on New England's streams, and by 1810 there were 200 fulling mills, which cleansed wool of oil and impurities by use of hot water and fuller's earth. At a Northampton cloth mill opened in 1809, fifty workmen turned out fine broadcloth 1¾ yards wide which sold for ten dollars a yard. Even in the new and rough northern sections more attention began to focus on sheep. After the losses of the Revolution, the offshore islands, namely Nantucket, Martha's Vineyard, and Block Island, built up their flocks again to scores of thousands, only to have them swept off once more in the War of 1812. Some said these transactions were not altogether involuntary.

Kendall, traveling through Connecticut in 1809, reported small flocks on every farm in Middletown, up to 16 or 20 sheep per farm. Newtown's sheep at that date added up to 4,145; Litchfield's, a decade later, to 6,784. Towns like these generally employed one or more town shepherds, to whose care the farmer could turn over his entire flock, if small, or whatever limited number his proprietor's rights permitted, to feed on the town's common lands. This custom continued for several decades into the 1800's.[12]

Aquidneck Island and the rest of eastern Rhode Island were especially noted for the size and fatness of their sheep. Their pastures were considered particularly nutritious. In South County, on the other side of Narragansett Bay, "Nailer Tom" Hazard puts down in his July 1805 diary: "Put three Sheep in Clover field to Fatt." Meat rather than wool would appear to have been his main object, for in 1816, 25 of his fleeces weighed but 81 pounds in all.[13] "Sandwich mutton," from the town of Sandwich on Cape Cod, had a reputation in Boston's market for eating quality. Contrary to the preserving of beef and pork, salt mutton did not work out well. Hence, success in raising sheep for meat depended on easy access to the markets of Boston and other large towns where people had special fondness for roast lamb.

Besides the desire to produce wool for cloth and flesh for the table or for sale, a sheep man might have a subsidiary objective in his breeding. Where the three southern New England states meet in the Quinebaug Valley and in central Massachusetts, a breed "of good flesh" called "otter sheep" is said to have become popular. Some say a Brimfield farmer developed it; others, a Charles River shepherd. The breed's short fore legs, bowed outward like those of an otter, appeared designed to prevent the jumping of fences, and were considered a desirable characteristic.[14]

In the new century, however, the attribute most sought after came to be a long-staple fleece. The Spanish Merino, now introduced, had this as its prime characteristic. In the next half century and more, the Merino was to make New England a national nucleus for breeding stock and for still another century the continent's center of wool marketing and woolen manufacture. The first purchase of a pair of the Spanish Merino breed to be successfully imported is credited to a Massachusetts man, Seth Adams, in 1801. The following year General David Humphreys, minister to Spain, brought over in the well-named sloop *Perseverance* to Derby, Connecticut, 75 ewes and 25 rams, to become the foundation stock for the breed in southern New England. In 1806 he followed up by starting a mill with a capital of half a million dollars in the Naugatuck Valley to make woolens.[15] Another early Merino importer was Robert Livingston of New York. Both sold stock at very high prices.

In 1807 Elkanah Watson, born in Plymouth and now a public spirited and progressive resident of Albany, bought a farm in Pittsfield in the Berkshires. He created a sensation among Western Massachusetts farmers by exhibiting under a great elm on Pittsfield's common a pair of superior Merinos from Livingston's flock with long fleeces. "All who examined the wool were delighted with its texture and fineness." His enterprise launched the Berkshires on a course of improved breeding that before long clothed its hillsides with thousands of long-staple sheep.[16] At Litchfield, Connecticut, General Humphreys continued to breed Merinos, and receive as much as $1,500 for a superior ram.

A great advance in the fortunes of the new breed came in 1811. William Jarvis of Boston, United States consul at Lisbon, received official permission to purchase animals from the royal Spanish flocks, hitherto with few exceptions jealously held intact. He selected 200 rams and shipped them to Boston along with 200–300 other sheep, and had them driven to his farm on the Connecticut River's oxbow at Weathersfield, Vermont. On the rich intervale land there, these and their offspring "throve incredibly," the cold winters adding length to their fleeces. Jarvis helped multiply superior animals in the area by selling purebreds to neighbors at moderate prices. Merinos spread west across the Green Mountains into the fertile Champlain Valley. All Vermont, for the next three quarters of a century became a cradle for superior sheep. They were taken east also into New Hampshire and Maine.[17]

Among the results of breeding superior sheep were increased prosperity and prestige for northern New England's farmers and added incentive to put capital into woolen manufactures all through the six states. In all this, at least as important to the well-being of farm people as the income derived was the eventual release of farm women and children from the burden of spinning and weaving to provide woolen clothing for their families.

29

Growth of the Land:
New Crops

FRUIT GROWING was not yet a business in itself, but important advances were in the wind. Practically every farmer grew some apples, for cider was the universal beverage and easy to market. A Hampstead, New Hampshire, farmer who kept accounts recorded in 1817 that his 20 barrels of cider cost him 140 man hours and 28 team hours. With cider at a dollar a barrel, labor and team each at 50 cents per day, he appears to have had some profit. Up to 1820 or 1830 most families used that quantity at home as beverage or for vinegar. Apples fresh and dried were highly valued in the kitchen also. Farm families cut great quantities into quarters, dried these on boards or hung slices on strings for pies. Trees would grow among rocks and along stone walls and highways on land otherwise unproductive. Some observers noted orchards in the older sections which were neglected, the prey of cankerworms.

John Lincklaen, however, in 1791–92 speaks of "superb orchards" in the Connecticut Valley of Vermont, "but a worm eats the fruit." Colonel John Bellows of Walpole, on the New Hampshire side of the river, in 1805 had 30 acres of apples and made 4,800 barrels of cider. A town such as Woodbury in the western Connecticut hills had "many valuable orchards, so that the making of cider and cider spirits are important agricultural interests," so reads a typical report. Cider making did not reach its climax in Connecticut till 1830. Northern Worcester County in Massachusetts, too, abounded in large, fine orchards in this period. "Many farmers pay particular attention to raising all kinds of fruit which they have in plenty and of the best quality," an observer stated.[1]

A few orchards received cultivation, but most were in grass. In Rhode Island an April morning job for "Nailer Tom" Hazard's son was to manure his father's trees. Settlers on New Hampshire's hills and in inland Maine took seeds and scions to their new homes to begin fresh plantings.

New England was already well on its way in selecting fruit varieties. To the Roxbury Russet, Rhode Island Greening, Westfield Seek-No-Further, and Williams apples had been added the Baldwin, and in 1790 came the Hubbardston Nonesuch, the Mother (1800), and Porter (1800), all locally developed. The famous New York apple, Northern Spy, is said to have been a seedling from Salisbury, Connecticut, though it did not return to New England until later.

Roxbury and Dorchester gentlemen farmers were trying out and improving European pears; the Bartlett, Clapp's Favorite, Sheldon, and Seckel among them.[2] John Kenrick in 1790 opened a peach nursery in Newton, Massachusetts, and about 1832 introduced the superior Beurre Bosc. Isaac Hill, New Hampshire governor in this period, speaks of various kinds of peaches, from the yellow and crimson-cheeked rareripe to the ordinary fall clingstone, as growing in his native town, West Cambridge (now Arlington), Massachusetts.[3]

One never-to-be-forgotten fruit enthusiast was John Chapman, "Johnny Appleseed." Born in 1774 in the fruit town of Leominster, Massachusetts, his passion for apples led him to travel by water and on foot through the new country of the Western Reserve, his pockets full of apple seeds. He planted them by the highway, gave them to settlers, and in the course of forty years started a wealth of apple trees and of legends as well, in the New West. Less noted but not perhaps of less consequence were the efforts of David Church of Newington, Connecticut, who in 1810 wrote back from Newington, Chenango County, New York:

"I have been carrying out appleseeds at the western little by little till I have carried out thirteen bushel and a half and put them in eighty nurseries and have got a hundred thousand trees I suppose." He had already sold 8,000 at 12½ cents each.[4]

Pedlars still hawked wild strawberries through the streets of the big towns in June; but near Boston and other large cities as the new century began, innovators were setting superior native plants in beds. Even in Western Vermont the historian of Salisbury mentions improved types brought there about 1810 from Salisbury, Connecticut. He states, however, that by 1860, when use of gypsum on the soil had become general, the quality and quantity of wild strawberries had improved, and as a result interest in strawberry cultivation flagged. Varieties propagated in early years by farmers included Early Hudson, Hudson's Bay, Hautboy, and Large Early Scarlet. Red and white field berry plants were set for cultivation also.[5]

Since colonial times cranberries had been harvested from eastern Massachusetts' natural bogs in marshy places in Norfolk, Middlesex, and other mainland counties. About the beginning of the century the purchaser of part of an island at Lincoln in the Sudbury Valley is reported to have sold enough berries the first year to pay for his real estate. In the year 1816 Captain Henry Hall of East Dennis, Cape Cod, began experiments in the cultivation of cranberries by transplanting to a neighboring bog vines from a marsh that produced extra fine berries. He also noticed the favorable effect of sand sifting in among the vines. His venture marked the start of an important present-day New England agricultural industry, the cultivation and processing of cranberries.[6]

By the end of the first quarter of the 1800's New England vegetable gardeners were growing great quantities of roots, especially potatoes, turnips, and parsnips, as well as onions, both for local use and for export. Greenwich, says Connecticut agricultural historian E. H. Jenkins, sent more potatoes to New York than did any other port, and became thereby a rich town. Johnston and other Rhode Island towns exported potatoes through Providence. The ship *Mary*, for example, in November 1810, put ashore at Richmond, Virginia, a shipment of 400 bushels (plus apples, cider, cheese, butter, onions, etc.). In 1812 the Providence packet ship *Rising States* landed 40 barrels as part of a cargo at Charleston, South Carolina.[7]

Coastal areas had the advantage of seaweed to manure their potato fields. In Madison, Connecticut, and other towns along the Sound, as has been noted, farmers spread whitefish on the land and plowed them in, a rich stimulant for this and other crops. Up country, on the fresh soil of new farms in New Hampshire and Vermont, potatoes might yield 400 bushels to the acre, their market frequently a whiskey distillery. In 1820 the Massachusetts Agricultural Society awarded a premium to Payson Williams of Fitchburg for a crop of 614 bushels from a single acre. The ordinary farmer's crop was on a much smaller scale, more like that of Deacon Amos Jewett of Rowley, who on March 30, 1816, planted "7 bushels of Red potatoes" in his sheep pasture. Each fall thereafter the deacon would sell a load of potatoes at Salem or Ipswich. The load in 1819, he noted, contained 41 bushels, sold for 30 cents a bushel. By 1829 his production had risen to 254 bushels. A farmer at Hampstead, New Hampshire, who in 1817 grew 442 bushels, at a valuation of twenty cents per bushel appeared to have a margin beyond expense of about one third. (Wheat at that time he valued at two dollars.) At Wilton, New Hampshire, Ezra Abbott is said to have worked out the process of making starch from the tubers, for sale to cotton manufacturers.

Maine had not yet turned to potatoes on any large scale, though Dr. Deane had earlier reported that even on poorly cultivated land a 100-bushel crop was not uncommon, and with better care 200. Maine already knew how to store them for later sale, for on April 7, 1825, the Maine sloop *Flora* delivered a cargo of 1,000 bushels at Boston from Orrington on the Penobscot.[8]

Wethersfield, Connecticut; Bristol, Rhode Island; and the farmer-fisher people of Barnstable on Cape Cod all continued to harvest quantities of onions. The Bristol ship *Juno*, outfitting in 1804 for the Pacific, had red onions among her supplies. Onions arrived at Boston and New York in single cargoes of as much as 18,000 bunches.

Close to Boston, where city manure or seaweed could be

hauled and the market was lively, market gardeners, as they came to be called, even before the end of the last century had begun to develop skill in growing early vegetables of many sorts on southern slopes and under hotbed glass. Their crops included forced early potatoes, peas, asparagus, snap beans, cucumbers, lettuce, radishes, parsley, sweet corn, celery, horseradish, and others. Rhubarb was becoming popular, and tomatoes had made a start. Stored winter vegetables included squash, cabbage, and all the cultivated roots and bulbs. Cape Cod turnips were a byword among vessel crews for excellence.[9]

Cranston, Little Compton, and other towns in its vicinity supplied Providence with vegetables; Portsmouth's market was Newport. A ship captain in 1813 even picked up 1,300 cabbages on Naushon Island off Buzzards Bay. East Hartford was especially noted for watermelons, marketed in Hartford; and New Haven drew on its nearby towns for produce.[10]

Native-grown vegetable seeds were now on sale by, among others, those skillful horticulturists the Shaker colonies, one of whose farms, at Enfield, Connecticut, included a thousand acres in all. Joseph Belden in 1811 advertised in the *Hartford Courant* pea, bean, beet, carrot, and asparagus seeds "with a variety of others," all the growth of 1810. In 1820 James L. Belden of Wethersfield began his seed business, and in the *Courant* the next season listed 60 vegetable varieties. This firm, now Comstock, Ferré & Co., and the Joseph Breck Co., which began in a small way to sell vegetable seed in Boston in 1818, were still in business a century and a half later. In 1825 a Derby farmer and an Orange farmer each started seed growing in New Haven County.

William Downing, of Hancock in Massachusetts' Berkshire Hills, in 1821 offered a list of 54 items raised there, "put up in papers." Among these were red, white, and yellow onions and two varieties of summer and two of winter squashes. In Boston in 1825, John B. Russell's catalogue of seeds for sale at his warehouse of agricultural implements included the "Tomato or Love-apple," fourteen kidney or dwarf beans, four pumpkins, four summer squashes and the "Akorn." In addition to field corn, he listed "Sweet or Sugar (best for boiling ears)." Hovey & Co., Boston seedsmen, in their 1834–35 catalogue offered twelve dwarf kidney or string beans, eight pole or running beans, eight squash varieties, two tomatoes ("small and large") four pumpkins, and three of rhubarb. Within five years their bush bean varieties had increased to twenty-one, pole beans to ten, and tomatoes to four.[11]

Not to be overlooked in any summary of the vegetables of this period are the general farmer's beans and field-sown pease. When thrashed out, they became mainstays in farm kitchens, as well as in the galleys of fishing vessels, cargo ships, and whalers. With the ordinary farmer, too, if Rodolphus Dickinson is to be believed, the kitchen garden, formerly often neglected, had "now become an object of great attention."

Several other specialty crops needing first-class land and manuring were grown for export. Flax, President Dwight of Yale thought to be "undoubtedly the most profitable crop which can be raised." Nearly every farmer had at least a small patch to provide raw material for his family's linens. Bronson Alcott, born in 1799 and brought up on Spindle Hill in northwest Connecticut, wrote: "Flax was cultivated by the farmers as generally as were oats and rye. Pulling flax was an employment in which women took part with the men. The linen manufacture was an important thing in every household. . . . My sisters were spinners both of wool and flax." [12]

The raw stalks, seed, and oil, all three, formed the basis of a substantial trade. Newport merchants made heavy shipments to Ireland. "Your flaxseed stands well in repute," a correspondent writes from Londonderry in 1785. Fairfield, Connecticut, on the Sound, alone in 1807 exported 20,000 bushels of seed, the product of about 3,000 acres. Nearby Milford sold yearly 100,000 pounds of flax and 4,000 bushels of seed, and Enfield was a heavy producer. In 1810 Connecticut could count 24 flaxseed oil mills within her borders. President Dwight mentions a New Bedford textile mill that annually twisted 50,000 pounds of Connecticut linen thread into twine. Household spinning was universal.[13]

The upper Connecticut Valley had been an important flax district since before the Revolution. Towns like Longmeadow, Sunderland, and Gill in Massachusetts; Walpole and Acworth, New Hampshire; and others in nearby Vermont now grew flax in quantity. Bennington was the market for western Vermont. Local mills crushed the seed. The oil and cake went east across the mountains to Hartford and Boston.

In Massachusetts, Worcester County towns such as Barre, Boylston, Lancaster, Lunenburg, and New Braintree were also big flax growers. The Merrimack Valley and eastern New Hampshire, where Scotch-Irish influence was strong, were heavily in flax. The little town of New Boston was nicknamed "Oil-Mill Village." Its mills crushed both flax and pumpkin seed. Portsmouth in 1796 had two oil mills. A bushel of seed made six quarts of linseed oil; the miller took one as toll. The oil cake residue found ready sale to fatten hogs and as feed for cattle.

Flaxseed was one of the few reliable sources of farm cash. Every storekeeper took it in trade. In the year October 1, 1790, to October 1, 1791, Massachusetts exported 6,036 hogsheads of the seed. Handmade linen goods produced beyond the needs of the family also furnished considerable farm income. Wansey, a visitor in 1794, mentions how the people of Northford, near New Haven, "raise a great deal of flax, and spin and weave it into sheeting, curtains, bed furniture Ec [etc.] of which I saw a great deal manufacturing." Newport got cloth from Western Massachusetts. Victor Clark, in his *History of Manufactures*, states that in 1788 Philadelphia was the market for 50,000 yards of New England linens, all hand-produced. In Vermont the Scotch at Ryegate built up a reputation for superior linens like that of the Scotch-Irish of Londonderry, New Hampshire.[14]

Another merchantable crop was hops. Judge Samuel Sewall records going "to View ye Hop-yards at Woburn" (Massachusetts), in 1702; and hop growing must have reached some magnitude before the Revolution, for shipping records show 3,000 pounds going to New York on the schooner *Bernard* in February 1763. To Massachusetts the crop became of such importance that in 1806 the state set strict standards of quality and required official inspection. A dozen towns, chiefly in northern Middlesex County, were the center of production not solely for New England but for the United States. "Tewksbury" (Massachusetts), says President Dwight, "yields more of this commodity than any other spot of equal extent in the United

States." Old kilns where hops dried over pine and oak charcoal fires are said still to be found in that town. Much of the crop went to Europe, which preferred the Massachusetts-inspected product, though Boston itself had two breweries. The port of Charlestown (now part of Boston) in three decades, 1806–37, inspected 76,860 bags weighing 16,467,162 pounds.[15]

The price was volatile. On September 30, 1802, a journal-keeper in the town of Shirley, Massachusetts, wrote: "Hops in great demand at six cents per pound; thousands bought and sold this day." In 1817 it is said that the price reached 37 cents. A hop fever set in, however, which by 1819 pushed the price back to 6 cents once more, or even less. The average price over these decades was 13 cents. Southern New England continued to grow the crop up to the time of the Civil War. Despite competition from other New England states and the West, in 1840 Massachusetts still produced one fifth of the nation's crop. A valuable benefit, just as in Kent, England, was the employment hop growing provided for local young people. To gauge the importance of the business, one family firm, the Blanchards of North Reading, between 1808 and 1837 brokered 16½ million pounds of hops.[16]

Western New England, in addition to cheese, dairy products, and fat stock, developed several marketable farm specialties. One reliable income producer was broomcorn. Cultivation of this grasslike form of maize began toward the end of the eighteenth century—first, it is claimed, in Connecticut. In the nineteenth century it became a staple for a tier of towns to the north in Hampshire and Franklin Counties, Massachusetts. Previously householders had relied on round brooms of birch twigs, hemlock tips, or split ash; some made by Indians, some by country people. Benjamin Franklin, that keen observer, is credited with planting America's first broomcorn seed. One story is that he brought it from England; another, that he picked a single stray seed from an imported whisk broom. The earliest recorded grower in New England seems to have been Samuel Hopkins of Hadley, who is said to have planted the seed in 1778. The broom trade's beginning has been credited to the year 1787.[17]

However, it was another Hadley farmer, Levi Dickinson, originally from Wethersfield, Connecticut, who developed the broomcorn industry. Beginning in 1797 and 1798, he gathered the straw from an experimental planting, bound it to handles with homegrown flax cord, and sold his few brooms to neighbors. His first brooms were circular, like those the Indians had made of birch brush, but of superior quality. Encouraged by their quick sale, he saved seed, the next year grew an acre, and peddled his brooms from a cart. From small beginnings he expanded operations till his sales route reached from Boston to Albany.

Noting Dickinson's success, other farmers in Hadley, Hatfield, Whately, and Northampton took up broomcorn growing and manufacture. Flat brooms replaced the round. Shops were opened where tiers became expert and the product uniform. Northfield took up the crop in 1813, then Deerfield; and Wethersfield in Connecticut was another center.

Broomcorn was grown much like field corn but required heavy manuring and more labor. It was planted in rows about $2\frac{1}{2}$ feet apart, with hills at $1\frac{1}{2}$ foot intervals. When nearing maturity, but before frost, the valuable upper two or three feet of the stalk was cut, allowed to dry, and the cuttings tied in bundles. The seed, if it had matured, was "hatcheled" out and the "brush" stored for manufacture. The stalks left standing in the field might be plowed in, burned, or cut as feed for young stock, any remainder trampled into manure. Each September, from Northampton to Northfield, the Connecticut Valley was said to look like one continuous broomcorn field.[18]

Between growing the raw material, and manufacturing and selling the finished products, country people had employment winter and summer. Nearby hill towns cut stock for the broom handles. "Broomcorn is valuable," commented John Harriott, an 1815 visitor, "and the seed is excellent for poultry"—a correct observation, though seed did not always mature.[19] Some farmers had the seed ground and fed it to cattle and hogs. The greatest virtue of all, from the farm point of view, was that for over three decades broomcorn became the money crop for the farm people of Hampshire and Franklin Counties of Massachusetts.

In this period the cigar industry developed also. Rhode

Island merchants had long been exporters of tobacco. When the Revolution ended, the business took on life once more. The brig *George* from Newport for Surinam in 1782 carried 29 hogsheads and two tierces—almost twelve tons in its lading. In 1783–84 the observant Spanish visitor Francisco de Miranda reported fields of very good tobacco on the light soils about Providence. Connecticut had also earlier grown tobacco in quantity, both for home consumption and for West Indies sales. Colonel Alexander Harvey of Scotland back in 1774 had noted excellent tobacco even at Ryegate, Vermont.[20]

About 1801 a Mrs. Prout of East Windsor, Connecticut, originally from Virginia, began to twist up tobacco leaves into cigars, whether from local or imported leaf is unclear—perhaps both. Previous local New England uses had been for pipe smoking and for chewing. Other women soon took up cigar making, exchanging cigars made in spare time for goods at local stores, or selling through traveling pedlars. These Connecticut Valley cigars got the name of "long nines"; in Massachusetts they were called "barnyard cigars."

In 1810 Simeon Viets of Suffield built a shop and started to roll cigar leaf in quantity. He also began pressing plug tobacco, called fudgeon. From Edward A. Kendall's description of a local church service, the chewing habit appears to have been already well established. Viets's brother Roswell built another shop at East Windsor, a town that had not only soil suitable for the crop but hog manure to fertilize it. The manure was a by-product from the large herds maintained on refuse grain at its distilleries.[21] Some leaf was imported from Cuba. The narrow, locally grown leaf known as "shoestring tobacco" was often bartered with village storekeepers.

Hadley, Sunderland, and Deerfield, Massachusetts, further north in the Connecticut Valley, were by 1835 growing leaf as a field crop, and town governments there (and even in the Merrimack Valley) accepted it in payment of taxes. Considerable leaf must have been exported, for among Hadley's regular town officials were Packers of Tobacco, an office known also in Connecticut at least as far back as the regulatory act of 1753.

Production increasing, a packing house to handle harvested

cigar leaf was built about 1825 at Warehouse Point, Connecticut. The leaf was then shipped in hundred-pound bales to New York. The enlarging tobacco trade opened what was to be a century and more of substantial prosperity for growers in the Great Valley and its neighborhood.

A quite different but likewise successful agricultural specialty became a reliance of farmers in the Franklin County hills northwest from Northampton. Peppermint had already, after the Revolution, been distilled in Agawam, across the river from Springfield. About 1812 Samuel Ranney, an Ashfield man from New York State, began to raise peppermint for which the stolons or shoots are thought originally to have been imported from England. He set up a small plant to distill the oil from his crop, for the success of which a moist soil rich in potash and long days for distillation were among the requirements.[22]

Sales of peppermint were good; growing expanded. By 1821 Ashfield's stills had increased to five; by 1830 to ten. Young salesmen from Ashfield and other hill towns set out each season in all directions bearing baskets, to quote Ashfield's historian, heavy not only with peppermint but with spearmint, hemlock, spruce, wintergreen, tansy, and other essences. Essence growing spread to Lanesboro, Pittsfield, and Lenox in the Berkshires; later to Warren, New Hampshire. Such products of their soil and labor, of high value in proportion to quantity, continued for years to afford welcome income to these hill towns. At length migration of experienced natives bore the skills and secrets of growing and distillation first to Western New York, later to Michigan. In both states superior conditions resulted in competition that the Massachusetts growers could no longer meet.

Another specialty crop to which gentleman farmers and home gardeners especially began to show marked attention was silk production. Though not destined for commercial success, the silk enthusiasm of this period and succeeding decades is one example of the determination of Americans of that era to search out every possible salable crop.

Propagating mulberry trees to feed silk worms had been an objective of the governments of Virginia and Georgia almost from the beginning; and, during the previous century, of other colonies also.[23] The Revolution over, the state of Connecticut in 1784 offered bounties for growing mulberry trees and producing raw silk from cocoons spun by silk worms feeding on their leaves. A Connecticut Silk Society, formed the next year, generated enthusiasm, and in 1789 the town of Mansfield produced 200 pounds of raw silk. At Northford, near New Haven, Henry Wansey in 1794 observed a great many plantations of mulberry trees and met a young lady who with her sister's help had the previous year raised and spun enough cocoons for 18 yards of Florentine silk. Mansfield, where by 1819 production of at least 2,500 pounds of raw silk was reported, and 3,000 in 1825, set up what is called the first silk mill in the United States. Sewing silk became part of the circulating medium. The following year Connecticut growers held a silk convention.[24]

Massachusetts and Rhode Island, even Vermont, also had their mulberry and silk enthusiasts. The sincere endeavors to establish a new type of crop for which the market was hungry, the speculative craze that grew from it, and the collapse that followed will be the subject for fuller discussion later. From the century's opening decades at least, the prospects appeared quite promising.

Meanwhile, wood and its products continued among the area's most reliable farm resources, although conditions as to forest products varied remarkably from one part of New England to another. While trees were being burned to clear land in the hills of Vermont and in interior Maine, providing potash as their only contribution to the economy, Cape Cod was already importing firewood, and in Truro pine seed was being planted in plough furrows to try to bring back a forest there. Eastham on the Cape had used up its oak and white pine to build vessels, and pitch pine was taking over. Orleans, lacking wood, was reduced to burning peat for cooking and heating, a custom long prevalent on Block Island. In interior Essex County, Middleton and Topsfield cut peat for fuel from 1800 on; and during the War of 1812 when the British shut off the Maine woodboats that ordinarily kept Boston and Salem warm, Essex County farmers sold peat outside at a great rate. At Bedford also, in Middlesex County, the extensive peat beds were highly valued for their coal-like quality.[25]

In southern New England, Rhode Island had little old-growth timber left. New Haven in 1806 imported 2,500 cords of firewood from Long Island, and drew on Maine for ship timber. Yet on that same Connecticut shore and further west, Guilford and Derby marketed in New York City both firewood and lumber. Up the Housatonic, the Salisbury iron works, their fifty blast furnaces fed by charcoal, devoured the woods for miles around. All in all, much of New England was rapidly clearing its original forest and changing its landscape to one of open country. Some sense of the importance of what in the twentieth century came to be called conservation is indicated by a letter home from Ambassador James Bowdoin of Boston, advising the sale of some timber on Naushon Island off Buzzards Bay. Though he is anxious that harvesting yield the greatest quantity of timber, he advises cutting the old and decaying trees only, leaving the rest for future growth. In New Hampshire, as early as 1822, the Board of Agriculture recommended what is now called selective cutting, and the propagation of forest trees. "If land be not useful for pasturage or tillage let it be forest." [26]

Maine's immense forests were the basis not only for the remarkable surge of shipbuilding that during the first years of the nineteenth century lined its shores with shipyards (an industry resumed after the War of 1812), but also for many of the keels laid down in Massachusetts. On Plymouth County's North River, shipbuilders reached continually further back for stock and masts. After they had taken out the oaks and hardwoods, white pine seed filtered in to replace them. This new crop was to become salable generations later. Up the Merrimack Valley in New Hampshire, lumbermen cut steadily into timber made marketable in Boston by the Middlesex Canal, completed to Concord, New Hampshire, in 1811. The great new mills and other structures of the new city of Lowell in 1822 also furnished a useful market. The upper Connecticut Valley floated its lumber down the great river, while the Champlain country shipped oak and pine as lumber by river north into Canada. Potash and pearlash (more refined and a source of baking soda) continued a chief source of outside income for mountainous areas away from water transport.

As the new century advanced, another forest crop began to contribute to the economy of hill farms: maple sugar. Goshen, Connecticut, settlers had made sugar there before the middle of the previous century. As early as 1754 a Hatfield, Massachusetts, farmer is recorded as having had a "sugar place" in the hills west of Northampton. By 1763 hill farmers were selling sugar in that shire town at five and six pence per pound, and maple "molasses" at two shillings five pence per gallon. Sugaring was also reported to the north, on the state line in Bernardston. This was just about the time that Reverend Samuel Hopkins was describing in print the process of sugar making as he observed it carried on by the Indians at Great Barrington in southern Berkshire.[27] A London publication of 1765 spoke of the method of getting sugar from trees as having been "lately" introduced into New England. About 1774 Norfolk, in the northwest Connecticut hills, was making 16,000 pounds a year; after another ten years 21,000, with three out of four families tapping trees. A decade later Dr. Stiles remarked that the process had been in use for forty years. Henry Wansey, passing the low mountains of Durham, Connecticut, in May of 1794, took note of taps still left in tree trunks and troughs beneath.[28]

In New Hampshire, Matthew Patten, a Bedford farmer, had his boys out "shugaring" in early April 1776. Later in the month they boiled sap to "molasses," but not to sugar. New Hampshire families often made as much as two to three hundred pounds. In newly opened Vermont, Pittsford's first settlers had made sugar in 1770. After the Revolution, John Lincklaen, traveling in the state's western section in 1791, had found to his surprise that the people did not seem to think the sugar maple of great advantage to them; chiefly, he suspected, from lack of a market for the sugar and the difficulty of getting utensils. Yet in Cavendish in eastern Vermont, 83 families are said to have made 80,000 pounds of sugar in 1793, and nearly as large a total the following year, selling much of it to storekeepers.[29]

In any case, early nineteenth-century western and northern

New England towns, far from the sources of imported cane sugar, began to produce tons of sugar for sale. Decade by decade the maple was to be of increasing importance to the whole hill country. In seaboard New England, on the other hand, the sugar maple tree was almost unknown. Even if available, at that period, its product could scarcely have competed for sweetening with molasses imports from the West Indies.

Another prime farm resource, often overlooked by historians, was the wealth of nut-bearing trees. The chestnut, hickory, black walnut, butternut, and beech grew thick on many a hillside. Their nuts made good eating in their natural state: dried and stowed away for winter use, they gave distinctive flavor to cakes and sweets. Swine throve on them, as the name "pignut" for one hickory variety attests. Of all forest species, hickory made one of the hottest fires. Properly shaped and smoothed it also became an excellent scythe or axe handle. Chestnut was easy to work, and popular with farmers for building timber and for fence rails; it would last for generations in all but moist situations. Walnut and butternut provided not only tool handles, gunstocks, and fine furniture, but also essential dyes to color textiles and clothing. These values were in addition to the food the nut trees furnished.

Every species of tree had its individual virtues. The several varieties of oaks and pines included numerous types of building and shipbuilding stock. Other trees had value right on the farm. The ash appeared to be especially designed by its straight smooth grain for long tool handles. Split into thin strips, ash was perfect for plaiting into baskets. The red cedar, which throve on the poorest gravel hillside pasture, served as a fence post that would last for generations; while the white cedar of the swamps, like white pine, became valuable for shingles. The cherry not only offered wild fruit, but was coveted by furniture makers. And no teeth for a hayrake or harrow were as tough as those made from hop hornbeam: a wood, when dry, almost as hard as iron. From even the soft gray birch, commonly considered a weed tree, the flexible small branches would make a good broom. When several of the long spidery branches were hitched so as to trail behind the width of a log, the result when this was drawn by a horse or ox was an excellent smoothing harrow.

These are but a few examples of the multitudinous uses that made the woods an invaluable asset to the New England husbandman, not only in the days of early settlement, but for generation on generation thereafter.

30

Tools and Tillage

Tillage methods had not changed much since the Revolution, nor the tools which did the work. Charles Newbold of New Jersey patented an iron plow in 1797. In 1814 Jethro Wood, born and brought up in Dartmouth, Massachusetts, but then of New York State, patented a cast iron plow with replaceable parts designed for more efficient soil breaking and scouring, and followed this five years later with an improved model. His plow was so superior that it was soon copied by numerous manufacturers without credit to the inventor. Despite his great contribution to agriculture he never reaped financial reward, though Congress in 1833 extended his patent. In 1822 Vermonter John Conant invented a lock coulter, and in 1825 Russell's Boston agricultural warehouse stocked a "greatly improved sidehill plow." Here and there a progressive farmer might hear of the novel all-iron plow, but of three plows entered at Berkshire County's first plowing match in 1818, two had wood mouldboards, though their shares were of wrought iron and the points steel. The exception was an imported iron plow. At a Brighton contest in 1825, four out of fifteen were of cast iron. For hay, a type of wooden horserake had been worked out, but its acceptance was yet to come.[1]

In hand tools the advance was greater. The wood shovel that a farmer could make himself remained useful for some purposes (handling grain, for example), especially when given a metal edge, but the Ames firm at North Easton, Massachusetts, in 1814 began to turn out nine to ten dozen a day of excellent iron shovels. Numerous small manufactories made greatly improved scythes, hay and manure forks, churns, and cheese presses.[2] An export trade in such tools was developing also. The cradle, of European origin, had begun since the Revolution to quicken grain harvesting, which for thousands of years had been dependent on the sickle. Any general use of it in New England was nevertheless still ahead.

With the improvement of roads leading to the large towns, horse wagons, some even with an eight-horse hitch, were practical for carrying produce to market. Though doubters at first labeled the one-horse wagon a horse-killer, it came into use to take people to church; and the sleigh shod with metal runners began to supplant the pung. The useful tipcart had made its appearance but was still uncommon. Yet the great advances in most farm tools were still to come.

One farm necessity, attention to which was continually required, was the stone wall. Not that walls were anything new. All through the previous century industrious farmers had been building walls and more or less permanent barriers of other sorts to replace original short-lived wood fences. As has been noted, on sandy Cape Cod and in alluvial plains where stone was scarce, ditches confined sheep and other animals—the banked earth that was thrown out forming an extra barrier on one side. Wherever stone was available, however, walls were preferred. A well-laid stone wall such as still surrounds many a barnyard and nearby lot is a work of skill, often of art. Most walls, however, were purely for utility, laid up to keep cattle out of a field or within it, or to mark a boundary. At the same time they rid cultivated land of a nuisance.

The end of common herding, marked by the division of proprietors' remaining common lands, and an increase in the number of sheep both helped to make the decades succeeding the Revolution an active period of wall building. A good man with a good team might build four rods a day. Such a statement illumines the investment of human labor involved in building and maintaining the thousands of miles of stone walls that, despite all efforts of modern bulldozers, still crisscross New

16. A noble stone wall serves to fence and clear a hundred-acre cornfield: (a) side view; (b) top view. Howard S. Russell collection.

England. Often they enclose one-time pastures, today become deep woods, or, as in Robert Frost's "Mending Wall," serve as boundaries: "Good fences make good neighbors," his next door farmer quoted.[3]

This enormous labor of clearing fields, building wall, and improving farm buildings and tillage was largely accomplished in farmers' slack periods, or, except in the case of gentleman farmers, by exchanging work with others. There was a minimum of hired labor.

In old-settled sections of New England, once the riches of the natural leaf mould were exhausted, farmers recognized the need to supplement the land's slim fertility. If they were within reach of salt water, they hauled rock-weed, kelp, and eelgrass in fall and winter for stable bedding, and again in spring as fertilizer for corn, potatoes, and roots. Industrious farmers were said to lay down from 30 to 60 loads to the acre. It was generally considered to be of great utility in enriching the land. Diaries of seaboard farmers like "Nailer Tom" Hazard of Rhode Island are full of seaweed hauling. Massachusetts' North Shore towns jealously guarded their beach rights against encroachments by inlanders seeking means for building up their soil. Rhode Island and Connecticut farmers at least were becoming great users of peat also. They dumped it on the land in piles to decompose, or put it in the pen for hogs to work into manure.[4]

Waterside cultivators had a second valuable manure, fish. Along the Sound, Connecticut farmers made immense hauls of whitefish, which they either spread directly on the land 10–12,000 to the acre before plowing, or composted with layers of earth for later use. This compost was deemed efficacious on all soils and for almost every type of vegetation. The lightest soils, enriched by fish, a writer maintained, have produced forty bushels of rye to the acre. Near Gloucester, Massachusetts, farmers obtained fish heads, the refuse of fish drying and the export business. At Plymouth and on the Merrimack, Mystic, and other estuaries leading to fresh water ponds, numerous reports of the early eighteenth century testify that the ancient Indian practice of putting herring in the cornhill still helped ensure an adequate crop.[5] Cape Cod had good returns from the king crab. The grain was reported to fill out well. Though the stalk was of low stature, it yielded twenty bushels to the acre on light land, one writer reports; another speaks of 35–45 bushels of corn and 20–30 of rye. On the shores of Buzzards Bay farmers plowed in what was locally called "menhaden," probably herring but perhaps whitefish.[6]

On most farms, if we are to believe available diaries, barnyard manure was ceaselessly hauled, spread, and valued. The ancient jibe about manure being allowed to accumulate till it was easier to move the barn than the manure pile, if it applied in New England at all, was possibly true only in the midst of new-land fertility or during hard winters. Eighteenth- and early nineteenth-century diaries abound in entries about carting, "beating," and spreading dung, though little thought was yet given to protecting it from the weather.

Travelers unanimously remark on the well-tilled, fertile appearance of country about Boston, New Haven, and other large ports. The many draymen's and private stables of such commercial centers were now the source of great quantities of manure. Nightsoil, brought from the city in tight covered wagons, was deposited in open basins and mixed with what Coleman calls "mould," presumably what would now be termed humus, to absorb the liquid parts and to put the whole into condition to apply to the soil. Slaughterhouse and tannery wastes also were hauled out for use in neighboring towns as these areas developed market gardening and commercial fruit growing. Near Boston a large farmer might contract for a stable's output by the year. Others bought manure by the load in winter, often hauling it on the return trip after sale of a load of wood or hay. In summer when Boston's Board of Health was hot after stable owners, forbidding accumulation of over two loads, farmers had to be "invited" to come in and clean the town.[7]

Presaging the coming of commercial fertilizer, trade sprang up in crop stimulants. Boston merchants sold French and Nova Scotia plaster of paris before the eighteenth century ended. In 1801 a Greenfield, Massachusetts, dealer offered plaster of paris by the ton or bushel. Soon President Dwight reported rich crops of clover and grain from treated fields in Massachusetts' Connecticut Valley. "The use of gypsum alone has wonderfully meliorated this soil," he concluded. Even in the limestone valleys of the Berkshires and Taconics plaster was used. Rodolphus Dickinson in his 1813 survey of Massachusetts remarked on the extensive spreading of plaster, which he considered especially useful on light soils. The idea was also abroad that after cropping land a few years a good farmer did well, as Eliot had advised, to sow clover and leave the field as a meadow to recover before planting again.[8]

Yet with all such additions to productiveness, and notwithstanding the praise of abundant crops that traveler after traveler gave the Connecticut Valley and the environs of Boston, Providence, Hartford, and other marketing centers, much of the older acreage was undoubtedly going downhill. Remaining native fertility was slight. Available manure and other soil complements went chiefly to fertilize corn land and money crops. Carelessness in conserving and returning fertility, however, might result more from lack of capital and the high cost of labor than from ignorance of the need to keep land in good heart.

As early as 1812 Provincetown was setting out beach grass to control its blowing sands. In 1826 Congress appropriated $28,000 for the purpose, while the state legislature forbade beaches to cattle, which might consume the vegetation that helped to anchor the sands.

With respect to farm labor, even in 1821 it was still not unknown, though no longer as common as earlier, for a country boy to be indentured until he was 21 to some good neighbor who agreed to teach him "the Art and Mystery of Husbandry." This was how Henry Wilson, destined to become a leading shoe manufacturer and merchant and Vice President of the United States, began his career. It was also the start for Nathaniel Stevens of Andover, who later founded a famous textile dynasty at North Andover, Massachusetts.[9]

At the expiration of his term of service the young man was likely, as in the case of Nathaniel King, of Sutton, New Hampshire (later a distinguished minister), to receive "two good suits of apparel both linen and woolen" plus 30 pounds lawful money. Or, after United States currency had been stabilized, the emancipated young man might be entitled to "two good suits, one for Lord's Day and one for working days and Eighty Dollars in good current money of this Commonwealth," an instance in Massachusetts (1820). From a satisfied employer the "suits" could include as many as twenty items. Henry Wilson received a pair of oxen and six sheep at the close of his tenure.[10]

Extra labor was scarce and usually high-priced. Though it might be needed by the grain farmer for harvest, "the real labor to the farmer and his family is severe; for additional hired help is not to be procured," John Harriott commented in 1815. Just to cut, pile, haul, and split the family's firewood took weeks of labor. If a job required more help than the farmer and his boys could supply, he would generally arrange with a brother, uncle, or neighbor to fill in, then return the favor when needed; or work out the value with his team at some other time, as did Peter Thacher of East Attleboro in 1831. Besides the help of a 19-year-old son and one hand for seven months, Thacher had to hire a boy and extra hands for haying. "We work out our team nearly or quite enough to pay our help," he said.[11]

For a big job such as a barn-raising the whole neighborhood would gather and hold a bee. The men and boys would unite their labor, and the women and girls provide a gigantic cookout for all. Until the temperance crusade discouraged its use, liquor would ordinarily be an added attraction.

On the frontier, women might have to help in outdoor toil, but following the tradition of the English yeomanry, New England farm women did not ordinarily work in the fields except in emergency, perhaps the illness of the farmer, as in the case of the mother of the distinguished clergymen Samuel and Eliphalet Nott of Connecticut. Matthew Patten of Bedford, New Hampshire, in the troubled times of 1776 had thought it worth diary notation that "all our women folk helped us husk from the time Bob went away." In August they "workt at the meadow." Exceptions were still to be found in Scotch-Irish and German communities, with their different tradition; and in the onion fields of Wethersfield, Connecticut, where even in the nineteenth century the local girls gained health, wealth, and fame by caring for that town's special crop.[12] (At Bristol, Rhode Island, in 1812 men did this work at 25 cents per day.)

The woman often looked after the poultry and calves. She would be in charge in the dairy. In some neighborhoods a woman might milk the family cows or care for the garden. Many must have already begun the home manufacture of hats from the abundant straw of the grain raised, for an 1819 report tells of this industry as producing in Massachusetts bonnets worth $550,000, 40 percent of them made in Norfolk County, southwest of Boston. Martha's Vineyard women, from the island's wool, in 1816 sent to market 9,000 pairs of stockings.

The woman's chief duty, however, was to the household. On most farms, between cooking, spinning, weaving, making clothing, molding candles, and discharging a score of other household tasks, long, full, and burdened days for women were the rule. Nevertheless, travelers of this period often comment with approval on the high quality and good health of New England's rural women. Adin Hodgson praised "Rhode Island's blooming beauties." But Lucy Stone's mother, who milked eight cows on their West Brookfield, Massachusetts, farm the night before Lucy was born in 1818, exclaimed: "Oh dear! I am sorry it is a girl. A woman's life is so hard!"

Like Mrs. Stone's, however, a New England farm woman's life might nevertheless be marked by quality. To quote that farmer-poet John Greenleaf Whittier, somewhat later, in "The Friend's Burial":

> And if her life small leisure found
>   For feasting ear and eye,
> And Pleasure, on her daily round,
>   She passed unpausing by,
>
> . . .
>
> She kept her line of rectitude
>   With love's unconscious ease;
> Her kindly instincts understood
>   All gentle courtesies.

An inborn charm of graciousness
Made sweet her smile and tone,
And glorified her farm-wife dress
With beauty not its own.[13]

31

Comfort and Struggle

ONCE MORE we come to a discussion and assessment of the farm people and their situation in the early nineteenth century, as the era of industrialization was about to begin.

Farm living continued to be laborious, but that did not necessarily imply discomfort or deprivation beyond that of other people. In new towns in northern New England the farmhouse might still be of squared logs, as Benjamin Silliman reported in 1819; but old people, questioned in a later era, looked back on life in them as very happy.[1] Or if framed and clapboarded, the house might still lack paint, especially in hill towns. But in 1809, of the dwellings he saw on the comparatively poor soils between Providence and Boston, English traveler Edward A. Kendall remarked: "the farmhouses (which are almost universally of wood, and painted either white or yellow) are frequently large, well built, and generally well furnished." Widespread production of linseed oil was one reason for the increasing use of house paint. John Lambert, traversing southern New England, gives further testimony: "A small town composed of these neat and ornamental edifices, and situated in the neighborhood of well-cultivated farms, large fields, orchards, and gardens . . . gives the traveller a high opinion of the prosperity of the country . . . The farms appear in excellent order, and the inhabitants sober, industrious, religious, and happy."[2] John Melish, a first decade English visitor, thought the white paint gave the country an appearance of great cleanliness and neatness.

Other improvements were beginning to appear. Most farms would for a long time depend for water on wells with their buckets and sweeps, but farmers near hillside springs were bringing in water through logs bored and fitted, to lighten the burden of the housewife as well as to water the stock. Here is the description of two farms advertised for sale in 1803 in the dairy town of Cheshire, Berkshire County, Massachusetts, source of the Great Cheshire Cheese: "They are situated one-half mile south of the meeting house, have all conveniences, have dairy, cheese, milk and press house, two dwelling houses, good barns, corn-houses, and two good fruit orchards. . . . Two aqueducts carry a plentiful supply of water to houses and barns." For village farms, as in 1798 at Keene, New Hampshire, a citizen might bring water in a wood pipe for several families; and soon aqueduct companies were being formed here and there to provide piped water for a whole neighborhood.[3] A Massachusetts gazetteer of 1813 said that wells were almost universal and subterranean aqueducts numerous.

By contrast, Horace Greeley later wrote of the struggles of farmers in the Scotch-Irish section where he grew up in southern New Hampshire. It was an area with strong but rocky soil and small struggling farms: "Its people all live by farming," Greeley wrote, "and own the land they cultivate; three-fourths of them were born where they live and there they expect to die . . . Poor as we were, no richer farmer lived within sight of our humble homestead, though our western prospect was only bounded by the Chestnut Hills, two or three miles away." For water supply Reverend Warren Cochrane, writing of another nearby town, tells us that even after wells were dug, water was drawn up with a pole, and well-curbs and well-sweeps were "precious inventions." "Many will remember when there was not a well-sweep in town," he says in 1845.[4]

As to food, except occasionally in the latest settled, most remote sections, it was seldom that a farm family suffered; and for most families the amount was ample, though variety was not always great. However, differences between areas and even within the same neighborhood might be considerable.

An observer in the town of Sandwich on Cape Cod, favored with marsh hay for stock, reports in 1802 that "the inhabitants in general are substantial livers." If a Sandwich farmer ran out of beef, lamb, pork, and cheese, he and every inhabitant had access to a supply of clams, flounders, and dried herring.[5] A surprising proportion of country people, even far inland, could also rely on fish for at least part of the year, as salmon, sturgeon, and herring sought ponds at the river sources to spawn.

During that same decade at the opposite corner of New England, John Lambert, from overseas, came ashore from a Lake Champlain craft in the early dawn of a snowy morning. He and his party knocked at the first farmhouse door they met and waked the family. Though the town of Shelburne was new and Vermont country rough, the household welcomed the visitors. The women stirred the fire, and with only a short delay, the travelers had the pleasure of sitting down to a substantial breakfast of eggs, fried pork, beefsteaks, apple tarts, pickles, cheese, cider, tea, and toast dipped in butter and milk![6]

Yet in that very same Vermont a native of Peacham, born in 1807, recalled that frequently during his childhood all that his father's household had for a meal was stewed pumpkins and milk. The historian of Francestown, New Hampshire, where the Scotch farmers mentioned earlier were for a time so poor that, lacking draft animals, they carried stable manure to the fields on their shoulders, comments: "A constant dish . . . was broth: corn broth, bean broth, barley broth and sometimes . . . a mixture." In New England as a whole the most common dishes seem to have been hasty pudding and pie. The diary of youthful Miss Elizabeth Fuller of a well-to-do family in Princeton, Massachusetts, records: "November 24. We baked two ovens full of pyes. . . . Nov. 25. Thanksgiving today. We baked three ovens full of pyes . . . They were better than last Thanksgiving for I made them all myself."[7]

Coming back once more to Cape Cod, but to the lower end, we are told that even among the poorest at this period a breakfast would include salt or fresh fish, brown bread generally with butter, and tea or coffee. At dinner, though the family would be likely to enjoy fresh butcher's meat not more than a dozen times a year, there would be fish of different kinds, salt pork baked with beans, "roots and herbs" (meaning, besides potatoes and very likely turnips, there might be carrots, parsnips, pumpkins, beans, and perhaps cabbage), followed by Indian pudding, and again tea and coffee. In rural Vermont at that period, however, the sole root mentioned in a store account book was turnips.[8]

An example applicable to many if not to most of the farm families of New England would be the recollection of Lucy Stone as she looked back at the West Brookfield hill farm where her mother had regretted the birth of a daughter because farm life was so hard. Lucy's recollection was of a copious larder: barrels of meat; milk, cream, butter, and eggs; several kinds of cultivated fruit and many wild berries; delicious honey; and fresh rye and Indian bread.* [9]

Independent, industrious, ingenious, shrewd, thrifty, often sagacious and active in the pursuit of knowledge; "raising [even in rural New Hampshire] ordinarily a little surplus with which to furnish their families the little necessaries which common custom or inclination invite them to procure"—the farm people of New England were the wonder of foreign travelers. "There is no class like that which the French call peasantry," William Cobbett wrote in 1818.[10]

President Dwight, leaving Yale to roam New England, is equally impressed. "Even a poor man," he says, "has usually a comfortable house, a little land, a cow, swine, poultry, a few sheep, and not infrequently a horse." The family eats well, has decent clothes, educates its children, and goes to church, he adds.[11] In the Housatonic town of New Milford ministers, doctors, lawyers, storekeepers all did some farming. One of

---

* As with numerous similar matters related to farm history it appears to this writer that despite the many popular and not too critical writings on undated "old times," the field deserves much more detailed and systematic attention than it has ordinarily received.

Dwight's Connecticut contemporaries acutely summed up the quality of New England's rural people: "Competence among the rocks," he called it.[12]

Nor should it be overlooked how many boys and girls destined to superior attainments, to become what the present generation priggishly designates as "intellectuals," were growing up during these years following the Revolution on farms among those rocks. As examples from those decades, set down Daniel Webster (born 1782), Horace Mann (1795), Mary Lyon (1797), William Cullen Bryant (1798), Bronson Alcott (1799), Dorothea Dix (1802), Hiram Powers (1805), John G. Whittier and Emma Hart Willard (1807), Theodore Parker and Asa Gray (1810), Horace Greeley and Henry Barnard (1811), Henry D. Thoreau and Sylvanus Thayer (1817), Lucy Stone (1818), Susan B. Anthony (1820), Clara Barton (1821), William Morris Hunt (1824).

In addition there was the host of inventors and innovators of these years, for whose practical, ingenious minds New England farm shops served as training ground—such men as Eli Whitney, inventor of the cotton gin and deviser of interchangeable parts for machines; John Fitch, who put steam to work for navigation; John Deere, father of the modern steel plow; Elias Howe, Jr., who devised the lockstitch sewing machine; William Howe, the truss bridge; Tyler Howe, the spring bed (all of one farm family); Simeon North, the revolver; and Eli Whitney Blake, who worked out the power stone-crusher with which it became possible to build all-weather roads. The list could continue.

For farm boys the options, besides farming, had for generations been the ministry, the law, teaching, a merchant's warehouse, or the sea, and these still attracted some of the best. But now almost limitless choices were opening. John Warren became a surgeon, and the father of Harvard Medical School; Oliver Hazard Perry, naval commander, and hero of the Battle of Lake Erie; and Henry Ellsworth, United States Commissioner of Patents and architect of the Department of Agriculture. Joseph Smith founded the Mormon Church. Collis P. Huntington was to build the Southern Pacific. More options were to open for girls also. The soil of New England farms might appear thin, but like the splendid forests that sprang from it, that granite soil nurtured a human harvest such as far richer ground might have been proud to sponsor.

In place of the term "subsistence farm," sometimes applied to the New England homestead of this half-century, a more accurate description would be "the multipurpose farm," and one of its primary purposes seems to have been the development of persons of superior capabilities and attainments.

Thus the first quarter of the nineteenth century, though interrupted by an unpopular war that for a time shattered New England's economic life and then by two years of climatic misfortunes, had been a time of seed-sowing: in trade, in transportation, in intellectual life and ingenuity.

Trade opportunities occasioned by the Napoleonic wars brought on a surge of shipbuilding, creating a market for forest products. Shipbuilders and the crews of vessels trading in the Atlantic and across the Pacific, and hunting cod and whales in many seas, had to be fed. Meanwhile, in their holds these ships carried not only barreled beef and pork, distilled spirits, lumber, staves and fish, but apples, cheese, lard, flaxseed, soap, onions, potatoes, and poultry; a diversity of minor products of the soil.

In assembling such cargoes merchants had the help of coasters from every little harbor, and of the first strands of a web of new turnpikes aiming straight at the ports from many directions.

Among the goods backflowing from port to farm was a trickle of blooded cattle, sheep, and poultry brought from foreign lands by observant travelers and sailors, and destined in time to come to make New England a seedbed of superior livestock.

Meanwhile, wars over and the new nation buoyant, the countryside showed increased well-being: paint shielded and decorated the wood of buildings, horse-drawn vehicles were more numerous, clothing more adequate, food less monotonous. Education was gaining, and ingenuity and thrift were creating on the farm and in the village a better life. For country people it had been a time of innovation, of seed sowing. Growing weather in both farming and intellectual life lay just ahead.

V. GOOD GROWING WEATHER, 1825–1860

32

Things to Come

IN THE EVENTFUL YEAR 1825 the waters of the newly dug Erie
Canal joined Albany, head of navigation of the tidal Hudson, to
Buffalo and the Great Lakes. That same year the new president
of the United States, John Quincy Adams of Massachusetts,
recommended to Congress exploration of the 2,000 miles of
unknown country that lay between the Mississippi and the
Oregon coast. The year following, 1826, was the fifty-first
anniversary of Bunker Hill. It saw one of the country's first
railways carry Quincy granite the few miles to the Neponset
shore, thence to be floated across the harbor for the 220-foot
memorial at Charlestown planned to commemorate the battle;
and 1829 saw incorporation of the Boston and Lowell, earliest
New England steam railroad company. These events were
harbingers of forces, historical and economic, destined in the four
decades ahead to transform New England farming—and the life
of the entire nation as well.

Of less national import yet examples of the striking changes
impending in agriculture were these: the first importation of
guano (the accumulated dried droppings of Pacific island
seabirds) and Chilean nitrate of soda, and a beginning in the
manufacture of ground bone, both of which would open the era
of extensive use of crop stimulants; the patenting by Silas
Lamson of Sterling, Massachusetts, of the graceful and effective
curved scythe snaith; the setting up at Canton, Connecticut, by

the Collins brothers and William Wells of the world's first axe factory; the publishing by Dr. Daniel Adams of the earliest American agricultural textbook; at Millbury, Massachusetts, the opening of the first Lyceum; and the establishment in Massachusetts and Vermont of the country's pioneer teacher-training institutes. At the new town of Lowell in these same few years the Merrimack Manufacturing Company started the machines in its great new brick mills, to turn out two million yards of cloth in its second twelvemonth; and at Sandwich on Cape Cod a new factory began to make attractive, inexpensive glassware available to American households everywhere.

This period also saw Boston open its monumental Quincy Market, unmatched in the New World. Worcester citizens, wishing to insure their dwellings and farm buildings, incorporated what has become Massachusetts' oldest fire insurance company. The Lake Champlain, the Blackstone, and the Farmington canals all began to transport freight. Lest the picture appear too rosy, a thousand miles away in Wisconsin the Colorado beetle began an eastward journey that presaged catastrophe for one of New England's most prized crops, potatoes.

Such crowding events were symptoms of the changes about to engulf New England farm people. Some of these farm folks would be made wealthy; some would be brought to national prominence. On the other hand, thousands of families would be uprooted from ancestral homes and occupations, and the ways of life of all would be altered at a hundred points.

The four keys (page 257, above) to the character of New England's agricultural history and the life of its farm people all increased their influence during these years preceding the Civil War. They are the rapid expansion of the means of transportation; marked improvement in education and information; a turning to better tools and machines; and a tremendous growth in industry and population in the area. Each brought benefits to New England farms; each created problems. Powerful additional factors exerted influence also, especially emigration from the hills; immigration of new peoples from Europe; the continual necessity to adapt to economic changes; and the beginnings of the era of farm as well as industrial organization.

By 1825 a widespread web of turnpikes and canals, the beginnings of which were mentioned earlier (page 264), had substantially reduced transportation costs for the back country, made travel more swift and comfortable, and the exchange of goods much easier. For interior towns they opened new markets for farm produce. Every state in New England benefited. Even Maine, though its rivers and sea routes made canals less necessary, and only a few turnpikes were built there, felt the influence. Military roads chopped through the woods linked Lincoln with Houlton and Houlton with Fort Fairfield. Thence a road eventually reached Calais, portending the opening of the Aroostook country. From the west, turnpikes through the White Mountains increased Portland's commerce.

From the Champlain Valley and western Vermont, butter, cheese, beef, pork, wool, and lumber flowed south by water to Albany and tidewater via the Champlain Canal and Lake George, in greater volume than they had ever gone north by the Richelieu River to Canada. In the decade 1823 to 1833, traffic south through Whitehall from both shores of the lakes increased greatly: in butter and cheese, five times; in sawed lumber, over three times; in wool, about fifty times. Most of this wool and half the dairy products came from the Vermont side.[1] On the Connecticut River a system of locks completed in 1835 by-passed the falls to help the produce and lumber of the great central valley reach tidal Connecticut. In turn, during the ice-free months, flatboatmen worked supplies north to the traders at Deerfield's Cheapside and as far as White River in Vermont. A sailing sloop, even, is reported to have unloaded freight at Brattleboro in 1837. Farmington Canal was extended from its Springfield terminal to Northampton, its total length 76 miles.[2] Maine, not to be left out, tied Lake Sebago with Portland. Directly or indirectly, each of these developments brought aid to interior farms.

The increasing mileage of through turnpikes stretching in all directions did even more to speed inland transportation.

Their centers were elevated for drainage. Ox-drawn scoops and tree-branch graders kept their surfaces smooth. In wet places willows planted alongside held fill and eliminated bogholes that had previously cursed travelers. The multi-horse team now superseded the plodding ox, though in an occasional tandem rig a horse might act as leader for a pair of oxen.[3]

Vermont's turnpikes tapped at least fifty towns. From Barre and vicinity eight-horse teams loaded with country produce headed south through the Williamstown Gulf to the Connecticut River Valley and thence east to Concord, New Hampshire, northern terminus of the Middlesex Canal. Southern Vermont traffic concentrated at the Bellows Falls bridge crossing the Connecticut River to Walpole and Keene, New Hampshire. Thence turnpikes led to Concord, and to Nashua and Lowell, canal ports still nearer Boston. Where the highway neared Lowell an eyewitness has left a word picture of huge canvas-topped wains called baggage-wagons entering the Merrimack Valley from the west drawn by six or oftener eight horses. In winter "two-horse pung sleighs" took their place. In these months, with the canal frozen, traffic had to continue the twenty further miles to Boston.

Every salable product of southern Vermont and New Hampshire was heaped on those wagons and pungs. In winter especially, when a bed of hard-packed snow made loads easy to haul and the climate provided automatic refrigeration, farm sleds came down from the back country piled with dressed beef, hogs, and fowl; with butter, cheese, lard, and apple sauce, as well as wool, flax, potash, feathers, and other nonperishables—all on their way to market. The load was likely also to include homespun tow-cloth, mittens, sox, and garments to be sold to provide a welcome bolster to family income. The load for the return trip might include salt and groceries for the household; and in addition a freight of barreled molasses or rum, salt cod, and dry goods, for a local merchant. Teaming such freight back was a common way for a farmer to help balance his running account at the general store.[4]

From northern New Hampshire and Vermont the pattern of highways leading to market was different. Though farmers in

New Hampshire's Haverhill region on the Connecticut River and those about Lake Winnepesaukee could reach Concord and the Middlesex Canal or even Boston, for towns further north the White Mountains loomed in the way. The opening through Crawford Notch of New Hampshire's Tenth Turnpike had given the north a practical route via Conway and the Saco River Valley to Portland, Dover, Portsmouth, and Newburyport, all thriving ports and markets. Another road through Dixville Notch offered the Colebrook area and northeast Vermont a means to reach Portland via the Androscoggin Valley, except that in winter snow closed this notch. By either road the plodding journey took ten to fifteen days. From new settlements in that northern country with fertility undiminished the load was likely to include wheat and other bulk grain.[5]

Not all highway traffic was by wagon and sleigh. In summer and fall drovers pushed east or south with cattle, sheep, and hogs destined for Brighton, at night putting their stock in rented pastures. On one November day in 1825 the toll-keeper at the Windsor-Cornish bridge on the Connecticut collected for 920 cattle crossing from Vermont. In a twelve-month period a dozen years later his count was 13,233 sheep and 2,420 cattle.

Great numbers of stock were driven down also from Maine, their destination either the slaughterhouses and tanneries of Essex County, the shoe and leather center of Massachusetts, or the Brighton market. If trade in these markets proved poor a drover might push on southeast as far as New Bedford. In 1827 a total of 10,000 cattle and 7,000 sheep crossed the Piscataqua and two other toll bridges into Massachusetts. Two thousand other cattle were driven over the highways in the opposite direction into New Brunswick.[6] Hogs, too, went over the same roads. In autumn flocks of gobbling turkeys would fill the highways. One keeper rode ahead on horseback, now and then dropping a few kernels of corn to tempt the birds. Another followed behind the flock. At night the attendants must pick a stopping place early, for with scant warning the approach of dark sent the turkeys to roost in trees. So much for the highways of the northern states and their contribution to farm and market economy.[7]

South of Boston the well-maintained turnpike to Providence

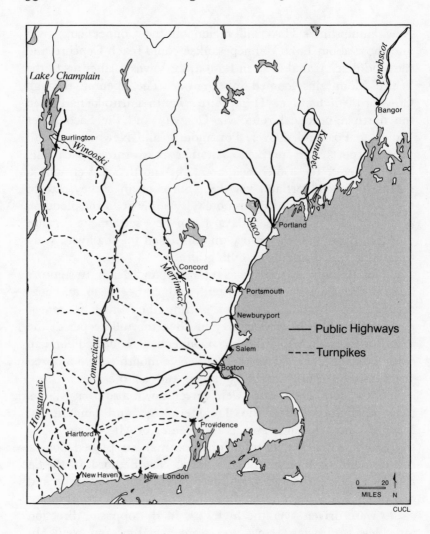

17. How the back country headed for market before the railroad: chief travel routes for stock, produce. In addition to these, all coastal areas made the sea their common route to market. Cartography Laboratory, Clark University.

got praise from foreign visitors. Not a piece of better macadam-
ized road was to be found in England, a Scottish traveler, James
Stuart, said of the tree-lined section between Pawtucket and
Providence. The Providence Coach, one of the hundred stage
lines centered at Boston, made its 40-mile runs twice daily each
way in the swift time of 7½ hours, called the fastest travel in
America. Yet in the same period in western Rhode Island, except
for the through turnpike toward Hartford, roads were wretched.
The west side of the bay clung long to coach travel. In 1829, 300
coaches a week were said to arrive and depart from Providence,
and a Cranston historian tells of Providence stage lines still
operating through that town at midcentury.[8]

Connecticut could count up to 3,000 miles of highway in
1812. Elias Boudenot back in 1809 had called the stretch from
New Haven to Hartford a fine turnpike road. By 1812 in western
Connecticut, Goshen cheese no longer went to New Haven for
export by ox-team but by 69 two-horse wagons. The town owned
324 horses in all. Connecticut historians concede, however, that
for ordinary highways cooperation between towns was often
lacking, and that despite the building of long stretches of
turnpike, most country roads were bad.[9] For inland New
England in general, long before the middle of the century,
highway travel on wheeled vehicles rather than horseback had
become the customary thing. In 1839, for example, A. Shumway,
a Massachusetts stagecoach driver, could count 15,000 trips that
he had driven during the previous quarter-century between
Belchertown and Hampshire's county seat at Northampton. His
mileage totaled 218,500, he claimed, and he had carried 25,000
passengers.[10]

Meanwhile, more than ever, coastal New England merchants and farmers used the sea for conveyance of goods to
market. Like automobile truckmen in the twentieth century,
regular coasters, small and large, connected every shore town
with larger ports.

From Portland, Wiscasset, Hallowell, and other Maine
harbors schooners christened *Sea Flower*, *Syren*, *Olive*, put off for
Boston with potash, clapboards, shovel handles, bedposts, apples,
cider, hay, butter, potatoes, sheepskins, cordwood. On New

Hampshire's sixteen-mile coast the *Sarah* or the *Polly and Clarissa* would leave Portsmouth or Rye for the big market loaded with potatoes, beans, butter, eggs, and cider. Cape Cod packets slipped across Massachusetts Bay bearing the Cape's fish, and along with it, thousands of ropes of onions. In 1835, from Portsmouth to Provincetown, Massachusetts Bay arrivals of coastwise vessels numbered 3,879.[11] In Narragansett Bay packets plied regularly from Newport, Bristol, and Warren to Providence, and others from the Bay's western shore. They bore to market the countryside's fresh eggs, poultry, onions, turnips, cheese, and butter. Even though by 1840 Rhode Island's direct foreign commerce was a thing of the past, the population and trade of Providence kept growing.[12]

Connecticut ports, today only minor factors in sea trade, continued their traffic with Boston and ever-expanding New York. Sloops and schooners bearing such imaginative names as *Eagle, Juno,* and *Harlequin* carried shiploads of corn, rye, and oats, often of from one to two thousand bushels a trip. "I have seen as many as 5,000 bushels of corn at one time going out of Southport Harbor in 1840," testified an elderly citizen, looking back.[13] Along with this bulk cargo went flax, cheese, cider, feathers, and other produce gathered from back towns or upriver in both Connecticut and western Massachusetts. All this traffic played its part in internal trade, but much of such freight eventually found its way into export. Most of it in either case had a bearing, direct or indirect, on farm prosperity.

If to farmers in interior New England canal and turnpike traffic was a boon, their effect was minor compared to the revolution that resulted from the coming of the railway. In 1835 the Boston and Worcester railroad opened; four years later it reached Springfield; and in 1842 by what was for that time superior engineering, the track was pushed up through high Berkshire valleys to the Hudson. By 1847 this "Western Railroad," linking Albany with Boston, carried 88,438 tons of freight. Meanwhile, the Boston and Lowell, completed in 1836, by lower rates and higher speed almost at once cut Middlesex Canal traffic by two thirds. Further south the Boston and Providence, and the Stonington and Providence railroads began business about the time Boston got its link to Worcester. In 1840 rails connected New Haven with Hartford, four years later with Springfield, in 1845 with Northampton, then in 1849 with New York.[14]

This was only the beginning. The railroad builders opened northern New England. The track crept up the Merrimack Valley into New Hampshire, then into Vermont. By 1845 the *Boston Cultivator* could report "an enormous train of 44 cars from the center of Vermont" arriving at Boston's Lowell depot. By 1850 Burlington on Lake Champlain was tied to Bellows Falls on the Connecticut. On November 13, 1851, Henry D. Thoreau, watching from Walden Pond, recorded in his journal: "The cattle train came down last night from Vermont with snow nearly a foot thick on it." [15] In 1853 Portland was connected to Montreal. Rails were reaching into Central Maine.

Canals and turnpikes found themselves superseded. The Middlesex Canal suspended operation in 1853. Dependent on tolls, most turnpikes lost money and eventually became public roads. The stages between the leading cities were given up, although certain short lines from interior towns to railway stations lasted through the rest of the century.

By the middle of the nineteenth century New England's network of railways surpassed in density anything to be found elsewhere in the United States. It was claimed that few farms in Massachusetts lay more than twelve miles from a railroad: the effects of "the steam train" reached every corner of New England. Towns previously important as stagecoach stops found themselves high and dry, while land values near the railways doubled and tripled. Before long the cost for freighting produce from Vermont to market dropped by three fourths from that of old teaming days.[16] Back-country farming towns, formerly a week distant from market, could now reach potential customers the next day. In the meantime, close-by farmers in Roxbury, the fruit and vegetable town nearest Boston, could get in and out by the new horse car if they wished.

As rails stretched west and south, the entire United States tended to become one vast market. This was a boon for New

England manufactures; and since nearly every town, however rural, provided at least some small portion of these, their industries promptly took eager advantage. Conversely, New England's commercial centers now became wide open to farm products and livestock from every direction, most importantly from the West with its rich virgin soils.

Despite the opening of the Erie Canal in 1825 New England farms had up to this time continued to grow considerable small grain. The Champlain Valley remained a wheat district until the midge appeared. The newly cleared intervales of northern New Hampshire grew wheat and rye for several decades more. Maine, spurred by a wheat bounty offered in 1837 by the state legislature, harvested over a million bushels the next year. Houlton in Aroostook claimed to produce 25 to 40 bushels to the acre.[17]

Western competition did not hit all farms at once. Fenced off as it was by the Berkshires from Erie Canal, Charles W. Eldridge in 1833 found the alluvial plain of Westfield, Massachusetts, "every inch cultivated" and "groaning under the weight of its rich but honest burden," principally of wheat and rye. East Windsor, Connecticut, produced 70,000 bushels of rye yearly for its distilleries. In Western Massachusetts straw from which the grain had been thrashed had a special market at $5 a ton at the paper mills.[18] At Winchendon in Worcester County a grower who got 31 bushels of wheat to the acre was able to sell his straw to local woodworkers for $20 a ton to pack woodenware in. Straw went also into mattresses, and near ports found use for bedding horses. The manufacture of straw bonnets grew important. Thus industry, if the loss of fertility to the soil is left out of consideration, for a time and in several minor respects was a help to local grain growers.

When, however, the Western Railroad in 1842 extended its track to the Hudson, Erie Canal terminus, western competition doomed any extensive New England wheat growing even more certainly than had the Hessian fly. Flour receipts at Boston increased from 530,000 barrels in 1840 to 761,000 barrels in 1850. By 1860 the amount of wheat produced in New England had sunk to a third of a bushel per capita. Maine's wheat crop dropped by over two thirds during these two decades.

Corn, though importations increased, proved less vulnerable. True, a historian of Plymouth by 1835 could already write that the principal part of the corn and rye and all the flour used there was imported by sea from the southern states or from Boston. At Sturbridge in central Massachusetts the record shows western corn coming in 1844 by railroad. Thoreau found one of his neighbors selling his own corn, and buying the corn from the South, and "shorts" or middlings from the flour mills. Yet between 1840 and 1860 production of corn in every New England state increased. In 1860, though less by a million bushels than that of a decade earlier (the largest crop ever), New England's total yield still went more than two million bushels beyond production of 1840.

It was otherwise with livestock, especially the hog market. Competition from rail shipments rose promptly. The decade previous to 1840 saw annual hog sales at the Brighton market average 22,700 head. By 1849 receipts of western hogs had pushed total sales to 80,120. Moreover, during the cold months bulk pork from interior New York began to arrive by rail. In the following decade, Western pork shipments tripled.[19] Though other factors entered, such rail competition forecast the eventual decay in New England not only of hog growing in quantity but of the cattle fattening that had been so lucrative for many productive corn and pasture areas. It helped to hasten the decline of the sheep industry also.

Yet, notwithstanding all the problems they brought to New England's agriculture, the railroads, as has been suggested, provided at least an equal freight of blessings. New, well-financed corporations were organized to take advantage of great river falls that had been too big to harness. A joint-stock company formed in 1822 dammed the Merrimack at East Chelmsford. In 1831 the Amoskeag Company, with a million dollars capital, threw a granite dam across the river to the north at Manchester in New Hampshire. At both locations the companies laid out new planned towns. For these industries, manufacturing cotton goods,

18. Family cow and farmer's daughter, York, Maine, 1883. Society for the Preservation of New England Antiquities.

the railroads provided the transportation essential both before and after fabrication. The mills offered employment and regular wages, and thousands of eager country people responded. In 1845 large-scale manufacture of woolens began further down the Merrimack where the river plunged again, and the vigorous textile city of Lawrence was born. These tremendous enterprises, at Lowell, Lawrence, Manchester, and elsewhere, unmatched in America up to this time, supplemented earlier but smaller factories at Waltham on the Charles and Pawtucket on the Blackstone, at Fall River, and at other sites which for a considerable time had been making fabrics by machinery.

Textile enterprises were not alone. Metal-working industries grew fast in Connecticut. On mountain streams in the Berkshires water power rolled out paper. In 1848 the white waters of the wide Connecticut were impounded at South Hadley for paper and more textiles, and the town of Holyoke grew beside the great dam. By means of the ever-expanding railways of the nation, the new mills found country-wide markets for their production.

To New England's farms, especially those inland from the sea, such enterprises offered new outlets; customers for food and fiber, with cash incomes, right at home. With regard to the textile factories at Palmer, Massachusetts, a gazetteer writer in 1846 put it thus: "The farmers are striving to meet the demands of factory villages for their productions. How much better this state of things is, than when they had to lug their beef, pork, butter and cheese to Boston to purchase foreign goods, at a dearer rate than such can now be made at their own doors, and of a better quality." [20]

Effects of the change appeared in countless directions. Water-powered machines, turning out inexpensive cottons and woolens, in a few decades freed farm women from the necessity to spin and weave which for generations had overburdened them. Farm girls, especially from New Hampshire and northeastern Massachusetts, released from home drudgery, thronged to the mills. At Manchester, Lowell, and Lawrence, for the first time in their lives, they could enjoy a reliable cash income. Despite the long factory hours, at a cost of but little more labor and time girls could now afford much better clothes, as well as comforts and luxuries previously out of reach.[21] At the same time, their fathers and brothers at home had found a brand new market not only for food products but for fiber and fuel and timber—one far easier to reach than the West Indies, the British Isles, or the Baltic: organized industry and its employees.

The new factory system might even help in the production of strictly agricultural products. At the nation's cheese capital, Goshen, Connecticut, for instance, Lewis M. Norton put machines to work to turn out factory-pressed cheese. Cream could now be set in Connecticut's machine-made tinware, and milk go to market in machine-rolled cans, while factories made scythes, forks, hoes, and axes better and lighter than any the local blacksmith had been able to turn out.

While the great mills produced textiles, Yankee inventors thought up new and improved tools, implements, and salable gadgets of a hundred sorts. Small but often vigorously expanding wood-, metal-, and leather-working industries, clinging to stream banks at every ten-foot waterfall, enlarged the income of rural people by providing seasonal employment and sometimes a market outlet as well for a surprising number of persons, even in very small towns. Here are a few such examples.[22]

Ashburnham, Massachusetts, and Windsor, Connecticut, started to make chairs. Leominster made combs. In the three northern states a swarm of small shops on small streams milled out bedsteads, blinds, bowls, churns, clothespins, firkins, matches, pails, rakes, rolling pins, spigots, spools, spoons, washboards, and similar articles of wood. Rhode Island turned wood into bobbins and spools for its cotton mills.

Besides wooden items, the town of Woodbury, Connecticut, in 1854 made tinware, buttons, shears, thimbles, tacks, and buckles. Hanover, Massachusetts, found profit in anchors, shafts, axles, tacks, machines, cranks, and similar hardware. Worcester was deep in wire and farm implements; Easthampton, in buttons; Bristol, Connecticut, turned to clocks; and a firm in a Maine village was said to hammer out more scythes than any other manufacturer in the world. St. Johnsbury, Vermont, was the center for platform scales. To all such items originating in country towns (there were quantities of others) as well as to the widespread household industrial products such as nails, shoes, and straw hats, the expanded outlets offered by the railroad proved a boon.

Still another of the almost countless side effects of the opening of the railroads and the accompanying industrial upsurge was a tremendous increase in the demand for wood for fuel to feed metal forges, railway engines, and furnaces of many sorts. Besides the enormous quantities used by locomotives to make steam, their balloon smokestacks caused fires along the right of way, to destroy more timber. To a farmer with salable wood, however, the advantages of a railroad siding as a market place and the additions to pasture that resulted from his cutting timber outweighed anxiety over future forest cover. Beyond all these factors, he and his family could enjoy the lifting of former rural isolation that attended each rail extension and each developing manufacturing community.

While new methods of land transportation were transforming inland life and commerce, New England's sea trade was growing rapidly also and ranging the globe. Consequently, supplying ship timber, provisioning the vessels, and furnishing cargo continued to be highly important to New England farms.

Though the needs of the shipyards were met partly from outside New England, the unmatched clippers rising on the stocks in the yards of Donald McKay of East Boston and other famous yards offered a hungry market for ship timber. Every inlet on the Sound, and the whole coast from Cape Cod to Machias, Maine, was laying down vessels. Their builders searched the countryside for oak knees, deck plank, and spars, providing not only a local outlet for woodland products, but winter employment for farmers and their ox-teams in hauling them to the waterside.

Once off the ways, every vessel required food supplies. Consider the fleet of 65 whalers that sailed out of New Bedford during 1858. Their provisions, doubtless largely from local farms and forests, included 10,400 pounds of beef, 7,150 of pork, 1,300 bushels of beans, 78,000 pounds of butter, 19,500 of cheese, 1,950 bushels of corn, 2,600 of potatoes, 1,300 of onions, 400 barrels of vinegar, 1,200 cords of wood, 260 cords of pine, 1 million staves, 260,000 feet heading (the last two items for barrels to contain the expected whale oil), 32,000 feet of boat boards.[23] The Nantucket and New London fleets and Stonington's sealers had proportionate needs, and the fishing vessels that harvested the offshore banks, likewise. A little fishing port such as Swampscott on Massachusetts Bay's North Shore counted 30 schooners. Though only a thimbleful compared to Marblehead, Gloucester, and Cape Cod harbors, a local historian relates how inland farmers drove thither to exchange butter, eggs, milk, and cheese for fresh fish and salt cod.[24] Fishermen's or even whalers' needs, however, were not to be compared to the requirements of the merchant vessels of the great ports which were engaged in foreign trade.

The importance of seaborne trade to agricultural prosperity becomes clearer with regard to such specialized items as onions and potatoes. From Barnstable and Danvers, Massachusetts; Bristol and Portsmouth, Rhode Island; and Wethersfield and Southport in Connecticut, coasters each fall loaded onions by the thousands of barrels as well as hundreds of thousands of ropes, to find their market in Boston, New York, and the South. Greenwich, Connecticut, grew wealthy shipping the potatoes of the neighboring countryside to New York and southern ports. Busy furnishing cotton for the world's spindles, Southerners came to rely on New England for their potatoes clear up to the Civil War. In Connecticut, growers responded with up to 200 bushels to the acre, and thousands of acres. In South County, Rhode Island, on Point Judith's excellent soil, one family grew from 16,000 to 20,000 bushels yearly, 300 bushels to the acre. South Kingstown's harvest, about 1839, was 75,000 bushels, its most profitable crop.[25]

Another offshoot of sea-borne trade was cartage in the big towns. Commerce stimulated demand for great quantities of hay and oats to feed city oxen and horses hauling goods to and from docks and warehouses. The thriving trade opened by Boston merchants in shipping ice harvested from local fresh-water ponds and rivers to the tropics provided a new and helpful source of winter employment for farmers and their teams;[26] and in season some vegetables and fruits went to market with the ice.

The succession of swift and startling changes of this period preceding the Civil War forced New England farms into continual adaptations. Constantly, farmers had to meet new conditions. The alert ones gained, some doubtless lost, all had to alter with the times.

33

The Eager Young

Nᴇᴡ Eɴɢʟᴀɴᴅ ꜰᴀʀᴍᴇʀꜱ in this first half-century might be reputed to be deeply conservative and subject to criticism for backwardness in agricultural practice, yet many, ambitious for their children in particular, placed high value on education. In 1827 the Massachusetts legislature, a majority of its members farmers, decreed that henceforth the public school system was to be supported by public taxation and open to all. Each town of 500 families or more was required to have a high school.

A decade later Harriet Martineau reported from New England to her English public: "All children go to school more or less." Her further observation was "nor . . . is there any farmer or citizen who is not more or less a student and thinker." James Stuart, another British visitor, asserted in 1841, perhaps optimistically, that in Massachusetts only 400 beyond childhood age were unable to read and write—a state of affairs, even allowing for exaggeration, unheard of in Europe.[1]

Still, the quality of general education was not high and in some places was called by local observers deplorable. Most conscious of the need for better schools was Horace Mann, a farm-raised boy, in 1837 a lawyer and president of the Massachusetts Senate. He persuaded the legislature to establish the country's first State Education Commission, and the next year abandoned his own prospects for higher office to become the Commission's secretary. Connecticut followed in 1839 with the similar appointment of Henry Barnard. Massachusetts next passed a law requiring at least six months schooling for all, appropriated two million dollars for better school buildings, and at Lexington set up its first normal school to train teachers.

The country schools sorely needed the improvements that Horace Mann and other innovators began. Yet despite the shortcomings of the schools, farm-bred boys and girls, spurred by ambition, were making their mark on the intellectual life of the time. William Cullen Bryant got his love of poetry from his Berkshire-farmer grandfather. In a neighboring hill town Bryant's schoolmate, Charles Dudley Warner, filled his memory with verses and Latin while he milked. At an Amesbury farm fireside John G. Whittier absorbed the history and legends of Indians, Quakers, and Essex County witches. Horace Greeley tells how on the New Hampshire farm and in country schools there and in Vermont, he learned, borrowed books, and laid the foundations for his editorial career. When he came to conduct the Concord School of Philosophy to which flocked that era's eager intellects, Bronson Alcott could look back to inspiration from his boyhood reading on the farm on Spindle Hill in Connecticut. Among Alcott's prized associates at Concord were country-born Henry Thoreau and Edward Everett, the latter's brothers still farming after he himself had become a leading orator and public figure.

Hawthorne, Salem reared, might twice in his "Note-Books" poke fun at the country graduates of Williams College, "great unpolished bumpkins, who had grown up farmer-boys"; but that very same year British-born Captain Frederic Marryat in his diary thought it remarkable how in New England a farmer with three or four sons would educate one to be a lawyer, another a doctor, a third a minister, while one stayed at home to take over the farm. "Thus, out of the proceeds of a farm, perhaps not containing fifty acres, all these young men shall be properly educated," and some started on the road to high position. Emerson in his essay "Self Reliance" holds up for praise the "sturdy lad from New Hampshire or Vermont, who teams it, farms it, peddles, keeps a school, preaches, edits a newspaper, goes to Congress, buys a township . . . and always like a cat falls

19. Ancient hay wain, Martha's Vineyard. Howard S. Russell collection.

on his feet." In 1847 Connecticut-born Henry Ward Beecher wrote: "Farmers' sons constitute three-fifths of the educated class." [2]

Nor were country-bred girls less eager. A Connecticut girl, Emma Hart Willard, pioneered women's education first at Middlebury, Vermont, then in the first woman's institution of college grade, at Troy, New York. Mary Lyon, "born upon a little rockbound farm" in Buckland in the western Massachusetts hills, founded Wheaton Seminary (now College), and in 1838 graduated the first class from what is now Mount Holyoke. Clara Barton's *Story Of My Childhood* warmly pictures the refined farm home at Oxford, Massachusetts, that nourished this teacher and nurse who was to found the Red Cross. Lucy Stone was later to recall in print her family's struggles on the West Brookfield farm that prepared her to fight for woman's rights. "There was a good farmer spoiled," she said, "when I went into reform." At Hatfield in the Connecticut Valley, reading, plus a season at an academy (in many country towns open to girls as well as boys), opened for

Sophia Smith a window on life that helped lead later to the bequest of her family fortune to found Smith College.[3]

The village "social libraries" already flourishing continued to grow in numbers and volumes; but an additional concept developed. In 1833 the New Hampshire farming town of Peterborough established the nation's first tax-supported public library, and in the middle of the century Massachusetts authorized tax support for a library by any town. A desire for strictly agricultural information led to organization of agricultural library associations. Deerfield farmers founded one in 1814, a second toward the middle of the century. Oxford, Massachusetts, farmers in 1854 raised $225 for 148 books on farming to be kept at their post office. Winchester, ten miles north of Boston, formed an Agricultural Library Association in 1856. In Vermont, Pomfret's Agricultural Library Association bought a hundred agricultural volumes in 1862. Undoubtedly careful local research would discover plenty of others across New England.

Another popular rural educator was the Lyceum. This type of forum originated in 1826 at Millbury, a farming and manufacturing town in southern Worcester County, and spread rapidly. By 1837 there were said to be 137 in Massachusetts alone. Local orators and pundits "debated everything: huge philosophical questions, trivialities, morals, religion, politics, farming, cattle raising. Excitement often ran high . . ." At Hubbardston debates led to a biweekly paper, *The Winter Wreath*, filled with original compositions by the ladies.[4] Benjamin Silliman, Yale Professor of Agriculture and Natural History, was one popular forum speaker on agricultural topics in the decades before the Civil War. The new scientific interest of the time found in the Lyceum a powerful means of extension.

Agricultural magazines began to appear—and to be read. Besides the *New England Farmer* published in Boston, already mentioned, in 1833 Ezekiel Holmes established the *Maine Farmer*, at first called the *Kennebec Farmer*, an excellent practical journal which enlisted farm support in that growing state and lasted nearly a century. Over in New York State, Jesse Buel from Connecticut founded the widely influential *Cultivator* at Albany in 1834, and published the *Farmer's Companion*, a book that also sold well in New England. A firm of Cambridge nursery and seed men, the Hoveys, in 1835 entered the horticultural field with the *American Gardener's Magazine*. By 1856 the Natick, Massachusetts, postmaster counted 59 copies of the *New England Farmer* and 22 of the *Massachusetts Ploughman* (founded 1841) to be distributed each week. Clarence Danhof estimates that in all New England agricultural publications may have had 50,000 subscribers.[5]

Such publications, however, failed to reach some who needed them most. The *New England Farmer* complained about the prejudice among ordinary farmers against agricultural periodicals. Many felt the methods and "fancy manures" they advocated to be impractical, and disbelieved in "the curculio and other new notions." Horace Greeley looked back late in life from his editorial desk in New York at the small, poor farms of the Scotch in southern New Hampshire and similar farms in Vermont among which he grew up. "I know," he declared, "that I had the stuff in me for an efficient and successful farmer," but "during the whole period, though an eager and omnivorous reader, I never saw a book that treated of Agriculture and the natural sciences . . . never saw even one copy of a periodical devoted mainly to farming; and I doubt that we ever harvested one bounteous crop." Plenty of farm people were readers, however. Lucy Stone's family took the *Massachusetts Spy*, the *Advocate of Moral Reform*, the *Liberator*, and others. Cyrus Hamlin, founder of Robert College at Constantinople, tells of much reading in his farm home. "My father and mother," he comments, "took great pains to keep up Massachusetts culture down in that new settlement in Maine," and despite the hardships in their new surroundings, the results showed in their children.[6]

A movement gathered force, though opposed by some farmers, for educational institutions to teach agricultural subjects specifically. To the two-year-old State of Maine, under the leadership of a prominent citizen, Robert Hallowell Gardiner, goes the honor of having in 1822 incorporated the nation's earliest school for teaching agriculture, chemistry, and the mechanic arts, the Gardiner Lyceum, and for making the earliest public appropriation in aid of agricultural education. The first class entered in 1823.[7]

In Connecticut, always educationally minded, Josiah Holbrook opened an agricultural school at Derby by the Housatonic a year later, but its life was short. In 1833 the Farm School on Thompson's Island in Boston Harbor began in a small way a long and useful life, its purpose "to teach indigent city boys mechanic arts and agriculture." The Manual Labor School at Shelburne Falls, Massachusetts, had "a considerable and valuable farm."

As a result of the 1842 bequest of Benjamin Bussey of Roxbury, Massachusetts, Harvard was enabled to found on his 200-acre Jamaica Plain tract (now the Arnold Arboretum) its Bussey Institution, designed to promote knowledge in agriculture, gardening, botany, and related subjects, as it still does. In 1845 Dr. Samuel Gold and his son Theodore opened at West Cornwall, Connecticut, the famous Cream Hill Agricultural School. In the next quarter-century this institution trained 272 boys, several of whom became distinguished leaders in agricultural and scientific education in New England and elsewhere.

Connecticut's interest in agricultural study caused Yale College in 1846 to appoint John P. Norton as the country's first professor of agricultural chemistry, and the next year to establish a School of Applied Chemistry with Professor Benjamin Silliman, Jr., at the head, where agricultural experiments became an important feature. From these came other advances, and eventually Yale's Sheffield Scientific School.[8]

Many agricultural enthusiasts wanted to go further. In state after state all through these decades proposals were offered for colleges to be devoted specifically to agricultural subjects. Governor John Ball of New Hampshire in 1828 even proposed a state experimental farm. There in 1856 Benjamin Thompson of Durham made his will bequeathing his property to the state for a school of agriculture and mechanic arts, now the seat of the University of New Hampshire. But despite agitation and debate real progress had to await the impetus of the Civil War, while the honor of opening the nation's earliest agricultural colleges went to Michigan and Pennsylvania.

A Connecticut man, Henry L. Ellsworth, was responsible for the first national agricultural report, made while he was U.S. Commissioner of Patents. There followed in 1840 the nation's first census of agriculture, a milestone in agricultural statistics.[9]

In the field of authorship in agriculture, in 1839 Connecticut-born Jesse Buel, of Albany, published in Boston his *Farmer's Companion*, which ran into eleven editions. A less pretentious work had been an *Essay on the Practicability of Cultivating the Honeybee*, by V. C. Smith, published in Boston in 1831. Three years after Buel's book, Alonzo Gray of Phillips Exeter Academy brought out *Elements of Scientific and Practical Agriculture*, and Thaddeus W. Harris of Harvard his valuable *Report on Insects Injurious to Vegetation*. In 1848 another farm-reared Harvard scientist, the famous Asa Gray, produced his *Manual of Botany of the Northern United States*, and in 1850 John P. Norton's influential *Elements of Scientific Agriculture* appeared. A science-minded minister, Rev. Benjamin Eastwood, in 1856 offered his well-prepared *Manual of the Cranberry*. On the distaff side, Mrs. Lydia Maria Child of Wayland, Massachusetts, opened a completely new publishing era with the nation's earliest magazine for children and published her *Frugal Housewife*, on home economics.

Further important influences of this era were the county, state, and local agricultural societies. County societies had sprung up in the early part of the century under the influence of Elkanah Watson, who in 1811 founded the Berkshire Agricultural Society. An autumn exhibition followed that drew thousands. In 1819, Watson persuaded the Massachusetts General Court to pass a general act for the incorporation of such bodies. The movement began to gain new impetus later when state legislatures were induced to appropriate funds to assist in financing such exhibitions, and county groups bought land for fair grounds. By 1857 there were said to be ninety-five such societies in New England.[10]

The exhibitions offered country people a chance to show their best stock, products, and handiwork, and provided a basis for comparison and competition. There were horse-racing and fun as well. Organization and management were usually in the hands of the well-to-do and gentlemen farmers; and they were often among the successful exhibitors and collected a considerable proportion of the prizes. This sometimes led to disparagement of the shows by ordinary farmers. Yet the opportunity to observe the best quality available in each phase of agriculture, livestock, and household manufactures, as well as to hear speakers of national repute, could hardly fail to stimulate new ideas and methods. Full reports in the local and agricultural press widened the influence of the speakers. State agricultural societies were revived or newly developed. The original Massachusetts Agricultural Society had in 1816 established the Brighton Cattle Fair. During the next decade this brought together yearly several hundred of the best livestock in New England for the edification of thousands of visitors, including Nathaniel Hawthorne. Maine organized a state society in 1818, New Hampshire one in 1822.

Agricultural enthusiasm spilled over into town organizations. Deerfield formed a Farmers Association in 1821; Middletown and West Cornwall, Connecticut, started Farmers Clubs in 1842; Lenox and Stockbridge, Massachusetts, in 1846; Newport and Bethel, Maine, by 1853. Such local groups put on their own educational meetings and shows. The Belmont, Massachusetts, club sponsored a highly successful local strawberry festival.

The new energy influenced state governments, which took steps to examine the resources and needs of their countrysides more carefully. First came geological surveys. Massachusetts opened the field with the nation's first, carried out by Edward Hitchcock. Connecticut followed in 1835 and the other New England states by 1844.[11] Next, Reverend Henry Colman of Deerfield was commissioned by Governor Edward Everett to survey the agriculture of Massachusetts. In 1838 he published the first of four official reports packed with information concerning practices on Massachusetts farms and markets and with suggestions on how they might be improved; two volumes more resulted from his observations of agricultural advances in England and on the Continent. People read and discussed these interesting and informative reports and the questions he raised.

The state agricultural societies (Massachusetts in 1852, and Maine in 1853) were influential in getting official state boards of agriculture appointed, which in turn appointed paid secretaries. The reports of these officials and the proceedings of the Boards, when published, contained authoritative essays and data. Among influential articles were those by Secretary Stephen L. Goodale of Maine on animal breeding, cultivated grasses, sheep, and fertilizers. The Massachusetts reports by Secretary Charles L. Flint on milch cows, dairy farms, and the state's first hundred years of agriculture were also eagerly read.

Destined in their special fields to have great influence on the course of New England agriculture were certain corollary organizations formed in this period. Most influential in their effects were the Massachusetts Horticultural Society, founded in 1829, its smaller sister the Worcester County Horticultural Society, and the Pomological Society of New Haven. The first two established permanent headquarters, with useful libraries, held public lectures, and frequent exhibitions with awards and prizes. Their efforts stimulated the development of improved fruits and plants. They assisted with imports of nursery stock and seeds from all quarters of the globe, and provided valuable public recognition to local innovators in the fields of fruits, plants, and flowers.

The decades preceding the Civil War saw also the formation of numerous mutual savings banks and fire insurance companies all through the six states. Among their corporators were the more well-to-do farmers. Both banks and insurance companies, organized without capital stock to meet the needs of their communities, were to prove towers of strength during the century that followed. The banks especially helped save rural New England, including its farm people, from the sharpest effects of recurring financial crises.

34

Sheep and Other Livestock

WHEN IN 1811 Consul William Jarvis had sent his purchase of Spanish Merino sheep from dockside to his Weathersfield acres in Vermont he started New England's hill country on a marked change in course. To many farmers it brought profit, even wealth; others it dispossessed. To many an upland community one longtime result was loss of population and a return of the woods.

As the blood of the Merinos and the related Saxony imports spread, the lengthy fleeces of these breeds offered a quality of wool that precisely met the needs of the increasing number of woolen mills, especially those producing high grade yarn and cloth. Thus sheep herding and woolen manufacturing complemented each other. Once the slump that followed the War of 1812 was over, both flourished under increased tariff protection.

When, however, the tariff on the poorer grades was removed and prices dropped, many growers became discouraged. Those near population centers, especially in Maine, eventually turned to the heavier-fleshed English meat breeds to take advantage of the growing city demand for roasts, chops, and spring lamb. The hill country reduced flock numbers for a time, and discouraged farmers left for the West; but the better-founded sheep men soon built up their flocks again and, as prospects improved, added land. A Vermonter sized it up: "As fast as one farmer caught the Western fever, his neighbor would buy him out, and . . . add to his flock of sheep. Thus we were depopulated and the West settled." [1]

With the 1830's, tariff protection had been increased for a time on both wool and woolens. During much of the next two decades long-staple Merinos and Saxonies became highly profitable. They multiplied in the Champlain Valley; in the hill country, too, sheep cropped nutritious mountain grasses from lands cleared to the summits.

Meanwhile skilled breeders were at work. In 1812 Vermont's average fleece had accounted for only 6 percent of the sheep's live weight. By 1844 the proportion of weight in fleece had been boosted to 15 percent, and by the end of the Civil War, in 1865, it reached 21. Though sheep numbers had dropped somewhat by 1850 when the United States published its first agricultural census, Vermont's wool production for the preceding year had been 3,400,717 pounds, almost half that of all New England and one third that of the great Empire State of New York. It was not uncommon in the 1850's for a prize ram to shear 12 pounds of wool, and Brigham rams from Cornwall turned in as much as 20 pounds or more. Vermont's reputation for superior stock brought buyers from all over the country seeking the rams and ewes of its noted breeders. Prices ran into the thousands for the best animals. Vermont sheep went west in great numbers. [2]

In the 1830's New England's three northern states between them could reckon almost three million sheep, and the number increased rapidly. In 1840 in Addison, Vermont's and the country's leading sheep county, there were eleven sheep for every human, or 1,681,000 in all. There beside Lake Champlain the density at one time reached 373 sheep per square mile. The town of Shoreham alone counted 26,584 in 1837 and Salisbury 81,166 in 1850. Springfield, on the opposite side of the state, had 17,872 in 1837.

Southern New England also showed some well populated sheep areas. In 1837 Newport, Rhode Island, had 37,340, and next door Portsmouth just short of 14,000. In 1840 the state of Connecticut counted over 250,000 and Massachusetts toward 400,000, mostly in their western counties, where several towns had 10,000 or more. In New Hampshire, wool shearings passed a million and a quarter pounds in 1840 and remained well over a million through 1860.[3] By contrast, Nantucket, once a big sheep county, was by that date down to 1,200 inferior animals.

At length loss of tariff protection, business depression, and increasing western competition knocked down wool prices. After the tariff changes of 1846, discouraged speculators sold whole flocks to the butcher the next season. Yet skillful selection for heavier fleeces by real sheep men continued. This held the loss of total clip to only 15 percent; and the healthy market for New England's high quality breeding stock lasted for decades after what was dubbed "the sheep mania" had subsided.[4]

Maine never became as enthusiastic over Merinos as Vermont. Flock sizes there were generally modest. Maine farms experimented with Leicesters, Cotswolds, Southdowns, and Dishleys. Farmers bred up the hardy common sheep so as to add half as much again to their fleece weight, but saw to it that their animals still ended with a good mutton carcass. Moreover, their breeding ran to a type that did well on rough pasture. When the 1850 census came, Maine, with 200,000 fewer sheep than its peak of 649,264 of a decade earlier, was nevertheless clipping almost as many pounds, and by 1860 showed an increase.[5]

Demand for mutton meanwhile constantly increased. Farmers with a good market for meat now bred and cared for their ewes so as to have them lamb in January and February to catch profitable early spring lamb prices. Though the peak in sheep raising was well past when the census figures of 1860 appeared, New England as a whole reported production of 6,578,000 pounds of wool, about two thirds as much as New York State. By this time, besides buying the local clip, New England mills were importing large amounts from the West and, when the tariff permitted, from overseas, so that to the larger woolen factories, local production became less important.

Sheep raising might flourish in favorable areas but for the majority of New England farms cattle remained the backbone. The small general farmer pridefully trained and used his yoke or two of oxen, which he might turn into beef after a few seasons' work, or more likely sell to a dealer to fatten. He also kept from three to ten milch cows (the common count in 1840 for Walpole, New Hampshire farmers, for example). Maine's farms in 1860 averaged seven cows each. The usual country cow gave perhaps five to six quarts of milk a day, mostly in warm weather. The surplus beyond family needs was turned into cheese or butter. Many villagers kept their own family cows. In Walpole in 1840 a hundred households had only a cow apiece, and 69 families kept two.[6] Usually such native cattle were descended chiefly from the original red Devon stock, which made excellent draft animals and gave a modest supply of milk.

Within reach of the great cheese market of Goshen, Connecticut, cheese making grew to the point where in 1844 Lewis Norton, of the enterprising cheese family, could open a factory—a new departure. Litchfield County as a whole was making $2\frac{3}{4}$ million pounds of cheese yearly, and Goshen had become wealthy on it. Here and among the Berkshire valleys of Massachusetts, herds of fifteen to twenty cows were not uncommon, with some larger. Eastern Connecticut was also a prolific cheese area, and in the middle of the century Vermont turned out almost 9 million pounds yearly.[7]

By midcentury competition from Vermont and from western cheese shipped in by rail gradually curtailed Connecticut's market. Next, New England's production, as a whole, instead of increasing from the 27 million pounds a year in the 1850 census report, dropped below 22 million in 1860, a decrease of toward 20 percent in a single decade. The largest percentage drop occurred for that formerly famous cheese producer, Rhode Island. Still, a lot of cheese continued to be made. In midcentury, for instance, the Berkshire town of Monterey sent 400,000 pounds to market yearly, and 25–30,000 pounds of butter in addition. The nearby mountain town of Sandisfield, where Durham, Ayrshire, and Devon blood had been infused into the native cattle, exported 300,000 pounds of cheese. By 1860 a thousand tons traveled to market over the Vermont and Canada Railway, quadrupling the freight load of 1851. In northern New Hampshire the new and fertile Lancaster area grew prosperous on cheese and butter, and some farmers there were termed rich. Nearer Boston, "Every farm had its cheesepress and every housewife her reputation in Faneuil Hall Market as a dairy woman." [8]

If, in the 1850's, New England dairy women decided to press less cheese, the amount of butter they churned grew by 7½ million pounds—the largest increase, 30 percent, being in Vermont—while Maine's total grew by over one quarter. At the end of the decade Vermont's butter production stood at 15,900,000 pounds, Maine's at 11,687,000, and the New England total almost 51,500,000. [9]

Most country stores took butter in exchange for groceries. It was likely to be heavily salted to make it keep, and of poor quality. Within reach of populated centers a market wagon might make the rounds of the neighborhood collecting butter and cheese, and along with these, poultry and eggs, for which cash returns were made the next week. As early as 1833 a traveler in Connecticut reported a hotel as icing the butter served on the table. By 1854 iced butter cars began to run to Boston by rail from as far as Franklin County in the northwest corner of Vermont. Butter dealers met farmers at the station, where the street would be packed with vehicles. [10] With icing, less salt was needed, and as a result light-salted butter of better quality reached Boston's tables from the three northern states. Another factor contributing to improvement in dairy returns was the practice—reported from Addison County, Vermont, and else-where—of growing beets, carrots, and similar roots for stock feed to supplement hay and corn fodder.

Butter and cheese production up to Civil War times was still largely on an individual basis, and usually the province of the women of the household. An Essex County, Massachusetts, farm boy, looking back to this period, wrote: "My mother's depart-ment on the farm was the dairy and no person took more pleasure than she in this line of work and the profits were all her own." (Clearly this was a farm more successful than the average.) "We always," he added, "had twelve to fifteen cows and we boys did the milking." [11]

As cities and manufacturing towns swelled in population, they called for more and more fresh milk. Farmers in town or within hauling distance turned from general farming to milk production and built up herd size to as many as 40 or 50 cows. They found it more practical to buy milkers from drovers bringing cattle from up country than to bother with raising calves. When purchased animals passed the stage of profitable milk production, they were sent to Brighton for beef and replaced with fresh milkers. It paid also to feed roots, cottonseed meal, and shorts (a type of milled grain) to supplement hay and pasture, so that the cows might average six quarts of milk daily for the year rather than four or perhaps five like neglected country stock.[12]

Often nearby dairies delivered the milk directly to consumers, but many farmers sold to milk dealers, whose cans the farmer filled and cooled in a well or with ice for delivery the following day. As railroads stretched out, dealers engaged farms at greater distances to supply their needs, at lower prices. The first New Hampshire milk flowed into Boston in 1845. The Fitchburg railway, a little later in the same decade, was daily delivering 14,400 quarts of up-country Massachusetts milk to Boston.[13]

Henry Colman in his *Fourth Report* in 1841 thought a good, nearby retail milk farm "profitable husbandry, where the milk brings 5 cents in summer and 6¼ cents in winter." [14] He had strong doubts, however, about any profit from milk that had to be sold at 3 cents to a milk dealer by a small farmer with only 4 to 6 cows.

Abuses in the cities, such as adulteration, dirt in milk, and the sale of unfit milk from cows fed on distillery slops led Massachusetts in 1856 to pass the nation's earliest pure milk law. Three years later Boston established the country's first systematic milk inspection.[15]

If the sale of fresh milk was to be a farm's objective, it became apparent that more attention needed to be given to selecting cows of superior milking characteristics. Patrick Shirreff, a Scottish farmer, entering New England via the Berkshires in 1833, thought the cattle he saw in the fields there invariably too thin, though at Northampton he met with "some beautiful cows apparently descended from the North Devon breed." [16] The "native" cattle, most of them originally of Devon blood, had remained for generations New England's favorites.

But in this first half of the nineteenth century forward-looking stockmen, often wealthy, here and there turned to animals of superior type from abroad. Selected imports: Devons, Herefords, Ayrshires, Alderneys; Shorthorns especially (even Longhorns were brought in), had succeeded and, according to the *Boston Cultivator* in 1848, had been of great advantage. Connecticut's Hurlburt family distributed as many as 1,500 of the progeny of their fine imported Devons.[17] Maine was keen on Devons as well as on the Shorthorns that had begun to arrive in the first quarter century. Two of the first Ayrshire importers were Massachusetts men, and the Massachusetts Society for Promoting Agriculture brought in two valuable Ayrshire bulls.

Connecticut got its first Jersey, or Alderney, from the Channel Islands in 1846; then in Massachusetts Thomas Motley's herd of 25 created a great impression at the 1858 Norfolk County Agricultural Show. Nevertheless, it was said in this decade that the whole number of Jersey cattle in the state was not over 75. Thirty of Maine's first Jerseys were shown at the State Fair in 1860, though only three were known to be in the state five years before.

In 1852 and at intervals in the next decade a Belmont, Massachusetts, farmer and fruit grower, Winthrop W. Chenery, imported Holstein or "Dutch" cattle that proved to be remarkable producers, and began to record them in a herd book.

New England farmers took great pride in their oxen. The native oxen were particularly adaptable to the combination of farm work, logging, and road hauling that local conditions made necessary. In Maine, Kennebec County in 1829 counted roughly one ox to each two cows, and two oxen to each horse. In long-settled York County, with the same proportion of oxen to cows, oxen were three times as numerous as horses. Admixture of imported Shorthorns and Devons with the native blood helped give Maine oxen a favorable reputation. Connecticut was equally proud of its red steers and oxen, while a Massachusetts speaker boasted that Norfolk and Worcester counties in his state could show working oxen superior to any to be found in Old England.

Fattening cattle for beef remained a special business. Maine,

New Hampshire, and Vermont finished thousands of cattle annually and drove them to Boston, or in later years slaughtered part of them locally. The Connecticut Valley, however, with its cornfields and skilled stockmen, continued for a time to be the center for fat beeves of high quality. Its cattlemen scoured the country for played out oxen and lean "stores" (many of them milked out females) to buy for fattening. They fed them grain, which by 1860 was coming in part from the West by rail, and in a few months had them in top condition for beef and the Boston butchers.[18] Some might be shipped even to New York or Philadelphia.

Week after week, from every direction, into the great Brighton Market with its hundred paved yards, poured thousands of animals of every kind. Collected by blue-frocked drovers who inspired Whittier to a poem, "The Drovers," large herds came by road. Others were brought by individual farmers. Some came long distances, from Northern Vermont and New Hampshire, from deep in Maine and from interior New York. After the building of the railroads, at a marked saving of time and of loss of weight in transit, one distant drover after another began to ship stock by car. After the Western Railroad in 1842 reached the Hudson, more and more came from outside New England, till altogether as many as 8,000 cattle might pile in at Brighton for the day or two of the main weekly market.[19]

Among them were fresh milch cows, destined for sale to nearby dairy farmers to replenish their herds of milkers, or to dealers who would peddle them out one by one to villagers as family cows. There were also dry cows and "stores," perhaps after purchase to be driven back for pasturage into the country areas from which they came. Calves were offered, to be turned into veal, and fine fat beeves whose quarters would end in the kitchens of Boston's famous hotels or at Faneuil Hall for the carriage trade. All were for sale by private bargaining on a cash basis, one week the credit limit. Forty thousand cattle of all grades had been the estimate of Brighton's cattle sales for 1819; 35,403 was the actual count in 1838; 66,550 in 1849; 70,650 in 1850.[20]

About 1834 a second cattle market was opened across the

20. *Thursday was top day at the great Brighton Cattle Market.* Ballou's Pictorial *(1856).*

Charles River in Cambridge, toward which three "great roads" from the north and west converged. Then in the course of the next two decades railroad tracks pushed north into New Hampshire. Boston was soon linked also with Bellows Falls, and the Central Vermont Railway connected Bellows Falls with Burlington on Lake Champlain. Nearby Cambridge now became the focus for cattle shipped by rail from both these northern states. On Wednesday, April 2, 1851, for example, the Fitchburg railroad, entering from the northwest, unloaded there 80 cars of livestock of all kinds; and the Boston and Lowell, 28 from the north.[21] The arrivals included 558 cattle, about 400 beeves, and 189 stores, consisting of working oxen, cows and calves, and 2–3 year olds. Brighton next day handled 875 beef cattle, no stores, 26 pair of oxen, 68 cows and calves (part, perhaps, driven across the river from Cambridge), 1,300 sheep and lambs, and 2,600 swine as well. Total carloads for a week at Cambridge might run as high as 270.

Besides cattle, these markets handled immense numbers of

21. A farm family's roast, ham, bacon, salt pork, and lard. Martin, Farm
Appliances *(1887)*.

sheep and lambs, hogs, horses, even fowl. Brighton disposed of
over 200,000 meat animals in 1830, and in 1849 about 300,000
large animals of all kinds, valued at over $1,419,000. The latter
figure included the receipts for almost 150,000 sheep and 80,000
hogs.[22] Though dressed meat was the principal product of the
butchers who were among the markets' big buyers, it was by no
means the only one. The hide went to the tanner, the hair to the
plasterer. "The slaughterer sells the feet and head to the
tallow-chandler and soap boiler who extracts the tallow and oil;
the horns go to the combmaker; the bones and pith . . . to the
bone-mill for manure, or . . . animal charcoal, and the blood to
the sugar refineries. A thorough system of economy pervades all
the branches of the business." [23] Brighton and vicinity was not
the sole center for slaughter. Topsfield, in Essex County, about
1850, killed 20,000 animals a year, largely sheep and calves.
These arrived mostly by road, partly from Boston. Their skins
became raw material for the tanners congregated in nearby
Danvers and Salem.[24]

Despite efforts to improve hog quality and the introduction
from England of the Berkshire breed in 1832 and of the Suffolk
in 1844, few New England farms bred superior swine or raised

hogs in a wholesale way. They were grown chiefly for family and local consumption. On farms that made butter and cheese in quantity, whey, boiled small potatoes, pumpkins, and other farm wastes could be turned into pork advantageously. Swine were useful also in composting peat, sand, seaweed, kelp, and straw into enriching manure. The ratio on dairy farms specifically was one hog to every four cows. One other type of pork production could be made profitable. Near Boston and Providence and in similar situations, garbage collected from city homes, hotels, and markets or refuse from distilleries provided food for hogs by the hundreds, though hog cholera sometimes played havoc. Five hundred to a thousand would be concentrated in some spot to which garbage could be delivered conveniently by road or rail, though this often caused local protests. The manure that resulted went to market gardens to grow vegetables.[25]

One good type of local hog, the Byfield, was developed in Essex County and spread into Rhode Island, but from lack of care in breeding soon ran out. A sea captain sponsored the Mackay breed. A few wealthy men imported Chester Whites, Poland Chinas, and Yorkshires, larger types that would dress five hundred pounds at sixteen months. Competition from the West, however, soon made large-scale production under ordinary farm circumstances uneconomical.[26] Before the railroads came, drovers brought hogs, two hundred or more in a herd, to market over the highways from New York State or even further. A day's journey would be about thirteen miles. The drover would have a dog to help, as Nathaniel Hawthorne recorded in his *Note-Books*, and would peddle some porkers by the way.[27] In 1849 one drover started his herd over the road in Kentucky. Buying and selling as he went, he eventually reached Albany. There he loaded his accumulated swine onto railroad cars and let the engine haul him and his charges the 170 miles to Brighton, where they all landed two months from the beginning.

With the coming of transportation, driving by road gradually ceased. Chilled hog carcasses began to arrive, in winter, from Western New York; in 1850 their number reached 37,778. In 1855 a processing plant opened at East Cambridge; it was enormous for that era and for a century was to be an important factor in packing both New England and western pork and dressed meat.

Between 1840 and 1860, however, western competition, plus greater opportunities in other lines, brought about a drop in hog numbers in southern New England of over 40 percent.[28] Maine and Connecticut farms showed the greatest stability. Hogs, except as they long persisted in domestic farm economy and garbage feeding, were never to become a major farm enterprise in New England.

With the advent of better roads and the use of the four-wheeled wagon, the buggy, the iron plow, and cultivating machines, the number of horses increased. They began gradually to displace oxen. The census report of 1860 counted 20 percent more horses in New England than in 1850. Though working oxen still outnumbered them by almost a third, Maine farms in 1859 had 60,637 horses, better than one apiece.[29] Vermont counted 69,071 on its farms that year.

Horse breeding in southern New England had dropped in importance with the decline of West Indies trade and the pacer. Coventry, Connecticut, farmers, however, keeping five to ten horses each, in the century's early decades continued to train medium-sized pacers. Harnessed to an ordinary rig, they were said to do the seventy-odd miles to Boston and back in a couple of days.[30]

In the three northern states Justin Morgan's progeny more and more made a name for themselves. From the strictly agricultural point of view, to quote a local historian: "Morgan horses were perfectly adapted for working on the small Vermont hill farms and for driving over the hilly roads." [31] They were special favorites of stage drivers. A regiment of British cavalry, sent to Canada in 1837 and there fitted out with Morgans, was so taken with them that it shipped many of its mounts back to England. "Black Hawk," a Morgan, was called by a writer for the *Louisville Journal* "the finest stallion I ever saw." [32] His son, "Ethan Allen," and other Morgan sires became famous. A six-year-old "Black Hawk" colt, accounted not too fast either (though doing a mile easily in three minutes), was reported sold in 1857 to an Illinois buyer for $5,000, to be driven west. Eager purchasers from as far away as California bought Morgan stock and drove or shipped them out. Western Vermont, touched by New York influence, bred Hambletonians also. When the Civil War came, army cavalry buyers almost stripped Vermont of mature horseflesh.

This was a period when county fairs were finding race tracks a popular drawing feature.[33] Increasing public interest in horses resulted in a three-day "First National Exhibition of Horses" at Springfield, Massachusetts, October 19–21 in 1853. The over 400 horses exhibited from eleven states and Canada brought visitors from nearly every state, and the event created a sensation. The exhibit, however, was considered more of a gentleman's than a farmer's affair. Not to be surpassed, the Maine Horse Association in 1860 exhibited a hundred at that state's capital, and Maine continued for some years to be a source of excellent driving horses, Drews, Eatons, and trotters, with Morgan and Messenger blood.[34] But for the long run, horse breeding was not to be New England's forte.

During these decades preceding the Civil War New England began to develop an interest in poultry that went beyond anything found elsewhere on this side of the water. This was in part because its population liked chicken and eggs and offered a good market for them, in part because of its world-wide trading.

Most farms had been in the habit of keeping some geese or turkeys, and a flock of nondescript hens; but as Yankee ships came back from harbors all over the world, their captains and crews, many of them farm-raised, brought home European and Asiatic fowl that caught their fancy. These were bred and cross-bred by the local folks. Poultry fanciers began to mate for special characteristics and to keep distinct the different breeds; though with the wealthier breeders, looks and plumage often counted more than laying records.

Instead of being left to roost haphazardly in barns or trees, as had often been the custom, fowl were now given better quarters, and improved care. "Nailer Tom" Hazard's South County, Rhode Island, diary, on June 3, 1830, records one development that was to be repeated again and again through the succeeding century: "helpt Son Benja. build a Hen House." On the 15th of November: "Glased the Hen House Window." All through the next few years his son Benjamin was carrying eggs to the packet landing to be picked up by the boat for Providence. Daughters, too, had a part. On December 7, 1835, the father records: "The Girls kild 29 Chickens Thay weight 48 lbs. carried them to Rodman's Pier and Sold them for 9 cents a lb." [35]

That the poultry business deserved attention became continually more apparent. In 1848 sales of poultry in Boston's Quincy Market reached a total of $694,483, and for the entire city went beyond a million dollars. The Market also handled well over a million dozen eggs that year at prices of from 11½ to 30 cents a dozen. From Maine, the Penobscot and Kennebec steamers were bringing to Boston $340,000 worth of eggs yearly. Three of the city's hotels alone used 200 dozen eggs a day. Even London steamers, after the Cunards in 1840 had established regular service, might take eggs on board for Great Britain. [36]

An incubator exhibited on School Street, Boston, in 1846 "delighted" the *New England Farmer*, but it would be another twenty or more years before use of these became practical. Meanwhile, farmers were experimenting on how best to feed birds. Besides providing corn from the fields, wastes from the kitchen, and pickings from the barnyard, we learn from Henry Thoreau's journal in 1851 that: "in Concord . . . they chop up young calves and give them to hens to make them lay, it being considered the cheapest and most profitable food for them." [37]

Many a farm still kept geese and turkeys. Deacon Jewett of Rowley, Massachusetts, on January 11, 1833, entered in his diary: "Kill & dress 8 turkies. I go to Ipswich P.M. Carry turkies 54 lbs. sold them for 10 per lb 5.40." At times thousands of turkeys were driven to market from the north over the turnpikes, their feet sometimes coated with tar to stand the long journey. [38] The German farmers at Waldoboro, Maine, raised peacocks.

Interest in poultry reached a peak in 1849 with a proposal from the editor of the *Boston Cultivator* and *Massachusetts Ploughman* for a convention of domestic fowl breeders and fowl fanciers. The response to this proposal surprised everyone. On November 15 and 16, 1849, the convention became a reality. In a marquee on Boston's new Public Garden, fowl fanciers exhibited 1,423 birds in 219 cages. The event attracted the unheard-of total of over 10,000 people (some said 20,000).

This first Boston Poultry Show, derisively called by critics "The Hen Convention," was the earliest such exhibit in the country, and the first in a series that was to last a century and more. Among the birds shown was a pen of the pioneer Plymouth Rock breeding, exhibited by Dr. John C. Bennett of Plymouth, a prime mover in the affair. The show resulted in the formation in the following February of the New England Society for the Improvement of Domestic Poultry. Books on poultry began to come out. Dr. Bennett in 1851 published *The Poultry Book, A Treatise on the Breeding and General Management of Domestic Fowl*. A periodical, the *New England Poultry Breeder*, fanned interest.

Not everybody was impressed, however. A skeptic wrote publicly: "We doubt if the archives of humbuggery has a chapter equal to the History of the Hen Fever." An interior farmer "living a little back from the center of influence" felt called on to "say a few words in favor of the common old-fashioned Yankee hens . . . yellow, blue, black, white, red, and speckled, with double and single combs, topknots, and mufflers, with roosters to match . . . the same now as they were so long ago as I can remember, nearly fifty years ago." [39]

Meantime down at Little Compton, Rhode Island, on the east shore of Narragansett Bay, two farmer marketmen, William Tripp, and a neighbor, John Macomber from across the Massachusetts line in Westport, teamed up. About 1854 they cross-bred certain of their best birds, good layers but meaty also, of Shanghai and Cochin-China blood. Within a dozen years the strain produced more and larger eggs, yet at the same time fowl whose carcasses dressed well. Though for the present, only the customers of Tripp and Macomber and neighboring poultry keepers were impressed, their selections for cross-breeding became the foundation for New England's second noted strain of poultry, the Rhode Island Red.[40]

35

Backbone Crops and New Departures

For GENERATIONS, to carry stock through the long winters, New England farmers had depended on hay, though corn fodder, now frequently cured in shocks, was a useful supplement. It had been considered good cultivation practice to plant crops for three years running and follow them with three years in herdsgrass and clover sod. With the common tendency to delay replowing, however, the period in hay might stretch on and on. Clover would disappear, weeds creep in, and land that cut two tons or more at the beginning would at length cease to yield enough to pay for cutting.

Pastures had often been neglected. Brush might be cut occasionally but that was all. The herbage would eventually become so slim that a report to the North Middlesex Agricultural Society in 1855 lamented: "Very few animals are now pastured in this section that do not find it necessary to labor as hard and as many hours per day . . . as do the farmers who own them." [1] To secure nutritious summer grazing, Massachusetts cattlemen often drove their dry stock to verdant mountain pastures in New Hampshire and Vermont. For hay, salt marshes remained a valuable asset to shore towns, while fresh marshes along the rivers were still a resource inland. Some diking was done to turn salt into fresh meadow. The better farmers manured, plowed, and reseeded their hayfields in regular rotation. Here and there hillside hayland got irrigation by cross channels gently sloping from a spring or brook above. Leading grasses cultivated for English hay continued to be herdsgrass, red clover, and redtop.

City dray and driving horses and work oxen offered farmers within hauling distance by wagon or by sea a cash market for their hay. Ipswich "green" hay topped the Boston market. Hay prices rose during the 1830's; and between 1840 and 1860 hay production in the six states increased one fourth. In the decade of 1850–60 its value rose in every New England state. The biggest jump was in Maine, from whose fresh fields farmers shipped hay to Boston in large quantities for sale. A report in 1857 warned them that many were exhausting their land by the practice. Yet it continued.[2]

Indian corn was always by far the leading grain, and frequently got the bulk of the farm's manure. As horse cultivators came more into use, level culture for corn began to replace hilling. With good care the average crop was around thirty bushels per acre. Fertile Connecticut Valley soils sometimes yielded seventy bushels year after year; and crops well over a hundred bushels on specially treated fields were by no means unknown. New Hampshire in particular reported high yields. Since early in the century separate corn-cribs had become customary farm buildings to store the ears. Jesse Buel's *Farmer's Companion* in 1839 urged leaving the entire cornstalk on the hill until fall, rather than topping above the ear to make the grain mature. At harvest the corn, stalk and all, was to be cut and allowed to cure in stooks (standing bundles). After husking, the stalk and leaves remained for winter fodder.

Importation of grain went on by the millions of bushels, not only through the ports but over the rails, to be unloaded at mills in towns well in the interior. Nevertheless, the harvest of New England's superior hard flint corn continued to grow through 1850, when the six states reported a crop of over ten million bushels. The 1860 census, however, showed a decrease in all except Connecticut. Yet Eastham, though on sandy Cape Cod, in 1860 raised enough for its own needs and exported 3,000 bushels besides.[3] Corn dishes were a cook's standby for farmers everywhere. Beyond that, the rest went to feed the livestock or was sold. Some farmers sold their own corn, then bought imported

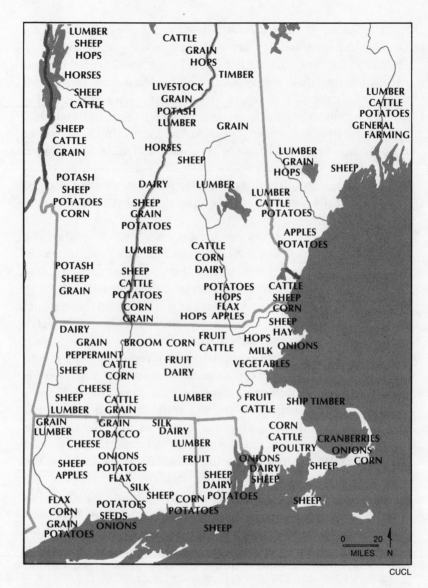

22. *The principal farm productions, by area, 1800–60. Cartography Laboratory, Clark University.*

grain at a lower price and had it ground to feed to their animals.

In contrast, wheat growing was in decline. The wheat midge, which arrived in the 1830's, made serious inroads. Yet despite a heavy drop in production in most places, northern New Hampshire and Vermont and interior Maine did well with wheat long after it had ceased to be of importance in southern New England. Upland valleys were green with wheat up to Civil War days and beyond. The finest wheat farms in New England, it was said, were to be found in the White Mountains.[4]

Rye held its own at about a million and a half bushels yearly, with Connecticut the largest producer. The growing of oats increased as farmers and draymen turned more and more to horses. New England's production expanded from 8,101,268 bushels in the 1850 census to 10,885,267 a decade later. Peas were a favorite companion crop. Perhaps a liking for oatmeal, developed from the admixture of Scots in parts of New England, also had an influence. In Barnet, Vermont, where Scots were strong, an 1838 diarist, sifting the meal from 57 bushels that the mill had ground for him, wrote: "Oatmeal constitutes one-fourth of the breadstuffs of this town." [5] Buckwheat was a useful catch crop, blossoming promptly to furnish food for bees, then grain for poultry. It was popular only in a few places. Norwich, Vermont, in the Connecticut Valley, for example, in the 1840 census reported a harvest of 11,119 bushels of corn, 20,727 of oats, and 11,182 of buckwheat. Down river, Amherst, Massachusetts, busy with brooms, tobacco, and dairying, five years later reported 18,930 bushels of corn but only 500 of buckwheat; and of wheat, rye, and oats a little less than 16,000 bushels. Added to its small grains, however, was an item of 4,526 bushels of broomcorn seed. By contrast, in the 1850 census Rochester, a large town in southeast New Hampshire, grew of small grain altogether only 4,000 bushels, while Indian corn totaled nearly 14,000. Back on the Connecticut River but on the opposite side from Norwich, as late as 1872 Walpole, New Hampshire, was topping its huge total of 38,000 bushels of corn with 33,000 bushels of barley. This variation in small grain was to be found within a circuit of seventy-five miles! [6]

Potatoes were a crop on nearly every farm, large or small. Like corn, the potato was a standby in the kitchen and good food for stock as well. From one to four acres was a common planting, but many farms grew up to a dozen acres for sale or export.

Potatoes for the South, according to James G. Bonner, writing on southern agriculture up to 1850, came almost wholly from New England. Connecticut's Greenwich area, growing 200 bushels to the acre, sent heavy shipments by water to New York. Smithfield and Johnston, towns in Rhode Island, were also among substantial exporters. Massachusetts, with a population by 1850 of almost a million, was growing three and a half million bushels for its own use and export. In all these states, towns near the shore, by fertilizing with fish, kelp, and rockweed, had excellent yields.[7]

In Maine, when wheat became unreliable, farmers turned to potatoes, often getting 250 bushels to the acre. A single year's production from the Kennebec Valley alone might reach a half million bushels. Where markets were too distant, newly built starch factories, opened in the 1840's, took up the slack, though at low prices. Starch was easily transported. It had only one tenth the bulk of whole potatoes and was salable both in textile cities and for export. In northern Maine Houlton already knew that it could grow potatoes; but to produce in quantity, Aroostook had to wait for rail transportation.[8]

Northern New Hampshire was making starch on a considerable scale. Some Vermont towns made starch, others turned potatoes into whiskey, which was salable and easily transported. Across the line in Massachusetts the town of Rowe in the Berkshires also had a potato still.[9] Near good markets, however, most potatoes were sold for food.

In all the northern states new land produced bountiful potato crops. On the wide Keene, New Hampshire, plain, yields in the century's first third were said often to reach 400 bushels per acre—in White Mountain valleys in the 1850's, 500 to 600. On older land, manure, muck, and turned-over sod helped production. In any case well-populated New England harvested double the amount per inhabitant that was grown by the country as a whole. There were, however, wide variations. Norwich,

Vermont, in 1840 harvested 53,480 bushels; yet only 90 miles south in the same rich Connecticut Valley and but five years later, Amherst, Massachusetts, grew a mere 1,691.[10] All through the middle decades a substantial factor in demand was the tremendous immigration of Irish to the mill towns of southern New England.

During the 1840 decade an unwelcome disease brought calamity, destroying whole crops either in the ground or after they were dug. Blight of some sort was not an altogether new phenomenon; it was said to have been reported several times, beginning in 1770, and control had been sought by reverting to the planting of potato seed balls. Now, in many sections, especially from 1843 to 1845, the effects of an imported disease, late blight, were disastrous. From over 35 million bushels in 1839 New England's production dropped by 40 percent in that decade. In Massachusetts the legislature offered $10,000 for a remedy. The only New England areas wholly to escape the blight appear to have been Martha's Vineyard and Nantucket.[11]

Recovery brought total production back to 21 million bushels in time for the 1860 census report. Maine's crop alone the previous year was 6,384,317 bushels, two thirds of the 1839 crop, yet its production nearly equaled that of the whole eleven states of the South and was almost double the amount reported in 1850.[12]

Among varieties grown about 1840, Henry Colman lists for Essex County, Massachusetts: English Whites, a round sort; Biscuits, round, with a rough skin but mealy and productive; La Plata, a long red; Chenango and Mercer, or Pennsylvania Blue, early and heavy producers which Clarence Day calls special favorites in Maine. There were half a dozen other sorts. The blight, however, was to cause radical changes in varieties planted.[13]

To a Vermonter, Albert Bresee of Hubbardton, is accorded the credit for developing a promising new variety, Early Rose. Its fame began about 1860, and shortly it became the leading American potato. Its ancestor was said to be Garnet Chili, one of thousands of seedlings grown from South American stocks by Reverend Chauncey Goodrich of Utica, New York. By selection and propagation Bresee fixed the type of his stock until, after the end of the Civil War, it was ready for introduction.[14]

Through the century's early years cider had continued to be a major product of New England apple orchards. As one instance, Hartford, Vermont, farmers worked together in a cider club, making twenty-four barrels average per member. However, the temperance crusade of the century's second quarter dealt a blow to old-fashioned, nondescript apple orchards. Yet long after rum and brandy fell into disfavor, cider drinking hung on in country towns. By 1840, nevertheless, many plantings started for cider had been cut down or abandoned. Good Baldwins, Greenings, Russets, and Pearmains continued to sell, and alert apple men top-grafted scions of these varieties on their ordinary trees, or, as Henry Thoreau noted, set new orchards in fenced plots. Baldwins especially were market favorites, but trees of this variety suffered severely in the hard winter of 1833–34 and were hurt again by cold in the 1850's.

In addition to the domestic market, apples went in coastwise vessels to Atlantic ports as far south as Mobile, as well as to the West Indies. Thousands of bushels also crossed to England, 120,000 from Boston alone in 1858–59. Iced, they were delivered to Calcutta.[15] In this period Massachusetts added the Sutton Beauty to the list of excellent varieties originated in New England, and at about the same time the Northern Spy was introduced from New York. Another fruit popular with apple growers and home gardeners alike was the quince, valuable for jelly.

Pear orchards were favorite projects both for gentlemen with estates in Roxbury and Dorchester (1,200 varieties on one such, it was said), and with ordinary farmers and householders. This fruit sold well in the markets. Farmers in the town of Lincoln, north of Boston, clothed their hillsides with peach trees, and did very well financially. The value of Massachusetts' fruit crop tripled in the quarter-century ending in 1860.[16]

Experiments with small fruits resulted at Lynn in the first domesticated native gooseberry variety; and in cultivated blackberry varieties at Beverly and Dorchester. At Concord, Ephraim

Bull, after years of patient experiment, in 1843 selected a seedling grape destined to become the most famous, popular, and useful of American grapes. He received the Massachusetts Horticultural Society's gold medal, and named the grape for his town.[17]

Demand for strawberries increased. To meet it, in 1838 the Hovey firm of nursery seedsmen in Cambridge introduced the first really successful American variety, the Hovey. The popular Wilson followed in 1853. Market gardeners began to grow berries in quantity; they even forced them under glass hotbed sash. Such early berries sold at sensational prices. From their field beds gardeners picked up to 4,000 quarts to the acre. The Farmers' Club of Belmont, Massachusetts, a market garden and fruit town, in 1859 invited the public to the first of what were to become innumerable strawberry festivals.[18] With rail transportation, specialization in early berries developed at Dighton, Massachusetts, near Providence, and at Concord. The railroad's coming forecast eventual trouble for local growers, however. Already a Connecticut farmer was at work in Alabama adapting strawberry growing to southern conditions.

On Cape Cod and in Plymouth County increasing interest in cranberries led in 1843 to the selection and propagation of the valuable Howes variety. Next came the Early Black by Cyrus Cahoon in 1847. As sales increased, towns had to adopt local bylaws for the preservation of the wild vines.[19]

The great bulk of the crop still came from the large natural meadows of the inland counties. A single bog of 25 acres in Franklin, Norfolk County, Massachusetts, was reported to yield 1,050 barrels in 1863. This was at a time when Harwich, with 2,697 barrels, was the only Cape Cod town picking more than a thousand barrels. A traveler to Portland, Maine, in October 1857 tells of a drained pond bed at Cape Elizabeth, bigger, he said, than Boston Common, with 50 to 60 pickers at work, and an expected crop of four to five hundred bushels. The owners of such natural bogs did very well financially.[20]

As population doubled, both in New England's cities and centers of manufacture and in the Atlantic states generally, much of the growth was in the families of workers receiving cash wages and those of businessmen active in trade and industry. They bought increasing quantities of vegetables of all kinds, and New England farms began to raise more, both of old staples and of novel sorts that grew popular.

By 1840 farmers in the Bristol area of Rhode Island, Wethersfield and Fairfield in Connecticut, and Barnstable and Danvers in Massachusetts were deep in onion growing. Their crops went to New York, Boston, and more distant markets. At Barrington and Warren, Rhode Island, about 1839, good growers working heavily manured land were producing 600 to 800 bushels per acre of onions, and of carrots up to a thousand bushels. Nearby Bristol grew not only these crops but rutabaga turnips as well. From Wethersfield, Connecticut, the South was said to get three fourths of all its onions. The cargo of a single outbound coaster that struck a Connecticut reef contained 65,000 ropes (about 4,000 bushels). Southport, in the town of Fairfield, had for years grown some onions for export. Now it increased its plantings to become for the next four decades, with its red, yellow, and white Globes, an important factor in the New York market. During the 1840's, the crop at Danvers, near Salem, increased from 25,000 bushels in 1838 to 120,000 in 1848. Despite the destructive onion maggot, this one town grew 200 acres in 1857, though producing only 300 to 400 bushels per acre. The crop for all Essex County was estimated to be worth several hundred thousand dollars annually.[21]

A demand for fresh produce had encouraged wide-awake farmers near the larger cities, particularly Boston, to grow a variety of vegetables. In addition, they extended the natural season at both ends. In early spring they used glass sash laid across plank frames. These were heated from beneath, at night and when sunlight failed, by fermenting horse manure. From these hotbeds they marketed radishes, lettuce, cucumbers, and melons months ahead of the outdoor season. In the fall, with underground pits and tight storages, they stored cabbages, squashes, potatoes, and all sorts of root vegetables far into winter and even the following spring. The pioneer Boston "market-gardeners," as this type of grower had also been called in England, were located in adjoining Brookline, Roxbury, and Jamaica

23. Boston's Faneuil Hall (or Quincy) Market, heart of New England meat and produce trade. Ballou's Pictorial (*1856–60*).

Plain. These towns, all in the area called by geologists the Boston Basin, enjoyed a frost-free season longer by a month than most of Massachusetts. Garden-farmers vied to be first in the market with green peas for June 17, Bunker Hill Day. They sprouted potato sections under glass and as soon as they dared set the started sections on warm south slopes so as to market new potatoes by July 1.[22]

For early spring transplanting outdoors, in late winter they sowed seeds of many vegetables under sash. A few gardeners experimented with greenhouses. By starting early and by companion-cropping of quick- with slow-growing vegetables, enterprising gardeners hustled two to four crops a season off each highly tilled and fertilized acre.[23] Most of this produce finally landed in South Market Street, beside Boston's imposing new Quincy Market. It was 535 feet long, all of granite, dedicated in 1826. "I know none that can equal it in any part of the world except one at Liverpool," wrote Henry Tudor, an English visitor. The open-air farmers' market, alongside, was entirely wholesale. It began its trade long before dawn. Later in the day the building's long corridor welcomed society matrons, hotel chefs,

24. The Boston hotbed: lettuce, radishes, even strawberries in March. Skilled market gardeners grew them in these beds, often hundreds of feet long, sheltered by tall fences, and kept warm at night by hot horse manure underneath and straw mats above the sash. New England Farmer *(1853).*

and ordinary householders to fill their needs from stalls full of choice meats, fowl, and fish as well as fruits and vegetables.[24]

Before the middle of the century, the city's growth had already turned some close-in market gardens into house lots. Growers then pushed farther out into Watertown, Newton, Arlington, and similar towns favored with the same long season. By ditching and heavy manuring, sometimes with seaweed to help, they turned poor, light sands and blueberry swamps into black loam on which to grow tennisball lettuce, white-stalked celery, and a dozen other vegetables, not only for Boston and New England's smaller cities but for New York.

Market gardens spread in a similar way in Rhode Island about Providence—where the great Budlong farm started business at Eden Park in 1854—and about Hartford and New Haven in Connecticut. By the 1850's Cape Elizabeth, close by Portland, Maine, was becoming a vegetable center. The 1860 census valued New England's market garden produce at over two million dollars, two thirds of it from Massachusetts. A Boston wholesale market report in February 1852 listed midwinter prices for nineteen different vegetables, including glass-grown lettuce and radishes.[25]

By that time new crops such as rhubarb and dandelions were well established in popular taste. Tomatoes had grown in favor for twenty years and sold in large quantities. Lima and sieva beans had been among the century's early arrivals. They are mentioned in the diary of Benjamin Goddard, a Brookline gardener, in 1812.

About 1835 John M. Ives of Salem introduced the Boston Marrow squash, said to have originated among New York State Indians. A decade later J. J. H. Gregory, Marblehead seedsman, brought out the Hubbard, which, he said, had been grown in a Marblehead garden since the end of the previous century. For at least the next century these two were to remain among New England's favorite winter vegetables. Improvements were taking place in sweet corn, another vegetable destined to become highly popular on New England tables and elsewhere. In 1839 Noyes Darling of New Haven crossed "sweet sugar corn," of the type that Captain Bagnall had brought from western New York in Revolutionary times, with white flint corn. The result, after selection, was "Darling's Early." This, the first variety specifically named, soon became popular. A decade later another New England variety appeared, "Old Colony," a cross with a dent corn. It was larger and held its sweet taste longer. A still better corn, "Crosby's Early," was the selection of an Arlington, Massachusetts, market gardener. This was destined to become for a half century the favorite both of vegetable consumers and of corn canners.[26] All these varieties had white kernels.

Increases in the production of vegetables and of flowers as well created a demand for reliable seed. The twenty-four Shaker colonies in New England continued to grow excellent seeds of both types, which they distributed in packets by wagon and through country stores.[27] James L. Belden, the Wethersfield, Connecticut, seedsman, in 1838 sold his business to Frank G. Comstock. The new proprietor began to decorate his packets with pictures of the hoped-for vegetables and flowers, a practice that seedsmen everywhere were prompt to take up. With his partner, Henry Ferré, Comstock sent seed wagons all through New England and into the Provinces. (This firm still publishes its annual catalogue.)[28] B. K. Bliss & Sons of Springfield, Massachusetts, are said to have published in 1853 the country's first catalogue illustrated with colored plates, and to have introduced the seed trade's mail order practice. By 1850 Connecticut contained at least ten seed farms; with neighboring New York it produced more seed for sale than all the rest of the United States.[29] About 1857 E. B. Clark of Milford, Connecticut, began to make sweet-corn seed his specialty. Several other growers entered this field, and corn seed became for years a valuable Connecticut product.

Though New England's soils have often been dismissed as inferior, their special qualities together with certain aspects of the region's climate have been determining factors in the flavor and crispness of apples, cranberries, and other fruits. Among field crops, and with cigar tobacco in particular, such local characteristics have had potent influence.

Southern New England had grown and sold tobacco from the beginning, but in the early nineteenth century Connecticut increased its plantings. About 1833 a grower at East Windsor brought in seed of the delicate-leaved Maryland Broadleaf. The variety did well, and acreage spread. In a shipment of leaf to Germany it was discovered that sweating in transit greatly improved its flavor and quality, making it of exceptional value as a binder for the outer layers of cigars. Taking this as a cue, growers dropped production of chewing and pipe-smoking varieties and began to concentrate on this type of cigar tobacco, which by selection came to be called Connecticut Broadleaf.[30]

The census of 1840 put Connecticut's tobacco crop at 471,000 pounds. Another source, an actual survey, put that of Hartford County alone at 417,380 pounds.[31] At the 1850 census the Connecticut crop had risen to 1,267,624 pounds, and cultivation had spread into the Housatonic Valley. By 1860 the total was just over 6,000,000 pounds. Further north, Massachusetts farmers in Hatfield and Whately, near Northampton, in place of their former modest plots began to set substantial acreages. The enthusiasm spread to Hadley, Amherst, and Granby. At Westfield two growers experimented successfully with another type, Havana Seed, destined to become the favorite variety for the upper Connecticut Valley. From 138,000 pounds in 1830, Massachusetts' harvest bounded up to 3,233,198 in 1860.

Prices paid by New York buyers varied widely from year to year, but on light soils suited to producing high grade leaf the returns to skilled growers were sometimes remarkable. This crop was not one for slovens, however. Its requirements were strict: early sowing in a seed bed, transplanting to the field, good manuring, careful cultivation, keeping the soil clear of weeds, continual expert attention to the curing process.

Details, especially fertilization, had a bearing on a crop's success. East Windsor, where Broadleaf got its start, was the seat of a number of distilleries. As a sideline, it will be recalled, distilleries kept large herds of hogs to profit from the grain waste. Their manure became an important factor in successful tobacco growing in the vicinity. Further up the Valley it was fertilizing the fields with the manure of sheep that on some tobacco farms added special quality to the local leaf. Farmers kept flocks of sheep or herds of cattle as much to benefit their tobacco crop as for the fleeces, milk, or meat that their stock provided. One consequence was that in order to feed the stock additional rough land had to be cleared of trees and sown to hay or used as pasture. Moreover, it was not tobacco alone that benefited from the liberal use of manure; subsequent crops grew bountifully.[32] Tobacco growing had effects on the general community also. By 1856 local cigar factories were employing 400 men and 200 women. The returns from this crop added to that air of comfort, even opulence, that visitors frequently noticed in Connecticut Valley farming towns. Eventually some modest fortunes built on tobacco growing went to the endowment of local schools, colleges, hospitals, and libraries.

For one group of Massachusetts towns in the Connecticut Valley, broomcorn continued during these decades to be largely the farmer's "money crop" to buy necessaries not readily bartered for with other farm produce. In 1845 Hadley reported a half-million pounds of broombrush and made almost 600,000 brooms. By 1850 with adjoining towns it had an output of 770,000 brooms and 70,000 brushes, with 41 shops doing the manufacturing. Ashfield, Goshen, and neighboring hill towns supplied wood handles for the brooms. Five years later Massachusetts' broomcorn crop was valued at $187,000, about equal to its onion crop and exceeding the worth of its wool clip by over $30,000.[33] There were other income producers, though less important. The center of production had already moved west, but in the Berkshire Hills a few farms still found peppermint, spearmint, and other oil-bearing and scented plants worth growing or collecting for essences. The expansion of woolen manufacture to large proportions created a ready market for teasels, the rough flower heads of a tall plant. When dried, they were employed to raise the nap on the cloth. New England's 1835 crop of teasel heads was 30 million, almost three fourths of the nation's production. At about that period Concord farmers in Massachusetts alone grew 880,000.

The effects of textile manufacture became evident in other directions. Flax growing for home use was on a steep downgrade. A linen mill with up-to-date machinery opened in Andover, Massachusetts, in 1836, another in Dudley in 1840, and one of 10,500 spindles at Fall River in 1852, to make linens by machinery. By 1860 local cultivation and household spinning of flax had nearly disappeared before the influx of inexpensive cotton goods from Pawtucket, Lowell, and Manchester. Farm people had little regret, however, at dropping the hard, dirty work of retting and swingling flax, or the monotonous grind of spinning and weaving that occupied every spare moment of the household.

Hops remained for some decades an important crop, especially in Middlesex County, Massachusetts, said to grow more than any similar area in the United States. In adjacent New Hampshire in the 1830's, Bedford in the Merrimack Valley was said to be the largest hop-growing town in New England. In the Connecticut Valley, Northfield, which began to raise the crop in 1833, was credited with nearly $30,000 worth in 1855; and in 1858 hopyards in Vermont's three northern counties

Brooks' Patent Silk Spinning Machine.

Brooks's silk spinning and reeling machine, which was invented by himself, is found to be a very simple and easy operating machine, and yet one of the most perfect that has been invented for the purpose of reeling and twisting silk from the cocoons, and manufacturing it into sewing silk. By the different arrangements of this machine, it will operate upon a single or double thread, as may be required, and prepare it for twisting or weaving. Experience has fully proved that by uniting the filaments of silk as they are drawn from the cocoons, wet in their natural glutinous substance before they are dry, the thread is more firm, smooth and stronger; from the simplicity of the machine, and the very easy way in which it is used, brings it within the comprehension and capacity of any person to use it. Mr Brooks has received a premium for his invention, from several societies, and of late, a premium and medal from the Scott's legacy, in Philadelphia.

25. Connecticut led the nation in mulberry trees and in silk production from cocoons grown by worms that had been fed on their leaves. Newell, Catalogue *(1836).*

produced 121,512 pounds, worth nearly as many dollars. The price, though high at times, was extremely volatile, and the crop was thought to rob the soil and absorb the bulk of a farm's manure, to the detriment of all else.[34]

By the second quarter of the nineteenth century the interest in producing silk from cocoons spun by worms fed on mulberry leaves, begun in the eighteenth century, had increased remarkably. The Cheney brothers in South Manchester, Connecticut,

William G. Comstock in Wethersfield, and Samuel Whitmarsh in Northampton, Massachusetts, were among the leaders in the movement. The Connecticut Valley, even as far up as New Hampshire and Vermont, was the area where enthusiasm became most intense, though the rest of New England shared the excitement. Connecticut, Massachusetts, Vermont, and Maine all offered bounties for silk production. (New Hampshire and Rhode Island refused.) Massachusetts published J. H. Cobb's *Manual . . . Respecting Growth of the Mulberry Tree, With Suitable Directions for the Culture of Silk.* Several states started silk societies. The federal government printed 6,000 copies of a *Manual of Silk Culture* to forward the movement. Special magazines whipped up what became a speculative mania.

One Wethersfield nurseryman grew mulberry trees in Cuba and shipped them home for sale. A Northampton stand was said to cover 500 acres: a Providence company grew 30,000 trees. Some nurserymen became rich. Householders filled their backyards. Plantings of a thousand were common; one of 6,500 trees is recorded as far north as Walpole, another of two acres in Sanbornton, New Hampshire. In Springfield, Vermont, enough were set to produce in one season a half ton of cocoons.[35]

Connecticut and Massachusetts were by far the greatest centers of interest. By 1825 the Mansfield area of Windham County had produced an estimated three to four tons, and its crop reached five tons in 1834. Its 1829 production was valued at $25,000. Silk was regularly accepted at stores in exchange for purchases or paid for in cash. Growing cocoons and spinning silk did not interfere with regular farm work, and it brought extra income.

The banking crisis of 1837 dampened the speculative fever. Terrible storms occurred in 1839, and the hard winter that followed killed thousands of mulberry trees. In the next year, 1840, to add discouragement, a mulberry blight set in and the boom faded. Still, on March 20, 1843, a grower in Vermont could record in his diary: "Bot 18¾ gallons of molasses of Mr. Willey [of Saxton's River] and paid him 300 skeins of silk." [36] Even a century later mulberry trees were occasionally to be found as reminders in city back yards and in country towns.

By far the most enduring result was that even though the mulberry boom soon faded, Manchester, Connecticut, and Northampton, Massachusetts, by importing raw materials, remained prosperous for a century as two of the three centers of silk manufacture for the United States. Manchester's large, successful mills were developed by able enterprising young local farmers and silk growers. Enough had been done also to prove that with due precautions raw silk production could be carried on as far north as Boston, should economic conditions ever warrant it.[37]

36

Marketing the Woods

THE HARVESTING of New England's woodland wealth went steadily on. Near railroads "the locomotives [were] sweeping away thousands upon thousands of acres yearly to say nothing of the millions upon millions of cords consumed for family and domestic purposes," a writer in the *Boston Cultivator* warned in 1848. (A cord is a horizontal pile of four-foot logs or split sections, four feet high and eight feet long.) Boston alone bought 120,000 cords in 1825, one sixth from nearby farms, the rest by sea from Maine, sledded to the waterside in winter. Salem in 1840 used 30,000 cords. Parts of Cape Cod might be sandy, but Falmouth marketed 5,050 cords of firewood in 1855. Lest all this seem exaggerated, Vermont's railways burned 63,000 cords yearly. (It was the late 1850's before Connecticut railways tried coal.) Rhode Island's lime producers burned 90 cords for each 500 barrels they made from the rock, and by 1839 they had been at it for eighty years. Glass factories, brickyards, and iron works burned wood or charcoal long after the 1830's, when cotton factories near the sea began rapidly to turn to mineral coal. The Boston & Sandwich Glass Works on Cape Cod, which owned 2,300 acres of woodland, used 3,000 cords a year. Like the foundries in western Connecticut, they employed farmers and their ox-teams off-season to haul the fuel.[1]

Up country the best stands were turned into lumber and shingles, defective trees into potash. Spring floods on the

Housatonic floated down pine and hemlock logs to be sawed at Derby on tidewater. In Massachusetts, with railroads handy, towns like Hubbardston, Middleboro, Milford, and Montague turned out over 2½ million board feet each a year; and in 1855 there were a dozen towns like Holland where fifteen mills each sawed a million feet.[2]

From eastern Maine to Cape Cod shipbuilders bought oak and hard pine knees for cash; and once the rails reached northern New Hampshire that area's knees and ship timber found a market in Maine's busy yards. Within drawing distance of Massachusetts Bay yards, a single, well-branched pasture white oak, skillfully cut up under the eye of a shipbuilder, might bring a farmer fifty dollars (a large sum then) and still leave him the minor branches for his own use. Nevertheless, as Thoreau and others commented, some farmers were not to be persuaded to part with a fine pasture oak for mere money.[3]

The results of deforestation showed, however. When Charles Dickens took the railroad north from Boston in 1842 he commented on the mile after mile of stunted growth that greeted him. Fires started by engines took heavy toll along all railway lines. In Petersham, now the seat of the Harvard Forest, in a bit over three decades the area in woods decreased by two thirds: from 9,270 acres in 1831 to 3,385 in 1865, the latter a mere 15 percent of the town's total area. The northern states had immense resources yet untouched; but Connecticut, which in 1844 still retained its impressive hemlock "Greenwoods" in the Taconics, was three fourths open land by 1860. Bronson Alcott, revisiting the Connecticut farmland of his boyhood, called the second growth there the most productive crop the owners could grow for the market. That market was the Naugatuck Valley, busy with clockmaking and copper and metal manufactures.[4]

All this available lumber brought certain concrete advantages. Histories of town after town in every state relate the amazing number of wood products, manufacture of which afforded income to farm people whose time at certain seasons was otherwise of small cash value. Endless wooden articles made with hand tools or in small mills during winter months were constantly being exported in all directions. Timber was the most

26. *Charcoal burning from 1650 to 1900 turned woods waste into wages and provided the fuel for metal manufacture (1884). Society for the Preservation of New England Antiquities.*

reliable cash resource for many a small farmer, though its cutting and sale might provide little beyond winter wages for himself and his team. If his own wood was gone, he could cut on shares for a larger owner, chopping perhaps as much as two cords of firewood a day. The clearing of woodland fortunately coincided with a steady increase in the market for dairy products, so that the added pasture, even though poor, became for a time a useful asset to the farms. On Cape Cod, however, it was not pasture that resulted, but sand dunes and wastes. Frederick Freeman, the Cape historian, in 1860 told of seeing large tree stumps on tidal flats a mile out from shore, apparently at Provincetown. At Eastham, just beyond the crook of the Cape, no forest remained except near its boundary with Wellfleet. Sand continually encroached.

Meanwhile recuperative forces were here and there beginning to appear. An occasional voice such as those of Theodore S. Gold of Connecticut and John Lowell of Massachusetts warned of waste or advocated reforestation.

Said one prophet in the *Massachusetts Agricultural Journal* in 1831: "We are fast consuming these rich treasures of our woods, and I fear that our prodigality will be followed . . . by the usual consequences of prodigality." Fifteen years later an official report commissioned by that state's legislature warned that unless pains were taken to replace the forests, manufacturers of products based on wood, with a payroll of over two millions, were likely to leave the state. "A prudent foresight may prevent this by planting [trees] in season."

Massachusetts and New Hampshire passed laws to protect shade trees. Far-sighted towns like Sheffield, Stockbridge, Lynn, Deerfield, Greenfield in Massachusetts, Walpole in New Hampshire, and numerous others were planting them along the highways. Already in places they were so plentiful that when architect Charles J. Latrobe in 1835 recorded his visit to the area, he called the great elms that frequently lined village streets on both sides and clustered about the dwellings "the glory of New England." [5]

What happened to fertility depended largely on location, on what could be found to augment manure made by the farm's livestock, and on whether available markets for the farm's products made worth while the labor and expense that extra manure entailed. Barnyard manure was likely to go largely to the crops that brought direct income.

Still, on many a farm, a large part of the manure's potential was lost through lack of care. Investment in a barn cellar to cover it from the weather commended itself to some, but Henry Colman in 1838 complained that one would go far to find one in Berkshire County, Massachusetts. Those who had cellars, though, in a few years began to sell hay, he said.[6] Many, nevertheless, pitched the manure out the window into the weather.

Near cities, market gardeners hauled from city stables every load of manure available. Colman said it cost about as much as good cordwood, and mentioned one gardener who paid out the (then) very large sum of a thousand dollars a year for city manure. Farms within smell of salt water had great advantages.

Two or three barrels of menhaden (a fish available in abundance), so a Bristol, Rhode Island, farmer testified in 1844, when spread on the land 6–10 inches apart and plowed in, were equal to a whole load of manure. The fish decomposed rapidly. Even on a poor, wornout sod an amazing growth of timothy and clover resulted, he continued, and cattle loved the sweetness of that grass and hay. The effects showed for years. For onions, when fish manure was plowed in during the fall, a great crop would be harvested next season. One Bristol, Rhode Island, farmer reported 800 bushels to the acre, plus some beets; another, 600. Crops of carrots went as high as 1,000.[7]

A compost pit or pile composed of earth, fish, peat, and salt mud, and covered with rockweed (called by Rhode Island farmers "fish pie") was best, said others, and avoided an offensive smell. For a heavy crop of corn, farmers dropped two half-pound fish into each hill at planting, or beside the hill at weeding time, and covered with the hoe. Farmers along the Merrimack backed carts up to the river bank to fill them with fish. Towns on Long Island Sound relied on broadcasting big dressings of whitefish; 20 million were used in Madison, Connecticut, in 1848, enough to manure 1,600 acres, at an expense of $20,000. However, if fish were used directly on the land, without composting, some Rhode Island farmers claimed that within a span of a few years crops failed to do well and the land became almost sterile or was covered by red sorrel.[8] (The imbalance may have been due to a lack of potassium or lime.)

Seaweed was an excellent feeder for potatoes, several Rhode Island farmers testified. At Newport on a one-and-a-quarter mile beach 3,000 wagon loads worth two dollars each were thrown up yearly. Sea wrack (flotsam and jetsam) did best "composted with rich, unctuous, and viscid" sand from along the shore or mixed with riverside sediment and broken shells ("coral"), a source of lime. Such a manure was often called mussel (or muscle) bed, sea mud, or flats, and might contain black clams. Like the Rhode Islanders, a Cape Cod farmer told of stacking all such materials in a pile and adding lime to the heap. When this mud plus seaweed, rockweed, and seamoss were put into the hog pen to be worked over, not only did excellent land dressing result, but the

27. *Gathering kelp for fertilizer, York, Maine, 1882. Society for the Preservation of New England Antiquities.*

hogs, feeding on the gelatinous sea plants, were healthy and ended in good shape for fattening.[9]

The British author Harriet Martineau was quick to note in 1837 how Gloucester farmers spread a compost made of seaweed and fishheads.[10] Henry Thoreau found seaweed being used to grow tomatoes at Marshfield. At South Dartmouth, beside Vineyard Sound, farmers reported using every variety of marine plant: eelgrass, rockweed, kelp. Some farmers spread eelgrass as top dressing on grass, but since it soon disappeared, the practice was thought wasteful. In Rhode Island eelgrass went into hog pens for litter and came out part of good compost.

Where slaughterhouses, tanners, and curriers were found, their waste and offal made a valuable manure for farmers nearby. Nightsoil (human excrement) from the large towns, mixed one part to four with loam or sand, had "extraordinary efficacy" on meadow land. At Hamden, Connecticut, in 1856 a factory began to press out fish oil and built up a fertilizer market among farmers for the waste. Other such factories opened in Rhode Island and near Boston. Peat dug from bogs in summer was hauled in winter by the hundreds of loads, spread directly on land to be cropped, or deposited in barnyards to be trampled into mud, which would be spread later. In his journal Thoreau describes this process.[11]

Everyone recognized the virtues of wood ashes, even after much of the potash had been leached from them, and plaster of paris had come into vogue well before 1830. A farmer in Poultney, Vermont, with a pailful in his hand, wrote his name in big letters with plaster on a piece of grassland, and let the results speak to his neighbors. By 1830 Boston received its first experimental Peruvian guano (sea bird droppings) which, placed under cornhills, was reported to do wonders. Thirty years later, three shiploads came into New London and a little began to be imported to Maine. Clarence Day states that in 1857 a Portland dealer advertised 150 tons.

Among the better-informed farmers, interest in chemical fertilizers grew. In 1848 the *Boston Cultivator* reported English experiments with phosphoric acid, lime, and potash, and in 1850 there were German trials of nitrate of soda and sulphate of ammonia. In the same year mixed fertilizer was produced at Baltimore, and Charles T. Jackson clearly outlined the properties of these and other sources of fertility before the Plymouth County Agricultural Association. A Berkshire farmer inquired of the *Cultivator* about poudrette (a dried product of human excrement). The important stimulus that commercial fertilizers were to offer New England crops was, however, still ahead.

Meanwhile, except near good markets, ordinary farmers often attempted to work too much land and, as one visitor after another pointed out, without sufficient labor or manure. On poor soils in long-settled areas plenty of fields—and farms—were by this time worn out. Visitors, however, continued to praise and to compare favorably with England the "delightful" farms and villages they met with near Hartford, in the Farmington Valley, about Springfield, and around Boston.[12]

Yet even in parts of the Connecticut Valley, said English visitor James F. W. Johnston in 1850, "rudeness still prevails and infantile husbandry almost everywhere—swamps undrained, thickets uncleared . . . wet land swarming with rushes." On long cleared fields in Maine, noted New York agricultural writer

Sylvester Judd, "might be seen the Danthonia, that wretched poverty-grass so common in the county of Hampshire." "With all our boasting in this country," he concluded, "we understand exhausting land much better than improving it, and in most of the states the exhausters are much more numerous than the improvers," an observation all too true in much of New England as well as the rest of the nation.[13] Over such neglected lands spread charlock, daisies, thistles, and others of a continually increasing list of weeds arrived from abroad.

Wallingford Plain, a light soil in Connecticut, had been called not worth cultivation back in 1819. Carolina Plain, in the southern Merrimack Valley, was depleted to the point that ten bushels of rye to the acre every third year was "its total production" (but the grain was said to be superior). Despite talk of "the golden hoof" (soil enrichment from sheep manure), the continued sale of wool and meat from New England's enormous population of sheep, a practice that had reached its peak in Vermont, could not fail to deplete the soil of pastures over wide areas of the hill country. Now the production of market milk and butter was systematically beginning a similar process on farms within reach of the railways, though its results would be slowed by the purchase of western grain as a feed supplement. Clearly, the arrival of chemical fertilizers was to be welcomed! Meanwhile, it was good practice, when grass ran out, to plow, and plant corn. Dressing the land with what manure was available, the second year's crop was potatoes. Then the land was laid down again to hay, with oats, barley, or rye as a nurse crop.[14]

The unprecedented advances in transportation, education, manufacturing and available markets, added to the populating of the West, continued to give New England life and farming in particular a tremendous shakeup, economically and socially.

In a farming town only one son, obviously, could take over the ancestral homestead. A second or third son would need considerable capital in order to buy and stock a local farm, assuming that he could find a good one for sale. On the other hand, a job in a factory, store, or school, or on a vessel, called for little or no investment. Wages or a share in trading or fishing profits offered a chance to accumulate money. This prospect appealed to many, for the farm, with its necessities and its variety of tasks, bred young people of industry and resourcefulness. Thousands of such eager youngsters, from the hill towns in particular, set out for the manufacturing and commercial centers of New England and New York. From a New Hampshire farm went Henry Wilson, to become a shoe manufacturer in Natick, Massachusetts, and to go on to be Vice President of the United States; Marshall P. Wilder left New Ipswich, New Hampshire, to build a leading Boston mercantile business and continue his agricultural bent as a farmer and president of the Massachusetts Horticultural Society; Jonas Chickering set forth from the same state to make famous pianos.

The West too was alluring.[15] It promised opportunity to take up a farm, on rich soil perhaps, with only a modest outlay; or to use education, skill, and ingenuity in trades and professions. So other thousands of farm boys—and girls—headed west to seek their fortunes. From a Vermont town John Deere set forth to Illinois to manufacture there steel plows to break the prairies. A Vermont farm boy, Stephen A. Douglas, went west to become Senator from Illinois and candidate for President; Marshall Field, to found Chicago's greatest mercantile house; and Gustavus Swift, from Cape Cod, to build a meat business in Chicago which, like Field's, still prospers. Farm-bred boys founded enduring colleges, churches, and institutions in Ohio, Michigan, and other new states. In 1830 Tocqueville was told that thirty-six of the nation's congressmen had been born in Connecticut. These sons were New England's most valuable farm export.

Girls, no longer tied to the spinning wheel, went by the hundreds into the new mills of Lowell and Manchester; in 1846, in Lowell, there were 1,200 Vermont girls at work. They and their "Lowell Offering" were the wonder of foreign visitors. Some taught school in the new states; some, like Mary Lyon, Lucy Stone, and Clara Barton, prepared for great public achievements and national and international fame.

By 1850 half of Vermont's natives were said to have removed. Hill towns lost not solely from outward emigration but by removal to valley towns with better soil, industries, and railroad service. There new villages grew up and old ones enlarged. Athens, Vermont, dropped from 507 in 1820 to 309 in 1850. Russell, in western Massachusetts, with 1,000 in 1840, counted only 532 a decade later; adjoining Montgomery decreased from 656 to 401. Foster, Rhode Island, dropped from 2,900 in 1820 to 1,935 in 1860. In those same years, however, railroad and mill towns doubled.

Yet it would be far from the truth to conclude, as some writers have done, that those who set forth were necessarily the ablest or most ambitious and that agriculture suffered. Nearly all really good farms remained occupied, and not infrequently in succeeding decades continued to breed superior men and women. Agricultural production in New England increased rather than decreased. Moreover, if a so-called farm had been treated actually as a mine, its timber and its natural fertility exhausted, or if it should never have been farmed at all, no private or public end was served by trying to exist there. Another farm was waiting to be exploited in the West, or the family members could better themselves by changing occupation while staying close by. Lewis D. Stilwell has acutely pointed out that "the bulk of the emigrants [from Vermont] were simply surplus . . ." In general this was true in every new England state. Swarms left the home hive regularly; yet a healthy nucleus remained, to swarm again and again.

37

Yankee Inventors

THE DECADES between the War of 1812 and the Civil War were years of amazing invention and improvement in farm tools. Of greatest import after the cotton gin was the development of the steel, self-scouring plow. The iron plow first in use was not wholly satisfactory, even with Jethro Wood's redesign and casting it in sections. A Hanover, Massachusetts, firm, Prouty & Mears, made a thousand iron plows a year that were reputed effective, and William Hussey of North Berwick, Maine, about 1825, began a line of Hussey plows that for years had a high local reputation. John Lane about 1833 put one together from sections of a steel saw. Then, four years later, John Deere, an emigrant to Illinois from Derby, Vermont (as noted), and a skilled blacksmith, succeeded in joining portions of discarded steel circular saw blades which he had painstakingly heated, bent, and bent again until the share automatically scoured away the sticky prairie earth; and the modern plow was born.[1]

Back in New England, Joel Nourse of Worcester offered five sizes of regular plows besides a swivel or side-hill plow and a cultivator. About 1842 he brought out his Eagle plow, its mouldboard skillfully shaped both to stand rough ground and gravelly fields and to turn tough sward. Nourse's Eagle not only remained for generations the local standard, but became an item of export. From Vermont, Cyrus Warren's and Frederick Holbrook's side-hill swivel plows proved a boon for hill farmers, though swivels had long been in use in England. Holbrook also invented a subsoil plow.[2]

By 1855 numerous New England foundries were manufacturing plows. Massachusetts was the core, in particular Worcester, which made Nourse's Eagle and was called the largest center for the manufacture of agricultural implements in the United States. The state had in 1830 turned out perhaps a few thousand plows (1,000 in Worcester that year); in 1845, 61,000. By 1855 its output, from 22 foundries, was 152,686. Of that year's production, worth over $700,000, one fifth stayed in the state and the rest were sold elsewhere, some in England.[3]

Other large tools made their way into use. For hauling manure and the omnipresent field stone, the dumpcart, which had become more common by the middle of the century, was a boon. A potato digger was tried out in 1833. Jesse Buel's *Farmer's Companion* in 1839 mentions the roller and drill-harrow as new implements. Buel thought that because of improved implements a farm could be run at half the expense of forty years earlier. George Page invented a revolving tillage tool in 1847, foretelling the disc harrow. The horse cultivator had begun to take over the job, formerly done by the plow, of eliminating the weeds between corn rows. It proved valuable also for other row crops. Charles W. Billings of South Deerfield invented a corn planter. Seed sowers were tried out for small seeds. In the barn, corn shellers, seed winnowing machines, and straw cutters began to come in. Nathaniel Hawthorne describes a hay chopper he saw about 1841; in 1855 Boston firms sold 11,900 hay cutters in that one year. Rhode Islanders patented a corn husker, grain drills, and haying machines.

Horse-drawn wooden rakes of various simple types locally invented, some in New England, had come into gradual use to handle the universal hay crop in the field. The first good riding rake was the idea of a Maine man, Calvin Delano, who patented it in 1849.[4] Mowers and reapers of various sorts began to appear. Nantucket-bred Obed Hussey had patented his reaper in 1833. The Walter A. Wood firm sold 500 such machines in 1853.

Hussey had worked out also the principle of the cutter bar which was to be used in the horse-drawn mower, and in Maine

28. *(a) Discharging and revolving horse rake; (b) Nourse's famous Eagle plow.* Sources: *(a) J. R. Newell,* Catalogue *(1836); (b) Russell, Nourse, and Mason,* Catalogue *(1846).*

R. T. Osgood conceived an even better arrangement, which the driver could raise and lower. Numerous other inventors were at work on mowers. Yet in 1847 it was said that in Norfolk County, south of Boston, not one farmer in ten used a mechanical mower. They were often crudely designed, always costly. From 1859 on, however, the close-cutting Wood mowing machine proved a thoroughly practical implement to help New England farmers through the war years.[5] The hay-tedder was scarcely known until the Massachusetts Society for Promoting Agriculture imported two English machines in 1858.

For grain, the Pitts brothers, Hiram and John, of Winthrop, Maine, concocted a combined thresher and separator. Though expensive, it would thresh 300 bushels a day, a wonderful advance over the flail.[6] In the hands of western farmers this combine, with McCormick's reaper, was to prove a boon on wide prairie landscapes. At the same time it made the growing of small grain in New England uneconomical except for local use. Worcester's Richardson Manufacturing Company claimed to be the oldest maker of the manure spreader, another machine destined for wide acceptance.

Improvement of small tools made great strides. They became more effective and in most cases lighter than any previously known. The Collins weighted axe, already mentioned; the Ames steel shovel and spade from North Easton, Massachusetts (2,400 made daily in 1857, one third of all shovels manufactured in the country); a cast steel garden hoe invented by C. Bulkeley of Colchester, Connecticut, and Buxton's onion hoe; Charles Goodyear's spring steel pitchfork, patented 1831; the Wyman Brothers' cast steel forks for horse manure—all were great improvements. From a small beginning in 1835, making steel pitchforks became for a century the big industry of the little village of Wallingford, Vermont, which exported large shipments to the Middle Atlantic states and England. In no more than a half century the efficiency of hand tools was doubled.

A gracefully curved ash snaith (or handle) for the scythe, patented in 1828, was the invention of Silas Lamson of Springfield, Vermont. A factory near Shelburne Falls, Massachusetts, came to put out 75,000 snaiths a year. Scythe factories dotted

CRANBERRY RAKE.

29. *(a) Grant's grain cradle (note the scythe at the lower edge); (b) grapevine grain cradle; (c) scythe snaith or handle (curved steel blade attached at right end); (d) cranberry rake, superseding hand picking. Sources: Newell,* Catalogue *(1836); Allen,* Catalogue *(1853).*

New England: one large producer in Litchfield, Connecticut; another at Smithfield, Rhode Island; a third at West Fitchburg, Massachusetts. In 1849 R. B. Dunn's factory at North Wayne, Maine, claiming to be the largest in the world, turned out 12,000 dozen annually.[7]

Grain cradles were slow in arriving in New England. A traveler records the cradling of oats at Leicester in central Massachusetts in 1820, but use of the cradle did not become general before 1840, and in a few years the harvester superseded it. A writer in the *Boston Cultivator* of August 26, 1848, advocated the use of wire for fences. "They will yet supersede all others," he correctly prophesied, for a quarter century later Joseph F. Glidden, farm hand and schoolteacher transplanted to the West from Charlestown, New Hampshire, patented barbed wire.

An especially valuable invention was the stone crusher worked out in 1852 by farm-born Eli Whitney Blake of Westborough, Massachusetts, nephew of the inventor of the cotton gin. It supplied not only the material for the hard surfaced roads so badly needed, but a market for the loose fieldstone with which the area's farms were all too well provided.

Other useful additions to farm equipment were the air-tight Mason fruit jar and a jar with a spring-fastened glass top patented by W. W. Lyman of Meriden, Connecticut (1858); the movable frame beehive (1852) designed by Lorenzo L. Langstreth of Pennsylvania, "father of modern beekeeping," who lived for a time in Massachusetts; the Eddy ice chest (1840's) and the ice cream freezer (1854); the hand-pushed wheelbarrow (1828); the platform scale, patented 1831 by Thaddeus Fairbanks of St. Johnsbury, Vermont; the steel square, credited to Silas Harris of Shaftsbury in that state; the safety fuse for blasting, conceived by Ensign Bickford of Granby, Connecticut, in 1836. Not to be forgotten for his influence on the household, Elias Howe, a clever farm-born mechanic, in 1846 patented his sewing machine.

Massachusetts could report in 1855 that five Boston agricultural warehouses sold 36,950 plows, 5,815 cultivators, 93,000 shovels, 60,000 hoes, 60,000 forks, 138,600 rakes, 33,600 scythes, 12,000 axes, 6,750 wheelbarrows, 11,900 haycutters, 12,165 corn shellers, 5,100 grain cradles, and 1,850 horse rakes: evidence of a

*30. A midcentury invention: Hussey's reaping and mowing machine. Allen,
Catalogue (1853).*

healthy desire for improved tools on the part of New England
farmers.[8]

Though these advances sound and are impressive, many a
small farmer lacked cash to buy the new implements; or,
recalling the depressions of the 1840's and 1857, thought it less
practical to spend money for them than to hang onto his savings
and deposit them in his trustworthy local savings bank. But the
Civil War just ahead was to cause swift changes in attitudes
toward machinery and other aspects of farming.

Toward the middle of the century the heavier-type soils
became more highly valued. Henry Thoreau in 1853 watched
one of his Concord neighbors clearing and ditching a piece of
level, naturally rich, but boggy land near Walden Pond. Instead
of the sharp comments he often made on local farming methods,
he voiced wondering approval.[9] Earlier generations, with inferior
tools, had preferred or been obliged to work chiefly the more
friable uplands. Now, with much upland robbed of its fertility
and baking in summer droughts, farmers turned to burning,
scraping, and draining peat bogs, to transform them into

31. Another midcentury invention: Wood's Reaper and Mower. Walter A. Wood Co., Catalogue *(1868)*.

haylands to grow food for dairy cattle. Near markets, the natural moisture and fertility of such land were assets for vegetable crops as well.

America's first drain tiles were made in New York in 1848, but their use spread slowly. In New England open ditches served for a long time. Then came drains laid up out of the abundant field stone. After the excavation had been dug and the side wall stones set in place, flat stones placed above these crosswise formed the roof. Then, to prevent the soil from silting in, brush was laid on above the stone conduit. The long ditch was refilled with earth and the field plowed. The cost of such drains was chiefly in spare-time labor. They lasted years, and they were still in use at the beginning of the twentieth century.

Other improvements came gradually. Every year more stone wall got laboriously built around pastures and feed lots. The farmer did it in slack time, or changed work with some neighbor to get his help, or hired a wall-builder. The builders would ordinarily lay up four rods a day, four feet high, at costs that varied from 16 to 75 cents a rod.[10] The stone might come from the very fields that the wall was to surround, or for stone-free marshland be hauled thither on a drag or stone boat in winter. Conversely, a never-ending late fall or early spring job was to pick stones off the planting land and spread them in low corners. With a few inches of swamp mud added on top, the area could then become excellent drought-proof mowing or pasture. For big boulders in the plowland, the farmer dug a hole and encircled the boulder with a chain; the oxen tugged, and the stone dropped in. The chain was released, the oxen then dragged in soil above, and all was ready for cultivation.

38

The Typical Farmer

To ATTEMPT an appraisal of the economic condition of the typical New England farm or farmer of this period would be bootless. Differences continued too marked. Read Horace Greeley on his boyhood among the poor, Scotch-Irish small farmers of southern New Hampshire, or the lugubrious description in an 1858 *Atlantic Monthly* of "Farming Life in New England" by "Timothy Titcomb" (Joshua G. Holland), who had grown up in Belchertown, Massachusetts; or listen to H. W. Collingwood, editor of the *Rural New Yorker*, on scratching a living as a boy on three stony acres in Bristol County, Massachusetts. The conclusion is hard to resist that the farmer's life and the farm home alike were "unloved" and "unlovable" as Holland maintains—a round of unenlightened drudgery.[1] Scientific farming had scarcely been thought of, as a southern New Hampshire visitor commented in 1852.

Against these set John Greenleaf Whittier's "Snowbound"; Cyrus Hamlin's description of how he and his brother took over on the Maine farm after his father's untimely death; Clara Barton's memoir of her youth on a hill farm in North Oxford, Massachusetts; Senator George F. Hoar's tribute to the Farrar household in Lincoln, where as a young man he spent a memorable year, or the stories for boys of Maine life by Elijah

Kellogg. From these one might conclude that farm life was not merely bearable but close to ideal.[2]

The plodding, niggardly type of farming of the first group was likely to result from poor soil and the difficult financial circumstances that many small farmers faced. Henry Thoreau compared such a farmer to a lichen that somehow sustains itself from a rock "and grows and thrives and cracks it and makes a vegetable mould" in which later plants find sustenance. One such in Connecticut, "Stingy Old Bacon" of Colchester, in 1854 left the town of Norwich $160,000 to found its free academy.[3]

On the other hand, one of New England's many town historians portrays a type of farmer that was at least as common. Despite the many boys who have gone into other callings, he says, enough sons, "all agricultural men," have succeeded their fathers to carry on the local farms generation after generation with "all the means for human enjoyment that humanity ought to crave." One of Colman's reports describes the agricultural population of an entire western Massachusetts county as comfortable, on the whole prosperous, and laying up money.[4]

Lucy Stone's are among the many recollections of farm-born women of this period. Her testimony, already quoted, was that money might be scarce on Coy's Hill, West Brookfield, but there was always plenty to eat, of many kinds and much of it delicious. She added: "We all worked hard, but we all worked together, and we had the feeling that everything was ours—the calves, the stock, the butter and cheese." [5] Secretary Stephen L. Goodale of Maine's Board of Agriculture, Editor Isaac Hill of New Hampshire's *Farmers Monthly Visitor*, and other contemporary writers offer similar assessments of the general thrift and comfort to be found in New England in the middle of the nineteenth century. We can only conclude that all these observers, whether they looked through dark or rosy glasses, told the truth, as they saw it, witnessing to the diversity that characterized farm life in various circumstances among the six states.

One important factor in the financial well-being of many farm families was supplementary income, particularly that from household industry. Shoemaking and the braiding of hats were common sources of cash in this period. Shoe manufacturers, some

ICE CUTTING AT SPY POND, WEST CAMBRIDGE, MASS.

32. Ice to cool summer's produce. Spy Pond, Arlington, Mass. Ballou's Pictorial Drawing Room Companion *(1854)*.

of them farmers themselves, furnished the stock. The farm people took out the materials, or a traveling agent distributed them through the countryside. There the farmer and his sons, in winter, rainy days, and any other available time, pegged and soled the boots or shoes on lapstones. The women cut and bound the uppers for women's shoes. The product was then returned to the factory for finishing and sale, or export. Boston was the boot and shoe market for the whole country and the West Indies. The centers of shoe manufacture were Lynn, Haverhill, Abington, Brookfield, Grafton, and Natick, and for shoemaking tools, Brockton. From these centers the work was spread all through eastern and central Massachusetts and southern New Hampshire.[6]

The extent and size of this rural occupation is amazing. In 1837 the towns of Holliston, Natick, and East Bridgewater, Massachusetts, each turned out a quarter-million pairs of boots and shoes; Grafton and Danvers over 600,000 each; and North

Brookfield almost as many. By 1860 North Brookfield, in western Worcester County, was making a million pairs yearly. In the little town of Wenham, in Essex County near Cape Ann, the work was spread among 226 persons. All these places, with numerous others of smaller production, were agricultural towns. Their product was only a modest proportion of the 33 million pairs of shoes and almost 12 million of boots that Massachusetts turned out in 1855; but it was a great help to farm income.[7]

One boy, brought up on a little stony place, put it this way later: "We were happy and care-free. What was our money crop? It was labor . . . Once a week they brought to the farm a case of uppers and a case of soles. We pegged them together with wooden pegs and they took them away for sale . . ." "Did not the world also lose something when those little shoe shops were nailed up?" he wondered as he looked back later, after the advent of complicated machinery made shoes a factory product.[8]

In similar fashion the hat manufacturer furnished materials, women and children braided the straw and sewed the hats and bonnets together at home, and the dealer finished them and sold the product wherever New England ships traded. Two hundred-fifty hats are said to have been a winter's work. At first all summer hats were of straw or grasses and the better quality had competition from imports. Then a New Hampshire dealer tried making some from poplar strips. Soon in place of these he and others were importing palm leaves from the West Indies for stock, and shipping hats that farm folks made from them as far as South America. In 1831 Massachusetts alone made two million, half in agricultural Worcester County. Petersham, for example, turned out 130,525 palm-leaf hats in 1836. The work spread to Connecticut and over much of rural New England.[9]

Hop-picking, where hops were grown, and broom-making elsewhere, offered piece work for young women and children with swift fingers. The ice business fitted in beautifully to provide winter occupation for farmers and farm laborers near Massachusetts ponds and later in Maine. Wenham, Massachusetts, cut 25,000 tons worth $40,000 in one winter of the 1850's.

In Vermont, New Hampshire, inland Massachusetts, and much of Maine it was wood-working; in Connecticut, metal products; in Rhode Island, parts for textile manufacture. All these occupations were largely carried on either in farm shops or by part-time farmers in mills at the hundreds of little water powers that came to border every ten-foot fall on New England's innumerable streams. Even the wooden bowls, in which placer miners washed California's gold, came from a tiny Berkshire Hills farming town. Candia, New Hampshire, farmers spent the winter making barrels to hold New England's mackerel catch and West Indies molasses.[10] Sharon and Watertown, Connecticut, turned out mouse traps by the thousands.

Such income bolstered many a farm's well-being. Later, these occupations were to become much more industrialized, as steam power, machinery, and the Civil War centralized manufacturing in larger places. But for the middle 1800's they were a potent help in meeting taxes, sending youngsters to academy and college, building accounts in local savings banks, paying off mortgages, and obtaining the little comforts that helped to make country life satisfying. Whether income came from field and livestock, household industry, or both, it was all hard work and hard work for all—men, women, and children—who had a hand in it.

Indenture or apprenticeship on farms had been quietly dropped in the century's early decades. As factories paying cash wages grew common, small farms had to rely largely on the assistance of children, on temporary help for haying and similar periods of stress, and on changing work with neighbors; older sons had gone where prospects were better.

The 1840's, with the tidal influx that resulted from Ireland's famine years, brought a new source of labor, a tremendous surge of immigrants. Cotton and woolen factories, tanneries, railroads, and similar employers of unskilled labor found the newcomers willing, adaptable, and ready to work for low wages, although "their experience with the impoverishing potato-patch seems to have given them a distaste for agriculture," a visiting Britisher commented.[11] One immediate effect was to divert the streams of local farm-raised boys and girls away from the large factories, and send more of them to skilled trades, teaching, and commerce, where wages or opportunities appeared greater.

Owners of gentlemen's estates, ready to spend money to develop them with select fruits, flowers, and landscaping, hired some of the newcomers. Thoreau came on one 350-acre estate at Marshfield on the South Shore that employed 15 or 16 laborers at $10.00 a month. This was average pay for these decades except in haying or harvest, when labor might demand as much as $1.25 a day. (Eggs in 1833 were 10 cents a dozen, beef and lamb 3 to 4 cents a pound.) By contrast a single man might be glad to work in midwinter solely for his board. Market gardeners, needing teamsters all year and in summer much extra labor, also employed immigrants, and frequently provided housing for them. In the Connecticut Valley some Canadian French came in, attracted to the broom-making towns. In general, however, the effects on the farms of the wave of immigration were likely to be indirect. The incoming hordes stuck chiefly to the cities, mill towns, and railroad points.[12]

In the midst of the bewildering cross-currents of these decades and despite increasing specialization in cash crops, the "general farm" remained characteristic of much of New England agriculture. Its three chief supports, corn, hay, and livestock, were all likely to be in modest proportion. Nevertheless, the pulls of economics continually worked to alter this pattern. In Vermont, New Hampshire, interior Maine, and western Massachusetts and Connecticut, as has been shown, sheep took over for several decades. Near populated centers and along railroads, dairying came to lead; within a dozen miles of the large ports such as Boston, Portland, Providence, and New Haven, market gardening, fruit growing, and retail milk farms flourished; while the Connecticut Valley, still growing broomcorn and feeding fat stock for market, grew ever more interested in tobacco. Both the general farm and individual trends, such as those outlined in the preceding chapter, as well as others less well known all deserve far more attention from historians than they have commonly received.

One of Henry Colman's reports, describing the agriculture of Essex County, about 1838, divides farms into three sorts. One is where farming is merely an accompaniment to a trade, business, or profession. The second is where a bare living is sought, and the family is "Content with the ordinary supplies and comforts of a farm without any view to improvement or gain." These two, he says, include most Essex farmers, "and their situation is almost universally comfortable and independent." "The third is where agriculture is pursued like any other business in the community, with a proper outlay of capital and labor, and with a main view to pecuniary advantage." This type he rightly expected to show increase in the years ahead.[13]

Among those numbered in both the first and the third groupings were the well-to-do men, often engaged in professions or business, who became fascinated with raising purebred stock, with improving fruits and ornamentals, or with other aspects of "high" farming. They had money, could hire labor for their experiments, and had leisure to attend meetings where new methods were advocated. Often they were leaders in the county agricultural societies that in this era held fall exhibitions all over New England; or members of the Massachusetts Society for Promoting Agriculture, or the State Boards of Agriculture in the various states. Critical as some were of customary farm methods, practical farmers frequently regarded their efforts skeptically, and not infrequently with good reason. Nevertheless their influence—especially in stock breeding and horticulture and in trying new crops, machinery, and methods—was in the long run of great benefit to all farmers.

Not infrequently they displayed more concern than did working farmers at the comparatively low esteem in which agriculture was said to be held even by farmers themselves, as compared to mercantile pursuits and the professions. They also worried about the great number of farm boys who left for other fields. This appears especially in the writings of ministers, some of them active and competent farmers in their own right. Rev. Ralph Waldo Emerson, however, was not among those who felt disturbed by either worry. Though careful not to paint the farmer in rose color, calling him "a slow narrow man," he concluded "he nevertheless had desirable stability, permanence." [14]

Emerson's good friend Bronson Alcott, the farm boy from Connecticut, who lectured, kept school, and wrote for publication, had no false pride. When money was short, he did not hesitate to work in his Concord neighbors' woodlots with his axe.[15]

It is at least open to doubt whether farmers as a whole felt a sense of social or political inferiority. Certainly the countryman cited by Van Wyck Brooks, who corrected Harvard's Charles Eliot Norton on a literary allusion to the French philosophical writer Montesquieu, was not thus encumbered! [16] Even in towns that became industrial, farmers, from their personal qualities, were likely then, and for generations to come, to continue to manage the public business long after they had become only a minority of the citizenry.

One evidence of the comfortable material condition of the farm people is the almost unanimous admiration of foreign observers for the white "cottages" with green blinds that they found along all the roads, and for the older saltbox homesteads the nineteenth century had inherited. "The villages of New England are proverbial for their neatness," wrote James Stuart in 1833. Patrick Shirreff, in his rival travelogue of the same year, failed to find the dooryard shrubs that Stuart remarked on, yet on his way east from Northampton he, too, exclaims over the white wood houses and says that he found "everything wearing the appearance of cleanliness, order, and comfort." In the dairy region of Brooklyn in eastern Connecticut, Edward Abdy was reminded of the snug English farmhouses at home.[17]

Harriet Martineau in her turn fell captive especially to what was apparently a working farm by the sea near Manchester, Massachusetts, "whose situation would make an envious person miserable," she said. The house, sheltered by a wooded hill, with fertile fields and wide pastures, "enjoys a glorious view of the bay." Of the farm woman and her children who were taking in a fine crop of apples she remarked: "We could only hope that they were sensible of their privilege of living in such a place." [18]

The Yankee eyes of Nathaniel Hawthorne on his way from Salem to the Brighton cattle fair in 1841 "Saw no absolutely mean or poor looking abodes. They were warm and comfortable farmhouses." [19] Usually a great elm or several maples shaded the south side and the yard; and often there were books within.

ARRANGEMENT OF FARMYARDS AND BUILDINGS
THE WILLIS K DANIELS FARM [JOSEPH FREEMAN~A·D·1800]
CORNISH N·H·

SCALE:

PACED MEASUREMENTS
ARTHUR A. SHURTLEFF
JUNE + SEPT~1917

COWS

BEE HIVES

FARM YARD

BARS

GATE

GARDEN

COW YARD

FARM YARD

DOOR YARD

GATE

GATE

11

GATE

GATE

T O W N   H I G H W A Y

1 – FIRST HOUSE ~ BUILT ABOUT 1800.
2 – NEW HOUSE ~ 1855
3 – MILKROOM ~ HONEY STORAGE~
4 – WOOD SHED
5 – CORN HOUSE, FEED, WOOD
6 – CARRIAGE HOUSE ~ BUILT 1850~
7 – WAGONS UNDER
8 – "LONG BARN" COWS~HORSES ~1805~
9 – HEN HOUSE~AFTERWARDS CARRIAGE SHED
10 – WAGON SHED ~ PASSAGEWAY
11 – SHEEP BARN~TOBACCO LOFT ~1805
12 – FIXED GRINDSTONES — 13 – HEN HOUSE
14 – SHED ~ 15 – SUGAR HOUSE + SOAP BOILING~1805~
16 – BEE HIVES, FRAMES, SUPERS, WAX, ETC.
17 – BRICK SMOKE HOUSE~STORAGE FOR WOOD ASHES~
18 – CLOTHES LINES~19 SUN DIAL~20~VEGETABLES~

33. A New Hampshire homestead arranged for efficiency, convenience, and comfort, winter and summer. Landscape Architecture *(1917).*

Wherever in Vermont, New Hampshire, or other hill country, springs bubbled from side hills, bored logs or bored soapstone were likely to bring water by gravity to both house and stock. If an open well served instead, it would have both bucket and sweep, or chain and sprocket; and perhaps supply an indoor iron pump. The washing was likely to be done in wood tubs on a bench outside.

To the original dwelling an ell might have been added to house the family of the son who would eventually take over. A woodshed connecting house and barn kept dry fuel handy and protected the yard in winter. Travelers from outside were quick to note that in New England it was usually the dwelling that received prime attention. The Scottish Robert Russell, who did not think highly of New England soil and agriculture, was glad to see even in the small farmhouses among the White Mountains so many signs of comfort.

Like dwellings, barns and outbuildings were greatly improved. Charles Russell told a Springfield audience in 1850: "The barn of today . . . is quite another affair from that of years ago. It assumes that cattle have breath to stifle, limbs to shiver, and nerves to feel, as well as men." [20] As dairying expanded, farmers added "linters" (lean-tos) to their barns to hold more cows, enlarged their haylofts, and often clapboarded the whole. In northern New England, in place of white lead barns and sometimes houses might get a coat of red ochre mixed with buttermilk or whey. This seldom needed renewal. A great elm by the barn might offer noonday shade for the oxen.

Appearances on well-traveled roads and in prosperous communities are often deceptive, however. Elsewhere, in houses ill-heated, ill-ventilated, and with little sanitation, many a farm family suffered from consumption, diarrhea or dysentery, diphtheria, or meningitis. Women and children often had to work excessively and many died young. In the north country up to the middle of the century some farm families lived in log houses and carried from a distance every gallon of water used. Many found life very hard, and existence drab.[21]

It was not alone strictly agricultural influences, climatic discouragements such as winter's severity or summer droughts, or competition from the West that affected farm prosperity. To a considerable extent the ups and downs of the general economy influenced farming also.

The panic of 1837 caused losses to people who had speculated in land. After better times came in the 1840's, another depression in the next decade made things difficult again. However, the effects of bankers' panics on farms were not always immediate or widespread, and they were so interwoven with other influences of the time as often in retrospect to be difficult to measure. In 1831 half the farms in one of Connecticut's most fertile towns were reported mortgaged; yet by 1855 a Ridgefield historian knew of no more than four such mortgages in his whole town. Maine agricultural historian Clarence Day estimates that in 1849, with potato blight, Maine farmers reached their lowest point; yet in Vermont, the coming of railroads about the same time was estimated to have increased the value of real estate by 31 million in a decade. The historian of Lancaster in northern New Hampshire calls the 1850–60 decade prosperous, with prices of farm produce high. Retail prices in Vermont declined almost continuously in the quarter-century preceding 1850. Yet a pound of maple sugar, equal in price to only half a pound of cane sugar in 1820, was of even value in 1850. In Dedham, Massachusetts, in 1837 a farmer could sell a load of wood for the price of a barrel of flour, a purchase that formerly would have represented for him several days of hard labor or a number of cords of wood.

Thus no clear pattern emerges. Despite light thrown on the period by Paul W. Gates and a few other scholars, much more study than has been possible within the limits of this discussion is needed for a proper evaluation of the interplay of economics with farming, and of agriculture with the various other public aspects of the economy of this period.

Looking back on these decades preceding the Civil War, it is possible to sense more clearly than could the New England country people who lived through it the remarkable fermentation of the time. Turnpikes and canals, hailed as great advances, in a few years were superseded by the network of railroads that left few farms more than a half day's drive from a station: great factory towns arose that opened new occupations and financial opportunities to country people, young women especially. The heaviest household burdens of spinning and weaving began to lift, and in their place appeared the chance at home for young and old to earn welcome cash income by piece work on shoes, brooms, hats, and wood products.

In farm homes and country towns education gained value. Social libraries and lyceums multiplied, daily and weekly papers and magazines circulated, more boys and girls studied in academy and college. Young people, farm trained, found welcome in other occupations. Despite such losses, the home farm, too, often prospered.

Agriculture was becoming less an all-inclusive calling than a diversity of occupations. Long-wooled sheep and Morgan horses took over the hill country. Farms near railways sent to market butter and cheese from improving dairy cows. For the Connecticut Valley fat cattle, broomcorn, and tobacco were income sources. Up country, potatoes went into starch, or nearer the sea into export. Around the large cities milk production, market gardening, poultry raising, and fruit growing clustered. A silk fever rose, flourished, vanished.

Mechanical ingenuity, born on farms and nurtured by necessity, burst forth in a remarkable list of tool inventions: plows, harrows, mowers, threshers, seeders, cultivators, a stone crusher, scales, corn shellers, axes, forks, ice tools; and for the household the sewing machine, ice chest, preserve jar, and ice cream freezer. Such aids, gradually acquired, made for comfort and content in the household; while outside, buildings for family, stock, and crops improved.

Above the farm country as in the rest of New England, however, gathered the shadow of national separation and tragedy. Some farms were becoming stations for the underground railway forwarding slaves to Canada. Other farm people while condemning slavery sought to keep the nation one and indivisible. The fierce storm of national division was about to beat upon all alike.

VI. WAR AND READJUSTMENT,

1861 AND AFTER

39

For Better and Worse

AGRICULTURALLY SPEAKING, the Civil War years 1861–65 were notable for trends rather than for changes in crops. Nor, except for a few products, were there such increases in prosperity or such profits as those in the world of manufacturing and commerce.

From the point of view of rural well-being the most striking aspect of the war was the departure of the finest young men of the villages, many of them called in the haying season. A disheartening number were never to return. Vermont saw 34,328 march off, one in nine of its whole population; New Hampshire, one in ten. Of Vermont's youth, 5,128 died in service; of Maine's 73,000, 7,322 were lost.[1] Jaffrey, in New Hampshire's green pasture area, sent 151: of these, 28 died, or 18.5 percent. Goshen, Connecticut, saw 146 go: 29, almost one in five, never came back. From Amherst, Massachusetts, 93 out of 345, about 27 percent, are said to have died of wounds or disease. These farm communities were typical of New England, though not all towns lost so heavily.

For those who returned, ties to the old town had been loosened by absence and travel. The urge to make a new start elsewhere was compounded by inducements to go West. Through the Homestead Act, passed in 1862 and liberalized in 1864, Congress offered 160 acres of public land for a small payment to any settler who would occupy it for five years: but in the case of a soldier who had served two years, four fifths of the residence requirement was waived. Railroads, pushing ever westward and anxious for settlers on the immense acreages granted them by Congress, held out lures of their own.

All this hastened the decline of the less favorably situated New England country villages. A town such as Sutton, in west central New Hampshire, which counted 1,431 people in the 1860 census before the war began, by 1870 was down to 1,153, and a decade later to 880. Ashfield, Massachusetts, in the Berkshire foothills, lost 122 inhabitants, almost a tenth in the 1860–70 decade, and another tenth by 1880. In a town such as Sanbornton, upriver from Concord, New Hampshire, its historian claimed in 1876 that a dozen contiguous farms there had each a record of three fourths of a century in the same family. In such cases, however, it was chiefly the older folks who remained.[2] Statistics alone may conceal what was happening. Half of Maine's counties and half of New Hampshire's in the two decades 1860–80 made population gains, and in Massachusetts all mainland counties except two had increases. Vermont's total stayed about even, while every Rhode Island and Connecticut county added inhabitants. Usually, however, it was the mill villages, railroad towns, and suburban and commercial communities that increased, perhaps even added farms; while at the same time the isolated, frosty, hilly towns and infertile areas gradually contracted and lost population.

A favorable feature of the war for agriculture was final success in establishing agricultural education of college grade. One of Vermont's representatives, Justin S. Morrill, a merchant-farmer, had the distinction of getting Congress in 1862 to endow every loyal state with a generous land grant from the national domain for establishing a college to teach "such branches of learning as are related to agriculture and the mechanic arts." For decades New England had talked of such colleges. Now four states promptly acted. Before the year ended, New Hampshire had accepted the grant; Massachusetts followed in 1863, Vermont in 1864, and Maine in 1865. All the new institutions except Vermont's opened for enrollment before the decade was out. Attempting to graft agricultural education on existing institutions, Connecticut waited until 1881, Rhode Island until 1888, before establishing separate agricultural colleges.

Agricultural progress came during the war in a related area of governmental action. Back in 1839, on recommendation of Henry L. Ellsworth of Connecticut, Commissioner of Patents, Congress had appropriated $1,000 to secure promising seeds and cuttings from foreign sources for trial, and to conduct agricultural investigations and assemble statistics. The first national agricultural report, a document of 59 pages, was one result. The public approved, and appropriations and activities increased. The Patent Office's annual report proved so popular that by the end of a quarter-century its edition exceeded a quarter-million copies. In 1862 with the war on, Congress advanced the agricultural bureau to the status of a government department. Divisions of chemistry, statistics, and entomology were soon set up.

Another decisive intervention of government, this time by a state, took place in the animal husbandry field. Resolutely meeting what might have become a frightful disaster to the whole nation's cattle, Massachusetts provided a precedent that was to prove highly valuable later.

It came about in this way. Winthrop W. Chenery, a progressive Belmont, Massachusetts, farmer, had for some years been importing superior Holstein cattle. Suddenly, in May 1859, deadly pleuropneumonia was discovered in Worcester County and traced to one of Chenery's importations. The disease spread. Consternation ensued. The Massachusetts legislature, acting promptly, set up a cattle control board with broad powers to quarantine and destroy, and made reporting of livestock diseases compulsory. Maine and the other states to the north promptly followed, so that the disease did not spread at all in that direction. In fighting the disease Massachusetts alone spent $20,000 and slaughtered hundreds of animals. So thoroughly was the situation met that by 1867 the plague had been wiped out in New England.[3] Moreover, a pattern of government action had been drawn that was to bear fruit nationally in control of foot and mouth disease, which appeared in Massachusetts in 1870, and for the later battle against bovine tuberculosis and other animal infections.

During the war years food processing, a field closely related to agriculture, opened a new era. Back in 1851 Gail Borden, a Texan transplanted to Connecticut, had patented a method to condense milk to a fraction of its normal bulk; but the process failed to gain popularity. Now, with war on, the need to feed troops put a different face on the innovation, and a hungry military outlet for the new product opened. In 1863 Borden's Condensed Milk Company was organized at Winsted, Connecticut. For a time it offered a market for local milk, but its stay in Connecticut lasted only a few years, then Borden moved his operations to the Harlem Valley, New York, later licensing another plant at Livermore Falls in Maine.[4]

In still another type of food processing the war brought advances. To some extent meat and other foods had been preserved in tin cans ever since Nicolas Appert discovered the process in France during the Napoleonic wars. The British had tinned meat and vegetables for their army and navy in the century's early decades. William Underwood, a young Englishman who came to Boston in 1822, had used Appert's methods to pack fruits in bottles, later in cans. In Maine about 1840, Isaac Winslow had tried canning sweet corn and in 1853 secured a patent on his process. Soon he was selling canned corn to S. S. Pierce, the Boston grocer. In the war's first year, a Baltimore canner, using a method invented in England, cut the boiling time for canning to a half hour.

The needs of the Northern forces and the difficulties of supplying great armies under southern field conditions opened the opportunity for canned rations of all kinds. Clarence Day recounts some of the effects in Maine. Though the best of Maine's beef continued to go to Boston, local canneries furnished a welcome nearby market for ordinary beef and for other farm products. One of these, the Portland Packing Company, put up mutton, veal, and sausage as well as beef. (The company is still active at this writing.) Quantities of Maine sweet corn went to the troops. When the war ended, wild blueberries by the hundreds of bushels also began to go off in cans. By the time the troops had dispersed, canning was well established, and thus began an important local industry.[5] By 1873, 13 Maine firms were turning out 5,700,000 cans of corn alone, as well as other vegetables. By 1881 the pack had almost doubled. That year it took 12,500 acres of Maine farmland to supply the canneries with vegetables.

During the war, between the draft and bounties to recruits, farmers unable to find help were forced to get along with youngsters and old men, and to turn to the new machines. Already, from 1850 to 1860, the value of farm tools produced in the nation had grown over 65 percent, more than one fifth of them made in New England. With the war demand soared. By 1864 mowing-machine production in the North had increased two and a half times. On one Norfolk County farm in Massachusetts an 1863 report mentions in addition to the mower, a hayspreader, a horse pitchfork, and a wheel horserake. The fork would unload a ton of hay in only six minutes, and with no sweat! Other wartime innovations included the checkrow corn planter, and a combined wheeled onion seed-drill and cultivator introduced by S. E. Harrington of North Amherst, Massachusetts. Connecticut inventors developed other seeders and special onion tools. On the less fortunate farms old standbys such as the bull rake and the wooden hand rake might still be the chief recourse in hay time, but the day of the blacksmith-made and home-whittled implement was past.

The war years saw also substantial advances in the volume of agricultural information and ways of spreading it. A gathering of notables attended the nation's first college "Short Course," the Yale Agricultural Lectures, from February 1 to 25 in 1860. A series of useful books was published. In 1862 George B. Emerson and Charles L. Flint printed a well-received *Manual of Agriculture*. The respected Fearing Burr of Hingham in 1863 brought out his excellent *Field and Garden Vegetables of America*. New York's Peter Henderson supplemented this in 1866 with his popular *Market Gardening for Profit*. For sheepmen, Henry S. Randall wrote *The Practical Shepherd*, published in 1863.

Toward the decade's end Professor Samuel Johnson of Yale tapped a new source of scientific information. He analyzed various fertilizers and told about the need for fertility in *How Crops Grow* (1868), and *How Crops Feed* (1870). Agricultural periodicals continued to circulate widely.

In dairy practice the midcentury saw continued changes. The compulsory reporting of diseases in cattle prompted by the pleuropneumonia epidemic was but the first of a series of official acts related to animal and human health. In 1859 Massachusetts led the nation with a law authorizing public inspection of milk. Boston promptly appointed an inspector of dairies, the first anywhere, and forbade feeding distillery slops (waste grain) to dairy cattle. Rhode Island, New Hampshire, and Maine followed. Five years later Massachusetts forbade the watering of milk, a practice previously not uncommon, and required all cities to set up milk inspection. Then in 1869 it led again by establishing the nation's pioneer Department of Public Health.[6] From the current farm viewpoint these actions affected chiefly the production and sale of whole milk, but they were the seed for an ever-expanding policy of public concern with food and health.

At the moment most of New England's milk went into farm-produced butter and cheese, 25,000 tons annually of butter alone as the decade came in. The war years had varied effects. Though Vermont cows usually got no grain except corn meal, sometimes mixed with oats, that state's butter production went up by almost two million pounds: the rest of New England remained static or lost ground. In all six states the cheese total dropped: in New Hampshire and Massachusetts the decline was tremendous.

Vermonters showed their concern for the future: assembled at Montpelier in 1869, they organized the nation's first state dairy association (none too soon, for railroads had begun to bring in Midwest butter). Interest grew in respect to breeding for production. Jersey cattle, already on trial in southern New England, commenced to gain favor among Maine and Vermont stockmen. When in 1868 George Waring of Ogden Farm, Newport, Rhode Island, arranged a meeting of Jersey breed fanciers at Farmington, Connecticut, the American Jersey Cattle Club was born and its herd register established.[7] Maine Jersey fanciers followed in 1870 with the Winthrop Jersey Association.

34. *Help for the farm wife's buttermaking: (a) cylindrical churn; (b) dash churn; (c) cylindrical butter worker; (d) lever butter worker.* Mapes Illustrated Catalogue *(1881).*

High-grade Guernseys and the first Brown Swiss were among other promising cattle imports. Undeterred by his experience with pleuropneumonia, Winthrop Chenery of Belmont continued his interest in Holsteins. Shorthorns were pushing north. In 1866 a group of twenty farmers about Springfield, Vermont, clubbed together to buy a purebred bull. Meanwhile in Maine, Herefords gained over Shorthorns. Despite such advances, by 1870 the number of milch cows reported for New England, 642,591, was less by 37,000 than it had been a decade before. Only Vermont had increased its cow numbers; Connecticut held steady, all the others dropped. Where possible, dairy farmers were shifting from butter and cheese to whole milk. By 1864 milk trains over the Worcester, Fitchburg, and Lowell railroads were bringing over 24 million quarts annually into Boston, a foretaste of greater changes ahead.[8]

Two of New England's staples, potatoes and onions, found hungry markets during the war years. Onions reached a top of $10.00 a barrel on the New York market. Southport, Connecticut, alone is said to have grown 100,000 barrels during the war. One vessel from that port, the *White Rock*, carried 1,100 to 1,200 barrels a trip to New York. Several others sailed each week carrying, along with the onions, pork, apples, and grain. Danvers, Massachusetts, was a big onion producer, and in the Connecticut Valley, Sunderland and Deerfield took up the crop.[9] By use of heavy dressings of fish manure, pig manure, kelp, and mussel-bed, except in the excessively dry year of 1864, yields in all these areas were generally good.

Responding to wartime demand, Connecticut increased its potato harvest by half in the war decade; Maine and Rhode Island each by a fifth. Bangor, Maine, is reported to have shipped out 300,000 bushels yearly in this period. If census figures are to be believed, however, the New England crop went up in total only about one eighth. In the 1870 census all New England was reported as producing close to 24 million bushels, over two thirds in the three northern states, where many went into starch. As early as 1833 a Maine inventor had patented a potato-digger,[10] but it was to be 1890 before any digger assumed importance.

When the war cut off the North's supply of cotton, the cities with cotton mills languished, while woolen mills and wool growers cashed in. Aside from civilian clothing needs, the army required immense numbers of uniforms and blankets. The yardage of woven wool cloth more than doubled, and the price of wool jumped. Sheep numbers had dropped substantially during the two previous decades, but in the three northern states careful attention to breeding had held the decline of the wool clip to a mere 10 percent. Now demand became for a time acute. Only in Maine, however, did the 1870 census report show an increase in total clip. The war did not prevent the exhibit at Hamburg, Germany, in 1863, by George Campbell of Vermont of a dozen fine Merinos. In competition with 1,761 European entries, these Vermont sheep captured two first prizes. Campbell's ewes and rams had proved superior in weight and length of fleece to some of Europe's best, and later sold for a total of $5,000.[11]

As demands encouraged wool growers in the West to expand, they often turned to New England for superior breeding stock. Prices rose, and the best local rams were quoted in thousands of dollars. A short period of prosperity ensued, but increases in the numbers of western flocks and the return of cotton to the markets following the war's end coincided to prevent permanent prosperity for sheepmen. Nevertheless sheep lingered on northern New England hillsides until long after, when undisciplined dogs became prevalent. New England diners retained a fondness for roast lamb, so that Maine and Berkshire Hills flock owners, who had turned early to mutton breeds, held out well toward the century's end—their animals of much greater value than those which composed the fine wooled flocks of their fathers. In 1890 Franklin County in the Bay State's hills, with only 11,000 sheep, raised 8,000 lambs, valued at $4.50 each.[12] As western stock flooded in, sales of sheep at Brighton grew from 250,597 animals in 1863 to 524,069 in 1885.

During the war decade, hog numbers, as reported by the census, slumped by a quarter—from 326,176 in the 1860 report to 241,000 in 1870—only to rise beyond the 1860 figure by 1880 and to increase further by 1890. Aside from the fact that the 1869 census count is suspect, the later increase may have reflected the

*35. Sheep dog, shepherd, and flock, Massachusetts, 1880's. Society for the
Preservation of New England Antiquities.*

practice of using cheap western corn to fatten native pork. It also
coincided with the rise in local butter and cheese making, with
surplus skim milk and whey going to the hogs. The change,
however, was of small significance, for with the growth of Boston
packing plants, the flood of western hogs increased. Local hog
growing had only a limited future, even though by 1886 the
Brighton Market handled more than ten times the number of
hogs sold there in 1863.[13]

The wartime leap in production of cigar tobacco was
spectacular. The crop pushed up the Connecticut Valley even
into New Hampshire and Vermont. New England yields per acre
were the highest in the nation, and its leaf brought the top price.
As cigar smoking gained wartime popularity, production grew
from 9¼ million pounds in 1860 to over 15¾ million in 1870. The
largest proportionate increase was in Massachusetts, where the

crop more than doubled. Hatfield, with only two acres in 1850, grew between seven and eight hundred when the 1869 census was taken. Crop value in 1865 ran from $275 to $405 per acre, and war prices lifted many a farm mortgage; yet there was opposition on moral grounds to using New England's best land for a crop that lacked food value.[14]

Hop growing ceased to be of importance in Massachusetts, its former stronghold. Between 1860 and 1870, if census figures are to be believed, Maine trebled its small crop. Vermont, the largest producer of this period, which had more than doubled between 1850 and 1860, dropped from 638,677 pounds to 527,927 in 1870; yet for some years production in that state was considerable. The census taken in 1869 is the last where hops appear to be significant in New England. New York and the West took over the crop.

That questionable 1870 census report indicated a substantial decrease from 1860 in corn production in all states except Vermont; there it showed a small increase. In average yield, New Hampshire led the Union with 40.8 bushels per acre. Popular field corn varieties now included New England Eight-Rowed, King Philip, Dutton (a high-producing Vermont strain selected by Salmon Dutton of Cavendish), Rhode Island Premium, and Northern White Flint. Some corn was being sown in drills and the stalks used for summer feed. The practice increased of gathering the mature stalks into standing bundles or stooks instead of lopping the tops above the ear.[15]

In the 1870 census all small grain harvests were reported down from ten years earlier, with rye the heaviest loser. Vermont, which had a slight gain in its small wheat harvest, was an exception.

The working oxen of which New England farmers had been so proud decreased in number: from 1850, when the count reported was 298,285, to 267,960 in 1860. By 1870 their number had slid down over one fourth more. That this was not merely the reflection of an inaccurate census count became clear in 1880. That year's report showed another drop of one third, to 137,581, just above half the 1860 total. Meanwhile, in these three decades, in every state horses on farms increased. In Maine,

36. Braiding next year's seed corn into long strings, called "traces": 1880's. Society for the Preservation of New England Antiquities.

former stronghold of the ox, they more than doubled. Some farmers still prized oxen, however. As late as 1938 the Worcester County fair was proud to show 101 yoke in procession.

The stall-fed beeves of Connecticut Valley stockmen sold well just before and during the war. Two big ones from Keene in 1866 weighed a total of 5,302 pounds and sold for $600. In 1865 Northfield, Massachusetts, twenty miles south, sold almost a hundred tons of beef. High beef prices made it profitable to bring in western grain for winter fattening. But western finished animals were themselves soon flooding into Brighton, and the fattening business in New England was doomed. In the quarter-century 1851 to 1877 Brighton's cattle sales, like its sheep sales, more than doubled.[16] In a single October week in 1872 Brighton and neighboring markets handled about 5,000 cattle, 1,500 of them from New England; plus 14,500 swine and over 10,000 sheep; again only 2,250 of them from New England.[17]

A new organization, The Butchers' Slaughtering and Melting Association, in 1870 erected at Brighton a large, modern abattoir. Here, close to the big market and with improved sanitation, all the varied processes connected with slaughter could be efficiently carried out. The whole livestock trade gained, and consumers benefited even more. Meanwhile at Portland new meat-packing facilities offered an advantage to the drovers and farmers of Maine.

At Brighton, bagged fertilizer became an important product. In the decade before the war, manufacturers had been making some chemical fertilizers, but these had played little part in New England's farming. Some manufactured bone phosphate had come into use, but mining of South Carolina's rock phosphate, which was to become one of the chief constituents of chemical fertilizers, began only in 1868. In Long Island and Maine factories, menhaden in tremendous amounts were turned into fertilizer as well as into feed for animals.[18] Some farmers bought guano from the dry Galapagos Islands off South America. Mixed fertilizers of various types were soon offered. Extravagant claims for them caused Connecticut to require the bags containing the goods to be labeled with a list of the contents. Maine also passed an act to prevent fraud in their sale. Really effective control, however, was still ahead.

The value of market-garden vegetables showed substantial growth in the war decade. Between the 1860 and the 1870 census reports the Massachusetts total increased from $1,397,000 to almost $2,000,000, Connecticut's from a third of a million to almost $600,000, while Rhode Island's more than doubled, from $140,000 to $316,000. Even considering wartime inflation, there were substantial gains.

By this time strawberries were grown in quantity near the larger cities. Providence was one such market center. Nearby Dighton had been growing some berries; but with the opening in 1866 of the Dighton and Somerset Railroad to Providence local farmers increased production. By 1881 the town was picking 10,000 bushels a year. At first the popular variety in Dighton was Old Virginia. By 1875 Massachusetts was credited with marketing 1,156,801 quarts, valued at about 20 cents a quart. Earlier, the berries had been grown on raised beds, but level, matted rows now took over.[19]

In the Boston suburban area yields of 4,000 quarts or more

per acre, packed in the wood veneer quart box which that market favored, were not unusual. In the 1870 report of the U.S. Commissioner of Agriculture a Maine grower near Bangor was cited for producing on 20 square rods 590 quarts of the popular Wilson variety. These sold for 21 cents a quart, a high price for the time. A favorite New England berry was Cutter's Seedling.

Maine's apple trees in 1860 bore a half million dollar crop. In Massachusetts the value of tree fruits of all kinds came to $925,000. In apples the next decade showed little change, but by 1875 Massachusetts reported a crop of about 3⅓ million bushels of tree fruits of all sorts, worth over 1½ millions. New England's apple exports to England were building up, and would soon become a big market factor.

Amid all the upheaval of the war, the shortage of labor, the inflation of the currency, and the demands of the army, there was no radical alteration in New England's type of farming. At its end, though many farmers had some more or less profitable specialty, the general farm, with several strings to its not very long bow, continued to be the most common type. By the time of the 1870 census report, however, some thousands of the poorer farms had gone out of production. In three New England states alone over 400,000 acres were dropped from the category of improved land.

40

Discouragement

THE THIRTY YEARS that followed 1870, including as they did the panic of 1873, seem to have been the most difficult that New England farmers had faced since Shays's Rebellion. "Decades of almost unrelieved gloom," a writer on Connecticut calls them.[1] Prices of many staples, especially grain, were in almost continuous decline from peaks reached at the war's end, as cheap western grain, helped by railroad rate cuts, flooded in. By 1895 the quoted price for wheat at New York had dropped 60 percent. Never again except under wartime necessity would it be practical to grow wheat in New England. By 1876 the corn harvested in a town like Rochester, New Hampshire, was only a little over half what its farmers had husked a quarter-century earlier, and small grains had all but disappeared there. Between 1870 and 1890 farm valuations in Vermont receded from 135 to 100 million, while in Maine cattle numbers lessened one eighth from 1870 to 1890, and dropped one fifth more in the next decade.

New England's wool shearings decreased one sixth between 1870 and 1880. By 1900 they were only two thirds those of 1870 and never again reached a total of real importance. Cheap western horses made it impractical for Vermont and Maine breeders to cater to any market except that for race horses; and some of the best Maine beef breeders found it expedient to leave for the prairies with their herds.

In the 70's and 80's all states lost in number of "census

farms." In the 1900 census report Massachusetts enumerators came up with a 9 to 10 percent gain and New Hampshire and Vermont showed slight increases. Yet the gain was of small significance, for between the 1880 and 1900 tallies, New Hampshire's farms had dropped by three fifths and Vermont's by half. Connecticut's cleared land reached its peak at the war's beginning, fell slowly till 1870, and receded fast thereafter. On Maine farms the woodlot had been relied on for cash income. When the last of it had been cut and sold, the farm owner had to get a job or move.

In 1890 New Hampshire's Commissioner of Agriculture reported 1,440 vacant or abandoned farms; Massachusetts' Commissioner, 1,576 in 1895. From 1870 on, fewer than two thirds of Vermont's natives were left to call that state home. It was the young in particular who took off. In 1871 at Northfield, Massachusetts, a group of ex-soldiers organized, sent a scout to spy out land in the New West, and planned to move as a body to settle there.

At home, as writer Rollin Lynde Hartt put it just as the century ended, "Steadily the river valleys, rich in water power, are robbing the uplands of their population. The people of New England are running down hill, Massachusetts has built the factory and mortgaged the farm. . . . Says Noah, 'All the spunkiest ones have up and got out.' " "Sweet Auburn," the town where Hartt was born, he considered now a skim-milk community. Tenancy increased in every New England state between 1880 and 1900, though it always remained of small proportions except in Rhode Island (19 percent there in 1899).[2]

Why indeed should a young man waste energy on a hill farm, say in the Sunapee region up half a mile from sea level with 90 days at the most for corn to mature between frosts, when as a peddler or soldier he had known the six-month season of the South or could obtain cheaply a virgin farm in the West? As a Vermonter who had long lived in the West pointed out in 1878, however, the proportion of unsuccessful farmers was quite as great in Illinois as in Vermont, and Governor Hoard of Wisconsin observed that the abandonment problem was every bit as serious in his state as in New England.[3]

One burden on farms in this postwar period was taxation. At the very time when farm prices were dropping, taxes were biting harder. A 1933 Maine study shows that the rate of taxation of farm property there reached its height for the whole nineteenth century in prosperous 1865, at .015. Though it dropped the next year to .0075, it continued to hover between .006 in 1870, .005 in 1880, and .004 in 1884, contrasted with prewar rates of only .002 and .003. Finally, after 1885, the rate dropped to .00275 for most of the rest of the century.[4]

At agricultural banquets captains of industry returning to the communities of their birth moaned over the farm situation, and city publicists shed tears in printers ink in current periodicals. Yet with sheep herding unprofitable and cattle prices low, decade by decade the poorer, stonier, frostier hill farms went relentlessly back to the woodland for which nature designed them. Houses that never would have been started had their builders known what lay west of the Hudson, burned or rotted, and back roads gradually filled with briers till timber took over. As the historian of Peterborough, New Hampshire, where many farms were tenantless, wrote in 1876: "We know not how these lands are to be recruited as long as the agricultural products of the West can be brought to us by a cheap transportation."[5]

Not everyone rushed to the wailing wall. In the 1870 report of the U.S. Commissioner of Agriculture, a correspondent in the Warner, New Hampshire, area, much further north in that same state, reported that there the majority of farmers made a good living, buildings were good, and "some accumulate very respectable fortunes."[6] Levi P. Warren of Sunderland, Massachusetts, in the Connecticut Valley, failed to share the usual alarm. Depopulation, he thought in the spring of 1871, was the result of progress in the art and science of agriculture. He saw "a youth of fourteen accomplish as much with a mower as a number of strong robust men formerly in the same time with scythes"; while the youth's younger brother ran the tedder and one younger still drove the hay rake. For the latter two, at any rate, it was a pastime.[7]

The statement held true also in regard to sowing seed for the Valley's crop of onions. Once this had been a backbreaking job lasting weeks, he said; now with a seeding machine a man could do two to three acres in a day. The time and effort once needed to get the crops to market over the road is cut, he noted; the railroad does it. If all those who used to be needed for farming had continued in it, the markets would be glutted. As to abandoned land, another farmer, just before the war, had pointed out that sterile land is "better left to the growth of wood." Let the poor lands go, and put time and manure on what will really produce—that seemed common sense to many.[8]

In any case, as Lewis Stilwell has admirably expressed it, New England farmers, Vermonters in particular, were never the plodding European peasant type that certain modern writers appear to believe they should have been, tied to the land; but a "climbing and creative stock." [9] In their new locations many with mechanical ability became craftsmen, some, such as Theodore N. Vail, heads of great new industries. More became teachers, college presidents, politicians; Hiram Powers was a sculptor. Connecticut-born Isaac Crary fathered Michigan's agricultural college, pioneer of the state university movement. New Englanders set the tone in large part for that state and for Wisconsin, Minnesota, and Kansas, as Lois Mathews points out. Emigrants with experience in the deep woods, Frederick Turner shows, harvested the pine belt of the northern Middle West, and sometimes became millionaires. Luther Burbank, born on the old Burbank Farm in Lancaster, Massachusetts, and doing well as a market gardener in nearby Lunenberg, set out for California to garner fame as a plant breeder.[10]

"The greatest crop raised hitherto on these farms," wrote George Loring in reply to Timothy Titcomb's prophecy of doom in the *Atlantic Monthly*, "is a host of active, thriving busy men in professions, business, commerce." In 1896 another writer concluded: "The average boy looking for something to do, sees about four openings in other directions to one in agriculture," and picks one of the four.[11]

Girls left as well as boys, and often beginning as schoolteachers, took their part in civilizing the new settlements. The historian of Guilford, Connecticut, quotes a settler who married one such: "Many a fireside in distant states has been graced and made happy by one of the daughters of Guilford, who carried with them the rich grace of truth, gentleness and Christian character." [12] Such young people not seldom helped parents at home to pay off a bothersome mortgage, very likely assumed in part for their education. Later they might return to endow a library in the home village or present a park or public building.

What about those who remained? A substantial number of observers differ from the opinion commonly expressed (for example, by Percy Bidwell) that it was the best, most energetic persons who left. Van Wyck Brooks thinks that the stay-at-homes "were much more real than the pioneers, and their lives . . . more interesting . . . [They were] superior types." The stayers were apt to be the more prosperous, with too much to lose by pulling up stakes. Stuart Holbrook's grandfather came to the conclusion that it wasn't necessarily the abler or more intelligent who migrated; the restlessness came from "something in the blood." Contrariwise, Page Smith, in a recent study, concludes that it was the most conservative who left.[13]

Harold Wilson decides that "the inheritance of fertile and well-located farms served to retain . . . many men and women of ability and initiative." [14] In such a judgment anyone familiar with rural life as demonstrated in the twentieth century must find great merit. Where the best were eventually forced to give up, however, the country village was left poor indeed; with inadequate leadership, capital, and, in some instances, a village community almost depopulated.

One loss to the country town that was never made up is seldom appreciated, even today. This was the constant drain of wealth in the form of taxes assessed for schools, and of contributions for country churches. This was money lost, invested in the abilities and character of those very young people whose talents went to build new cities and new states elsewhere.[15] Another setback was the curtailment of town appropriations as resources diminished, resulting in poorer care for back roads, the closing of outlying schools, and general loss of confidence.

John Black calls attention to one point often overlooked, however.[16] Very little land in New England was actually abandoned. Some neighbor bought the old fields and added them to his cow pasture or woodland holdings. It was cultivation that ceased, not ownership, when the land reverted to nature. As a visiting Scot had observed in the decade before the war: "It is nonsense to talk of the soil being exhausted. There was never anything to exhaust." On many a rocky hillside, when the seeds of pine or birch sifted into old fields, nature was quietly returning the soil to its highest use, natural and economic.

At least one New Englander took action to offset the emigration: Wilbur W. Thomas, a Maine native, consul at Gothenburg, Sweden. With the backing of Maine's government, beginning in 1870, he brought in 600 hardworking Swedish farmer families. In three years they cleared 22,000 acres of prime Aroostook land and established the prosperous town of New Sweden.

41

Adapt or Perish

THERE WAS a second side to the coin. Untoward developments helped bring into play the capacity for adaptation to circumstances that had always distinguished New England's country people.

In the years after the war, from natural increase and the flood of immigrants, New England's population count shot up from just under 3½ million in 1870 to a total of 4,700,000 by 1890, a boost of over a third in two decades. Except for a 0.1 percent loss in Vermont in the 1890 census report, quite possibly due to a miscount, every state made at least a small gain each decade.

Of the immigrants whose numbers bulked heavily in the addition, most stayed in the tenements of cities and mill towns to earn cash wages and become consumers of food rather than producers. For with the help of these newcomers New England was making more than half of the nation's boots and shoes, a large proportion of its textiles and textile machinery, and manufactured goods of many other sorts. It also became more and more a center for banking and insurance, and at the same time a market for the best in food, with money to buy it. Its flour and much of its beef and pork might come from the West, but milk, butter, eggs, poultry, vegetables, and fruit came chiefly from local farms. Growing population spelled farm opportunity, and the local farmers grasped it.

To the up-country farmer looking for a product to replace the wheat, sheep, or fat cattle that the West now produced more cheaply, nothing could appeal more strongly than the hungry dairy-products markets of Boston, Providence, and the Connecticut cities, with their concentrations of people. Even with the new Hoosac Tunnel route opened in 1875, the cost and difficulty of transportation from the West of milk, butter, even cheese provided an umbrella to protect nearby producers. New Englanders were used to handling cattle; they had pasture and hay fields.

The demand for fresh milk in particular was growing. Within driving distance of the cities local farms had long been selling it. Now hundreds more situated within a few hours by rail were added to the "milkshed," as the fresh milk area came to be called. By 1864 nearly 25 million quarts of milk annually came by rail into Boston alone. Between 1870 and 1880 Massachusetts dairymen almost doubled the amount of milk they sent to market. Further out, butter buyers took the farm wife's production: and where transportation was even more distant, she made cheese. By 1880, every New England state except New Hampshire reported an increase in milch cows, 66,426 of them, almost 10 percent, added in twenty years.

In these same two decades rail service made it practical also to increase butter production by more than one fourth. The New England total of farm-churned butter rose to 65,453,000 pounds. In the 1880 census even small Rhode Island was credited with over a million pounds of farm-made butter. Much of it was put up in five and ten pound boxes or crocks.

Butter, especially if well made, was a sure means of getting cash or at least credit at the country store or through a commission merchant. But farm-churned butter was not always of high quality. By 1870 excellent Midwest butter, sometimes shipped on by emigrant New Englanders, began to appear on eastern markets. It was the product of Iowa, Illinois, and Wisconsin creameries and took prizes at exhibitions; because of superior quality the best sold at as much as a 10 percent premium over local butter. Yet to the end of the century, the expanding markets absorbed all, both local and imported.[1]

Creameries were soon organized in New England also. They assembled the milk of a whole neighborhood, turned it into butter (or cheese), and sold the product. The farmer was paid for the fat or solids, and the skim milk or whey went back with him to feed his calves and swine.

Advances in related fields held promise for the dairy business. In 1881 the Mechanical Refrigerating Company opened in Boston the nation's earliest mechanical refrigeration plant. That same year the Maine Central Railroad started refrigerator service, Bangor to Boston. By 1884 use of the newly invented De Laval centrifugal machine began in Vermont. This separated the cream content of milk mechanically. Setting milk overnight in pans for the cream to rise and the skimming that followed were no longer necessary. The proportion of cream secured was greater, also. Soon all dairy plants used it. By 1890 a St. Albans, Vermont, butter factory was making two million pounds a year. In New Hampshire 40 cooperative creameries made three million pounds. Only one cloud shadowed butter's future: by 1888 Boston wholesalers were handling five and a half million pounds of oleomargarine, and some of it was sold as butter.[2]

While butter-making increased, farm cheese production dropped by three fourths between 1860 and 1880. In part this may have been due to growth of local cheese factories (the first one had opened in war time), which reduced farm cheese making, or it may have represented a shift to butter or selling whole milk. In any case the home cheese vat was on the way out. Cheese factories were often small, at first usually cooperatively owned, and not always capably managed. Together with the butter plants they did, however, relieve farm women of that hard labor in the dairy which, added to other duties, had often been too much for their health.

As a result of these shifts in practice at least one country industry prospered, the making of butter tubs and cheese boxes. Farm pigs also benefited. In the 1890 census report, Vermont, Maine, and Massachusetts swine population reached its highest point in forty years.

While consumption of fresh milk gained, swifter rail transport and increasing use of ice soon made it possible to draw fresh milk from greater distances. Massachusetts farmers shipped cityward 61 million quarts in 1870; a decade later they had almost doubled it. In New Hampshire one river meadow town, Milford, sent down 880,000 quarts a year to the big city. In 1890 Bellows Falls made the first shipment of fresh Vermont milk to Boston. By 1895 that city was getting milk by rail from an area spread out like the fingers of a hand: from Vermont and New Hampshire; from Willimantic in northeast Connecticut; from Charlemont, Massachusetts, at the edge of the Berkshires on the Hoosac Tunnel route; via the Central Massachusetts Railroad from Northampton, in the Connecticut Valley; as well as from many nearer stations on each rail line. Besides supplying local New England markets, some Connecticut and Berkshire milk went to New York City.[3] Then in 1887 (the very year that the ice-cream soda was introduced), Maine's Turner Center Creamery began to ship iced fresh cream by rail. Meanwhile, the population of New England's largest city had grown from 177,840 in 1860, to 560,892 in 1900.

One notable effect of milk-shed extension was the incentive for farmers along rail routes to build larger barns, which held the increased numbers of milkers that an assured market made possible and stored the hay needed to keep them through the winter. Even before the fresh milk era, an occasional farm might tie up 60 cows; but with whole milk shipment, large herds became practical in many places.[4] So the decades following the Civil War saw the erection of numbers of the tall, combined hay and stock barns which became a characteristic of New England's countryside. In the northern tier of states where winter was hard, a milk room, wagon shed, and wood shed would tie the barn to the farmhouse. Doors opening between provided an inside passageway, and the whole sheltered the barnyard from the north wind.

While farmers thus added cows to increase New England's milk supply, city dealers were accused of extending it still further from their water taps; also of skimming off cream then recoloring what remained with caramel; and of treating milk with boracic acid to make it keep longer.[5] Such practices householders did not always mind, but in this decade Massachusetts passed stringent control legislation, and in 1891 made illegal another abuse, the sale of oleomargarine as butter.

If census figures are reliable, despite all intervening agricultural and monetary fluctuations, the total value in money of livestock in the six New England states at the century's end remained practically what it had been in 1860. The slight change was an increase of about 3 percent or a little over $3,000,000. Almost two thirds of this was in Massachusetts, the other third in Vermont.

However, an important change was taking place in the feeding of cattle. This was the chopping of green corn, stalks and all, or green clover into ensilage to provide succulent feed all winter. The chopped-up fodder was stored in silos, where it fermented but did not spoil. The first ensilage in America has been variously claimed to have been made in Maryland, New York, and Illinois in 1876, but two local silos were described in the Vermont Agricultural Report of 1869–70, and the subject was at least discussed at a meeting in 1875 of New Hampshire's State Board of Agriculture. J. M. Bailey of Billerica, Massachusetts, had a silo before 1880. By 1881 there were said to be 50 silos in New Hampshire (one of them 20 × 20 × 12½ feet), a larger number in Vermont and Massachusetts. By 1888 Vermont claimed to have 100, while farmers all over New England experimented with the new method. Originally silos were square, their walls made of stone, and were sometimes wholly or partly below ground. Occasionally a barn still contains one of the masonry silos of this period. In 1887 "the silo system" had been termed "best adapted to high-priced lands and so-called high farming." Yet in that very year a Vermont professor, speaking to Rhode Island farmers, advocated them for general use. He advised building them of the less expensive wood rather than stone.[6] Succeeding decades were to see circular wooden construction become most common, and the silo brought to nearly every practical dairy farm.

Excitement and great uneasiness developed in 1880 with regard to tuberculosis in cattle. Isolated cases of tubercular cattle had been found earlier in several Massachusetts towns. Now the

selectmen of Grafton, south of Worcester, called to the attention
of the state's Cattle Commission the unhealthy condition of a
local herd. It was housed in a tight, unventilated barn. One
animal had died, two were emaciated, several coughing. When
the Commission had one of the sickest animals slaughtered, its
lungs were found to be almost solid with tubercles.[7]

This happening was especially unsettling because for human
tuberculosis, "consumption," which had become very prevalent
in New England, on farms as well as in cities, no certain cure was
known. Villemin in Paris in 1865 had proved that tuberculosis
could be transmitted by inoculation, but not till 1882 did Robert
Koch find that among humans the bacillus was spread by
sputum. Yet leading American physicians long remained skepti-
cal of the bacillus explanation for the disease. A stay at a
sanitarium at some elevated spot in rural surroundings appeared
the most practical expedient.[8]

In 1885 Frank S. Billings, a Boston veterinary surgeon,
alarmed the Massachusetts Board of Agriculture by reporting
how widespread the disease had become among the state's cattle.
He recommended public control at Brighton and other abattoirs
and prohibition of the sale of meat and milk from diseased
animals. The following year the Board besought the legislature to
ask Congress for federal controls. Within two years the Board was
told that one fourth of all cattle in eastern Massachusetts were
infected.[9] To add to public alarm, pleuropneumonia had reap-
peared in cattle brought from the West. Foot and mouth disease
in 1884 had been discovered in Maine but had been stamped out
there. That same year the United States Congress took note of
the prevalence of animal diseases and added a Bureau of Animal
Industry to the Department of Agriculture, two years later
authorizing payment of indemnity to owners of stock condemned
for disease and slaughtered by official order. Meanwhile in 1885
a number of animals in Maine's state college herd were found to
be infected with tuberculosis. Amid wide public agitation and
criticism, the entire herd was slaughtered.[10]

Worried at the danger represented by the constant uncon-
trolled influx to the great cattle mart at Brighton of animals from
many directions, the Massachusetts legislature passed a law

requiring inspection of all cattle entering the state. Going further in 1892, it directed all towns to inspect their local cattle and to slaughter suspected animals, and authorized compensation to the owner for the occasional animal found, after slaughter, to have been free from disease. Town officials were very slow to act and had to be prodded again and again. That year Rhode Island destroyed 207 cattle, all but 5 diseased, yet the milk from these cows was sold up to the day of slaughter! Unprincipled butchers were even said to collect diseased cattle in the northern states and ship them to Massachusetts markets to be killed for beef.

Lacking adequate federal control, all New England states now set up quarantines. One prompt result was that cattle from the West suspected of being diseased were diverted from New England to New York, which had no inspection law.

In 1890 Dr. Koch found that by testing suspected animals with a bacillus extract, the presence of tuberculosis could be determined with reasonable accuracy. Tightening control, in 1894 Massachusetts adopted this tuberculin test, licensed slaughterers, and began branding cattle pronounced tubercular. The same year Vermont began inspection. Nevertheless it was still only at the owner's request that cattle were tested. Of 3,325 inspected in Massachusetts in 1895, 26 percent proved diseased; of 1,639 quarantined by local inspectors, 802 were condemned. Up to this time, of 26,958 in all examined by the Massachusetts Board of Cattle Commissioners and given the tuberculin test, 4,389 had been condemned. With milk a popular food, the number of milch cows in New England had been rising steadily; 75,345 were added between 1880 and 1890 alone. Now the increasing tuberculosis agitation cast a cloud over the future of the dairy business. By 1895 one weakness in tuberculosis control was in part remedied: all states except Vermont provided some compensation to owners of animals condemned. However, the futility of relying on physical inspection alone became clearer when the herd of 33 at an experiment station was tested. The entire herd, the report said, seemed to be in prime condition except for two; but under the tuberculin test 21 more reacted. Where was all this to end? [11]

Even though infection in the three northern states was much

less than in the southern tier, in 1895 New England's cattle
commissions jointly decided to require inspection for all interstate shipments. Meanwhile, across the long three-state border,
New York was still without controls against diseased animals. Its
state veterinary association asserted that the common practice
there was to test cattle arriving from the West, send sound
animals into New England, and sell the reactors in New York
State. Much criticism appeared in the farm press, however, to the
effect that the tuberculin test was proving inaccurate. Upon
slaughter some condemned animals showed no sign of the
disease; others passed as healthy might be found full of tubercles.
In 1897 a special committee of the Massachusetts legislature was
appointed to check on the testing of 140 cows in the Lowell area,
138 of which reacted to the test. Its report questioned the test's
reliability and the dangers to health involved. Already Massachusetts was spending a quarter-million yearly, with no end in
sight. At times legislatures refused appropriations for the work.
Connecticut in 1897 repealed all laws except one forbidding the
sale of milk from an infected animal. Two years later, half
the herd at the state college were found to be tuberculous. Thus
the century ended. Progress had been made, but still much
confusion and difference of opinion remained. As long as
physicians continued to doubt that bovine tuberculosis could
affect humans, full control was a long way ahead. Meanwhile,
many children and others on farms and elsewhere were to
suffer.[12]

Paralleling the growth of dairy farming came an upsurge in
interest in poultry. Poultry raising was no longer the pursuit of
gentleman fanciers, interested as they continued to be, or solely a
matter of barnyard flocks, cared for by farm wives, boys, and
girls. Enthusiastic poultrymen experimented with improved
housing, ventilation, and feeding; with new types of birds; with
methods of selection and breeding. All this was preparation for
the poultry leadership New Englanders were to show in the
succeeding century. For several decades after the war, as cereal
prices kept slipping, the relative cheapness of shipped-in western
grain for feed offered a distinct advantage to close-to-market

producers of both eggs and meat. New Englanders responded by increasing farm flocks and developing specialized poultry farms. The new incubators helped to make larger flocks practical.

As a single local instance of poultry's increasing status, Waldoboro, Maine, farmers in the year ending April 1, 1874, shipped by rail to Boston 1,600 boxes of 125 dozen eggs each, as well as 200 boxes that went by steamer. Poultrymen there were well started on what was to continue for a century an important local enterprise.[13] They were not alone. In the 1880 federal census report, the first for poultry separately, the six New England states held the country's six top positions in egg yield, Maine in the lead. New England's egg output was almost 7 dozen per bird, against a national average of $4\frac{1}{2}$ dozen. (This figure in the twentieth century would appear small indeed. For 1925–29 the New England average was to be $11\frac{1}{2}$ dozen, for 1945–49 almost $16\frac{1}{2}$ dozen; both totals surpassed those of every other section of the nation except the Pacific states.)[14]

Between the 1880 and the 1900 censuses the numbers of New England's "chickens" (the census term) and eggs rose far faster than its human population: an increase of over 60 percent for the birds, 100 percent in eggs. In every state, bird numbers and egg production increased. Rhode Island and New Hampshire each doubled its bird population and more than doubled its egg total. Massachusetts and Maine, the two largest producers, were not far behind. The figures reflected not only increased demand but also breeding for egg production and the growing use of incubation to get early layers. By 1885 in Massachusetts alone, between 35,000 and 40,000 people, on a large or small scale, were said to be in the poultry game. That year eggs brought them $1,600,000; within twenty years an additional million dollars was added. By the time of the 1900 census, New England's hens were laying more than 52,000,000 dozen eggs annually. This figured out as nine dozen apiece or better for every man, woman, and child in the six states and was not far from an egg every third day for each New England inhabitant. At the farm these eggs were worth $9,000,000, nearly the same value as the whole New England apple crop.

Apart from eggs, some poultry keepers made a business of

fattening chickens for roasting. Vermont and southern Rhode Island were noted for fat turkeys, and Plymouth County grew Pekin ducks for Boston hotels. South County, Rhode Island, still fancied geese. Roast duckling was becoming fashionable. One Bristol County poultryman sent 5,000 ducks to market each year at the age of eight weeks (and had 2,000 white Wyandotte and Plymouth Rock chicks besides). Another duck grower in southeast Massachusetts claimed in 1897 to have sold 50,000 duck eggs for hatching. He kept 2,500 birds for breeding, scattering his flocks over greensward for health. With the aid of the manure the birds made in their winter housing, he grew carrots and hay for the next season, and these helped to supply food and keep healthy fifty to sixty horses that he boarded. An ingenious farmer could make circumstances serve him.[15]

Here and there poultrymen began to raise chicks for sale. Rhode Island's largest breeder in 1899 claimed to house 4,000 layers and breeders, all scattered in a hundred colony houses. He hatched and sold thousands of chicks each year, as well as 1,500 to 2,000 goslings.[16] The ordinary poultry keeper was like the neighboring hen man who raised 600 layers and 1,000 incubated chicks. He found that feeding and housing the flock and retailing the eggs gave him all he could do, with a little help needed at times, and provided him a satisfactory income. This was termed, in 1898, a large and successful Rhode Island poultry farm.[17] The great majority of poultry, however, were still to be found in small farm flocks. The Plymouth Rock, originated in New England and developed into two main strains, Barred and White, was the most popular type, but the Rhode Island Red and several other breeds each had its advocates.

These closing years of the century saw also the beginning of publicly sponsored experimental work in poultry. In 1886 Rhode Islanders formed a state poultry association. By 1890 the new Rhode Island Agricultural College set to work at scientific development of the Rhode Island Red. In 1898 it offered the nation's first college course in poultry husbandry, which attracted students from as far as Illinois and Nebraska.[18]

Interest grew in poultry health, including better construction and ventilation of poultry houses as well as the colony system. The century's last year was marked, fortunately, by the discovery of the bacillus of that scourge of young chicks, pullorum (white diarrhea), a disease that had carried off thousands every year.

42

How the Gardens Grew

Beckoned by a continually rising population, vegetable growers expanded. There were occasional setbacks. Potato production, plagued by disease and competition, scarcely held its own from 1870 to 1880. To make matters worse, the Colorado beetle arrived. As a result, by 1890 the harvest showed a big dip in every state, even Maine. By 1900, however, it had rebounded strongly; Maine in particular reported an increase. The Bangor & Aroostook Railroad was opened in 1894 to Houlton, then to Caribou and Fort Fairfield. It brought an immediate boom to Aroostook County. Though Aroostook's summer was short, it was one of New England's most fertile spots. On its fresh limestone soils with their weekly rains potato acreage leaped forward, rising in that decade from 16,641 to almost 42,000 acres. Newly designed and increasingly effective sprayers and diggers assisted by commercial fertilizer helped the "Empire of Aroostook" to produce potatoes on a scale and of a quality that opened markets down and around the coast as far as Texas.[1] The potato was one of New England's important exports. In the 1890 census report Maine topped the nation with an average yield of 300 bushels per acre, a little beyond Ohio's. New Hampshire, in third place, averaged 240 bushels; Massachusetts, fifth, reported 233. New Hampshire's leading potato towns were for a long time in the north, the starch-factory area.

New varieties helped. In 1876 J. J. H. Gregory, a Marblehead seedsman, announced the breeding by a Massachusetts youth of the new Burbank's Seedling, which was later to become the ancestor of the Idaho baking potato. In 1885 three Vermont growers, Brownell, Rand, and Alexander, bred a new variety, which was to become famous. They called it "Green Mountain"; it was destined for almost as wide cultivation and acclaim as that state's Early Rose of two decades earlier, and became the special favorite of Aroostook County.[2]

New England's second most important export vegetable, the onion, was undergoing certain shifts in location. Danvers and Peabody on the Massachusetts coast, despite insects and disease, continued to get heavy yields and to enjoy the advantage of the Boston market. Barnstable is no longer mentioned. Bristol, Rhode Island, had lost its overseas trade but continued to grow onions for Providence, now its market. In the decades just after the war, the Wethersfield and Southport, Connecticut, areas were at their height, growing 500–900 bushels per acre, and 80,000 to 100,000 barrels annually, to supply New York and more distant markets. To do this, growers imported New York City horse manure to supplement local supplies and seaweed. Prices fell, and disease increased there, but until the end of the century Southport was New England's leading producer.

Up the Great Valley in Massachusetts, Deerfield, Sunderland, Hadley, and Whately farmers began to expand in onion-growing. For labor, recruiters brought in hundreds of hard-working, aspiring Polish families to take over the stooping monotonous field work. Eventually the Poles were to acquire ownership of many of the farms, and handle merchandising of the crop.[3] In 1900 the federal census credited Connecticut with 422,000 bushels of onions, Massachusetts with 748,000, and Rhode Island with 116,000, over 1¼ million bushels in all New England. The yellow Danvers Globe was the favorite.

A third export specialty was canned sweet corn and other canned vegetables. Maine canners, selling countrywide, annually contracted for heavy acreages of corn, beans, and soup vegetables: 12,500 acres in 1882 for seventy-one factories. In the year preceding they had processed a pack of 11,350,000 cans of sweet corn alone. Canners provided a market for nearly $300,000 worth of Maine's dry beans also. Toward the end of the century, a half-dozen Vermont factories canned the corn from five to six thousand acres.[4]

The most striking change in vegetable growing was in the rapid strides made by market gardeners near cities. Their production of fresh vegetables constantly increased. (The Census Bureau's inattention to local deviations from nationwide crop categories prevents federal figures from reflecting this fully.)

Concord, Massachusetts, farmers had begun in the 1850's to fill their sandy plains with asparagus roots. By 1874, 35 or more large growers together with numerous smaller ones were in the business. Within a decade they produced nearly 75,000 bunches, half the Massachusetts crop, with an income of $200 to $300 per acre. Cucumbers and rhubarb were new Concord crops, grown under glass. One farm sold 25,000 cucumbers a year, together with two indoor crops of fresh rhubarb.[5] Pickle factories, opened in Cranston, Rhode Island, Lincoln, Massachusetts, and the Deerfield area, together with some in Vermont and New Hampshire, offered an outlet for what one grower called "as profitable a crop as I ever raised." [6]

Irrigation of upland meadows by sloping furrows from springs above is mentioned in Rhode Island in 1839. Irrigation to keep summer vegetables constantly growing goes back to Arlington, Massachusetts, at least to 1873, perhaps beyond. By 1877 a number of growers around Boston were using large-size hose and hand watering for cabbage, lettuce, celery, and cauliflower. In 1883 one grower declared water as essential for success for growing vegetables as for washing them. In Rhode Island the Budlong family enterprise at Cranston irrigated 180 acres of cucumbers. Most of these, along with horseradish, cauliflower, and small onions, 50,000 bushels a year in all, went into the firm's pickle products. By 1886 at least one strawberry grower near Providence and others near Boston used water to get full production from that crop. Some gardeners built windmills with elevated tanks, others provided artesian wells and steam pumps. Market gardening of such a type called for substantial capital, full equipment, and heavy manuring. Suburban land is "taxed highly and costs us very dear," one said. Dear also was the city horse manure that made the soil productive. But it all paid. Their highly tilled fields sometimes yielded a thousand dollars worth per acre of vegetables and small fruits.[7]

The "Boston hotbed," covered with glass sashes to force crops, was one productive resource. As long before as February 9, 1753, Reverend Edward Holyoke in his Salem diary had told of planting gourds, cucumbers, and lettuce in his hotbed; and well before the Revolution Boston newspapers advertised glass sash for them. The sides were thick plank staked up parallel and banked outside, the bed running east and west, with a slight slope south to catch the sun. A foot or more of the soil between was dug out and the excavation filled with steaming, fermenting horse manure, bought at a high price, up to a dollar per sash, from large city stables. A few inches of fine soil were filled in on it so as to leave a foot of air space, then the sash were laid across the planks. The sun warmed the soil by day and straw mats over the sash held in the manure's heat by night. Shielded by windbreak fencing, the market gardener's beds might run to hundreds of feet in length. In them gardeners grew vegetables such as lettuce, radishes, cucumbers, and greens to market size. To gain the early market they also started thousands of seedlings for transplanting to sunny outside slopes.

Real greenhouses had till the nineteenth century been the province of wealthy amateurs to force grapes and tropical fruits and flowers; but by 1839 at least one Arlington market gardener had a greenhouse in use to start early plants for transplanting outside.[8]

About 1872 a Newton, Massachusetts, commercial grower named Morse erected on a south exposure a low, inexpensive, but practical greenhouse of wood and glass. It was about 350 feet long, of the ridge and furrow type, heated by hot water circulating in pipes from two coal furnaces. Morse marketed his greenhouse lettuce successfully by rail in New York City, where Boston's hotbed lettuce had a high reputation. Greenhouse violets, which he also grew, toward the century's end charmed Boston ladies. Sensing the opportunity for winter income, growers with capital began to build greenhouses on a large scale in the towns about Boston. On the Fitchburg Railroad at

Templeton, in Worcester County, a distinct group of winter
cucumber greenhouse men established themselves. Experimenters turned winter tomatoes and rhubarb into profitable crops
also. Partly as a result, between 1885 and 1895 Massachusetts
greenhouse production increased over 150 percent.[9]

In the meantime, outdoor vegetable growing also expanded
as vegetable producers profited from a gradual change in
popular food habits. More and more people found employment
indoors in heated buildings. They turned to vegetables in place of
the heavier foods of former years. Production centered around
the large city markets: Boston, Worcester, Providence, Hartford,
and New Haven. In Maine, Cape Elizabeth, close to Portland,
also went extensively into gardening, and each of the growing
smaller cities acquired its nucleus of farmer-gardeners. The U.S.
census report of 1880 assigned Connecticut's vegetables a total
value $2\frac{1}{2}$ times that of 1870; between 1889 and 1899 this state's
vegetable value grew $2\frac{1}{3}$ times again. The Massachusetts 1895
census report, more detailed than the federal, showed for that
one state a fresh vegetable production total of almost $5\frac{1}{4}$ million
dollars. From 1889 to 1899 census enumerators noted at least a
doubling of vegetable production in each of the six states except
Rhode Island, and a tripling in Vermont.

Marketing of greenstuffs and roots was simplified and
standardized by the development at Boston of a uniform reusable
package. The square, flat Boston bushel box took the place of the
barrel and the nondescript bag that long remained in use
elsewhere in the country. Its open face encouraged more honest,
uniform, and attractive packing. Holding eighteen heads of
lettuce or two dozen bunches of beets or carrots, it helped New
England produce to ship well. Thus it became popular with
buyers in New York and elsewhere, and contributed to the
development of a considerable outside trade. Toward the end of
the century a winter visitor to Florida complained that the only
vegetables offered in stores there were shipped down from
Boston! [10]

Increasingly, greenhouse men saw opportunities in growing
flowers for sale as well as vegetables. Between the 1880 and the

1890 census reports the number of florists rose substantially in all the states. To provide better sales facilities, Boston area growers in 1892 organized the Boston Flower Exchange and set up their own market place. The Massachusetts state census of 1895 gave a half million value to its commercial flowers. In Connecticut by 1900 the U.S. census reported almost as much, and the Massachusetts value by then was up to $1,639,000. Along with the flowers, growers built up a substantial sale in started plants.

Gardeners found small fruits excellent companions to vegetables. As markets expanded and better varieties were brought out, strawberry production became increasingly important. The Wilson was popular and the large and delicious Marshall, originated in Marshfield, Massachusetts, was acclaimed in 1890. By that time Concord and the Dighton area east of Providence had become considerable centers of production. Yet as early as 1878, Concord had been able to count 100 or more growers and over 50 acres of berries, the leading producer marketing 25,000 quart boxes. In 1885 for the whole state of Massachusetts the total reached 4,000,000 quarts with a value of $400,000, twenty times the crop reported two decades before. Connecticut also was marketing large crops. Ledyard, in the New London area, was one production center, single farms there selling up to 6,000 baskets; while in 1900 one New Haven market gardener picked 50,000 quarts.

Cranberry growing gained favor steadily also, helped by the recently invented cranberry scoop. In its most prosperous year, 1895, growers harvested a crop of 150,000 barrels, worth an estimated million dollars.[11] By the end of the century, Cape Cod had invested $1,400,000 in bogs that totaled 3,500 acres, many of the owners men who had previously followed the sea; Plymouth County next door, however, was the crop's center. An acre of well-made bog, fruiting properly and served with adequate water, might be worth $1000. Severe troubles, unfortunately, lay ahead for this fruit.

A modest development took place in grapes. Moore's Early was a new (1871) Massachusetts variety. One Worcester County fruit town, in 1885, reported 20,000 vines with a yield of 128,000 pounds, while the whole state produced almost 3,000,000, half of them hothouse grown.

The invention in 1852 by Rev. L. L. Langstreth of Pennsylvania of the moveable-frame hive became the foundation for all future bee-keeping. Five years later he was living in Greenfield, Massachusetts. Aside from producing honey the bees were the means of fertilizing apples and other fruit blooms. As greenhouse men and market gardeners turned to growing cucumbers, bees being indispensable for their crop also, they hired bee colonies from apiarists. Though bees were never destined to great numbers in New England, they had enthusiastic devotees in all its states. By 1876 James Wood, an apiarist in Prescott, Massachusetts, had gained a national reputation as a breeder of pure Italian queens. Total value of bees in 1900 was $206,000; Maine and Vermont the leaders.

The gravel hills of southern Maine, southern New Hampshire, Connecticut, western Rhode Island, Massachusetts, and parts of Vermont, set largely with orchards of Baldwins, Russets, and Greenings, produced crisp tasty apples that not only New England but Old England welcomed. "The foreign market for our fruit is as well established as for our wheat," Colonel Wilder, leading horticulturist, commented in 1876. The price off the steamer at Liverpool in 1878 was a pound sterling per barrel. The year 1880, with its big apple crop, saw especially huge shipments go abroad. Steamers with Maine apples left Portland every week. In 1896 almost a million barrels went across from Boston. As time went on, Maine orchardists turned considerably (and mistakenly) to the huge, handsome Ben Davis as an export variety; although easily raised, it was of inferior quality. In the rest of New England, Baldwins and Russets remained popular.

Immense quantities of apples, especially those from minor orchards on general farms, went into cider and vinegar, or to canners and evaporators who prepared dried apples for the hotel and grocery trade as well as for export "to the remotest nations." Gloucester's fishing fleet alone, to feed its 4,300 fishermen, made

37 tons of dried apples into pies and apple sauce in the course of a year. Farm families continued to slice and dry apples on strings in the kitchen around the fire, a tedious job.[12]

Every state was interested in apple growing. Between 1890 and 1900 New Hampshire's orchards shrank somewhat, while Massachusetts was doubling its production. In 1900 Maine had over four million apple trees. Vermont developed profitable orchards about Lake Champlain and in its southern section but did not become an important apple state. Even in small Rhode Island the crop was considerable. Nevertheless one observer claimed that a large proportion of New England orchards made a sorry picture of disease and neglect.

The San Jose scale, a sucking insect noticed first in California in 1870, was found in Connecticut by 1885 and reported in Massachusetts a decade later. Eventually it spread everywhere and damaged fruit trees of many types. Within three years of its appearance the Connecticut Experiment Station was advising the use of chemical sprays to counteract such unwelcome intrusions. Though as early as 1878 Paris green is said to have been used against canker worm in New York State, the Connecticut action was the start of pesticide control for New England orchards.

Not only apples but pears, peaches, quinces, cherries, and currants continued to be of market importance. New England's first large commercial peach orchard was the work of J. H. Hale. His plantings at South Glastonbury and those of other growers in that area were said to number three million trees and made Connecticut for several decades New England's peach state. Hale gave to horticulture the excellent peach variety that bears his name. Except in years of extreme cold, peaches became a market crop well north in New England. In 1898 Wilbraham, east of Springfield, had an orchard of 3,000 trees. A fertile hill fruit town such as Harvard, Massachusetts, could claim 13,743 peach trees, a number substantial even when compared with its 27,717 apple trees. But winterkilling, disease, and increasing rail shipments from the South and New York eventually limited New England's production. Along with peaches, many a hilly acre, especially in

Connecticut, was set to Luther Burbank's new hybrid Japanese plums.[13] Burbank had started his horticultural career on a farm in Lunenburg, Massachusetts, then transferred to California.

Cigar tobacco was for the rest of the century the leading money crop of the Connecticut Valley. The fields extended north into southern New Hampshire and Vermont, and into Connecticut's Housatonic Valley. Volatile prices and poor seasons weeded out soils and growers unsuited to the crop; but as cigars grew more popular, Connecticut's production increased from 8,328,000 pounds, the 1870 census figure, to over 14,000,000 at the next report. In Massachusetts the single town of Whately in 1870 produced leaf of an estimated value of $275,000, but production in the state as a whole dropped back almost 2,000,000 pounds in the next decade. In the 1880 census report the value of its entire 5,369,000-pound pack was given as just under $700,000 but was only half that received at the war's end.

One important cause of tobacco trouble was that manufacturers discovered on the island of Sumatra in the East Indies a superior light-colored wrapper tobacco leaf that they could import cheaply. Tobacco leaf sells by the pound. Two pounds of the excellent Sumatra leaf would furnish the outside wrappers for a thousand cigars. To wrap that number in Connecticut Valley leaf required four pounds or more. Dismayed at loss of their market the local farmers in 1883 organized a Connecticut Valley Tobacco Growers Association. They persuaded Congress to enact a tariff of $2.00 per pound. From 1890 on, this slowed importation and helped the local market.

Then the new state experiment stations went to work on tobacco. Charles Goessman at the Massachusetts station studied and advised on soil conditions, which varied widely. In 1900 Connecticut investigated the possibility of growing fine leaf under artificial shade, making studies that were to save the growing of wrapper tobacco for New England for another half century. Invention of a transplanting machine in the 1880's was a step toward efficient and more profitable production. To meet one hazard of the business the growers themselves formed the

Tobacco Growers Mutual Insurance Company, which issued the nation's first hail insurance policy.[14]

General farmers continued to raise some small grain, even wheat, but as horses replaced oxen both on farms and in cities, oats gained favor. Vermont led in 1880, raising 3,742,282 bushels. By 1890 Maine, which reported 2,265,595 in the 1880 census, had boosted production to 3,668,909; Vermont stayed nearly even. By 1900, however, all states save Maine showed a decline in oats. Except that its straw was salable, rye was no longer important anywhere, and barley only in Maine and Vermont. Buckwheat had seldom been popular except in Maine. There its production continued, especially among the Aroostook French.

Yet to the century's end, despite heavy imports of cheap western grain, conservative general farmers found it practical to grow a substantial volume of Indian corn. Connecticut, Vermont, and Massachusetts each reported larger corn production in 1900 than in 1870. Rhode Island and New Hampshire were not far behind. In 1894 a corn husking at Walpole, New Hampshire, could still attract a barnful of people to enjoy an oyster supper, husk the ears, and dance all night. Maine farmers, on the other hand, turned to sweet corn for the canneries, and to ensilage. Meanwhile a change long in process gained favor: the practice of topping cornstalks above the ear was given up. Stalks and ears were harvested together; if carefully handled, well cured stalks made good feed for dairy cows where there was no silo.

Production of New England's most widespread crop, hay, remained important throughout the century's final decades. Nearly every state made a modest gain of 10 to 20 percent, the largest in Maine. This may have reflected, in part, the increase in dairying, in part, the increasing city demand for hay and its ready transport by either rail or water. Durham, New Hampshire, for example, sent 1,500 tons of hay annually to Boston. The Belfast, Maine, area shipped large quantities by sea, some of it for cows kept in crowded city and suburban dairies. Day calls attention to another money crop, a substantial production in eastern Maine of clover seed for sale.[15]

Salt hay from the thousands of acres of coastal marshes retained its importance. This "harvest of the sea" actually improved in quality, as the nutritious "black grass," good fodder even for milkers, spread more widely. Black grass, cutting about a ton per acre, made up half the crop along Massachusetts Bay's North Shore. At Green Harbor on the South Shore, a dike 1,800 feet long, finished in 1873, reclaimed over 1,400 acres of marsh for valuable English grass.[16] Yet much of New England's hayland unquestionably was starved. In the areas of farm abandonment, the grass was merely cut annually until it was no longer worth cutting and birches and red cedars took over. For good farmers, however, hay remained a valuable and necessary crop.

Maple products had for a century been the year's first harvest for thousands of upland farmers, especially in Vermont, New Hampshire, and western Massachusetts and Connecticut. A farmer might tap from 1,000 to 1,500 trees. The maple orchard supplied farm families with sweets, making purchase of cane sugar unnecessary. Maple sugar had been sold in competition with cane, at first for a lower price. During the Civil War, with cane sugar cut off, maple gained popularity and reached higher prices. Vermont was the leading producer, reporting almost 9 million pounds in 1870, increasing to 11¼ million in 1880, and to over 14 million in 1890, about one fourth of the nation's supply. New Hampshire's totals ran from just under 2 million to 2 ¾ million pounds; several of its towns harvested 40,000 to 80,000 pounds, Acworth setting the pace. The town of Sandisfield, the leading Massachusetts producer, made 200,000 pounds in 1855, and continued substantial crops for years.

By the end of the century there was a change in popular demand. More and more maple was sold each decade as syrup, Vermont alone producing 160,000 gallons in 1900. Passage of the Pure Food Act in 1906 strengthened its position, choking off the common practice by food distributors of adulterating maple with glucose.[17] By 1910 the value of Vermont's harvest was to pass a million dollars; by 1920, 3½ millions, as maple syrup came to be generally appreciated as a table delicacy. Though the crop required much hard work—and sometimes in years when sap flowed poorly was a disappointment—maple products were a welcome source of cash for thousands of hill farmers.

New England's combination of soils of only meager natural fertility with proximity to the hungriest markets on the continent for foodstuffs led farmers in this half century into effective use of artificial fertilizers. Not that natural fertilizers were in the least downgraded or their use diminished: by now a growing number of barn cellars protected the manure of the stock from the weather. Nor were other natural manures neglected. An 1880 report to the Massachusetts Board of Agriculture, for example, tells of one farmer applying 5,000 oxcart loads of swamp mud to 25 acres in the course of 15 years. Off the end of Long Island 100 vessels with 300 men in 1869 caught 67,500,000 menhaden. After their oil was extracted and the residue ground, they supplied 7,105 tons of fish manure for the fertilizer trade.[18] Farmers in Guilford, Connecticut, still applied whitefish direct to the land. In Essex County, Massachusetts, seaweed and "mussel bed" remained prime favorites for compost to grow big crops of onions. The Massachusetts state census of 1885 reported 25,546 cords of sea manure used in that state. Up-country, plaster of paris continued to have advocates.

Influenced by the publications of the German chemist Justus Von Liebig and by those of local scientists, bagged mixed fertilizers were put on the market in a flood. Some were outright frauds, many of only minor aid to crop production. The original control laws proving of little value, Massachusetts in 1872 passed an effective act requiring guarantees of chemical contents. Connecticut, which had been doing a first-rate analysis job, followed in 1881. Before these laws were passed, however, some brands contained as much as 15 percent sand and moisture. Some furnished scarcely any nutrients. Seventeen brands, sold in Massachusetts at an average cost of $51.25 per ton, averaged only $16.35 in the value of the ingredients.[19]

Enforcement and publicity brought honesty into the business and encouraged honorable manufacturers. Bowker Fertilizer Company in 1872 started making bagged goods with meat waste from the Brighton Stockyards as a base. Mining of South Carolina phosphate rock jumped each year. From the rock came acid phosphate, an important mineral fertilizing constituent. In 1880 a leading gentleman farmer, Joseph Burnett, commented on one of the new brands: "Stockbridge Fertilizers are of incalculable value. Indirectly, I suppose, we are indebted to the Agricultural College, which gave to Professor [Levi] Stockbridge the opportunity to experiment on and produce them." [20]

By the time of the 1890 census report, New England topped the entire country in expenditure per acre for manures and fertilizers. The leading uses were these: for celery, $92.80 per acre; for cabbage and onions, about $68.00; asparagus, $52.78; sweet corn, $37. Rhode Island led in the use of fertilizer for potatoes, at $38. Massachusetts spent $36 and Maine $30.[21] Nonetheless, the richest fertilizer used in Maine in the 80's was of only 2–8–2 percentage analysis; low in nitrogen and potassium, both desirable but costly; high in the less expensive phosphoric acid.

The decade of the Civil War marked New England's high point for cultivated land and the low point for its forest cover. Connecticut in 1870 was three fourths "improved land"; Massachusetts, Vermont, and New Hampshire roughly two thirds. Even Maine reached its highest point of clearance in 1880. The "improvement," nevertheless, may often have been only that the wood was cut off and cattle turned in to browse on the herbage.

During the sixties for more and more factories and railways coal took over as fuel, yet Civil War demands boosted prices of cordwood. A growing population still used great quantities of wood to cook and keep warm. Iron forging, glass making, and other industries demanded immense supplies of charcoal and cordwood. At Lancaster, New Hampshire, in 1874, wood brought more income than potatoes and half as much again as butter. Where the local market was good, farm woodlots might be cut every 15 or 20 years. Trees were sometimes sold standing, by auction in eighth-acre lots. Lumber mills were as busy as ever.

Altogether in each of the larger states, the woods in 1870 added from one to one and three fourths million dollars to rural income and one fourth million even in Rhode Island. At the same time they supplied material for important local wood manufactories, tanneries, shipbuilders, and farm use.

Steadily, as people left the hills, young forest began to take over. Petersham, Massachusetts, for example, saw its woodlands almost double between 1865 and 1885, and double again by 1905, when trees again covered 55 percent of the town's area.[22] Such changes did not inevitably decrease cultivated land. While poor areas of the farm were allowed to return to woods, tillage might even increase.

One discouraging development for the forest was the accidental introduction into New England from Europe in 1868 of the gypsy moth. A decade later this pest came to public notice with widespread defoliation of forest and shade trees in eastern Massachusetts. From there, carried by the winds, the moths spread rapidly. In 1897 appeared the brown-tail moth, to add to the destruction. Great areas of woodland and thousands of street trees were ruined and cut down. After the value of lead arsenate as a spray was discovered in 1892, reasonable control was established. Biological controls eventually displaced spraying, but no permanent remedy has yet been found.

As an offset, hundreds of village improvement societies all over the six states were busy lining principal highways with elms, maples, and oaks. State legislatures passed new acts for protection of street trees and required the election of tree wardens. In 1900 Yale established its famed School of Forestry, and the practice of forestry became a profession.

43

Any Way to Make a Dollar

THE PERIOD WHEN the farm shop had supplemented family finances was drawing to a close. By 1882 the historian of Sanbornton, New Hampshire, was commenting on the buildings, now empty, "in which the former occupants were wont to engage in their mechanical works—upon wood, iron, or leather." [1] Still, a good many country people continued to gain added income by doing piecework on boots and shoes, brooms, straw hats; and to make spare hours yield support by manufacturing small items, especially of wood, in winter using local water power. Sanbornton's own peddlers bartered that town's tinware for sheepskins all through the countryside. As G. Stanley Hall told Worcester's American Antiquarian Society, there were many grades of progress and versatility.

In 1875 Fogg's *New Hampshire Gazetteer* reported Sandown in the east part of the state as making 120,000 pairs of shoes out of stock brought from Haverhill and Lynn, Massachusetts. Across the state in the Connecticut Valley Walpole made 30,000 pairs. Acworth's output brought in $31,000, Fogg estimated. Acworth's other by-products, aside from sawn lumber, included 200,000 hoops; 5,000 bushels of shoe pegs; 4,000 boxes of clothespins; 56,000 hoehandles; and 175 dozen rakes. These added $23,200 in income to the town's $90,000 returns from products of the soil. Nearby Alstead turned out leatherboard, straw wrapping-paper, scythe nibs, and pail handles. Hinsdale on the Ashuelot River shipped out cashmeres, paper, boxes, chisels, spokeshaves, mowing machines, leather, bolts, shooks, waterwheels, boots, and shoes—and managed to farm. To the north beyond the mountains, Littleton on the Ammonoosuc wove woolen goods and made machinery and foundry products, as well as starch, churns, scythes, carriages, harnesses, and boots and shoes. "Many men . . . rated as farmers do considerable mechanical work during the year," says Fogg.[2]

The roll of small local plants in Vermont in 1878 included 34 butter-tub and 10 cheese-box makers, 13 of dairy apparatus, and 6 of sugar utensils. The long list of farm tools manufactured there ranged from hand forks to horse rakes (5 makers), hand and drag rakes (12), oxbows (2), whetstones (5), and many others. Page Smith points out how valuable the combination of farm and mill was to a country town when the mill cut down or shut down. With nearly everyone a part-time farmer, the town was able to go on with everyone eating while awaiting better fortune.[3]

In Massachusetts, in 1873, Athol, in northern Worcester County, made cottons, woolens, hollow ware, castings, farm implements, boots, shoes, shoe pegs, cabinet ware, palm leaf hats, pocketbooks, boxes, doors, sashes, blinds. At Fitchburg, Amherst, Barre, and Palmer, palm leaf hat factories were still operating in the 1870's. The manufacturers sent around imported leaf to be processed by farm wives and daughters, who then returned the hats to the factory for finishing. Three Waldoboro, Maine girls, ten to fourteen, in 1873 boosted family income by knitting eight pairs of stockings and thirty-six pairs of double mittens. Massachusetts shoe factories continued to farm out work widely in that state and New Hampshire. On Martha's Vineyard half the farmers were reported to be fishermen as well.

Maine farmers had plenty of winter industries besides the perennial forest crafts. Once the principles of cooling were worked out, refrigerated shipment of dairy products, meat, fruits, and vegetables gained importance, and as the home ice chest grew popular and cream shipment came into practice, demand for ice strengthened. At first the source was Massachusetts ponds, then Maine rivers. Occasionally a killing frost would destroy

Florida's winter products and curtail demand for ice to refriger-
ate fruit sent north to market. Maine furnished much of this ice
(1,300,000 tons in 1870; 2,000 cargoes in 1880; over 3 million
tons in 1889–90); sent its apples and potatoes along with it; and
built ships (346 vessels in the 1880's) to carry it all south.
Farmers from far and near, with their teams of oxen and horses,
concentrated at the great Kennebec ice houses. During the bitter
late winter they worked for ice companies, marking, cutting, and
elevating the ice into storage. Local farmers boarded the workers,
getting income from extra rooms, pork, milk, butter, and eggs.
The companies bought marsh hay and sawdust to insulate the ice
in storage and on vessels. Discarded cakes iced farm milk. The
1880's were years of prosperity for Maine. In Massachusetts
likewise, farm people and seasonal laborers shared extra income
from this winter work. Even from the western part, ice went
down to New York.[4] Arlington, Massachusetts, made the indispensable ice tools.

By contrast, Connecticut seems to have had little employment to provide farm people extra winter income except for
tobacco sorting shops and sewing for shirt manufacturers. The
state's thriving metal industries, though often directly related to
the needs of agriculture, generally called for continuous employment. A few of this type of industry deserve particular mention,
however. Collins Brothers' lightweight chopping axe had become
popular worldwide. East Hampton made cowbells; New Britain,
sleighbells; and Watertown, the nation's bull rings. Mousetraps
came by the thousands from Watertown and Sharon; New
Britain and other metal-working towns were expert in the steel
hand tools and hardware that every farmer needed; and about
1880, Charles A. Meeker's smoothing harrow, a horse-drawn
substitute for the steel hand rake and a great advance in
preparing topsoil for sowing onions and small vegetable seeds,
began to be made in Southport.

At every ten-foot fall, Rhode Island's squirming little
streams provided power for some cotton factory, 148 of them in
1860. To these, said a local historian in 1875, "we owe the
present prosperity of the villages along [their] banks, and in a

large measure, their very existence." [5] For farm people they were important as furnishing a market: though not one at high prices, for the labor force was increasingly made up of low-paid immigrants.

As to country manufacturing in general, however, the heyday of small plants was over, as industry concentrated around large waterpowers or cheap water-borne coal. The historian of New London, New Hampshire, tells of a decline from 90 manufacturing plants in that and neighboring towns in 1870 to only a third of that number by 1900.

Though the tremendous advances in grain harvesting machinery no longer meant much to New England farms directly, invention and improvement in farm tools continued. Farms benefited more from a corn cutter and binder developed about 1880; vegetable seed sowers and wheeled onion hoes with steel blades; the stationary gasoline engine which began to come in during the 1890's; increasing use of the silo and the centrifugal cream separator. All these meant labor saved and more efficient farming. Two inventions by New England natives, barbed wire by Joseph F. Glidden, born in Charlestown, New Hampshire, and the self-governing windmill that had been patented in 1854 by Daniel Halladay of Ellington, Connecticut, though useful, were proving of greater importance to Great Plains farmers than to those of New England.

Worcester had developed into a great center for making agricultural tools. In 1860 the Ames Plow Company took over the old Nourse firm, which already made 3,000 plows a year. Before the end of the century Ames had offered 225 different models of plows alone. The Walter A. Wood Company was said to have sold 84,000 agricultural machines and implements in 1884. In 1890 one firm there, the Richardson Manufacturing Company, shipped out 7,000 mowing machines, 3,000 hay tedders, and 1,000 manure spreaders. In Vermont the little town of Wallingford prospered by making Batchellor spring-steel hay and other forks to serve not only New England's farms but for export across this country and to England.[6]

During these difficult transition decades a new source of income for country people became important: the summer visitor.

To Newport, Rhode Island, the summer guest had long been an old story. Planters from the West Indies and the Carolinas and visitors from humid Philadelphia had been going there for the warm months since decades before the Revolution. Some lodged with townspeople: some, after a time, drawn by the equable climate and the considerable social life, bought property. Under the new nation Newport came into favor again. Across Narragansett Bay, Westerly's first summer hotel dated from 1840, and after the war, cottages multiplied at Watch Hill and Weekapaug. Narragansett Pier by 1890 was becoming a cottage city like Newport.

The White Mountains too attracted visitors. By the middle of the century the Glen House at Mt. Washington's base could accommodate 350 persons. Jackson with two hotels was popular. At Gorham the railroad built a large hotel. By 1875 the value of Bethlehem's tourist trade, $160,000, considerably exceeded that of its soil productions. The "large influx" of visitors afforded a "fine opportunity to market surplus produce at advance rates." Franconia, equally popular, counted three hotels and eight large boarding houses, and almost every house took guests; while Conway's 2,000 permanent summer guests and thousands of visitors, like Bethlehem's, left considerably more money than was derived from its traditional crops. Lake Champlain's southern end became a fashionable resort in the middle of the century, and the Green Mountains, even before the Civil War, were beckoning visitors. Brattleboro had its first summer hotel in 1845. Newport on Memphramagog had a hotel and an iron lake steamer in 1870; and at Sheldon, mineral springs attracted many.[7] Woodstock's famous Inn dates from 1892.

On Lake Winnepesaukee, by 1870 it was reported that "The inhabitants are generally engaged in farming and keeping summer boarders." Wolfeboro's summer visitors were worth $125,000 to that community. Center Harbor entertained 600 summer guests in 1875, in addition to transients by the thousands. Around New London, summer people began to arrive in the 1880's. They continued to come, for long stays, right up through the end of the century. Some boarded (1,200 registered in 1900); others bought property. The Monadnock region had been popular since long before the Civil War. Farmers near Dublin Lake were taking boarders by 1840. Organized camping is said to have had its inception at Squam Lake in 1888, and the original ski club was born at Berlin in 1900. On the larger lakes "elegant steamboats" added to the attractions. Massabesic, near Manchester, its shores dotted with cottages, in 1893 boasted four steamers. On the coast at Hampton almost every house had a few boarders by 1875, and there was said to be a home market there for all the farmers' surplus.[8]

In Maine the Ricker family had been entertaining guests at Sabbathday Lake since 1794. By the 1840's their Poland Spring water had attained a reputation that brought increasing numbers of guests. Moosehead Lake got its first excursion steamer in 1836. On the coast, Old Orchard Beach about 1840 developed entertainment facilities. A large three-story hotel opened in the Portland, Maine, area in 1849, followed by numerous others. Bar Harbor began to attract about the same time, but it was later in the century before it gained society recognition. At Cape Elizabeth the first summer hotel dated from 1875.

Lenox and Stockbridge, Massachusetts, drew the wealthy and fashionable of New York decades before the Civil War; while Connecticut's Sound and lakes and Massachusetts' shore resorts attracted artists and sojourners long before the century's end. By 1870 Princeton, beside Mt. Wachusett, had a half dozen hotels besides farm boarding houses.

This increasing influx of visitors brought many an up-country farm family a lucrative market for milk (cream especially), eggs, vegetables, and farm cooking, and a welcome income also from surplus rooms in the farm dwelling. The hotel trade bought supplies largely from city dealers, yet even so, formed an important outlet for market gardeners, growers of small fruits, and dairymen, though they might be one or two hundred miles away. New Hampshire claimed 1,400 summer hotels and boarding houses by 1890, "annually filled to overflowing." A Vermont report said, regarding cream, "We shall be strangely blind, if we fail to . . . cater to this new demand which has come to our very doors." [9]

The time for summer people to take over abandoned farms was still largely ahead, but already, though not always welcomed, they formed an important stabilizing factor, increasing farm and community income for many a hill and shore town, and, equally important, stirring the social and intellectual life of neighborhoods that were losing population and might be inclined to lethargy.[10] Governor W. J. Bachelder was to say in 1905 that for New Hampshire, the summer business was worth as much as the state's hay crop—three million dollars. Some resented the intrusion, but in general farm people benefited from both, not only in New Hampshire but in every New England state.

44

Agriculture Organizes

WIDESPREAD ORGANIZATION, both governmental and voluntary, characterized agriculture during the last half of the nineteenth century. Partly this was the result of economic pressures, partly it arose from an urge to improve animals, crops, methods of production and sale, and community life as well.

The Civil War was one year along when President Lincoln signed the act creating the United States Department of Agriculture. In 1889 its Commissioner was made a member of the cabinet. Meanwhile, the Bureau of Animal Industry had been set up in 1884 and several other bureaus and divisions added, including by 1888 the Office of Experiment Stations. In 1890 the Weather Bureau was transferred to Agriculture.

In certain respects organization by New England state governments preceded federal legislation. One timely step had been the creation of cattle commissions to meet the pleuropneumonia crisis. This had made possible also Maine's successful confinement of a foot-and-mouth disease outbreak in 1884. Massachusetts next set up a Dairy Bureau in 1892.

Official state organization on behalf of agriculture had begun even earlier. Massachusetts formed a State Board of Agriculture in 1852; Maine (after a short-lived earlier attempt) followed in 1856; Connecticut, in 1866; New Hampshire, 1870; Vermont, 1872; and Rhode Island, 1892. These boards were usually composed of one representative from each of the state's county or regional agricultural societies, in some cases with other state officials or appointees added. They met at the state capital, and from time to time in other central locations. Prominent speakers, persons of agricultural and scientific attainment, presented papers on timely subjects, often before a considerable audience besides board members. These papers and discussions— example, William S. Clark's articles on "The Circulation of Sap in Plants" and "Observations on the Phenomena of Plant Life"— received wide publicity. They were customarily gathered by the board's paid secretary and printed in an annual volume, distributed in some states by the thousands. The secretaries of the state boards, devoted men such as Stephen L. Goodale of Maine, Theodore S. Gold of Connecticut, and Charles L. Flint of Massachusetts, also wrote important contributions of their own.

The boards made grants from public funds to local groups for holding agricultural exhibitions where the best in stock, crops, and home products were entered in competition. They encouraged county societies to set up Farmers' Institutes. These offered winter courses of lectures, often lasting several days, at which staff members from agricultural colleges and experiment stations, farm publication editors, and visiting notables were instructors. Attendance was general, and, as Day makes clear for Maine, the institutes opened the scientific and theoretical aspects of agriculture to ordinary farm people under circumstances such that they could learn, yet feel at ease.

Through the century's closing decades the state governments also gave increasing financial support to their agricultural colleges, though not infrequently against apathy and opposition. Connecticut added an agricultural school at Storrs, which in 1893 became a college.

These efforts were effective, as W. H. Jordan of Geneva, New York, commented in 1898: "What a vast amount of scientific, well-organized, useful facts and principles have been assimilated by New England agriculture during the past 25 years." "The college," he said, "has been the local interpreter of the lessons of modern science." [1]

Connecticut in 1875 became the first state in the country to appropriate public funds for an agricultural experiment station, "to be used in employing competent scientific men," as the act provided. It opened at Wesleyan's Middletown campus with Wilbur O. Atwater as director, and two years later moved to New Haven, where Samuel W. Johnson was appointed to head it. Wholly financed by the state after its first year, by 1877 it was issuing analysis reports that exposed shady practices in the booming commercial fertilizer industry, was beginning tests of seeds offered for sale, and soon started testing 1500 varieties of grasses. In 1881–82 Atwater and Charles D. Woods provided, and in 1889 published, what is believed to be the earliest proof of the assimilation of nitrogen from the air by clover.

Massachusetts, its Agricultural College already versed in scientific experimentation, funded its station in 1882, Maine, in 1885; New Hampshire and Vermont, in 1886. With the passage of the Hatch Act by Congress in 1887, federal finance and organized support came to the aid of all the stations.

Connecticut's stations soon went deep into studies of human and animal nutrition. Among important results, this pioneering led to the development of diabetic foods. At Amherst, Massachusetts, Professor Charles H. Fernald began his notable work in entomology, while Professor Charles A. Goessman was specializing in soil fertility, plant growth, sugar-beet and tobacco-crop research. Rhode Island in 1890 began its work on poultry. Maine in 1891 came up with a recommendation for Bordeaux mixture for apple scab and worked on field crops, feeds, and egg fertility; New Hampshire, on milk quality and fertilizers; Vermont, on wool, milk, and potatoes. The contributions of New England stations to the nation's and the world's well-being have been notable indeed, and those of the entire nation of a value incalculable.[2]

Meanwhile, Harvard University, aided by a bequest from James Arnold of New Bedford, established on the site of its Bussey Farm its famed Arnold Arboretum and soon began to assemble the most comprehensive tree and shrub collection of the western world. Professor Storrs in 1887 published there *Chemistry and Its Relation to Agriculture* and put out the country's first experiment station bulletin. Harvard scientists Dr. Theobald

Smith and Dr. Daniel Salmon offered new and valuable information on the cause and prevention of hog cholera.

In the dairy field, organization took two paths, one the formation of breed associations and state stockmen's groups, the other the development of local enterprises, many of them cooperative, to manufacture butter and cheese and to collect cream for shipment.

Vermont farmers honored their calling by organizing in 1869 at Montpelier the country's first dairy association. Maine followed in 1874, and Connecticut, in 1882. Breeders of individual types of cattle gathered also in associations. Several of these had their birth in New England but became national in scope. Their purpose was to improve dairy blood lines and keep records of purebred and superior animals and their progeny.

From the home of its secretary at South Wilbraham, Massachusetts, the Association of Breeders of Thorough-Bred Neat Stock in 1863 published the earliest American Devon herd book. This included pedigrees of 501 Devons, from 58 breeders in 15 states. A second volume followed five years later. At Farmington, Connecticut, in 1868, Jerseymen set up the American Jersey Cattle Club; two years later at Winthrop, Maine, what was to become the Maine State Jersey Cattle Club was formed. W. W. Chenery of Belmont, Massachusetts, in 1871 took the lead in organizing the Association of Breeders of Thoroughbred Holstein Cattle. In 1885 this was to unite with a Friesian group to become the Holstein-Friesian Association of America. Next, in 1875, came the American Ayrshire Breeders' Association. This group, reorganized in 1886, still has headquarters at Brandon, Vermont. In 1877 the American Guernsey Cattle Club was founded in Massachusetts and its herd register set up. The breed's national headquarters remains in New England, at Peterborough, New Hampshire. The Brown Swiss Cattle Breeders' Association followed, formed at Worcester in 1880.[3]

Up to this time the milk from a farmer's dairy cows had been turned into butter chiefly at home. The census report of 1880 marked the high point for butter made on farms, as that of 1850 had for cheese. But Midwest butter of excellent, uniform quality had for a decade or so begun to top New England markets. Eastern farmers soon concluded that combining their butter-making efforts should yield better results than a multitude of small operations.

Cheese factories had been established during the Civil War. Maine's first started at Sandy River in 1872. What is said to have been the first New England butter creamery opened in 1879 at Shelburne in Vermont's Champlain Valley. The following year, at Hatfield in Massachusetts' Connecticut Valley, local farmers united to set up a cooperative butter factory, and across the river in Easthampton another began in 1881. Maine farmers sent a scout to observe, and in 1883 opened that state's first cooperatives at Wales, Winthrop, New Gloucester, and Machias. Turner Center, destined to become best known of all, began business the next February.[4] Soon, in addition to butter, this plant was selling the sweet cream for which it was to become famous. Some creameries proved too small to be efficient, but Maine's butter production kept growing through 1900. The other states gradually turned more to the sale of whole milk.

Individuals with capital also opened commercial creameries, some of them growing to large size. By the 1900's in each of the butter-making states the number of independent creameries equaled the total of cooperatives.

Some local plants achieved a good deal of success. The Franklin County, Vermont, creamery, serving 1,200 farmers milking 16,000 cows, made 2¾ million pounds of butter in a single year. By 1890 it was claimed to be the largest butter manufacturer anywhere. A cooperative creamery in the Quinebaug Valley at the Massachusetts-Connecticut line, formed in 1887, supplied Boston's Adams House, Parker House, and Young's Hotel for years, as well as the famous S. S. Pierce grocery firm. It claimed to be the most prosperous in New England.[5]

In the field of whole milk, effective organization was not to come till later. An Old Colony Milk Producers Association in Plymouth County is recorded in 1877. In the 1891 report of the Massachusetts Board of Agriculture a speaker credited a Milk Producer's Union with gaining a cent on the price of milk. The successful Springfield Cooperative Milk Association handled about 8,000 quarts daily before the close of the century. But not till the organization of the New England Milk Producer's Association in 1917 was there to be an effective counterweight to the power of the Boston milk dealers, five of whom gradually concentrated control of the retail milk business of that area and dictated prices paid farmers and the territory from which milk was imported. In the New York milkshed, which came to include western Connecticut and a part of Massachusetts, conditions were chaotic. The Five States Milk Producers Association, organized in 1898, strove with small success to surmount them.

Organization went on in other branches of agriculture. Orchardists began with the Connecticut Pomological Society in 1871, the Maine State Pomological Society in 1873, and the Massachusetts Fruit Growers' Association in 1895. All are still active.

In poultry husbandry the Boston Poultry Show continued its successful annual exhibitions. The American Poultry Association dated from 1873. Maine and Rhode Island poultrymen had organized by 1886.

A New England Tobacco Association gathered members in 1883 to fight for tariff protection, but it was shortlived. Eighteen eighty-six saw the formation of the Boston Market Gardeners Association, the earliest body in the country in the field of vegetable growing. Eighty years later it was to evolve into the New England Vegetable Growers Association. The seed growers of Connecticut and their competitors of other areas got together at Hartford in 1892 to form the American Seed Trade Association. The Society of American Florists was organized in 1885, and in the depression year of 1894 the Boston Flower Exchange set up business in the basement of the Park Street Church. In 1894 forty-four citizens of Windsor, Connecticut, and nearby towns set up a vegetable cannery that in two seasons put up 20,000 cases of tomatoes, 1,200 barrels of ketchup, 15,000 cases of squash, and large amounts of bottled juices. Under various managements this cannery was to last beyond World War I.

Community farmers' clubs, which before the war had enjoyed a slow growth, now spread widely. Sometimes, as at Industry, Maine, mechanics were also members. These held frequent meetings and discussions, often assembled their own libraries, and held exhibitions of local products. Besides their agricultural value, as Jarvis M. Morse points out, they quickened social life in country communities and softened jealousies and bickerings. From discussions at "the wide-awake club" in Woodstock, Connecticut, a local history states, new interest in farming arose and this club led its members to improvement on traditional practices. Greens Farms Club, organized in the winter of 1860, was known for 50 years for its progressiveness. It was the Belmont, Massachusetts, club that introduced the strawberry festival custom. Between 1860 and 1875 Maine alone counted as many as 75 such local farmers' clubs. They flourished in farming communities in the other states, some into the next century. In more than one town the Farmers' Club became for decades the leading community organization. Harvest clubs that included both sexes became leaders in the Connecticut Valley. There, in 1898, the Hampden County club was discussing immigration and the future of the Philippines.[6]

Important in the impression that it made on rural living as well as on agriculture as a means of livelihood was the rise during the last quarter of the century of the Grange. Oliver Kelley of Washington conceived of a new secret order, distinctively rural, to include both men and women.[7] The time was ripe and the movement widened to include all the northern states. At the beginning the idea spread slowly. The first local grange organized in New England is said to have been that at St. Johnsbury, in northeastern Vermont, formed July 1, 1871, its State Grange exactly a year later. In 1873 Massachusetts, Maine, and New Hampshire followed with State Granges; Connecticut did the same in 1874, and Rhode Island in 1889.

These early organizing steps began just as the great panic and depression of 1873 gripped the nation. Amid the general disaster farm people felt the need of a powerful, effective instrument to protect themselves and their interests. Soon the growth of the new Grange order became electric. Important political effects resulted nationally, among them control of railway transportation through the Interstate Commerce Commission.

The comparative stability and wealth of New England, the lighter burden of mortgage debt on its farms, and their closeness to market spared the farm people of these six states the worst effects of the depression and the political extremism that convulsed the West. The New England granges did act in both political and economic fields. However, both the original mushroom growth of the order and the downward plunge in membership that succeeded it when economic hopes were not realized were less spectacular in New England than in newer states lacking industry and far from market.

For a decade or two the Grange's future looked uncertain. But the New England Grange movement took root; membership stabilized, then began a steady increase. By 1897 populous Worcester County, Massachusetts, for example, could list fifty local granges with 4,889 members. Some of the organization's newly developed cooperative ventures failed. Others, however, including successful insurance companies and community stores, weathered all difficulties and settled down to long and useful lives. For their members and other country people these enterprises often made substantial savings.[8]

More important than their business aspect, however, was the value of the local and county granges as rural social centers. Something on the lines of the old Lyceum and farmer's clubs, they served as a focus for education, for excellence in handicrafts and gardening, and as a means of community betterment. The Grange was powerful in support of agricultural education and active in sponsoring local fairs and exhibitions of farm products and handicrafts.

County pomonas and state granges often became ladders to political preferment, a development not necessarily unfortunate in its results. In states in other parts of the country the Grange mushroomed, then almost vanished. In New England, which came to be called the Gibraltar of the order, it took root and became an important and helpful rural influence.

45

The Farm Wife

Nᴇᴡ Eɴɢʟᴀɴᴅ's ꜰᴀʀᴍ ᴘᴇᴏᴘʟᴇ, true to their history, continued to exhibit wide variations of method, habit, and progress. A farm family could still be found here and there like one described in Barnet, Vermont, about 1875, who "though well-to-do and hospitable, had not in [sixty] years bought a pound of sugar or meat or flour." The farm had produced all that the household required, and this was not an uncommon case. Henry Ward Beecher saw farm life darkly. In 1874 his judgment was that the great majority of farmers in New England fared coarsely, "not half as well clothed and housed as the average mechanic." Calvin Coolidge's Vermont hilltop neighbors, however, had no mortgages, paid their debts promptly, and had money in the savings bank. J. H. Hale, always inclined toward optimism, in 1890 told of his travels to other states. He came back impressed that in no other part of the nation did the farmhouses have so many comforts or were the farm people so well dressed and intelligent. Yet in the very same period a country parson reported that in remote communities a large number of farmers were running steadily behind.[1]

As time passed, changes came to both poor and well-to-do. The well-to-do farmer increasingly concentrated on the specialties that did best in his location, and prospered. Sometimes he took over the land of the less fortunate. Censuses of this period show some enlargement in average acreage even as total farms decreased. The farmer who fared poorly would be likely to have the good sense to enter full-time employment of some other sort. Then he confined his farming to a garden and a cow, or moved into an industrial community. With the influx of western meat and grain, and in the face of continuously dropping prices for staples, he was better off working for someone else and buying his food.

Thoreau's town of Concord offers a fair example of the changes. The famed philosopher and observer of nature did not think highly of commercial farming. Yet on his town's sandy acres it was the change in the second half of the century from general farming to dairying, to growing asparagus, strawberries, and, later, greenhouse crops that helped arrest Concord's decline in population and made its farm families prosperous.

Fifteen miles north of Concord there was another example. The farmers of the progressive upland town of Harvard turned to milk and fruit. They made almost half a million gallons of milk in 1890; several of the town's farms marketed a thousand barrels or more apiece of apples. While maintaining the traditional crops of corn and potatoes, they worked into peaches and small fruits. Even in Williamstown's Berkshire valley, although farmers still relied on corn, oats, grass, and potatoes, now orchards, small fruits, and horticulture rounded out the scene.[2]

Though the trend was in another direction, in much of the back country the "general" farm continued to be common. The country store still took its production of butter, eggs, and salt pork. Such a farm was likely to have a pair of oxen or horses, a few cows, a few hogs, a few hens, some potatoes, a few acres of corn, a few of rye or oats, considerable hay and pasture, plus woodland and a first-class garden. The farm family "got along"; thrifty, it appeared comfortable. It took public affairs seriously and sent its children to the academy and its contributions to foreign missions.

One factor that contributed importantly to the well-being of New England farm people, especially those producing fruits, vegetables, and eggs, was the superiority of the area's marketing facilities.

Each of its larger cities maintained some type of wholesale

market, often with only mediocre accommodations; traveling small dealers picked up supplies, and so did country grocers. Connecticut, Rhode Island, and Western Massachusetts were linked by rail and boat with New York. For the rest of New England, however, Boston was the great market. On Boston all roads, railroads, and steamship lines converged. About Faneuil Hall were concentrated every type of food merchant and great cold storages. From it supplies of fresh food headed to all parts of the six states, the Canadian provinces, and New York.

Aside from milk (a separate class of operation), fresh food dealers fell into three categories: butter, cheese, and eggs; fruits and vegetables; and meat dealers. Most of the three bought and sold on their own account and also handled produce on commission for up-country shippers, both farmers and local dealers. Their customers ranged from other dealers to hotels and steamships. They included grocers, peddlers, and, with some firms, retail customers. The chain store was as yet scarcely known; the few pioneers handled chiefly nonperishables.

In the midst of these, alongside the great Quincy Market, for six mornings a week buyers and sellers struggled with a mountain of fresh produce in the farmers' market on wide South Market Street. No set prices prevailed: farm salesmen and wholesale buyers bargained. Each day's, sometimes each hour's, prices varied according to the goods available, their pack and quality, the competition of daily arrivals from the South, and the bargaining strength of the contenders. By the time prices appeared in print, though they might be informative to a distant shipper, the market had often superseded them. These transactions governed returns to producers over much of New England.

Often in this period and the opening decades of the 1900's the special burdens of the times fell disproportionately on the farm woman. If income was low or a mortgage payment had to be met, it was likely that to her ordinary responsibilities she added more poultry raising or increased butter making. If, in the effort to find a livelihood, the farm advertised for summer visitors, as many did, she toiled through the hot months to serve them fresh biscuits and strawberry shortcake, while she coped with mountains of washing.

Home canning in glass jars had come in; so the housewife could now vary the family's winter diet and make the garden last through the year. Yet this added extra hot hours of canning to her summer schedule. On a dairy farm in haying time, or where, near a city, the farmer turned to vegetables, these months might mean the extra burden of immigrant helpers also to be housed and fed. As countryman Robert Frost recognizes in his poem "A Servant to Servants," such a cross was quietly borne, and not seldom the farm woman added a blessing. Whittier had described the quiet, saintly country woman of his time in "The Friend's Burial." Frost, in his "Death of the Hired Man," was to portray again her gentle influence.

The housewife did get relief, helped by several inventions. The iron cookstove was far better than the fireplace and brick oven, not only for preparing meals but for providing comfort in the kitchen in winter. To complement the stove came the ice chest, often kept cold by ice from a pond on the farm, and with it the ice-cream freezer, which a son was always ready to turn. Tinware, china, and washboards also became commonplace.

In more and more farmhouses running spring water or at least a pump from the well lightened woman's kitchen work and washing, and an iron or soapstone sink and set tubs received the water. The men piped in water from the spring or above the well erected a self-governing windmill. Near cities, prosperous farmers put in bathrooms. To help the woman in another branch of her duties, Elias Howe, Jr.—a Spencer, Massachusetts, farmer—had patented the lock-stitch sewing machine, and on a Sterling farm in that state Ebenezer Butterick originated Butterick dress patterns. The spinning wheel could now gather cobwebs in the attic, while machine-made sewing thread, pins and needles, cottons, and dress goods came within the means of almost all. Speaking in 1895 before Vermont's State Board of Agriculture on "Farm Life in the Vermont Hills," Mrs. Ellen C. Stearns dwelt on some of these changes: the coming of the big cookstove, the sewing machine, the conveniences for dairy work: "a hundred things," she said, "for use or beauty that our grandmothers never dreamed of." Moreover, as contemporary writers

Fig. 3.   Fig 1   P

DESCRIPTION.—Fig. 410 shows the implement set up and in operation. *a* is the tub, 26 inches high, and 24 inches in diameter at the top, and 21 inches at the bottom. The tub stands upon the base-board, *b*. The pounder, *c*, is made up of a series of 16 smaller pounders or pestles, *p*. One of them is shown enlarged at *P*. These pass loosely through *c*, being held from dropping out by small brass pins. A strong spiral brass spring, *w*, keeps them down as far as the spring across the top will permit. It will readily be seen that when brought down forcibly upon clothing in the tub, the small pestles or pounders will yield, by compressing the springs, *w*.

37. The "Metropolitan Washing Machine." Mapes, Illustrated Catalogue (1861).

point out, the use of haying and other machines cut sharply the number of harvest hands the farm wife had to feed.[3]

So it was not altogether true, as one ministerial observer charged in 1889, that the introduction of machinery had done nothing to take the strain off the farmer's wife. Nevertheless, despite the improved lot of farm women, daughters were still leaving the old homestead. In 1896 Harriet M. Rice told the Vermont Board of Agriculture why. The daughter, she said, wants to be independent. "If she has a letter to mail she doesn't have to ask Pa for . . . two cents. She doesn't want to be obliged to tease for a new dress . . . hat . . . or shoes." Fortunately, either many fathers were less grudging, or many daughters more dutiful, for Vermont farm houses never ceased to remain farm homes.[4]

Where a farm was doing well, the wife's duties could also be lightened by hiring at small wages one of the Irish, Swedish, or Polish girls that every steamer brought; or a smart country girl from Nova Scotia. This was a frequent arrangement beneficial to both parties. If immigration created problems, in this respect at least it appeared a benefit. In any case its effects on New England as a whole during the century's second half, and particularly on the southern tier of states, were profound. Yet in the country districts, except for a remarkable increase in food demand, in only a few localities did farms see great changes arise from it. Lacking capital, most of the newcomers herded in cities or manufacturing towns where they could get wage jobs.

Among exceptions were the Polish who were drawn into the labor shortage of the Connecticut Valley as tobacco and onion growers increased acreage. A modest number of French Canadians, attracted by the broom trade, had filtered in earlier. In the 1880's enterprising recruiters began to bring Slavs into the tobacco towns from New York where they had landed. Though the immigrants distressed local people by overcrowding to save money, also because the women neglected the house for the fields, they proved hard workers.[5]

On the large market gardens in city suburbs and on small-fruit and asparagus farms, Irish immigrants filled the labor forces, living usually in quarters provided by the farmer.

Eventually, however, many of them also would get farms of their own, though not in the proportion of the land-loving Polish. But the great bulk of small farms continued to get along with family labor and, if needed, the help of the proverbial "hired man." He was often as competent as the farm owner, sometimes more so. His advice was worthy of respect. If single, he lived with the family as one of them. Sometimes for years, in case of accident, death, or widowhood, he held the farm and family together.

The town as a corporation had long since ceased to govern the course of its farmers' agriculture. Nonetheless, as the twentieth century approached, the town had a deep impact on the lives of farm people, and they on the town. Writers might flock to Concord's School of Philosophy and publishers seek out the village's famous authors, but in 1865 five of that town's nine school committeemen were farmers. In a manufacturing town like Waltham, Massachusetts, and many another, respected farmers remained generation after generation as selectmen, assessors, and representatives at the state capital. Town meetings voted taxes and roads. On these and similar matters the voice of the farmers continued strong.

When the unsatisfactory condition of highways in Massachusetts reached the point of agitation, it was to the State Board of Agriculture that the General Court in 1870 gave a mandate for study. The Board's investigations led in 1893 to a pioneering state law which provided state assistance for building through highways, with $300,000 to start it off. Mile-long sections were built as starters, then connected. Within three years the state was spending a million a year on this project. In 1895 Connecticut also began a systematic program, the cost evenly divided between state, county, and town. Other states followed, so that by 1903 state aid for roads was offered all over New England.

Parallel with improvement of the roads by the states, after a year or two of experiment, the federal government in 1900 inaugurated systematic free delivery of rural mail in New England by horse-drawn postal wagon, with fifteen routes each the first year in Connecticut, Maine, Massachusetts, and New Hampshire, thirteen in Vermont, and nine in Rhode Island. In southern New England electric car lines multiplied, joining the principal centers and passing through numerous smaller ones. Rural isolation was disappearing.

In an 1897 *Atlantic Monthly* article Alvan F. Sanborn describes a country community that he calls "Indian Ridge." It is a town of thrifty farms, with little wealth but scarcely any real poverty. Food, dress, and home furnishings are all of the simplest, yet the town has forty miles of good roads, and adequate public buildings and schools. A church with an able minister plays a prominent part in the well-being of the place, and there is a lively country store where local sages foregather. Some inhabitants work in mills, farming a little on the side. The young people staff the canning factory in season. The village takes pride in former residents who have gone elsewhere and done well. The place has its faults, Sanborn admits, but life in Indian Ridge is by no means the utterly empty affair that existence in a farming village is popularly supposed to be.[6]

Without for a moment ignoring the many villages, in the hills especially, where the spark of life glowed now but dimly, Sanborn's appears a realistic description of hundreds of farming communities across all six New England states as the nineteenth century drew toward its end; and from them were still appearing distinguished persons, such as the Concord sculptor Daniel Chester French, whom his daughter described as always a farmer at heart.

VII. A FOURTH CENTURY

46

Seven Million to be Fed

THE PAST FOUR DECADES had been in many respects the most difficult for country people since the ten years following the Revolution. They had seen the loss of young men and women leaving for the cities and the West; abandonment of thousands of hill farmsteads, of once lively communities; the creeping back of forest; the invasion of orchard, field, and wood by foreign pests.

Yet on any accurate balance sheet the gains far outweighed the losses. An immense population increase had gone far toward doubling the local market. Instinctive selection by farm people of crops and stock for which nearness to local markets offered advantage had resulted in concentration on dairying, fruits, potatoes, fresh vegetables and flowers, maple products, and other specialties that appeared promising.

The founding of the agricultural colleges had already shown profound effects on New England rural life. From the six New England experiment stations came added gains, not only toward local production but to human health and nutrition, to scientific knowledge, of a value simply incalculable. These benefited not merely farm people, not agriculture alone, not solely New England, but the well-being of the nation, and, to some extent, of the world.

Meanwhile, organization among farm and country people gave more generous proportions to life in country towns, helped solve economic problems locally and beyond, resulted in better livestock, village improvement, marketing advances.

Nor was the decline of the hill farms as unmixed an evil as some viewed it. The coming of the summer visitor and his tendency to like what he found made for a healthy intermingling of life patterns and often brought tangible benefits in the form of libraries, parks, and street trees. This tendency was to grow in future decades until any differences in manners, speech, and ways of life were to become minor, and a common culture the fruit.

In the countryside, therefore, the nineteenth century could well end on a note of hopefulness and good cheer.

As New England's farming in 1900 entered the final two decades of its third century of history, the key factor continued to be its ever-expanding local market. No longer was its market only the distant West Indies and the Southern river towns of the previous century's beginnings, but also, now, the 7,400,000 people within its own perimeter, augmented by millions more only 200 miles away. The region's farmers could not afford to grow much bread grain, or fatten stock, but for the fresh milk, fruits, vegetables, eggs, and other high-value produce which the well-paid populace that surrounded its farms demanded, distance and transportation costs would for another generation afford New England a protective shield.

Sensing this, the Yankee farmer built larger barns for cattle and hay; silos for corn fodder; storages for potatoes, tobacco, and onions; greenhouses for vegetables and flowers. He paid out cash for fertilizers and in general so conducted his operations as to make life on the farm not only endurable but in the majority of cases comfortable. Poor hill farms, it is true, went begging for a few years yet, and woodland continually encroached on pastures, but good farmers resisted stubbornly, and those well located for community life and transportation increased production.

A favorite conception of the New England farmer has been of a person of rock-ribbed independence, beholden to nobody, neither seeking nor receiving favors from government or any other source. If this had ever been true, the wall of self-sufficiency was breached in the Civil War, with establishment of the Department of Agriculture at Washington and authorization of the nationwide system of agricultural education and research. In all this improvement New England was alert to share. By the end of the century dividends from these ventures were clearly manifest in advances in agriculture and chemistry which benefited the entire nation.

The first move has already been described, the landmark Morrill Act passed in the midst of civil war, affording federal funds to educate boys in agricultural and mechanic arts. By 1888 every New England state had taken advantage of the act to set up a college of agriculture. From time to time these ran into indifference or active opposition, yet their momentum increased as the years passed. It even spilled over to a foreign nation, for Japan called on the experience of the Massachusetts college to establish a similar system. In 1876 President William S. Clark organized the college at Sapporo, in Hokkaido, the northern island, since become a great university and one of the most important education centers of the Japanese nation. His name is still held in high respect in Japan. In New England itself, by the end of the nineteenth century, ever larger groups of serious students were graduating from each of its six agricultural colleges. Many went on to take posts of leadership not only in New England, but in education and in such new fields as entomology and agricultural chemistry, all across the nation and in other countries.

One path that beckoned these graduates led to the second landmark institution, the agricultural experiment station, born at Middletown and New Haven. A gift of $1,000 by Professor Levi Stockbridge initiated the Massachusetts station in 1878, the first public appropriation being made five years later. In 1887 the Hatch Act provided national funds and supervision for the support of such stations in each state of the republic. The Adams Act which was to follow in 1906 increased federal financing.

Connecticut's Storrs station inaugurated its famous egg-laying contest in 1911. After pioneering in the nature of vegetable proteins, in 1913 came the discovery by Thomas B. Osborne and L. B. Mendel of Vitamin A; and identification of the amino acids and of two more vitamins in foodstuffs followed. Donald F. Jones, Edward M. East, Herbert K. Hayes, and others worked out the principles underlying the double-cross hybridization of corn, destined so tremendously to increase the corn crops of the nation and the world. Jones' theory of genetics was published in a Connecticut station bulletin in 1918, and the first cross-bred seed was made available in 1921.[1]

The Rhode Island station emphasized the need of New England's sour soils for lime, and fixed the desirable qualities of the Rhode Island Red as a poultry breed. In 1908 its researchers determined that the fatal blackhead in young turkeys was a coccidial disease spread by sparrows and other wild birds.[2]

While this went on, Massachusetts was busy on egg genetics; and in 1905 began work on cranberry pests that resulted in 1910 in the cranberry experiment station at Wareham. In 1916, through the influence of the Boston Market Gardeners Association, the state set up at Lexington the nation's first experiment station for vegetable growing, a move that was to result in important improvements in varieties and in insect and disease control. The Amherst station continued to study tobacco and onion diseases. Meanwhile at Concord with the help of the federal Department of Agriculture, skilled farmers brought forth two disease-resistant asparagus strains, Martha and Mary Washington, on which that vegetable's nationwide future was to be built.

In 1913 the Maine experiment station, which had originated a trapnest and an open-front house for poultry, began to investigate breeding and feeding problems in cattle and poultry, and studied apple insects. The legislature appropriated funds to buy "Highmoor Farm," where both potato and apple experiments were to yield important fruit.

New Hampshire's station began a variety of investigations. Enthusiastic young scientists tried such crops as beans and sweet corn under glass, made variety tests of potatoes, delved into soils, studied the life of the forest caterpillar, and went after that enemy of apples, the codling moth. In the poultry field its staff developed the Barred Plymouth Rock, destined to serve as the foundation for an ever-expanding broiler business.

Vermont investigators naturally kept a close eye on milk and cream problems; worked on that animal closely allied to dairy manufactures, the hog; and emphasized truthful branding of seeds. All the stations had as regular useful chores the analysis of fertilizers, feeds, and seeds sold within their borders, in addition to the prevention of fraud.

The value of such experimental work, its results often published in scientific journals, went far beyond any dividends to agriculture itself. The Connecticut station's studies in dietary nutrition, digestion, and metabolism, for example, were of worldwide importance. Its exposures of false claims in labeling concoctions offered for human use (392 misbrandings, adulterations, and failures to meet quantities out of 1,369 samples in the 1916 report alone) helped bring honesty into the food and drug business.[3]

The problems of the country's tremendous growth in population and production seemed to call more and more for the intervention of government in agriculture and rural affairs, if not for the benefit of rural people themselves, in the interest of the physical and economic health of the nation. President Theodore Roosevelt's White House Conservation Conference in 1908 opened to the nation an enlarged conception of its duty to its basic resource, the land itself, to the abuses of soil and forest that had become a thoughtless habit, and to the obligation to preserve the nation's natural heritage. The disclosure of fraud and disregard of health that resulted in the Pure Food and Drug Act and the Meat Inspection Act of 1906 helped rivet public attention on food and the necessity for its healthful production and distribution. In New England, with its heavy burden of tuberculosis in both humans and livestock, Dr. Theobald Smith's reports on the transmissability of hog cholera and tuberculosis between animals and man offered examples of farm problems with ramifications so wide that only sustained and expensive public action could solve them.[4]

The century's second decade saw the Congress enact two more major pieces of agricultural legislation; (1) the Smith-Lever Act, to become the foundation of the county extension system:

agricultural advice, home economic instruction and 4-H clubs; (2) the Federal Farm Loan Act, on which a far-ranging structure of rural credit was to be erected. This decade's legislation included also in 1911 a federal insecticide law; in 1912, establishment of nationwide parcel post; and the Smith-Hughes Act for vocational agricultural training. In addition, the Department of Agriculture was authorized to set up a market-reporting service and a Bureau of Roads.

Of all these, establishment of the agricultural extension services by the agricultural colleges had the most immediate import for farm families, and the greatest influence on farm production. This was particularly true in areas such as New England, where farm people had a good general education and some experience in organization.

Extension teaching of a sort by the colleges had been going on for years, as President Kenyon L. Butterfield of the Rhode Island college pointed out in 1905. Correspondence courses reached farmers too old or too busy to study at college, and helped young farmers not able to spare four years of college residence. Farmers' winter institutes took instruction to the snowbound town halls of New Hampshire. About 1900 the Rhode Island college organized a "Nature Guard" of boys and girls, forerunner of the 4-H Club movement. Summer field meetings were in vogue, and agricultural professors addressed farmers' clubs and pomona granges in all states. By 1913 J. L. Hills, seeking state aid, could truthfully tell Vermont dairymen, not keen to spend the state's money, "The agricultural college, experiment station, and the national Department of Agriculture are the main purveyors of direct information and instruction." [5]

To Vermont's Bennington, Windsor, and Caledonia counties goes the honor of appointing in 1911 the first county agricultural or farm demonstration agents in New England, a step forward shared for the rest of the nation with Broome County, New York. Four Maine counties, with a grant from the General Education Board, a Rockefeller foundation, followed in 1912 to 1914.[6] By 1915 Connecticut could show a county agent in each of its six counties. Meanwhile, in 1914 the federal Smith-

Lever Act had authorized federal support of state and county agricultural extension work.

Soon agricultural agents were joined by home demonstration agents, to assist countrywomen in their domestic sphere. Work with farm boys and girls began in Maine in 1913 and in Vermont the following year. By 1918 Vermont had enrolled 3,800 enthusiastic youngsters in 152 towns into calf, lamb, garden, and similar clubs. If these educational experiments were to have a continuing impact, it became plain that country people themselves must participate in management. So organizations called county farm bureaus appeared, sponsored not only by farm people but others interested in rural affairs, to set direction and provide financial aid for the work of the county extension agents. Membership included both men and women; general farmers, gentlemen farmers, and leaders in the specialized farm fields that were more and more becoming separate branches of agriculture. The college-trained young men and women who took county agent positions had a true missionary spirit. No day was too long. They might be chief attractions at an evening meeting in a far corner of the county, yet be on call at the office by eight next morning to give advice on a sick cow; and woe to the agent not at hand ready to respond! Their state extension directors were men such as Joseph Carrigan of Vermont, Arthur Deering of Maine, John Kendall of New Hampshire, Willard Munson of Massachusetts, and other leaders of vision—their goal a healthy, vigorous, well-informed countryside.

Private organization in New England's specialized farm fields went on also. One more national breed association had its birthplace there—the American Devon Cattle Club, formed in 1918 at Agawam, Massachusetts. In dairying, though many farmers and small dealers had their own milk routes, control of the Boston and New York milk markets had gradually become concentrated in the hands of a few large dealers. These decided both the price to consumers and the return to producers. If opposed, they secured supplies by extending the "milk shed" or supply zone further up country. Tactics that farmers thought oppressive in 1910 brought on a "Boston Milk War," led for the farmers by the newly formed Boston Cooperative Milk Producers Union. In the following year the dealers succeeded in having the courts declare the Union an illegal combination in restraint of trade. One factor favoring the dealer was the gradual introduction of pasteurization, a process requiring capital and expensive equipment.

Undiscouraged, New Hampshireman Richard Pattee traveled farm to farm and town to town in that state, Vermont, and Massachusetts, convincing dairymen of the necessity for a legal bargaining association powerful enough to secure fair wholesale prices for their production. The resulting New England Milk Producer's Association reached a membership of 20,000 in 1920, and became for the next half century the strongest influence for the farmers at the bargaining table.[7] It formed an alliance with Maine's well-managed Turner Center Creamery. The Creamery pioneered in offering premium payments for off-season milk, a move designed to reduce the demoralizing spring flood of milk and increase the winter supply. Under the management of Edward L. Bradford, Turner Center grew to have twenty-three receiving stations, a headquarters plant, and distributing stations in Massachusetts and Rhode Island; do a business close to five million dollars a year; and own property worth nearly half that figure. Meanwhile, by 1920 in Vermont five cooperative creameries had federated.

Farmers were working into other cooperative ventures. In addition to Grange stores and insurance companies, as well as cooperative butter plants, by 1920 a half dozen farmers' exchanges in New Hampshire were buying farm supplies for members. Four canning cooperatives in Maine by 1922 canned half the blueberry crop. The Flower Exchange in Boston continued to afford its members an effective outlet for flowers. But the Eastern States Farmers Exchange and similar groups that were to systematize the wholesale purchase of farm supplies were still ahead.

Dairying now had become the most important branch of New England agriculture. With the advent of the Babcock test to determine butterfat content of milk, it was possible to contrast the fat yield of individual cows and of different breeds of cattle.

Testing, however, proved economical only when a substantial number of dairy animals warranted a full-time tester. The country's first cow-test association is said to have been formed in Michigan in 1905. Waterford, Maine, dairymen took up the plan in 1907. Windsor, Vermont, in 1909, formed a dairy herd improvement association, followed in 1911 by one in Massachusetts.[8]

Constant improvement continued in making and handling milk. Pasteurization had no sooner begun to make milk safe from typhoid and tuberculosis germs than a Torrington, Connecticut, creamery in 1915 by accident discovered how milk could be homogenized. The easily cleaned glass delivery bottle superseded the tin quart can; and in 1921 the first shipment of milk bottled in the country for retail delivery left Vermont's Bellows Falls Creamery for a Boston grocery chain. An agreement made under the spur of Food Administrator Herbert Hoover kept the market price stable during the war years.

Though New England's dairy cow total remained between eight and nine hundred thousand all through this period, except for a temporary rise during the war, the proportion of milk that went into butter and cheese (especially the latter) shrank. By contrast, sales of fresh milk grew almost continuously. By 1920 the large Connecticut cities alone consumed about 350,000 quarts a day.

Milksheds expanded. It became uneconomical for each individual farmer to carry his milk to the railway station. Instead dealers arranged for teamsters, later truckmen, to pick up the 8½ quart cans at farm roadside points. As a result even farmers with as few as a half dozen cows could market milk.

Control of tuberculosis remained a vexing problem for farmers and public alike. In 1917, with the cooperation of the United States Livestock Sanitary Association, the federal Bureau of Animal Industry inaugurated a program of accrediting entire herds, later entire counties, as free from tuberculosis, a promising forward step. The first area of the nation accredited as completely free from bovine tuberculosis in its dairy cows was the District of Columbia. Tuberculin testing had been going on there since 1906; its first entire herd was accredited in 1918. The next year Congress appropriated a half-million dollars to partly indemnify owners of cattle slaughtered as diseased. In New England, Vermont took the lead in accreditation, followed by Maine, Connecticut, and New Hampshire. In the northern states, which bred their own cattle, the disease affected a much smaller proportion than in Massachusetts and Rhode Island, supplied with cows largely by the great Brighton market, where the situation was worst. By 1920, 2,161 Vermont herds containing 38,839 cattle were under supervision, of which 1,343 herds with 16,082 cattle had been found free of the disease.[9] Only Minnesota (with five times the total cattle population) was ahead of Vermont in animals tested.

The long and extremely costly battle to wipe out the tuberculosis scourge nationwide had opened. It would involve the slaughter of cows by the scores of thousands, purebreds and grades alike, and last a whole generation. Sometimes the struggle meant destruction of a famous herd, built up through a lifetime—a bitter tragedy and perhaps financial ruin to the farmer. It involved public appropriations enormous for the time, and seemingly without end. In the long run, however, success in the fight was to prove a tremendous benefit to both the health of the great consuming public and to the dairy industry itself.

During the gradual shift from making butter and cheese to marketing whole milk, the number of New England's dairy cows reached almost a million in 1905, then dropped slightly. Generally speaking, however, any numbers the three southern states and New Hampshire lost, Vermont and Maine gained. During these years, breed associations were gathering prestige and experience. Gradual increases in production per cow resulted as the Babcock test came into general use and herd improvement associations made records of production reliable. However, like other pioneer efforts in agriculture, the early associations suffered severely after 1916 because of World War I restrictions and dislocations. No great change took place in feeding cows, except that the urge to make winter milk tended to increase the purchase of grain from the West, while silos for the storage and fermentation of corn fodder and other green crops continually grew in favor. By 1921 Vermont could count 9,445 silos, one to every 30 cows. In all states, as Clarence Day truly says of Maine, the silo became the visible badge of the good dairyman. Yet the capital expense involved in such improvements tended to discourage and weed out the small general farmer. He continued to depend on hay, which in most towns still surpassed every other farm crop in value. Meanwhile, many a farmer who turned to fruit or vegetables continued to keep a family cow or two, for daily milk and Sunday ice cream.

Other than the dairy cow, large animals on New England farms receded in importance. Oxen grew steadily fewer. Horses took their place, but of these more and more came from the West, bred and raised cheaply there. For New England, except on professional stud farms which bred race horses or saddle horses, they had become farm tools rather than farm products.

What with dog devastation, Western competition, and imports of foreign wool, the number of sheep dropped also. Despite improved breeding, Vermont's wool clip in 1920 was but one eighth of its 1850 total: it had dropped by two thirds in two decades. Maine, growing sheep with an eye largely for the spring lamb market, led the six states in wool clip in the 1920 census figures; but the 665,453 pounds produced was less than half the figure reported in 1900. Farmers could do better making milk.

Swine numbers, never great in New England, had varied but slightly in sixty years. They held their average of two per farm only by virtue of the large herds maintained to fatten on city garbage and the farm porkers kept on dairy and kitchen wastes, the latter usually butchered at home. Though a cholera serum had been developed in 1905, disease continued to cause severe losses.

Hay was still the most widespread farm crop, but tonnage dropped after 1900 except in Maine and Vermont. Most was consumed right on the farm. A town such as Gorham, Maine, west of Portland, however, could ship out 5,000 tons in 1903 to feed city horses and help cash income.[10]

Indian corn production had substantially decreased in New England as a whole, yet held its own surprisingly in the area's three southern states. Partly as a result of the World War, Connecticut's 1919 crop of over two million bushels equaled that of 1860. Massachusetts' corn harvest had dropped only one fourth in sixty years; Rhode Island's, one third. Although the northern states turned more to sweet corn for canneries and fodder corn for cattle, 1910 saw at Worcester what was termed a "magnificent display" of field corn at a New England Corn Exhibit.

Maine and Vermont still grew a considerable amount of oats. Aroostook County with its short season kept on with oats (4,500 acres in Presque Isle in 1936) and buckwheat as rest crops from potatoes. Except for a spurt of wheat grown in wartime for poultry feed, all other grains, by the end of New England's third century of farming, had become minor factors.

Tree fruits, especially apples, continued largely to be the product of general farms, though orchardists with a thousand or more trees were becoming common. Orchard pests were not yet such a problem that spraying was an absolute necessity, and the great freeze of 1933–34 was still ahead. Uniformly graded and packed fancy apples from the new Northwest were topping New England's markets; but ordinary apples, poured into flour barrels and old bushel boxes and well topped out, were still readily salable. The poorest went into cider or dried apples (delicious in pies), stocked by every grocer. Maine was now the leading apple state, its crop running from a million to a million and a quarter barrels a year; Massachusetts was next; and New Hampshire and Connecticut about even in their production. In 1904 the central New Hampshire town of Bristol shipped out 10,000 barrels. Yet New England's total crop did not equal that of the Empire State of New York. Professional orchardists, allied in state pomological societies, began to plant trees in blocks and to use sprays recommended by the state experiment stations. They were destined in the next few decades to take over New England's apple production and the cream of the market. These men backed new state inspection laws for nursery stock, designed to keep out a horde of pests and diseases that imported trees and plants might bring in. Some of the very worst of these pests, alas—gypsy and brown-tail moths, railroad worm, codling moth, and San Jose scale—were already established and spreading.

Commercial peach growing, along with Japanese plums,

had in the late 1800's begun to cut a substantial figure, especially in Connecticut. It boomed in the next decade. By 1896 there were said to be a million and a half peach trees in that state, with returns of two to five hundred dollars per acre received for superior local fruit. Their number doubled by 1900. In 1901 Connecticut's crop was said to be worth as much as two million dollars. A severe winter in 1917–18, however, killed trees on hundreds of acres and gave local enthusiasm a crushing setback.[11]

Urged on only by his deep interest in plants, a Belchertown, Massachusetts farmer, Everett Howard, with his son, was seeding and breeding strawberries and flowers on his rocky 35-acre farm. In 1908 the firm introduced the Dighton berry, named for a leading strawberry town in southeast Massachusetts. Already in 1906 they had fruited another new berry, to which they gave the number "17". Besides yielding bountifully, it had the great advantage of being virus-free. Plants sent to a midwestern state experiment station for trial caught the attention of a local nurseryman there. In the absence of a plant copyright law the new variety was introduced as "Premier" by midwestern firms, so that the true originator received little financial benefit. However, Mr. Howard's son was eventually able to prove that his firm was the source of what became for decades the country's most valuable strawberry, the "Howard 17" or "Premier." [12]

Commercial strawberry growing in New England attained its height at the opening of the twentieth century, when receipts for the berries sold reached ten million dollars, only a million less than the value of New England's fifty-two million dozen eggs. Concord, Dighton, and Falmouth in Massachusetts, Cape Elizabeth in Maine, and some Rhode Island and Connecticut towns continued for several decades to grow large acreages of the berries and to hold part of the market in the face of a flood of berries crowding in from other regions by rail and coastwise boat. Two hundred Portuguese growers in Falmouth, Massachusetts, with the help of the state's Department of Agriculture, made a name in the market for their 600,000 quarts of berries annually by buying supplies, grading carefully, and selling together.[13]

Further north, fresh Maine and New Hampshire blueberries

went to market in round veneer boxes packed in crates. Blueberry growing expanded beyond Maine's Washington County, and packing plants to handle the crop appeared in the new areas. Harvesting the berries and growing dry beans for the canners helped many a family in eastern Maine to piece out a living. Maine canned blueberries sold coast to coast, now meeting competition from those of other sections but still the largest crop in any state. In 1922 Washington County harvested 184,050 bushels, giving employment to 541 persons just to process them.[14] A portent of things to come was a first exhibit in 1913 at the Massachusetts Horticultural Society of cultivated blueberries.

The Massachusetts cranberry crop reached 575,000 barrels in the heavy year of 1893, and 600,000 in 1899. It ran at about 400,000 to 500,000 in the early 1900's, while experiments in disease control and bog management went forward. One important result of these investigations was the discovery by Dr. H. J. Franklin, head of the Wareham Experiment Station, of a way to forecast a threatened frost by noon of the preceding day. For this innovation in 1920 he received the gold medal of the Massachusetts Horticultural Society. This station also developed controls for the disease known as "false blossom," believed to have been imported from Wisconsin.[15] Meanwhile in 1912, Ocean Spray began the commercial canning of cranberry sauce, opening a valuable new outlet for that fruit.

47

An Artful Adjustment

As THE NINETEENTH CENTURY turned into the twentieth, vegetable growing increased by leaps and bounds. Maine's average yield per acre of potatoes soon surpassed that of any other state in the nation. Its production of 9,813,748 bushels in 1899, two thirds of them from Aroostook's 42,000 acres, was tripled a decade later. Meanwhile, the crop of every other New England state except Vermont declined. The exigencies of World War I reduced the harvest; yet in 1919 Maine still reached the enormous yield of 25,531,470 bushels. During this very period, however, farms in some of Maine's older towns were being abandoned and cultivated land reverted to forest.

Aroostook's sixty starch factories took part of the potato crop, in years of low prices especially; yet Maine's market, reached by cheap ocean freight, included the entire Atlantic coast. Wherever shipping costs permitted, its potatoes went inland as well. It was a chancy business, income dependent on price and weather. Aroostook farmers gained a reputation as gamblers, trusting in good years to overcome the losses and debts of the bad. Yet as a whole the county prospered and gained population.

Southern and western farmers came to value Maine potatoes for seed. They found that Maine seed yielded better than their own. This reputation had its dangers, for some Maine tubers carried an imported disease, powdery scab, as well as other troubles. The appearance of potatoes, sold for seed by commercial brokers, might offer few clues as to infection or inheritance, and disappointment sometimes resulted. To prevent loss of Maine's seed market scientists were called in from the recently formed Bureau of Plant Industry at Washington. They suggested establishing (1) standards of excellence for potatoes sold for seed and (2) a guarantee of practical freedom from disease. They proposed inspection for disease in the field even before harvest, and attachment of an official government statement as to quality. Maine people listened and acted. Henceforth a blue tag on the bag would certify that Maine's Department of Agriculture had inspected the seed and approved it as safe to plant.

The seed from the first few hundred acres inspected and certified soon built a reputation. Bags marked with the blue tag began to command a commensurate premium. All these measures were costly, but by pioneering such certified seed Maine opened a new era in potato growing. More and more growers joined the campaign; succeeding decades brought ever higher standards. The innovation spread to Vermont, which by 1922 was certifying 110,600 bushels from 553 acres, then to other states and to the Canadian provinces. For Maine the result was ever greater competition, but the state held its own. Thus New England had pioneered another agricultural advance, of the highest value to the food supply of the whole nation.[1]

As potatoes were to Aroostook, cigar tobacco was to the Connecticut and Housatonic valleys. The threat from Sumatra's high-grade leaf had to be overcome, and it was, by the Connecticut Experiment Station in cooperation with the U.S. Department of Agriculture. In 1901 scientists proved that for use as wrappers on the outside of cigars local leaf grown under the shade of cotton cheesecloth tents could equal the imported leaf in quality, even excel it. Cigar manufacturers were enthusiastic at the samples submitted. Congress granted tariff protection. From a modest beginning of a few acres, plantings of shade-grown tobacco mushroomed. By 1910 the yield had reached 1,800,000 pounds; by 1923, 8,600,000. Two thirds of the shade crop was grown in Connecticut. Overproduction and other difficulties ensued, yet shade-tobacco growing continued to be a prosperous minor branch of New England agriculture. Partly because of the heavy capital involved, production of this specialized type became largely the field of corporations and cigar manufacturers rather than of individual farmers. Yet it provided work and helped local income.[2]

Cigar sales kept rising. The ordinary Valley outdoor grower, despite disappointing years, kept boosting his production of the broad and Havana-seed leaf. Beneath the light-colored, expensive shade-grown cigar wrapper, the best of these types formed the second layer, "the binder," which held together the lower quality "filler."

Farmers fed their tobacco fields lavishly with stable manure (in 1906 they imported a thousand cars from Boston and New York) and with cottonseed meal, ground bone, potash, and lime. The soil responded with excellent crops, much of the production high-grade tobacco.

Harvest came in August. Workers cut the plants at the base and hung them on portable frames. A low wagon bore these frames to long, side-ventilated barns for curing. In four to six weeks during some short period of "tobacco damp" when they were pliable, the tobacco was taken down and borne to warehouses for sorting, packing, and fermentation. Every step required skill and judgment. Only a handful of soils elsewhere in the nation could produce cigar leaf of a quality to compare with that grown in the Connecticut and Housatonic valleys.

Prices fluctuated widely from year to year according to economic conditions, weather, and size and quality of crop, but between 1900 and 1920 production in both Connecticut and Massachusetts doubled. It was not uncommon for tobacco farmers to become wealthy, especially in the war years; and the whole countryside prospered with them. In 1920 Hartford was the leading tobacco county in the nation. Depression was soon to deal tobacco farmers some sad blows, but for a time the goose hung high.

The light loams of the Valley, highly fertilized and carefully tilled, were as well suited for onions as for tobacco. Polish immigrant families imported to grow the tobacco crop proved equally adept in onion fields. In 1900 Connecticut still grew over 400,000 bushels of onions; but by that time the Massachusetts area, centered about South Deerfield on both sides of the Connecticut River bridge, had nearly doubled Connecticut's production figure to become onion headquarters for the next two generations. By 1910 the single town of Hatfield was shipping out 500 to 600 carloads yearly. The highest yield came in 1920, with a 450 bushel per acre average for Massachusetts (including the fields of the Danvers market gardeners on the Essex County coast); but a yield of only 280 bushels in 1921 brought the growers almost twice as much money. The value of the Massachusetts onion crop, $748,309 in 1899, with war's inflation increased to $1,913,000 in 1923, the income from 3,360 acres.[3]

Outfitted in straw hats and blue jeans, and in bare feet, boys and girls of Polish families did the kneeling jobs in the onion fields. Through hot summer days they planted the sets and later weeded the seeded rows, while their elders with horse-hoes took care of the tobacco and cut the hay. Little by little these families accumulated money, bought farms, and at length came to own much of the best land in the tobacco-onion towns of Hatfield, Hadley, Whately, (North) Amherst, Sunderland, and Deerfield. A few of the most enterprising became onion brokers, supply dealers, and respected businessmen in other lines. In time both in Massachusetts and Connecticut, farmers bearing Polish surnames were elected selectmen and school committeemen.[4]

Other immigrants were progressing. In central New England, Finns began to take over the inexpensive, gravelly hill farms of Worcester County, Massachusetts, and southern New Hampshire. They raised berries and poultry. Bringing with them European cooperative ideas, in 1907 they established the United Cooperative Society of Maynard and the United Farmers at Fitchburg to do their buying and selling. In southern Worcester County, on better soil, a group of Holland dairymen and mechanics bought farms. Norwegians and Swedes concentrated in the Concord River Valley to raise berries and asparagus. Italian workers were making their start in suburban market gardens and florists' greenhouses in Rhode Island, Connecticut, and Massachusetts. Portuguese had long been taking up dairy and vegetable farms in eastern Rhode Island and southeastern Massachusetts. In Grand Isle County, Vermont, and Aroostook County, Maine, it was French Canadian farmers who became numerous. One Aroostook town was very properly named New Sweden. In the southern Berkshires a Jewish colony from New York City tried their hand at farming. From all these manifold European strains many proved good farmers and citizens, in time taking their places with descendants of earlier comers in all the enterprises of the countryside.

Growing fresh vegetables was increasingly such an enterprise. By the time of the Twelfth Census report in 1900, over one third of Rhode Island's farm income came from vegetables; for Massachusetts and Maine, with potatoes included, the proportion was one fourth, and for Connecticut almost one fifth. Yet vegetables used only one tenth of Rhode Island's farm land, and in Massachusetts only a little over one acre in fifteen. The largest acreage by far was within twenty miles of Boston. For crop value per acre, Massachusetts, Rhode Island, Connecticut, and New Hampshire led all states of the nation.[5]

Market gardeners in these areas had become highly skilled, their experience often running back in families for several generations. Glass-grown crops reached large proportions. The earlier, simple, wood-frame greenhouses had developed into rows of capacious steel and glass structures, heated by steam. Under heavy manuring and irrigation, greenhousemen harvested as many as four crops of lettuce during the colder months. A more common practice was a fall crop of tomatoes, then two crops of lettuce in midwinter, followed with the returning sun by another of tomatoes or cucumbers. North Leominster and Baldwinsville on the Hoosac Tunnel route were heavy shippers of cucumbers. New England's high-quality greenhouse products topped the market in New York and other centers.

Out-of-doors, market gardeners generously fertilized their fields with manure and chemicals, and made them yield two, three, even four crops a year by intercropping lettuce, spinach, radishes, and beans among long-season crops. Cabbages, carrots, beets, and parsnips followed lettuce and quick-growing leaf vegetables. Marshy land proved excellent for celery, a Boston

38. Corn and pumpkins have fed New England through three centuries. Food Marketing in New England *(1955).*

specialty known far and wide for quality. One unwelcome visitor
was discovered near Boston in 1917, the European corn borer.
This insect damaged first the locally popular sweet corn, but was
destined to become a menace also to the nation's immense field
corn production. Vegetable prices fluctuated according to supply
and demand as well as with the general economy, but vegetable
market transactions were universally for cash, a great advantage
to farmers. Pickle factories, processing cucumbers, onions, and
specialties flourished in the central Connecticut Valley even into
Vermont, with local farmers growing for picklers under contract.

Numerous greenhousemen had turned to growing commercial flowers, at first hardy violets, pansies, and sweet peas, then,
with more reliable heating, more tender varieties. By 1937 the
Budlong Farm at Cranston, Rhode Island, with thirteen acres
under glass, each day cut 18,000 roses, mostly White Killarney.[6]
Enterprising growers originated new varieties and before long
made New England the nation's headquarters for carnations. At
Cromwell, Connecticut, a Swedish newcomer, product of thorough training in European methods, had put up his first
greenhouse in 1872. By the century's end the A. N. Pierson
"Cromwell Gardens" had ten acres under glass, with 25 greenhouses in roses alone; four in carnations with 35,000 plants; and
2,400,000 lilies of the valley (a then popular wedding flower);
with other plants in proportion. By 1920 Cromwell Gardens had
achieved national notice for its hardy chrysanthemums. Thus
New England's greenhouse flowers found markets all over the
East.

Irrigation, both for glass and for field vegetables, had
become common in the high-priced market garden districts.
There were now automatic sprinklers fed by municipal systems,
under pressure, or by water pumped from private ponds and
wells—sometimes both.

In 1910 Hartford provided space for a local produce market.
Not long afterward, organized Boston market gardeners defeated
an attempt to limit their centuries-old right to sell produce in the
market streets about Faneuil Hall. The nation's Department of
Agriculture set up an Office of Markets in 1917. Market
gardeners about Providence in 1918 formed the Providence

Farmers Exchange. New Hampshire was the earliest state to begin publishing prices for farm produce, and to search out markets locally. In 1919 Boston's first daily produce report was inaugurated, a valuable summary of supplies and prices. Two years later the Massachusetts legislature was persuaded to adopt a standard for the wooden bushel-box in which most fresh produce there and in other New England centers went to market.[7]

Connecticut continued to be an important headquarters for vegetable seeds, especially sweet corn and onion seed. When diseases discouraged local growers, the state's enterprising seedsmen served their customers with seed grown on new land in the Far West.

In central and western Maine, sweet corn for the canners remained a leading crop. Annual plantings ran 11,000 acres or more, and the pack filled over 20,000,000 cans. Beans for the baked bean trade, green peas, squash for bakeries, and apples helped to keep seventy factories busy. Growing and processing these crops brought income to hundreds of farm families, while the vines and waste afforded fodder for their stock.[8]

48

Back to the Woods

THE BARNYARD FLOCK of forty or fifty hens, frequently of a nondescript type that one writer called "All American," living in summer largely on bugs, worms, chickweed, and kitchen scraps, had long remained the backbone of the poultry enterprise on most general farms.

Some observers claimed that the poultry, often supervised by the women of the family, was the farm's best-paying venture and, if truth were known, provided most of the grocery money. Feeding and housing the flock added little to farm expense, and the income secured many extras. Despite trainloads of white eggs that began to reach eastern markets, eventually from as far away as California, housewives preferred the traditional brown "strictly fresh" eggs and paid extra for them. Every month in the year New England prices for poultry, meat, and eggs ran higher than those reported from any other part of the nation except the new states of the Far West.

Poultry and egg production on a much larger scale and in a professional manner was claiming the attention of more and more New England specialists. Distinct local poultry breeds became the leaders: Plymouth Rocks, White Wyandottes, Rhode Island Reds. Kerosene-warmed 200-egg incubators and coal-fired brooders made it easier to raise chicks. Large flocks of a thousand birds, even three or four thousand, became practical. One Rhode Island poultryman needed five helpers. A southeastern Massachusetts town in 1916 could count 26,229 fowl in all.[1] Birds did best, it was found, in open front houses and in colony units spread over wide fields to minimize disease. Between 1900 and 1910 poultry and egg totals rose in all states except Rhode Island but dropped when grain prices soared during the grain stringency of World War I. Portents of the future for New England as a poultry center included in 1904 the admission of the Rhode Island Red to the American Poultry Association's Standard of Perfection; and at the Storrs, Connecticut, Experiment Station egg-laying contest, an increase in average annual production of eggs per bird from 153.5 in 1911–12 to 159.7 in 1920. At the Amherst station Dr. H. D. Goodale doubled the Red flock's production in the course of eight years. (It was to reach 183 per bird in 1930–31 and 229.5 at mid-century).[2] At New Hampshire's college (to become in 1923 a university), Professor A. R. Richardson developed the vigorous strain of birds that came to be known by that state's name. Experimenters at Connecticut and Massachusetts had found methods for control of white diarrhea: a remarkable contribution to poultry health.

The forest remained, as always, a farm resource. Connecticut had been three fourths open land as the Civil War began. By 1910 it was back halfway to woods, but was cutting heavily. Western Rhode Island's rocky terrain, though growing excellent orchards, was largely green with young forest. Until coal finally destroyed its market, southern New Hampshire added to its income by selling thousands of cords of firewood. Bangor was now the focus of Maine's great lumber industry and a center of winter employment for hundreds of summer farm hands. Many a farm boy "born with an axe in his hand" still went to college from the lumber off a farm pine lot, or on money from winter wood-chopping. In Massachusetts, Plymouth County water mills turned native oak into barrels to hold the local cranberries. Up-country butter went to Boston and New York in native white pine firkins, Cambridge candies crossed the country in twenty-pound wooden pails of native lumber. However, New England was slowly waking to the importance of conserving its forests. In 1897 Dr. B. E. Fernow offered the nation's earliest technical forestry course at Massachusetts Agricultural College. After Yale opened its forestry school in 1900, Harvard followed in 1906 and John S. Ames, Easton horticulturist, enabled the University to buy 2,000 acres of woods in Petersham to serve as a laboratory. Maine's State College of Agriculture opened its forestry school the next year. Already the Massachusetts Forest and Park Association, born in 1898, had whetted public interest in that state, and in 1906 the Commonwealth appointed a State Forester and began the acquisition of forest lands.[3]

Interest was not confined to scholars and well-to-do landowners, however. The lead article in a widely circulated farm paper, the *New England Homestead*, on November 24, 1900, was a savage attack on huge deforesting operations said to be going on in the White Mountains. It charged tax-title grabs and efforts by land companies to squeeze out small holders. Deforestation, it warned, means loss of summer tourists. Changes in the Merrimack's watershed were affecting the operation of Manchester's great mills, it claimed.

A conservation wave was stirring. In 1908 President Theodore Roosevelt called a conference at Washington and set up a national Conservation Commission. New Hampshire appointed a State Forestry Commission. It was none too soon. In 1909 in Connecticut 420 mills sawed nearly 170 million board feet. Vermont's State Forester asserted that up to the century's end New England had been self-supporting in lumber but was now importing one third of its needs. By 1913 the Massachusetts State Forester put the native production of that state at only 10 percent of its lumber use.

In 1911, with an appropriation of eleven million dollars the U.S. Congress intervened and passed the Weeks Bill, authorizing purchase of land to form the White Mountain National Forest and to preserve this scenic area with its spectacular views of a thousand-mile landscape as a permanent national asset. In five years more, the area of the Forest had expanded to 260,000 acres, some of which, however, was badly denuded. A Green Mountain National Forest in central Vermont was to follow. Both were vital contributions to New England's ecology and economy.

In Vermont the single most valuable tree was the rock maple. Owners of maple groves (called "sugarbush") formed a Maple Sugar Makers Association, which soon had 800 members. Returns from 41 towns in 1913 showed over 1½ million Vermont trees tapped. During the war the state's total tap reached 5½ million, yielding almost 12½ million pounds, equal to the state's entire sugar requirements! [4]

A European disease, white-pine blister rust, arrived in nursery importations to threaten destruction to one of New England's most valuable trees. To combat it, the states had to sacrifice two favorite small fruits, currants and gooseberries, whose bushes were found to winter the spores. Another unwelcome import, chestnut blight, spread north from the Middle States to doom completely one of southern New England's most highly prized forest trees. The chestnut was especially useful to farmers both for nuts and for posts and rails, because of the resistance to decay of its lumber, a characteristic that made chestnut also the favorite wood for railroad ties. Too late to forestall these disastrous visitations, the year 1912 brought enactment of a federal Plant Quarantine Act, a Seed Act, and prohibition of interstate transportation of insect-infested plants. Ignoring the law, windborne gypsy and brown-tail moths, among others, paid no attention to town and state lines. Only discovery by F. L. Moulton of Massachusetts of the value of lead arsenate as a spray had so far proved able to offset their spread. The moths stripped almost every broad-leafed tree. They spared solid pine forests, but in stands mixed with deciduous trees they killed the pines with a single stripping. Large areas, especially in eastern Massachusetts, were denuded.

The First World War produced an acute shortage of coal and a heavy demand for lumber. Homes, even factories, which had burned coal for decades had to turn to cordwood. The trees killed by moth infestation and disease were thus put to use, and farmers had a market for both cordwood and dimension lumber. Yet the chestnut blight and insect pests were heavy misfortunes.

A minor seasonal forest industry grew in these decades. The sale to city people of Christmas trees offered the northern states a market for thousands of young spruce that filtered into pastures. In addition, a continuing demand for wreaths and forest greens brought many a dollar into back towns where even small additions to income were welcomed.

49

Close of the Third Century

Nᴜᴍᴇʀᴏᴜs ꜰᴀᴄᴛᴏʀs, both on farms and off, made the final decades of New England's third century of farming a time of flux, the end of old ways and the opening of new.

World War I proved one of the most potent. Because of the immense destruction of ships and cargoes by submarines, one of the nation's prime objectives had to be feeding England as well as its own armies in France. Western grain, which normally nourished New England's people and livestock, had to be sent overseas. The Kaiser's submarine campaign destroyed much, and shipments to Europe were three times the usual. As far as possible home-grown food and feed had to fill its place. Home canning of vegetables boomed; but to can fruit, sugar was lacking, so rhubarb and some fruit went to waste. If poultry were to eat grain, New England farms had to raise much of it. Indian corn became again a mainstay crop. Some farmers went back to wheat, and it did well. As in the Civil War, with labor short, farmers found labor-saving devices indispensable. All young men 21 to 30 had to register, though where need was shown, young farmers could be deferred to help in food production.

War dislocations made essential a degree of national economic control never before conceived of. Daylight saving became mandatory, and gasoline-less days cut automobile use. Florists had to curtail as coal became too precious to grow winter flowers. Under such rigorous conditions of public planning, the newly established system of county agricultural and home demonstration agents, trained to advise and now forced to lead, proved of tremendous worth. These new professionals established themselves solidly in the esteem of farm people and the public.

Only temporarily slowed by the war, innovations continued to revolutionize country life and habits. Henry Ford had introduced his Model T automobile in 1908, and in 1916 the Goodyear Company had developed the pneumatic truck tire. Though use of the tire had to await the end of the war, both Ford's economical automobile and the pneumatic tire were to prove of immense value to farm people. By 1920 one Vermont farm in four had an automobile; a decade later the ratio was two out of three. (The farm tractor was still in its infancy.) Telephone wires lined village roads, often pushing far out through the country. Occasionally the farmers of a town organized their own company and gradually extended its service.

In 1920, even in the rural state of Vermont, one farm family in ten had elecricity, at first for light only.[1] Its use was to triple in the next decade. Later came welcome assistance to many an overworked farm woman as the current made possible reliable refrigeration for both kitchen and dairy. A gasoline engine was likely to saw up the stove wood. One labor-saving appliance after another followed. Clarence Birdseye's discovery of how to process frozen foods was just ahead—to come in 1924.

With state, then federal appropriations, main roads vastly improved. By 1905 Massachusetts was appropriating almost a half million dollars in state aid. New Hampshire was voting $10,000 for a highway map. In 1916 the federal government had set up in the Department of Agriculture a Bureau of Public Roads and authorized aid to the states in building rural post roads. Gradually, for farm-to-market roads, well-drained crushed stone surfaces began to take the place of mud and gravel. It would be another generation before stone fill and "tarvia" would make the ordinary country road passable in mud time, but these beginnings were important.

With better roads and the use of automobiles and trucks increasing, the village general store gradually lost importance as an outlet for farm produce and became merely a source of necessary supplies. Farmers turned to more efficient outlets. The introduction of parcel post in 1912 and the organization of more adequate sources of credit both helped the decline of the village merchant.

With each succeeding decade the number of New England farms listed by census takers diminished. For example, Rhode Island's "census farms" dropped from 5,292 in 1909 to 4,083 in 1919, and the number mortgaged fell even more precipitously. For New England as a whole the reduction in twenty years amounted to 35,324, more than the total of all farms counted in Vermont at the 1899 enumeration. Many a farm continued to be occupied chiefly because its buildings were good: its fields went largely unused, except perhaps that the hay was cut by a neighbor. By contrast, in the nineteenth century's first decade New England's total population grew over 17 percent and almost 13 percent again in the second, the size of the local farm market continually expanding. This growth, and the higher prices for farm products that often looked tempting, attracted shipments of farm produce from every quarter of the nation and from Canada. Competition increased year after year. More and more it forced the poorly located, ill-conducted, now economically unjustified general farm to drop out. The better situated, better managed farms, however, concentrated on products in special demand, and prospered. From replies by farmers to a questionnaire, one of the able new county agents in the Connecticut Valley in 1920 reached the following conclusions: of 21 dairy farms, 15 were profitable; of 7 onion farms, 5 paid; of 5 tobacco farms, 4; of 5 poultry farms, 4; of 3 potato farms, 2 paid; and of 2 each in sheep and maple sugar enterprises, both did well. His prize farm exhibit was 13 apple growers; only one considered his business unsuccessful. Large and medium-sized farms did best, he found. Among the small ones, almost half considered farming a losing game.[2]

Enterprising farmers on good farms, in many cases members of dairy, fruit, vegetable, and similar associations, found in the county extension system an inviting rallying point. Rapid growth of a new and parallel organization, the county Farm Bureau, was a natural consequence. Bureau membership soon came to include most practical farmers in every branch of agriculture.

Once organized by counties, these sensed their need for making known their views on the great public issues arising from the war and the depression that promptly succeeded it. Conventions of county delegates speedily organized state Farm Bureau federations. These in 1920 launched the American Farm Bureau Federation.[3] With memberships of many thousands in each state, and supported by more adequate finance than any previous farm organizations, these national and state groups became for the next three generations powerful factors in deciding public questions. They developed leaders of commanding ability who attained national respect. Among such were "Uncle George" Putnam, president for over a quarter-century of the New Hampshire Farm Bureau Federation, and Arthur Packard, who headed the Vermont organization for an equal period. They employed staff to investigate farm problems and seek practical solutions, often by new legislation. They raised capital to provide cooperative sales, insurance, and purchasing facilities of many types. The American Farm Bureau Federation took its place as one of the most influential of the nation's business organizations. Local county Farm Bureaus gave needed support and balance to the system of agricultural education and experiment, and helped agriculture overcome the war's dislocations and readjust into a modern business.

Meanwhile, many more small farmers who in the nineteenth century had taken in shoe parts or hat-making to add income, went to work full time in a local mill or factory. The farm, however, now down to a single cow and garden, and chiefly a home, remained a valued recourse when the mill work slacked in the 1921 depression. Like small farms, small country industries were casualties of economic change, leaving fewer openings for part-time labor, long a small farmer's resource.

One offset to economic dislocations was continued rapid growth in "summer business" in every state, especially New Hampshire. That state offered an excellent example of what a wide-awake government can do to meet economic dislocations.

Empty farms blessed with decent buildings and sites passed continually into the possession of summer visitors from the cities, persons who had begun as boarders and to whom a country home of their own appealed. The popular "Old Home Week" movement inaugurated in 1899 by Governor Rollins helped; the 4,000 copies of the state's *New Hampshire Farms for Summer Homes*, issued annually from 1902 on, sent visitors scouring the countryside for the bargains. President Theodore Roosevelt's Country Life Commission of 1908 added momentum.

The summer vacation boom brought visitors by the thousands. In 1920 New Hampshire counted summer hotels in 59 towns. One town of only 100 people in 1918 entertained 3,000 guests; another of 300 claimed to put up 10,000 visitors. Cornish was described as a little New York; Washington people congregated at Springfield; Montclair visitors at Littleton; St. Louis folks in Cheshire County. Bostonians had for decades found the Monadnock region enticing. Eastman's cheap Kodak was called an incentive. A state report asserted that the economic lift from this development had doubled assessed values in many towns. Literally hundreds of farmers were said to pay off mortgages and accumulate property by taking advantage of a two-to-three-month market right at hand, "better than Boston for everything that their town could produce."

A Vermont farmer described how through these two decades, with two or three helpers, he had gardened for 80 to 90 guests. Vegetables were what they wanted. He couldn't give them asparagus too often—until peas arrived! Princeton, Massachusetts, beside Wachusett Mountain, gloried in the buildings erected by summer residents on discontinued farms. On the Maine, Connecticut, and Rhode Island shores, demand for cottages mounted. Their occupants, often distinguished persons, were reported to pay well for fruits, vegetables, and dairy and poultry products. All this helped rural New England adjust to a new economic era, and sparked local improvements. "A town cannot be found that has not felt its quickening influence," was an official New Hampshire comment.[4]

A new government-sponsored system of farm credit eased the readjustments that followed the war. Because of the wide distribution of mutual savings banks, which farmers had often helped form, New England's farmers had long been better served as to mortgage credit than those of most parts of the nation. Yet as a result of the difficulties that marked the closing years of the nineteenth century, farm mortgages had fallen out of favor. Hence, organization in 1917 of the Federal Land Bank at Springfield to provide farm credit for farmers of New England and New York came as an important stabilizing factor for farm enterprise. That same year saw the Eastern States Exposition launched in Springfield to begin a fruitful career of exhibitions and prizes for the next half century and longer.

So as a whole, and sometimes painfully, New England farming adjusted. Backwoods and hilltop farm buildings, especially unused barns, were burning, decaying, slumping into cellars; on the contrary, good dairy, fruit, and garden farms, especially near transportation, exhibited an outlook quite different. Substantial farm dwellings, thousands of them, well clapboarded and painted white or buff with lead and oil, bordered country roads in every state. On their south sides or in front rose great elms and maples to cool the dwelling in summer and shade the well-kept lawn. The New England farmer was often accused of being tight-fisted and insensitive to aesthetic considerations; yet there stood the ample, comfortable farmstead, an obvious refutation too often taken for granted by all because so common.

Outbuildings, too, were often good. Dairymen needing shelter for increasing numbers of cattle and the hay to keep them through the winter had built sturdy barns, a hundred feet long or more, with wide doors opening at each end for the haywagon to enter and leave, and smaller side doors for cattle. Ordinarily they stood on stone wall foundations, enclosing a manure cellar and hogpen, perhaps floored with cement.

Though siding might be only wide vertical boards, more often both walls and roof were shingled, walls even painted. A cupola for hay ventilation crowned the whole. North of the Massachusetts line, house and barn were likely to be connected by a shed or two, offering a covered walkway for bad weather and providing a sheltered yard for family and stock. Everything reflected characteristic adaptation to climate and circumstances.

Thus the year 1921 approached, and with it the beginning of the fourth century of New England farming. Like the year which saw the long-ago Pilgrim fathers harvest their first crop, the outlook had its features both of hope and of difficulty.

50

The Earth Remains

THIS ACCOUNT of three centuries began with an excursion into prehistory and a description of the locality now titled New England according to the impressions of the first comers. It may appropriately end with a review of how soil and landscape had fared in the course of three hundred years and how the character of New England stood as a new generation inherited it.

Contrary to often repeated assertions, it has been shown that the land the first immigrants entered from overseas was not a gloomy, unending primeval forest, alive with wild beasts, some of them ferocious. It was instead an inhabited land, adapted in the course of centuries to the uses of an intelligent, capable branch of the human race.

From the westernmost limit of the Connecticut shore in what is now New England to the Saco River on the Maine coast, level treeless salt marsh fringed much of the shore. Fresh meadows bordered the edges of the great rivers and several of their interior tributaries.

Alongside the numerous sheltered harbors, bays, and estuaries and on offshore islands the native inhabitants had cleared substantial areas to provide village sites, and fields for their crops. They had cut the neighboring trees for firewood. Most of the early explorers of the coast who have left records—Verrazano, Champlain, John Smith, George Waymouth, Van der Donck, De Vries—were as much impressed by the open spaces that they found near the shore and up the great rivers, even the Kennebec in Maine, as with the noble forest trees that they also describe. These open plains and uplands, cleared by their Indian inhabitants, were the chief factor that made it possible for the Pilgrims to exist at Plymouth, for the Puritans to settle down comfortably about Boston Harbor and Massachusetts Bay, and for certain dissident or uneasy groups among them to colonize the southern Connecticut Valley, the shores of Narragansett Bay, and coastal New Hampshire.

Not even in the interior was unending woodland the rule. To the Indian village sites and cultivated fields that the settlers found alongside many interior ponds and tributaries scores of local historians attest. Villages dotted the territory occuped by the inland Nipmuck, Pocumtuck, Pennacook, Abenaki, and similar tribes. Besides village sites and cultivated fields every tribe had its own carefully delineated hunting grounds. For example, the Wampanoags, Massasoit's people, hunted in what are now Rehoboth and Raynham. In Connecticut the Naugatuck Valley and the Litchfield hills were hunting grounds, and in central Massachusetts so were the Brimfield-Monson neighborhood and the Ware River Valley. Such areas had been kept free of large timber by Indian fires. The purposes were at least threefold. First, the deer herd and the bears served the natives in place of livestock as a prime source of meat, clothing, and wigwam covering. Such game animals are not habitants of the deep forest, but increase where in the seasons following a fire, herbage is tender and easy to browse or penetrate. Besides providing a source of meat and skins, these scorched clearings served a second purpose: burning them over brought successive years of raspberries, blueberries, strawberries, and later black cherries, all important food for the natives (and for game). A third motive for periodic burning, the colonial writer Edward Johnson states, was to clear underbrush so as to make travel and hunting easier. Anyone who has ever fought a way through masses of laurel, bullvine, or ground juniper can appreciate the importance of this aspect.

Spring fires, however, ordinarily left undamaged the extensive swales where cedars, maples, and often some pine grew thick, and the miles-long plains where mature pine soared. Fallen leaves burned but oaks and nutbearing trees, sources of food for both men and game, remained unharmed.

By modern standards, however, at the time of white settlement population was light. Even the better inhabited southern portions of New England were thinly peopled. Northern New England—except for parts of the Champlain, Connecticut, and Merrimack, and certain Maine valleys—was almost total wilderness.

It is easy to exaggerate the immediate effects on such a landscape of the coming of the English. Keep in mind, for one detail, that handling an axe was a skill unknown to most of the newcomers. Recall also that for the first half century and more the chief goal in farming at Massachusetts Bay was livestock and its products. Grain was grown mostly for family food. For cattle the scythe, not the axe, was the primary implement, and the natural salt and fresh marshes of coast and river, not cultivated fields, the source of feed. Besides cattle the other important domestic animals at first were hogs and goats. These made the woods and native vegetation their feeding ground.

So, at first, tillage to grow bread grain and roots for human food was confined largely to long-cultivated former Indian fields. Forest cutting was chiefly for housing and shipbuilding, until export demand made it profitable to cut and merchandise lumber, spars, and staves. Moreover, the English set up their villages largely on Indian sites, some of them left vacant by fatal epidemics, others deeded to the colonists by the original possessors.

The landscape, therefore, would for decades show few totally new clearings. English dwellings, laid out on village plans, had indeed taken the place of dome-shaped Indian wigwams. Fences, occasionally a wall, surrounded the old fields. Apple trees now blossomed in spring. Nevertheless, noticeable changes in the landscape were few and to be found almost entirely near salt water and on the open lands of inland valleys. In only one area, along the Piscataqua River where New Hampshire and Maine now meet, was there in the first half century lumbering on a scale sufficient to alter substantially the existing ecology.

One change in natural surroundings, however, deadly serious to the farming colonists yet easy for moderns to forget, resulted from the coming of the cattle, hogs, sheep and poultry of the colonists. There appears to have been an alarming increase in predatory wild animals and birds. Town records are full of measures against wolves and bears, which, finding domesticated European livestock greatly to their liking and easy to hunt, rapidly multiplied. One consequence was the designation of numerous insular spots off the coast as "hog islands" and "calf pastures," valuable because safe from predators. From the air, crows, blackbirds, and passenger pigeons plundered the new cereal crops of the English. Unlike maize, these grains had no tough protective husk. Frequent votes of bounties in town records attest their damage. Thus matters continued for nearly a half century.

The end of King Philip's War, in 1676, opened large additional tracts of confiscated Indian lands to white settlement. However, the French and Indian wars that began only fifteen years later ushered in six decades of intermittent but deadly raids on outlying New England villages and blocked English expansion elsewhere. Northern Worcester County at this period was called a howling wilderness, a dreary waste. In the quarter-century of 1700–25, fewer than twenty new towns were incorporated by Massachusetts. Up to 1750 any growth was chiefly a filling-in of territory, new parishes formed from or near older ones, mostly in the settled parts of the provinces. Meanwhile, in Maine, New Hampshire, and the upper Connecticut Valley, what had promised to become flourishing villages lay burnt—deserted and reverting to nature. Connecticut and Rhode Island alone were for the most part physically unscathed.

Yet within reach of the coast, timber was being constantly felled. Despite wars, shipbuilding and export went forward. Almost every cargo included shingles, staves, and hoops. White pines, oaks, and cedars were cut increasingly; pitch pines were bled.

In the older towns much cultivated land had already been depleted. Growing small grain year after year led to gullies in the upland. As forest decreased and wolves and wildcats were exterminated, sheep more and more took over the cleared pastures. New England's population was growing, its forest receding, its landscape opening.

Lower Cape Cod was cutting its forests and found sand dunes filling anchorages and burying salt marsh. To hold blowing sand, towns there were forced to control cutting and grazing, and to plant beach grass. River towns elsewhere took measures to ensure free passage of fish upstream for spawning to conserve this valuable resource. Jared Eliot of Connecticut warned in print that irreplaceable upland topsoil was washing down from unclothed grainfields, to muddy clear brooks. Massachusetts in 1743 legislated to restrain the firing of woodland, which destroyed fences, wasted soil fertility, and prevented reproduction of desirable timber. The first manifestations of what is today called conservation had been voiced.

Meanwhile, all through settled southern New England new features appeared on the land. Miles of stone wall laced the cleared pastures, orchards bloomed and fruited, neat dwellings filled villages, and to travelers the landscape appeared civilized. In 1760 a visitor likened Connecticut's fertile valley to one continuous town.

The year 1763, when the Treaty of Paris ended the French and Indian War, is a watershed in New England ecological history. Within the bounds of the older towns of Connecticut and Massachusetts the land was already fully distributed. Meanwhile a numerous third or fourth generation of native-born grew up. How were they to be accommodated? Once the treaty had removed the menace of Indian attack, the expansive forces burst old bounds. Connecticut's young people poured west into the Housatonic Valley and north up the Connecticut into Vermont. From Massachusetts' older towns settlers streamed into New Hampshire and the Berkshire Hills.

By 1775 the whole unsettled remainder of Connecticut had been divided into townships. In 1762 Massachusetts auctioned off its western wilderness for township sites. By the end of 1775 it had incorporated close to sixty new towns. New Hampshire in fifteen years set up a hundred new townships. Its own farmers pushed north as far as Lancaster and the Coos country. Some

Massachusetts settlers found easy access to Maine by water and went east in swarms.

Unlike their forefathers, except for the few fortunate enough to find meadows or a very few spots where land had been Indian-cleared, all these newcomers had to chop their homesteads out of the forest. But by now the English were used to the axe. With skillful methods of preparation and good help, a whole acre of trees might fall in a single day. Then the next season, either with or without help of fire, the opening thus made became a sunlit corn or wheat field. When, a few years later, bread and housing for the family were secure, further clearing might result in merchantable potash, and provide English pasture grasses for cattle which could reach market on their own hooves. Moreover, salable wheat throve on the rich new soil, twenty to forty bushels to the acre.

But so for some years did bears and raccoons, grateful to the settlers for sweet young corn ears. Deer cropped fruit-bearing trees. Wolves, bears, and wildcats from the adjoining forest found the newcomers' hogs and young stock to their taste. One Thetford, Vermont, farmer claimed to have killed three bears in his corn in a single night. It took time for the settlers to tame both the land and its native wild life.

These pioneers commonly built their towns and farmsteads on high land, avoiding damp places and valley plains darkened by white-pine stands. Hillsides offered the best pasturage also. About Lake Champlain and the Connecticut and Maine rivers on which the logs could be floated to mills for export, logging went on.

Thus for a full half-century after the American Revolution took the New England states into the new republic, the pattern continued. Then a transformation came to upland New England. The sheep craze began. By this time, predators were under control. Insects, disease, soil mining, and the Erie Canal had taken the profit out of wheat. Now tariff protection and a strong demand for fiber from the fast-expanding woolen industry made it profitable to breed by thousands the recently introduced Merino sheep. To provide pasture, Vermont and New Hampshire hills were cleared and grassed to their summits. Flock owners added farm to farm, until in the sheep towns, except in the roughest areas, accessible woods almost disappeared. The former occupants moved west. Sheep moved in.

It was in the same era that the through turnpikes cut across the landscape, then the canals and railways. Next came the gold rush and the opening of the prairies. All these forces enticed families from hill farms, many of them cleared less than a century but now lacking promise for the future. The Civil War brought even more displacements. In all New England except Maine and northern New Hampshire, land clearing had reached its zenith; Connecticut by 1860 was three fourths open land. In Massachusetts, in three of its westernmost counties, the proportion of land cleared was still greater. With 1,159 sawmills operating in 1865, Massachusetts harvested 140 million board feet of lumber. Each year left more thousands of its acres unclothed.

Still, even in 1851 Henry Thoreau, passing through first-settled Plymouth, reported forest that axe had never touched. In the Connecticut Valley the English traveler Johnston commented on what he called the less promising portions where, he said, "the Saxon woodsman" had only begun. The chopper had as yet scarcely entered northern Maine, except for Aroostook, and much of it was to remain permanently in forest.

Meanwhile, faint signs of a change in attitude toward the forest appeared. At Enfield, Connecticut, the Shaker colony in 1866 was planting a pine grove. George P. Marsh was in print protesting the destruction of the woods. More impelling, at the very time that Colebrook, New Hampshire, was burning peat, New England's factories and railroads were turning to mined coal. Soon its dwellings also would be heated by anthracite; the market for cordwood was gradually curtailed, and cutting immature woods for fuel would eventually sink to small proportions. The rage for sheep raising had tapered off. On mountainsides and rough lands nature was taking over once more. The gradual return to woodland often took the form of "pasture pine." Pine seeds sifted into the uncropped herbage to become solid acreages. These were eventually to yield a welcome and valuable box and board lumber harvest in the twentieth century, and here and there a popular picnic grove.

Besides the gradual return of the forest, more effective means of draining and utilizing land were altering the farm landscape. Swales that had once produced only cattails and bunch grass were now drained and leveled to become productive hay meadows. In southeast Massachusetts hundreds of acres of natural bog were ditched and leveled at great expense, then set with cranberry vines, to provide a marketable crop of increasing value.

On every active farm, however, some proportion of cultivated land, most often in corn, was always to be found. After a few years this gave way to grass, so that extensive soil washing became unusual. "You don't know the first meaning of the word erosion," an Ohio speaker told an audience of Connecticut farmers.

On the uplands the labors of a half dozen generations had cleared farm fields of rocks and concentrated them in unnumbered miles of stone wall that became a hallmark of the New England countryside. Apple trees by the thousands lined the walls or were enclosed within them, lending to the landscape both fragrance and fruitfulness. In the air Italian bees hummed all summer, enjoying both native blossoms and imported clovers. A wealth of small birds—robins, sparrows, swallows, bluebirds— had multiplied, to replace the wild turkeys and passenger pigeons that had welcomed the first explorers.

During the decades that followed the Civil War millions in added population had filled up New England cities and manufacturing towns, and suburbs had spread. Responding to the craving of their people for milk and butter, meadows, some of which had pastured sheep, now fed a million dairy cows. Wheat fields became hay fields. Corn more and more was cut green into silos rather than shocked. Deer were now protected by law, bears and wolves found only in the wildest places.

The herbage of lane and hayfield had subtly altered from colonial times. Clovers and timothy were now the rule. Buttercups, daisies, dandelions, burdocks, tansy, literally a thousand new field plants edged roadsides and filtered into meadows. Following in the white farmer's footsteps, they had increased until most persons thought them native. Overseas shrubs, the barberry, and the lilac had also managed to scatter widely. Meanwhile, ragweed and goldenrod, weeds that Indian farmers had fought, continued to find to their liking the vastly enlarged cornfields of their successors.

In further ways the landscape had been altered. Though the automobile had as yet by no means fully taken over, the network of highways had expanded tremendously. Roads reached almost every part of the six states. The greatest rivers no longer flowed unhindered, but at every considerable fall dams, interrupting their plunge, had created new lakes. Spawning fish could no longer reach their headwaters to reproduce. The effluent from paper mills, lumber mills, wool-cleaning plants, and cotton-print works polluted many streams. Yet in the great majority of smaller streams water still flowed free, often with less obstruction than in earlier days when every brook supported a series of useful local industries.

Despite all changes, in the face of the constant presence of seven and a half million humans living in the midst of one of the busiest workshops and playrooms of a mighty nation, the beginning of its fourth century, like its first, found New England's a beckoning landscape. Buildings and roads and people in reality covered but a small proportion of its surface. For the rest, three fourths was once more forest. About and between and amongst the whole lay the green and pleasant pattern of the farmlands. These filled most of its valleys and reached long fingers into its unnumbered hills.

After three centuries the soil was no better and no worse. Never, except in a few favored areas where forest mold, accumulated through thousands of years, offered a temporary illusion of riches had most of it been really fertile. The Pilgrims in 1621 had enriched the sandy Plymouth slopes with fish and harvested a grain that gave them reason for Thanksgiving. Their successors in 1921 were still forced to enrich the soil. It was corn that the Pilgrims had harvested. Their successors did the same, but in addition husbanded livestock and enjoyed the meat, milk,

39. The original "homestall" granted 1636 to John Coolidge, the president's ancestor, at Mt. Auburn, near the Cambridge–Watertown line. Still being farmed in the 1880's, when this photograph was taken. Society for the Preservation of New England Antiquities.

butter, and eggs that stock supply. The Pilgrim farmers gave thanks for bare necessities; nineteenth-century farmers grew potatoes, vegetables, fruits, tobacco, and flowers, and offered them for sale, to supply their other needs. Such crop alterations, as John Black has pointed out, were not haphazard developments but deliberate selections on the part of the farm people. Thus, despite the economic depression that marked 1921, the three-hundredth year of New England agriculture, the modern farmer, like the first, could appropriately celebrate Thanksgiving.

Alongside descendants of Pilgrims, Puritans, and Indians, New England farms now offered home and livelihood to numerous families of Nova Scotian, French, German, Irish, Italian, Polish, Lithuanian, Scandinavian, Scottish, Portuguese, and other blood. Yet the requisites for survival and success continued virtually unaltered. After three centuries, farm prosperity and contentment remained the fruit of intelligence and industry.

One other condition remained unchanged. In this new generation the promise for the future still beckoned chiefly such men and women as look to the soil for life as well as for a living. Among them was one of the century's most discerning poets, Robert Frost. Also among them, despite the vicissitudes of the passing years, were hundreds of families in each state who still possessed and found a livelihood on farms that their ancestors had originally acquired from the Indians or hewn out of the green forest. It was a record of continuity of enterprise unmatched in any other calling. Beyond all that, New England's farms continued to nurture men and women of a quality capable of reaching the highest distinction in the professional, business, artistic, and political life of the nation. In just two years beyond the three-hundredth anniversary of the first stirring of Plymouth soil, one of these, born on a farm in the Plymouth in Vermont, would receive there from his father the oath of President of the United States. His blood and surname would be those of the John Coolidge who in 1636 received the allotment of a "homestall of twelve acres" and "Lott 1" with thirty acres in Watertown, in the new colony of Massachusetts Bay. He would come of a family to whom some New England farm had ever since been home and occupation.

The path had been a long, deep furrow.

Notes

PART I. THE ROOTS

1. New England's First Farmers

1. Alvin M. Josephy, Jr., *The Indian Heritage of America* (New York, 1968), p. 83. Douglas S. Byers, "Radio Carbon Dates from Bull Brook," *Mass. Arch. Soc. Bull.*, 20 (1959), 33. William S. Fowler, *Ten Thousand Years in America* (New York, 1957), p. 109. Walton F. Galinat, *Plant Habit and Adaptation of Corn*, Bulletin 565, U. of Mass. Exp. Sta. (Waltham, 1967), p. 4.

2. Roger Williams, *An Helpe to the Native Language of That part of America Called New-England* ("Williams' Key,"), Narragansett Club (Providence, 1866), p. 144.

3. John de Verrazano, "Voyage along the Coast of North America from Carolina to Newfoundland, A.D. 1524," Joseph G. Coggswell, tr., *New York Hist. Soc. Coll.*, 2nd ser., 1 (1811), 48.

4. W. L. Grant, ed., *Voyages of Samuel de Champlain 1604–1618* (New York, 1907), pp. 61–72, 95. G. P. Winship, ed., *Sailors' Narratives of Voyages along the New England Coast 1524–1624* (Boston, 1905), p. 240.

5. Henry M. Dexter, ed., *Mourt's Relation* (Boston, 1865), pp. 103, 136.

6. Laurence S. Mayo, *John Endecott* (Cambridge, 1936), p. 96. John W. DeForest, *History of the Indians of Connecticut from the Earliest Known Period to 1850* (Hartford, 1851), pp. 92, 169, 171.

7. Clarence A. Day, *A History of Maine Agriculture 1604–1860*, U. of Me. *Bull.* 56 (1954), p. 20.

8. Galinat, p. 5.

9. John Winthrop, *The History of New England 1630–1649*, ed. James Savage (Boston, 1825), 1: 147.

10. William Wood, *New England's Prospect* (London, 1639), Prince Soc. Reprint (Boston, 1865), p. 106. Lyman Carrier, *The Beginnings of Agriculture in America* (New York, 1923), p. 95.

11. I have enlarged on certain aspects of Indian agriculture and food economy in the following: Howard S. Russell, "New England Indian Agriculture," Mass. Arch. Soc. *Bull.*, 22 (1961), 58–61; ibid., "How Aboriginal Farmers Stored Food," 23 (1962), 47–49; and "New England Agriculture from Champlain and Others," 31 (1969–70), 11–16.

2. Corn: Teachers and Pupils

1. Verrazano, *Voyage*, 1: 58.

2. Gabriel Archer, *Relation of Captain Gosnold's Voyage to the North Part of Virginia*, Old South Leaflets, Vol. 5, No. 120 (Boston, 1920), 7.

3. Justin Winsor, ed., *Narrative and Critical History of America* (Cambridge, 1884), 3: 173–74. Grant, *Voyages*, pp. 40, 41, 64, 89.

4. Henry S. Burrage, ed., *Rosier's Relation of Waymouth's Voyage to the Coast of Maine* (Portland, 1887), p. 105. Samuel Maverick, *A Briefe Description of New England and the Severall Townes Therein* (Boston, 1885), p. 7.

5. Winship, *Sailors' Narratives*, p. 230.

6. For light on the Pilgrims' agricultural experience the following works, supplementing their own accounts, are helpful (listed alphabetically by author): Charles M. Andrews, *The Colonial Period of American History* (New Haven, 1934–38), 1: 291; Edward Arber, *The Story of the Pilgrim Fathers 1606–1623* . . . (Boston, 1897), pp. 58–164; Warren A. Ault, "Open Field Husbandry and the Village Community," Am. Phil. Soc. *Trans.*, new ser. 55, Pt. 7 (1965), 11; Charles E. Banks, *The English Ancestry and Homes of the Pilgrim Fathers* (New York, 1929), pp. 25, 33, 37, 99, 116, 127; John A. Boyle, *The English In America* (London, 1887), 1: 45; Martin S. Briggs, *Homes of the Pilgrim Fathers in England and America* (London, 1932), pp. 29, 30; John M. Brown, *The Pilgrim Fathers of New England and Their Puritan Successors* (New York, 1895), pp. 69, 126; Henry M. and Morton Dexter, *The England and Holland of the Pilgrims* (Cambridge, 1905), pp. 379, 390; Darrett B. Rutman, *Husbandmen of Plymouth: Farms and Villages in the Old Colony 1620–1692* (Boston, 1969), p. 4; Roland G. Usher, *The Pilgrims and Their History* (New York, 1918), pp. 10, 35, 63, 69, 75.

7. William Bradford, *Bradford's History "Of Plimoth Plantation": From the Original Manuscript* (Boston, 1898), p. 18.

8. Usher, p. 75.

9. Ibid., p. 91. Bradford, p. 121. *Mourt's Relation*, ed. Henry M. Dexter (Boston, 1865), p. 132. Fulmer Mood, "John Winthrop, Jr. on Indian Corn," *New England Quarterly*, 10 (1937), 125. How Squanto and the southern New England Indians may have acquired the practice of fertilizing cornhills with herring is a matter of dispute. I believe that the straightforward assertions of the colonial writers are to be taken at face value. Any other conclusion ignores too many agricultural and historical realities.

3. Massachusetts Bay

1. Winsor, *Narrative*, 3: 311, 326. Frances Rose-Troup, *Roger Conant and the Early Settlements on the North Shore of Massachusetts* (n.p., 1926), pp. 11, 12. Herbert L. Osgood, *The American Colonies in the Seventeenth Century* (New York, 1904–07), 1: 129. Clifford K. Shipton, *Roger Conant, A Founder of Massachusetts* (Cambridge, 1944), pp. 62, 65.

2. Francis Higginson, "New-England's Plantation," in Alexander Young, ed., *Chronicles of the First Planters of the Colony of Massachusetts Bay in New England 1623–1636* (Boston, 1846), p. 259. Rose-Troup, pp. 11, 12.

3. Nathaniel B. Shurtleff, ed. *Records of the Governor and Company of Massachusetts Bay in New England, 1628–1686* (Boston, 1853–54), 1: 24–40. Young, *Chronicles*, p. 14.

4. Young, *Chronicles*, pp. 246, 247. James D. Phillips, *Salem in the Seventeenth Century* (Boston, 1933), p. 72.

5. The views expressed result from study of many sources, including Charles E. Banks, "English Sources of Emigration to the New England Colonies in the Seventeenth Century," Mass. Hist. Soc. *Proc.*, 60 (1926–27), 366–72; Banks, *The Winthrop Fleet of 1630* (Boston, 1930); Banks, *The Planters of the Commonwealth* (Boston, 1930), preface, pp. viii, 12–14, 30, 31; Allen French, *Charles I and the Puritan Upheaval* (Boston, 1955), pp. 342, 362, 375; Richard H. Frothingham, *History of Charlestown, Mass.* (Boston, 1852), pp. 22, 78 (and numerous other local histories); Andrews, *Colonial Period*, 1: 496 ff.

6. Among works on contemporary English agriculture helpful toward understanding the background of New England's agriculture are Warren O. Ault, "Open-Field Husbandry and the Village Community: A Study of Agrarian By-Laws in Medieval England," Am. Phil. Soc. *Trans.*, New Ser., 55, Pt. 7 (Philadelphia, 1965) pp. 1–102; Carl Bridenbaugh, *Vexed and Troubled Englishmen* (New York, 1968); George G. Coulton, *The Medieval Village* (Cambridge, England, 1925); H. C. Darby, ed., *An Historical Geography of England before 1800* (Cambridge, England, 1936); Thomas Davis of Longleat, *A General View of the*

Agriculture of the County of Wiltshire (London, 1794); George L. Gomme, *The Village Community* (New York, 1890); H. P. R. Finberg, ed., *The Agrarian History of England and Wales*, Vols. 1, 4 (Cambridge, England, 1972, 1967); Norman S. B. Gras and Ethel Culbert, *The Economic and Social History of an English Village* (Cambridge, 1930); Howard L. Gray, *English Field Systems* (Cambridge, 1915); Herbert Hall, "The Romance of Marshland Farming," *Contemporary Review* (June 1933); John Hatcher, *Rural Economy and Society in the Duchy of Cornwall 1300–1500* (Cambridge, England, 1970); W. G. Hoskins, *The Midland Peasant* (London, 1957); Frederick W. Maitland, *Township and Borough* (Cambridge, England, 1898); John Norden, *Essex Described* (London, 1840); Wallace Notestein, *The English People on the Eve of Colonization 1603–1630* (New York, 1954); Rowland E. Prothero, *English Farming, Past and Present* (London, 1912); Michael Robbins, *Ancient Middlesex* (London, 1953); Frederick Seebohm, *The English Village Community*, 4th ed. (London, 1890); M. E. Seebohm, *The Evolution of the English Farm* (Cambridge, Mass., 1927); Robert Trow-Smith, *A History of British Livestock Husbandry to 1700* (London, 1957); Thomas Westcote, *A View of Devonshire* (1630) (Exeter, England, 1845).

7. Charles E. Banks, however, considers that Winthrop's decision was heavily weighted by economic considerations: *Winthrop Fleet*, pp. 19–23.

4. *Livestock the Key*

1. Frothingham, *Charlestown*, pp. 19, 20.

2. Banks, *Winthrop Fleet*, p. 47.

3. Ibid., p. 41. Winthrop, *History*, 1: 339.

4. Justin Winsor, *Memorial History of Boston, 1630–1880* (Boston, 1880), 1: 116.

5. Winthrop, *History*, 1: 39.

6. Shurtleff, *Bay Colony Records*, pp. 86, 89.

7. Winthrop, *History*, p. 61.

8. Young, *Chronicles*, p. 415.

9. Edward Johnson, *Wonder Working Providence of Sion's Saviour in New England* (London, 1654), ed. William F. Poole (Andover, 1867), p. 84.

10. Winthrop, *History*, p. 147.

11. Young, *Chronicles*, pp. 396, 404. Cambridge, *Proprietors' Records of the Town* (Cambridge, 1896), pp. 2, 6, 7, 8, 16. *Bay Colony Records*, 1: 388.

5. *Stirring the Soil*

1. Johnson, *Wonder Working Providence*, pp. 56, 83. John White,

"The Planter's Plea," *American Colonial Tracts Monthly,* 1 (Rochester, N.Y., 1898), 14.

2. Johnson, p. 56. Wood, *New England's Prospect,* p. 78.

3. Young, *Chronicles,* p. 403 n. Winthrop, *History,* 1: 87.

4. Phillips, *Salem,* p. 93. Thomas Lechford, *Plaine Dealing or News from New England,* 1642, reprint ed. J. H. Trumbull (Boston, 1861), p. 109. John Underhill, *News from America* (London, 1638), p. 65.

5. William B. Weeden, *Economic and Social History of New England 1620–1789* (Boston, 1890), 1: 331. Sylvester Judd, *History of Hadley,* new ed. (Springfield, 1905), p. 354.

6. Fulmer Mood, ed., "John Winthrop, Jr. on Indian Corn," *New England Quarterly,* 10 (1937), 128. Jasper Dankers and Peter Sluyter, "Journal of a Voyage to New York," Long Island Historical Society *Mem.* (Brooklyn, 1867), 1: 394. Edmund Browne, "Report on Massachusetts," Col. Soc. of Mass. *Trans.,* 8 (1900), 77.

7. Johnson, *Wonder Working Providence,* pp. 56, 120. Mood, "John Winthrop, Jr.," p. 127. J. B. Felt, *Annals of Salem* (Salem, 1845), 1: 243.

8. Edmund S. Morgan, "Masters and Servants in Early New England," *More Books,* 17, No. 7 (Boston Public Library, 1942), p. 311. Gerald W. Johnson, *Our English Heritage* (Philadelphia, 1949), p. 57.

9. Shurtleff, *Bay Colony Records,* 2: 181.

10. Thomas Wiggin letter, quoted by Willard H. Clark, *History of Winthrop, Mass.* (Winthrop, 1952), p. 50. James D. Knowles, *Memoir of Roger Williams,* (Boston, 1834), p. 119.

11. John Josselyn, *An Account of Two Voyages to New England* (London, 1674/5), p. 182.

12. Mildred Campbell, "Social Origins of Some Americans," in James M. Smith, *Seventeenth Century America* (Durham, N.C., 1959), p. 73. Alice Clark, *Working Life of Women in the Seventeenth Century* (London, 1919), p. 46.

6. *Distance Beckons the Uneasy*

1. For motives and methods leading to new settlements, see Archer B. Hulbert, *Soil: Its Influence on the History of the United States* (New Haven, 1930), pp. 105 ff.; Charles M. Andrews, *The River Towns of Connecticut* (Baltimore, 1889), pp. 30, 78; George L. Haskins, *Law and Authority in Early Massachusetts* (New York, 1960), pp. 48–77; and Lois M. Mathews, *The Expansion of New England* (Boston, 1909), pp. 1–36.

2. Bradford, *History*, pp. 361–63. Frederic W. Cook, *Historical Data Relating to Counties, Cities and Towns* (Boston, 1948).

3. Winsor, *Narrative*, 3: 326. Byron Fairchild, *Messrs. William Pepperell, Merchants at Piscataqua* (Ithaca, N.Y., 1954), p. 65. Wilbur O. Spencer, *Pioneers of Maine Rivers* (Portland, 1930), p. 65.

4. Ralph May, *Early Portsmouth History* (Boston, 1926), p. 99.

5. Boyle, *English in America*, 1: 275. Spencer, pp. 86, 128, 131. Edwin L. Sanborn, *History of New Hampshire . . . to 1874* (Manchester, 1875), p. 40. Day, *Maine Agriculture*, p. 10.

6. Edward A. Charlton, *New Hampshire as It Is* (Claremont, 1857), pp. 19, 37.

7. Day, pp. 10, 11. Spencer, p. 47.

8. Winsor, *Boston*, 1: 84.

9. Samuel G. Arnold, *History of the State of Rhode Island and Providence Plantations* (New York, 1859), p. 98.

10. James D. Knowles, *Memoir of Roger Williams* (Boston, 1834), pp. 102, 119.

11. J. Russell Bartlett, *Letters of Roger Williams* (Providence, 1874), pp. 71, 85.

12. Peter J. Coleman, *The Transformation of Rhode Island . . . 1790 to 1860* (Providence, 1963), p. 5. W. L. Watson, "A Short History of Jamestown . . . R.I.", R.I. Hist. Soc. *Coll.*, 26 (1933), 42.

13. Oliver P. Fuller, *History of Warwick, Rhode Island* (Providence, 1875), p. 19. Arnold, p. 132. Bernard Bailyn, *The New England Merchants in the Seventeenth Century* (Cambridge, 1955), p. 117. Ralph H. Brown, *Historical Geography of the United States* (New York, 1968), p. 33.

14. Daniel Howard, *A New History of Old Windsor, Connecticut* (Windsor, 1935), pp. 7–14. Winthrop, *History*, 2: 132, 184. Louis B. Mason, *The Life and Times of Major John Mason of Connecticut, 1600–1672* (New York, 1935), p. 78.

15. Winthrop, 1: 187. Perry Miller, *Errand into the Wilderness* (Cambridge, 1956), pp. 16–47.

16. Walter Hard, *The Connecticut* (New York, 1947), p. 55. William DeLove, *The Colonial History of Hartford* (Hartford, 1914), p. 156.

17. John G. Palfrey, *History of New England* (Boston, 1858–90), 1 (1858), 534. Lois K. Mathews, *The Expansion of New England 1620–1865* (Boston, 1909), pp. 14–30. Winsor, *Narrative*, 3: 332. Charles H. Walcott, *Concord in the Colonial Period* (Boston, 1884), p. 35.

18. George Sheldon, *History of Deerfield* (Deerfield, 1895–96), 1: 52. Harry A. Wright, *The Genesis of Springfield: The Development of the Town*

(Springfield, Mass., 1936), pp. 41–44. Ruth A. McIntyre, *William Pynchon, Merchant and Colonizer* (Springfield, Mass., 1961), p. 15.

19. John W. Oliver, *History of American Technology*, (New York, 1956), p. 41.

7. *To Market, to Market*

1. William Bradford, "A Description and Historical Account of New England in Verse," Mass. Hist. Soc. *Coll.*, 3 (1794), 78. Winthrop, *History*, 2: 21, 31. Johnson, *Wonder Working Providence*, p. 172. Marion H. Gottfried, "The First Depression in Massachusetts," *New England Quarterly*, 9 (1936), 655. William Hubbard, "General History of New England," Mass. Hist. Soc. *Coll.*, 2nd ser., 5 (1815), 140.

2. Alan Everitt, "The Marketing of Agricultural Produce," in Finberg, *Agrarian History*, 4: 466–591.

3. Winthrop, *History*, 2: 31.

4. Samuel Maverick, *Briefe Description*, p. 26. Bailyn, *Merchants*, pp. 96–100. *Essex County Probate Records*, 1 (1633–44); 2 (1665–74) (Salem, 1916, 1917). *Suffolk County Estates 1675–1696.*

5. Maverick, pp. 13–22.

6. Rutman, *Husbandmen of Plymouth*, pp. 204, 231.

7. *Diary of Thomas Minor of Stonington, Connecticut, 1653–1684* (New London, 1899), p. 90.

8. Deane C. Phillips, *Horse Raising in Colonial New England* (Cornell Exp. Sta., Ithaca, 1922), p. 896.

9. J. Franklin Jameson, ed., *Narratives of New Netherland, 1609–1664* (New York, 1909), p. 423. Amelia Forbes Emerson, *Early History of Naushon Island* (privately printed, 1935), p. 197.

10. Stackpole, *History of New Hampshire* (New York, 1916), 1: 128. May, *Early Portsmouth*, p. 169. William M. Carleton, "Masts and the King's Navy," *New England Quarterly*, 12 (1939), pp. 4–18. Bailyn, *Merchants*, p. 100.

11. First Ironworks Assn., *The Saugus Restoration* (Saugus, Mass., 1951). Samuel E. Morison, *Builders of the Bay Colony* (Boston, 1930), p. 279.

12. Dexter, *England and Holland of the Pilgrims*, p. 10. H. C. and Eila Darby and M. J. Campbell, *The Domesday Geography of South-East England* (Cambridge, 1962), pp. 33–599. Westcote, *Devonshire*, p. 37. Norden, *Essex*, p. 9.

13. Noah A. Phelps, *History of Simsbury, Granby and Canton* (Hartford, 1840), p. 89. William S. Tilden, *History of the Town of Medfield* (Boston, 1887), p. 45.

14. W. Storrs Lee, *The Yankees of Connecticut* (New York, 1957), p. 190.

15. A. Hyatt Verrill, *The Heart of Old New England* (New York, 1936), p. 147. George F. Dow et al., *History of Topsfield* (Topsfield, Mass., 1940), p. 14. Louis E. Roy, *Quaboag Plantation Alias Brookefeild: A Seventeenth Century Massachusetts Town* (West Brookfield, 1965), p. 165. Joshua Coffin, *A Sketch of the History of Newbury, Newburyport and West Newbury, 1635–1845*, (Boston, 1845), p. 140. Peleg Sanford, *The Letter Book of a Newport Merchant . . . 1666–1668* (R.I. Hist. Soc., Providence, 1928). Federal Writers Project, *Connecticut* (Cambridge, 1938), p. 30.

16. Charles M. Ellis, *The History of Roxbury Town*, Pt. I (Boston, 1867), p. 63.

17. Gottfried, "First Depression," p. 676. See the illuminating discussion in Curtis P. Nettels, *The Money Supply of the American Colonies before 1720*, U. of Wisconsin Studies, 20 (1934), 208 ff.

18. Samuel Danforth, *An Almanack for the Year of Our Lord 1648* (Cambridge, 1648).

8. *Patterns from Home*

1. For the Colony charter, its transfer to Massachusetts Bay, and the government of the early colonies, these works are useful: C. M. Andrews, *Colonial Period*, Vol. 1, chaps. 17, 18; Samuel E. Morison, *The Oxford History of the American People* (New York, 1965), pp. 65–67; and Haskins, *Law and Authority*, pp. 10–20.

2. Shurtleff, *Bay Colony Records*, 1: 157. Lemuel Shattuck, *History of the Town of Concord . . . to 1832* (Concord, 1835), p. 3. Townsend Scudder, *Concord, American Town* (Boston, 1947), pp. 4–8. C. H. Walcott, *Concord in the Colonial Period* (Boston, 1884), p. 17.

3. Among works on the development of town government, the following, with the colony records, are enlightening: Roy Hidemichi Akagi, *Town Proprietors of the New England Colonies* (Philadelphia, 1924); Charles M. Andrews, *The River Towns of Connecticut* (Baltimore, 1889); Finberg, *English Agrarian History*, Vol. 1; Anthony N. B. Garvan, *Architecture and Town Planning in Colonial Connecticut* (New Haven, 1951); George L. Gomme, *The Village Community* (New York, 1890); George L. Howard, *An Introduction to the Local Constitutional History of the United States* (Baltimore, 1889), Vol. 1; George L. Langdon, Jr., *Pilgrim Colony: A History of New Plymouth 1620–1691* (New Haven, 1966); Frederick W. Maitland, *Township and Borough* (Cambridge, England, 1898); Edna Scofield, "The Origin of Settlement Patterns in New England,"

Geographical Review, 28 (1938); and Michael Zuckerman, *Peaceable Kingdoms: New England Towns in the Eighteenth Century* (New York, 1970). Among studies of early communities are Philip J. Greven, Jr., *Four Generations: Population, Land and Family in Colonial Andover, Massachusetts* (Ithaca, N.Y., 1970); Sumner C. Powell, *Puritan Village: The Formation of a New England Town* (Middletown, Conn., 1963); Kenneth A. Lockridge, *A New England Town: The First Hundred Years. Dedham, Massachusetts, 1636–1736* (New York, 1970).

4. Besides the lists above and the wealth of town histories, valuable viewpoints appear in the following: Herbert B. Adams, "The Germanic Origin of New England Towns," in Vol. 1 of *Local Institutions* (Baltimore, 1882); Richard L. Bushman, *From Puritan to Yankee: Character and the Social Order in Connecticut 1690–1765* (Cambridge, 1967); Boyle, *English in America*, Vol. II; Melville Egleston, *The Land System of the New England Colonies* (Baltimore, 1886); Wm. E. Foster, ed., "Early Attempts at Rhode Island History," R.I. Hist. Soc. *Coll.*, 7 (1885), 5–109; Wallace Notestein, *The English People on the Eve of Colonization 1603–1690* (New York, 1954); and Page Smith, *As a City upon a Hill: The Town in American History* (New York, 1966).

5. Frothingham, *Charlestown*, p. 103.

6. *Colonial Laws of Mass.*, p. 35.

7. Maitland, *Township and Borough*, p. 79; Bernard C. Steiner, *History of the Plantation of Manunkatuck and of the Original Town of Guilford* (Baltimore, 1897), p. 238.

8. Thomas F. Waters, *Ipswich in the Massachusetts Bay Colony 1633–1700*, (Ipswich, 1905), 1: 63 ff.

9. Erastus Worthington, *History of Dedham, Mass. to 1827* (Boston, 1827), p. 54. Joseph B. Felt, *History of Ipswich, Essex, and Hamilton* (Cambridge, 1834), p. 58.

10. Merrill, *Amesbury*, p. 47.

11. *Cambridge Town Records*, p. 123.

12. Charles H. Bell, *Exeter, N.H.* (Exeter, 1888), p. 54.

13. Merrill, *Amesbury*, p. 49.

14. *Cambridge Town Rec.*, p. 123.

15. Fuller, *Warwick, R.I.*, entry of Jan. 6, 1641.

16. Portsmouth, R.I., *Early Records 1639–1697* (Providence, 1901), p. 120.

17. Spencer P. Mead, *Ye Historie of ye Town of Greenwich . . . Connecticut* (New York, 1911), p. 29.

18. Phillips, *Salem*, p. 98. George P. Winship, ed., *Boston in 1682 and 1699: A Trip to New England by Edward Ward . . .* (Providence, 1905), p. 57.

9. *A Few Tools*

1. Charles L. Flint, "A Hundred Years' Progress of American Agriculture," Mass. Board of Agriculture (1873), *Report*, p. 18. Edward H. Jenkins, *A History of Connecticut Agriculture*, Conn. Agric. Exper. Station (New Haven, n.d.), pp. 306, 313.

2. Felt, *Annals of Salem*, 1: 243.

3. F. L. Newton, "Notes on Old Plows," *Agricultural History*, 17 (1933), 62. W. P. Woodward, *The Way Our People Lived* (New York, 1945), p. 51.

4. Albert H. Sanford, *The Story of Agriculture in the United States* (Boston, 1916), p. 52.

5. Carrier, *Beginnings of Agriculture*, p. 265.

6. Percy W. Bidwell and John I. Falconer, *History of Agriculture in the Northern United States 1620–1860*, Reprint (New York, 1941), p. 36. Shurtleff, *Plymouth Records*, 2: 78. Mellen Chamberlain, *Documentary History of Chelsea 1624–1824* (Boston, 1908), p. 55. Felt, p. 47.

7. Weeden, *Economic and Social History*, 1: 183.

8. Compiled from various sources, including *Essex County Probate Records*; *Suffolk County Estates*; *Plymouth Scrap Book*, ed. Charles H. Pope (Boston, 1918); Bidwell and Falconer, p. 34; Amos E. and Emily M. Jewett, *Rowley, Massachusetts, Mr. Ezechi Rogers' Plantation, 1639–1850* (Rowley, 1946), p. 201; and Josselyn, *Two Voyages*, pp. 9, 11, 16, 18.

9. Willard DeLue, *The Story of Walpole, 1724–1924* (Norwood, Mass., 1925), p. 21. James R. Newhall, *Lin or Jewels of the Third Plantation* (Lynn, 1868), p. 58. Francis M. Thompson, *History of Greenfield, Mass.* (Greenfield, 1904), 1: 74.

10. *Settling In*

1. For the genesis and character of farm buildings, besides original records, see Sidney O. Addy, *The Evolution of the English House* (London, 1898); M. W. Barley, *The English Farmhouse and Cottage* (London, 1961); M. S. Briggs, *Homes of the Pilgrim Fathers*, p. 36; John Demos, *A Little Commonwealth: Family Life in the Plymouth Colony* (New York, 1970), pp. 25, 27, 47; Fiske Kimball, *Domestic Architecture of the American Colonies and of the Early Republic* (New York, 1927), p. 6; *Quarter-Millennial Celebration of Sandwich and Bourne 1639–1889* (Falmouth, Mass., 1890), p. 36; and Henry C. Kittredge, *Cape Cod: Its People and Their History* (Boston, 1930), p. 76.

2. Thomas Weston, *History of the Town of Middleboro, Massachusetts* (Boston, 1906), p. 30.

3. Roger Clap, *Memoirs* (Boston, 1731, reprinted 1844), p. 42. Johnson, *Wonder Working Providence*, pp. 23, 38, 83, 174. Winthrop, *History*, 1: 38 ff. Anne Bush MacLear, *Early New England Towns: A Comparative Study of Their Development* (New York, 1908), p. 37.

4. Alfred S. Hudson, *History of Concord* (Concord, 1904), p. 69. Adams, *Weathersfield*, p. 725. Prothero, *English Farming*, p. 83.

5. Atwater, *New Haven*, pp. 71, 532. Howard, *Old Windsor*, p. 14. Crofut, *Guide to Connecticut*, 2: 574. John C. Pease, "An Historical Sketch of Enfield," in Francis P. Allen, ed., *History of Enfield, Connecticut* (Lancaster, Pa., 1900), p. 113. E. B. O'Callaghan, ed., *Documentary History of the State of New York* (Albany, 1849–51), 4: 31. Addy, *Evolution of the English House*, pp. 12–15.

6. George L. Clark, *A History of Connecticut, Its People and Institutions* (New York, 1914), p. 104. Garvan, *Architecture in Colonial Connecticut*, pp. 94, 96, 99, 120, 128.

7. J. Frederick Kelly, "A Seventeenth Century Connecticut Log House," Soc. of N.E. Antiquities *Bull.* 31 (1940), 19–40.

8. Weeden, *Early R.I.*, p. 73. Kimball, p. 14.

9. Douglas E. Leach, *The Northern Colonial Frontier 1607–1673* (New York, 1966), inset opp. p. 162. Thomas T. Waterman, *The Dwellings of Colonial America* (Chapel Hill, 1950), pp. 239, 242.

10. Garvan, p. 98. Kimball, p. 25.

11. Hudson, *Sudbury*, p. 15. Demos, p. 66. Greven, *Four Generations*, chap. 2. Clap, *Memoirs*, p. 353.

12. Winthrop, *History*, 1: 39.

13. Cambridge, *Proprietors' Records*, pp. 3, 7, 73–90. Crofut, *Guide to Connecticut*, 1: 243. Briggs, p. 98. Minor, *Diary*, p. 65.

14. Garvan, p. 82. Hudson, *Concord*, p. 301. Hudson, *Sudbury*, p. 80. Kimball, p. 13. *Sandwich Anniversary*, p. 36. William Barry, *A History of Framingham, Mass.* (Boston, 1847), p. 4.

15. Lucien R. Paige, *History of Cambridge, Mass. 1630–1877* (Cambridge, 1877), p. 95 n.

16. Johnson, *Wonder Working Providence*, p. 84. Young, *Chronicles*, p. 246. James M. Usher, *History of Medford* (Boston, 1886), p. 29.

17. Mass. Hist. Soc. *Coll.*, 4th ser. 6 (1863), 146–7. L. C. Corbett, et al., "Fruits and Vegetables," USDA *1925 Yearbook*, p. 120.

18. Winthrop, *History*, 1: 331 n. Shipton, *Roger Conant*, p. 43.

19. Usher, p. 29.

20. Alice G. Lapham, *The Old Planters of Beverly in Massachusetts* (Cambridge, 1930), p. 93.

21. S. G. Arnold, *Rhode Island*, pp. 98, 137.

22. Henry R. Stiles, *History of Ancient Windsor, Connecticut* (Albany, 1863), 1: 478. Hedrick, *Horticulture*, p. 36. Minor, *Diary*, p. 57. Maverick, *Briefe Description*, p. 217.

11. *The Farm Family*

1. Quoted in Sir Evelyn Wrench and Stewart B. Anthony, "Founders of New England," *National Geographic*, 103 (1953), 832.

2. Mood, "John Winthrop, Jr. on Indian Corn," *New England Quarterly*, 10 (1937), 129. Josselyn, *Rarities*, ed. Tuckerman, p. 101.

3. Johnson, *Wonder Working Providence*, p. 173. Prothero, *English Farming*, p. 84.

4. Dow, *Everyday Life*, p. 98. Adams, *Weathersfield*, p. 950. Freeman, *Cape Cod*, 1: 185.

5. Winship, *Boston in 1682 and 1699*. Benjamin Tompson, *New England's Crisis* (Club of Odd Volumes reprint, 1894), p. 6.

6. John Dunton, "Journal," *Mass. Hist. Soc. Coll.* 2nd ser., 2 (1846), 120. Ann Hardy, "How to Boil Meat Successfully," *The Listener*, Jan. 28, 1954.

7. Edmund Browne, "Massachusetts," *Col. Soc. of Mass. Trans.*, 7 (1900), 78.

8. Charles F. Swift, *Cape Cod, the Right Arm of Massachusetts* (Yarmouth, 1897), p. 66. George F. Daniels, *History of the Town of Oxford* (Oxford, Mass., 1892), p. 9 n. E. Alexander Bergstrom, "English Game Laws and Colonial Food Shortages," *New England Quarterly*, 3 (1939), 686–90.

9. Josselyn, p. 103. Dow, *Everyday Life*, pp. 42 ff.

10. Dow, p. 64. Woodward, *The Way Our People Lived*, p. 11. Adams, *Weathersfield*, p. 951.

11. Johnson, *Wonder Working Providence*, p. 174.

12. Ibid., p. 208.

13. *Essex Probate Records*; *Suffolk County Estates*; DeLove, *Hartford*, p. 156; and similar local records.

PART II. WAR AND TRADE, 1675–1800

12. *Toil and Trouble*

1. Douglas Edward Leach, *Flintlock and Tomahawk* (New York, 1958), pp. 43 ff., gives a general view of the war. Samuel Eliot Morison's *Story of the Old Colony of New Plymouth* (New York, 1956), pp.

251–284, offers a lively account of struggle as it affected that area. For New Hampshire losses, see Sanborn, *History*, pp. 67 ff.

2. Town histories detail local incidents and losses. A best seller in its time, often reprinted, is *The Narrative of the Captivity and Restoration of Mrs. Mary Rowlandson*, reprint (Lancaster, Mass., 1903).

3. Leach, *Northern Frontier*, p. 59. Epaphras Hoyt, *Antiquarian Researches, Comprising a History of the Indian Wars in the Country Bordering the Connecticut River* . . . (Greenfield, Mass., 1824), pp. 110 ff. Benjamin Trumbull, *A Complete History of Connecticut* (New Haven, 1797), 1: 350. Stackpole, *New Hampshire*, 1: 98.

4. Spencer, *Maine Rivers*, p. 285.

5. Quoted in Waters, *Ipswich*, 1: 167.

6. William B. Weeden, *Early Rhode Island, A Social History of the People* (New York, 1910), p. 97.

7. Sanborn, *New Hampshire*, p. 73.

8. Verrill, *Heart of Old New England*, p. 103.

9. Sources of data on the war's effects on Indian agriculture include Daniel Gookin, "An Historical Account of the Sufferings of the Christian Indians," Am. Ant. Soc. *Trans.*, 2 (1836), 423–533; Leach, pp. 43 ff.; Vaughan, *New England Frontier: Puritans and Indians 1620–1675* (Boston, 1965); Mason, *Life and Times*; George Howe, *Mount Hope* (New York, 1959); Morison, *New Plymouth*; Langdon, *Plymouth Colony*; and Elizabeth H. Schenck, *History of Fairfield, Conn. 1639–1818* (New York, 1889), 1: 200.

10. Sanborn, p. 91.

11. Henry S. Nourse, *History of the Town of Harvard* (Clinton, Mass., 1894), p. 36.

12. J. H. Temple, *History of North Brookfield* (North Brookfield, 1887), p. 203. Abijah P. Martin, *History of the Town of Lancaster, Massachusetts* (Lancaster, 1879), p. 137.

13. Simon G. Griffin, *A History of the Town of Keene* (Keene, 1904).

13. *A Surplus to Sell*

1. Edward Randolph, "Report to the Committee for Trade and Plantations," Oct. 12, 1676 (Prince Society Reprint, Boston, 1898), 2: 248.

2. Robert Mason, quoted in Stackpole, *New Hampshire*, 1: 121. Clark, *Manufactures*, pp. 90–94.

3. William D. Miller, *The Narragansett Planters* (Worcester, 1934), pp. 160, 328. Sanford, *Letterbook*, p. 30. Frances M. Caulkins, *History of*

New London (New London, Conn., 1852), pp. 232, 234 ff. Roland M. Hooker, *Colonial Trade of Connecticut* (New Haven, 1936), p. 13.

4. Adams, *Weathersfield*, p. 541. For illuminating discussions of New England's agricultural commodities in foreign trade see Bailyn, *New England Merchants*, and Weeden, *Economic and Social History*.

5. Johnson, *Wonder Working Providence*, p. 208.

6. Joshua Hempstead of New London, *Diary, 1711–1758* (New London, 1901), entry, June 26, 1724. Robert W. Howard, *The Horse in America* (New York, 1965), p. 41. Caulkins, *New London*, p. 483. Thomas Allen, of New London, MS Account Books, Am. Antiq. Soc., Worcester.

7. Carl R. Woodward, "Rural Economy in R. I.", *R.I. History*, 5 (1946), 121.

8. Weeden, *Economic and Social History*, 1: 376.

9. Allen, Account Books.

10. Hempstead, *Diary*, p. 83 and dates listed. Weeden, *Early R.I.*, p. 320.

11. English Shipping Records Relating To Massachusetts Ports, 1756–1763, Pt. III, nos. 1144–1417, at Peabody Museum, Salem.

12. Mass. Hist. Soc., Belcher Papers, "To the Lords of Trade," Pt. I, p. 71. James Birket, *Some Cursory Remarks . . . in His Voyages to North America 1750–51* (New Haven, 1896), pp. 11, 20, 24. Weeden, 2: 503.

13. Clark, *Manufactures*, 1: 82. *Commerce of Rhode Island 1726–1800* (Boston 1915), 1: 486. Bidwell and Falconer, p. 98.

14. William C. Langdon, *Everyday Things in American Life, 1607–1776* (New York, 1941), p. 215. Birket, p. 24. Richard J. Frothingham, *History of Charlestown, Mass.* (Boston, 1852), p. 257. Ezra Stiles, *Extracts from the Itineraries 1755–1794*, ed. Franklin B. Dexter (New Haven, 1916), pp. 79, 111. Curtis P. Nettels, *The Money Supply of the American Colonies before 1720* (Madison, Wisc., 1934), p. 103. William H. Rowe, *The Maritime History of Maine* (New York, 1948), p. 102.

15. Charles E. Banks, *History of Martha's Vineyard* (Boston, 1911–25), 1: 436. Daniel Ricketson, *History of New Bedford, Mass. . . . including Westport, Dartmouth and Fairhaven* (New Bedford, 1858), p. 65. Bridenbaugh, *Cities*, p. 177. Timothy Pitkin, *A Statistical View of the Commerce of the United States . . .* (Hartford, 1816), p. 43.

16. Calculated from provisioning of Allen vessels out of New London, 1758–68; Allen, Account Books, Nov. 9, 1768.

17. Edward P. Hamilton, *The French and Indian Wars* (New York, 1962), p. 109.

18. Bidwell and Falconer, p. 142.

19. See *Randolph Report*, p. 248; Neal, *History of N.E.*, 2: 584; and Albert E. Van Duzen, *Connecticut* (New York, 1961) pp. 111, 114.

20. Amos E. Brown, *Faneuil Hall and Faneuil Hall Market* (Boston, 1900), pp. 66 ff. Winsor, *Boston*, 1: 232, 539 ff.

21. Brown, pp. 67, 69, 97–100. Karen J. Friedman, "Victualling Colonial Boston," *Agricultural History*, 44 (1973), 189–205.

22. Birket, *Cursory Remarks*, p. 9.

23. Leonard A. Morrison, *History of Windham in New Hampshire* (Boston, 1883), pp. 292, 294. Edward L. Parker, *History of Londonderry . . . New Hampshire* (Boston, 1851), p. 62.

14. *Growth of the Land: Grass and Grain*

1. Richard Bradley, *A General Treatise of Husbandry and Gardening* (London, 1724), p. vii. Davis, *Agriculture of Wilts.*, p. B-2.

2. Hubbard, "Hist. of N.E.," Mass. Hist. Soc. *Coll.*, 2nd ser., 5 (1848), 23.

3. Birket, *Cursory Remarks*, p. 19.

4. Paul Coffin, "Memoir and Journals: A Tour to the Connecticut River," Maine Hist. Soc. *Coll.*, 4 (Portland, 1856), 264. Newton D. Mereness, *Travels in the American Colonies* (New York, 1916), p. 447. Stackpole, *New Hampshire*, 2: 156.

5. Neal, *New England*, 2: 212.

6. Jared Eliot, *Essays on Field Husbandry in New England* (Boston, 1760), 2nd Essay. Boyle, *English in America*, 2: 500.

7. Winthrop, *History*, 1: 46. Samuel Sewall, *History of Woburn* (Boston, 1868), p. 119. Joseph Andrews, MS Journal, 1753–1787, Mass. Hist. Soc. Timothy Walker, "Diaries 1730–1782," ed. Joseph B. Walker, N. H. Hist. Soc. *Coll.*, 9 (1889), 123–91. Zaccheus Collins, *Diary of Farming and Malting 1726–1769*, 2 MSS at Essex Institute, Salem, Vol. 2, May 1672 entries.

8. Thomas Hutchinson, "Journal," Mass. Hist. Soc. *Proc.*, 15 (1887), 332.

9. Quoted in Carrier, *Beginnings of Agriculture*, p. 147.

10. Bartlett, *Roger Williams, Letters*, p. 146. John Chipman Gray, *Essays Agricultural & Literary* (Boston, 1856). Judd, *Hadley*, p. 362.

11. The date of introduction of both white and red clover is uncertain. Some claim white to be indigenous. See Fergus and Hallowell, "Red Clover," in *Advances in Agronomy*, 12 (New York, 1960), pp. 369, 370. "It must be that it [introduction of clover species] preceded written documentation" (personal communication of Sept. 5,

1969, from Robert C. Leffel, Leader, Clover Investigations, USDA Ag. Research Service, Beltsville, Md.).

12. Josselyn, *Two Voyages*, p. 188. Emerson, *Naushon Island*, p. 157.

13. Hempstead, *Diary*, April 22, 1725. Thomas Hutchinson, *The History of the Colony and Province of Massachusetts-Bay*, ed. Lawrence S. Mayo (Cambridge, 1936), 1: 403 n. Fergus and Hallowell, p. 369. Jared Eliot, *Essays upon Field Husbandry in New England and Other Papers*, new ed. (New York, 1967), p. 233.

14. G. E. Fussell, "The Grasses and Grassland Cultivation of Britain, I: Before 1700", British Grassland Soc. *Journal*, 19–20 (1964–65), 19, 50, 212.

15. Hempstead, *Diary*, April 20, 1757. Charles L. Flint, *Grasses and Forage Plants*, 5th ed. (Boston, 1860), p. 34. Bidwell and Falconer, p. 104. Eliot, Third Essay.

16. John Josselyn, *New England's Rarities Discovered*, ed. Edward Tuckerman (Boston, 1865), p. 91.

17. Charles L. Flint, *A Hundred Years' Progress*, Mass. Board of Agric., *1873 Report*, p. 21.

18. Minor, *Diary*. Solomon Lincoln, Jr., *History of Hingham* (Hingham, 1827), p. 83.

19. Grant Powers, *Historical Sketches of the Coos Country 1754–1785* (Haverhill, N.H., 1847, reprint 1880), p. 74.

20. Mass. Hist. Soc. *Proc.*, Vol. 4 (1858–60), p. 295.

21. William Douglass, *A Summary Historical and Political of the British Settlements in North America* (Boston, 1755), 2: 207; Lord Adam Gordon, "Journal," in Mereness, *Travels*, p. 451.

22. Paul Dudley, "Observations on Some of the Plants in New England," Royal Soc. of London *Trans.* (1724), p. 198. Edith and Frank Shay, *Sand in Their Shoes* (Boston, 1951), p. 183.

23. Edmund Hersey, "Agriculture," in *History of the Town of Hingham* (Hingham, 1893), 1: 182. George F. Dow, *The Holyoke Diaries* (Salem, 1911), p. 88 n.

24. Thomas Anburey, *Travels through The Interior Parts of America* (London, 1789), 2: 218.

25. Hempstead, *Diary*, October 1711 and October 1723, 1724 entries. Berthold Laufer, "American Plant Migration," *Scientific Monthly*, 28: 239–51.

15. *Growth of the Land: Vegetables and Fruits*

1. Winthrop, *History*, entry of Jan. 8, 1636. Shipton, *Conant*, p. 76.

2. Parker, *Londonderry*, pp. 35–49. Day, *Maine Agriculture*, p. 35.

H. B. & Harvey E. D. Wright, *The Settlement and Story of Oakham, Mass.* (Oakham, 1947), 1:5 ff. *Cyclopedia*, 2: 520. Charles K. Bolton, *Scotch Irish Pioneers in Ulster and America* (Boston, 1910), p. 200. Arthur L. Perry, *Origins of Williamstown* (Williamstown, Mass., 1900), pp. 81, 91. Mary T. Wilson, "Americans Learn to Grow the Irish Potato," *New England Quarterly*, 32 (1959), 334.

3. Jenkins, *Conn. Ag.*, p. 328. Allen, Acct. Books, November 1759 entry.

4. Douglass, *Summary*, 2: 181. Francis S. Drake, *The Town of Roxbury: Its Memorable Persons and Places* (Roxbury, 1878), p. 57. Samuel Deane, *The New England Farmer or Georgical Dictionary* (Worcester, 1790), p. 224. William Willis, ed., *Extracts from the Diary of Rev. Samuel Deane 1761–1814* (Portland, 1849), p. 318.

5. Birket, p. 11. V. S. Clark, *Manufactures*, 1: 82.

6. Stiles, *Itineraries*, p. 215.

7. Adrian F. McDonald, *The History of Tobacco Production in Connecticut* (New Haven, 1936), pp. 4 ff. Elizabeth Ramsey, *The History of Tobacco Culture in the Connecticut Valley* (Northampton, 1930), p. 114.

8. U.S. Dept. of Interior, Census of 1880, Vol. 3, *Manufactures of Tobacco.* Adams, *Weathersfield*, pp. 623, 946.

9. Weeden, *Early R.I.*, p. 321. James B. Hodges, *The Browns of Providence Plantation* (Cambridge, 1952), pp. 6, 23, 31, 249.

10. Wilfred H. Munro, *The History of Bristol, Rhode Island* (Providence, 1880), p. 337. Charles O. F. Thompson, *Sketches of Old Bristol* (Providence, 1942), p. 118. Adams, *Weathersfield*, pp. 615, 948.

11. U. P. Hedrick, *A History of Horticulture in America* (New York, 1950), p. 42. A. J. Pieters, "Seed Selling, Seed Growing, and Seed Testing," USDA *1899 Yearbook*, p. 550; *1925 Yearbook*, p. 325. Judd, *Hadley*, p. 363.

12. Dow, *Holyoke Diaries*, pp. 7, 13, 20, 59. Anne Hulton, *Letters of a Loyalist Lady* (Cambridge, 1927), p. 34. Stiles, *Itineraries*, p. 217. John W. Hanson, *History of the Town of Danvers* (Danvers, 1848), p. 93.

13. Charles J. Taylor, *History of Great Barrington* (Great Barrington, 1882), p. 52.

14. Walker, *Diaries*, 1764 entries. Lord Gordon, *Diary*, p. 451.

15. Bidwell & Falconer, p. 99. Nourse, *Harvard*, p. 99. Daniels, *Oxford*, p. 775.

16. Marshall P. Wilder, *The Horticulture of Boston and Vicinity* (Boston, 1881), pp. 35, 37, 62. Edgar M. Bacon, *Narragansett Bay: Its Historic and Romantic Associations* (New York, 1904), p. 285. Hedrick, *Horticulture*, p. 35. Erston V. Miller, "The Natural Origins of Some

Popular Varieties of Fruit," *Economic Botany*, 8 (1954), 340. Carl R. Woodward, *Plantation in Yankeeland* (Wickford, R.I., 1971), p. 106.

17. Drake, *Roxbury*, p. 119. Josselyn, *Two Voyages*, p. 190. Maverick, *Briefe Description*, p. 27.

18. Sarah C. Sedgwick and Christina S. Marquand, *Stockbridge 1739–1939: A Chronicle* (n.p. 1939), p. 68.

16. *Growth of the Land: Livestock*

1. Stackpole, *New Hampshire*, 2: 39.

2. A. P. Usher, "Colonial Business and Transportation," in *Commonwealth History of Massachusetts*, ed. Albert Bushnell Hart (Boston, 1927–30), 2: 392.

3. Compiled from Abbott L. Cummings, *Rural Household Inventories 1675–1775*, (Boston, 1964). Edward P. Hamilton, *A History of Milton* (Milton, Mass., 1957), pp. 221–41. Sarah L. Bailey, *Historical Sketches of Andover, Mass.* (Cambridge, 1880), p. 20.

4. Joseph Green, of Salem Village, Diary, Essex Inst. Hist. Coll., 2nd ser., 10 (1869), 73–104. Anburey, 2: 220.

5. Matthew Patten, of Bedford, New Hampshire, *Diary 1754–1788* (Concord, 1903), p. 117.

6. Samuel Orcutt, *History of the Old Town of Derby, Connecticut 1642–1880* (Springfield, 1880), p. 125. Ezekiel Read, Book of Accounts 1712–1733, MSS in possession of the family of H. F. Tompson, Seekonk, Mass. Glenn Weaver, *Jonathan Trumbull, Connecticut's Merchant Magistrate* (Hartford, 1956), pp. 14 ff.

7. Bacon, *Narragansett Bay*, pp. 249, 283.

8. Elisha R. Potter, Jr., "The Early History of Narragansett," R.I. Hist. Soc. *Coll.*, 3 (1885), 111, 131.

9. Andrew Burnaby, *Travels through the Middle Settlements in North America in the Years 1759 and 1767* (2nd ed., London, 1775), p. 137. "Boston in 1740," Mass. Hist. Soc. *Proc.*, 5 (1861), 111.

10. Birket, *Cursory Remarks*, p. 13. Usher, *Commonwealth History*, 2: 392.

11. William S. Pattee, *History of Old Braintree and Quincy . . .* (Quincy, 1878), p. 550. Henry M. Burt, *The First Century of the History of Springfield* (Springfield, 1898), 2: 442.

12. Ebenezer Parkman, *Diary*, ed. Harriet E. Forbes (Westboro, Mass., 1899), p. 42. Benjamin W. Hall, *History of Eastern Vermont . . . to the Close of the 18th Century* (New York, 1858), p. 98. Federal Writers Project, *Connecticut*, p. 469. *American Husbandry*, London, 1775; ed. Harry J. Carman (New York, 1939), p. 59.

13. Collins, *Diary*. Patten, *Diary*. Read, *Accounts*.

14. Caroline Hazard, *Thomas Hazard, Son of Robert, Called College Tom* (Boston, 1893), p. 78. Douglass, *Summary*, 2: 100. Bacon, *Narragansett Bay*, p. 242. Edward Channing, *The Narragansett Planters* (Baltimore, 1886), p. 10. Miller, *Narragansett Planters*, p. 22.

15. Weeden, *Early R.I.*, p. 157. Alice Morse Earle, *Customs and Fashions in Old New England* (New York, 1890), p. 189. Federal Writers Project, *Rhode Island*, p. 93. Channing, *Narragansett Planters*, p. 9. Albert S. Bolles, *Industrial History of the United States* (Norwich, Conn., 1879), p. 147. Dean C. Phillips, *Horse Raising*, p. 894.

16. Bacon, *Narragansett Bay*, p. 247. J. E. A. Smith, *History of Pittsfield, Mass. 1734–1800* (Boston, 1869), 2: 34.

17. Weeden, p. 157. Hempstead, *Diary*. Douglass, 2: 214.

18. Josselyn, *Two Voyages*, p. 191. Josiah Paine, *A History of Harwich, Barnstable Co., Mass. 1620–1800* (Rutland, Vt., 1937). Coffin, *Newbury*, p. 122.

19. Robert R. Walcott, "Husbandry in Colonial New England," *N.E. Quart.*, 9 (1936), 243. Anburey, 2: 217.

20. Usher, *Commonwealth History*, 2: 412, 413.

21. R. W. Howard, *Horse in America*, p. 80.

22. Samuel Sewall, *Diary*, ed. Mark Van Doren (New York, 1927), p. 17.

23. Douglass, 2: 218.

24. Deane, p. 240. Philip Padelford, *Colonial Panorama 1775: Dr. Robert Honyman's Journal for March and April* (San Marino, Cal., 1939), p. 54.

25. Henry White, *Indian Battles, with Incidents in the Early History of New England* (New York, 1859), p. 349.

26. Green, Diary, entry for Aug. 31, 1711. John H. Lockwood, *Westfield and Its Historic Influences* (Westfield, 1922), 1: 390.

27. Thaddeus W. Harris, *Insects of Massachusetts Injurious to Vegetation* (Cambridge, 1841), p. 136.

28. Timothy Dwight, *Travels in New England and New York, 1796–1815* (New Haven, 1821–22), 1: 49. Powers, *Coos Country*, pp. 153, 159.

17. *Wealth from Forests*

1. *Watertown Records*, p. 14. Waters, *Ipswich*, p. 66. Steiner, *Guilford, Conn.*, p. 181.

2. John J. Currier, *History of Newbury, Mass.* (Boston, 1902), pp. 128, 129.

3. Day, *Maine Agriculture,* p. 40. Frederick Freeman, *History of Cape Cod* (Boston, 1860–62), 2: 112.

4. See enlightening discussions in William M. Carleton's "Masts and the King's Navy," *N.E. Quart.,* 12 (1939), 4–18. Joseph J. Malone, *Pine Trees and Politics,* (Seattle, 1964). B. F. Hall, *Eastern Vermont,* p. 143; and local histories.

5. Weeden, *History,* 1: 356.

6. Burnaby, *Travels,* p. 151.

7. J. E. A. Smith, *Pittsfield,* p. 42.

18. *Probing the Wilderness*

1. For development of new towns, an excellent monograph is Clifford K. Shipton, "The New England Frontier 1607–1763," *N.E. Quart.,* 10 (1937), 25–36.

2. Stackpole, *New Hampshire,* 1: 350. Parker, *Londonderry,* pp. 97 ff. Thomas Smith, *Extracts from Journals, 1719–1788,* ed. William Willis (Portland, Me., 1849), pp. 53, 143. Rising Lake Morrow, *Connecticut Influences in Western Massachusetts and Vermont* (New Haven, 1936), pp. 10–14. Marcus Lee Hansen, *The Mingling of the Canadian and American Peoples* (New Haven, 1940), 1: 30–35.

3. Cutter, *History of Arlington, Mass.,* p. 151.

4. D. Hamilton Hurd, ed., *History of Cheshire and Sullivan Counties* (Phila., 1886), p. 231.

5. Ellen M. Raynor and Emma L. Petitclerc, *History of the Town of Cheshire, Berkshire County, Massachusetts* (Holyoke, 1885), pp. 30, 61.

6. Henry H. Vail, *Pomfret, Vermont,* ed. Emma C. White (Boston, 1930), 1: 102. Eliot, *Field Husbandry,* p. 2.

7. Samuel Williams, *The Natural and Civil History of Vermont* (Walpole, N.H., 1794), p. 312.

19. *The Ways and the Means*

1. Estate inventories such as those in *Essex County Probate Records* correct erroneous impressions.

2. Hempstead, *Diary,* entry of March 22, 1742.

3. Merrill, *Amesbury,* p. 237. Cummings, *Rural Household Inventories.*

4. Warren R. Cochrane and George K. Wood, *History of Francestown, N.H. . . . 1759–1891* (Nashua, 1895), p. 381.

5. Sidney Perley, *History of Salem, Mass.* (Salem, 1924), 1: 238. Hempstead, p. 104. J. B. Felt, *Annals of Lynn* (Nashua, N.H., 1891), p. 131.

6. Portsmouth, R.I., Town Records, April 16, 1671. J. P. Brissot de Warville, *New Travels in the United States of America, Performed in 1788* (2nd ed., London, 1794), p. 102.

7. Carl Bridenbaugh, ed., *Gentleman's Progress: The Itineraries of Dr. Alexander Hamilton, 1744* (Chapel Hill, 1945), p. 97. Birket, *Cursory Remarks*, p. 30.

8. Leonard B. Ellis, *History of New Bedford and its Vicinity* (Syracuse, 1892), p. 114.

9. Judd, *Hadley*, pp. 192, 439, 440. Quotation from Chard P. Smith, *Housatonic, Puritan River* (New York, 1946), p. 235.

20. *Life on the Farm*

1. Quoted by Marshall B. Davidson, *Life In America* (Boston, 1951), p. 492.

2. Andrews, *Journal.* Collins, Walker, and Hempstead, diaries for dates noted.

3. Clarence W. Bowen, *Woodstock: An Historical Sketch* (New York, 1886), p. 60. Raynor, *Cheshire*, p. 61.

4. Parkman, *Diary*, p. 172.

5. Green, Diary, and Walker, *Diary*, for dates mentioned. Miller, *Narragansett Planters*, p. 22. Bacon, *Narragansett Bay*, p. 242. Morison, *American People*, p. 149. C. H. S. Davis, *History of Wallingford* (Meriden, Conn., 1870), p. 339.

6. Data for the following paragraphs on health come from diverse sources. Among the more informative, in addition to town and regional histories, are John B. Blake, *Public Health in the Town of Boston* (Cambridge, Harvard University Press, 1959); Zabdiel Boylston, *An Historical Account of the Small Pox Inoculation in New England* (2nd ed., London 1784); John Demos, *A Little Commonwealth: Family Life in Plymouth Colony* (New York, Oxford University Press, 1970); Philip J. Greven, Jr., *Four Generations . . . in Colonial Andover* (Ithaca, Cornell University Press, 1970); Johnson, *Our English Heritage*, pp. 30 ff.; and Nathaniel S. Shaler, "Physiography of North America," in Winsor, *Narrative and Critical History*, 4: x–xxi. The quotation is from Ralph D. Smith, *History of Guilford, Connecticut* (Albany, 1877).

7. Paine, *Harwich*, p. 118.

8. Benjamin Chase, *History of Old Chester, New Hampshire* (Auburn, N.H. 1867), p. 425. Samuel Orcutt, *History of the Towns of New Milford and Bridgewater, Conn. 1703–1882* (Hartford, 1882), p. 106.

9. Patten, *Diary*, dates 1772 ff. Read, Account Book. William R. Bliss, *Colonial Times on Buzzards Bay* (Boston, 1888), p. 30.

10. Robert E. Brown, *Middle-Class Democracy and the Revolution in Massachusetts, 1691–1780* (Ithaca, N.Y., 1955), pp. 14, 16, 18.

11. Edmund B. Barton, *Brief History of . . . Braintree 1640–1940* (Braintree, 1940), p. 28.

12. Jackson T. Main, *The Social Structure of Revolutionary America* (Princeton, N.J., 1965), p. 254.

13. Charles S. Thompson, *Evolution of the American Public Library, 1653–1876* (Washington, D.C., 1952), p. 42. Louis B. Wright, *The Cultural Life of the American Colonies* (New York, 1957), p. 148.

14. George L. Kittredge, *The Old Farmer and His Almanack* (Boston, 1904), pp. 59, 60. Joseph T. Buckingham, *Personal Memoirs* (Boston, 1852), 1: 12.

15. Eliot, *Essays upon Field Husbandry* (Boston, 1760). Eliot, *Essays . . . and Other Papers*, ed. Harry J. Carman et al. (New York, 1967).

16. Charles S. Grant, *Democracy in the Connecticut Frontier Town of Kent* (New York, 1961), pp. 135, 167.

17. Zuckerman, *Peaceable Kingdoms*, pp. 200–17. E. Brown, *Middle-Class Democracy*, p. 93. David Hawke, *The Colonial Experience* (New York, 1966), p. 474.

PART III. THE REVOLUTION AND ITS AFTERMATH, 1775–1800

21. *Patriotic Fervor*

1. It seems unnecessary to enter deeply into the political and constitutional aspects of the crisis leading to the Revolution—already the subject of an immense body of historical investigation and description by distinguished scholars.

2. "Diary of Thomas Nowell," *Mass. Hist. Soc. Proc.*, 15 (1876–77), 354.

3. Samuel Cooper to Thomas Pownal, Aug. 17, 1774, *Am. Hist. Rev.*, 7 (1924), 328.

4. George C. Mason, "The British Fleet in Rhode Island," *R.I. Hist. Soc. Coll.*, 7 (1885), 315.

5. Stephen E. Patterson, *Political Parties in Revolutionary Massachusetts* (Madison, University of Wisconsin Press, 1973), pp. 98–113. *Extracts from the Account Book of John Goddard of Brookline*, Brookline Hist. Soc., Pub. 15 (Brookline, 1900); Experience Richardson, Sudbury, Mass., Diary, copy in possession of author.

6. James T. Adams, *Revolutionary New England 1691–1776* (Boston, 1923), p. 434. Bacon, *Narragansett Bay*, p. 285. W. L. Watson, "Jamestown," *R.I. Hist. Soc. Coll.*, 26 (1933), 83.

7. David Hawke, *The Colonial Experience* (New York, 1966), p. 611. Wallace Brown, "The American Farmer during the Revolution: Rebel or Loyalist?", *Ag. Hist.*, 42 (1968), 329–34.

8. Banks, *Martha's Vineyard*, 1: 372–81. William Baylies, "Description of Gay Head," *Memoirs Am. Ac. Arts and Sciences*, 2 (1793), 150–55. Charles F. Elkins, ed., *Early History of Falmouth* . . . (Falmouth, 1889), p. 85.

9. George Bancroft, *History of the United States* (Boston, 1885), 5: 330. Mead, *Greenwich*, pp. 144, 159.

10. Day, *Maine Agriculture*, p. 58.

11. Frederick P. Wells, *History of Newbury* (St. Johnsbury, Vt., 1902), p. 90. Samuel Swift, *History of Middlebury* (Middlebury, Vt., 1859), pp. 181–90.

12. Bancroft, *United States*, 5: 125.

13. David Wilder, *The History of Leominster* . . . (Fitchburg, Mass., 1853), p. 47. Abijah P. Martin, *History of Lancaster, Mass.* . . . (Lancaster, 1879), p. 310.

14. J. M. Stowe, *History of Hubbardston* (Hubbardston, Mass., 1881), p. 67.

15. Olson, *Agricultural Economy and Population*, p. 17.

16. William Lincoln, *Journals of the Provincial Congress of Massachusetts in 1774 & 1775* (Boston, 1838), p. 317. Merrill, *Amesbury*, p. 254.

17. Benjamin L. Mirick, *History of Haverhill, Mass.* (Haverhill, 1832), p. 177.

18. Van Duzen, *Connecticut*, p. 158. Payne K. Kilbourne, *Sketches and Chronicles of* . . . *Litchfield, Conn.* (Hartford, 1859), p. 120. I. W. Stuart, *Life of Jonathan Trumbull, Senior, Governor of Connecticut* (2nd ed., Hartford, 1878), p. 468. Vail, *Pomfret*, p. 177.

19. Crofut, *Guide to Connecticut*, 2: 396. Stiles, *Windsor*, p. 403.

20. George F. Clark, *History of Norton* (Boston, 1859), p. 406. Ralph V. Harlow, "Economic Conditions in Massachusetts during the American Revolution," *Col. Soc. of Mass. Trans.*, 20 (1920), 166 ff. Mack E. Thompson, "Moses Brown's Account of a Journey to Distribute Donations," *R.I. History*, 15 (1956), 97–121. Thomas Vernon, *Diary*, R.I. Hist. Tracts, 13 (Providence, 1881).

21. Day, *Maine Agriculture*, p. 62. Harlow, pp. 179, 181. Oscar and Mary Handlin, *Commonwealth: Massachusetts 1774–1861* (New York, 1947), p. 11. Smith, *Pittsfield*, p. 471. David Willard, *History of Greenfield* (Greenfield, Mass., 1838), p. 63.

22. Samuel Lane, *A Journal for the Years 1739–1803*, ed. Charles L Hanson (Concord, N.H., 1937), p. 51. Hanson, *Danvers*, p. 97. Merrill

Jensen, "The American Revolution and American Agriculture," *Ag. Hist.*, 43 (1969), 114–19.

23. Robert A. East, *Business Enterprise in the American Revolutionary Era* (New York, 1938), pp. 74–81. Van Duzen, p. 160. Harlow, 182–84.

24. Samuel E. Morison, *Maritime History of Massachusetts* (Boston, 1921), p. 29. J. Franklin Jameson, *The American Revolution Considered as a Social Movement* (Beacon Press, reprinted 1963), pp. 61–64. Parkman, *Diary*, p. 79.

25. Wallace W. Brown, "The American Farmer during the Revolution," *Ag. Hist.* 42 (1968), 330. Frederic Denison, *Westerly and Its Witnesses, 1626–1876* (Providence, 1878), p. 118.

26. Powers, *Coos Country*, p. 146.

27. John G. Holland, *History of Western Massachusetts* (Springfield, 1855), 2: 341.

28. Ellen D. Larned, *History of Windham County, Connecticut* (Worcester, 1874), p. 208. Grace Graylock Niles, *The Hoosac Valley: Its Legends and Its History* (New York, 1912), p. 199.

29. William R. Bliss, *Colonial Times on Buzzards Bay* (Cambridge, 1888), p. 140.

30. Merrill Jensen, *The New Nation: The United States during the Confederation* (New York, 1950), pp. 238 ff.

31. Hawke, *Colonial Experience*, p. 662. Harlow, in Col. Soc. of Mass. *Trans.*, p. 183. Joseph Hadfield, *An Englishman in America 1785 . . .* , ed. Douglas S. Robertson (Toronto, 1933), p. 185.

32. Smith, *Pittsfield*, 1: 393.

33. Marion L. Starkey, *A Little Rebellion* (New York, 1955), is a lucid, interesting, well-authenticated account of the whole affair. Taylor, *Western Mass. in the Revolution*, is also valuable.

34. Starkey, p. 65. James E. Clauson, *Cranston: A Historical Sketch* (Providence, 1904), p. 25.

35. Jensen, "The American Revolution," p. 119.

22. The New States

1. Brissot de Warville, *New Travels*, p. 106. Francis Jean de Chastellux, *Travels in North America in the Years 1780, 1781 and 1782* (London, 1787), 1: 37. Grant, *Kent*, p. 34.

2. Betty F. Thomson, *The Changing Face of New England* (New York, 1958), p. 44.

3. Isabel Mitchell, *Roads and Road Making in Connecticut*, Conn. Tercentenary Commission (1933), pp. 24–31. Olson, *Agricultural Economy in Conn.*, pp. 7, 25.

4. Chard P. Smith, *Housatonic*, p. 209. Noah Porter, Jr., *Historical Discourse in Commemoration of the Original Settlement of Farmington in 1640* (Hartford, 1841).

5. John Drayton, *Letters Written during a Tour through the Northern and Eastern States of America* (Charleston, S.C., 1794), p. 43. *Commerce of R.I.*, 2: 167–308.

6. Brissot, p. 117. Francisco de Miranda, *Travels in the United States 1783–1784*, ed. John J. Ezell (Norman, Okla., 1963), pp. 133, 155.

7. In this field, Morison's *Maritime History of Massachusetts* is incomparable. Day, *Maine Agriculture*, p. 80. W. Winterbotham, *An Historical Geographical, Commercial and Philosophical View of the United States* (New York, 1796), 2: 160.

8. *Massachusetts Centinel*, March 28, 1787. John B. Blake, *Public Health in the Town of Boston, 1630–1822* (Cambridge, 1959), pp. 156, 163. Henry Wansey, *An Excursion to the United States of America in the Summer of 1794* (Salisbury, England, 1798), p. 22.

9. William Bentley, *Diary* (Salem, 1905–14), entry for July 28, 1790. George F. Dow, *Two Centuries of Travel in Essex Co., Mass.* (Topsfield, 1921), pp. 178, 184.

10. Mass. Hist. Soc. *Coll.*, 2 (1793), 204.

11. Peter Whitney, *History of the County of Worcester, Mass.* (Worcester, 1793), pp. 51, 59, 145, 155, 196, 209, 234, 311.

12. Wansey, p. 55. Samuel Davis, "Journey from Plymouth to Connecticut," Mass. Hist. Soc. *Proc.*, 11 (1869–70), 11.

13. Robertson, *Hadfield Diary*, p. 175.

14. Lord Adam Gordon, "Journal 1764 and 1765," in Mereness, *Travels*, p. 447. Smith, *Pittsfield*, 2: 35. La Rochefoucauld, *Travels through the United States of North America* (London, 1799), 2: 175, 206.

15. Chastellux, *Travels*, 2: 225, 226, 237.

16. Stiles, *Extracts from Itineraries*, p. 200. Joslyn, *Poultney, Vt.*, p. 23. Nathan Perkins, *Narrative of a Tour through Vermont . . . 1789* (Woodstock, 1930), p. 17. Swift, *Middlebury*, p. 204.

17. John Lincklaen, *Travels in the Years 1791 and 1792 in Pennsylvania, New York and Vermont* (New York, 1897), p. 86. J. A. Graham, *A Descriptive Sketch of the Present State of Vermont* (London, 1797), pp. 31–37.

18. Rowe, *Maritime Maine*, pp. 102, 103.

19. Dan Stiles, *Land of Enchantment: The Penobscot Bay–Mt. Desert Area of the Maine Coast*, pp. 14 ff. Dwight, *Travels*, 3: 221.

20. Maine Hist. Soc. *Coll.*, 4 (1856), 312, 320, 345, 389.

21. Day, *History*, p. 69. La Rochefoucauld, *Travels*, 1: 427.

23. *A New Century Approaches*

1. Porter E. Sargent, *A Handbook of New England* (Boston, 1916), p. 62. Jedediah Morse, *The American Geography* (2nd ed., London, 1792), p. 145.

2. Assembled from Cummings, ed., *Rural Household Inventories 1675–1775.*

3. James T. Adams, *Provincial Society 1690–1763* (New York, 1927), pp. 305 ff.

4. Kittredge, *Old Farmer's Almanack*, p. 18.

5. Day, *Maine Agriculture*, p. 235.

6. Mass. Soc. for Promoting Agriculture, *Centennial Report* (1892), p. 7. William H. Child, *History of Cornish, New Hampshire* (Concord 1912), 1: 214. Mirick, *Haverhill*, p. 184.

7. Frederick J. Wood, *Turnpikes of New England* (Boston, 1919), p. 35.

8. N. Porter, Jr., *Historical Discourse*, p. 81. Winterbotham, *Historical View*, 2: 163.

9. Quoted by Carrier, p. 151.

10. S. L. Bailey, *Historical Andover*, p. 403.

11. Deane, *N. E. Farmer*, 2nd ed., 1797, intro.

12. Day, *Maine Agriculture*, p. 83.

13. Brissot, *New Travels*, p. 390.

14. Padelford, *Honyman's Journal*, p. 49.

15. Whitney, *Hist. of Worcester Co.*, p. 314.

16. See, for example, "The Account of the Emigration of Capt. William Allen from Martha's Vineyard to Maine," in William C. Hatch, *History of Industry* (Farmington, 1893), pp. 72–89.

PART III. ANOTHER BEGINNING, 1800–1825

24. *Lines of Force*

1. *Compendium, U. S. 10th Census*, June 1, 1880 (revised ed., Washington, 1885), Part I, pp. 4, 5.

2. Edward A. Kendall, *Travels through the Northern Parts of the United States in 1807–1808* (New York, 1809), 2: 259, 3: 28. John C. Pease and John M. Niles, *A Gazetteer of Connecticut and Rhode Island* (Hartford, 1819), pp. 13, 186, 196, 203, 246. Daniel W. Teller, *History of Ridgefield, Connecticut* (Danbury, 1878), p. 171.

3. George Howe, *Mount Hope*, p. 136.

4. R. H. Brown, *Historical Geography*, p. 156. James Stuart, *Three*

Years in North America (Edinburgh, 1833), p. 310. Blanche E. Hazard, *Organization of the Boot & Shoe Industry in Massachusetts* (Cambridge, 1921), pp. 135, 138, 204–07. Rodolphus Dickinson, *A Geographical and Statistical Survey of Massachusetts* (Greenfield, 1813), pp. 68–75.

5. Richard J. Purcell, *Connecticut in Transition, 1775–1818* (new ed., Middletown, 1963), p. 83. Pease and Niles, pp. 13, 36, 183. Federal Writers Project, *Vermont* (Cambridge, 1937), p. 30. Lewis D. Stilwell, "Migration from Vermont (1776–1860)," Vt. Hist. Soc. *Proc.*, 5 (1937), 109. Andrew N. Adams, *History of Fair Haven, Vermont* (Fair Haven, 1870), pp. 183.

6. Pease and Niles, p. 14. Dickinson, p. 69.

25. Turnpikes, Canals, and Bridges

1. Henry M. Fenner, *History of Fall River* (New York, 1906), pp. 12, 13.

2. For specific information on the turnpike movement see Frederick J. Wood, *The Turnpikes of New England* (Boston, 1919). Struik, *Yankee Science*, pp. 99–102.

3. Struik, pp. 102–12, is excellent on bridge-building.

4. Wansey, *Excursion*, p. 22. Struik, pp. 114–20. Stackpole, *New Hampshire*, 2: 252.

5. Griffin, *Keene*, pp. 350, 363.

6. Ellis, *New Bedford*, p. 170.

7. John Harriott, *Struggles through Life* (3rd ed., London, 1815), 2: 171. Jospeh T. Buckingham, *Personal Memoirs* (Boston, 1852), 1: 12.

8. Nourse, *Harvard*, p. 40. Holland, *Western Mass.*, 1: 480.

9. Kendall, *Travels*, 1: 136, 264, 266.

10. Larned, *Windham County*, 2: 377. Day, *Farming in Maine*, p. 125.

11. Quoted in Hedrick, *Agriculture of New York*, p. 65.

12. James Drayton, *Letters*, p. 64.

13. Quoted by Percy W. Bidwell, "Rural Economy in N.E.," in Conn. Academy of Sciences *Trans.*, 4 (1916), 20, 348.

26. Combing the Back Country

1. Allen, Account Books.

2. *Commerce of R.I.*, 2: 111. J. E. A. Smith, *Pittsfield*, p. 47. Larned, *Windham Co.*, 2: 47.

3. Chase, *Haverhill*, pp. 451 ff. Sheldon, *Deerfield*, pp. 919 ff. Thompson, *Greenfield*, 1: 295. Martha McD. Frizzell, *History of Walpole, N.H.* (Walpole, 1963), 1: 24, 42.

4. Bowen, *Woodstock, Conn.* 1: 213.

5. Augustine G. Hibbard, *History of Goshen, Connecticut* (Hartford, 1877), p. 365. Lewis M. Norton, *Goshen in 1812* (Acorn Club of Conn., Pub. 21 (1949). Jarvis M. Morse, *A Neglected Period of Connecticut History, 1818–1856* (New Haven, 1933), p. 256.

6. Holland, *Western Mass.*, 2: 10. Jasper J. Stahl, *History of Old Broad Bay and Waldoboro* (Portland, Me., 1956), 2: 10, 13. Federal Writers Project, *Massachusetts*, p. 433.

7. Earle Newton, *The Vermont Story* (Montpelier, 1949), p. 120. Cochrane, *Francestown, N.H.*, p. 273.

8. Percy W. Bidwell, "The Agricultural Revolution in New England," *Hist. Rev.*, 26 (1921), 685.

9. Sidney Perley, *Historic Storms of New England* (Salem, 1891), pp. 187–213.

10. Mathews, *Expansion of N.E.*, pp. 160, 183. Stuart H. Holbrook, *The Yankee Exodus* (New York, 1950), p. 48.

27. Ways with Grass and Grain

1. Lord Gordon, quoted in Mereness, *Travels*, p. 413.

2. Edward Enfield, *Indian Corn: Its Value, Culture and Uses* (New York, 1866), p. 60.

3. See local accounts, such as Edward Miller and Frederic P. Wells, *History of Ryegate, Vermont* (St. Johnsbury, 1913), p. 97. Swift, *Middlebury*, p. 94. Day, *Maine Agriculture*, p. 156.

4. Arria S. Huntington, *Under a Colonial Roof-Tree* (Boston, 1891), p. 41.

28. Horses, Cheese, and Sheep

1. In discussing Justin Morgan, the trainer, and his horse "Figure," later known as "Justin Morgan," I have relied chiefly on Margaret Gardiner and Alexander Mackay-Smith, "The Great Justin Morgan Pedigree Controversy," *The Chronicle of the Horse*, 30 (1967), Nos. 18: 26–28; 19: 20–22; 20: 20–21, and 21: 22. Among other sources consulted are D. C. Linsley, *Morgan Horses: A Premium Essay on Their Origin, History, and Characteristics* (New York, 1837); Robert W. Howard, *The Horse in America* (New York, 1965); review of Howard by Mackay-Smith, *Ag. Hist.*, 40 (1966), 312–13; Dorothy C. Fisher, *Vermont Tradition* (Boston, 1953), pp. 211 ff.; Samuel Swift, *Statistical and Historical Account of the County of Addison, Vermont* (Middlebury, 1859), pp. 103, 110; and Gates, *Agriculture and Civl War*, passim.

2. For more extended discussion I recommend Raynor and Petitclerc, *Cheshire*, pp. 86–88; and C. A. Browne, "Elder John Leland and the Mammoth Cheshire Cheese," *Ag. Hist.,* 19 (1944), 145–53.

3. Chester Dewey, et al., *History of the County of Berkshire* (Pittsfield, Mass., 1829), pp. 90, 401.

4. Hibbard, *Goshen*, pp. 365, 366. Federal Writers Project, *Connecticut*, p. 470.

5. George F. Lemmer, "The Spread of Improved Cattle through the Eastern United States to 1850, *Ag. Hist.,* 21 (1947), 86. S. W. Pomeroy, "Dairy Stock," *Mass. Ag. Repository*, 6 (1821), 89.

6. Blake, *Public Health in Boston*, p. 208.

7. Powers, *Coos Country*, p. 225.

8. Olson, *18th Century*, p. 3.

9. Jewett, *Rowley*, p. 284 ff. Nathaniel Bouton, *History of Concord* (Concord, N.H., 1856), p. 474. John G. Curtis, *History of Brookline, Mass.* (Boston, 1933), p. 176. Dickinson, *Geog. and Stat. View*, pp. 68, 73.

10. Winterbotham, *Historical View*, 2: 87.

11. P. P. F. De Grand, *Boston Weekly Report of Public Sales and Arrivals*, for April 1, 1825. Birket, *Cursory Remarks*, p. 13. Benjamin F. Parker, *History of Wolfeborough* (Wolfeborough, N.H., 1901), p. 190.

12. Kendall, *Travels*, 1: 88. Jane E. Johnson, ed., *Newtown's History and Historian* (Newtown, Conn., 1917), p. 181.

13. Thomas B. Hazard, *Nailer Tom's Diary, of Kingstown, R.I., 1778–1840* (Boston, 1930), p. 261.

14. Kendall, 1: 309. Dwight, *Travels*, 3: 134.

15. J. E. Wing, "Merino Sheep," *Cyclopedia*, 3: 619; also "Humphreys," *Dict. of Am. Biography.* Van Dusen, *Connecticut*, p. 186.

16. Elkanah Watson, *History of . . . the Berkshire Agricultural Society . . .* (Albany, 1819), p. 9.

17. Harold F. Wilson, "The Rise and Decline of the Sheep Industry in Northern New England," *Ag. Hist.,* 9 (1935), 25. Federal Writers Project, *Vermont*, p. 166.

29. *Growth of the Land: New Crops*

1. Anonymous, Daily Journal, 1817–25 (Hampstead, N.H.), Old Sturbridge Village Library, Sturbridge, Mass. Lincklaen, *Travels*, p. 93. Whitney, *County of Worcester*, p. 155.

2. Fruit varieties and dates: I have distilled the facts from numerous sources, sometimes conflicting, including Hedrick, *Hist. of Horticulture*; Worcester Co. Hort. Soc., *Fruit List of Old Varieties* (Worces-

ter, 1968); Stowe, *Hubbardston*, p. 7; Robert Manning, *Book of Fruits* (Salem, 1838), p. 51; Jenkins, *Conn. Agr.*, p. 403; Marshall P. Wilder, *The Horticulture of Boston and Vicinity* (Boston, 1881), pp. 29, 31, 70; and *American Gardener's Magazine*, 1 (1835), 92.

3. Henry K. Rowe, *Tercentenary History of Newton* (Newton, 1930), p. 45. *Farmers Monthly Visitor* (Concord, N.H., 1838), 1: 170.

4. Hedrick, *Horticulture*, p. 310. Van Wyck Brooks, *The World of Washington Irving* (New York, 1944), p. 93. MS letter in possession of John C. Willard, Wethersfield, Conn.

5. Stephen W. Fletcher, *The Strawberry in North America* (New York, 1917), pp. 12–20. John M. Weeks, *History of Salisbury, Vermont* (Middlebury, 1860), p. 84.

6. Swift, *Cape Cod*, p. 283. Albert E. Benson, *History of the Massachusetts Horticultural Society* (Boston, 1929), p. 409.

7. Jenkins, p. 410. Malcolm Keir, "The March of Commerce," *Pageant of America* (New Haven, 1925–29), 4: 41. George L. Miner, "A Providence Packet Ship of 1812," R.I. Hist. Soc. *Coll.*, 26 (1933), 39.

8. Jewett, *Rowley*, pp. 285 ff. Hempstead, *Journal*. De Grand's *Report*, 1824–25.

9. Benjamin Goddard, "Daily Occurrences" (1812 diaries) at Brookline Public Library. Dwight, *Travels*, 1: 21, 28. Kittredge, *Almanack*, p. 84.

10. Hedrick, p. 204. Barber, *Connecticut Historical Collections* (improved ed., New Haven, 1856), p. 85. Jenkins, 407, 408.

11. James L. Belden, Wethersfield, Conn., *Seed List for 1821*. John C. Willard, of Wethersfield, MSS in the author's possession. William Downing, Hancock, Mass. *Seed List*, at Old Sturbridge Village Library, Sturbridge, Mass. Barber, as above. Mass. Hort. Soc., Boston, Collection of Seed Catalogues.

12. Dwight, 1: 23. Bronson Alcott, *New Connecticut* (Boston, 1881), p. 12 n.

13. *Commerce of R.I. 1775–1800*, p. 269. Jenkins, pp. 351, 417.

14. Winterbotham, *Historical View*, 2: 85; Wansey, *Excursion*, p. 48. Clark, *Manufactures*, 1: 440. Miller and Wells, *Ryegate*, p. 93.

15. Sewall, *Woburn*, p. 176. Dwight, 1: 357. Bidwell and Falconer, p. 244.

16. Ethel S. Bolton, *Shirley Uplands and Intervales* (Boston, 1914), p. 29. *N.E. Farmer*, 8 (1856), 463. Federal Writers Project, *Massachusetts*, p. 433.

17. Judd, *Hadley*, pp. 360, 361. John H. Martin, "Broom Corn, the Frontiersman's Cash Crop," *Economic Botany*, 7 (1953), 166.

18. Colman, *Fourth Report*, p. 30. Adams, *Weathersfield*, p. 615. Herbert C. Parsons, *A Puritan Outpost: A History . . . of Northfield, Mass.* (New York, 1937), p. 260. Wells and Field, *Hatfield*, p. 219. Mass. Board of Ag., *1882 Report*, p. 155.

19. Harriott, *Struggles*, 2: 125.

20. *Commerce of R.I.*, 2: 167. Miranda, *Travels*, p. 147. Alexander Harvey "Journal," Vt. Hist. Soc. *Proc. (1921)*.

21. This discussion is based largely on the following, plus pertinent local histories: George K. Holmes, "Some Features of Tobacco History," Am. Hist. Soc., *1919 Report*, 1: 385–407; "Three Centuries of Tobacco," USDA, *1919 Yearbook*, 151–75; Jenkins, *Conn. Ag.*, p. 412; Ramsey, *Tobacco in the Conn. Valley*, pp. 119–28; Joseph C. Robert, *The Story of Tobacco in America* (New York, 1952), pp. 57, 95, 102; Garner, Moss, et al., "History and Status of Tobacco Culture," USDA, *1922 Yearbook*; A. F. McDonald, *Tobacco Production in Connecticut*; and Kendall, *Travels*, 1: 317.

22. Frederic G. Howes, *History of Ashfield* (Ashfield, Mass., 1910), p. 104. Dewey, *Berkshire*, p. 86. N. K. Ellis, "Peppermint and Spearmint Production," *Economic Botany*, 14 (1960), 280–85.

23. *Mass. Ag. Repository*, "History of Silk in the United States," 9 (1826), 128–30; 10 (1827), 145–54.

24. Wansey, p. 48. Nelson Klose, "Sericulture in the United States," *Ag. Hist.*, 37 (1963), 226.

25. Lura W. Watkins, "When They Burned Peat in Middleton," *Old Time New England*, 52: 75–80. Pease and Niles, pp. 116, 198. Louise K. Brown, *Wilderness Town: The Story of Bedford, Massachusetts* (1968), p. 167.

26. *New Hampshire Agricultural Repository* (Concord, 1822), pp. 45, 50. Lee, *Yankees of Conn.*, p. 129. Emerson, *Naushon Island*, p. 390.

27. Judd, *Hadley*, p. 378. Samuel Hopkins, *Historical Memoirs Relating to the Housatonnuck Indians* (Boston, 1753), pp. 25–27.

28. C. P. Smith, *Housatonic*, p. 236. Wansey, p. 74.

29. Patten, *Diary*, p. 380. Lincklaen, *Travels*, p. 88. S. Williams, *Hist. of Vt.*, p. 314.

30. Tools and Tillage

1. Leo Rogin, *The Introduction of Farm Machinery in Relation to the Productivity of Labor in the Agriculture of the United States . . .* (Berkeley, 1931), pp. 22–27. Bidwell and Falconer, p. 208. Frank Gilbert, *Jethro Wood, Inventor of the Modern Plow* (Chicago, 1882). Holland, *Western Massachusetts*, p. 397.

2. Struik, *Yankee Science*, p. 101. Joseph C. G. Kennedy, *Agriculture of the United States in 1860* (Govt. Printing Office, 1864), pp. xxiii, xxv.

3. *Vermont History*, 23 (1955), 314. Norton, *Goshen in 1812*. Arthur W. Peach, ed., "As The Years Pass: The Diaries of Seth Shaler Arnold (1784–1871) Vermonter," Vt. Hist. Soc. *Proc.*, new ser., 7, No. 2 (1940), entries for 1835. Robert Frost, *Complete Poems* (New York, 1936), p. 47.

4. Harriott, *Struggles*, 2: 386. Hanson, *Danvers*, p. 113. Pease and Niles, pp. 172, 365.

5. Pease and Niles, p. 98. Barber, *Conn. Hist. Coll.*, p. 533. Kendall, 2: 39, 148.

6. Mass. Hist. Soc. *Coll.*, 8 (1802), 156, 189. Ricketson, *New Bedford*, p. 269.

7. Blake, *Health in Boston*, pp. 156, 163. Colman, *Fourth Report*, p. 329.

8. R. Dickinson, *Geographical View*, p. 8. Sheldon, *Deerfield*, 2: 919. Dwight, *Travels*, 1: 315.

9. Augusta H. Worthen, *History of Sutton* (Concord, N.H., 1830), p. 275. Hazard, *Shoe Industry*, p. 69. Langdon, *Everyday Things in American Life*, p. 253.

10. Worthen, pp. 276, 283. Bolton, *Shirley Uplands*, p. 37. Main, *Social Structures of Revolutionary America*, p. 21, appears misinformed in stating that there were no longer indentured servants in Massachusetts country towns. The indenture even of young females occurred.

11. *Mass. Agric. Journal*, 10 (1827), 370.

12. Mildred Campbell, "Social Origins of Some Early Americans," in J. M. Smith, ed., *Seventeenth Century America* (Chapel Hill, N.C., 1959), p. 73. James S. Grinnell, "History of Sheep Husbandry in Mass.," Mass. Board of Agric., *1891 Rpt.*, p. 106. William Tudor, *Letters on the Eastern States* (Boston, 1821), p. 211. Patten, *Diary*, entry of Oct. 17, 1776. Kittredge, *Almanack*, p. 182. For exceptions see Cochrane and Wood, *Francestown*, p. 360, and Miller and Wells, *Ryegate*, p. 207.

13. John Lambert, *Travels through Canada and the United States* (3rd. ed., London, 1816), 2: 323. Adam Hodgson, *Letters from North America* (London, 1824), 2: 136. Alice Stone Blackwell, *Lucy Stone, Pioneer of Woman's Rights* (Boston, 1930), p. 9.

31. *Comfort and Struggle*

1. Benjamin Silliman, *Remarks on a Short Tour between Hartford and Quebec . . . 1819* (New Haven, 1824), p. 412. Miller and Wells, *Ryegate*, p. 94.

2. A. N. Somers, *History of Lancaster* (Concord, N.H., 1899), p. 127. Kendall, *Travels*, 2: 35. Lambert, *Travels*, 2: 307.

3. Howes, *Ashfield*, p. 147. Raynor and Petitclerc, *Cheshire*, p. 88. Griffin, *Keene*, p. 302. Fisher, *Vermont Tradition*, p. 60. Larned, *Windham Co.*, 2: 413. Dickinson, *Geographical View*, p. 7.

4. Horace Greeley, *Recollections of a Busy Life* (New York, 1868), p. 50. Cochrane, *Francestown*, p. 371.

5. Mass. Hist. Soc. *Coll.*, 8 (1802), 121, 151; 8 (1803), 121.

6. Lambert, 2: 14.

7. Ernest L. Bogart, *Peacham: The Story of a Vermont Town* (Montpelier, 1948), p. 74 n. Cochrane, p. 37. Francis E. Blake, *History of Princeton* (Princeton, 1915), 1: 303.

8. Mass. Hist. Soc. *Coll.*, 7: 151. Vermont Hist. Soc. *Proc.*, 7: 140.

9. Blackwell, *Lucy Stone*, p. 12.

10. J. Farmer and J. B. Moore, eds., *Collections, Relating Principally to New Hampshire* (Concord, 1822), 1: 14. Cobbett, quoted by Van Wyck Brooks, *The World of Washington Irving* (New York, 1944), p. 22.

11. Dwight, *Travels*, 2: 254. Samuel Orcutt, *History of New Milford and Bridgewater* (Hartford, 1882), p. 448.

12. Levi H. Clarke, "Haddam in 1808," *Connecticut Towns*, (Acorn Club of Conn., Pub. 22 (1949), 10.

PART IV. GOOD GROWING WEATHER, 1825–1860

32. *Things to Come*

1. Edward C. Kirkland, *Men, Cities, and Transportation: A Study in New England History 1820–1900* (Cambridge, 1948), 1: 89, 90. Stilwell, *Migration*, p. 134.

2. Bidwell, *Rural Economy*, pp. 307 ff. R. H. Brown, *Historical Geography*, p. 105. Stilwell, p. 105. Griffin, *Keene*, p. 382.

3. Lambert, *Travels*, 2: 306. Worthen, *Sutton*, p. 568.

4. D. Hamilton Hurd, *History of Cheshire, Sullivan Counties* (Phila. 1886), p. 393. T. M. Adams, *Prices Paid by Vermont Farmers . . . 1790–1940* (Vermont Agric. Exp. Sta., Burlington, 1944), pp. 46–48. Wilkes Allen, *History of Chelmsford 1653–1820* (Haverhill, 1882), p. 442. Lambert, 2: 562. Griffin, *Keene*, pp. 337, 350, 360.

5. William Little, *History of Warren: A Mountain Hamlet* (Manchester, N.H., 1870), p. 386. Benjamin G. Willey, *History of the White Mountains* (new ed., Cambridge, 1870), pp. 60, 111, 119. Somers, *Lancaster*, pp. 60, 119. Stackpole, *New Hampshire*, 2: 353. Rowe, *Maritime History*, p. 112.

6. William H. Child, *Cornish, N.H.*, p. 214. Day, *Maine Agriculture*, p. 183. Moses Greenleaf, *Survey of the State of Maine* (Portland, 1829), pp. 212–15.

7. Eugene M. Graves, "History of Maine's Nineteenth Century Beef Industry" (M.A. thesis, U. of Me., Orono, 1967) pp. 7, 9. Bouton, *Concord, N.H.*, p. 474.

8. James Stuart, *North America*, 1: 359. DeLue, *Walpole*, p. 230. J. Coleman, *Transformation of R.I.*, p. 163. Clauson, *Cranston*, p. 33.

9. Milton H. Thomas, ed., *Elias Boudinot's Journey to Boston* (Princeton, 1955), p. 18. Jenkins, *Conn. Agric.*, p. 344.

10. John Hayward, *Gazetteer of Massachusetts* (Boston, 1846), p. 33.

11. De Grand's Reports, 1825. Kirkland, *Men, Cities*, 1: 7.

12. Pease and Niles, *Gazetteer of Conn. & R.I.*, p. 324.

13. De Grand's Reports, 1824, 1825. Charlotte A. Lacey, *An Historical Story of Southport* (Fairfield, Conn. 1927), p. 44.

14. Richard B. Morris, *Encyclopedia of American History* (New York, 1950), p. 426. Sidney Withington, *First Twenty Years of Railroading in Connecticut* (New Haven, 1935), p. 29.

15. *Boston Cultivator*, Nov. 25, 1848. Henry D. Thoreau, *Writings* (Boston, 1906), 3: 114.

16. Charles Russell, *Address before the Hampden Co. Hort. Soc.* (Oct. 3, 1850), p. 19. Swift, *Middlebury*, p. 111. Adams, *Farm Prices*, p. 46.

17. Day, p. 156. Willey, p. 58.

18. Charles W. Eldridge, "Journal of a Tour in 1833," Vt. Hist. Soc. *Proc.*, 2: 54. Barber, *Conn. Hist. Coll.*, p. 76.

19. Bidwell and Falconer, pp. 226, 340. E. Hasket Derby, *Boston: A Commercial Metropolis* (Boston, 1850). Carl N. Degler, *Out of Our Past: The Forces That Shaped America* (New York, 1959), p. 120.

20. Hayward, *Gazetteer*, p. 229.

21. Larned, *Windham Co.*, 2: 400. Bidwell, *Agric. Revolution*, p. 696. Johnston, *North America*, 2: 422.

22. Examples that follow are but a few in scores of local histories, gazetteers, and similar sources.

23. Ellis, *New Bedford*, pp. 420.

24. *Christian Science Monitor*, "Sketch of Swampscott, Mass., History," May 27, 1952.

25. Jenkins, *Conn. Agric.*, p. 410. Charles T. Jackson, *Agricultural Survey of Rhode Island* (Providence, 1840), p. 166. James C. Bonner, "Advancing Trends in Southern Agriculture, 1840–1860," *Agric. Hist.*, 22 (1948), 255.

26. Richard O. Cummings, *The American Ice Harvests* (Berkeley,

Cal., 1949), pp. 15–63. Oscar E. Anderson, Jr., *Refrigeration in America* (Princeton, 1953), pp. 11–26.

33. *The Eager Young*

1. Harriet Martineau, *Society in America* (New York, 1837), 2: 99. Stuart, *Three Years in America*, p. 323.

2. Nathaniel Hawthorne, *Passages from the American Note-Books* (Boston, 1884), 1: 162, 164. Frederick Marryat, *A Diary In America* (Indiana U. Press, 1960), p. 77. Ralph Waldo Emerson, *Essays* (revised ed., Boston, 1888), 2: 75. Henry Ward Beecher, *Pleasant Talks about Fruits, Flowers and Farming* (New York, 1874), p. 99.

3. Ray Bearse, *Vermont Guide* (Boston, 1966), p. 281. Holland, *Western Mass.*, 2: 384. Clara Barton, *The Story Of My Childhood* (New York, 1907). Blackwell, *Lucy Stone*, p. 233. Wells, *History of Hatfield*, pp. 271, 352, 354.

4. Ethel S. Bolton, *Farm Life: A Century Ago* (privately printed, 1909), p. 22. J. M. Stowe. *History of Hubbardston* (Hubbardston, Mass., 1881), p. 83.

5. *Cyclopedia*, 4: 78. Clarence A. Day, *Farming in Maine 1860–1940* (Orono, 1963), pp. 12–16, 240. Oliver A. Bacon, *History of Natick* (Boston, 1856), p. 105; Clarence H. Danhof, *Change in Agriculture in the Northern United States 1820–1870* (Cambridge, Harvard University Press, 1969), p. 57.

6. *New England Farmer*, 9: 405. Greeley, *Recollections*, pp. 56, 59. Cyrus Hamlin, *My Life and Times* (Boston, 1893), pp. 12, 41.

7. *Cyclopedia*, 4: 367–370. Struik, *Yankee Science*, p. 357.

8. *Cyclopedia* 4: 369, 404.

9. Ibid., pp. 479, 569.

10. Elkanah Watson, *Berkshire Co. Agric. Soc.*, p. 73. *Cyclopedia*, 4: 292.

11. Struik, *Yankee Science*, p. 188.

34. *Sheep and Other Livestock*

1. Joslyn et al., *Poultney, Vt.*, p. 81.

2. Wilson, *Sheep Industry*, p. 27. Kennedy, *Agriculture in the U.S. in 1860*, intro. Swift, *Addison Co.*, p. 104. Fisher, *Vermont Tradition*, p. 192.

3. Stilwell, *Migration*, pp. 172, 173. C. Benton and S. F. Barry, *Statistical View of the Number of Sheep in . . . Maine, New Hampshire,*

Vermont, Massachusetts, Connecticut (Cambridge, 1837), p. 33. Weeks, *Salisbury*, p. 81. John Hayward, *Gazetteer of New England* (4th ed., Boston, 1839).

4. Paul W. Gates, *The Farmer's Age: Agriculture 1815–1860* (New York, 1960), p. 225.

5. Day, *Maine Agric.*, pp. 186–94.

6. Frizzell, *Walpole*, p. 549.

7. Jenkins, *Conn. Agric.*, p. 395. Dewey, *Berkshire*, p. 401.

8. Holland, *Western Mass.*, pp. 527, 575. Somers, *Lancaster*, p. 228. Mass. Bd. of Agric., *1886 Rpt.*, p. 34.

9. *Compendium, U.S. 10th Census*, Rev. ed., Pt. I, p. xxxiii.

10. Edward Wiest, *The Butter Industry in the United States* (New York, 1916), p. 140.

11. Nathaniel C. Bradstreet, "Recollections," Mass. Audubon Soc. *Bull.*, (October 1951), p. 29.

12. Colman, *First Report*, p. 255.

13. Gates, *Farmer's Age*, p. 239.

14. Colman, *Fourth Report*, p. 252.

15. USDA, Commissioner's *1870 Rpt.*, p. 316.

16. Patrick Shirreff, *A Tour through North America* . . . (Edinburgh, 1835), p. 37.

17. *Boston Cultivator*, Sept. 23, 1848. Jenkins, *Conn.*, p. 392.

18. Bidwell and Falconer, pp. 224–26. Wells, *Hatfield*, p. 219. Colman, *Fourth Report*, pp. 5, 298–301.

19. The subject is given extended treatment in E. M. Graves' unpublished "History of Maine's Nineteenth Century Beef Industry," (from which part of these figures are quoted by author's permission). *Agric. Repository*, 10: 292. Hayward, *Gazetteer*, pp. 113, 296.

20. James A. Gourgouras, "Brighton: Oldest Cattle Market in U.S.," *The Breeder-Stockman*, 14 (1953), 9. *Boston Globe*, Jan. 31, 1967.

21. *Boston Cultivator*, Apr. 5, 1851. Graves, p. 151.

22. *Agric. Repository*, 10: 292.

23. Colman, *Fourth Report*, p. 298.

24. George F. Dow et al., *History of Topsfield* (Topsfield, Mass., 1940), p. 365.

25. Colman, p. 315.

26. *Agric. Repository* 9: 19, 10: 211. James S. Grinnell, "Agriculture of Massachusetts," Mass. Bd. of Agric., *1881 Report*, p. 371. Bolles, *Industrial History*, p. 258.

27. Hawthorne, *American Note-Books*, 1: 200, 251. Graves, p. 357.

28. Bidwell and Falconer, p. 231.

29. Day, *Maine Agric.*, p. 275.

30. Jenkins, *Conn. Agric.*, p. 390. Federal Writers Project, *Connecticut*, p. 389.

31. Allen W. Thompson, *The Horses of Woodstock* (Riverside Press, 1881), p. 3.

32. Mass. Bd. of Agric., *1882 Rpt.*, p. 296.

33. Frizzell, *Walpole*, p. 552. *N.E. Farmer*, 9: 73. Gates, *Farmer's Age*, p. 229. *Vt. Hist.*, 23 (1955), 231.

34. *Cyclopedia*, 4: 100. Day, *Maine Agriculture*, pp. 195–200.

35. "Nailer Tom" Hazard, *Diary*, pp. 716 ff.

36. *Boston Cultivator*, Nov. 10, 1849. John C. Bennett, *The Poultry Book: A Treatise on the Breeding and General Management of Domestic Fowls* (Boston, 1851), p. 286.

37. Thoreau, *Writings*, 2: 325.

38. Jewett, *Rowley*, p. 293. Graves, p. 79.

39. *Boston Cultivator*, Oct. 27; Nov. 10, 24; Dec. 1, 1849. Bennett, pp. 217, 296.

40. Arthur A. Brigham, "Notes on Rhode Island Reds," R.I. Agric. Exp. Sta., *Fourteenth Rpt.*, Pt. II, pp. 324–28. "The Rhode Island Red," *N.E. Farm Finance News*, 9 (1954), 8.

35. *Backbone Crops and New Departures*

1. Mass. Bd. of Agric., *1855 Rpt.*, p. 109.

2. *N.E. Farmer*, 9: 395.

3. Freeman, *Cape Cod*, 2: 354.

4. Willey, *White Mts.*, p. 58.

5. Vt. Hist. Soc. *Proc.*, new ser., 2 (1931), 115, Jan. 18 entry.

6. Franklin McDuffie, *History of Rochester, N.H.* (Manchester, 1892), p. 328. Frizzell, *Walpole*. M. E. Goddard and H. V. Partridge, *History of Norwich, Vermont* (Hanover, N.H., 1805), p. 183.

7. Bonner, *Southern Agriculture*, p. 255. Jenkins, *Conn.*, p. 410. Pease and Niles, p. 342.

8. Day, *Maine Agric.*, pp. 163–65.

9. H. Blake, "Fifty Years of Farm Life in Northern Vermont," Vermont State Bd. of Agric. *4th Report* (1877), p. 93.

10. Edward W. Carpenter and Charles F. Morehouse, *History of Amherst, Mass.* (Amherst, 1896), p. 285. Goddard and Partridge, *Norwich*, p. 133.

11. Alonzo and James R. Newhall, *History of Lynn* (Boston, 1865), pp. 416, 426, 432. Bidwell, *Agric. Rev.*, p. 693. Gates, *Farmer's Age*, pp. 264, 266.

12. Gates, p. 318.

13. Colman, *First Report*, p. 33. Day, *Maine Agric.*, pp. 132, 167.

14. Harold M. Bailey, "Vermont in the Potato Lineage Book," *Vt. Hist.*, 23 (1955), 120. Michel Oren with Janet Greene, "The Only Potato Fit to Eat," *Vt. Life*, 15 (1960), 54.

15. Day, *Maine Agric.*, p. 208.

16. Gates, *Farmer's Age*, p. 261. Charles F. Adams, Jr., *The Town of Lincoln 1754–1904* (Lincoln, Mass., 1905), p. 204.

17. Hedrick, *Horticulture*, pp. 437, 444.

18. Ibid., p. 440. MSS Records (Belmont, Mass. Hist. Soc.). Benson, *Mass. Hort. Soc.*, p. 107.

19. "Cranberry Lore," *Food Marketing In N.E.* (November 1954), p. 7.

20. Mass. Bd. of Agric., *1863 Rpt.*, pp. 103, 108. William B. Jordan, Jr., *A History of Cape Elizabeth, Maine* (Portland, 1965), p. 71.

21. Letter dated 11/27/1837 at Wethersfield, Conn., Hist. Soc. *N.E. Farmer*, 23 (1845), p. 381; *N.E. Farmer*, Second Ser., 9 (1857), 326, 474, 381. George P. Jennings, *Greens Farms, Connecticut: The Old West Parish of Fairfield* (Greens Farms, 1933), pp. 18, 131.

22. *Mass. Repository*, 7: 41. Colman, *Fourth Report*, p. 219. Jackson, *Survey of R.I.*, pp. 153–56.

23. "A Morning in a Market Garden," *N.E. Farmer*, Second Ser., 7 (1855) p. 444. Colman, *Fourth Report*, p. 353. Isaac Hill, "Two Days in West Cambridge, Mass.," *Farmer's Monthly Visitor*, 1: (1839), 169–71.

24. Amos E. Brown, *Faneuil Hall and Faneuil Hall Market* (Boston, 1900), pp. 173–84. Henry Tudor, *Tour in North America* (London, 1834), 1: 358.

25. *Boston Cultivator*, Feb. 28, 1852.

26. Fearing Burr, *Field and Garden Vegetables of North America* (Boston, 1865), p. 203. James J. H. Gregory, *Squashes: How to Grow Them* (New York, 1867), p. 45. Goddard, "Daily Occurrences." Walton C. Galinat, *The Evolution of Sweet Corn*, U. of Mass. Agric. Exp. Sta. *Bull.* 591 (Amherst, 1971), p. 10.

27. Coolidge and Mansfield, *New England*, p. 435. Hedrick, *Horticulture*, p. 285.

28. Hedrick, p. 251. Milford W. Atwood, "The Seed Catalogue," *N.E. Homestead* (Jan. 10, 1959), p. 10. Communications from John C. Willard, Wethersfield, Conn. (formerly of Comstock, Ferre & Co.): "Indian Corn," "Hybrid Corn," and "Seed Trade."

29. U.S. Census, 1890 *Rpt. of the Statistics of Agriculture of the United States at the Eleventh Census*, p. 575.

30. "Tobacco Culture," USDA *1922 Yearbook*, p. 408. McDonald, *Tobacco Production in Conn.*, pp. 6–8. Jenkins, *Conn. Agric.*, p. 413. Mass. Bd. of Agric., *1892 Rpt.*, pp. 140–58; *1893 Rpt.*, p. 355.

31. T. M. Woodford, *Smith's 1855 Map of Hartford Co., Conn.* (Hartford 1855).

32. Bidwell and Falconer, p. 246. U.S. Census, *1880 Rpt.*, 3: 244.

33. John H. Martin, "Broomcorn—The Frontiersman's Cash Crop," *Economic Botany*, 7 (1953), 166. Mass. Bd. of Agric., *1882 Rpt.*, p. 155. Bidwell and Falconer, p. 245.

34. Coolidge and Mansfield, *New England*, p. 420. *Food Marketing in N.E.*, 27 (1967), 31.

35. Adams, *Weathersfield*, p. 617. Bolles, *Industrial History*, p. 438. Holland, *Western Mass.*, 2: 256. Klose, *Sericulture in the U.S.*, p. 226.

36. "Arnold Diaries," Vt. Hist. Soc. *Proc.*, new ser., 8 (1940), 140.

37. Alpheus S. Packard, Jr., *Our Common Insects* (Boston, 1873), pp. 60, 61.

36. Marketing the Woods

1. *Boston Cultivator*, Dec. 9, 1848. Kirkland, *Men, Cities*, p. 26. Colman, *First Report*, p. 13. Jackson, *Survey of R.I.*, pp. 67, 144. Felt, *Salem*, 1: 257.

2. Francis DeWitt, *Statistical Information Relating to Industry in Massachusetts for Year Ending June 1, 1855* (Boston, 1856).

3. Somers, *Lancaster, N.H.*, p. 142. Rowe, *Maritime Maine*, p. 120. Bradstreet, "Recollections," p. 292. Thoreau, *Writings*, 4: 431, 465.

4. Hugh M. Raup and Reynold E. Carlson, *The History of Land Use in the Harvard Forest* (Petersham, Mass., 1941), p. 25. Barber, *Hist. Coll., Conn.*, p. 502. Alcott, *New Connecticut*, p. 89.

5. Charles J. Latrobe, *The Rambler in North America* (London, 1835), 1: 44.

6. Colman, *Second Report*, p. 80.

7. Colman, *First Report*, p. 327. *N.E. Farmer*, Dec. 6, 1844.

8. Jackson, *Survey of R.I.*, pp. 149–81, 208–65. Barber, *Conn.*, pp. 224, 553. Pease and Niles, p. 97. *Boston Cultivator*, Nov. 18, 1848. Frank D. Smith, *History of Guilford, Connecticut* (Albany, 1877), p. 42.

9. *N.E. Farmer*, 24: 197, 9: 341. *Mass. Agric. Journal*, 10 (1831), 276.

10. Martineau, *Society in America*, 1: 283.

11. Pease and Niles, pp. 98, 172. Danhof, *Change in Agriculture*, p. 266. Charles Hudson, *History of Lexington, Mass.* (Boston, 1868), p. 414.

12. Edward S. Abdy, *Journal of a Residence and Tour of the United States 1833–34* (London, 1835), 1: 89. Tudor, *Tour* 1: 355, 376.

13. James F. W. Johnston, *Notes on North America, Agricultural, Economical, and Social* (Boston, 1851), 2: 500. *N.E. Farmer*, 9 (1857), 395.

14. Clark, *History of Conn.*, p. 539.

15. Illuminating views on aspects of emigration are found not solely in Frederic Jackson Turner's well-known essay *The Frontier in American History*, but also in Holbrook's *Yankee Exodus*, especially pp. 73 and 108; Van Wyck Brooks, *Sketches in Criticism*: "The Tradition of Rootlessness" and especially "Thoughts on History"; Fulmer Mood, "A British Statistition of 1854 Analyzes the Westward Movement in the United States," *Agric. Hist.*, 19 (1945), pp. 142–51; Mathews, *Expansion of New England*; Stilwell, *Migration From Vermont*; and numerous other studies. The matter will receive further attention in a later chapter.

37. *Yankee Inventors*

1. *Cyclopedia*, 1: 388, 4: 63. Danhof, *Changes in Agriculture* pp. 182–241; Frank Gilbert, *Jethro Wood, Inventor of the Modern Plow* (Chicago, 1882), pp. 10 ff. John S. Barry, *A Historical Sketch of Hanover, Mass.* (Boston, 1853), pp. 148–50. Frank L. Remington, "When John Deere Engineered Efficiency into Tilling the Land," *C.S. Monitor*, Aug. 21, 1971.

2. F. L. Newton, "Notes on Old Plows," *Agric. Hist.*, 17 (1933), 9.

3. George P. Smith, "Evolution of Farm Machines," Mass. Bd. of Agric., *1899 Rpt.*, p. 249. James W. Grinnell, "Agricultural Implements and Machines," ibid., *1882 Rpt.*, p. 240. Charles G. Washburn, *Industrial Worcester* (Worcester, 1917), pp. 130–36.

4. C. L. Flint, "A Hundred Years' Progress," Mass. Bd. of Agric., *1873 Rpt.*, p. 28. DeWitt, *Mass. Industry for 1855*. Gates, *Civil War*, p. 281.

5. Day, *Maine Agric.*, pp. 229, 282. Clarence A. Danhof, "Gathering the Grass," *Agric. Hist.*, 30 (1956), 170. Jesse Buel, *The Farmer's Companion* (Boston, 1839), p. 125.

6. Flint, *Grasses*, pp. 342, 345. G. P. Smith, "Farm Machines," p. 255. Bidwell and Falconer, p. 296.

7. Day, *Maine Agric.*, p. 220.

8. Kennedy, *Agriculture in the U.S.*, intro., p. xxv. *N.E. Farmer* (January 1857), p. 39.

9. Birney C. Batcheller, *People of Wallingford* (Brattleboro, Vt., 1937), pp. 45, 224, 227. Kennedy, p. xxiii. Day, *Maine Agric.*, p. 270.

10. DeWitt. Thoreau, *Writings*, 4: 483. Peach, *Arnold Diaries*, Oct. 19, 1835. *Vt. Hist.*, 22 (1954), 314.

38. *The Typical Farmer*

1. Greeley, *Recollections*, pp. 28, 36–39. Joshua G. Holland (Timothy Titcomb), "Farming Life in New England," *Atlantic*, 2 (1858), 334–41. H. W. Collingwood, "Market Gardening with Limited Capital," Mass. Bd. of Agric., *1899 Rpt.*, pp. 30, 68.

2. John G. Whittier, "Snowbound, A Winter Idyll," *Complete Works*, pp. 487–99. Hamlin, *Life and Times*, pp. 30–52. Barton, *Story of My Childhood*, pp. 12, 17, 51–73. George F. Hoar, *Autobiography* (New York, 1903), 1: 81.

3. Thoreau, *Works*, 3: 352. Lee, *Yankees of Conn.*, p. 161.

4. Cutter, *History of Arlington*, p. 148. Colman, *Fourth Report*, p. 155.

5. Blackwell, *Lucy Stone*, p. 12.

6. Bidwell and Falconer, p. 254. Bidwell, *Agric. Rev.*, p. 697. The best account of the shoe trade is Hazard's *Boot and Shoe Industry*, especially pp. 52, 69–71, 113, 135, 136–38, 174. Many Mass. and N.H. town histories describe local shoemaking—for example, J. Bailey Moore, *History of Candia, N.H.* (Manchester, 1893), p. 270.

7. Hazard, pp. 207–10.

8. Collingwood, p. 67.

9. Benjamin Chase, *History of Old Chester* (Auburn, N.H., 1869), p. 434. Elizabeth W. Lord and Ethel M. Eaton, eds., *The Story of Templeton, Mass.*, Narragansett Hist. Soc. (Templeton, 1946), p. 24. J. Leander Bishop, *History of American Manufactures from 1608 to 1860* (Phila. 1861–68), 2: 78, 157, 285, 311.

10. Fed. Writers Project, *Mass.*, p. 456. Moore, p. 267.

11. Mood, "A British Statistician," *Agric. Hist.*, 19 (1945), 147.

12. Thoreau, *Works*, 2: 350. Abdy, *Journal* 1: 116. Johnston, *Notes*, 2: 463. U.S. Patent Office, *1847 Rpt.*, p. 361.

13. Colman, *First Report*, p. 36.

14. Emerson, *Essays*, 1: 75. *Society and Solitude* (rev. ed., Boston, 1889), p. 135.

15. Odell Shepard, ed., *The Journals of Bronson Alcott* (Boston, 1938), p. 139.

16. Van Wyck Brooks, *New England: Indian Summer, 1865–1915* (New York, 1945), p. 84.

17. Stuart, *Three Years*, p. 295. Shirreff, *Tour*, pp. 40, 52. Abdy, *Journal*, 1: 214.

18. Martineau, *Society in America*, 1: 284.

19. Hawthorne, *American Note-Books*, 2: 248.

20. Robert Russell, *North America, Its Agriculture and Climate* (Edinburgh, 1857), p. 12. Charles T. Russell, *Address*, p. 10.

21. Paul A. Chadbourne, "The Farmer's Home," Mass. Bd. of Agric., *1881 Rpt.*, pp. 206–08. Cochrane and Wood, *Francestown*, p. 371.

PART V. WAR AND READJUSTMENT, 1861 AND AFTER

39. *For Better and Worse*

1. Federal Writers Project, *Vermont*, p. 33. Newton, *Vermont Story*, p. 182. Cochrane, *Francestown*, p. 273. Elias Mason, *Gazetteer of the State of Massachusetts* (Boston, 1874), p. 57.

2. Moses T. Runnels, *History of Sanbornton, N.H.* (Boston, 1882), p. 331.

3. Gates, *Agriculture and Civil War*, p. 219.

4. Joe B. Frantz, *Gail Borden, Dairyman to a Nation* (Norman, Okla., 1951), pp. 51, 229–37, 264.

5. Int. Tin Research and Development Council, *Historic Tinned Foods* (Middlesex, England, Pub. 85, 2nd ed., 1939), p. 9. Wm. Underwood Co. Watertown, Mass., *The Red Devil*, 1 (April 1968), 2–3; 2 (August 1969), 3–9. Clarence Francis, *A History of Food and Its Preservation* (Princeton, N.J., 1937), pp. 9–11. Day, *Farming in Maine*, pp. 28–32, 157.

6. USDA, *1870 Rpt.*, p. 317. Struik, *Yankee Science*, p. 236.

7. *Cyclopedia*, 3: 365.

8. Gates, *Civil War*, p. 198.

9. Jenkins, *Conn. Agric.*, p. 411. Lacey, *Southport*, p. 44. *N.E. Farmer*, 9: 326.

10. Day, *Farming in Maine*, p. 119. USDA, *1870 Rpt.*, p. 402.

11. Wilson, *Sheep Industry*, pp. 28, 29. *Genesee Farmer*, 24 (1863), 333.

12. Mass. Bd. of Agric., *1850 Rpt.*, p. 402.

13. Graves, "Maine Beef Industry," table II.

14. A. F. McDonald, *Tobacco Production*, pp. 12 ff. U.S. Commissioner of Agric., *1870 Rpt.*, p. 451. Gates, *Civil War*, pp. 143, 145. J. M. Smith, *Tobacco Culture*, p. 168.

15. Enfield, *Indian Corn*, pp. 60–65. Flint, *Grasses*, p. 338. Sanborn, *New Hampshire*, p. 358. *Vt. Life*, 23 (1955), 64. Donovan and Woodward, *Lyndeborough, N.H.*, p. 478.

16. Graves, table II. Parsons, *Puritan Outpost*, p. 311.

17. *Homestead*, Oct. 19, 1872.

18. Wayne D. Rasmussen, "Scientific Agriculture," in Melvin Kranzberg and Carroll W. Pursell, Jr., eds., *Technology in Western Civilization* (London, 1967), 2: 348.

19. Fletcher, *Strawberry in America*, pp. 126–30. Mass. Bd. of Agric., *1881 Rpt.*, p. 15. Gates, *Civil War*, p. 374.

40. *Discouragement*

1. Van Duzen, *Connecticut*, pp. 250–52. Lee Benson, "The Historical Background of Turner's Frontier Essay," *Agric. Hist.*, 25 (1951), 59–82, offers a helpful analysis of the period.

2. Rollin Lynde Hartt, "A New England Hill Town," *Atlantic*, 83 (1899), 572. Fred A. Shannon, *The Farmer's Last Frontier: Agriculture 1860–1877* (New York, 1945), p. 418.

3. Vermont Bd. of Agric., *1878 Rpt.*, p. 141. Mass. Bd. of Agric., *1890 Rpt.*, p. 121.

4. Charles H. Merchant and Merton S. Parsons, *Farm Property Taxation in Maine*, Me. Agric. Exp. Sta., *Bull.* 366 (Orono, 1933), pp. 268, 269.

5. Albert Smith, *History of Peterboro . . . New Hampshire* (Boston, 1876), p. 211.

6. U.S. Commissioner of Agric., *1870 Rpt.*, p. 260.

7. *Homestead* (April 29, 1871), p. 404.

8. *N.E. Farmer*, 8 (1856), 523. Mass. Bd. of Agric, *1889 Rpt.*, p. xvii.

9. Stilwell, *Migration From Vt.*, p. 65.

10. Mathews, *Expansion of N.E.*, pp. 229–44. Turner, *Frontier*, p. 143. Luther Burbank with Wilbur Hall, *The Harvest of the Years* (Cambridge, 1927), pp. 1–12.

11. G. B. Loring, "New England Farming," Mass. Bd. of Agric., *1859 Rpt.*, p. 51. G. W. Atherton, "Future of N.E. Agriculture," Mass. Bd. of Agric., *1896 Rpt.*, p. 112.

12. Steiner, *Guilford*, p. 139.

13. Bidwell, *Agric. Revolution*, p. 701. Brooks, *Sketches*, p. 119. Holbrook, *Yankee Exodus*, p. 268. Page Smith, *City upon a Hill*, p. 53.

14. Harold F. Wilson, *The Hill Country of Northern New England* (New York, 1936), p. 150.

15. George Hill, "Market Gardening," Mass. Bd. of Agric., *1883 Rpt.*, p. 104.

16. John D. Black, *The Rural Economy of New England* (Cambridge, 1950), p. 20.

41. *Adapt or Perish*

1. Mass. Bd. of Agric., *1881 Rpt.*, pp. 7–9; *1884 Rpt.*, p. 19. Howes, *Ashfield*, p. 121.

2. O. E. Anderson, *Refrigeration*, p. 82. Newton, *Vermont Story*, p. 194. Mass. Bd. of Agric., *1888 Rpt.*, p. xiii. N.H. Bd. of Agric., *1891 Rpt.*, p. 92.

3. Adams, *Farm Prices*, p. 132. Mass. Bd. of Agric., *1895 Rpt.*, chart opp. p. 48.

4. *Vt. Hist.*, 23 (1954), 147. Vt. Bd. of Agric., *1900–01 Rpt.*, p. 124.

5. Mass. Bd. of Agric., *1880 Rpt.*, p. 9; *1883 Rpt.*, p. xiii.

6. Day, *Farming in Maine*, p. 59. N.H. Bd. of Agric., *1881 Rpt.*, p. 357. Vt. Bd. of Agric., *1869–70 Rpt.*, p. 174. Mass. Bd. of Agric., *1887 Rpt.*, p. 161. R.I. Bd. of Agric., *1887 Rpt.*, p. 108.

7. Mass. Bd. of Agric., *1880 Rpt.*, p. 190.

8. Edward L. Trudeau, *Autobiography* (New York, 1916), p. 184.

9. Mass. Bd. of Agric., *1887 Rpt.*, p. 228.

10. Day, *Farming in Maine*, p. 84.

11. Mass. Bd. of Agric., *1895 Rpt.*, pp. xxv, 192, 509. Mass. Senate, *Doc. 5*, 1893. R.I. Bd. of Agric., *1892 Rpt.*, p. 14.

12. USDA, Bureau of Animal Industry, *Legislation [re] Bovine Tuberculosis* (Washington, 1901). *Relation of Bovine Tuberculosis to Public Health*, Bull. 33 (Washington, 1901). Mass. House, *Doc. 1341*, 1897. *Homestead*, (Aug. 29, 1897), p. 104.

13. Vt. Bd. of Agric., *1895 Rpt.*, pp. 189, 240. Mass. Bd. of Agric., *1896 Rpt.*, p. 512. Stahl, *Waldoboro*, 2: 383.

14. *N.E. Farm Finance News*, August 1954.

15. *Homestead* (Feb. 25, 1894), p. 227.

16. Ibid. (April 29, 1899), p. 552.

17. Ibid. (Aug. 13, 1898), p. 151.

18. *Farm Finance News* (n. 14, above). USDA, Bureau of Animal Industry, *American Breeds of Fowls: The Plymouth Rock* (Washington, 1901).

42. *How the Gardens Grew*

1. Kirkland, *Men, Cities*, 1: 492. Helen Hamlin, *Pines, Potatoes and People* (New York, 1948), pp. 102, 144.

2. *Food Marketing*, 31, No. 1 (1971), 5. H. M. Bailey, "Vermont in the Potato Lineage Book," *Vt. Hist.*, 33 (1955), 120. Oren, *Only Potato Fit to Eat*, p. 57.

3. Emily G. Balch, *Our Slavic Fellow Citizens* (Charities Pub. Committee, New York, 1910), p. 240.

4. Day, *Farming in Maine*, pp. 30, 32. Vt. Bd. of Agric., *1900–01 Rpt.*, p. 24.

5. *Homestead* (Aug. 13, 1898), p. 147. Edward Jarvis, "Traditions and Reminiscences of Concord 1779–1878," MSS, Concord, Mass., Public Library.

6. Mass. Bd. of Agric., *1877 Rpt.*

7. J. B. Moore, "Market Gardening," Mass. Bd. of Agric., *1873 Rpt.*, p. 87. Richard Hittinger, "Irrigation," *1897 Rpt.* W. W. Rawson, ibid., *1891 Rpt.*, pp. 104–35; *1882 Rpt.*, pp. 95, 98.

8. Thomas G. Fessenden, *New American Gardener* (Boston, 1828), p. 152. *Farmer's Monthly Visitor*, 1 (1839), 170.

9. Correspondence from Mary M. Morse and Elizabeth Philbrick, Newton, Mass., in author's file. *Hort. Register and Gardener's Mag.*, 1 (1835), 345. B. T. Galloway, "Commercial Growing of Plants Under Glass," USDA, *1899 Yearbook*, p. 583. W. C. Strong, "Winter Gardening and Glass Structures," Mass. Bd. of Agric., *1874 Rpt.*, pp. 93, 105.

10. *Homestead* (March 27, 1897), p. 396.

11. Swift, *Cape Cod*, p. 284. *Homestead* (Aug. 27, 1898), p. 198.

12. Day, *Farming in Maine*, pp. 93–98. Mass. Bd. of Agric., *1880 Rpt.*, p. 105; *1881*, p. 95; *1896*, p. 413. J. W. Clark, "Growing and Marketing Apples," Vt. Bd. of Agric., *1895 Rpt.*, p. 102.

13. T. S. Gold, *Handbook of Conn.*, pp. 64–67.

14. Ramsey, *Tobacco Production*, p. 149 ff. Federal Writers Project, *Connecticut*, p. 115.

15. Day, *Farming*, p. 167.

16. J. Q. Evans, Mass. Bd. of Agric., *1894 Rpt.*, p. 50. Charles Goessman, ibid., *1874–75 Rpt.*, p. 335.

17. Adams, *Prices Paid by Vt. Farmers*, pp. 19, 36. *Cyclopedia*, 2: 425.

18. U.S. Comm. of Agric., *1870 Rpt.*, p. 440.

19. Mass. Bd. of Agric., *1871–72 Rpt.*, p. 92.

20. Ibid., *1880 Rpt.*, p. 20.

21. U.S. Census, *1890 Rpt.*, "Statistics of Agriculture," p. 578.

22. Raup and Carlson, *Harvard Forest*, p. 25.

43. *Any Way to Make a Dollar*

1. Runnels, *Sanbornton*, p. 236, 253.

2. Fogg, *N.H. Gazetteer*, Descriptions of towns noted.

3. Vt. Bd. of Agric., *1878 Rpt.*, pp. 173–75. Page Smith, *City upon a Hill*, p. 91.

4. Anderson, *Refrigeration*, pp. 38, 53, 109. Jennie G. Everson, *Tidewater Ice on the Kennebec River* (Maine State Museum, Freeport, 1970), pp. 5–124. Kirkland, *Men, Cities*, 2: 192.

5. Fuller, *Warwick*, p. 136. Bishop, *Manufactures*, 2: 787.

6. Mass. Bd. of Agric., *1890 Rpt.*, p. 7. Batcheller, *Wallingford*, p. 277. Bishop, 2: 701.

7. Fogg, *N.H. Gazetteer*, for towns named, p. 328. Robert Russell, *North America*, p. 18. *Vt. Hist.*, 23 (1955), 169, 247.

8. *Gazetteer*, pp. 87, 378. James D. Squires, *Mirror to America: A History of New London, N.H.* (Concord, 1952), pp. 15, 146. N.H. Bd. of Agric., *1891 Rpt.*, p. 205. Moore, *Candia*, p. 444.

9. N.H. Bd. of Agric., *1891 Rpt.*, p. 203. Vt. Bd. of Agric., *1885–86 Rpt.*, p. 81.

10. Julius A. Ward, "The Revival of our Country Towns," *N.E. Magazine* (November 1889), p. 245.

44. *Agriculture Organizes*

1. Day, *Farming in Maine*, 205–10. Mass. Bd. of Agric., *1898 Rpt.*, p. 170.

2. *Cyclopedia*, 4: 422, 423. Jenkins, *Connecticut*, 378–82. Gold, *Handbook*, p. 25. Storrs School, 2nd annual *Rpt.* (1889), pp. 11–51.

3. *Cyclopedia*, 3: 337, 357, 365. Mass. Bd. of Agric., *1865 Rpt.*, "Guernsey Cattle in America." E. Parmelee Prentice, *American Dairy Cattle: Their Past and Future* (New York, 1942), pp. 144, 238, 374, 385. *Homestead* (Nov. 12, 1955), p. 14.

4. Bogart, *Peacham, Vt.*, p. 355. Day, *Farming*, pp. 48, 54. Mass. Bd. of Agric., *1899 Rpt.*, p. vii.

5. Adams, *Farm Prices*, p. 128. Newton, *Vermont Story*, p. 194. Quinebaug Hist. Soc. *Leaflets*, 2 (1901), 69. N.H. Bd. of Agric., *1891 Rpt.*, p. 203.

6. Morse, *Neglected Period*, p. 226. Day, *Farming*, p. 183. *Homestead* (Dec. 24, 1898), p. 709.

7. *Cyclopedia*, 4: 294, 297.

8. Vt. Bd. of Agric., *1896 Rpt.*, pp. 110, 203. Day, *Farming*, p. 191.

45. *The Farm Wife*

1. Miller and Wells, *Ryegate, Vt.*, p. 207. Beecher, *Pleasant Talks*, p. 60. Coolidge, *Autobiography*, p. 17. Mass. Bd. of Agric., *1890 Rpt.*, p. 15. Julius A. Ward, *N.E. Mag.* (Nov. 1889), p. 243.

2. Nourse, *Harvard*, pp. 408–09. Perry, *Williamstown*, p. 65.

3. Vt. Bd. of Agric., *1895 Rpt.*, p. 125. R.I. Bd. of Agric., *1886–87 Rpt.*, p. 159.

4. Ward, p. 243. Vt. Bd. of Agric., *1896 Rpt.*, p. 195.

5. Balch, *Slavic Fellow Citizens*, pp. 240–42, 329–30. Ralph J. Harlow, "The Pole in the Land of the Puritan," *N.E. Mag.*, new ser., 29 (1933), 162–66.

6. Alvan F. Sanborn, "A Farming Community," *Atlantic*, 79 (1897), 588–98.

PART VI. A FOURTH CENTURY

46. *Seven Million to be Fed*

1. Jenkins, *Conn. Agric.*, pp. 378–82. Conn. Agric. Exp. Sta., *1910 Rpt.*, p. 75; *1900 Rpt.*, p. 322; *1916 Rpt.*, pp. xviii, 323; *1919 Rpt.*, p. 4. Rasmussen, "Scientific Agriculture," 2: 341.

2. R.I. Agric. Exp. Sta., *1908 Rpt., 1910 Rpt.*

3. Conn. Agric. Exp. Sta., *1916 Rpt.*, Pt. IV, p. 185. USDA, *1925 Yearbook*, p. 447. USDA *Exp. Sta. Record* for the period.

4. Morris, *Encyclopedia*, p. 715.

5. R.I. Bd. of Agric., *1905 Rpt.*, p. 222. *Agriculture of Vt.* for 1913.

6. Newton, *Vt. Story*, p. 190. Day, *Farming in Maine*, p. 263.

7. Newton, p. 195.

8. Day, pp. 65, 70. *Agric. of Vt.* (1913), p. 78.

9. Vt. Comm. of Agric., *1920–22 Rpt.*, "Dairymen," p. 13.

10. Hugh D. McLellan, *History of Gorham, Maine* (Portland, 1903), p. 252.

11. T. S. Gold, *Handbook of Conn. Agric.*, pp. 64–67. *Food Marketing*, 5 (1946), 3.

12. *Homestead* (Nov. 12, 1960). USDA, *1925 Yearbook*, p. 260.

13. Wilfred Wheeler, "Cooperative Work in Grading and Marketing Fruits," Vt. Comm. of Agric., *Hort. Rpt.* (1920–22), 21.

14. *Food Marketing*, 26 (1957), 6. Day, p. 161.

15. Benson, *History Mass. Hort. Soc.*, pp. 409, 483. USDA, *1931 Rpt.*, p. 174.

47. *An Artful Adjustment*

1. Day, *Farming In Maine*, pp. 140–48, 222. Vt. Comm. of Agric. *1920–22 Rpt.*, p. 12.

2. Conn. Exp. Sta., *1900 Rpt.*, pp. 322–29. McDonald, *Tobacco Production*, pp. 18 ff. Meyer Jacobstein, *Tobacco Industry of the United States* (New York, 1907), p. 60. Ramsey, *Tobacco Production*, p. 169.

3. USDA, *1925 Yearbook*, p. 907. Mass. Bd. of Agric., *1915 Rpt.*, Pt. II, p. 257. Wells, *Hatfield*, p. 235.

4. Paul Fox, *The Poles in America* (New York, 1922), pp. 61, 73. Harlow, "Pole, Puritan," *N.E. Mag.*, new ser., 29 (1933), 162–66.

5. U.S. *12th Census*, Vol. VI, Pt. II, p. 281.

6. Federal Writers Project, *Rhode Island*, p. 352.

7. *Food Marketing*, 22, No. 1 (1961), p. 9; ibid., No. 3, p. 29. Mass. Dept. Agric., *1921 Rpt.*, p. 57.

8. John W. Winslow, "Canning Industry of Maine," *Homestead* (Jan. 19, 1901), p. 94.

48. *Back to the Woods*

1. James E. Rice, "The Poultry Industry," R.I. Bd. of Agric., *1905 Rpt.*, p. 157. George H. Tilton, *History of Rehoboth, 1643–1918* (Boston, 1918), p. 253. Roy E. Jones, "100 Years of Poultry House Construction," *Homestead* (June 11, 1955), p. 6.

2. Ryan, "Storrs Egg Laying Contest." Gay T. Klein, "One Hundred Years of Our Poultry Industry," *Homestead* (Feb. 26, 1955), pp. 8–27.

3. Harold O. Cook, *Fifty Years a Forester*, Mass. Forest and Park Assn. (Boston, 1961), pp. 18–20.

4. Vt. Comm. of Agric., *1913 Rpt.*, p. 19; *1916–18 Rpt.*, p. 7.

49. *Close of the Third Century*

1. Newton, *Vermont Story*, p. 192. *Homestead* (Dec. 1, 1900), p. 540.

2. J. H. Putnam, "Poultry as a Cash Crop," Conn. Bd. of Agric., *1920–21 Rpt.*, p. 42.

3. USDA, *Chronology of American Agriculture 1790–1965*, revision of 1965.

4. N.H. Bd. of Agric., *1905–07 Rpt.*, pp. xii–xv; *1918–20 Rpt.*, p. 53. Vt. Comm. of Agric., *1916–18 Rpt.*, p. 7. *Homestead* (Aug. 4, 1900), pp. 108, 116. R.I. Agric. Exp. Sta., *1899 Rpt.*, p. 115.

Bibliography

GENERAL

(Biographies, Manuscript Collections and Diaries, Literary Works, Statistics)

Alcott, A. Bronson. *New Connecticut: An Autobiographical Poem*, Boston, 1881.

———. *The Journals of Bronson Alcott*, ed. Odell Shepard, Boston, Little Brown, 1938.

Allen, Nathaniel and Thomas (merchants of New London). Pre-Revolutionary Account Books, American Antiquarian Society, Worcester.

American Statistical Association. *Collections*, ed. Joseph B. Felt, Vol. 1, Pts. I–III, Boston, 1847.

American Agriculturist Yearbook and Almanac, 1905 edition.

Anderson, George P. "Highgate as Seen from an Old Account Book," Vermont Historical Society, *Proceedings*, New Ser., 7, No. 3 (1939), 122–60.

Andrews, Joseph. Journal, 1752–1787, Massachusetts Historical Society, Boston.

Arnold, Seth Shaler. "As the Years Pass: The Diaries of Seth Shaler Arnold (1788–1871), Vermonter," ed. Arthur W. Peach, Vermont Historical Society, *Proceedings*, New Ser., 8,2 (1940), 107–93.

Bartlett, J. Russell. *The Letters of Roger Williams*, Providence, Narragansett Club Pub'ns., 1874.

Barton, Clara. *The Story of My Childhood*, New York, 1907.

Barton Family. Account Book, 1830–37, Gill, Massachusetts, copy in possession of Howard S. Russell.

Beecher, Henry Ward. *Pleasant Talks about Fruits, Flowers and Farming,* New York, 1874.

Belcher Papers. Massachusetts Historical Society, Boston.

Belden, James. Seed List for 1821, Wethersfield, Conn., Historical Society.

Bentley, William. *Diary,* 4 vols., Salem, 1905–14.

Blackwell, Alice S. *Lucy Stone, Pioneer of Woman's Rights,* Boston, Little Brown, 1930.

Blodget, Samuel. *Economica: A Statistical Manual for the United States of America* (1774–1808), Washington, 1808.

Botkin, Benjamin A. *A Treasury of New England Folklore,* New York, Crown, 1944.

Brookline, Mass., Historical Society, "More Early Notices of Local Events," Pub. No. 16 (1899).

Brooks, Van Wyck. *The Flowering of New England,* New York, Dutton, 1936.

——. *New England, Indian Summer, 1865–1915,* New York, Dutton, 1945.

——. *Sketches In Criticism,* New York, Dutton, 1932.

——. *The World of Washington Irving,* New York, Dutton, 1944.

Buckingham, Joseph T. *Personal Memoir,* Boston, 1852.

Burbank, Luther, with Wilbur Hall. *The Harvest of the Years,* Cambridge, Mass., Houghton Mifflin, 1927.

Clap, Roger. *Memoirs,* Boston, 1731; reprint, 1844.

Clark, Horace. Diary 1836–37 (East Granby, Conn.), Old Sturbridge Village Library.

Collins, Zaccheus. Diary of Farming and Malt Business, 1726–69, 2 vols., Essex Institute, Salem.

Connecticut, *Register and Manual,* Helen E. Sellers, ed., Hartford, 1942.

Coolidge, Calvin. *Autobiography,* New York, Cosmopolitan Book Co., 1929.

Cooper, Samuel. Letter to Thomas Pownall, *American Historical Review,* 8 (1924), 328.

Cummings, Abbott L., ed. *Rural Household Inventories, 1675–1778,* Boston, Soc. for the Preservation of New England Antiquities, 1964.

Deane, Rev. Samuel. *Extracts From Diary, 1761–1814,* ed. William Willis, Portland, Me., 1849.

De Grand, P. P. F. *Weekly Report of Public Sales and Arrivals*, Boston, 1824–25.

Derby, Elias. Invoice of Merchandise, "Grand Turk" for Calcutta, 1792, Peabody Museum, Salem.

De Witt, Francis, ed. *Statistical Data Relating to Certain Branches of Industry in Massachusetts for 1854–55*, Boston, 1856.

Dow, George F. *The Holyoke Diaries*, Salem, Essex Institute, 1911.

Downing, William. *Seed List for 1821*, Hancock, Mass., Old Sturbridge Village Library.

Dunton, John. Journal, Massachusetts Historical Society *Collections*, 2nd Ser. 2 (1846), 97–124.

Dyer, Elisha. *Valuation of the Cities and Towns in the State of Rhode Island from 1860 to 1869 . . . together with the Census of the Colony in 1730 and 1775 . . .* , Providence, 1871.

Emerson, Ralph W. *Essays, First Series*, revised ed., 2 vols., Boston, 1888.

"English Shipping Records Relating to Massachusetts Ports," Peabody Museum, Salem.

Essex County Probate Records, 1633–1674, 2 vols., Salem, Essex Institute, 1916.

Felt, Joseph B. *Statistics of Towns in Massachusetts*, Boston, 1843.

Fenner, Arthur, and Co. 1742 Shipping Book, Rhode Island Historical Society *Collections*, 23 (1930), 74–80.

Fisher, Dorothy C. *Vermont Tradition: The Biography of an Outlook on Life*, Boston, Little Brown, 1953.

Frantz, John B. *Gail Borden, Dairyman to a Nation*, Norman, Okla., 1951.

Frost, Robert. *Collected Poems*, New York, Holt, 1930.

Gilbert, Frank. *Jethro Wood, Inventor of the Modern Plow*, Chicago, 1882.

Goddard, Benjamin. "Daily Occurrences," Diary, 1812, Brookline, Mass., Public Library.

———. *Extracts from Account Book*, Pub. 15, Brookline Historical Soc.

Goodale, Elaine. *Journal of a Farmer's Daughter*, New York, Putnam, 1881.

Greeley, Horace. *Recollections of a Busy Life*, New York, 1868.

Green, Joseph, of Salem Village. Diary, Essex Institute, *Historical Collections*, Second Ser., 10 (1869), 10–104, Salem, 1869.

Green, S. A. *Groton Records*, Cambridge, 1880.

Hall, G. Stanley. "A Boy's Life in a Massachusetts Town Thirty Years

Ago," Worcester, American Antiquarian Soc. *Proceedings*, New Ser., 7, Part I (1890), 107–28.

Hamlin, Cyrus. *My Life and Times*, Boston, 1893.

Hawthorne, Nathaniel. *American Note-Books*, Complete Works, Vols. 17 and 18, Boston, 1884.

Hazard, Thomas B. *Nailer Tom's Diary, of Kingston, Rhode Island, 1778–1840*, Boston, Merrymount, 1930.

Heath Papers, Massachusetts Historical Society, Boston.

Hempstead, Joshua. *Diary*, New London Historical Society, New London, Conn., 1901.

Hoar, George F. *Autobiography of Seventy Years*, 2 vols., New York, Scribner, 1903.

Hodges, Benjamin and John. Accounts 1784–1801; Ledgers; Cargo Lists. Peabody Museum, Salem.

Howes, David S. Account Book, 1830–1842 (Ashfield and Roxbury, Mass.), Old Sturbridge Village Library.

Hulton, Anne. *Letters of a Loyalist Lady . . . Boston 1767–1776*, Cambridge, Harvard University Press, 1927.

Huntington, Arria S. *Under A Colonial Rooftree . . . Diary of Elizabeth Porter Phelps of Hadley, Mass., 1763–1812*, Boston, 1891.

Jarvis, Edward. "Traditions and Reminiscences of Concord, Mass., 1779–1878," manuscripts, Concord Public Library.

Jewell, Margaret H. "Country Life in Maine a Century Ago. Gleanings from the Diary of Gen. Samuel Leighton of Alfred, Maine," *Old Time New England*, Bulletin, Society for the Preservation of N.E. Antiquities, 23 (July 1932), 28–38.

Knowles, James D. *Memoir of Roger Williams*, Boston, 1834.

Lane, Samuel. *A Journal for the Years 1753–1803, By Samuel Lane of Stratham, New Hampshire*, ed. Charles L. Hanson, Concord, N.H., Historical Society, 1937.

Mason, Louis B. *The Life and Times of Major John Mason of Connecticut, 1600–1672*, New York, Putnam, 1935.

Massachusetts, Census of the Commonwealth, *1855 Abstract*.

———. 1885, Vol. 2, *Agricultural Products and Property*.

Massachusetts, *Colonial Laws to 1672*, 2 vols., City of Boston, 1882.

Massachusetts, *Journal of the Provincial Congress, 1774–75*, Boston, 1838.

Massachusetts Horticultural Society, Boston. Seed Catalogue Collection, 1770 to the present.

Mayo, Lawrence S. *John Endecott*, Cambridge, Harvard University Press, 1936.

McIntyre, Ruth A. *William Pynchon, Merchant and Colonizer*, Springfield, Conn. Valley Historical Society, 1961.

Minor, Thomas, of Stonington, Conn. *Diary, 1653–1684*, prepared by S. H. Miner and G. D. Stanton, New London, 1899.

Morris, Richard B. *Encyclopedia of American History*, New York, Harper, 1953.

Moses, Asa, and Jabez Richards. Account Book for 1816, Old Sturbridge Village Library.

Parkman, Ebenezer. *Diary*, ed. Harriette E. Forbes, Westborough, Mass., Historical Society, 1899.

Patten, Matthew, of Bedford, New Hampshire. *Diary, 1754–1788*, Concord, N.H., Rumford Press, 1903.

Peach, Arthur W., ed. *See* Arnold, Seth Shaler.

Philbrick, Eliza, of Newton, Mass. Correspondence on early greenhouses, in file of Howard S. Russell.

Pitkin, Timothy, *Statistical View of the Commerce of the United States of America: Its Connection with Agriculture and Manufactures*, Hartford, 1816.

Pope, Charles H., ed. *The Plymouth Scrap Book*, Boston, Goodspeed, 1918.

Portsmouth, R.I. *Early Records 1639–97*, Rhode Island Historical Society, Providence, 1901.

Prince, Hezekiah, Jr. *Journals 1822–1828*, Maine Historical Society, New York, Crown, 1865.

Read, Ezekiel, of Seekonk, Mass. "Book of Accounts, 1712–33" in possession of Harold F. Tompson family, Seekonk, Mass.

Rhode Island, Commerce of, 1726–1800. Boston, Massachusetts Historical Society, 1915.

Richardson, Experience, of Sudbury, Mass. Excerpts from Diary 1705–86, in file of Howard S. Russell.

Rose-Troup, Frances. *Roger Conant and the Early Settlements on the North Shore of Massachusetts*, Roger Conant Family Assn., 1926.

Salem Town Records, 1634–59. Essex Institute *Historical Collections*, 2nd Series 1:1–242.

Sanford, Peleg. *The Letter Book of Peleg Sanford of Newport, Merchant, 1666–1668*, Providence, R.I. Historical Society, 1928.

Sewall, Samuel. *Diary*, ed. Mark Van Doran, New York, Macy Massins, 1927.

Shurtleff, Nathaniel B., ed. *Records of the Governor and Company of Massachusetts Bay in New England (1620–92)*, 5 vols., Boston, 1853–54.

Shurtleff, Nathaniel B. et al., eds. *Records of the Colony of New Plymouth in New England (1620–92)*, 12 vols., Boston, 1855–61.

Smith, Thomas. *Extracts from the Journals, 1719–1788*, ed. William Willis, Portland, Me., 1849.

Stevens, Henry. Fragments of Diary, 1838, Vermont Historical Soc. *Proceedings*, New Ser. 2 (1931), 115–18.

Stuart, I. W. *Life of Jonathan Trumbull, Sr., Governor of Connecticut*, 2nd ed., Hartford, 1878.

Thoreau, Henry D. Journal, in *Writings*, ed. Bradford Torrey, Vols. 3–14, Boston, 1906.

Trudeau, Edward L. *Autobiography*, Garden City, N.Y., Doubleday, Page, 1916.

Vernon, Thomas. Diary, *A Loyalist Banished from Newport . . . in 1776*, Providence, R.I., Historical Tracts, 13 (1881).

Walker, Timothy. "Diaries of Rev. Timothy Walker, the First and Only Minister of Concord, New Hampshire . . . 1730–1782," New Hampshire Historical Society, *Collections*, 9 (1889), 123–91.

Watertown Records, Comprising the First and Second Books of Town Proceedings, Watertown, Mass., 1884.

Weaver, Glenn. *Jonathan Trumbull, Connecticut's Merchant Magistrate*, Hartford, Connecticut Historical Society, 1956.

Whittier, John G. *Complete Works*, Household Edition, Boston, Houghton Mifflin, 1893.

Willard, John. Manuscripts and correspondence on the history of Wethersfield, Connecticut, and the seed industry, in possession of Howard S. Russell.

Winslow, Ola E. *John Eliot, Apostle to the Indians*, Boston, Houghton Mifflin, 1968.

Woodward, Carl R. "Rural Economy in Rhode Island 200 Years Ago . . . Account Books of Benoni Waterman . . . 1733–1740," *Rhode Island History*, 4 (1945), 97–106; 5 (1946), 119–128.

Historical Works

Ackerman, Edward. "Sequent Occupance of a Boston Suburban Community," *Economic Geography* (1941), pp. 61–74.

Adams, Andrew N. *A History of the Town of Fair Haven, Vermont,* Fair Haven, 1870.

Adams, Charles F., Jr. *The Town of Lincoln, 1754–1904,* Lincoln, Mass., 1905.

Adams, Herbert B. *The Germanic Origin of New England Towns,* Johns Hopkins University *Studies,* 1st Ser., No. 2, Baltimore, 1882.

———. "Village Communities of Cape Ann and Salem," in Vol. I, *Local Institutions,* Johns Hopkins University *Studies,* 1st Ser., No. 2, Baltimore, 1882.

Adams, James T. *Provincial Society, 1690–1763,* New York, Macmillan, 1927.

———. *Revolutionary New England, 1691–1776,* Boston, Atlantic Monthly Press, 1923.

Adams, Sherman A., revised by H. R. Stiles. *History of Ancient Weathersfield,* New York, 1904.

Addy, Sidney O. *The Evolution of the English House,* London, 1898.

Akagi, Roy H. *The Town Proprietors of the New England Colonies,* Philadelphia, University of Pennsylvania Press, 1924.

Allen, T. Warren, et al. "Highways and Highway Transportation," U.S. Dept. of Agriculture, *Yearbook,* (1924), pp. 97–184.

Allen, Wilkes. *History of Chelmsford, 1653–1820,* Haverhill, Mass., 1872.

American Husbandry, London 1775; reprint, ed., Harry J. Carman, New York, Columbia University Press, 1934.

Anderson, Oscar E. *Refrigeration in America: A History of a New Technology and Its Impact,* published for the University of Cincinnati by Princeton University Press, Princeton, 1953.

Andrews, Charles M. *The Colonial Period of American History,* 4 vols., New Haven, Yale University Press, 1934–38.

———. *The River Towns of Connecticut,* Johns Hopkins University *Studies,* Ser. 7, Nos. 7–9, Baltimore, 1889.

Annett, Albert, and Alice E. E. Lehtinen. *History of Jaffrey (Middle Monadnock), New Hampshire,* Jaffrey, 1937.

Arber, Edward. *The Story of the Pilgrim Fathers, 1606–1623: As Told by Themselves, Their Friends and Their Enemies,* Boston, 1897.

Arnold, Samuel G. *History of the State of Rhode Island and Providence Plantations,* 2 vols., New York, 1859.

Atwater, Edward E. *History of the Colony of New Haven to Its Absorption into Connecticut,* New Haven, 1881.

Bacon, Edgar M. *Narragansett Bay: Its Historic and Romantic Associations,* New York, Putnam, 1904.

Bacon, Oliver M. *History of Natick, Massachusetts*, ed. James Savage, Boston, 1825.

Bailey, Sarah L. *Historical Sketches of Andover, Massachusetts*, Cambridge, Houghton Mifflin, 1880.

Bailyn, Bernard. *The New England Merchants of the Seventeenth Century*, Cambridge, Harvard University Press, 1955.

Baker, J. N. C. "England in the Seventeenth Century," in H. C. Darby, ed., *Historical Geography of England and Wales before A.D. 1900*, pp. 387–442.

Bancroft, George. *History of the United States*, 10 vols., Boston, 1885.

Banks, Charles E. "English Sources of Emigration to the New England Colonies," Mass. Historical Society *Proceedings*, 60 (1926–27), 366–72.

————. *The English Ancestry and Homes of the Pilgrim Fathers*, New York, Grafton Press, 1929.

————. *The Planters of the Commonwealth*, Boston, Houghton Mifflin, 1930.

————. *The Winthrop Fleet of 1630*, Boston, Houghton Mifflin, 1930.

————. *The History of Martha's Vineyard*, 3 vols., Boston, 1911–25.

Barber, John W. *Connecticut Historical Collections*, New Haven, 1836, "Improved Edition," 1856.

————. *Historical Collections of Massachusetts*, Worcester, 1844.

————. *History and Antiquities of New England, New York and New Jersey*, Worcester, 1841.

Barry, John S. *Historical Sketch of the Town of Hanover, Massachusetts*, Boston, 1853.

Barry, William. *History of Framingham, Massachusetts*, Boston, 1847.

Barton, Edward B. "Braintree Historical Sketches," in *A Brief History of the Town of Braintree 1640–1940*, Braintree, Mass., 1940.

Batcheller, Birney C. *People of Wallingford*, Brattleboro, Vt., Stephen Daye Press, 1937.

Baylies, William. "Description of Gay Head," American Academy of Arts and Sciences *Memoirs*, 2 (1793), 150–155.

Beard, Charles and Mary. *The Rise of American Civilization*, Vol. 1, *The Agricultural Era*, New York, Macmillan, 1927.

Belknap, Jeremy. *History of New Hampshire*, Vol. 3, Boston, 1792.

Bell, Charles H. *History of the Town of Exeter, New Hampshire*, Exeter, 1888.

Benson, Albert E. *History of the Massachusetts Horticultural Society*, Boston, 1929.

Benson, Lee. "The Historical Background of Turner's Frontier Essay," *Agricultural History*, 25 (1951), 59–82.

Bidwell, Percy W. "The Agricultural Revolution in New England," *American Historical Review*, 26 (1921), 683–702.

———. "Rural Economy in New England at the Beginning of the Nineteenth Century," *Connecticut Academy of Arts and Sciences Transactions*, 20 (1916), 241–399.

——— and John I. Falconer. *History of Agriculture in the Northern United States, 1620–1860*, Washington, Carnegie Inst., 1925; New York, Peter Smith, 1941.

Bishop, J. Leander. *History of American Manufactures from 1608 to 1860*, 3 vols., Philadelphia, 1861–68.

Blake, Francis E. *History of the Town of Princeton*, Princeton, Mass., 1915.

Blake, John B. *Public Health in the Town of Boston 1630–1822*, Cambridge, Harvard University Press, 1959.

Bliss, William R. *Colonial Times On Buzzards Bay*, Cambridge, 1888.

Bloch, Marc. *French Rural History: An Essay on Its Basic Characteristics*, tr. Janet Sondheimer, Berkeley, University of California Press, 1966.

Bogart, Ernest L. *Peacham: The Story of a Vermont Town*, Vermont Historical Society, Montpelier, 1948.

Bolles, Albert S. *Industrial History of the United States*, Norwich, Conn., 1879.

Bolton, Charles K. *Scotch-Irish Pioneers in Ulster and America*, Boston, Little Brown, 1920.

Bolton, Ethel S. *Farm Life a Century Ago*, privately printed, 1909.

———. *Shirley Uplands and Intervales*, Boston, 1914.

Bonham-Carter, Victor. *The English Village*, Penguin Books, Harmondsworth, Middlesex, 1952.

Bonner, James C. "Advancing Trends in Southern Agriculture," *Agricultural History*, 22 (1948), 248–59.

Bouton, Nathaniel. *History of Concord . . . 1725–1853*, Concord, N.H., 1856.

Bowen, Clarence W. *Woodstock: An Historical Sketch*, New York, 1886.

Boyle, John A. *The English in America*, Vol. 1, London, 1887.

Bradford, Alden. *New England Chronology*, Boston, 1842.

Bradford, William. "A Descriptive and Historical Account of New England in Verse," Massachusetts Historical Society *Collections*, 3 (1810), 77–84.

———. *Of Plimoth Plantation*, "Printed from the Original Manuscript," Boston, 1898.

Bridenbaugh, Carl. *Cities in the Wilderness: The First Century of Urban Life in America, 1625–1702*, New York, Ronald Press, 1938.

———. "The New England Town, A Way of Life," American Antiquarian Society *Proceedings* 56 (1947), 19–48.

————. *Vexed and Troubled Englishmen, 1590–1642*, New York, Oxford University Press, 1968.

Briggs, Martin S. *Homes of the Pilgrim Fathers in England and America*, London, Oxford University Press, 1932.

Brown, Amos E. *Faneuil Hall and Faneuil Hall Market*, Boston, 1900.

Brown, John. *The Pilgrim Fathers of New England and Their Puritan Successors*, New York, 1895.

Brown, Louise K. *Wilderness Town: The Story of Bedford, Massachusetts*, privately printed, 1968.

Brown, Robert E. *Middle Class Democracy and the Revolution in Massachusetts, 1691–1780*, Ithaca, Cornell University Press, 1955.

Brown, Wallace, "The American Farmer during the Revolution: Rebel or Loyalist?" *Agricultural History*, 42 (1968), 327–38.

Browne, C. A. "Elder John Leland and the Mammoth Cheshire Cheese," *Agricultural History*, 18, No. 4 (1944), 145–53.

Burt, Henry M. *The First Century of the History of Springfield: The Official Records, 1636–1736*, 2 vols., Springfield, 1898.

Bushman, Richard R. *From Puritan to Yankee: Character and the Social Order in Connecticut, 1690–1765*, Cambridge, Harvard University Press, 1967.

Cambridge, Mass. *Proprietors' Records*, Cambridge, 1896.

————. *Records of the Town of Cambridge (formerly Newtowne), 1633–1703*, Cambridge, 1901.

Campbell, Mildred. *The English Yeoman under Elizabeth and the Early Stuarts*, New Haven, Yale University Press, 1942.

————. "Social Origins of Some Early Americans," in *Seventeenth Century America*, ed. James M. Smith, Chapel Hill, University of North Carolina Press, 1959.

Carleton, William M. "Masts and the King's Navy," *New England Quarterly*, 12 (1939), 1–18.

Carpenter, Edward W., and Charles F. Morehouse. *History of the Town of Amherst, Massachusetts, 1731–1896*, Amherst, 1896.

Carrier, Lyman. *The Beginnings of Agriculture in America*, New York, McGraw Hill, 1923.

Cary, Harold W. *The University of Massachusetts: A History of One Hundred Years*, Amherst, University of Massachusetts Press, 1962.

Caulkins, Frances M. *History of New London . . . 1612–1852*, New London, Conn., 1895.

Chamberlain, Mellen. *A Documentary History of Chelsea, 1624–1824*, Boston, 1908.

Channing, Edward. *The Narragansett Planters: A Study of Causes*, Baltimore, Johns Hopkins University *Studies*, 4th Series, No. 3, 1886.

Chase, Arthur. *History of Ware, Massachusetts*, Cambridge, University Press, 1911.

Chase, Benjamin. *History of Old Chester, 1709–1869*, Auburn, N.H., 1869.

Chase, George W. *History of Haverhill*, Haverhill, 1861.

Chickering, Jesse. *A Statistical View of the Population of Massachusetts*, Boston, 1840.

Child, William H. *History of the Town of Cornish, New Hampshire*, Concord, Rumford Press, 1912.

Clarence, Francis. *A History of Food and Its Preservation*, Princeton, Princeton University Press, 1937.

Clark, Alice. *The Working Life of Women in the Seventeenth Century*, New York, Dutton, 1919.

Clark, George F. *History of Norton*, Boston, 1859.

Clark, George L. *History of Connecticut: Its People and Institutions*, New York, Putnam, 1914.

Clark, Victor S. *History of Manufactures in the United States, 1607–1860*, Washington, rev. ed., 1870.

Clark, Willard H. *History of Winthrop, Massachusetts*, Winthrop, 1952.

Clarke, Levi H. *Haddam in 1808*, Acorn Club of Connecticut, Pub. 22, Hartford, 1949.

Clauson, James E. *Cranston: An Historical Sketch*, Providence, 1904.

Cochrane, Warren R., and George K. Wood. *History of Francestown, New Hampshire, 1758–1891*, Nashua, 1895.

Coffin, Joshua. *A Sketch of the History of Newbury, Newburyport and West Newbury From 1635 to 1845*, Boston, 1845.

Coleman, Peter J. *The Transformation of Rhode Island, 1790–1860*, Providence, Brown University Press, 1963.

Cook, Frederic W., ed. *Historical Data Relating to Cities and Towns* (Massachusetts), Boston, 1948.

Cook, Harold O. *Fifty Years a Forester*, Massachusetts Forest and Park Assn., Boston, 1961.

Coulton, George G. *The Medieval Village*, Cambridge, at the University Press, 1925.

Craven, Wesley F. *The Colonies in Transition, 1660–1713*, New York, Harper and Row, 1968.

Crawford, Mary C. *Social Life in Old New England*, Boston, Little Brown, 1914.

Cummings, Richard O. *The American Ice Harvests: A Historical Study in Technology, 1800–1918*, Berkeley, University of California Press, 1949.

Currier, John J. *History of Newbury, Massachusetts, 1635–1902*, Boston, 1903.

Curtis, John G. *History of the Town of Brookline, Massachusetts*, Boston, Houghton Mifflin, 1933.

Cutter, Benjamin, and William R. *History of the Town of Arlington, Formerly West Cambridge, 1675–1869*, Boston, 1869.

Daniels, George F. *History of the Town of Oxford*, Oxford, Mass., 1892.

Darby, H. C., ed., *An Historical Geography of England before A.D. 1800*, Cambridge, at the University Press, 1962.

Davis, Charles H. S. *History of Wallingford, Connecticut*, Meriden, Conn., 1870.

Day, Clarence A. *A History of Maine Agriculture, 1604–1860*, Orono, University of Maine Studies, 68, 1954.

———. *Farming in Maine 1860–1940*, Orono, University of Maine Studies, 2nd Ser., No. 78, 1963.

Deane, Samuel. *History of Scituate*, Boston, 1831.

DeForest, John W. *History of the Indians of Connecticut*, Hartford, 1851.

Degler, Carl N. *Out of Our Past: The Forces That Shaped Modern America*, New York, Harper and Row, 1957.

DeLue, Willard. *The Story of Walpole, 1724–1924*, Norwood, Mass., 1925.

Demos, John. *A Little Commonwealth: Family Life in Plymouth Colony*, New York, Oxford University Press, 1970.

Denison, Frederic. *Westerly and Its Witnesses*, Providence, 1878.

Dewey, Chester. *History of the County of Berkshire*, Pittsfield, 1829.

Dexter, Henry M., ed. *Mourt's Relation*, Boston, 1865.

———. and Morton Dexter. *The England and Holland of the Pilgrims*, Boston, Houghton Mifflin, 1905.

Donovan, Dennis J., and Jacob C. Woodward. *History of the Town of Lyndeborough, New Hampshire*, Medford, Tufts College Press, 1906.

Dorfman, Joseph. *The Economic Mind in American Civilization*, 3 vols., New York, Viking Press, 1946–49.

Dow, George F. *Everyday Life in the Massachusetts Bay Colony*, Boston, Society for the Preservation of New England Antiquities, 1935.

——— et al. *History of Topsfield*, Topsfield, Mass., 1940.

Drake, Francis F. *The Town of Roxbury: Its Memorable Persons and Places*, Roxbury, 1878.

Earle, Alice M. *Customs and Fashions in Old New England*, New York, 1890.

East, Robert A. *Business Enterprise in the American Revolutionary Era*, New York, Columbia University Press, 1938.

Elkins, Charles W., ed. *The Early History of Falmouth . . . to 1812*, Falmouth, Mass., 1889.

Ellis, Charles M. *History of Roxbury Town*, Part I, Boston, 1847.

Ellis, Leonard M. *History of New Bedford and Its Vicinity, 1602–1872*, Syracuse, 1872.

Emerson, Amelia F. *Early History of Naushon Island*, privately printed, 1939.

Everitt, Alan. "Farm Laborers," in Joan Thirsk, ed., *The Agrarian History of England and Wales*, Vol. 4, Cambridge, at the University Press (1967), 396–454.

———. "The Marketing of Agricultural Produce," ibid., pp. 466–589.

Everson, Jennie G. *Tidewater Ice of the Kennebec River*, Maine Heritage Series, No. 1, Freeport, Maine State Museum, 1970.

Fairchild, Byron. *Messrs. William Pepperell, Merchants at Piscataqua*, Ithaca, Cornell University Press, 1954.

Faulkner, Harold U. *American Economic History*, New York, Harper, 1924.

Felt, Joseph B. *Annals of Salem*, 2 vols., Salem, 1845.

———. *Customs of New England*, Boston, 1853.

———. *History of Ipswich, Essex and Hamilton*, Cambridge, 1834.

Fenner, Henry M. *History of Fall River*, New York, 1906.

Finberg, H. R. R., "Anglo-Saxon England to 1042," in *The Agrarian History of England and Wales*, ed. Finberg, Vol. 1, *A.D. 43–1042* (London, Cambridge University Press, 1972), pp. 385–525. Ibid., Vol. 4, *A.D. 1500–1640*, ed. Joan Thirsk (1967).

Fisher, Dorothy C. *Vermont Tradition: The Biography of an Outlook on Life*, Boston, Little, 1953.

Fite, Emerson D. *Social and Industrial Conditions in the North during The Civil War*, New York, Macmillan, 1910.

Foster, William C., ed. "Early Attempts at Rhode Island History," Rhode Island Historical Society *Collections*, 7 (1885), 5–134.

Fowler, William S. *Ten Thousand Years in America*, New York, Vantage, 1957.

Fox, Paul. *The Pole in America*, New York, Doran, 1922.

Francis, Clarence A. *A History of Food and Its Preservation*, Princeton, Princeton University Press, 1937.

Freeman, Frederick. *History of Cape Cod*, 2 vols., Boston, 1860–62.

French, Allen. *Charles I and the Puritan Upheaval*, Boston, Houghton Mifflin, 1955.

Frizzell, Martha M. *A History of Walpole, New Hampshire*, Walpole, 1963.

Frothingham, Richard J. *History of Charlestown, Massachusetts*, Boston, 1852.

Fuess, Claude M. *Andover, Symbol of New England: The Evolution of a Town*, Vol. 1, Andover, Mass., 1959.

Fuller, Oliver P. *History of Warwick, Rhode Island*, Providence, 1875.

Fussell, G. E. "The Agricultural Revolution, 1600–1850," in Kranzberg and Purcell, eds. *Technology in Western Civilization*, Vol. 1, London, Oxford University Press (1967), 128–42.

———. "The Traffic in Farm Produce in Seventeenth Century England," *Agricultural History*, 20 (1946), 77–86.

Gabriel, Ralph H. *Toilers of Land and Sea*, Vols. 2 and 3, Pageant of America Series, New Haven, Yale University Press, 1926–29.

Garraty, John A. *The New Commonwealth*, New York, Harper and Row, 1968.

Garvan, Anthony N. B. *Architecture and Town Planning in Colonial Connecticut*, New Haven, Yale University Press, 1951.

Goddard, M. E., and Henry V. Partridge. *History of Norwich, Vermont*, published by authority of the town, Hanover, N.H., Dartmouth Press, 1905.

Goodhue, Josiah F. *History of the Town of Shoreham, Vermont*, Middlebury, 1861.

Gottfried, Marion H. "The First Depression in New England," *New England Quarterly*, 9, No. 4 (1936), 655–78.

Governor Endicott, An Horticulturist, Danvers, Mass., 1919.

Grant, Charles S. *Democracy in the Frontier Town of Kent*, New York, Columbia University Press, 1961.

Gras, Norman S. B. *The Economic and Social History of an English Village*, Cambridge, Harvard University Press, 1930.

Graves, Eugene. "A History of Maine's Nineteenth Century Beef Industry," M.A. thesis, University of Maine, Orono, 1967.

Greven, Philip J. *Four Generations: Population, Land, and Family in Colonial Andover, Massachusetts*, Ithaca, Cornell University Press, 1970.

Griffin, Simon G. *History of the Town of Keene, 1732–1874*, Keene, N.H., 1904.

Hall, Benjamin H. *History of Eastern Vermont from Its Earliest Settlement to the Close of the Eighteenth Century*, New York, 1858.

Hall, H. B. "A Description of Rural Life and Labor in Massachusetts, at Four Periods." Ph.D. thesis, Harvard University, 1917.

Hamilton, Edward P. *The French and Indian Wars*, Garden City, N.Y., Doubleday, 1962.

———. *A History of Milton*, Milton, Mass., 1957.

Hamlin, Helen. *Pines, Potatoes and People: The Story of Aroostook*, New York, Norton, 1948.

Handlin, Oscar et al., eds. *Harvard Guide to American History*, Cambridge, Harvard University Press, 1934. New Edition, New York, Athenaeum, 1967.

Handlin, Oscar, and Mary F. *Commonwealth: A Study of the Role of Government in the American Economy, 1774–1861*, New York, New York University Press, 1947.

Hansen, Marcus L. *The Mingling of the Canadian and American Peoples*, Vol. I, New Haven, Yale University Press, 1940.

Hanson, John W. *History of the Town of Danvers to 1840*, Danvers, Mass., 1848.

———. *History of Norridgewock and Canaan*, Boston, 1849.

Harlow, Ralph V. "Economic Conditions in Massachusetts, 1775–1783," Colonial Society of Massachusetts *Transactions*, 20 (1920), 163–192.

———. "The Pole in the Land of the Puritan," *New England Magazine*, New Series, 29 (1933), 162–66.

Hart, Albert B., ed. *Commonwealth History of Massachusetts*, 5 vols., New York, State History Co., 1927–30.

Haskins, George L. *Law and Authority in Early Massachusetts*, New York, Macmillan, 1960.

Hatch, William C. *History of the Town of Industry, Franklin County, Maine*, Farmington, 1893.

Hawke, David. *The Colonial Experience*, New York, Bobbs-Merrill, 1966.

Hayes, Lyman S. *History of the Town of Rockingham, Vermont*, Bellows Falls, 1907.

Hazard, Blanche E. *Organization of the Boot and Shoe Industry in Massachusetts*, Harvard Economic Studies, Cambridge, Harvard University Press, 1921.

Hedges, James B. *The Browns of Providence Plantation*, Providence, Brown University Press, 1968.

Hedrick, Ulysses P. *History of Agriculture in the State of New York*, Albany, New York State Agricultural Society, 1933.

———. *History of Horticulture in America to 1860*, New York, Oxford University Press, 1950.

Hibbard, Augustine G. *History of the Town of Goshen, Connecticut*, Hartford, 1877.

Hinckley, Anita W. "Wickford Tales," *American Heritage*, 16 (1965), 80–90.

Hobart, Benjamin. *History of the Town of Abington*, Boston, 1866.

Hodges, James B. *The Browns of Providence Plantation*, Cambridge, Harvard University Press, 1952.

Holbrook, Stuart H. *The Yankee Exodus: An Account of Migration from New England*, Macmillan, New York, 1950.

———. "Why Did They Go Away?" *American Heritage*, 6 (1955), 226–35.

———. *Machines of Plenty: Pioneering in American Agriculture*, New York, Macmillan, 1920.

Holland, John G. *History of Western Massachusetts*, 2 vols., Springfield, 1855.

Hooker, Roland M. *The Colonial Trade of Connecticut*, For the Tercentenary Commission, New Haven, Yale University Press, 1936.

Hopkins, Samuel. *Historical Memories Relating to the Housatonnuck Indians*, Boston, 1753.

Hoskins, W. G. *The Midland Peasant: The Economic and Social History of a Leicestershire Village*, London, Macmillan, 1957.

Howard, Daniel. *A New History of Old Windsor, Connecticut*, Windsor, 1935.

Howard, George E. *Introduction to the Local Constitutional History of the United States*, Baltimore, 1884.

Howe, George. *Mount Hope: A New England Chronicle*, New York, Viking, 1959.

Howe, Henry E. *Prologue To New England*, New York, Farrar, Strauss, 1943.

———. *Salt Rivers of the Massachusetts Shore*, New York, Rinehart, 1951.

Howe, M. A. DeWolfe. *Bristol, Rhode Island: A Town Biography*, Cambridge, Harvard University Press, 1930.

Howes, Frederick G. *History of the Town of Ashfield, Massachusetts, 1742–1910*, Ashfield, 1910.

Hoyt, Epaphras. *Antiquarian Researches: Comprising a History of the Indian Wars in the Country Bordering the Connecticut River*, Greenfield, Mass., 1824.

Hubbard, William. "A General History of New England," Part I, "Events . . . to 1641," Massachusetts Historical Society *Collections*, 2nd Ser., No. 5 (1848), 1–304.

———. *Narrative of the Indian Wars of New England, 1607–1677*, Worcester, 1801.

Hudson, Alfred S. *History of Concord, Massachusetts*, 2 vols., Concord, 1904.

Hudson, Charles. *History of Lexington, Massachusetts*, Boston, 1868.

———. *History of Sudbury, Massachusetts*, Sudbury, 1889.

Hulbert, Archer B. *Soil: Its Influence on the History of the United States*, New Haven, Yale University Press, 1930.

Hurd, D. Hamilton, ed. *History of Cheshire and Sullivan Counties, New Hampshire*, Philadelphia, 1886.

Hutchinson, Thomas. *The History of the Colony and Province of Massachusetts Bay*, ed. Thomas S. Mayo, Vol. 1, Cambridge, Harvard University Press, 1936.

Jacobstein, Meyer. *The Tobacco Industry in the United States*, Columbia University Studies, 26 (1907), 1–208.

Jameson, J. Franklin. *The American Revolution Considered as a Social Movement*, Princeton, Princeton University Press, 1926; Boston, Beacon Press, 1963.

———. *Narratives of New Netherland, 1609–1664*, New York, 1909.

Jenkins, Edward H. *A History of Connecticut Agriculture*, New Haven, Connecticut, Agric. Exp. Station, n.d.

Jennings, George P. *Greens Farms, Connecticut: The Old West Parish of Fairfield*, Greens Farms, Modern Books, 1933.

Jensen, Merrill. "The American Revolution and American Agriculture," *Agricultural History*, 43 (1969), 107–24.

———. *The New Nation: A History of the United States during the Confederation 1781–1789*, New York, Knopf, 1950.

Jewett, Amos E. and Emily M. A. *Rowley, Massachusetts: Mr. Ezechi Rogers' Plantation, 1639–1850*, Rowley, 1946.

Johnson, Edward. *Wonder Working Providence of Sion's Saviour in New England*, Andover, 1867.

Johnson, Gerald. *Our English Heritage*, Philadelphia, Lippincott, 1949.

Johnson, Jane E., ed. *Newtown's History and Historian, Ezra Levan Johnson*, Newtown, Conn., 1917.

Jones, Matt B. *History of Waitsfield, Vermont, 1782–1908*, Boston, 1909.

Jordan, William B., Jr. *A History of Cape Elizabeth, Maine*, Portland, House of Falmouth, 1965.

Joslin, J. B. Frisbie, and F. Ruggles. *History of the Town of Poultney, Vermont*, Poultney, 1875.

Judd, Sylvester. *History of Hadley, Massachusetts*, new ed., Springfield, 1905.

Keir, Malcolm. "The March of Commerce," Vol. 4, Pageant of America Series, New Haven, Yale University Press, 1926–29.

Kelly, J. Frederick. "A Seventeenth Century Log House," Society for the Preservation of New England Antiquities *Bulletin*, 21 (1940), 19–40.

Kilbourne, Payne K. *Sketches and Chronicles of the Town of Litchfield, Connecticut,* Hartford, 1859.

Kimball, Fiske. *Domestic Architecture of the American Colonies and the Early Republic,* New York, Scribner, 1927.

Kirkland, Edward C. *Men, Cities, and Transportation: A Study in New England History,* 2 vols., Cambridge, Harvard University Press, 1948.

Kittredge, George L. *The Old Farmer and His Almanac,* Boston, Ware and Co., 1904.

Kittredge, Henry C. *Cape Cod: Its People and Their History,* Boston, Houghton Mifflin, 1930.

Kranzberg, Melvin, and Carroll W. Pursell, Jr., eds. *Technology in Western Civilization,* 2 vols., London, Oxford University Press, 1967.

Kull, Irving S. and Nell M. *Chronological Encyclopedia of American History,* 1969 ed., New York, Popular Library.

Lacey, Charlotte A. *An Historical Story of Southport,* Fairfield, Conn., 1927.

Lapham, Alice J. *The Old Planters of Beverly in Massachusetts and the Thousand Acre Grant of 1635,* Beverly Historical Assn. (Printed at Riverside Press), 1930.

Larned, Ellen D. *Historic Gleanings in Windham County, Connecticut,* Providence, 1899.

———. *History of Windham County, Connecticut,* 2 vols., Worcester, 1874.

Leach, Douglas E. *Flintlock and Tomahawk,* New York, Macmillan, 1958.

———. *The Northern Colonial Frontier,* New York, Holt, Rinehart, 1966.

Lee, W. Storrs. *The Yankees of Connecticut,* New York, Holt, 1957.

Lewis, Alonzo, and James R. Newhall. *History of Lynn,* Boston, 1865.

Lincoln, Solomon. *History of Hingham, Massachusetts,* Hingham, 1827.

Little, William. *History of Warren, A Mountain Hamlet,* Manchester, New Hampshire, 1870.

Lockridge, Kenneth A. *A New England Town, The First Hundred Years: Dedham, Massachusetts, 1636–1736,* New York, Norton, 1970.

Lockwood, John H. *Westfield and Its Historic Influences,* Westfield, Massachusetts, 1922.

Lord, Elizabeth W. *The Story of Templeton, Massachusetts,* ed. Ethel M. Eaton, sponsored by Narragansett Historical Soc., Templeton, 1946.

Lounsbury, Ralph G. "Yankee Trade at Newfoundland," *New England Quarterly,* 3 (1930), 607–26.

Maclear, Anne B. *Early New England Towns: A Comparative Study of Their*

Development, Columbia University Studies, Vol. 29, New York, Longmans Green, 1908.

Macy, William F. *The Story of Old Nantucket*, Boston, Houghton Mifflin, 1938.

Main, Jackson T. *The Social Structure of Revolutionary America*, Princeton, Princeton University Press, 1965.

Maine, University of, *Bulletin*, see Day, Clarence A.

Maitland, Frederick W. *Township and Borough*, Cambridge, at the University Press, 1898.

Malone, Joseph J. *Pine Trees and Politics: The Naval Stores and Forest Policy of New England, 1691–1775*, Seattle, University of Washington Press, 1964.

Marshfield . . . The Autobiography of A Pilgrim Town, ed. Joseph C. Hagar, Marshfield, Mass., 1940.

Martin, Abijah P. *History of the Town of Lancaster, Massachusetts*, Lancaster, 1879.

Martin, Margaret E. *Merchants and Trade in the Connecticut River Valley, 1750–1820*, Smith College Studies in History, Northampton, 1939.

Mason, George C. "The British Fleet in Rhode Island," Rhode Island Historical Society *Collections*, 7 (1885), 299–325.

Mathews, Lois K. *The Expansion of New England, 1620–1865*, Boston, 1909.

May, Ralph. *Early Portsmouth History*, Boston, Goodspeed, 1926.

McDuffie, Franklin. *History of Rochester, New Hampshire*, Manchester, 1892.

Mead, Spencer P. *Historie of ye Town of Greenwich, Connecticut*, New York, 1911.

Merrill, Joseph. *History of Amesbury and Merrimac*, Haverhill, Mass., 1880.

Miller, Edward, and Frederic P. Wells. *History of Ryegate, Vermont*, St. Johnsbury, 1913.

Miller, Perry. *Errand into the Wilderness*, Cambridge, Harvard University Press, 1956.

Miller, William D. *The Narragansett Planters*. Worcester, American Antiquarian Society, 1934.

Mirick, Benjamin F. *History of Haverhill, Massachusetts*, Haverhill, 1832.

Mitchell, Isabel. *Roads and Roadmaking in Connecticut*, for the Connecticut Tercentenary Commission, New Haven, Yale University Press, 1933.

Moore, J. Bailey. *History of the Town of Candia, New Hampshire*, Manchester, 1893.

Morgan, Edmund S. "Masters and Servants in Colonial New England," Boston Public Library, *More Books*, 17, No. 7 (1942), 311–28.

Morison, Samuel E. *Builders of the Bay Colony*, Boston, Houghton Mifflin, 1930.

——. *The Maritime History of Massachusetts, 1783–1860*, Boston, Houghton Mifflin, 1921.

——. *The Oxford History of the American People*, New York, Oxford University Press, 1965.

——. *The Story of the Old Colony of New Plymouth*, New York, Knopf, 1956.

Morrison, Hugh. *Early American Architecture: From the First Colonial Settlements to the National Period*, New York, Oxford University Press, 1952.

Morrow, Rising Lake. *Connecticut Influences in Western Massachusetts and Vermont*, New Haven, Yale University Press, 1933.

Morse, Jarvis M. *A Neglected Period of Connecticut History, 1818–1850*, New Haven, Yale University Press, 1933.

Morton, Thomas. *The New English Canaan*, ed. Charles F. Adams, Jr., Boston, Prince Society, 1883.

Munro, Wilfred H. *History of Bristol, Rhode Island: The Story of the Mount Hope Lands*, Providence, 1880.

Neal, Daniel. *The History of New England To 1700*, 2 vols., London, 1720.

Nettels, Curtis P. *The Money Supply of the American Colonies before 1720*, University of Wisconsin *Studies*, 20, Madison, 1934.

——. *The Roots of American Civilization: A History of American Colonial Life*, New York, Appleton, 1938.

Newhall, James R. *Lin or Jewels of the Third Plantation*, Lynn, Mass., 1862.

Newton, Earle. *The Vermont Story: A History of the People of the Green Mountain State, 1749–1949*, Montpelier, Vermont Historical Society, 1949.

Niles, Grace G. *The Hoosac Valley: Its Legends and History*, New York, Putnam, 1912.

Notestein, Wallace. *The English People on the Eve of Colonization, 1603–1630*, New York, Harper and Row, 1954.

Nourse, Henry S. *History of the Town of Harvard*, Clinton, Mass., 1894.

O'Callaghan, E. B. *Documentary History of the State of New York*, Albany, 1849–51.

Oliver, John W. *History of American Technology* (New York, 1956), p. 41.

Orcutt, Samuel D. *History of the Towns of New Milford and Bridgewater, Connecticut*, Hartford, 1882.

Orcutt, William D. *Good Old Dorchester: A Narrative History*, Cambridge, 1893.

Osgood, Herbert L. *The American Colonies in the Seventeenth Century*, 3 vols., New York, Macmillan, 1904–07.

Otis, Charles P., Translator. *The Voyages of Sieur de Champlain*, Boston, Prince Society, 1878.

Paige, Lucius R. *History of Cambridge, Massachusetts*, Boston, 1877.

Paine, Josiah. *History of Harwich, Barnstable County, Massachusetts, 1600–1800*, Rutland, Vt., Tuttle, 1937.

Palfrey, John G. *History of New England*, Vol. 1, Boston, 1858.

Pares, Richard. *Yankees and Creoles: The Trade between North America and the West Indies before the American Revolution*, Cambridge, Harvard University Press, 1956.

Parker, Benjamin. *History of Wolfeborough, New Hampshire*, Wolfeborough, 1901.

Parker, Edward L. *History of Londonderry, New Hampshire*, Boston, 1851.

Parsons, Herbert C. *A Puritan Outpost: A History of the Town and People of Northfield, Massachusetts*, New York, Macmillan, 1937.

Pattee, William S. *History of Old Braintree and Quincy*, Quincy, Mass., 1878.

Patterson, Stephen E. *Political Parties in Revolutionary Massachusetts*, Madison, University of Wisconsin Press, 1973, pp. 98–113.

Payne, Kenyon K. *Sketches and Chronicles of the Town of Litchfield, Connecticut*, Hartford, 1859.

Pease, John C. "Historical Sketch of the Town of Enfield," in Francis P. Allen, *History of Enfield, Connecticut*, Lancaster, Pa., 1900.

Perley, Sidney. *History of Salem, Massachusetts*, Salem, 1924.

——. *Historic Storms of New England*, Salem, 1891.

Perry, Arthur L. *Origins of Williamstown*, Williamstown, Mass., 1900.

Peters, Samuel. *A General History of Connecticut*, ed. Samuel J. McCormick, New York, 1877.

Phelps, Noah A. *History of Simsbury, Granby, and Canton*, Hartford, 1845.

Phillips, James D. *Salem in the Seventeenth Century*, Boston, Houghton Mifflin, 1933.

Pickard, Eldridge A. "Re-Introducing Boston's Stockyards," *Boston Business*, 32, No. 11 (1941).

Porter, Noah, Jr. *Historical Discourse in Commemoration of the Original Settlement of Farmington in 1640*, Hartford, 1841.

——. *Historical Discourse at Centennial of Farmington Congregational Church Building, 1872*, Hartford, 1873.

Potter, Elisha R. "The Early History of Narragansett," Rhode Island Historical Society *Collections*, Vol. 3 (1835).

Powell, Sumner C. *Puritan Village: The Formation of a New England Town*, Middletown, Conn., Wesleyan University Press, 1963.

———. "Seventeenth Century Sudbury, Massachusetts," Soc. Architectural Historians *Journal*, 11, No. 1 (1952), 3–15.

Powers, Grant. *Historical Sketches of the Discovery, Settlement, and Progress . . . in the Coos Country, 1754–1795*, Haverhill, N.H., 1847, reprint 1880.

Pratt, Enoch. *Comprehensive History . . . of Eastham, Wellfleet and Orleans, Massachusetts*, Yarmouth, 1844.

Pratt, Harvey H. *The Early Planters of Scituate*, Scituate, Mass., 1929.

Price, Robert. "The Origins of Johnny Appleseed," *New England Quarterly*, 12 (1939), 454–69.

Prince, Thomas. "Chronological History of New England in the Form of Annals," Boston, 1736, reprint, Mass. Historical Society *Collections*, 2nd Ser., 7 (1818), 189–295.

Purcell, Richard J. *Connecticut in Transition, 1775–1818*, new edition, with foreword by S. Hugh Bruchner, Middletown, Wesleyan University Press, 1963.

Putnam, Ralph W. "Vermont's Part in Industry," Vermont Historical Society *Proceedings*, 8 (1940), 357–73.

Raynor, Ellen M., and Emma L. Petitclerc. *History of the Town of Cheshire, Berkshire County, Massachusetts*, Holyoke, 1885.

Rhode Island Agricultural Experiment Station, *One Hundred Years of Rhode Island Agriculture*, Bulletin 378, 1965.

Ricketson, Daniel. *History of New Bedford, Massachusetts, Including Westport, Dartmouth and Fairhaven*, New Bedford, 1848.

Robert, Joseph C. *The Story of Tobacco in America*, New York, Knopf, 1952.

Roberts, Christopher. *The Middlesex Canal, 1793–1860*, Cambridge, Harvard University Press, 1938.

Roberts, George. *The Social History of the People of the Southern Counties of England in Past Centuries*, London, 1856.

Rowe, Henry K. *Tercentenary History of Newton, 1630–1930*, Newton, Mass., 1930.

Rowe, William H. *The Maritime History of Maine*, New York, Norton, 1948.

Roy, Louis E. *Quabaug Plantation, Alias Brookefeild: A Seventeenth Century Massachusetts Town*, West Brookfield, 1965.

Runnels, Moses T. *History of Sanbornton, New Hampshire*, Boston, 1882.

Rutman, Darrett B. *Husbandmen of Plymouth: Farms and Villages in the Old Colony, 1620–1692*, Boston, Plimoth Plantation by Beacon Press, 1967.

Sanborn, Edwin D. *History of New Hampshire*, Manchester, 1874.

Sandwich and Bourne, Quarter-Millennial Celebration, 1639–1889, Falmouth, Mass., 1890.

Sanford, Albert H. *The Story of Agriculture in the United States*, Boston, Heath, 1916.

Schafer, Joseph. *The Social History of American Agriculture*, New York, Macmillan, 1936.

Schenck, Elizabeth H. *History of Fairfield, Connecticut, 1639–1818*, New York, 1889.

Schlesinger, Arthur M. *The Birth of the Nation*, New York, Knopf, 1968.

———. *The Colonial Merchants and the American Revolution*, Columbia University *Studies*, 75, New York, 1918.

———. "Food in the Making of America," in *Paths to the Present*, New York, 1949.

Scofield, Edna. "The Origin of Settlement Patterns in Rural New England," *Geographical Review*, 28 (1938), 652–63.

Scudder, Townsend. *Concord, American Town*, Boston, Little Brown, 1947.

Sedgwick, Sarah C., and Christina S. Marquand. *Stockbridge, 1738–1939: A Chronicle*, privately printed, 1939.

Seebohm, Frederick. *The English Village Community*, 4th ed., London, 1890.

Seebohm, Mabel E. *The Evolution of the English Farm*, London, Allen and Unwin, 1927.

Semple, Ellen C. *American History and Its Geographic Conditions*, Boston, Houghton Mifflin, 1903.

Sewall, Samuel, *History of Woburn*, Boston, 1868.

Shannon, Fred A. *The Farmer's Last Frontier: Agriculture 1860–1897*, Vol. 5 of *Economic History of the United States*, New York, Farrar, Rinehart, 1945.

Shattuck, Lemuel. *History of the Town of Concord*, Boston, 1835.

Sheldon, George. *History of Deerfield, Massachusetts*, Deerfield, 1895–96.

———. "Old Time Traffic on the Connecticut," Pocumtuck Valley Memorial Assn. *History and Proceedings*, 3 (1901), 117–29.

Shipton, Clifton K. "The New England Frontier, 1607–1763," *New England Quarterly*, 10 (1931), 25–36.

———. *Roger Conant: A Founder of Massachusetts*, Cambridge, Harvard University Press, 1944.

Smith, Albert. *History of the Town of Peterboro, Hillsborough County, New Hampshire*, Boston, 1860.

Smith, Frank D. *History of Guilford, Connecticut: From Its First Settlement in 1639*, ed. Ralph D. Smith, Albany, 1877.

Smith, J. E. A. *History of Pittsfield, Berkshire County, Massachusetts, 1734-1800*, Boston, 1869.

Smith, James Morton, ed. *Seventeenth Century America*, Chapel Hill, University of North Carolina Press, 1958-59.

Smith, John. *Generall Historie of New England*, 1629 edition, Richmond, 1819.

Smith, Page. *As a City upon A Hill*, New York, Knopf, 1966.

Somers, A. N. *History of Lancaster, New Hampshire*, Concord, 1899.

Spencer, Wilbur D. *Pioneers of Maine Rivers, with Lists to 1651*, privately printed, Portland, 1930.

Squires, James D. *Mirror to America: A History of New London, New Hampshire, 1900-1950*, Concord, N.H., Evans, 1952.

Stackpole, Everett S. *History of New Hampshire*, 4 vols., American Historical Society, New York, 1916.

Stahl, Jasper J. *History of Old Broad Bay and Waldoboro*, 2 vols., Portland, Bond Wheelwright, 1956.

Starkey, Marion L. *A Little Rebellion*, New York, Knopf, 1955.

Steiner, Bernard C. *History of the Plantation of Menunkatuck and of the Original Town of Guilford, Connecticut*, Baltimore, 1897.

Stiles, Henry R. *History and Genealogies of Ancient Windsor, Connecticut*, Albany, 1833.

Stilwell, Lewis D. "Migration From Vermont," Vermont Historical Society *Proceedings*, 5 (1937), 63-245.

Stowe, J. M. *History of the Town of Hubbardston*, Hubbardston, Mass., 1881.

Struik, Dirk J. *Yankee Science in the Making*, Boston, Little Brown, 1948.

Swift, Charles F. *Cape Cod: The Right Arm of Massachusetts*, Yarmouth, 1897.

———. *History of Old Yarmouth*, Yarmouth Port, 1884.

Swift, Samuel. *History of the Town of Middlebury, in the County of Addison, Vermont*, Middlebury, 1859.

Taylor, Charles J. *History of Great Barrington*, Great Barrington, Mass., 1882.

Taylor, Robert J. *Western Massachusetts in the Revolution*, Providence, Brown University Press, 1954.

Teller, Daniel W. *History of Ridgefield, Connecticut*, Danbury, 1878.

Temple, J. H. *History of Framingham, Massachusetts*, Framingham, 1887.
———. *History of North Brookfield*, North Brookfield, Mass., 1887.
Thompson, Charles O. F. *Sketches of Old Bristol*, Providence, R.I., 1902.
Thompson, Charles S. *Evolution of the American Public Library 1653–1876*, Washington, D.C., Scarecrow Press, 1952.
Thompson, Francis M. *History of Greenfield, Massachusetts, 1682–1900*, Greenfield, 1904.
Tilden, William S. *History of the Town of Medfield*, Boston, 1887.
Tilton, George H. *History of Rehoboth, 1643–1918*, Boston, 1918.
Tompson, Benjamin. *New England's Crises*, reprint by Club of Odd Volumes, 1894.
Trewortha, Glenn T. "Types of Rural Settlement in the United States," *Geographic Review*, 36 (1946), 568–96.
Trumbull, Benjamin. *A Complete History of Connecticut*, 2 vols., New Haven, 1797 and 1818.
Tryon, Rolla M. *Household Manufactures in the United States, 1640–1860: A Study in Industrial History*, Chicago, University of Chicago Press, 1917.
Turner, Frederick J. "The Frontier in American History," American Historical Assn. *Annual Report* (1893), pp. 119–227.

Usher, A. P. "Colonial Business and Transportation," in Albert B. Hart, ed., *Commonwealth History of Massachusetts*, Vol. 2 (New York, 1928), chap. 8.
Usher, James M. *History of Medford*, Boston, 1886.
Usher, Roland G. *The Pilgrims and Their History*, New York, Macmillan, 1918.

Vail, Henry H. *Pomfret, Vermont*, ed. Emma C. White, Boston, Cockayne, 1930.
Van Duzen, Albert E. *Connecticut*, New York, Random House, 1961.
Van Wagener, Jared J. *The Golden Age of Homespun*, Ithaca, Cornell University Press, 1953.
Vaughan, Alden T. "The Horrid and Unnatural Rebellion of Daniel Shays," *American Heritage*, 17 (1966), 50–53, 77–81.
———. *New England Frontier: Puritans and Indians, 1620–1675*, Boston, Little Brown, 1965.

Walcott, Charles H. *Concord in the Colonial Period*, Boston, 1884.
Washburn, Charles G. *Industrial Worcester*, Worcester, Davis, 1917.
Waterman, Thomas T. *The Dwellings of Colonial America*, Chapel Hill, University of North Carolina Press, 1950.

Waters, Thomas F. *Ipswich in the Massachusetts Bay Colony, 1633–1700*, 2 vols., Ipswich, 1905–17.

Waters, W. *History of Chelmsford, Massachusetts*, Lowell, 1917.

Watkins, Lura W. "When They Burned Peat in Middleton," Soc. for the Preservation of New England Antiquities *Bulletin*, 52, No. 3 (1962).

Watson, W. L. "A Short History of Jamestown . . . Rhode Island," Rhode Island Historical Society *Collections* 26 (1933), 40–59.

Weeden, William B. *Early Rhode Island: A Social History of the People*, New York, Grafton Press, 1910.

———. *Economic and Social History of New England*, 2 vols., Boston, 1896.

Weeks, John W. *History of Salisbury, Vermont*, Middlebury, 1868.

Wells, Daniel W., and Reuben Field. *History of Hatfield*, Springfield, Mass., 1910.

Wells, Frederic W. *History of Newbury, Vermont*, St. Johnsbury, 1902.

Weslager, C. A. *The Log Cabin in America*, New Brunswick, N.J., Rutgers University Press, 1969.

Weston, Thomas. *History of the Town of Middleboro, Massachusetts*, Boston, 1906.

White, Henry. *Indian Battles, with Incidents in the Early History of New England*, New York, 1859.

White, John. "The Planter's Plea," in *The Founding of Massachusetts* (Boston, Massachusetts Historical Society, 1930), pp. 138–201.

Whitney, Peter. *History of the County of Worcester*, Isaiah Thomas, Worcester, 1793.

Wilder, David. *History of Leominster*, Fitchburg, Mass., 1853.

Willard, David. *History of Greenfield*, Greenfield, Mass., 1838.

Willey, Benjamin G. *History of the White Mountains*, new ed., Cambridge, 1870.

Williams, Haynes. *Stonington Chronology*, Stonington, Conn., 1949.

Williams, Roger. *An Helpe to the Native Language of That Part of America Called New England* (Williams' "Key"), ed. J. H. Trumbull, Providence, 1864.

Williams, Samuel. *The Natural and Civil History of Vermont*, Walpole, N.H., 1794.

Williamson, William D. *History of the State of Maine*, 2 vols., Hallowell, 1832.

Willis, William. *Journals of the Rev. Thomas Smith and the Rev. Samuel Deane, Pastors of the First Church of Portland*, Portland, Me., 1849.

Wilson, Harold F. *The Hill Country of Northern New England*, New York, Columbia University Studies, History of Agriculture Series, 1936.

Winship, John P. C. *Historical Brighton*, Boston, 1899.

Winslow, Edward. "Good News From New England," Massachusetts Historical Society *Collections*, 1st Ser., 8 (1802), 239–76; 2nd Ser., 9 (1832), 74–104.

Winsor, Justin, ed. *Memorial History of Boston, 1630–1880*, 4 vols., Boston, 1880–81.

———, ed. *Narrative and Critical History of America*, 8 vols., Cambridge, Mass., 1884–89.

Winthrop, John. *The History of New England, 1630–1649*, ed. James Savage, 2 vols., Boston, 1825.

Withington, Sidney. *The First Twenty Years of Railroading in Connecticut*, published for the Tercentenary Commission by Yale University Press, New Haven, 1935.

Wood, Frederick J. *The Turnpikes of New England*, Boston, Marshall Jones, 1919.

Woodard, Florence M. *The Town Proprietors of Vermont: The New England Town Proprietorship in Decline*, New York, Columbia University Studies, 1936.

Woodward, Carl R. *Plantation in Yankeeland: The Story of Cocumscussoc, Mirror of Colonial Rhode Island*, Cocumscussoc Assn., Wickford, R.I., 1971.

Woodward, W. F. *The Way Our People Lived*, New York, Dutton, 1945.

Worthen, Augusta H. *History of Sutton, New Hampshire*, Concord, 1830.

Worthington, Erastus. *History of Dedham*, Boston, 1827.

Wrench, Sir Evelyn. "Founders of New England," *National Geographic*, 103 (1953), 803–38.

Wright, Harry A. *The Genesis of Springfield: The Development of the Town*, Springfield, Johnson's Bookstore, 1936.

Wright, H. B., and E. A. Harvey, *The Settlement and Story of Oakham, Massachusetts*, Oakham, 1947.

Wright, Louis B. *The Cultural Life of the American Colonies, 1607–1693*, New York, Harper, 1957.

Wright, Richardson, *Hawkers and Walkers in Early America*, Philadelphia, Lippincott, 1927.

Young, Alexander, *Chronicles of the First Planters of the Colony of Massachusetts Bay in New England, 1630–1636*, Boston, 1841.

———. *Chronicles of the Pilgrim Fathers*, Boston, 1844.

Zuckerman, Michael. *Peaceable Kingdoms: New England Towns in the Eighteenth Century*, New York, Knopf, 1970.

Agricultural Works

Adams, T. N. *Prices Paid by Vermont Farmers 1790–1940*, Burlington, Vermont, Agricultural Experiment Station, 1944.

Agriculture of Vermont. Reports of Commissioner and State Societies.

Atwood, Milford W. "The Seed Catalogue," *New England Homestead* (Jan. 10, 1959), pp. 18, 19.

Ault, Warren O. "Open Field Husbandry and the Village Community," American Philosophical Soc. *Transactions*, New Ser., 55, Pt. VII (Philadelphia, 1965), 1–102.

Bailey, Harold M. "Vermont in the Potato Lineage Book," *Vermont History*, 23 (1955), 118–23.

Bailey, Liberty H. *Cyclopedia of American Agriculture*, 5th ed., 4 vols., New York, Macmillan, 1917.

Barley, M. W. *The English Farmhouse and Cottage*, Routledge and Kegan Paul, London, 1961.

———. "Rural Housing in England," in *The Agrarian History of England and Wales, 1500–1640*, ed. Joan Thirsk, Vol. 4 (Cambridge, at the University Press, 1967), 696–761.

Bassett, T. D. Seymour. "A Case Study of Urban Impact on Rural Society," *Agricultural History*, 30 (1956), 29–34.

Bennett, John C. *Treatise on the Breeding and General Management of Domestic Poultry*, Boston, 1851.

Benton, C., and S. F. Barry. *Statistical View of the Number of Sheep* (in the New England States), Cambridge, 1837.

Bergstrom, E. Alexander. "English Game Laws and Colonial Food Shortages," *New England Quarterly*, 12 (1939), 681–90.

Billings, E. R. *Tobacco, Its History, Varieties, Culture, Manufacture, and Commerce*, Hartford, 1875.

Blake, H. "Fifty Years of Farm Life in Northern Vermont," Vermont State Board of Agriculture Fourth Biennial *Report* (Montpelier, 1877), pp. 81–95.

Bradley, Richard. *A General Treatise on Husbandry and Gardening*, 2 vols., London, 1724.

Briggs, Martin S. *The English Farmhouse*, London, Botsford, 1963.

Brigham, Arthur A. "Notes on Rhode Island Reds," Rhode Island Agricultural Experiment Station *Report* (1901), pp. 324–33.

Buel, Jesse. *The Farmer's Companion*, Boston, 1839.

Bullen, Ripley P. "Forts, Boundaries and Ha-has," Massachusetts Archaeological Society *Bulletin*, 4 (1942), 1–11.

Burr, Fielding. *Field and Garden Vegetables of North America*, Boston, 1865.

Collingwood, H. W. "Market Gardening With Limited Capital," Massachusetts Board of Agriculture *Report* (1897), pp. 65–83.

Comstock, William G. "Early History of the Seed Trade in Wethersfield, Connecticut," American Seed Trade Assn., Tenth Annual Convention *Report* (1892).

Connecticut Agricultural Experiment Station, *Annual Reports*. Connecticut Board of Agriculture, *Annual Reports*.

Corbett, L. C., et al. "Fruit and Vegetable Production," U.S. Dept. of Agriculture *Yearbook* (1925), pp. 151–452; ibid., "Fruits and Vegetables," pp. 107–49.

Cutler, Manasseh. "An Account of Some of the Vegetable Productions Naturally Growing in This Part of America, Botanically Arranged," American Academy of Arts and Sciences *Memoirs*, 1 (1785), 396–493.

Danhof, Clarence H. *Change in Agriculture in the Northern United States, 1620–1870*, Cambridge, Harvard University Press, 1969.

———. "Gathering the Grass," *Agricultural History*, 30 (1956), 169–73.

Davis, Thomas. *General View of the Agriculture of the County of Wilts*, London, 1794.

Deane, Samuel. *The New England Farmer or Georgical Dictionary*, Worcester, 1790; 3rd ed., Boston, 1822.

Dudley, Paul. "Observations on Some of the Plants in New England," Royal Society of London, *Philosophical Transactions* (London, 1724), pp. 193–200.

Eastwood, B. *Complete Manual of the Cranberry*, New York, 1856.

Edwards, Everett E. *A Bibliography of the History of Agriculture in the United States*, USDA Misc. Pubn. 84, Washington, 1930. *References on American Colonial Agriculture*, USDA Library, 1938. *References on Agriculture in the Life of the Nation*, USDA Library, 1939.

Egleston, Melville. *The Land System of the New England Colonies*, Johns Hopkins University *Studies*, 4th Ser., Nos. 40–41, Baltimore, 1886.

Eliot, Jared. *Essays upon Field Husbandry in New England*, Boston, 1760.

———. *And Other Papers*, ed. Harry J. Carman and Rexford G. Tugwell, New York, A.M.S. Press, 1967.

Ellis, N. K. "Peppermint and Spearmint Production," *Economic Botany*, 14 (1960), 280–85.

Enfield, Edward. *Indian Corn: Its Value, Culture and Uses*, New York, 1866.

Fergus, E. N., and E. P. Hallowell. "Red Clover," in *Advances in Agronomy*, Vol. 12 (New York, Academic Press, 1960), 365–436.

Fessenden, Thomas G. *New American Gardener*, Boston, 1828.

Fletcher, Stephen W. *The Strawberry in North America*, New York, Macmillan, 1917.

Friedman, Karen J. "Victualling Colonial Boston," *Agricultural History*, 47 (1973), 189–205.

Flint, Charles L. *Grasses and Forage Plants: A Practical Treatise*, 5th ed., Boston, 1860.

――――. "A Hundred Years' Progress of American Agriculture," Massachusetts Board of Agriculture *Report* (1873), pp. 11–64.

Food Marketing in New England. George L. Moore, ed. Somerville, Mass. First National Stores, 1940–71.

Fussell, G. E. "The Grasses and Grassland Cultivation of Britain, I, Before 1700" and "II, 1700–1900," British Grassland Soc. *Journal*, 19–20 (1964–65), 49–54, 212–17.

――――. "The Traffic in Farm Produce in Seventeenth Century England," *Agricultural History*, 20, No. 2 (1946), 77–86.

Galinat, Walton C. "The Evolution of Sweet Corn," University of Massachusetts Agricultural Experiment Station *Bulletin* 591 (1971).

Galloway, B. T. "Progress of Commercial Growing of Plants under Glass," U.S. Dept. of Agriculture *Yearbook* (1899), 575–90.

Gardiner, Margaret, and Alexander Mackay-Smith. "The Great Justin Morgan Pedigree Controversy," *The Chronicle of the Horse*, Vol. 30, Nos. 18–21 (Dec. 23, 1966 – Jan. 13, 1967).

Garner, W. W., and E. G. Moss. "The History and Status of Tobacco Culture," U.S. Dept. of Agriculture *Yearbook* (1922), pp. 395–468.

Gates, Paul W. *Agriculture and the Civil War*, New York, Knopf, 1965.

――――. *The Farmer's Age: Agriculture 1815–1860*, New York, Holt, Rinehart and Winston, 1960.

Gold, Theodore. *Handbook of Connecticut Agriculture*, Hartford, 1901.

Goode, G. Browne. "The Use of Agricultural Fertilizers by the American Indians and the Early Colonists," *American Naturalist*, 14 (1880), 473–79.

Gomme, George L. *The Village Community*, New York, 1890.

Gourgouras, James A. "Brighton, Oldest Cattle Market in the United States," *Breeder-Stockman*, 14, No. 9 (1953), 9–10, 60–61.

Graves, Eugene M. "A History of Maine's Nineteenth Century Beef Industry," M.A. thesis, University of Maine, Orono, 1967.

Gray, Howard L. *English Field Systems*, Cambridge, Harvard University Press, 1915.

Gregory, James J. H. *Squashes: How to Grow Them*, New York, Judd, 1867.

Grinnell, James S. "Agricultural Machinery and Implements," Massachusetts Board of Agriculture *Report* (1882), pp. 231–55.

Harris, Thaddeus W. *Insects of Massachusetts Injurious to Vegetation*, Cambridge, 1841.

Hersey, Edmund. "Agriculture," in Vol. 1 of *History of Hingham* (Hingham, Mass., 1893), 181–92.

Holland, Joshua G. "Farming Life in New England," *Atlantic Monthly*, 2 (1858), 334–48.

Holmes, George K. "Some Features of Tobacco History," American Historical Assn. *Annual Report*, 1 (1919), 385–407.

Howard, Robert W. *The Horse in America*, New York, Fuller, 1965.

Jull, M. A., et al. "The Poultry Industry," U.S. Dept. of Agriculture *Yearbook* (1924), pp. 377–456.

Klose, Nelson. "Sericulture in the United States," *Agricultural History*, 37 (1963), 225–34.

Laufer, Berthold. "American Plant Migration," *Scientific Monthly*, 28 (1927), 239–51.

Lummer, George F. "The Spread of Imported Cattle through the Eastern United States," *Agricultural History*, 21 (1947), 79–93.

Linsley, D. C. *Morgan Horses: A Premium Essay on the Origin, History, and Characteristics of This Remarkable American Breed of Horses*, New York, 1857.

Loring, George B. "New England Farming," Massachusetts Board of Agriculture *Report* (1859), pp. 46–56.

Markham, Gervase. *A Way to Get Wealth*, London, 1676.

Martin, John H. "Broomcorn: The Frontiersman's Cash Crop," *Economic Botany*, 7 (1953), 163–81.

Massachusetts, Department of Agriculture. *Agricultural Statistics for Massachusetts and New England*, Boston, 1921.

Massachusetts Society for Promoting Agriculture, *Centennial Report, 1792–1892*, Salem, 1892.

Massachusetts Agricultural Repository and Journal, Boston, 1798–1832.

McDonald, Adrian F. *History of Tobacco Production in Connecticut*, New Haven, Yale University Press, 1936.

McDonald, Angus. *Early American Soil Conservationists*, USDA Misc. Publication No. 449 (Oct., 1941).

McGrew, T. F. "The Real Origin and Development of Poultry in Modern Times," Connecticut State Board of Agriculture *Report* (1905), pp. 147–57.

Merchant, Charles H., and Merton S. Parsons. *Farm Property Taxation in Maine*, Maine Agricultural Experiment Station, Bulletin 366, Orono, 1933.

Mood, Fulmer. "John Winthrop, Jr. on Indian Corn," *New England Quarterly*, 10 (1937), 163–81.

Needham, Walter, and Barrows Mussey. *A Book of Country Things*, Brattleboro, Stephen Greene Press, 1965.

New England Cultivator, Boston, 1852.

New England Farm Finance News, Boston.

New England Farmer, Boston.

New England Homestead, Springfield, Mass.

New Hampshire Agricultural Repository, Concord, 1822.

Olson, Albert L. *Agricultural Economy and the Population of Eighteenth Century Connecticut*, Tercentenary Pamphlet 40, New Haven, Yale University Press, 1935.

Oren, Michel and Janet Greene. "The Only Potato Fit to Eat," *Vermont Life*, 15 (Autumn 1960), 54–57.

Packard, Alpheus S., Jr. *Our Common Insects*, Boston, 1873.

Phillips, Deane C. *Horse Raising in Colonial New England*, Cornell Experiment Station *Memoir* 34, Ithaca, N.Y., 1922.

Pieters, A. J. "Seed Selling, Seed Growing, and Seed Testing," U.S. Dept. of Agriculture *Yearbook* (1899), pp. 549–74.

Porter, B. A., and C. H. Alden. "The Cankerworms," U.S. Dept of Agriculture *Bulletin* 1238 (1924).

Prentice, E. Parmelee. *American Dairy Cattle: Their Past and Future*, New York, Harper, 1942.

Prothero, Rowland E. *English Farming, Past and Present*, London, 1912.

Putnam, J. H. "The Depopulation of Our Rural Districts," Vermont Board of Agriculture *Report* (1878), pp. 132–41.

Rasmussen, Wayne D. "Scientific Agriculture," and "Food For the Future," in Vol. 2 of *Technology of Western Civilization*, ed. Melvin Kranzberg and Carroll W. Purcell, Jr. (London, Oxford University Press, 1967), pp. 337–53, 414–37.

Remington, Frank L. "When John Deere Engineered Efficiency into Tilling the Land," *Christian Science Monitor*, Aug. 16, 1971.

Rogin, Leo. *The Introduction of Farm Machinery in Its Relation to the*

Productivity of Labor . . . during the Twentieth Century, Berkeley, University of California Press, 1931.

Russell, Charles T. *Address, before the Hampden Horticultural Society*, Boston, 1850.

Rutman, Darrett B. "Governor Winthrop's Garden Crop: The Significance of Agriculture in the Early Commerce of Massachusetts Bay," *William and Mary Quarterly*, 20 (1963), 396–415.

Safford, William. "The Potato of Romance and Reality," Smithsonian Institution 1925 *Report* (1926), pp. 509–32.

Sanborn, Alvan F. "A Farming Community," *Atlantic Monthly*, 79 (1897), 588–98.

Sanford, Albert H. *The Story of Agriculture in the United States*, Boston, Heath, 1916.

Schorger, A. W. *The Wild Turkey: Its History and Domestication*, Norman, Okla., University of Oklahoma Press, 1946.

Schuette, H. A. "Maple Sugar: A Bibliography of Early Records," Wisconsin Society of Sciences, Arts, and Letters *Transactions*, 29 (1935), 209–36.

—— and A. J. Ihde. Ibid., Part II, *Transactions*, 38 (1946), 89–184.

Shannon, Fred A. *The Farmer's Last Frontier: Agriculture 1860–1897*, New York, Farrar Rinehart, 1945.

Simmons, Amelia. *American Cookery*, Hartford, 1796; Prospect Press reprint, 1937.

Smith, George P. "The Evolution of Farm Machines," Massachusetts Board of Agriculture *Report* (1899), pp. 246–57.

Smith, J. M. "Tobacco and Its Culture," Massachusetts Board of Agriculture *Report* (1882), pp. 136–60.

Strong, William C. "Market Gardening and Glass Structures," Massachusetts Board of Agriculture *Report* (1874–75), pp. 88–140.

Sturtevant, E. Lewis. "Notes on Edible Plants," ed. U. P. Hedrick, Albany, New York State Experiment Station *Report*, Vol. 2, Pt. II (Albany, 1919).

Sutton, G. P. "Forty Miles of Stone Fencing," *Yankee* (September 1968), pp. 88–93.

Tapley, William T. "Sweet Corn," in *The Vegetables of New York*, Albany, New York State Experiment Station *Report*, 1, Pt. III (1933–34).

Tawney, Richard. *The Agrarian Problem in the Sixteenth Century*, London, 1912.

Thirsk, Joan. "The Farming Regions of England" and "Farming

Techniques," in *The Agrarian History of England and Wales*, Vol. 4, 1500–1640 (Cambridge 1967), pp. 1–109; 161–197.

Thomas, Gertrude I. *Foods of Our Forefathers*, Philadelphia, Davis, 1941.

Thompson, Allen W. *The Horses of Woodstock* (Vt.): *With Sketches of the Different Breeds of New York Horses*, Cambridge, Mass., 1887.

Thompson, James W. *A History of Livestock Raising in the United States, 1607–1860*, U.S. Dept. of Agriculture, Agricultural History Series, No. 5, Washington, 1942.

Trow-Smith, Robert. *A History of British Livestock Husbandry to 1700*, London, Routledge and Kegan Paul, 1957.

True, A. C. "Agricultural Education in the United States," and "Agricultural Experiment Stations in the United States," U.S. Dept. of Agriculture *Yearbook* (1899), pp. 137–90, 513–48.

United States Dept. of Agriculture, Washington: Annual *Reports* and *Yearbooks*. *Bibliography of the History of Agriculture in the United States*. Misc. Publication No. 84, Washington, 1930.

———. Bureau of Animal Industry: *American Breeds of Fowls, The Plymouth Rock*, Bulletin No. 29, 1901. *Legislation with Reference to Bovine Tuberculosis*, 1901. *The Relation of Bovine Tuberculosis to Public Health*, 1901.

———. Economic Research Service, *A Chronology of American Agriculture, 1790–1965*.

———. *Experiment Station Record*.

———. *References on American Colonial Agriculture*. Library Bibliographical Contributions, No. 33, 1938.

United States Department of the Interior. *Census Reports, Statistics of Agriculture*.

United States Patent Office. *Report for 1847* (Agriculture).

Walcott, Robert R. "Husbandry in Colonial New England," *New England Quarterly*, 9 (1936), 218–52.

Ward, Julius A. "The Revival of Our Country Towns," *New England Magazine*, New Ser. (November 1889), 242–48.

Watson, Elkanah. *History of the Rise, Progress and Existing State of the Berkshire Agricultural Society*, Albany, 1819.

Wiest, Edward. *The Butter Industry of the United States*, Columbia University Studies, New York, 1916.

Wilder, Marshall P. *The Horticulture of Boston and Vicinity*, Boston, 1881.

Willard, John A. "Indian Corn"; "Hybrid Seed Corn and the Seed Trade"; "Sweet Corn for Seed": unpublished articles, Wethersfield, Conn.

Williams, Edward B. "The Present Condition of the Farmer," *New England Magazine*, New Ser. 3 (1890), 10–15.

Williams, Thaddeus. *Report on Insects Injurious to Vegetation*, Cambridge, Mass., 1841.

Wilson, Harold F. *The Hill Country of Northern New England*, Columbia University Studies in the History of American Agriculture, Vol. 3, New York, AMS Press, 1936.

———. "The Rise and Decline of the Sheep Industry in Northern New England," *Agricultural History*, 9 (1935), 12–14.

Wilson, Mary T. "Americans Learn to Grow the Irish Potato," *New England Quarterly*, 32 (1959), 333–50.

Worcester County Horticultural Society. "Fruit List of Old Varieties" (Apples), ed. S. Lothrop Davenport, Worcester, Mass., 1968.

Zelinsky, Wilbur. "The New England Connecting Barn," *Geographical Review*, 48 (1958), 540–53.

Works of Travel and Description

Abdy, Edward S. *Journal of a Residence and Tour of the United States, 1833–34*, 3 vols., London, 1835.

Alsberg, Henry G. *American Guide*, New York, Hastings, 1949.

Anburey, Gabriel. *Travels through the Interior Parts of America*, 2 vols., London, 1789.

Archer, Gabriel. *Relation of Captain Gosnold's Voyage to the North Part of Virginia*, Old South Leaflets, 120, Boston, 1920.

Bacon, Edgar M. *Narragansett Bay: Its Historic and Romantic Associations*, New York, Putnam, 1904.

Bakeless, John. *The Eyes of Discovery*, Philadelphia, Lippincott, 1950.

Bearse, Ray. *Vermont Guide*, Boston, Houghton Mifflin, 1966.

Birket, James. *Some Cursory Remarks Made . . . in His Voyage to North America, 1750–51*, New Haven, 1896.

Black, John O. *The Rural Economy of New England: A Regional Study*, Cambridge, Mass., 1950.

Bolton, Ethel S. *Shirley Uplands and Intervales*, Boston, 1914.

Boudinot, Elias. *Journey to Boston in 1809*, ed. Milton H. Thomas, Princeton, Princeton University Library, 1955.

Bradstreet, Nathanael C. "Recollections of Bradstreet Hill," Massachusetts Audubon Society *Bulletin*, 35, No. 7 (1951), 290–91.

Bridenbaugh, Carl E., ed. *Gentleman's Progress: The Itineraries of Dr. Alexander Hamilton, 1744*, Williamsburg, Va., Institute of Early American History and Culture, 1948.

Browne, Edmund. "Report on Massachusetts," Colonial Society of Massachusetts *Transactions*, 7 (1900), 76–80.

Burnaby, Andrew, *Travels through the Middle Settlements of North America . . . 1759 and 1760*, 2nd ed., London, 1775.

Burrage, Henry S., ed. *Rosier's Relation of Waymouth's Voyage to the Coast of Maine*, Portland, Gorges Society, 1851.

Champlain, Samuel de. *Voyages*, ed. W. L. Grant, New York, Scribner, 1902.

Charlton, Edmund A. *New Hampshire as It Is*, Claremont, 1857.

Chastellux, Francois, Marquis de. *Travels in North America in the Years 1780, 1781, and 1782*, 2 vols., London, 1787.

Cobbett, William. *A Year's Residence in the United States of America*, Pt. I, New York, 1818.

Coffin, Paul, of Buxton, Me. "Tours," Maine Historical Soc. *Collections*, 4 (1856), 261–405.

Comer, William R. *Landmarks in the Old Bay State*, Wellesley, Mass., privately printed, 1911.

Coolidge, Austin J., and J. B. Mansfield. *A History and Description of New England, General and Local*, Vol. 1, *Maine, New Hampshire, and Vermont*, Boston, 1859.

Crofut, Florence S. M. *Guide to the History and Historic Sites of Connecticut*, 2 vols., New Haven, Yale University Press, 1937.

Dankers, Jasper, and Peter Sluyter. "Journal of a Voyage to New York in 1679–80," Long Island Historical Society *Memoirs*, Brooklyn, 1867.

Davidson, Marshall B. *Life in America*, Vol. 1, Boston, Houghton Mifflin, 1951.

Davis, Samuel. "Journey from Plymouth to Connecticut," Massachusetts Historical Society *Proceedings*, 11 (1869–70), 9–32.

Derby, E. H. *Boston: A Commercial Metropolis in 1850*, Boston, 1850.

Dickinson, Rodolphus. *A Geographical and Statistical View of Massachusetts Proper*, Greenfield, 1813.

Douglass, William. *A Summary, Historical and Political, of the British Settlements in North America*, 2 vols., Boston, 1755.

Dow, George F. *Two Centuries of Travel in Essex County, Massachusetts*, Topsfield Historical Society, 1921.

Drayton, John. *Letters Written during a Tour through the Northern and Eastern States of America*, Charleston, S.C., 1794.

Dwight, Timothy. *Travels in New England and New York* (1796–1815), 4 vols., New Haven, 1821–22.

Eldridge, Charles W. "Journal of a Tour through Vermont to Westmoreland, Quebec, in 1833," Vt. Historical Society *Proceedings*, 2 (1931), 53–81.

Ezell, John S., ed., and Judson P. Wood, tr., *The New Democracy in America: Travels of Francisco de Miranda in the United States, 1783–84*, Norman, Okla., 1963.

Farmer, J., and J. B. Moore. *Collections Typographical, Historical and Biographical, Relating Principally to New Hampshire*, Vol. 1, Concord, 1822.

Faux, William. *Memorable Days in America: Being a Journal of a Tour of the United States*, London, 1823.

Federal Writers Project, American Guide Series, Cambridge, Riverside Press:
Connecticut, 1938.
Maine, A Guide "Down East," 1937.
Massachusetts, A Guide to its Places and People, 1937.
New Hampshire, A Guide to the Granite State, 1938.
Rhode Island, A Guide to the Smallest State, 1937.
Vermont, 1937.

First Ironworks Assn. *The Saugus Restorations*, Saugus, Mass., 1951.

Fogg, Alonzo J. *Statistics and Gazetteer of New Hampshire*, Concord, 1875.

Gorges, Ferdinand (The Younger). "A Description of New England," in *America Painted to the Life* . . . , London, 1657.

Graham, J. G. *A Descriptive Sketch of the Present State of Vermont*, London, 1797.

Greenleaf, Moses. *A Survey of the State of Maine*, Portland, 1829.

Hadfield, Joseph. *An Englishman in America 1785, Being the Diary of Joseph Hadfield*, ed. Douglas S. Robertson, Toronto, Hunter Rose Co., 1933.

Harmon, Daniel W. *A Journal of Voyages and Travels in the Interior of North America*, New York, 1903.

Hard, Walter. *The Connecticut*, Rivers of America Series, New York, Holt, Rinehart, 1947.

Harriott, John. *Struggles through Life: Various Travels and Adventures in Europe, Asia, Africa, and America*, 3rd ed., Vol. 2, London, 1815.

Hartt, Rollin Lynde. "A New England Hill Town," *Atlantic Monthly*, 93 (1899), 561–74, 712–20.

Harvey, Col. Alexander, of Scotland and Barnet, Vt. "Journal" (1774), Vt. Historical Society *Proceedings*, (1921–23), 199–262.

Hayward, John. *Gazetteer of Massachusetts*, Boston, 1846.
————. *Gazetteer of New England*, 4th ed., Boston, 1839.
Higginson, Francis. "New England's Plantation," and "A True Relation of the Last Voyage to New England," in Alexander Young, *Chronicles of Massachusetts Bay* (Boston, 1841), pp. 213–67.
Hodgson, Adam. *Letters from North America*, London, 1824.

Jackson, Charles T. *Report on the Geological and Agricultural Survey of the State of Rhode Island*, Providence, 1840.
Johnston, James F. W. *Notes on North America, Agricultural, Economical, and Social*, 2 vols., Boston, 1851.
Josselyn, John. *An Account of Two Voyages to New England*, London, 1670–75.
————. *New England's Rarities Discovered*, London, 1672, ed. Edward Tuckerman, Boston, 1865; facsimile edition, Berlin, 1926.

Kalm, Peter. "Travels into North America," tr. John R. Foster in *Pemberton's Travels* (London, 1812), pp. 374–700.
Kendall, Edward A. *Travels through the Northern Parts of the United States in 1807–08*, 3 vols., New York, 1809.
Knight, Sarah K. *Private Journal of a Journey from Boston to New York in the Year 1704*, Albany, 1865.

La Rochefoucauld-Liancourt, François Alexandre Frédéric, Duc de. *Travels through the United States of North America*, London, 1799.
Lambert, John. *Travels through Canada and the United States . . . in the Years 1806, 1807, and 1808*, 3rd ed., Vol. 2, London, 1816.
Langdon, William C. *Everyday Things in American Life, 1607–1776*; ibid., *1776–1876*, New York, 1937, 1941.
Latrobe, Charles J. *The Rambler in North America*, 2 vols., London, 1835.
Lechford, Thomas. *Plaine Dealing, or News From New England*, ed. J. Hammond Trumbull, reprint, Boston, 1867.
————. *Note Book*, reprint, Cambridge, 1885.
Lincklaen, John. *Travels in the Years 1791 and 1792 in Pennsylvania, New Jersey, and Vermont*, New York, 1897.

Marryat, Frederic. *A Diary in America*, 3 vols., London, 1839.
Martineau, Harriet. *Society in America*, Vols. 1–3, London, 1837.
Maverick, Samuel. *A Briefe Description of New England . . . From a Manuscript Written in 1660*, ed. John W. Dean, Boston, 1885.
Melish, John. *Travels through the United States . . . 1806–11*, London, 1818.
Mereness, Newton D., ed. *Travels in the American Colonies*, New York, Macmillan, 1916.

Merrill, Eliphalet and Phineas. *Gazetteer of New Hampshire*, Exeter, 1817.
Morgan, Philip A. "A Remote Village," *Atlantic Monthly*, 79 (1897), 578–87.
Morse, Jedediah. *The American Geography*, 2nd ed., London, 1792.

Norden, John. *Essex [England] Described*, London, 1840.
Norton, Lewis M. *Goshen in 1812*, Pub'n. 21, Acorn Club of Connecticut, Hartford, 1949.

Observations on the Agriculture, Manufactures, and Commerce of the United States, New York, 1789.

Padelford, Philip, ed. *Colonial Panorama, 1775: Dr. Robert Honyman's Journal for March and April*, San Marino, Cal., Huntington Library, 1939.
Pease, John C., and John M. Niles. *A Gazetteer of the States of Connecticut and Rhode Island*, Hartford, 1819.
Perkins, Nathan (of Hartford). *A Narrative of a Tour through the State of Vermont from April 27 to June 12, 1789*, Woodstock, Vt., Elm Tree Press, 1930.
Pory, John. *Lost Description of Plymouth*, ed. Champlin Burrage, Boston, Houghton Mifflin, 1918.

Relation of a Voyage to Sagadahoc, 1607–08, Boston, Massachusetts Historical Society, 1962.
Robbins, Michael. *Ancient Middlesex* (England), London, 1953.
Randolph, Edward, *Report to the Committee for Trade and Plantations*, Boston, Prince Society Reprint, 1898.
Robertson, Douglas S., ed. *An Englishman in America, 1785, Being the Diary of Joseph Hadfield*, Toronto, Hunter Rose, 1933.
Rosier, James. *A True Relation of Captain George Waymouth, His Voyage . . . the Discovery of the North Part of Virginia*, reprint with notes by George Prince, Maine, 1860.
Russell, Robert. *North America, Its Agriculture and Climate*, Edinburgh, 1859.

Sargent, Porter E. *A Handbook of New England*, Boston, 1916.
Scales, John. *Historical Memoranda Concerning Persons and Places in Old Dover, New Hampshire*, Dover, 1900.
Shay, Edith and Frank. *Sand in Their Shoes*, Boston, Houghton Mifflin, 1951.
Shelton, Jane DeF. *The Salt-Box House: Eighteenth Century Life in a New England Hill Town*, New York, Baker and Taylor, 1900.

Shirreff, Patrick, Farmer. *A Tour through North America . . . As Adapted for Agricultural Emigration*, Edinburgh, 1835.

Silliman, Benjamin. *Remarks Made on a Short Tour between Hartford and Quebec in . . . 1819*, 2nd ed., New Haven, 1824.

Smith, Chard P. *Housatonic, Puritan River*, New York, Holt, Rinehart, 1946.

Smith, J. Russell. *North America*, New York, 1895.

State of the British and French Colonies in North America, London, 1755.

Stiles, Ezra. *Extracts from the Itineraries, 1755–84: With a Selection from His Correspondence*, ed. Franklin B. Dexter, New Haven, Yale University Press, 1916.

Stuart, James D. *Three Years in North America*, 2 vols., Edinburgh, 1833.

Thompson, Mack E. "Moses Brown's Account of a Journey to Distribute Donations, 12th month, 1775," *Rhode Island History*, 15 (1956), 97–121.

Thomson, Betty F. *The Changing Face of New England*, New York, Grafton Press, 1958.

Tudor, Henry. *Narrative of a Tour in North America*, Vol. 1, London, 1834.

Underhill, Captain John. *News from America* (London, 1638), ed. Charles Orr, Cleveland, 1897.

Van der Donck, Adriaen, "Description of New Netherland," New York Historical Society *Collections*, 2nd Ser., 1 (1841), 125–242.

Verrill, A. Hyatt. *The Heart of Old New England*, New York, Dodd Mead, 1936.

Verrazano, Giovanni de. "Voyages Along the Coast of North America," tr. J. G. Coggswell, New York Historical Society *Collections*, 2nd Ser., 1 (1811), 37–63.

Wansey, Henry. *An Excursion to the United States of America in . . . 1794*, Salisbury (England), 1798.

Warville, Jacques Pierre de. *New Travels in the United States of America Performed in 1788*, 2nd ed., London, 1794.

Westcote, Thomas. *A View of Devonshire*, Exeter, England, 1845.

Winship, George P., ed. *Boston in 1682 and 1699: A Trip to New England by Edward Ward, and A Letter from New England by J. W.*, Providence, 1905.

————. *Sailors' Narratives of Voyages along the New England Coast, 1524–1624*, Boston, Houghton Mifflin, 1905.

Winterbotham, W. *An Historical, Commercial, and Philosophical View of the United States of America*, Vol. 2, New York, 1792.

Wood, Judson P. *See* Ezell, John S.

Index